A Guide to Instructional Materials

Speech & Language Development

Communication Skill Builders ↗*®

3130 N. Dodge Blvd. / P.O. Box 42050
Tucson, Arizona 85733
(602) 327-6021

Published by:

**Communication
Skill Builders, Inc.** ®
3130 N. Dodge Blvd./P.O. Box 42050
Tucson, Arizona 85733
(602) 327-6021

ISBN 0-88450-745-9
Catalog No. 3139

Introduction

The Speech and Language Development Guide to Instructional Materials addresses the long-standing need on the part of educators and speech professionals to identify materials according to specific speech and language skills. The Guide was developed for Communication Skill Builders, Inc., by VORT Corporation from its instructional materials data base. This simple pupil-based format includes information on more than 4,300 supplemental materials, each indexed to specific skills. The Skills Index can be used for individual student planning.

The specific information on each material has been derived from literature and samples provided by the publishers. Speech and language professionals have acknowledged that materials can teach more than the specific skills that publishers list for them. Therefore, in some cases, materials have been listed in skill areas where it will be necessary for the speech and language professionals to adapt the material to achieve the most for their students.

The Guide does not include all the information available on a given material, nor is the representation of a publisher's products all-inclusive. We have included only those materials which will serve as a stimulating and motivating force for the speech and language professional's practice.

Communication Skill Builders, Inc., and VORT Corporation have exercised their best judgment in compiling information for the Guides, and have no legal responsibility for errors in, or omission of, information on any given material. They will continue to revise, improve, and expand the Guide, and recommendations or suggestions for modification are most welcome.

Development Staff

Thomas Holt, Managing Editor (VORT Corporation)

Linda Nadell, Editorial Manager (Communication Skill Builders, Inc.)

Joanne Gilles, Editor/Materials Analyst (VORT Corporation)

Mary Baldwin, Materials Analyst (VORT Corporation)

Carolyn Ausberger, Materials Analyst (Communication Skill Builders, Inc.)

Vickie Robins, Data Processing (VORT Corporation)

Matilda Shields, Typist (Communication Skill Builders, Inc.)

Ricky Bourque, Typist (Communication Skill Builders, Inc.)

INSTRUCTIONS

1. Identify individual pupil or group needs. This can be done utilizing standardized tests, criterion-referenced instruments, or this Guide's Skills Index.

2. Determine the pupil's interest level. Interest level as used in this Guide is structured according to grade placement and reflects the content level of interest and not necessarily the reading level.

3. Review the Skills Index and identify the skill(s) that best matches the pupil's needs. The Skills Index contains 94 skill areas. Only the portion of those 94 skills applicable to this Guide are included herein.

4. For the identified skill, turn to the page indicated by the Skills Index. Review the materials starting on the designated page for the selected skill. Be sure to screen all the materials since materials for a given skill may appear on more than one page.

5. Review the materials based on the determined interest level. The interest levels are sequenced from Readiness (R) through Secondary (S). In cases where a material is appropriate for more than one interest level, two or more levels are indicated (e.g., PI). Refer to the Code Tables (page viii) for accurate interpretation of the interest level and format abbreviations. In some cases additional information is provided for each title (e.g., RL - Reading Level). Reading levels are the designated grade level as determined by the publisher.

6. Based upon the identified skill and interest level, review the different materials formats (e.g., MULTIM: SKLKIT: WKBOOK). Formats are grouped

alphabetically within each interest level. Select those materials which, based on skill, interest level, and format, will best meet the pupil's needs.

7. Use Appendix A to determine other skills that are taught by the selected title(s). Appendix A provides an alphabetical list of titles and the number(s) of each skill taught by each title.

8. Use the alphabetical publisher's listing (Appendix B) for ordering materials or for securing additional information. In most cases, only the original publisher/source for a given material is shown. VORT Corporation recommends that you contact the publisher for additional information on a given material.

9. The price for each material has been coded according to one of twelve different price ranges. The price of the material at the time of printing fell within the indicated price range (e.g., 151-200 means that the material's price is somewhere between $151 and $200).

10. The NT column indicates the number of subtitles available. This appears only for those titles that are sets and have subtitles.

TABLE OF CONTENTS

ALPHABETICAL
Skills Index - Speech and Language Development

PAGE SEQUENCE
Skills Index - Speech and Language Development

TYPE CODES

Code	Type	Definition
ACTCRD	Activity Cards	Collection of individual cards each containing a separate activity or a small group of related cards (e.g., picture sequence cards, etc.).
AUDCAS	Audio Cassette	Audio tape in a standard cassette, any length.
AUDCRD	Audio Card	Audio tape on card used with audio card reading machine (i.e., Language Master).
AUDKIT	Audio Kit	Series of materials in audio form (record or cassette); may include a teacher's guide.
AUDTAP	Audio Tape, Reel	Audio tape of unspecified speed.
A/VKIT	Audio/Visual Kit	Collection of materials in several media or forms which requires use of playback or viewing equipment. Print materials not included.
CHART	Chart/Poster/Display	Meant for wall/easel/floor display. Distinguished from individually used study prints or pictures.
CL SET	Classroom Set	May contain multiple copies of one or more books, single copies of many books, or enough manipulatives for use by an entire class.
DITTO	Ditto Master/Stencil	Commercially prepared duplicating materials.
EQUIPM	Equipment	Hardware used with instructional media; includes playground and other physical development equipment. .
FILMST	Filmstrip	Silent, distinguished from sound filmstrip.
FLASH	Flash Cards	Cards used for individual or group activities for memorizing basic sight words/math facts.
FLNLBD	Flannel Board Materials	Cut-outs made from materials which will adhere to a flannel board surface.
GAME	Game	Materials used by individual or small groups in gameboard/cards or other manipulative format.
GUIDE	Guide	Teacher's manual, curriculum guide, or course of study.
HI INT	High Interest, Controlled Vocabulary	Materials with stated reading level featuring high interest topics for use with students reading below grade level.

Code	Type	Definition
MANIPU	Manipulatives	Materials such as puzzles, blocks, cubes, etc.
MOVIEL	Movie, Loop	Motion picture in a film cartridge. Requires use of a film loop projector.
MULTIM	Multimedia Kit	Collection of materials in several forms, some of which require use of playback and/or viewing equipment (i.e., transparencies, dittos, records or cassettes, etc.). Does not include manipulative materials.
MULTIU	Multi-Use Kit	Collection of materials in several forms, one or more of which may require use of hardware. Kit also contains one or more manipulative (e.g., games, puzzles, activity cards, etc.).
OLFACT	Olfactory	
PICTUR	Picture/Study Prints	Prints, pictures, etc. for individual class use.
PI/PRT	Programmed Instruction, Print	Printed programmed instructional materials sequenced so pupil can move from one step to the next at his own rate, usually self-checking.
PROMA	Professional Material	Teacher resource material (print/non-print).
PUPILB	Pupil Book	Single copy, hardbound or paperback, distinguished from student textbook.
RECORD	Record	Phonograph record of unspecified speed.
REFBK	Reference Book	Material used by pupil (i.e., dictionary, encyclopedias, etc.).
SKLKIT	Skills Kit	Collection of materials designed to develop skills in specific areas (e.g., using the context, fractions, etc.). Generally comprised of individual pupil booklets or activity cards and teacher's guide.
SND FS	Sound Filmstrip	Filmstrip with internal or separate sound-carrying medium.
SP EQT	Special Equipment Required	Materials which are specifically designed to be used on special equipment (e.g., Controlled Reader, tachistoscope, special machines, etc.).
TEXTBK	Textbook	Used by the pupil as the basic text in a course of study or a subject area.

Code	Type	Definition
TRANSP	Transparency	For use on overhead projector.
TUTORL	Tutorial	Material that can be used by a classroom aide, tutor, or parent with an individual requiring more extensive practice in a given area.
VISKIT	Visual Kit	Collection of materials in different forms, one or more of which may require use of viewing equipment (i.e., silent filmstrip, transparencies, etc.). Does not include audio materials.
WORKBK	Workbook	Write-on material (i.e., workbook, worksheet, write-on cards, etc.). Some may be reuseable.

INTEREST LEVELS

R - Readiness
  PreK - 1

P - Primary
  1 - 3

I - Intermediate
  4 - 6

J - Junior High
  7 - 9

S - Secondary
  10 - Adult

SKILLS LISTINGS SECTION

LEVEL	FORMAT	TITLE	PUBLISHER	NT	$PRICE

1 - SKILL: SPEAKING SKILLS - GENERAL

LEVEL	FORMAT	TITLE	PUBLISHER	NT	$PRICE
R	ACTCRD	LEARNING LANGUAGE AT HOME, LEVEL I	COUNCIL FOR EXCEPTIONAL CHILDREN		31-50
RP	GUIDE	TIME FOR PHONICS, BOOK R, T.E.	WEBSTER DIVISION/MCGRAW-HILL		<5
RP	MULTIU	LISTENING TO THE WORLD	AMERICAN GUIDANCE SERVICE, INC.		101-150
RP	REFBK	STORY TELLING	CREATIVE STORYTIME PRESS		<5
RP	WKBOOK	TIME FOR PHONICS, BOOK R	WEBSTER DIVISION/MCGRAW-HILL		<5
RPI	SKLKIT	PEEL & PUT READING PROGRAM	COMMUNICATION SKILL BUILDERS, INC		51-75
P	ACTCRD	LEARNING LANGUAGE AT HOME, LEVEL II	COUNCIL FOR EXCEPTIONAL CHILDREN		31-50
P	GUIDE	TIME FOR PHONICS, BOOK A, T.E.	WEBSTER DIVISION/MCGRAW-HILL		<5
P	GUIDE	TIME FOR PHONICS, BOOK B, T.E.	WEBSTER DIVISION/MCGRAW-HILL		<5
P	GUIDE	TIME FOR PHONICS, BOOK C, T.E.	WEBSTER DIVISION/MCGRAW-HILL		<5
P	MULTIM	LANGUAGE EXPERIENCES IN READING (LEIR), LEVEL I	ENCYCLOPEDIA BRITANNICA		201-300
P	MULTIM	LANGUAGE EXPERIENCES IN READING (LEIR), LEVEL II	ENCYCLOPEDIA BRITANNICA		201-300
P	MULTIM	LANGUAGE EXPERIENCES IN READIN (LEIR), LEVEL III	ENCYCLOPEDIA BRITANNICA		201-300
P	WKBOOK	TIME FOR PHONICS, BOOK A	WEBSTER DIVISION/MCGRAW-HILL		<5
P	WKBOOK	TIME FOR PHONICS, BOOK B	WEBSTER DIVISION/MCGRAW-HILL		<5
P	WKBOOK	TIME FOR PHONICS, BOOK C	WEBSTER DIVISION/MCGRAW-HILL		<5
PI	ACTCRD	GOT TO BE ME, 48 CARDS	DEVELOPMENTAL LEARNING MATERIALS		11-20
PI	MULTIM	LISTEN, SPEAK, READ, & SPELL	DEVELOPMENTAL LEARNING MATERIALS		76-100
PI	WKBOOK	GOT TO BE ME, WORKBOOK	DEVELOPMENTAL LEARNING MATERIALS		6-10
I	MULTIM	LANGUAGE EXPERIENCES IN READING (LEIR), LEVEL IV	ENCYCLOPEDIA BRITANNICA		201-300
IJS	WKBOOK	ACQUIRING LANGUAGE SKILLS, BOOK A	WEBSTER DIVISION/MCGRAW-HILL		<5
IJS	WKBOOK	BUILDING LANGUAGE SKILLS, BOOK B	WEBSTER DIVISION/MCGRAW-HILL		<5
IJS	WKBOOK	CONTINUING LANGUAGE SKILLS, BOOK C	WEBSTER DIVISION/MCGRAW-HILL		<5
IJS	WKBOOK	DIRECTING LANGUAGE SKILLS, BOOK D	WEBSTER DIVISION/MCGRAW-HILL		<5
JS	AUDCAS	POWER OF WORDS	EBSCO CURRICULUM MATERIALS		6-10

2 - SKILL: BASIC LANGUAGE SKILLS

LEVEL	FORMAT	TITLE	PUBLISHER	NT	$PRICE
R	GAME	BODY PARTS CARDS & GAMEBOARD	COMMUNICATION SKILL BUILDERS, INC		11-20
R	GUIDE	ATTENDING	COMMUNICATION SKILL BUILDERS, INC		6-10
R	GUIDE	COLOR RECOGNITION	COMMUNICATION SKILL BUILDERS, INC		6-10
R	GUIDE	THE COMMUNICATION SCREEN	COMMUNICATION SKILL BUILDERS, INC		6-10
R	MULTIU	SMALL WONDER	AMERICAN GUIDANCE SERVICE, INC.		51-75
R	MULTIM	CONCEPTS & LANGUAGE	NATIONAL EDUCATIONAL LABORATORY		301-400
R	RECORD	THIS IS YOUR YEAR	FOLKWAYS RECORDS & SERVICE CORP.		11-20
RP	ACTCRD	KINDERGARTEN KEYS: LANGUAGE DEVELOPMENT CARDS, GROUP B	ECONOMY COMPANY		31-50
RP	AUDCAS	PROGRAMMED ENRICHMENT SONGS FOR EXCEPTIONAL CHILDREN	CONCEPT RECORDS		21-30
RP	AUDKIT	LITTLE TROLLY BOOKS & TAPES	ECONOMY COMPANY		101-150
RP	AUDKIT	WORDWORLD	ECONOMY COMPANY		101-150
RP	AUDKIT	SPACETALK	ECONOMY COMPANY		151-200
RP	CHART	CONCEPTO-CHARTS	EDUCATIONAL PERFORMANCE ASSOC.		21-30
RP	CHART	LANGUAGE ASSOCIATION BOARD NO. 1	MODERN EDUCATION CORPORATION		11-20
RP	CHART	LANGUAGE ASSOCIATION BOARD NO. 2	MODERN EDUCATION CORPORATION		11-20
RP	CHART	LANGUAGE ASSOCIATION BOARD NO. 3	MODERN EDUCATION CORPORATION		11-20
RP	CL SET	LANGUAGE SKILLS STEP BY STEP, KIT A	CONTINENTAL PRESS, INC.		51-75
RP	CL SET	CROSSTIES PROGRAM	ECONOMY COMPANY	11	76-100
RP	CL SET	CROSSTIES PROGRAM: GRAND CENTRAL BOOKS, SEPTEMBER	ECONOMY COMPANY		201-300
RP	CL SET	CROSSTIES PROGRAM: GRAND CENTRAL BOOKS, OCTOBER	ECONOMY COMPANY		31-50
RP	CL SET	CROSSTIES PROGRAM: GRAND CENTRAL BOOKS, NOVEMBER	ECONOMY COMPANY		31-50
RP	CL SET	CROSSTIES PROGRAM: GRAND CENTRAL BOOKS, DECEMBER	ECONOMY COMPANY		31-50
RP	CL SET	CROSSTIES PROGRAM: GRAND CENTRAL BOOKS, JANUARY	ECONOMY COMPANY		31-50
RP	CL SET	CROSSTIES PROGRAM: GRAND CENTRAL BOOKS, FEBRUARY	ECONOMY COMPANY		31-50
RP	CL SET	CROSSTIES PROGRAM: GRAND CENTRAL BOOKS, MARCH	ECONOMY COMPANY		31-50
RP	CL SET	CROSSTIES PROGRAM: GRAND CENTRAL BOOKS, APRIL	ECONOMY COMPANY		31-50
RP	CL SET	CROSSTIES PROGRAM: GRAND CENTRAL BOOKS, MAY	ECONOMY COMPANY		31-50
RP	CL SET	CROSSTIES PROGRAM: GRAND CENTRAL BOOKS, SUMMER	ECONOMY COMPANY		31-50
RP	CL SET	LEARNING LANGUAGE SKILLS 1	AEVAC, INC.		51-75
RP	CL SET	LEARNING LANGUAGE SKILLS 2	AEVAC, INC.		51-75
RP	FLASH	DESCRIPTO CARDS	COMMUNICATION SKILL BUILDERS, INC		11-20
RP	GAME	GAMEBOARDS FOR SPEECH & LANGUAGE DEVELOPMENT	COMMUNICATION SKILL BUILDERS, INC		31-50
RP	GAME	GAMEBOARDS FOR EARLY CHILDHOOD EDUCATION	COMMUNICATION SKILL BUILDERS, INC		31-50
RP	GUIDE	EMERGING LANGUAGE 2	COMMUNICATION SKILL BUILDERS, INC		6-10
RP	GUIDE	101 LANGUAGE ARTS ACTIVITIES	COMMUNICATION SKILL BUILDERS, INC		6-10
RP	MANIPU	SEASON LOTTO	NIENHUIS MONTESSORI, INC.		31-50
RP	MANIPU	MONSTER LACING CARDS	DEVELOPMENTAL LEARNING MATERIALS		6-10
RP	MANIPU	PICTURE LACING BOARD	DEVELOPMENTAL LEARNING MATERIALS		6-10
RP	MANIPU	IDENTIFICATION PUZZLES	MODERN EDUCATION CORPORATION		21-30
RP	MULTIU	BASIC LANGUAGE STIMULATOR	EDUCATIONAL PERFORMANCE ASSOC.		76-100
RP	MULTIU	PEABODY LANGUAGE DEVELOPMENT KIT, LEVEL #P	AMERICAN GUIDANCE SERVICE, INC.		201-300
RP	MULTIU	PEABODY LANGUAGE DEVELOPMENT KIT, LEVEL #1	AMERICAN GUIDANCE SERVICE, INC.		76-100
RP	PICTUR	TR LARGE PICTURE CARDS, SET 1	TEACHING RESOURCES CORPORATION		31-50
RP	PICTUR	TR LARGE PICTURE CARDS, SET 2	TEACHING RESOURCES CORPORATION		31-50
RP	PICTUR	TELL AGAIN NURSERY RHYMES CARDS	AEVAC, INC.		11-20
RP	PICTUR	IDENTIFICATION CARDS	MODERN EDUCATION CORPORATION		11-20
RP	PICTUR	PROBLEM SOLVING CARDS, SET 1: S SOUND	MODERN EDUCATION CORPORATION		11-20
RP	PICTUR	PROBLEM SOLVING CARDS, SET 2: R SOUND	MODERN EDUCATION CORPORATION		11-20
RP	RECORD	1, 2, 3 & A ZING, ZING, ZING	FOLKWAYS RECORDS & SERVICE CORP.		6-10
RP	RECORD	SONGS TO GROW ON, VOLUME 2: SCHOOL DAYS	FOLKWAYS RECORDS & SERVICE CORP.		6-10
RP	RECORD	SING CHILDREN'S SONGS & GAMES FROM THE SOUTHERN MOUNTAINS	FOLKWAYS RECORDS & SERVICE CORP.		6-10
RP	RECORD	OLD TIME SONGS FOR CHILDREN	FOLKWAYS RECORDS & SERVICE CORP.		6-10

LEVEL	FORMAT	TITLE	PUBLISHER	NT	$PRICE

2 - SKILL: BASIC LANGUAGE SKILLS

LEVEL	FORMAT	TITLE	PUBLISHER	NT	$PRICE
RP	RECORD	NEW HOUSE & HOW MONEY HELPED	FOLKWAYS RECORDS & SERVICE CORP.		6-10
RP	RECORD	MUSIC TIME WITH CHARITY BAILEY	FOLKWAYS RECORDS & SERVICE CORP.		6-10
RP	RECORD	SONG & PLAY TIME	FOLKWAYS RECORDS & SERVICE CORP.		6-10
RP	RECORD	LADYBUG, LADYBUG & MORE CHILDREN'S SONGS	FOLKWAYS RECORDS & SERVICE CORP.		6-10
RP	RECORD	MY STREET BEGINS AT MY HOUSE	FOLKWAYS RECORDS & SERVICE CORP.		6-10
RP	RECORD	AND ONE AND TWO	FOLKWAYS RECORDS & SERVICE CORP.		6-10
RP	RECORD	ACTIVITY RHYTHMIC MOVEMENTS OF ZOO ANIMALS	FOLKWAYS RECORDS & SERVICE CORP.		6-10
RP	REFBK	NATURAL LANGUAGE	COMMUNICATION SKILL BUILDERS,INC		<5
RP	SKLKIT	STEPTEXT	FOLLETT PUBLISHING COMPANY		31-50
RP	SKLKIT	PIPER: WHISPERS UNIT	READERS DIGEST SERVICES, INC.		31-50
RP	SKLKIT	MWM PROGRAM FOR DEVELOPING LANGUAGE ABILITIES	EDUCATIONAL PERFORMANCE ASSOC.		201-300
RP	TUTORL	DEVELOPMENTAL STORY BOOKS	DEVELOPMENTAL LEARNING MATERIALS		6-10
RP	WKBOOK	MY EVERYTHING PRACTICE BOOK	EDUCATIONAL PERFORMANCE ASSOC.		<5
RPI	MULTIU	PEEL & PUT (SPEECH THERAPY & LANGUAGE DEVELOPMENT)	COMMUNICATION SKILL BUILDERS,INC		51-75
RPIJS	GUIDE	SCHOOL & HOME PROGRAM	COMMUNICATION SKILL BUILDERS,INC		11-20
RPIJS	PICTUR	PICTURES, PLEASE!	COMMUNICATION SKILL BUILDERS,INC		31-50
RPIJS	SKLKIT	TEACHING MORPHOLOGY DEVELOPMENTALLY	COMMUNICATION SKILL BUILDERS,INC		31-50
P	AUDKIT	SPEECH THERAPY	EBSCO CURRICULUM MATERIALS		51-75
P	AUDKIT	BASIC COMMUNICATION SKILLS	LEARNING TREE FILMSTRIPS		51-75
P	CL SET	LEARNING LANGUAGE SKILLS 3	AEVAC, INC.		51-75
P	CL SET	LEARNING LANGUAGE SKILLS 4	AEVAC, INC.		51-75
P	DITTO	LISTEN & SPEAK TO READ	HAYES SCHOOL PUBLISHING COMPANY		<5
P	GAME	ANIMALS CAN TEACH	COMMUNICATION SKILL BUILDERS,INC		6-10
P	GAME	CONCEPTO-SORT	EDUCATIONAL PERFORMANCE ASSOC.		6-10
P	GAME	BACKPACK: A LANGUAGE DEVELOPMENT GAME	DEVELOPMENTAL LEARNING MATERIALS		6-10
P	GUIDE	SPEAK FOR YOURSELF	PEEK PUBLICATIONS		<5
P	GUIDE	HELPING CHILDREN LEARN	T.S. DENISON & COMPANY		6-10
P	GUIDE	INDIVIDUAL CORRECTIVE ENGLISH, GRADES 2 - 3, T.M.	MCCORMICK-MATHERS PUBLISHING CO.		<5
P	MANIPU	SPORTS LOTTO	NIENHUIS MONTESSORI, INC.		31-50
P	MANIPU	PROGRESSION LOTTO	NIENHUIS MONTESSORI, INC.		21-30
P	MANIPU	PERCEPTION LOTTO	NIENHUIS MONTESSORI, INC.		21-30
P	MANIPU	COUNTING LOTTO	NIENHUIS MONTESSORI, INC.		21-30
P	MANIPU	GO TOGETHER LOTTO	NIENHUIS MONTESSORI, INC.		21-30
P	MANIPU	CONCEPTO-PUZZLES	EDUCATIONAL PERFORMANCE ASSOC.		6-10
P	MULTIU	DISTAR ACTIVITY KIT: LANGUAGE	SRA		101-150
P	MULTIU	PEABODY LANGUAGE DEVELOPMENT KIT, LEVEL #2	AMERICAN GUIDANCE SERVICE, INC.		101-150
P	PICTUR	MOTOR EXPRESSIVE LANGUAGE PICTURE CARDS I	DEVELOPMENTAL LEARNING MATERIALS		<5
P	PICTUR	MOTOR EXPRESSIVE LANGUAGE PICTURE CARDS II	DEVELOPMENTAL LEARNING MATERIALS		<5
P	PUPILB	INDIVIDUAL CORRECTIVE ENGLISH, GRADE 2	MCCORMICK-MATHERS PUBLISHING CO.		<5
P	PUPILB	INDIVIDUAL CORRECTIVE ENGLISH, GRADE 3	MCCORMICK-MATHERS PUBLISHING CO.		<5
P	RECORD	SONGS TO GROW ON, VOLUME 3: AMERICAN WORK SONGS	FOLKWAYS RECORDS & SERVICE CORP.		6-10
P	SKLKIT	DEVELOPMENTAL LANGUAGE LESSONS	TEACHING RESOURCES CORPORATION		31-50
P	SND FS	FIRST CONCEPTS FILMSTRIP LIBRARY	TROLL ASSOCIATES		101-150
PI	ACTCRD	COMMUNICARDS	COMMUNICATION SKILL BUILDERS,INC		11-20
PI	ACTCRD	LANGUAGE	FRANK SCHAFFER PUBLICATIONS, INC		<5
PI	CL SET	LANGUAGE SKILLS STEP BY STEP, KIT B	CONTINENTAL PRESS, INC.		51-75
PI	DITTO	WHO, WHAT, WHEN, WHERE, WHY	FRANK SCHAFFER PUBLICATIONS, INC		<5
PI	FILMST	NEW ADVENTRURES IN LANGUAGE	TROLL ASSOCIATES		101-150
PI	GAME	BE A STAR	COMMUNICATION SKILL BUILDERS,INC		6-10
PI	GUIDE	LEARNING ACTIVITIES FOR THE LEARNING DISABLED	FEARON PITMAN PUBLISHERS, INC.		<5
PI	GUIDE	LEARNING THROUGH SONG	TEACHING RESOURCES CORPORATION		21-30
PI	PICTUR	LAC CARDS, SET 1: VERBS, SPORTS IN ACTION	MODERN EDUCATION CORPORATION		11-20
PI	PICTUR	LAC CARDS, SET 2: GENERAL VERBS	MODERN EDUCATION CORPORATION		11-20
PI	VISKIT	COLA (CONCEPTUAL ORAL LANGUAGE ACTIVITY KIT)	ACADEMIC THERAPY PUBLICATIONS		21-30
PI	WKBOOK	WHO, WHAT, WHEN, WHERE, WHY	FRANK SCHAFFER PUBLICATIONS, INC		<5
PI	WKBOOK	ADVENTURES IN READING COMPREHENSION	FRANK SCHAFFER PUBLICATIONS, INC		<5
PI	WKBOOK	CONCEPT UNDERSTANDING PROGRAM: VOCABULARY OF DIRECTIONS	PAUL S. AMIDON & ASSOC., INC.		11-20
PIJ	FLASH	PHOTO RESOURCE KIT	MODERN EDUCATION CORPORATION		31-50
PIJS	MULTIU	COMMUNICATIVE COMPETENCE	COMMUNICATION SKILL BUILDERS,INC		201-300
PIJS	MULTIU	LANGUAGE DEVELOPMENT PROJECT	SPECIAL LEARNING CORPORATION		6-10
PIJS	WKBOOK	SPACE ADVENTURES READING SERIES	COMMUNICATION SKILL BUILDERS,INC		11-20
I	ACTCRD	ALTERNATIVE CARDS	DEVELOPMENTAL LEARNING MATERIALS		<5
I	FILMST	PRONUNCIATION SKILLS	EDUCATIONAL PROJECTIONS COMPANY		21-30
I	GUIDE	INDIVIDUAL CORRECTIVE ENGLISH, GRADE 4, T.M.	MCCORMICK-MATHERS PUBLISHING CO.		<5
I	GUIDE	INDIVIDUAL CORRECTIVE ENGLISH, GRADE 5, T.M.	MCCORMICK-MATHERS PUBLISHING CO.		<5
I	GUIDE	INDIVIDUAL CORRECTIVE ENGLISH, GRADE 6, T.M.	MCCORMICK-MATHERS PUBLISHING CO.		<5
I	PUPILB	INDIVIDUAL CORRECTIVE ENGLISH, GRADE 4	MCCORMICK-MATHERS PUBLISHING CO.		<5
I	PUPILB	INDIVIDUAL CORRECTIVE ENGLISH, GRADE 5	MCCORMICK-MATHERS PUBLISHING CO.		<5
I	PUPILB	INDIVIDUAL CORRECTIVE ENGLISH, GRADE 6	MCCORMICK-MATHERS PUBLISHING CO.		<5
IJ	A/VKIT	SPEAKING OF LANGUAGE	GUIDANCE ASSOCIATES		51-75
IJ	CL SET	SEMANTICS	CHANNING L. BETE COMPANY, INC.		76-100
IJ	GAME	K-SPEECH NEWS	COMMUNICATION SKILL BUILDERS,INC		11-20
IJ	MULTIM	DISNEYLAND LANGUAGE ARTS SKILL BUILDING KIT	WALT DISNEY EDUCATIONAL MEDIA		201-300
IJ	WKBOOK	SEMANTICS	CHANNING L. BETE COMPANY, INC.		<5
IJS	PICTUR	CONSUMER SEQUENTIAL CARDS	DEVELOPMENTAL LEARNING MATERIALS		<5
JS	GUIDE	REALLY READING	CHARLES E. MERRILL PUBLISHING CO		<5
JS	PUPILB	REALLY READING	CHARLES E. MERRILL PUBLISHING CO		<5
JS	REFBK	WHAT TO DO ABOUT BILL?	COMMUNICATION SKILL BUILDERS,INC		11-20
S	FLASH	PICTURE COMMUNICATION CARDS	COMMUNICATION SKILL BUILDERS,INC		11-20

LEVEL	FORMAT	TITLE	PUBLISHER	NT	$PRICE

---

2 - SKILL: BASIC LANGUAGE SKILLS

LEVEL	FORMAT	TITLE	PUBLISHER	$PRICE
S	FLASH	WHAT'S THE SOLUTION?	COMMUNICATION SKILL BUILDERS,INC	11-20
S	GAME	BASIC COMMUNICATION GAMES	LANSFORD PUBLISHING COMPANY	151-200
S	PROFMA	WORKSHOPS FOR PARENTS & TEACHERS	COMMUNICATION SKILL BUILDERS,INC	11-20

3 - SKILL: NON-VERBAL COMMUNICATION

LEVEL	FORMAT	TITLE	PUBLISHER	$PRICE
R	GUIDE	ATTENDING	COMMUNICATION SKILL BUILDERS,INC	6-10
RP	CL SET	CREATING CHARACTERIZATION	COMENIUS, INC.	76-100
RP	GAME	TEDDY BEAR BINGO	MILTON BRADLEY/PLAYSKOOL	6-10
RP	GUIDE	101 LANGUAGE ARTS ACTIVITIES	COMMUNICATION SKILL BUILDERS,INC	6-10
RP	REFBK	NATURAL LANGUAGE	COMMUNICATION SKILL BUILDERS,INC	<5
RPIJ	GUIDE	TEACHING SPEECH TO A NONVERBAL CHILD	H & H ENTERPRISES, INC.	<5
RPIJ	GUIDE	TEACHING A CHILD TO IMITATE	H & H ENTERPRISES, INC.	<5
RPIJS	GUIDE	PLANNING INDIVIDUALIZED SPEECH & LANGUAGE INTERVENTION PROG.	COMMUNICATION SKILL BUILDERS,INC	11-20
RPIJS	PICTUR	PICTURES, PLEASE!	COMMUNICATION SKILL BUILDERS,INC	31-50
RPIJS	PI/PRT	HANDS ON	COMMUNICATION SKILL BUILDERS,INC	31-50
RPIJS	SKLKIT	NON-SLIP KIT	H & H ENTERPRISES, INC.	201-300
PIJ	SKLKIT	ON LOCATION WITH LANGUAGE	XEROX EDUCATION PUBLICATIONS	201-300
PIJS	GAME	PLAY IT BY SIGN	EDMARK ASSOCIATES	11-20
IJ	CL SET	SEMANTICS	CHANNING L. BETE COMPANY, INC.	76-100
IJ	WKBOOK	SEMANTICS	CHANNING L. BETE COMPANY, INC.	<5
IJS	CHART	SIGN LANGUAGE ALPHABET WALL CARDS	EDMARK ASSOCIATES	6-10
IJS	GUIDE	SIGN LANGUAGE FOR EVERYONE	EDMARK ASSOCIATES	11-20
IJS	PICTUR	SIGN LANGUAGE	EDMARK ASSOCIATES	11-20
IJS	REFBK	SIGN LANGUAGE THESAURUS	EDMARK ASSOCIATES	11-20
JS	GUIDE	NON-VERBALL COMMUNICATION	NATIONAL TEXTBOOK COMPANY	6-10
JS	PUPILB	PATHWAYS TO SPEECH	GLOBE BOOK COMPANY, INC.	<5
S	FLASH	PICTURE COMMUNICATION CARDS	COMMUNICATION SKILL BUILDERS,INC	11-20
S	FLASH	WHAT'S THE SOLUTION?	COMMUNICATION SKILL BUILDERS,INC	11-20
S	MULTIM	NONVERBAL COMMUNICATION & INTERACTION	LANSFORD PUBLISHING COMPANY	151-200
S	TRANSP	NONVERBAL COMMUNICATION	LANSFORD PUBLISHING COMPANY	151-200
S	TRANSP	BODY LANGUAGE	LANSFORD PUBLISHING COMPANY	101-150

4 - SKILL: ORAL LANGUAGE WORD VOCABULARY

LEVEL	FORMAT	TITLE	PUBLISHER	$PRICE
R	CHART	STORY BOARDS	CHILDCRAFT EDUCATION CORPORATION	21-30
R	GAME	BODY PARTS CARDS & GAMEBOARD	COMMUNICATION SKILL BUILDERS,INC	11-20
R	GUIDE	COLOR RECOGNITION	COMMUNICATION SKILL BUILDERS,INC	6-10
R	MULTIU	PEABODY EARLY EXPERIENCES KIT	AMERICAN GUIDANCE SERVICE, INC.	201-300
R	PUPILB	LADYBIRD BOOK: ANIMALS	IDEAL SCHOOL SUPPLY COMPANY	<5
R	PUPILB	LADYBIRD BOOK: HOME	IDEAL SCHOOL SUPPLY COMPANY	<5
R	PUPILB	LADYBIRD BOOK: THE BEACH	IDEAL SCHOOL SUPPLY COMPANY	<5
R	PUPILB	LADYBIRD BOOK: SHOPPING	IDEAL SCHOOL SUPPLY COMPANY	<5
R	PUPILB	LADYBIRD BOOK: BABY	IDEAL SCHOOL SUPPLY COMPANY	<5
R	PUPILB	LADYBIRD BOOK: CLOTHES	IDEAL SCHOOL SUPPLY COMPANY	<5
R	PUPILB	LADYBIRD BOOK: THE PARK	IDEAL SCHOOL SUPPLY COMPANY	<5
R	PUPILB	LADYBIRD BOOK: GARDENS	IDEAL SCHOOL SUPPLY COMPANY	<5
R	PUPILB	LADYBIRD BOOK: STARTING SCHOOL	IDEAL SCHOOL SUPPLY COMPANY	<5
R	PUPILB	LADYBIRD BOOK: HOLIDAYS	IDEAL SCHOOL SUPPLY COMPANY	<5
R	PUPILB	LADYBIRD BOOK: BEDTIME	IDEAL SCHOOL SUPPLY COMPANY	<5
R	VISKIT	CREATIVE READING PROGRAM I	HARPER & ROW PUBLISHERS, INC.	101-150
R	VISKIT	READY STEPS	HOUGHTON MIFFLIN COMPANY	151-200
RP	ACTCRD	KINDERGARTEN KEYS: LANGUAGE DEVELOPMENT CARDS, GROUP A	ECONOMY COMPANY	76-100
RP	ACTCRD	KINDERGARTEN KEYS: LANGUAGE DEVELOPMENT CARDS, GROUP B	ECONOMY COMPANY	31-50
RP	ACTCRD	LEARNING ACTIVITY CARDS FOR CHILDREN	LOVE PUBLISHING COMPANY	6-10
RP	ACTCRD	CREEPING RUG CARD PROGRAMS: ALPHABET-LANGUAGE DEVELOPMENT	MOSIER MATERIALS	21-30
RP	AUDKIT	WORDWORLD	ECONOMY COMPANY	101-150
RP	AUDKIT	KIT 23: READING READINESS STORY STARTERS	EDUCATIONAL RESEARCH, INC.	101-150
RP	A/VKIT	IMPROVING COMMUNICATION SKILLS THROUGH SPEECH CORRECTION	EYE GATE MEDIA	76-100
RP	A/VKIT	LEARNING TO LEARN SERIES, SET 1	EDL/MCGRAW-HILL	51-75
RP	A/VKIT	LEARNING TO LEARN SERIES, SET 2	EDL/MCGRAW-HILL	76-100
RP	CHART	NAMING NAMES	IDEAL SCHOOL SUPPLY COMPANY	<5
RP	CHART	NAMING ACTIONS	IDEAL SCHOOL SUPPLY COMPANY	<5
RP	CHART	LANGUAGE ASSOCIATION BOARD NO. 1	MODERN EDUCATION CORPORATION	11-20
RP	CHART	LANGUAGE ASSOCIATION BOARD NO. 2	MODERN EDUCATION CORPORATION	11-20
RP	CHART	LANGUAGE ASSOCIATION BOARD NO. 3	MODERN EDUCATION CORPORATION	11-20
RP	CHART	STORY BOARDS	HOUGHTON MIFFLIN COMPANY	11-20
RP	CL SET	CREATING WORD PICTURES	COMENIUS, INC.	76-100
RP	CL SET	BREAKTHROUGH TO LITERACY	BOWMAR/NOBLE PUBLISHERS, INC.	201-300
RP	DITTO	LANGUAGE STIMULATION: VERBS	MODERN EDUCATION CORPORATION	6-10
RP	DITTO	LANGUAGE STIMULATION: ADJECTIVES	MODERN EDUCATION CORPORATION	6-10
RP	DITTO	LANGUAGE STIMULATION: NOUNS, ANIMALS & INSECTS	MODERN EDUCATION CORPORATION	6-10
RP	DITTO	LANGUAGE STIMULATION: NOUNS, FOOD	MODERN EDUCATION CORPORATION	6-10
RP	DITTO	LANGUAGE STIMULATION: NOUNS, HOUSEHOLD ITEMS	MODERN EDUCATION CORPORATION	6-10
RP	FLNLBD	ANIMAL CUT-OUTS	CREATIVE STORYTIME PRESS	<5
RP	FLNLBD	OLIVE THE OSTRICH	CREATIVE STORYTIME PRESS	<5
RP	GAME	PICTURE CARD GAMES, SET I	MILTON BRADLEY/PLAYSKOOL	6-10
RP	GAME	PLAY SCENES LOTTO	MILTON BRADLEY/PLAYSKOOL	<5
RP	GUIDE	EMERGING LANGUAGE 2	COMMUNICATION SKILL BUILDERS,INC	6-10
RP	GUIDE	FUNTACTICS: MOVEMENT & SPEECH ACTIVITIES FOR YOUNG CHILDREN	FEARON PITMAN PUBLISHERS, INC.	<5

LEVEL	FORMAT	TITLE	PUBLISHER	NT	$PRICE

4 - SKILL: ORAL LANGUAGE WORD VOCABULARY

LEVEL	FORMAT	TITLE	PUBLISHER	NT	$PRICE
RP	GUIDE	101 LANGUAGE ARTS ACTIVITIES	COMMUNICATION SKILL BUILDERS, INC		6-10
RP	MANIPU	CHATTERBOARDS: ANIMALS	IDEAL SCHOOL SUPPLY COMPANY		6-10
RP	MANIPU	CHATTERBOARDS: TOYS	IDEAL SCHOOL SUPPLY COMPANY		6-10
RP	MANIPU	IDENTIFICATION PUZZLES	MODERN EDUCATION CORPORATION		21-30
RP	MULTIU	ALPHA TIME PRE-READING PROGRAM	ARISTA CORPORATION		201-300
RP	MULTIU	ALPHA PHONICS PROGRAM	ARISTA CORPORATION		201-300
RP	MULTIU	PEABODY LANGUAGE DEVELOPMENT KIT, LEVEL #P	AMERICAN GUIDANCE SERVICE, INC.		201-300
RP	MULTIU	PEABODY LANGUAGE DEVELOPMENT KIT, LEVEL #1	AMERICAN GUIDANCE SERVICE, INC.		76-100
RP	OLFACT	USE YOUR SENSES	COMMUNICATION SKILL BUILDERS, INC		31-50
RP	PICTUR	LANGUAGE VISUALS	COMMUNICATION SKILL BUILDERS, INC		31-50
RP	PICTUR	IDENTIFICATION CARDS	MODERN EDUCATION CORPORATION		11-20
RP	PICTUR	PROBLEM SOLVING CARDS, SET 1: S SOUND	MODERN EDUCATION CORPORATION		11-20
RP	PICTUR	PROBLEM SOLVING CARDS, SET 2: R SOUND	MODERN EDUCATION CORPORATION		11-20
RP	PUPILB	FUN SOUNDS (RL K-3)	BENEFIC PRESS		<5
RP	PUPILB	GAY SOUNDS (RL K-3)	BENEFIC PRESS		<5
RP	REFBK	NATURAL LANGUAGE	COMMUNICATION SKILL BUILDERS, INC		<5
RP	SKLKIT	SWEET PICKLES READING READINESS PROGRAM	BFA EDUCATIONAL MEDIA		101-150
RPI	GAME	GAMES & MORE GAMES KIDS LIKE	COMMUNICATION SKILL BUILDERS, INC		11-20
RPIJ	GUIDE	TEACHING SPEECH TO A NONVERBAL CHILD	H & H ENTERPRISES, INC.		<5
RPIJ	GUIDE	TEACHING A CHILD TO IMITATE	H & H ENTERPRISES, INC.		<5
RPIJ	REFBK	FUNCTIONAL SPEECH & LANGUAGE TRAINING	H & H ENTERPRISES, INC.		31-50
RPIJS	REFBK	30,000 SELECTED WORDS ORGANIZED BY LETTER, SOUND & SYLLABLE	COMMUNICATION SKILL BUILDERS, INC		11-20
RPIJS	SKLKIT	NON-SLIP KIT	H & H ENTERPRISES, INC.		201-300
P	ACTCRD	CAREER AWARENESS STICKERS	COMMUNICATION SKILL BUILDERS, INC		6-10
P	ACTCRD	ACTION CARDS, SET 1	LAKESHORE CURRICULUM MATERIALS		6-10
P	ACTCRD	ACTION CARDS, SET 2	LAKESHORE CURRICULUM MATERIALS		6-10
P	ACTCRD	ACTION CARDS, SET 3	LAKESHORE CURRICULUM MATERIALS		6-10
P	ACTCRD	SENTENCE-BUILDING SEQUENTIAL CARDS	DEVELOPMENTAL LEARNING MATERIALS		<5
P	ACTCRD	PICTURE CARDS	MILTON BRADLEY/PLAYSKOOL		6-10
P	ACTCRD	VEGETABLES & FRUITS POSTER CARDS	MILTON BRADLEY/PLAYSKOOL		6-10
P	AUDKIT	BASIC COMMUNICATION SKILLS	LEARNING TREE FILMSTRIPS		51-75
P	DITTO	EARLY WORDS	MILTON BRADLEY/PLAYSKOOL		<5
P	FLNLBD	ORAL LANGUAGE SKILLS THROUGH "BRAVE THE DRAGON"	LESWING PRESS		6-10
P	GAME	ANIMALS CAN TEACH	COMMUNICATION SKILL BUILDERS, INC		6-10
P	GUIDE	ORAL LANGUAGE CONTINUUM CHECKLIST	CHILD FOCUS COMPANY		11-20
P	MANIPU	MIX & MATCH MONSTER PUZZLES	DEVELOPMENTAL LEARNING MATERIALS		6-10
P	MULTIU	ALPHA ONE	ARISTA CORPORATION		>450
P	MULTIU	ALPHA TIME PLUS	ARISTA CORPORATION		151-200
P	MULTIU	PEABODY LANGUAGE DEVELOPMENT KIT, LEVEL #2	AMERICAN GUIDANCE SERVICE, INC.		101-150
P	MULTIU	PEABODY LANGUAGE DEVELOPMENT KIT, LEVEL #3	AMERICAN GUIDANCE SERVICE, INC.		76-100
P	MULTIU	ORAL LANGUAGE EXPANSION	EDUCATIONAL ACTIVITIES, INC.		101-150
P	MULTIM	LET'S TALK WITH WINNIE THE POOH	WALT DISNEY EDUCATIONAL MEDIA		101-150
P	PICTUR	WHAT'S WRONG HERE?, LEVEL 1	TEACHING RESOURCES CORPORATION		6-10
P	PICTUR	LOOK-LISTEN-SAY STORY CARDS	AEVAC, INC.		11-20
P	PICTUR	WHAT'S GOING ON?	LEARNING STUFF		6-10
P	PUPILB	HAPPY SOUNDS (RL 1-3)	BENEFIC PRESS		<5
P	PUPILB	GLAD SOUNDS (RL 1-3)	BENEFIC PRESS		<5
P	PUPILB	SAY & HEAR (RL 1-3)	BENEFIC PRESS		<5
P	RECORD	WITCH'S BREW	EDUCATIONAL ACTIVITIES, INC.		6-10
P	VISKIT	CREATIVE READING PROGRAM II	HARPER & ROW PUBLISHERS, INC.		101-150
P	VISKIT	CREATIVE READING PROGRAM III	HARPER & ROW PUBLISHERS, INC.		101-150
P	VISKIT	CREATIVE READING PROGRAM IV	HARPER & ROW PUBLISHERS, INC.		101-150
P	WKBOOK	TALK ABOUT IT	ST. JOHN SCHOOL FOR THE DEAF		<5
P	WKBOOK	LAUGH & LEARN WITH JACK & JULIE	ST. JOHN SCHOOL FOR THE DEAF		<5
PI	ACTCRD	BOOK REPORTING	FRANK SCHAFFER PUBLICATIONS, INC		<5
PI	ACTCRD	SEE HOW YOU FEEL	LAKESHORE CURRICULUM MATERIALS		11-20
PI	CHART	CARTOON STORY STARTERS	CREATIVE TEACHING ASSOCIATES		<5
PI	CHART	CARTOON BOARDS	MODERN EDUCATION CORPORATION		11-20
PI	CHART	CARTOON BOARD POSTERS	MODERN EDUCATION CORPORATION		11-20
PI	CL SET	ORAL READING & LINGUISTICS PROGRAM (RL 1-6)	BENEFIC PRESS	8	11-20
PI	DITTO	FAR OUT STORY STARTERS	CREATIVE TEACHING ASSOCIATES		<5
PI	GAME	ARE YOU LISTENING?	JUDY COMPANY		6-10
PI	GAME	SOUND DOMINO GAME	JUDY COMPANY		6-10
PI	GAME	SPIN-A-WORD	JUDY COMPANY		6-10
PI	GAME	SPEECH LINGO	MODERN EDUCATION CORPORATION		11-20
PI	GAME	PS: PREFIX-SUFFIX LANGUAGE-BUILDING GAME	COMMUNICATION SKILL BUILDERS, INC		6-10
PI	MANIPU	POPEYE'S SPECIAL LANGUAGE BUILDER: BALLOON PUZZLES (SP.ED.)	KING FEATURES		11-20
PI	MANIPU	POPEYE'S SPECIAL LANGUAGE BUILDER: STORY BUILDERS (SP.ED.)	KING FEATURES		21-30
PI	MULTIU	W L N K J C G V Q Y Z X KIT	LESWING PRESS		31-50
PI	MULTIU	LARC (LANGUAGE ARTS RESOURCE CENTER) PROGRAM	ARISTA CORPORATION	5	>450
PI	MULTIM	UNDERSTANDING WHAT WE READ, LEVEL A	NYSTROM		151-200
PI	MULTIM	ALICE IN COMMUNICATION LAND	WALT DISNEY EDUCATIONAL MEDIA		76-100
PI	PICTUR	TELL-A-TALE CARDS, SET 1	TEACHING RESOURCES CORPORATION		6-10
PI	PICTUR	TELL-A-TALE CARDS, SET 2	TEACHING RESOURCES CORPORATION		6-10
PI	PICTUR	LAC CARDS, SET 1: VERBS, SPORTS IN ACTION	MODERN EDUCATION CORPORATION		11-20
PI	PICTUR	LAC CARDS, SET 2: GENERAL VERBS	MODERN EDUCATION CORPORATION		11-20
PI	PICTUR	STIMULATION CARDS, SET 2: R SOUND	MODERN EDUCATION CORPORATION		6-10
PI	PICTUR	STIMULATION CARDS, SET 3: TH SOUND	MODERN EDUCATION CORPORATION		6-10
PI	PICTUR	STIMULATION CARDS, SET 4: L SOUND	MODERN EDUCATION CORPORATION		6-10

LEVEL	FORMAT	TITLE	PUBLISHER	NT	$PRICE

4 - SKILL: ORAL LANGUAGE WORD VOCABULARY

LEVEL	FORMAT	TITLE	PUBLISHER	NT	$PRICE
PI	PICTUR	STIMULATION CARDS, SET 5: SH SOUND	MODERN EDUCATION CORPORATION		6-10
PI	PICTUR	STIMULATION CARDS, SET 6: K SOUND	MODERN EDUCATION CORPORATION		6-10
PI	PICTUR	STIMULATION CARDS, SET 7: G SOUND	MODERN EDUCATION CORPORATION		6-10
PI	PICTUR	STIMULATION CARDS, SET 8: CH SOUND	MODERN EDUCATION CORPORATION		6-10
PI	PICTUR	STIMULATION CARDS, SET 9: Z SOUND	MODERN EDUCATION CORPORATION		6-10
PI	SKLKIT	EDMARK READING PROGRAM (FOR NONREADERS)	EDMARK ASSOCIATES		301-400
PI	SND FS	AN ADVENTURE IN OPEN EDUCATION	EDUCATIONAL ENRICHMENT MATERIALS		31-50
PI	WKBOOK	CONCEPT UNDERSTANDING PROGRAM: VOCABULARY OF DIRECTIONS	PAUL S. AMIDON & ASSOC., INC.		11-20
PIJ	ACTCRD	REBUS GLOSSARY CARDS	AMERICAN GUIDANCE SERVICE, INC.		51-75
PIJ	AUDKIT	SPEAK OUT!	MAFEX ASSOCIATES, INC.		N/A
PIJ	DITTO	PORTFOLIO OF RUB-ON REBUSES	AMERICAN GUIDANCE SERVICE, INC.		11-20
PIJ	FLASH	SEE IT, SAY IT	ADDISON-WESLEY PUBLISHING CO.		31-50
PIJ	FLASH	PHOTO RESOURCE KIT	MODERN EDUCATION CORPORATION		31-50
PIJ	PICTUR	PICTURES FOR SOUNDS	TEACHING RESOURCES CORPORATION		31-50
PIJ	REFBK	STANDARD REBUS GLOSSARY	AMERICAN GUIDANCE SERVICE, INC.		<5
PIJ	SKLKIT	ON LOCATION WITH LANGUAGE	XEROX EDUCATION PUBLICATIONS		201-300
PIJS	FLASH	LINES 'N DOTS CARD GAME	COMMUNICATION SKILL BUILDERS, INC		11-20
PIJS	MULTIU	COMMUNICATIVE COMPETENCE	COMMUNICATION SKILL BUILDERS, INC		201-300
PIJS	REFBK	LANGUAGE REMEDIATION & EXPANSION	COMMUNICATION SKILL BUILDERS, INC		11-20
I	ACTCRD	WRITTEN LANGUAGE CARDS, GENERAL	DEVELOPMENTAL LEARNING MATERIALS		6-10
I	A/VKIT	LET'S COMMUNICATE	BARR FILMS		76-100
I	PUPILB	LOUD & CLEAR (RL 4-6)	BENEFIC PRESS		<5
I	PUPILB	HEAR YE! HEAR YE! (RL 4-6)	BENEFIC PRESS		<5
I	PUPILB	NOW HEAR THIS (RL 4-6)	BENEFIC PRESS		<5
IJ	A/VKIT	WHY DON'T PEOPLE SAY WHAT THEY MEAN?	BARR FILMS		76-100
IJ	A/VKIT	LEARNING COMMUNICATION SKILLS	BARR FILMS	5	201-300
IJ	A/VKIT	LET'S TALK ABOUT FAMILIES	BARR FILMS		51-75
IJ	A/VKIT	LET'S TALK ABOUT RULES	BARR FILMS		51-75
IJ	A/VKIT	LET'S TALK ABOUT LEARNING	BARR FILMS		51-75
IJ	A/VKIT	LET'S TALK ABOUT MAKING FRIENDS	BARR FILMS		51-75
IJ	CL SET	SEMANTICS	CHANNING L. BETE COMPANY, INC.		76-100
IJ	FILMST	ENGLISH COMES ALIVE: ADVENTURES IN COMMUNICATION	UNITED LEARNING		31-50
IJ	FILMST	ENGLISH COMES ALIVE SERIES	UNITED LEARNING	6	151-200
IJ	MULTIM	COMMUNICATION POWER SERIES	UNITED LEARNING	5	201-300
IJ	MULTIM	COMMUNICATION POWER SERIES: ORAL COMMUNICATION	UNITED LEARNING		51-75
IJ	PICTUR	WHAT'S WRONG HERE?, LEVEL 2	TEACHING RESOURCES CORPORATION		6-10
IJ	WKBOOK	SEMANTICS	CHANNING L. BETE COMPANY, INC.		<5
IJS	GAME	SCARECROW CARD GAME	COMMUNICATION SKILL BUILDERS, INC		11-20
IJS	GUIDE	KALEIDOSCOPE	TEACHING RESOURCES CORPORATION		11-20
IJS	MULTIU	PUZZLERS	LESWING PRESS		11-20
IJS	MULTIU	PUZZLES & SUCH	LESWING PRESS		6-10
IJS	PICTUR	WHAT'S HAPPENING?	TEACHING RESOURCES CORPORATION		6-10
J	MULTIM	COMMUNICATION: PROBLEMS APPROACH	PAUL S. AMIDON & ASSOC., INC.		76-100
JS	AUDCAS	VOICE, VOCABULARY DELIVERY	ASSOCIATED EDUCATIONAL MATERIALS		21-30
JS	AUDCAS	POWER OF WORDS	EBSCO CURRICULUM MATERIALS		6-10
JS	AUDCAS	SPEECH: AN IMPORTANT SKILL AUDIO PACK (RL 4-6)	BENEFIC PRESS		21-30
JS	A/VKIT	COMMUNICATION SKILLS (ORAL)	INTERPRETIVE EDUCATION		31-50
JS	CL SET	PLAN: LITERATURE, LANGUAGE & COMMUNICATION	WESTINGHOUSE LEARNING CORP.		101-150
JS	DITTO	WRITE-ON WORKSHEETS AA	EDL/MCGRAW-HILL		21-30
JS	DITTO	WRITE-ON WORKSHEETS BA	EDL/MCGRAW-HILL		21-30
JS	DITTO	WRITE-ON WORKSHEETS CA	EDL/MCGRAW-HILL		21-30
JS	PICTUR	40-FOURS, SET 1: S SOUND	MODERN EDUCATION CORPORATION		11-20
JS	PICTUR	40-FOURS, SET 2: R SOUND	MODERN EDUCATION CORPORATION		11-20
JS	PUPILB	SPEAKING BY DOING	NATIONAL TEXTBOOK COMPANY		<5
JS	PUPILB	PATHWAYS TO SPEECH	GLOBE BOOK COMPANY, INC.		<5
JS	TEXTBK	SPEECH & PUBLIC SPEAKING: COMMUNICATION GAMES	MACMILLAN PUBLISHING CO., INC.		<5
S	AUDCAS	COMMUNICATIONS: THE BUSINESS OF ORAL COMMUNICATIN	SOUTH-WESTERN PUBLISHING CO.		201-300
S	GUIDE	COMMUNICATION: INTERACTING THROUGH SPEECH	CHARLES E. MERRILL PUBLISHING CO		<5
S	TEXTBK	WORD STUDIES	SOUTH-WESTERN PUBLISHING CO.		6-10
S	TEXTBK	COMMUNICATION: INTERACTING THROUGH SPEECH	CHARLES E. MERRILL PUBLISHING CO		6-10

5 - SKILL: ARTICULATION

LEVEL	FORMAT	TITLE	PUBLISHER	NT	$PRICE
R	AUDCAS	SPEECH THERAPY WITH BEGINNING SOUNDS	MEDIA MARKETING, INC.		51-75
R	GUIDE	THE COMMUNICATION SCREEN	COMMUNICATION SKILL BUILDERS, INC		6-10
R	MULTIU	SMALL WONDER	AMERICAN GUIDANCE SERVICE, INC.		51-75
RP	ACTCRD	FORM-A-SOUND	IDEAL SCHOOL SUPPLY COMPANY		11-20
RP	ACTCRD	WORD MAKING CARDS	WORD MAKING PRODUCTIONS, INC.		31-50
RP	AUDKIT	SPACETALK	ECONOMY COMPANY		151-200
RP	A/VKIT	IMPROVING COMMUNICATION SKILLS THROUGH SPEECH CORRECTION	EYE GATE MEDIA		76-100
RP	CL SET	LEARNING LANGUAGE SKILLS 1	AEVAC, INC.		51-75
RP	CL SET	LEARNING LANGUAGE SKILLS 2	AEVAC, INC.		51-75
RP	FLASH	DESCRIPTO CARDS	COMMUNICATION SKILL BUILDERS, INC		11-20
RP	FLASH	PEABODY ARTICULATION DECKS	AMERICAN GUIDANCE SERVICE, INC.	10	31-50
RP	FLASH	PEABODY ARTICULATION DECKS: DECK 1, (B-M-P)	AMERICAN GUIDANCE SERVICE, INC.		<5
RP	FLASH	PEABODY ARTICULATION DECKS: DECK 2, (CH-SH)	AMERICAN GUIDANCE SERVICE, INC.		<5
RP	FLASH	PEABODY ARTICULATION DECKS: DECK 3, (F-V)	AMERICAN GUIDANCE SERVICE, INC.		<5
RP	FLASH	PEABODY ARTICULATION DECKS: DECK 4, (G,K)	AMERICAN GUIDANCE SERVICE, INC.		<5
RP	FLASH	PEABODY ARTICULATION DECKS: DECK 5, (L)	AMERICAN GUIDANCE SERVICE, INC.		<5
RP	FLASH	PEABODY ARTICULATION DECKS: DECK 6, (R)	AMERICAN GUIDANCE SERVICE, INC.		<5

LEVEL	FORMAT	TITLE	PUBLISHER	NT	$PRICE

5 - SKILL: ARTICULATION

LEVEL	FORMAT	TITLE	PUBLISHER	$PRICE
RP	FLASH	PEABODY ARTICULATION DECKS: DECK 7, (S)	AMERICAN GUIDANCE SERVICE, INC.	<5
RP	FLASH	PEABODY ARTICULATION DECKS: DECK 8, (TH)	AMERICAN GUIDANCE SERVICE, INC.	<5
RP	FLASH	PEABODY ARTICULATION DECKS: DECK 9, (Z)	AMERICAN GUIDANCE SERVICE, INC.	<5
RP	FLASH	PEABODY ARTICULATION DECKS: DECK 10, (L-R-S BLENDS)	AMERICAN GUIDANCE SERVICE, INC.	<5
RP	GAME	GAMEBOARDS FOR SPEECH & LANGUAGE DEVELOPMENT	COMMUNICATION SKILL BUILDERS,INC	31-50
RP	GUIDE	SUGGESTIONS FOR TEACHING LANGUAGE SKILLS	WORD MAKING PRODUCTIONS, INC.	6-10
RP	PICTUR	PROBLEM SOLVING CARDS, SET 1: S SOUND	MODERN EDUCATION CORPORATION	11-20
RP	PICTUR	PROBLEM SOLVING CARDS, SET 2: R SOUND	MODERN EDUCATION CORPORATION	11-20
RP	PROFMA	ACTION PHOTOS	IDEAS	11-20
RP	PUPILB	MORE PROGRAMMED ARTICULATION SKILLS CARRYOVER STORIES	COMMUNICATION SKILL BUILDERS,INC	11-20
RP	PUPILB	PROGRAMMED ARTICULATION SKILLS CARRYOVER STORIES	COMMUNICATION SKILL BUILDERS,INC	11-20
RP	PUPILB	SEQUENCE PICTURES FOR STORY TELLING	WHITEHAVEN PUBLISHING COMPANY	11-20
RP	SKLKIT	GOLDMAN-LYNCH SOUNDS & SYMBOLS DEVELOPMENT KIT	AMERICAN GUIDANCE SERVICE, INC.	151-200
RP	VISKIT	PATTERNS	C.C. PUBLICATIONS, INC.	31-50
RPI	ACTCRD	PEEL & PUT: SIBILANT PHONEMES	COMMUNICATION SKILL BUILDERS,INC	11-20
RPI	ACTCRD	PEEL & PUT: DIALECTAL PHONEMES	COMMUNICATION SKILL BUILDERS,INC	11-20
RPI	GAME	GAMES & MORE GAMES KIDS LIKE	COMMUNICATION SKILL BUILDERS,INC	11-20
RPI	GUIDE	STIMULUS SHIFT ARTICULATION KIT	IDEAS	11-20
RPI	GUIDE	ARTICULATION MODIFICATION /1/ AMP	C.C. PUBLICATIONS, INC.	21-30
RPI	GUIDE	ARTICULATION MODIFICATION /S/ /Z/ AMP	C.C. PUBLICATIONS, INC.	21-30
RPI	GUIDE	ARTICULATION MODIFICATION /S/ AMP	C.C. PUBLICATIONS, INC.	21-30
RPI	GUIDE	ARTICULATION MODIFICATION /TS/ /D3/ AMP	C.C. PUBLICATIONS, INC.	21-30
RPI	GUIDE	ARTICULATION MODIFICATION /E/ /A/ AMP	C.C. PUBLICATIONS, INC.	21-30
RPI	MULTIU	PEEL & PUT (SPEECH THERAPY & LANGUAGE DEVELOPMENT)	COMMUNICATION SKILL BUILDERS,INC	51-75
RPI	MULTIU	B T M P D R H S F KIT	LESWING PRESS	31-50
RPI	PICTUR	WHAT'S FUNNY CARDS	MODERN EDUCATION CORPORATION	11-20
RPI	VISKIT	PROGRAMMED ARTICULATION CONTROL KIT	IDEAS	11-20
RPIJ	EQUIPM	TOK-BACK	INCENTIVES FOR LEARNING, INC.	6-10
RPIJ	GUIDE	TEACHING SPEECH TO A NONVERBAL CHILD	H & H ENTERPRISES, INC.	<5
RPIJ	GUIDE	TEACHING A CHILD TO IMITATE	H & H ENTERPRISES, INC.	<5
RPIJ	REFBK	FUNCTIONAL SPEECH & LANGUAGE TRAINING	H & H ENTERPRISES, INC.	31-50
RPIJ	VISKIT	MULTIPLE PHONEME APPROACH	IDEAS	11-20
RPIJS	CHART	TONGUE POSITION CHARTS	COMMUNICATION SKILL BUILDERS,INC	6-10
RPIJS	REFBK	30,000 SELECTED WORDS ORGANIZED BY LETTER, SOUND & SYLLABLE	COMMUNICATION SKILL BUILDERS,INC	11-20
RPIJS	SKLKIT	NON-SLIP KIT	H & H ENTERPRISES, INC.	201-300
P	ACTCRD	HAPPY BIRTHDAY CARDS	WORD MAKING PRODUCTIONS, INC.	<5
P	ACTCRD	LANGUAGE MAKING ACTION CARDS	WORD MAKING PRODUCTIONS, INC.	31-50
P	AUDKIT	SPEECH THERAPY	EBSCO CURRICULUM MATERIALS	51-75
P	AUDKIT	KIT 30: IMPROVING SPEECH PATTERNS	EDUCATIONAL RESEARCH, INC.	101-150
P	CHART	PICTURE COMPOSITE CHART	SOUND MATERIALS	<5
P	CL SET	LEARNING LANGUAGE SKILLS 3	AEVAC, INC.	51-75
P	CL SET	LEARNING LANGUAGE SKILLS 4	AEVAC, INC.	51-75
P	CL SET	REBUS SOUND-CENTERED PICTURE PUZZLES	WORD MAKING PRODUCTIONS, INC.	11-20
P	DITTO	SPEECH THERAPY WORKBOOKS: S SOUND	MODERN EDUCATION CORPORATION	6-10
P	DITTO	SPEECH THERAPY WORKBOOKS: R SOUND	MODERN EDUCATION CORPORATION	6-10
P	DITTO	SPEECH THERAPY WORKBOOKS: L SOUND	MODERN EDUCATION CORPORATION	6-10
P	DITTO	SPEECH THERAPY WORKBOOKS: TH SOUND	MODERN EDUCATION CORPORATION	6-10
P	DITTO	SPEECH THERAPY WORKBOOKS: CH SOUND	MODERN EDUCATION CORPORATION	6-10
P	DITTO	SPEECH THERAPY WORKBOOKS: SH SOUND	MODERN EDUCATION CORPORATION	6-10
P	DITTO	SPEECH THERAPY WORKBOOKS: K SOUND	MODERN EDUCATION CORPORATION	6-10
P	DITTO	SPEECH THERAPY WORKBOOKS: G SOUND	MODERN EDUCATION CORPORATION	6-10
P	DITTO	SPEECH THERAPY WORKBOOKS: P SOUND	MODERN EDUCATION CORPORATION	6-10
P	DITTO	SPEECH THERAPY WORKBOOKS: B SOUND	MODERN EDUCATION CORPORATION	6-10
P	DITTO	SPEECH THERAPY WORKBOOKS: T SOUND	MODERN EDUCATION CORPORATION	6-10
P	DITTO	SPEECH THERAPY WORKBOOKS: D SOUND	MODERN EDUCATION CORPORATION	6-10
P	DITTO	SPEECH THERAPY WORKBOOKS: F SOUND	MODERN EDUCATION CORPORATION	6-10
P	DITTO	SPEECH THERAPY WORKBOOKS: V SOUND	MODERN EDUCATION CORPORATION	6-10
P	DITTO	SPEECH THERAPY WORKBOOKS: Z SOUND	MODERN EDUCATION CORPORATION	6-10
P	DITTO	SPEECH THERAPY WORKBOOKS: J SOUND	MODERN EDUCATION CORPORATION	6-10
P	DITTO	LISTEN & SPEAK TO READ	HAYES SCHOOL PUBLISHING COMPANY	<5
P	FLASH	PICTURE FLASHCARD SET	SOUND MATERIALS	<5
P	FLASH	PEABODY ARTICULATION CARDS KIT	AMERICAN GUIDANCE SERVICE, INC.	31-50
P	FLNLBD	ORAL LANGUAGE SKILLS THROUGH "BRAVE THE DRAGON"	LESWING PRESS	6-10
P	GAME	SOUND CHECKERS /S/ (SP. ED.)	WHITEHAVEN PUBLISHING COMPANY	<5
P	GAME	SOUND CHECKERS /R/ (SP. ED.)	WHITEHAVEN PUBLISHING COMPANY	<5
P	GAME	SOUND CHECKERS /L/ (SP. ED.)	WHITEHAVEN PUBLISHING COMPANY	<5
P	GAME	SOUND CHECKERS /SH/ (SP. ED.)	WHITEHAVEN PUBLISHING COMPANY	<5
P	GAME	PLAY & SAY, SET A	STANWIX HOUSE, INC.	6-10
P	GAME	PLAY & SAY, SET B	STANWIX HOUSE, INC.	6-10
P	GAME	PLAY & SAY, SET C	STANWIX HOUSE, INC.	6-10
P	GAME	PLAY & SAY, SET D	STANWIX HOUSE, INC.	6-10
P	GUIDE	ORAL LANGUAGE CONTINUUM CHECKLIST	CHILD FOCUS COMPANY	11-20
P	GUIDE	SPEECH FUN WITH A CHALKBOARD (SP. ED.)	WHITEHAVEN PUBLISHING COMPANY	<5
P	MANIPU	BLOCK BASICS	WORD MAKING PRODUCTIONS, INC.	6-10
P	MANIPU	TOK-BACH	DEVELOPMENTAL LEARNING MATERIALS	N/A
P	PICTUR	PICTURE COMPOSITE	SOUND MATERIALS	6-10
P	PICTUR	ARTICK CARDS, SET 1: S SOUND	MODERN EDUCATION CORPORATION	11-20
P	PICTUR	ARTICK CARDS, SET 2: R SOUND	MODERN EDUCATION CORPORATION	11-20
P	PUPILB	READ-THE-PICTURE STORYBOOKS	WORD MAKING PRODUCTIONS, INC.	21-30

LEVEL	FORMAT	TITLE	PUBLISHER	NT $PRICE

5 - SKILL: ARTICULATION

LEVEL	FORMAT	TITLE	PUBLISHER	NT $PRICE
P	PUPILB	SNOOPY SNAKE & OTHER STORIES	WORD MAKING PRODUCTIONS, INC.	6-10
P	SKLKIT	KING LOUIE HOLIDAY STORIES FOR SPEECH & LANG. REMEDIATION	COMMUNICATION SKILL BUILDERS, INC	31-50
P	SND FS	LEARNING SPEECH SOUNDS, SET 1	AEVAC, INC.	51-75
P	SND FS	LEARNING SPEECH SOUNDS, SET 2	AEVAC, INC.	51-75
P	SND FS	LEARNING SPEECH SOUNDS, SET 3	AEVAC, INC.	51-75
P	TEXTBK	HANDBOOK FOR SPEECH THERAPY	WORD MAKING PRODUCTIONS, INC.	11-20
P	WKBOOK	WORD LISTS	SOUND MATERIALS	6-10
P	WKBOOK	MERRY CHRISTMAS CARDS	WORD MAKING PRODUCTIONS, INC.	<5
P	WKBOOK	MORE SEQUENCE PICTURES FOR STORY TELLING	WHITEHAVEN PUBLISHING COMPANY	11-20
P	WKBOOK	MY SOUND BOOK: S	STANWIX HOUSE, INC.	<5
P	WKBOOK	MY SOUND BOOK: R	STANWIX HOUSE, INC.	<5
P	WKBOOK	MY SOUND BOOK: TH	STANWIX HOUSE, INC.	<5
P	WKBOOK	MY SOUND BOOK: L	STANWIX HOUSE, INC.	<5
P	WKBOOK	MY SOUND BOOK: K	STANWIX HOUSE, INC.	<5
P	WKBOOK	MY SOUND BOOK: G	STANWIX HOUSE, INC.	<5
P	WKBOOK	MY SOUND BOOK: SH	STANWIX HOUSE, INC.	<5
PI	ACTCRD	WORD FAMILIES	TEACHING RESOURCES CORPORATION	31-50
PI	ACTCRD	DI-TRI BLENDER	ACADEMIC THERAPY PUBLICATIONS	6-10
PI	ACTCRD	LANGUAGE: VERB ACTION PICTURES	WHITEHAVEN PUBLISHING COMPANY	11-20
PI	ACTCRD	LANGUAGE: PLURAL ACTION PICTURES	WHITEHAVEN PUBLISHING COMPANY	11-20
PI	DITTO	ASSIST ONE & TWO & THREE	COMMUNICATION SKILL BUILDERS, INC	11-20
PI	DITTO	STAR TRAILS /r/-/s/-/l/-/th/-/sh/-/ch/	COMMUNICATION SKILL BUILDERS, INC	11-20
PI	FILMST	IMPROVING COMMUNICATION SKILLS THROUGH SPEECH CORRECTION	EYE GATE MEDIA	76-100
PI	GAME	TALK & TURN	COMMUNICATION SKILL BUILDERS, INC	11-20
PI	GAME	CHECKER GAME BOOK NO. 1 /S/ SOUND	WHITEHAVEN PUBLISHING COMPANY	<5
PI	GAME	CHECKER GAME BOOK NO. 2 /S/ SOUND	WHITEHAVEN PUBLISHING COMPANY	<5
PI	GAME	STUCK NO. 1 (SP. ED.)	WHITEHAVEN PUBLISHING COMPANY	<5
PI	GAME	STUCK NO. 2 (SP. ED.)	WHITEHAVEN PUBLISHING COMPANY	<5
PI	GAME	SOUND WHEEL (SP. ED.)	WHITEHAVEN PUBLISHING COMPANY	11-20
PI	GAME	SPEAKEASY /S/ (SP. ED.)	WHITEHAVEN PUBLISHING COMPANY	<5
PI	GAME	CONFUSION, SET 1	WHITEHAVEN PUBLISHING COMPANY	<5
PI	GAME	CONFUSION, SET 2	WHITEHAVEN PUBLISHING COMPANY	<5
PI	GAME	CONFUSION, SET 3	WHITEHAVEN PUBLISHING COMPANY	<5
PI	GAME	INSTEAD, SET 1	WHITEHAVEN PUBLISHING COMPANY	<5
PI	GAME	INSTEAD, SET 2	WHITEHAVEN PUBLISHING COMPANY	<5
PI	GAME	INSTEAD, SET 3	WHITEHAVEN PUBLISHING COMPANY	<5
PI	GAME	MOTIVATIONAL CARD GAMES /s/-/r/-/l/	COMMUNICATION SKILL BUILDERS, INC	11-20
PI	GUIDE	TO THE STUTTER	SPEECH FOUNDATION OF AMERICA	<5
PI	GUIDE	IF YOUR CHILD STUTTERS	SPEECH FOUNDATION OF AMERICA	<5
PI	GUIDE	THERAPY FOR STUTTERS	SPEECH FOUNDATION OF AMERICA	<5
PI	GUIDE	SELF-THERAPY FOR THE STUTTER	SPEECH FOUNDATION OF AMERICA	<5
PI	GUIDE	PHONEME BASELINE RECORDING FORMS	COMMUNICATION SKILL BUILDERS, INC	11-20
PI	MULTIU	W L N K J C G V Q Y Z X KIT	LESWING PRESS	31-50
PI	MULTIM	UNDERSTANDING WHAT WE READ, LEVEL A	NYSTROM	151-200
PI	PERIOD	STUTTERING WORDS	SPEECH FOUNDATION OF AMERICA	<5
PI	PICTUR	FREQUENT ERROR PAIRS	COMMUNICATION SKILL BUILDERS, INC	31-50
PI	PICTUR	STIMULATION CARDS, SET 1: S SOUND	MODERN EDUCATION CORPORATION	6-10
PI	PICTUR	STIMULATION CARDS, SET 2: R SOUND	MODERN EDUCATION CORPORATION	6-10
PI	PICTUR	STIMULATION CARDS, SET 3: TH SOUND	MODERN EDUCATION CORPORATION	6-10
PI	PICTUR	STIMULATION CARDS, SET 4: L SOUND	MODERN EDUCATION CORPORATION	6-10
PI	PICTUR	STIMULATION CARDS, SET 5: SH SOUND	MODERN EDUCATION CORPORATION	6-10
PI	PICTUR	STIMULATION CARDS, SET 6: K SOUND	MODERN EDUCATION CORPORATION	6-10
PI	PICTUR	STIMULATION CARDS, SET 7: G SOUND	MODERN EDUCATION CORPORATION	6-10
PI	PICTUR	STIMULATION CARDS, SET 8: CH SOUND	MODERN EDUCATION CORPORATION	6-10
PI	PICTUR	STIMULATION CARDS, SET 9: Z SOUND	MODERN EDUCATION CORPORATION	6-10
PI	PROFMA	PERSONALIZED FLUENCY CONTROL THERAPY	TEACHING RESOURCES CORPORATION	51-75
PI	PROFMA	TONGUE THRUST THERAPY	TEACHING RESOURCES CORPORATION	101-150
PI	SKLKIT	ARTICULATION WORKSHEETS	COMMUNICATION SKILL BUILDERS, INC	11-20
PIJ	ACTCRD	MILLER PICTURE INDEX	WHITEHAVEN PUBLISHING COMPANY	31-50
PIJ	ACTCRD	REBUS GLOSSARY CARDS	AMERICAN GUIDANCE SERVICE, INC.	51-75
PIJ	CHART	GOOD SPEECH POSTERS, SET 1	WHITEHAVEN PUBLISHING COMPANY	6-10
PIJ	CHART	GOOD SPEECH POSTERS, SET 2	WHITEHAVEN PUBLISHING COMPANY	6-10
PIJ	CL SET	R-SOUND WORKBOOK	MAFEX ASSOCIATES, INC.	31-50
PIJ	DITTO	PORTFOLIO OF RUB-ON REBUSES	AMERICAN GUIDANCE SERVICE, INC.	11-20
PIJ	GAME	MILL /S/ SOUND	WHITEHAVEN PUBLISHING COMPANY	<5
PIJ	GAME	MILL /R/ SOUND	WHITEHAVEN PUBLISHING COMPANY	<5
PIJ	GAME	MILL /L/ SOUND	WHITEHAVEN PUBLISHING COMPANY	<5
PIJ	GAME	PERPLEXITY	WHITEHAVEN PUBLISHING COMPANY	<5
PIJ	GUIDE	SYMPTOMATIC VOICE THERAPY	MODERN EDUCATION CORPORATION	31-50
PIJ	MANIPU	SPEECH PENCILS	IDEAS	6-10
PIJ	MULTIU	SAY IT RIGHT: ARTICULATION KIT FOR "R"	EDUCATIONAL ACTIVITIES, INC.	11-20
PIJ	MULTIU	SAY IT RIGHT: ARTICULATION KIT FOR "S"	EDUCATIONAL ACTIVITIES, INC.	11-20
PIJ	MULTIU	SAY IT RIGHT: ARTICULATION KIT FOR "L"	EDUCATIONAL ACTIVITIES, INC.	11-20
PIJ	PICTUR	BOMB-SCARE MYSTERY	STANWIX HOUSE, INC.	<5
PIJ	PROFMA	UNIVERSAL ARTICULATION PROGRAM	TEACHING RESOURCES CORPORATION	201-300
PIJ	PROFMA	VOICE DISORDERS	TEACHING RESOURCES CORPORATION	101-150
PIJ	PROFMA	FIVE COMPONENTS FOR ARTICULATION MODIFICATION	IDEAS	6-10
PIJ	REFBK	STANDARD REBUS GLOSSARY	AMERICAN GUIDANCE SERVICE, INC.	<5
PIJ	VISKIT	TEACHING OF /R/ BY A SEQUENCED METHOD	MAFEX ASSOCIATES, INC.	51-75

LEVEL	FORMAT	TITLE	PUBLISHER	NT	$PRICE

---

5 - SKILL: ARTICULATION

LEVEL	FORMAT	TITLE	PUBLISHER	$PRICE
PIJ	WKBOOK	PICTURE WORKBOOKS: HOLIDAY SOUNDS	WHITEHAVEN PUBLISHING COMPANY	<5
PIJ	WKBOOK	PICTURE WORKBOOKS: CIRCUS SOUNDS	WHITEHAVEN PUBLISHING COMPANY	<5
PIJ	WKBOOK	PICTURE WORKBOOKS: SOUNDS IN FANTASY LAND	WHITEHAVEN PUBLISHING COMPANY	<5
PIJS	GUIDE	SPEECH & HEARING	SPECIAL LEARNING CORPORATION	6-10
PIJS	PROFMA	A PROGRAM TO ESTABLISH FLUENT SPEECH	IDEAS	11-20
PIJS	REFBK	LANGUAGE REMEDIATION & EXPANSION	COMMUNICATION SKILL BUILDERS,INC	11-20
I	GUIDE	STRAIGHT TALK	STANWIX HOUSE, INC.	6-10
I	PICTUR	STRAIGHT TALK CARD SET	STANWIX HOUSE, INC.	6-10
IJ	GAME	K-SPEECH NEWS	COMMUNICATION SKILL BUILDERS,INC	11-20
IJ	SKLKIT	UN "FAMILIAR" FABLES FOR /S/ CARRYOVER	COMMUNICATION SKILL BUILDERS,INC	11-20
IJ	WKBOOK	WORDS	CHANNING L. BETE COMPANY, INC.	<5
IJS	GAME	MULTI-SOUNDS	WHITEHAVEN PUBLISHING COMPANY	<5
JS	AUDCAS	VOICE, VOCABULARY DELIVERY	ASSOCIATED EDUCATIONAL MATERIALS	21-30
JS	AUDCAS	POWER OF WORDS	EBSCO CURRICULUM MATERIALS	6-10
JS	AUDKIT	S-I PROGRAM TO INCREASE FLUENCY	IDEAS	11-20
JS	CHART	COMMUNICATING THROUGH SYMBOLS	LEARNING HANDBOOKS	<5
JS	PICTUR	40-FOURS, SET 1: S SOUND	MODERN EDUCATION CORPORATION	11-20
JS	PICTUR	40-FOURS, SET 2: R SOUND	MODERN EDUCATION CORPORATION	11-20
S	AUDCAS	AUDIO CASSETTES AS SUPPLEMENTARY THERAPY FOR ADULT APHASICS	COMMUNICATION SKILL BUILDERS,INC	51-75
S	GUIDE	COMMUNICATION: INTERACTING THROUGH SPEECH	CHARLES E. MERRILL PUBLISHING CO	<5
S	TEXTBK	WORD STUDIES	SOUTH-WESTERN PUBLISHING CO.	6-10
S	TEXTBK	COMMUNICATION: INTERACTING THROUGH SPEECH	CHARLES E. MERRILL PUBLISHING CO	6-10

---

6 - SKILL: ORAL LANGUAGE SENTENCE STRUCTURE

LEVEL	FORMAT	TITLE	PUBLISHER	$PRICE
R	PUPILB	LADYBIRD BOOK: ANIMALS	IDEAL SCHOOL SUPPLY COMPANY	<5
R	PUPILB	LADYBIRD BOOK: HOME	IDEAL SCHOOL SUPPLY COMPANY	<5
R	PUPILB	LADYBIRD BOOK: THE BEACH	IDEAL SCHOOL SUPPLY COMPANY	<5
R	PUPILB	LADYBIRD BOOK: SHOPPING	IDEAL SCHOOL SUPPLY COMPANY	<5
R	PUPILB	LADYBIRD BOOK: BABY	IDEAL SCHOOL SUPPLY COMPANY	<5
R	PUPILB	LADYBIRD BOOK: CLOTHES	IDEAL SCHOOL SUPPLY COMPANY	<5
R	PUPILB	LADYBIRD BOOK: THE PARK	IDEAL SCHOOL SUPPLY COMPANY	<5
R	PUPILB	LADYBIRD BOOK: GARDENS	IDEAL SCHOOL SUPPLY COMPANY	<5
R	PUPILB	LADYBIRD BOOK: STARTING SCHOOL	IDEAL SCHOOL SUPPLY COMPANY	<5
R	PUPILB	LADYBIRD BOOK: HOLIDAYS	IDEAL SCHOOL SUPPLY COMPANY	<5
R	PUPILB	LADYBIRD BOOK: BEDTIME	IDEAL SCHOOL SUPPLY COMPANY	<5
R	VISKIT	CREATIVE READING PROGRAM I	HARPER & ROW PUBLISHERS, INC.	101-150
RP	AUDKIT	WORDWORLD	ECONOMY COMPANY	101-150
RP	A/VKIT	LEARNING TO LEARN SERIES, SET 1	EDL/MCGRAW-HILL	51-75
RP	A/VKIT	LEARNING TO LEARN SERIES, SET 2	EDL/MCGRAW-HILL	76-100
RP	CHART	STORY BOARDS	HOUGHTON MIFFLIN COMPANY	11-20
RP	CL SET	BREAKTHROUGH TO LITERACY	BOWMAR/NOBLE PUBLISHERS, INC.	201-300
RP	DITTO	LANGUAGE STIMULATION: VERBS	MODERN EDUCATION CORPORATION	6-10
RP	DITTO	LANGUAGE STIMULATION: ADJECTIVES	MODERN EDUCATION CORPORATION	6-10
RP	DITTO	LANGUAGE STIMULATION: NOUNS, ANIMALS & INSECTS	MODERN EDUCATION CORPORATION	6-10
RP	DITTO	LANGUAGE STIMULATION: NOUNS, FOOD	MODERN EDUCATION CORPORATION	6-10
RP	DITTO	LANGUAGE STIMULATION: NOUNS, HOUSEHOLD ITEMS	MODERN EDUCATION CORPORATION	6-10
RP	GUIDE	EMERGING LANGUAGE 2	COMMUNICATION SKILL BUILDERS,INC	6-10
RP	MANIPU	CHATTERBOARDS: ANIMALS	IDEAL SCHOOL SUPPLY COMPANY	6-10
RP	MANIPU	CHATTERBOARDS: TOYS	IDEAL SCHOOL SUPPLY COMPANY	6-10
RP	PICTUR	LANGUAGE VISUALS	COMMUNICATION SKILL BUILDERS,INC	31-50
RPI	GAME	GAMES & MORE GAMES KIDS LIKE	COMMUNICATION SKILL BUILDERS,INC	11-20
P	MANIPU	MIX & MATCH MONSTER PUZZLES	DEVELOPMENTAL LEARNING MATERIALS	6-10
P	PICTUR	LOOK-LISTEN-SAY STORY CARDS	AEVAC, INC.	11-20
P	SKLKIT	FOKES SENTENCE BUILDER	TEACHING RESOURCES CORPORATION	51-75
P	SKLKIT	FOKES SENTENCE BUILDER EXPANSION	TEACHING RESOURCES CORPORATION	31-50
P	SP EQT	AUDITORY SKILLS: SYNTHESIS	INSTRUCTIONAL INDUSTRIES (G.E.)	51-75
P	SP EQT	AUDITORY SKILLS: SYNTAX A	INSTRUCTIONAL INDUSTRIES (G.E.)	101-150
P	SP EQT	AUDITORY SKILLS: SYNTAX B	INSTRUCTIONAL INDUSTRIES (G.E.)	101-150
P	VISKIT	CREATIVE READING PROGRAM II	HARPER & ROW PUBLISHERS, INC.	101-150
P	VISKIT	CREATIVE READING PROGRAM III	HARPER & ROW PUBLISHERS, INC.	101-150
P	VISKIT	CREATIVE READING PROGRAM IV	HARPER & ROW PUBLISHERS, INC.	101-150
PI	A/VKIT	USING GOOD ENGLISH	SVE	51-75
PI	GAME	SPEECH LINGO	MODERN EDUCATION CORPORATION	11-20
PI	MULTIM	UNDERSTANDING WHAT WE READ, LEVEL A	NYSTROM	151-200
PIJ	SKLKIT	SYSTEMATIC SENTENCE BUILDER, LEVEL ONE	MODERN EDUCATION CORPORATION	51-75
PIJ	SKLKIT	SYSTEMATIC SENTENCE BUILDER, LEVEL TWO	MODERN EDUCATION CORPORATION	51-75
PIJ	SKLKIT	SYSTEMATIC SENTENCE BUILDER, LEVEL THREE	MODERN EDUCATION CORPORATION	51-75
PIJ	VISKIT	SYNTAX CODES IS, IS VERBING	C.C. PUBLICATIONS, INC.	21-30
PIJ	VISKIT	SYNTAX CODES ARE, ARE VERBING	C.C. PUBLICATIONS, INC.	21-30
PIJ	VISKIT	SYNTAX CODES SINGULAR NOUN PRESENT TENSE VERB	C.C. PUBLICATIONS, INC.	21-30
PIJ	VISKIT	SYNTAX CODES REGULAR PAST TENSE VERBS	C.C. PUBLICATIONS, INC.	21-30
PIJ	VISKIT	SYNTAX CODES IRREGULAR PAST TENSE VERBS, I	C.C. PUBLICATIONS, INC.	21-30
PIJ	VISKIT	SYNTAX CODES IRREGULAR PAST TENSE VERBS, II	C.C. PUBLICATIONS, INC.	21-30
PIJ	VISKIT	SYNTAX CODES IRREGULAR PAST TENSE VERBS, III	C.C. PUBLICATIONS, INC.	21-30
PIJ	VISKIT	SYNTAX CODES IRREGULAR PAST TENSE VERBS, IV	C.C. PUBLICATIONS, INC.	21-30
PIJ	VISKIT	VIP NOUNS, BOX 1	C.C. PUBLICATIONS, INC.	31-50
PIJ	VISKIT	VIP VERBS, BOX 1	C.C. PUBLICATIONS, INC.	31-50
PIJ	VISKIT	VIP ADJECTIVES	C.C. PUBLICATIONS, INC.	31-50

LEVEL	FORMAT	TITLE	PUBLISHER	NT	$PRICE

6 - SKILL: ORAL LANGUAGE SENTENCE STRUCTURE

LEVEL	FORMAT	TITLE	PUBLISHER	$PRICE
PIJS	MULTIU	COMMUNICATIVE COMPETENCE	COMMUNICATION SKILL BUILDERS,INC	201-300
PIJS	SKLKIT	SYNTAX ONE	COMMUNICATION SKILL BUILDERS,INC	51-75
PIJS	SKLKIT	SYNTAX TWO	COMMUNICATION SKILL BUILDERS,INC	51-75
IJ	SKLKIT	INDIVIDUALIZED ENGLISH, SET J	FOLLETT PUBLISHING COMPANY	101-150
IJS	GUIDE	LESSONS IN SYNTAX: TEACHER'S MAUNAL	DORMAC, INC.	6-10
IJS	SKLKIT	INDIVIDUALIZED ENGLISH, SET H	FOLLETT PUBLISHING COMPANY	101-150
IJS	WKBOOK	LESSONS IN SYNTAX: STUDENT'S WORKBOOK	DORMAC, INC.	6-10
JS	AUDCAS	VOICE, VOCABULARY DELIVERY	ASSOCIATED EDUCATIONAL MATERIALS	21-30
JS	AUDCAS	SPEECH: AN IMPORTANT SKILL AUDIO PACK (RL 4-6)	BENEFIC PRESS	21-30
JS	CL SET	PLAN: LITERATURE, LANGUAGE & COMMUNICATION	WESTINGHOUSE LEARNING CORP.	101-150
JS	PUPILB	PATHWAYS TO SPEECH	GLOBE BOOK COMPANY, INC.	<5
JS	TEXTBK	SPEECH - AN IMPORTANT SKILL PUPIL TEXT (RL 4-6)	BENEFIC PRESS	6-10

7 - SKILL: ORAL LANGUAGE USAGE

LEVEL	FORMAT	TITLE	PUBLISHER	$PRICE
R	CHART	STORY BOARDS	CHILDCRAFT EDUCATION CORPORATION	21-30
R	VISKIT	CREATIVE READING PROGRAM I	HARPER & ROW PUBLISHERS, INC.	101-150
RP	AUDKIT	WORDWORLD	ECONOMY COMPANY	101-150
RP	A/VKIT	CREATIVE DRAMATICS PROGRAM	CHILDREN'S PRESS, INC.	51-75
RP	CL SET	CREATING CHARACTERIZATION	COMENIUS, INC.	76-100
RP	FLASH	DESCRIPTO CARDS	COMMUNICATION SKILL BUILDERS,INC	11-20
RP	FLNLBD	ANIMAL CUT-OUTS	CREATIVE STORYTIME PRESS	<5
RP	FLNLBD	OLIVE THE OSTRICH	CREATIVE STORYTIME PRESS	<5
RP	GUIDE	EMERGING LANGUAGE 2	COMMUNICATION SKILL BUILDERS,INC	6-10
RP	GUIDE	CONCEPT FORMATION: STEPS UP TO LANG. FOR LEARNING IMPAIRED	COMMUNICATION SKILL BUILDERS,INC	6-10
RP	GUIDE	FUNTACTICS: MOVEMENT & SPEECH ACTIVITIES FOR YOUNG CHILDREN	FEARON PITMAN PUBLISHERS, INC.	<5
RP	MANIPU	CHATTERBOARDS: ANIMALS	IDEAL SCHOOL SUPPLY COMPANY	6-10
RP	MANIPU	CHATTERBOARDS: TOYS	IDEAL SCHOOL SUPPLY COMPANY	6-10
RP	MANIPU	MONSTER LACING CARDS	DEVELOPMENTAL LEARNING MATERIALS	6-10
RP	PICTUR	PEOPLE, PLACES & THINGS: OCCUPATIONS	TEACHING RESOURCES CORPORATION	6-10
RP	PICTUR	PEOPLE, PLACES & THINGS: STORIES	TEACHING RESOURCES CORPORATION	6-10
RP	PICTUR	STORY STIMULUS CARDS	MAFEX ASSOCIATES, INC.	11-20
RP	PUPILB	FUN SOUNDS (RL K-3)	BENEFIC PRESS	<5
RP	PUPILB	GAY SOUNDS (RL K-3)	BENEFIC PRESS	<5
RP	RECORD	ACTION SONGS FOR RHYTHMIC ACTIVITIES: SING A SONG OF ACTION	KIMBO EDUCATIONAL	11-20
RP	RECORD	NURSERY RHYMES FOR LITTLE PEOPLE	KIMBO EDUCATIONAL	6-10
RPI	MULTIU	PEEL & PUT (SPEECH THERAPY & LANGUAGE DEVELOPMENT)	COMMUNICATION SKILL BUILDERS,INC	51-75
RPIJ	REFBK	FUNCTIONAL SPEECH & LANGUAGE TRAINING	H & H ENTERPRISES, INC.	31-50
RPIJS	GUIDE	PLANNING INDIVIDUALIZED SPEECH & LANGUAGE INTERVENTION PROG.	COMMUNICATION SKILL BUILDERS,INC	11-20
P	ACTCRD	STORIES TO FINISH PRIMARY GRADES	KENWORTHY EDUCATIONAL SERVICE	<5
P	ACTCRD	ASSOCIATION PICTURE CARDS 4	DEVELOPMENTAL LEARNING MATERIALS	<5
P	AUDKIT	SPEECH THERAPY	EBSCO CURRICULUM MATERIALS	51-75
P	AUDKIT	LANGUAGE CENTER 1	EDUCATIONAL PROGRESS CORPORATION	151-200
P	AUDKIT	BASIC COMMUNICATION SKILLS	LEARNING TREE FILMSTRIPS	51-75
P	DITTO	PRACTICE IN BASIC LANGUAGE SKILLS, BOOK 1 (GRADE 1)	INSTRUCTOR PUBLICATIONS, INC.	<5
P	DITTO	PRACTICE IN BASIC LANGUAGE SKILLS, BOOK 2 (GRADE 2)	INSTRUCTOR PUBLICATIONS, INC.	<5
P	DITTO	PRACTICE IN BASIC LANGUAGE SKILLS, BOOK 3 (GRADE 3)	INSTRUCTOR PUBLICATIONS, INC.	<5
P	FLNLBD	ORAL LANGUAGE SKILLS THROUGH "ALMOST JUST ALIKE"	LESWING PRESS	6-10
P	FLNLBD	ORAL LANGUAGE SKILLS THROUGH "BRAVE THE DRAGON"	LESWING PRESS	6-10
P	GAME	DOG TALES GAME	CHILD FOCUS COMPANY	<5
P	GAME	BACKPACK: A LANGUAGE DEVELOPMENT GAME	DEVELOPMENTAL LEARNING MATERIALS	6-10
P	GUIDE	ORAL LANGUAGE CONTINUUM CHECKLIST	CHILD FOCUS COMPANY	11-20
P	MANIPU	PEOPLE PUPPETS & SCRIPTS, BLACK	DEVELOPMENTAL LEARNING MATERIALS	21-30
P	MANIPU	PEOPLE PUPPETS & SCRIPTS, WHITE	DEVELOPMENTAL LEARNING MATERIALS	21-30
P	MANIPU	HOUND DOG PUPPET	DEVELOPMENTAL LEARNING MATERIALS	11-20
P	MANIPU	TURTLE PUPPET	DEVELOPMENTAL LEARNING MATERIALS	11-20
P	MANIPU	ANIMAL PUPPETS & TAPE	DEVELOPMENTAL LEARNING MATERIALS	21-30
P	MOVIEL	TALK ABOUT IT SERIES	AEVAC, INC.	>450
P	MULTIU	PEABODY LANGUAGE DEVELOPMENT KIT, LEVEL #2	AMERICAN GUIDANCE SERVICE, INC.	101-150
P	MULTIU	PEABODY LANGUAGE DEVELOPMENT KIT, LEVEL #3	AMERICAN GUIDANCE SERVICE, INC.	76-100
P	MULTIM	LET'S TALK WITH WINNIE THE POOH	WALT DISNEY EDUCATIONAL MEDIA	101-150
P	PICTUR	PEOPLE, PLACES & THINGS: RECREATION	TEACHING RESOURCES CORPORATION	6-10
P	PICTUR	PEOPLE, PLACES & THINGS: SPORTS	TEACHING RESOURCES CORPORATION	6-10
P	PICTUR	TELL-A-STORY CARDS	AEVAC, INC.	11-20
P	PICTUR	THINK AWHILE STORY CARDS	AEVAC, INC.	11-20
P	PUPILB	HAPPY SOUNDS (RL 1-3)	BENEFIC PRESS	<5
P	PUPILB	GLAD SOUNDS (RL 1-3)	BENEFIC PRESS	<5
P	PUPILB	SAY & HEAR (RL 1-3)	BENEFIC PRESS	<5
P	RECORD	LET'S SING & ACT TOGETHER	CLASSROOM MATERIALS CO.	6-10
P	RECORD	ACTION SONGS FOR RHYTHMIC ACTIVITIES: HOLIDAY ACTION SONGS	KIMBO EDUCATIONAL	11-20
P	REFBK	DISCOVER NEW WAYS	DISCOVERY LEARNING	<5
P	TEXTBK	HANDBOOK FOR SPEECH THERAPY	WORD MAKING PRODUCTIONS, INC.	11-20
P	VISKIT	CREATIVE READING PROGRAM II	HARPER & ROW PUBLISHERS, INC.	101-150
P	VISKIT	CREATIVE READING PROGRAM III	HARPER & ROW PUBLISHERS, INC.	101-150
P	VISKIT	CREATIVE READING PROGRAM IV	HARPER & ROW PUBLISHERS, INC.	101-150
P	WKBOOK	MORE SEQUENCE PICTURES FOR STORY TELLING	WHITEHAVEN PUBLISHING COMPANY	11-20
P	WKBOOK	CREATIVE STORY STARTERS I	DEVELOPMENTAL LEARNING MATERIALS	<5
P	WKBOOK	CREATIVE STORY STARTERS II	DEVELOPMENTAL LEARNING MATERIALS	<5
P	WKBOOK	CREATIVE EXPRESSION: DINOSAUR BONES	SCHOLASTIC BOOK SERVICE	<5

LEVEL	FORMAT	TITLE	PUBLISHER	NT	$PRICE

7 - SKILL: ORAL LANGUAGE USAGE

LEVEL	FORMAT	TITLE	PUBLISHER	NT	$PRICE
P	WKBOOK	CREATIVE EXPRESSION: JUNGLE SOUNDS	SCHOLASTIC BOOK SERVICE		<5
PI	ACTCRD	MULTI-STORY SEQUENCE PADS	MAFEX ASSOCIATES, INC.		11-20
PI	ACTCRD	LANGUAGE ARTS ACTIVITIES	EDUCATIONAL INSIGHTS, INC.		6-10
PI	ACTCRD	READING BOX	EDUCATIONAL INSIGHTS, INC.		6-10
PI	CL SET	ORAL READING & LINGUISTICS PROGRAM (RL 1-6)	BENEFIC PRESS	8	11-20
PI	DITTO	ASSIST ONE & TWO & THREE	COMMUNICATION SKILL BUILDERS,INC		11-20
PI	GAME	TALK & TURN	COMMUNICATION SKILL BUILDERS,INC		11-20
PI	GAME	CONFUSION, SET 1	WHITEHAVEN PUBLISHING COMPANY		<5
PI	GAME	CONFUSION, SET 2	WHITEHAVEN PUBLISHING COMPANY		<5
PI	GAME	CONFUSION, SET 3	WHITEHAVEN PUBLISHING COMPANY		<5
PI	GAME	MOTIVATIONAL CARD GAMES /s/-/r/-/l/	COMMUNICATION SKILL BUILDERS,INC		11-20
PI	GUIDE	ROLE-PLAYING UNIT FOR GRADES K-6	CHILD FOCUS COMPANY		<5
PI	MULTIU	W L N K J C G V Q Y Z X KIT	LESWING PRESS		31-50
PI	MULTIM	UNDERSTANDING WHAT WE READ, LEVEL A	NYSTROM		151-200
PI	MULTIM	ALICE IN COMMUNICATION LAND	WALT DISNEY EDUCATIONAL MEDIA		76-100
PI	PICTUR	WALKING INTO THE PICTURE	CHILD FOCUS COMPANY		<5
PI	SND FS	STORY STARTERS	CLEARVUE, INC.	12	76-100
PI	SND FS	STORY STARTERS: FIREHOUSE	CLEARVUE, INC.		11-20
PI	SND FS	STORY STARTERS: IT'S MAGIC	CLEARVUE, INC.		11-20
PI	SND FS	STORY STARTERS: BIRTHDAY PARTY	CLEARVUE, INC.		11-20
PI	SND FS	STORY STARTERS: MYSTERY HAT	CLEARVUE, INC.		11-20
PI	SND FS	STORY STARTERS: UP, UP, UP	CLEARVUE, INC.		11-20
PI	SND FS	STORY STARTERS: SECRET MESSAGE	CLEARVUE, INC.		11-20
PI	SND FS	STORY STARTERS: LOST DOG	CLEARVUE, INC.		11-20
PI	SND FS	STORY STARTERS: WAITING	CLEARVUE, INC.		11-20
PI	SND FS	STORY STARTERS: PLAYGROUND	CLEARVUE, INC.		11-20
PI	SND FS	STORY STARTERS: CARNIVAL	CLEARVUE, INC.		11-20
PI	SND FS	STORY STARTERS: WINTER HIKE	CLEARVUE, INC.		11-20
PI	SND FS	AN ADVENTURE IN OPEN EDUCATION	EDUCATIONAL ENRICHMENT MATERIALS		31-50
PIJ	ACTCRD	REBUS GLOSSARY CARDS	AMERICAN GUIDANCE SERVICE, INC.		51-75
PIJ	CHART	GOOD SPEECH POSTERS, SET 1	WHITEHAVEN PUBLISHING COMPANY		6-10
PIJ	CHART	GOOD SPEECH POSTERS, SET 2	WHITEHAVEN PUBLISHING COMPANY		6-10
PIJ	DITTO	PORTFOLIO OF RUB-ON REBUSES	AMERICAN GUIDANCE SERVICE, INC.		11-20
PIJ	FLASH	SEE IT, SAY IT	ADDISON-WESLEY PUBLISHING CO.		31-50
PIJ	GUIDE	TELEPHONE TALK	MAFEX ASSOCIATES, INC.		6-10
PIJ	REFBK	STANDARD REBUS GLOSSARY	AMERICAN GUIDANCE SERVICE, INC.		<5
PIJ	SKLKIT	ON LOCATION WITH LANGUAGE	XEROX EDUCATION PUBLICATIONS		201-300
PIJS	FLASH	LINES 'N DOTS CARD GAME	COMMUNICATION SKILL BUILDERS,INC		11-20
I	DITTO	PRACTICE IN BASIC LANGUAGE SKILLS, BOOK 4 (GRADE 4)	INSTRUCTOR PUBLICATIONS, INC.		<5
I	DITTO	PRACTICE IN BASIC LANGUAGE SKILLS, BOOK 5 (GRADE 5)	INSTRUCTOR PUBLICATIONS, INC.		<5
I	DITTO	PRACTICE IN BASIC LANGUAGE SKILLS, BOOK 6 (GRADE 6)	INSTRUCTOR PUBLICATIONS, INC.		<5
I	PUPILB	LOUD & CLEAR (RL 4-6)	BENEFIC PRESS		<5
I	PUPILB	HEAR YE! HEAR YE! (RL 4-6)	BENEFIC PRESS		<5
I	PUPILB	NOW HEAR THIS (RL 4-6)	BENEFIC PRESS		<5
I	PUPILB	SPEAKING EFFECTIVELY	HOLT, RINEHART AND WINSTON, INC.		11-20
I	WKBOOK	CREATIVE EXPRESSION: GHOST SHIPS	SCHOLASTIC BOOK SERVICE		<5
I	WKBOOK	CREATIVE EXPRESSION: COOK-UP TALES	SCHOLASTIC BOOK SERVICE		<5
I	WKBOOK	CREATIVE EXPRESSION: ADVENTURES OF A 3-SPINED STICKLEBACK	SCHOLASTIC BOOK SERVICE		<5
IJ	ACTCRD	CREATIVE DIALOGUE	KENWORTHY EDUCATIONAL SERVICE		<5
IJ	ACTCRD	STORIES TO FINISH MIDDLE GRADES	KENWORTHY EDUCATIONAL SERVICE		<5
IJ	MULTIM	DISNEYLAND LANGUAGE ARTS SKILL BUILDING KIT	WALT DISNEY EDUCATIONAL MEDIA		201-300
IJ	MULTIM	COMMUNICATION POWER SERIES	UNITED LEARNING	5	201-300
IJ	MULTIM	COMMUNICATION POWER SERIES: ORAL COMMUNICATION	UNITED LEARNING		51-75
IJ	SND FS	RHETORIC READINESS	EYE GATE MEDIA		51-75
IJS	GAME	SCARECROW CARD GAME	COMMUNICATION SKILL BUILDERS,INC		11-20
J	AUDKIT	LANGUAGE CENTER 2	EDUCATIONAL PROGRESS CORPORATION		151-200
JS	AUDCAS	VOICE, VOCABULARY DELIVERY	ASSOCIATED EDUCATIONAL MATERIALS		21-30
JS	AUDCAS	POWER OF WORDS	EBSCO CURRICULUM MATERIALS		6-10
JS	AUDCAS	SPEECH: AN IMPORTANT SKILL AUDIO PACK (RL 4-6)	BENEFIC PRESS		21-30
JS	CL SET	PLAN: LITERATURE, LANGUAGE & COMMUNICATION	WESTINGHOUSE LEARNING CORP.		101-150
JS	GUIDE	LET'S TALK	REGENTS PUBLISHING COMPANY		<5
JS	PUPILB	SPEAKING BY DOING	NATIONAL TEXTBOOK COMPANY		<5
JS	PUPILB	PATHWAYS TO SPEECH	GLOBE BOOK COMPANY, INC.		<5
JS	TEXTBK	SPEECH - AN IMPORTANT SKILL PUPIL TEXT (RL 4-6)	BENEFIC PRESS		6-10
JS	TEXTBK	SPEECH & PUBLIC SPEAKING: COMMUNICATION GAMES	MACMILLAN PUBLISHING CO., INC.		<5
S	AUDCAS	COMMUNICATIONS: THE BUSINESS OF ORAL COMMUNICATIN	SOUTH-WESTERN PUBLISHING CO.		201-300
S	CL SET	MODCOM: MODULES IN SPEECH COMMUNICATIONS	SRA		31-50
S	CL SET	SHORT PLAYS: THE ADULT SCENE, KIT A	JABBERWOCKY		31-50
S	CL SET	SHORT PLAYS: FRIENDS INDEED, KIT B	JABBERWOCKY		31-50
S	CL SET	SHORT PLAYS: SCRIPTS ON SOCIETY, KIT C	JABBERWOCKY		31-50
S	CL SET	SHORT PLAYS: FUN WITH FANTASY, KIT D	JABBERWOCKY		31-50
S	GUIDE	VERBAL ABILITIES	NATIONAL LEARNING CORPORATION		6-10
S	GUIDE	COMMUNICATION: INTERACTING THROUGH SPEECH	CHARLES E. MERRILL PUBLISHING CO		<5
S	MULTIM	SKITS FOR SKILLS: THE ADULT SCENE, KIT A	JABBERWOCKY		101-150
S	MULTIM	SKITS FOR SKILLS: FRIENDS INDEED, KIT B	JABBERWOCKY		101-150
S	MULTIM	SKITS FOR SKILLS: SCRIPTS ON SOCIETY, KIT C	JABBERWOCKY		101-150
S	MULTIM	SKITS FOR SKILLS: FUN WITH FANTASY, KIT D	JABBERWOCKY		101-150
S	PUPILB	R.E.A.C.H. (READING EXERCISES AND COMPOSITION HELP)	BARRON'S EDUCATIONAL SERIES,INC.		<5
S	TEXTBK	WORD STUDIES	SOUTH-WESTERN PUBLISHING CO.		6-10

LEVEL	FORMAT	TITLE	PUBLISHER	NT	$PRICE

7 - SKILL: ORAL LANGUAGE USAGE

LEVEL	FORMAT	TITLE	PUBLISHER	$PRICE
S	TEXTBK	PATTERNS IN COMMUNICATION	HARPER & ROW PUBLISHERS, INC.	6-10
S	TEXTBK	COMMUNICATION: INTERACTING THROUGH SPEECH	CHARLES E. MERRILL PUBLISHING CO	6-10
S	TRANSP	PUBLIC SPEAKING	LANSFORD PUBLISHING COMPANY	76-100
S	TRANSP	DO'S & DON'T'S FOR BEGINNING SPEAKERS	LANSFORD PUBLISHING COMPANY	76-100

8 - SKILL: VISUAL SKILLS - GENERAL

LEVEL	FORMAT	TITLE	PUBLISHER	$PRICE
R	ACTCRD	LEARNING LANGUAGE AT HOME, LEVEL I	COUNCIL FOR EXCEPTIONAL CHILDREN	31-50
R	AUDCAS	WHAT IS BIG? WHAT IS SMALL?	ASSOCIATED EDUCATIONAL MATERIALS	11-20
R	AUDCAS	MANY & FEW	ASSOCIATED EDUCATIONAL MATERIALS	11-20
R	MULTIM	CONCEPTS & LANGUAGE	NATIONAL EDUCATIONAL LABORATORY	301-400
R	VISKIT	TASK CARDS: KINDERGARTEN VISUAL PERCEPTION	DIVERSIFIED PRODUCTION RESOURCES	6-10
RP	ACTCRD	ACTIVITY CARDS: KINDERGARTEN VISUAL PERCEPTION	DIVERSIFIED PRODUCTION RESOURCES	<5
RP	ACTCRD	KINDERGARTEN KEYS: LANGUAGE DEVELOPMENT CARDS, GROUP A	ECONOMY COMPANY	76-100
RP	ACTCRD	SAME OR DIFFERENT PROPORTION CARDS	DEVELOPMENTAL LEARNING MATERIALS	<5
RP	ACTCRD	LEARNING CENTER PAK (GRADES K - 3)	WISE OWL PUBLICATIONS	31-50
RP	MANIPU	VERSA-TILES	LAURI, INC.	21-30
RP	MULTIM	ALPHABET MOTOR ACTIVITIES, BOOK & TAPE	DEVELOPMENTAL LEARNING MATERIALS	11-20
RP	REFBK	BEGINNING DISCOVERY	DISCOVERY LEARNING	<5
RP	SKLKIT	MWM PROGRAM FOR DEVELOPING LANGUAGE ABILITIES	EDUCATIONAL PERFORMANCE ASSOC.	201-300
RP	SND FS	PRIMARY CONCEPTS II	TROLL ASSOCIATES	101-150
RP	SP EQT	CONCEPT DEVELOPMENT: BEGINNING LANGUAGE CONCEPTS, KIT C	BORG-WARNER EDUCATIONAL SYSTEMS	101-150
RP	SP EQT	CONCEPT DEVELOPMENT: BEGINNING LANGUAGE CONCEPTS, KIT D	BORG-WARNER EDUCATIONAL SYSTEMS	101-150
RP	SP EQT	CONCEPT DEVELOPMENT: BEGINNING LANGUAGE CONCEPTS, KIT E	BORG-WARNER EDUCATIONAL SYSTEMS	101-150
RP	SP EQT	CONCEPT DEVELOPMENT: BEGINNING LANGUAGE CONCEPTS, KIT H	BORG-WARNER EDUCATIONAL SYSTEMS	101-150
RP	WKBOOK	BEGINNING READINESS	JENN PUBLICATIONS	<5
P	ACTCRD	LEARNING LANGUAGE AT HOME, LEVEL II	COUNCIL FOR EXCEPTIONAL CHILDREN	31-50
P	ACTCRD	SOUND, PICTURE MATCH-UP	DEVELOPMENTAL LEARNING MATERIALS	6-10
P	CL SET	REBUS SOUND-CENTERED PICTURE PUZZLES	WORD MAKING PRODUCTIONS, INC.	11-20
P	CL SET	SEMEL AUDITORY PROCESSING PROGRAM (BEGINNING BASE)	FOLLETT PUBLISHING COMPANY	21-30
P	CL SET	SEMEL AUDITORY PROCESSING PROGRAM (INTERMEDIATE BASE)	FOLLETT PUBLISHING COMPANY	21-30
P	CL SET	SEMEL AUDITORY PROCESSING PROGRAM (ADVANCED BASE)	FOLLETT PUBLISHING COMPANY	21-30
P	FILMST	DEVELOPING LANGUAGE SKILLS: CAN YOU DESCRIBE IT?	ENCYCLOPEDIA BRITANNICA	31-50
P	GUIDE	MERRILL PHONICS SKILL TEXT: COSTUME BOOK, LEVEL R	CHARLES E. MERRILL PUBLISHING CO	<5
P	MULTIU	SEE-LISTEN-THINK	MCCORMICK-MATHERS PUBLISHING CO.	51-75
P	MULTIU	LANGUAGE PATTERNS/SELF-INSTRUCTIONAL MODALITIES APPROACH	MILTON BRADLEY/PLAYSKOOL	76-100
P	MULTIM	BLENDING SOUNDS WITH COCO & CHARLIE	EDUCATIONAL ACTIVITIES, INC.	31-50
P	WKBOOK	LOOK SHARP	CREATIVE TEACHING ASSOCIATES	<5
P	WKBOOK	MERRILL PHONICS SKILL TEXT: COSTUME BOOK, LEVEL R	CHARLES E. MERRILL PUBLISHING CO	<5
PI	ACTCRD	BUILDING AUDITORY & VISUAL PERCEPTION SKILLS	B. L. WINCH & ASSOCIATES	6-10
PI	ACTCRD	LEARNING CENTER PAK (GRADES 2 - 4)	WISE OWL PUBLICATIONS	31-50
PI	GUIDE	100 INDIVIDUALIZED ACTIVITIES FOR READING	FEARON PITMAN PUBLISHERS, INC.	<5

9 - SKILL: VISUAL DISCRIMINATION - GENERAL

LEVEL	FORMAT	TITLE	PUBLISHER	$PRICE
R	ACTCRD	TUTORGRAM: SIMILARITIES & DIFFERENCES	ENRICHMENT READING CORP OF AMER.	11-20
R	AUDCAS	DISCOVERING LETTERS	ASSOCIATED EDUCATIONAL MATERIALS	11-20
R	AUDCAS	USING LETTERS	ASSOCIATED EDUCATIONAL MATERIALS	11-20
R	AUDKIT	GETTING READY TO READ	MEDIA MATERIALS, INC.	6-10
R	MANIPU	GEOMETRIC SORTING BOARD	CHILDCRAFT EDUCATION CORPORATION	6-10
R	MANIPU	DISNEY PUZZLES: DOPEY	PLAYSKOOL, INC.	<5
R	MANIPU	DISNEY PUZZLES: DONALD DUCK	PLAYSKOOL, INC.	<5
R	MANIPU	DISNEY PUZZLES: PLUTO	PLAYSKOOL, INC.	<5
R	MANIPU	DISNEY PUZZLES: MICKEY MOUSE	PLAYSKOOL, INC.	<5
R	MANIPU	DISNEY PUZZLES: GOOFY	PLAYSKOOL, INC.	<5
R	MANIPU	DISNEY PUZZLES: MICKEY & DONALD	PLAYSKOOL, INC.	<5
R	MANIPU	DISNEY PUZZLES: HUEY, DEWEY & LOUIE	PLAYSKOOL, INC.	<5
R	MANIPU	DISNEY PUZZLES: THREE LITTLE PIGS	PLAYSKOOL, INC.	<5
R	MANIPU	DISNEY PUZZLES: MINNIE MOUSE	PLAYSKOOL, INC.	<5
R	MANIPU	FIRST PUZZLES: THINGS THAT FLY	PLAYSKOOL, INC.	<5
R	MANIPU	FIRST PUZZLES: COLORS I SEE	PLAYSKOOL, INC.	<5
R	MANIPU	FIRST PUZZLES: THINGS WITH WHEELS	PLAYSKOOL, INC.	<5
R	MANIPU	FIRST PUZZLES: FARM ANIMALS	PLAYSKOOL, INC.	<5
R	MANIPU	FIRST PUZZLES: FAVORITE FRUITS	PLAYSKOOL, INC.	<5
R	MANIPU	FIRST PUZZLES: FOR MY BATH	PLAYSKOOL, INC.	<5
R	MANIPU	FIRST PUZZLES: MY PETS	PLAYSKOOL, INC.	<5
R	MANIPU	FIRST PUZZLES: MY TOYS	PLAYSKOOL, INC.	<5
R	MANIPU	PEANUTS PUZZLES: SMAK!	PLAYSKOOL, INC.	<5
R	MANIPU	PEANUTS PUZZLES: SIGH!	PLAYSKOOL, INC.	<5
R	MANIPU	PEANUTS PUZZLES: BE A FRIEND	PLAYSKOOL, INC.	<5
R	MANIPU	PEANUTS PUZZLES: NATIONAL DOG WEEK	PLAYSKOOL, INC.	<5
R	MANIPU	PEANUTS PUZZLES: SCHROEDER & SNOOPY	PLAYSKOOL, INC.	<5
R	MANIPU	PEANUTS PUZZLES: HEAD BEAGLE	PLAYSKOOL, INC.	<5
R	MANIPU	PEANUTS PUZZLES: SMILE!	PLAYSKOOL, INC.	<5
R	MANIPU	PEANUTS PUZZLES: SNOOPY SUPERSTAR	PLAYSKOOL, INC.	<5
R	MANIPU	PEANUTS PUZZLES: I CAN CURE ANYTHING	PLAYSKOOL, INC.	<5
R	MANIPU	PLAY TRAY PUZZLES	PLAYSKOOL, INC.	21-30
R	MANIPU	SESAME STREET LOOK-INSIDE PUZZLES: GROVER'S BLOCKS	PLAYSKOOL, INC.	<5
R	MANIPU	SESAME STREET LOOK-INSIDE PUZZLES: BIG BIRD PRESENTS COLORS	PLAYSKOOL, INC.	<5
R	MANIPU	SESAME STREET LOOK-INSIDE PUZZLES: PEOPLE IN NEIGHBORHOOD	PLAYSKOOL, INC.	<5
R	MANIPU	SESAME STREET LOOK-INSIDE PUZZLES: GOIN' FOR A RIDE	PLAYSKOOL, INC.	<5

LEVEL	FORMAT	TITLE	PUBLISHER	NT	$PRICE

```
                    -----------------------------------------------------
                            9 - SKILL:   VISUAL DISCRIMINATION - GENERAL
                    -----------------------------------------------------
```

LEVEL	FORMAT	TITLE	PUBLISHER	NT	$PRICE
R	MANIPU	SESAME STREET LOOK-INSIDE PUZZLES: WHERE DO THINGS COME FROM	PLAYSKOOL, INC.		<5
R	MANIPU	SESAME STREET LOOK-INSIDE PUZZLES: COOKIE'S NUMBER TRAIN	PLAYSKOOL, INC.		<5
R	MULTIU	EXPERIENCES WITH PERCEPTION	MILTON BRADLEY/PLAYSKOOL		76-100
R	SKLKIT	COLOR, SHAPE, TEXTURE, SIZE	DELTA EDUCATION, INC.		21-30
R	VISKIT	VERSA-TILES, EARLY CHILDHOOD SET	EDUCATIONAL TEACHING AIDS		11-20
R	WKBOOK	FROM COLOR TO WORDS	CREATIVE TEACHING ASSOCIATES		<5
RP	ACTCRD	TUTORGRAM: CONCEPTUAL DISCRIMINATION	ENRICHMENT READING CORP OF AMER.		11-20
RP	ACTCRD	SAME OR DIFFERENT DESIGN CARDS	DEVELOPMENTAL LEARNING MATERIALS		<5
RP	ACTCRD	SYMMETRICAL MATCH-UP	DEVELOPMENTAL LEARNING MATERIALS		<5
RP	ACTCRD	DESIGN DOMINOES	DEVELOPMENTAL LEARNING MATERIALS		<5
RP	ACTCRD	BUZZER BOARD PATTERN CARDS	DEVELOPMENTAL LEARNING MATERIALS		<5
RP	ACTCRD	HOW ARE THEY ALIKE?	MILTON BRADLEY/PLAYSKOOL		<5
RP	ACTCRD	OPPOSITES	MILTON BRADLEY/PLAYSKOOL		<5
RP	ACTCRD	STORY CARDS TELL WHAT PART IS MISSING	MILTON BRADLEY/PLAYSKOOL		<5
RP	AUDCRD	SOUNDS AROUND US	AUDIOTRONICS CORPORATION		21-30
RP	AUDKIT	EARLY PRIMARY SKILLS SERIES	MEDIA MATERIALS, INC.	7	51-75
RP	A/VKIT	READING READINESS	EYE GATE MEDIA		101-150
RP	A/VKIT	SIGHTS & SOUNDS, SET 1	EDL/MCGRAW-HILL		101-150
RP	A/VKIT	SIGHTS & SOUNDS, SET 2	EDL/MCGRAW-HILL		76-100
RP	DITTO	VISUAL DISCRIMINATION GAMES	CHILDREN'S LEARNING CENTER, INC.		<5
RP	DITTO	VISUAL DISCRIMINATION	CHILDREN'S LEARNING CENTER, INC.		<5
RP	DITTO	I CAN DO IT, PART ONE	GEL-STEN, INC.		<5
RP	DITTO	DECODING SKILLS 1	ACTIVITY RESOURCES COMPANY, INC.		<5
RP	FILMST	READING READINESS	ENCYCLOPEDIA BRITANNICA		76-100
RP	GAME	READINESS DISCOVERY	DISCOVERY LEARNING		<5
RP	GAME	GAMEBOARD KIT F	READING JOY, INC.		6-10
RP	GAME	CHIP MATES	MILTON BRADLEY/PLAYSKOOL		6-10
RP	GAME	PLAY SCENES LOTTO	MILTON BRADLEY/PLAYSKOOL		<5
RP	GUIDE	PHONICS IS FUN, BOOK 1	MODERN CURRICULUM PRESS		<5
RP	MANIPU	KEYS & LOCKS KNOB PUZZLE	CONSTRUCTIVE PLAYTHINGS		6-10
RP	MANIPU	PUZZLE CUBES	CHILDCRAFT EDUCATION CORPORATION		6-10
RP	MANIPU	VISUAL CLOSURE & DISCRIMINATION PUZZLE KIT	EDUCATIONAL TEACHING AIDS		31-50
RP	MANIPU	VISUAL DISCRIMINATION BOARDS	EDUCATIONAL TEACHING AIDS		11-20
RP	MANIPU	ETA VISUAL DISCRIMINATION INSTRUCTION SET	EDUCATIONAL TEACHING AIDS		6-10
RP	MANIPU	ADVANCED PUZZLES: THE AQUARIUM	PLAYSKOOL, INC.		<5
RP	MANIPU	ADVANCED PUZZLES: CIRCUS ELEPHANT	PLAYSKOOL, INC.		<5
RP	MANIPU	ADVANCED PUZZLES: A BIRTHDAY PARTY	PLAYSKOOL, INC.		<5
RP	MANIPU	ADVANCED PUZZLES: PUPPIES	PLAYSKOOL, INC.		<5
RP	MANIPU	ADVANCED PUZZLES: PLAYING DOCTORS	PLAYSKOOL, INC.		<5
RP	MANIPU	ADVANCED PUZZLES: PLAYING DRESS-UP	PLAYSKOOL, INC.		<5
RP	MANIPU	ADVANCED PUZZLES: FLYING HIGH	PLAYSKOOL, INC.		<5
RP	MANIPU	ADVANCED PUZZLES: AT THE BEACH	PLAYSKOOL, INC.		<5
RP	MANIPU	ADVANCED PUZZLES: THE BALLOON MAN	PLAYSKOOL, INC.		<5
RP	MANIPU	STORYBOOK PUZZLES: TORTOISE & THE HARE	PLAYSKOOL, INC.		<5
RP	MANIPU	STORYBOOK PUZZLES: RUB-A-DUB-DUB	PLAYSKOOL, INC.		<5
RP	MANIPU	STORYBOOK PUZZLES: CINDERELLA	PLAYSKOOL, INC.		<5
RP	MANIPU	STORYBOOK PUZZLES: THREE BEARS	PLAYSKOOL, INC.		<5
RP	MANIPU	STORYBOOK PUZZLES: HUMPTY-DUMPTY	PLAYSKOOL, INC.		<5
RP	MANIPU	STORYBOOK PUZZLES: RUMPELSTILTSKIN	PLAYSKOOL, INC.		<5
RP	MANIPU	STORYBOOK PUZZLES: HANSEL & GRETEL	PLAYSKOOL, INC.		<5
RP	MANIPU	STORYBOOK PUZZLES: LITTLE RED RIDING HOOD	PLAYSKOOL, INC.		<5
RP	MANIPU	STORYBOOK PUZZLES: OLD WOMAN IN THE SHOE	PLAYSKOOL, INC.		<5
RP	MANIPU	SESAME STREET PUZZLES: BERT'S "B"	PLAYSKOOL, INC.		<5
RP	MANIPU	SESAME STREET PUZZLES: COOKIE'S "C"	PLAYSKOOL, INC.		<5
RP	MANIPU	SESAME STREET PUZZLES: NIGHT & DAY	PLAYSKOOL, INC.		<5
RP	MANIPU	SESAME STREET PUZZLES: BIG & LITTLE	PLAYSKOOL, INC.		<5
RP	MANIPU	SESAME STREET PUZZLES: WE'RE FRIENDS	PLAYSKOOL, INC.		<5
RP	MANIPU	SESAME STREET PUZZLES: FOUR MONSTERS	PLAYSKOOL, INC.		<5
RP	MULTIM	HELP: PERCEPTUAL DIFFERENCES	CENTER FOR EARLY LEARNING		6-10
RP	MULTIM	PHONICS FOR FUN	ARISTA CORPORATION		201-300
RP	MULTIM	WHAT'S YOUR STORY?	HARCOURT BRACE JOVANOVICH, INC.		101-150
RP	PICTUR	CAMOUFLAGED ANIMAL CARDS	DEVELOPMENTAL LEARNING MATERIALS		6-10
RP	PI/PRT	SESAME STREET PUZZLES: ERNIE	PLAYSKOOL, INC.		<5
RP	PUPILB	FINTON THE FISH	ANN ARBOR PUBLISHERS		<5
RP	PUPILB	KINDERGARTEN KEYS: THE CATERPILLAR CAPER	ECONOMY COMPANY		<5
RP	SND FS	PERCEPTUAL TRAINING FILMSTRIPS	TROLL ASSOCIATES		101-150
RP	WKBOOK	ABC MAZES	ANN ARBOR PUBLISHERS		<5
RP	WKBOOK	SYMBOL DISCRIMINATION SERIES, BOOK I	ANN ARBOR PUBLISHERS		<5
RP	WKBOOK	SYMBOL DISCRIMINATION SERIES, BOOK II	ANN ARBOR PUBLISHERS		<5
RP	WKBOOK	SYMBOL DISCRIMINATION SERIES, BOOK III	ANN ARBOR PUBLISHERS		<5
RP	WKBOOK	SYMBOL DISCRIMINATION SERIES, BOOK IV	ANN ARBOR PUBLISHERS		<5
RP	WKBOOK	SYMBOL DISCRIMINATION SERIES, BOOK V	ANN ARBOR PUBLISHERS		<5
RP	WKBOOK	SYMBOL DISCRIMINATION SERIES, BOOK VI	ANN ARBOR PUBLISHERS		<5
RP	WKBOOK	PHONICS IS FUN, BOOK 1	MODERN CURRICULUM PRESS		<5
P	ACTCRD	PERCEPTION CARDS: COGITO	INVICTA PLASTICS LTD.		6-10
P	ACTCRD	PERCEPTION CARDS: TOM TURNIP	INVICTA PLASTICS LTD.		6-10
P	ACTCRD	PERCEPTION CARDS: CLOWNS	INVICTA PLASTICS LTD.		6-10
P	ACTCRD	PERCEPTION CARDS: BUSES	INVICTA PLASTICS LTD.		6-10
P	ACTCRD	PERCEPTION CARDS: TRUCKS	INVICTA PLASTICS LTD.		6-10

LEVEL	FORMAT	TITLE	PUBLISHER	NT	$PRICE

9 - SKILL: VISUAL DISCRIMINATION - GENERAL

LEVEL	FORMAT	TITLE	PUBLISHER	$PRICE
P	ACTCRD	VISUAL DISCRIMINATION LEARNING- MATCHING LETTERS N	EDUCATIONAL PERFORMANCE ASSOC.	31-50
P	ACTCRD	LANGUAGE ARTS-SKILL DRILLS WITH MOTIVATORS	SVE	31-50
P	ACTCRD	PICTURE CARDS	MILTON BRADLEY/PLAYSKOOL	6-10
P	AUDKIT	VISUAL DISCRIMINATION	EBSCO CURRICULUM MATERIALS	51-75
P	CHART	PICTURE COMPOSITE CHART	SOUND MATERIALS	<5
P	DITTO	PRE-READING EXERCISES & PERCEPTUAL SKILLS	BOOK-LAB, INC.	6-10
P	DITTO	READING STEP BY STEP, KIT A	CONTINENTAL PRESS, INC.	51-75
P	DITTO	MY ALPHABET BOOK	FRANK SCHAFFER PUBLICATIONS, INC	<5
P	DITTO	WORD RELATIONSHIPS: CUT & PASTE	FRANK SCHAFFER PUBLICATIONS, INC	<5
P	DITTO	CATEGORY WORD HUNT I	DEVELOPMENTAL LEARNING MATERIALS	<5
P	DITTO	CATEGORY WORD HUNT II	DEVELOPMENTAL LEARNING MATERIALS	<5
P	DITTO	BEGINNING SOUND WORD HUNT I	DEVELOPMENTAL LEARNING MATERIALS	<5
P	DITTO	BEGINNING SOUND WORD HUNT II	DEVELOPMENTAL LEARNING MATERIALS	<5
P	DITTO	VISUAL DISCRIMINATION	INSTRUCTO/MCGRAW-HILL	<5
P	DITTO	CONFUSED WORDS	MILTON BRADLEY/PLAYSKOOL	<5
P	FILMST	DEVELOPING BASIC SKILLS: WHAT DO YOU SEE?	ENCYCLOPEDIA BRITANNICA	31-50
P	FILMST	DEVELOPING BASIC SKILLS: WHERE IS IT?	ENCYCLOPEDIA BRITANNICA	31-50
P	FILMST	DEVELOPING BASIC SKILLS: WHAT IS IT?	ENCYCLOPEDIA BRITANNICA	31-50
P	FLASH	PICTURE FLASHCARD SET	SOUND MATERIALS	<5
P	GAME	PHONICS WHEEL	TEACHING RESOURCES CORPORATION	11-20
P	MANIPU	MATCH & CHECK, LEVEL 2	SCOTT, FORESMAN & CO.	6-10
P	MANIPU	MATCH & CHECK, LEVEL 3	SCOTT, FORESMAN & CO.	6-10
P	MANIPU	MATCH & CHECK, LEVEL 4	SCOTT, FORESMAN & CO.	6-10
P	MANIPU	SKETCH-A-PUZZLE	EDUCATIONAL PERFORMANCE ASSOC.	6-10
P	MANIPU	LARGE SYMMETRICAL MATCH-UPS	DEVELOPMENTAL LEARNING MATERIALS	<5
P	MANIPU	TWO PART MATCH-UPS: ANIMAL, VEGETABLE, MINERAL	DEVELOPMENTAL LEARNING MATERIALS	<5
P	MANIPU	ANIMALS IN PLACE	DEVELOPMENTAL LEARNING MATERIALS	6-10
P	MULTIU	ALPHA TIME PLUS	ARISTA CORPORATION	151-200
P	MULTIU	PERCEPTION TASK CARDS	MILTON BRADLEY/PLAYSKOOL	21-30
P	MULTIM	DEVELOPING READING SKILLS, PART I: WORD RECOGNITION	EDUCATIONAL ENRICHMENT MATERIALS	101-150
P	PICTUR	PICTURE COMPOSITE	SOUND MATERIALS	6-10
P	SND FS	SEEING CLEARLY: VISUAL READINESS	TROLL ASSOCIATES	51-75
P	WKBOOK	SYMBOL DISCRIMINATION & SEQUENCING	ANN ARBOR PUBLISHERS	<5
P	WKBOOK	WORD LISTS	SOUND MATERIALS	6-10
P	WKBOOK	NEW PHONICS WORKBOOK, BOOK A	MODERN CURRICULUM PRESS	<5
PI	ACTCRD	READING FUN FACTORY	KIDS & COMPANY	<5
PI	DITTO	FIND-A-WORD	FRANK SCHAFFER PUBLICATIONS, INC	<5
PI	MULTIU	GOAL, LEVEL II: LANGUAGE DEVELOPMENT	MILTON BRADLEY/PLAYSKOOL	151-200
PI	REFBK	SPECIAL NEEDS: SPECIAL ANSWERS	BOOK-LAB, INC.	11-20
PI	WKBOOK	READING ACTIVITIES FOR LEARNING CENTERS	FRANK SCHAFFER PUBLICATIONS, INC	<5
PIJ	DITTO	RESCUE, VOLUME I	EDUCATIONAL SERVICE, INC.	6-10
IJ	VISKIT	VERSA-TILES, BEGINNING READING SET	EDUCATIONAL TEACHING AIDS	11-20
JS	AUDKIT	PRE- READING SKILLS SERIES	MEDIA MATERIALS, INC.	21-30

10 - SKILL: VISUAL DISCRIMINATION - COLOR

LEVEL	FORMAT	TITLE	PUBLISHER	$PRICE
R	ACTCRD	TUTORGRAM: PUZZLES I	ENRICHMENT READING CORP OF AMER.	11-20
R	AUDCAS	COLORS WE SEE	ASSOCIATED EDUCATIONAL MATERIALS	11-20
R	AUDCAS	COLORS AT A PARTY	ASSOCIATED EDUCATIONAL MATERIALS	11-20
R	AUDKIT	VISUAL DISCRIMINATION	MEDIA MATERIALS, INC.	6-10
R	GUIDE	AUDITORY VISUAL MOTOR SKILLS: STARTING OFF W/PHONICS, BOOK 1	MODERN CURRICULUM PRESS	<5
R	MANIPU	RAINBOW ROLLS	COMMUNITY PLAYTHINGS	76-100
R	MANIPU	PRIMARY COLOR BOX	DICK BLICK COMPANY	11-20
R	MANIPU	CIRCLE-SQUARE FIT-INS	EDUCATIONAL TEACHING AIDS	6-10
R	MANIPU	COLOR & SHAPE BOARD	EDUCATIONAL TEACHING AIDS	6-10
R	MULTIU	EXPERIENCES IN READING READINESS	MILTON BRADLEY/PLAYSKOOL	76-100
R	SKLKIT	PERCEPTION OF COLOR	DELTA EDUCATION, INC.	11-20
R	WKBOOK	AUDITORY VISUAL MOTOR SKILLS: STARTING OFF W/PHONICS, BOOK 1	MODERN CURRICULUM PRESS	<5
RP	ACTCRD	COLORCOLOR	COLORCO	6-10
RP	ACTCRD	CUBES IN COLOR	INCENTIVES FOR LEARNING, INC.	6-10
RP	A/VKIT	STARTER SET: SHAPES, COLORS, SIZES, LETTERS, NUMBERS	EYE GATE MEDIA	76-100
RP	A/VKIT	BASIC COLORS	SVE	76-100
RP	CHART	FUN WITH COLORS	CREATIVE TEACHING ASSOCIATES	<5
RP	CHART	FUN WITH COLORS	ENRICH, INC.	<5
RP	CHART	COLOR CATS	TREND ENTERPRISES, INC.	<5
RP	CHART	LEARNING COLORS	TREND ENTERPRISES, INC.	<5
RP	CHART	COLORS & SHAPES	CHILD'S WORLD	6-10
RP	CL SET	STAR BOOKS	ARISTA CORPORATION	51-75
RP	DITTO	LEARN THE COLORS	CHILDREN'S LEARNING CENTER, INC.	<5
RP	DITTO	VISUAL PERCEPTION	ACTIVITY RESOURCES COMPANY, INC.	<5
RP	DITTO	LOOK SHARP	ACTIVITY RESOURCES COMPANY, INC.	<5
RP	GAME	LINE GAME CUBES	NIENHUIS MONTESSORI, INC.	101-150
RP	GUIDE	COLOR DISCRIMINATION	EDUCATIONAL PROGRAMMERS, INC.	6-10
RP	MANIPU	FORM BLOCKS	COMMUNITY PLAYTHINGS	151-200
RP	MANIPU	SHAPES, COLORS & FORMS	CONSTRUCTIVE PLAYTHINGS	6-10
RP	MANIPU	FIT-A-SHAPE	CONSTRUCTIVE PLAYTHINGS	6-10
RP	MANIPU	COLOR TABLETS: SECOND BOX	CONSTRUCTIVE PLAYTHINGS	11-20
RP	MANIPU	COLOR TABLETS: THIRD BOX	CONSTRUCTIVE PLAYTHINGS	31-50
RP	MANIPU	DOTS & COLOR	CHILDCRAFT EDUCATION CORPORATION	11-20
RP	MANIPU	CUBES IN COLOR DESIGN CARDS	INCENTIVES FOR LEARNING, INC.	6-10

LEVEL	FORMAT	TITLE	PUBLISHER	NT	$PRICE

10 - SKILL: VISUAL DISCRIMINATION - COLOR

LEVEL	FORMAT	TITLE	PUBLISHER	$PRICE
RP	MANIPU	SEQUENCING BEADS & DESIGN CARDS	INCENTIVES FOR LEARNING, INC.	11-20
RP	MANIPU	ETA PICTURE & SHAPE SORTING CARDS	EDUCATIONAL TEACHING AIDS	11-20
RP	MANIPU	ETA WHAT-IS-MY-COLOR? MATCHING CARDS	EDUCATIONAL TEACHING AIDS	<5
RP	MANIPU	FIRST BOX OF COLORS	NIENHUIS MONTESSORI, INC.	6-10
RP	MANIPU	SECOND BOX OF COLORS	NIENHUIS MONTESSORI, INC.	11-20
RP	MANIPU	THIRD BOX OF COLORS	NIENHUIS MONTESSORI, INC.	31-50
RP	MANIPU	COLOR DOMINOES	NIENHUIS MONTESSORI, INC.	11-20
RP	MANIPU	GRAPHIC DOMINOES	NIENHUIS MONTESSORI, INC.	31-50
RP	MANIPU	COLOR & SHAPE SET	DEVELOPMENTAL LEARNING MATERIALS	31-50
RP	MANIPU	PARQUETRY DESIGN BLOCKS	MILTON BRADLEY/PLAYSKOOL	6-10
RP	MULTIU	ALPHA TIME PRE-READING PROGRAM	ARISTA CORPORATION	201-300
RP	MULTIU	DOODLE DOLLY & HER DAO GAN DISCOVER COLORS	EDUCATIONAL DIMENSIONS CORP.	31-50
RP	MULTIM	COLORS EVERYWHERE	SPOKEN ARTS, INC.	151-200
RP	PICTUR	SAME OR DIFFERENT COLOR CARDS	DEVELOPMENTAL LEARNING MATERIALS	<5
RP	PICTUR	COLOR ASSOCIATION PICTURE CARDS	DEVELOPMENTAL LEARNING MATERIALS	<5
RP	PICTUR	COLOR DISCOVERY CARDS	DEVELOPMENTAL LEARNING MATERIALS	<5
RP	PUPILB	COLORS	BRADBURY PRESS, INC.	6-10
RP	PUPILB	A WORLD OF COLOR	CHILDREN'S PRESS, INC.	6-10
RP	PUPILB	CALICO CAT'S RAINBOW	CHILDREN'S PRESS, INC.	6-10
RP	PUPILB	COLORS FLIP BOOK	TREND ENTERPRISES, INC.	<5
RP	PUPILB	A WORLD OF COLOR	CHILD'S WORLD	6-10
RP	PUPILB	MAGIC MONSTERS LOOK FOR COLORS	CHILD'S WORLD	6-10
RP	SND FS	COLOR CONCEPTS	EDUCATIONAL ENRICHMENT MATERIALS	101-150
RP	SND FS	STORIES ABOUT COLORS	CORONET MULTI MEDIA	101-150
RP	SP EQT	PERCEPTUAL TRAINING, SET 6: BEGINNING ADDITIONS	INSTRUCTIONAL INDUSTRIES (G.E.)	51-75
RP	WKBOOK	COLOR, CUT & READ	ACADIA PRESS, INC.	<5
RP	WKBOOK	TELL & DRAW STORIES	CREATIVE STORYTIME PRESS	6-10
RP	WKBOOK	MORE TELL & DRAW STORIES	CREATIVE STORYTIME PRESS	6-10
RP	WKBOOK	LOTS MORE TELL & DRAW STORIES	CREATIVE STORYTIME PRESS	6-10
RP	WKBOOK	MATCH & MEMORY, BOOK 2: VISUAL DISCRIMINATION & PERCEPTION	EDUCATIONAL PROGRAMMERS, INC.	6-10
RP	WKBOOK	BEGINNING READINESS	JENN PUBLICATIONS	<5
RPI	MANIPU	COLOR TABLETS: FIRST BOX	CONSTRUCTIVE PLAYTHINGS	6-10
RPI	MULTIU	B T M P D R H S F KIT	LESWING PRESS	31-50
P	ACTCRD	COLOR MIX & MATCH	IDEAL SCHOOL SUPPLY COMPANY	11-20
P	ACTCRD	PEG PADS	DEVELOPMENTAL LEARNING MATERIALS	<5
P	ACTCRD	PEGBOARD DESIGNS	DEVELOPMENTAL LEARNING MATERIALS	11-20
P	AUDKIT	SOUND IT!	EDUCATIONAL TEACHING AIDS	101-150
P	AUDKIT	READING CASSETTES: READING READINESS	IDEAL SCHOOL SUPPLY COMPANY	51-75
P	AUDKIT	HAPPY WORLD OF COLOR	EDUCATIONAL ACTIVITIES, INC.	11-20
P	CHART	COLOR RECOGNITION CHART	IDEAL SCHOOL SUPPLY COMPANY	<5
P	CHART	COLOR TRAIN	IDEAL SCHOOL SUPPLY COMPANY	<5
P	FLASH	COLOR NAME CARDS	IDEAL SCHOOL SUPPLY COMPANY	<5
P	FLASH	COLOR GRADATION CARDS	IDEAL SCHOOL SUPPLY COMPANY	<5
P	FLASH	COLORS & SHAPES: FLIP & LEARN FLASHBOOK	MILTON BRADLEY/PLAYSKOOL	<5
P	GAME	COLOR RECOGNITION	FRANK SCHAFFER PUBLICATIONS, INC	<5
P	GAME	ETA COLOR BINGO	EDUCATIONAL TEACHING AIDS	6-10
P	GAME	BALLOON GAME	JUDY COMPANY	6-10
P	GAME	ALPHA, MATCH	JUDY COMPANY	6-10
P	MANIPU	COLOR PADDLES	INVICTA PLASTICS LTD.	<5
P	MANIPU	DESIGN BOARD	NIENHUIS MONTESSORI, INC.	21-30
P	MANIPU	PEGBOARD	DEVELOPMENTAL LEARNING MATERIALS	<5
P	MANIPU	PEGS	DEVELOPMENTAL LEARNING MATERIALS	<5
P	MANIPU	COLORED INCH CUBES	DEVELOPMENTAL LEARNING MATERIALS	11-20
P	MANIPU	COLORED INCH CUBE DESIGNS	DEVELOPMENTAL LEARNING MATERIALS	<5
P	MANIPU	COLOR LOTTO	JUDY COMPANY	6-10
P	MULTIU	COLOR	EDUCATIONAL DIMENSIONS CORP.	76-100
P	MULTIM	OBSERVING & DESCRIBING COLOR	ENCYCLOPEDIA BRITANNICA	31-50
P	VISKIT	COLOR CHARTS	INSTRUCTOR PUBLICATIONS, INC.	6-10
P	WKBOOK	TALK TALK TALK	ST. JOHN SCHOOL FOR THE DEAF	<5
PI	CHART	COLOR WHEEL	MILTON BRADLEY/PLAYSKOOL	<5
PIJ	MULTIM	VISUAL AURAL DISCRIMINATIONS, BOOK I	ANN ARBOR PUBLISHERS	<5

11 - SKILL: VISUAL DISCRIMINATION - SIZE

LEVEL	FORMAT	TITLE	PUBLISHER	$PRICE
R	ACTCRD	TUTORGRAM: PUZZLES I	ENRICHMENT READING CORP OF AMER.	11-20
R	AUDCAS	WHAT IS BIG? WHAT IS SMALL?	ASSOCIATED EDUCATIONAL MATERIALS	11-20
R	AUDKIT	VISUAL DISCRIMINATION	MEDIA MATERIALS, INC.	6-10
R	MANIPU	CIRCLE-SQUARE FIT-INS	EDUCATIONAL TEACHING AIDS	6-10
R	SKLKIT	RECOGNIZING & USING SHAPES	DELTA EDUCATION, INC.	31-50
RP	ACTCRD	READINESS: SIZE DISCRIMINATION & CLASSIFICATION	INSTRUCTIONAL FAIR	<5
RP	ACTCRD	ALIKE & NOT ALIKE, SET 1: SIZE PICTURE CARDS	IDEAL SCHOOL SUPPLY COMPANY	<5
RP	ACTCRD	ALIKE & NOT ALIKE, SET 2: PROPORTION PICTURE CARDS	IDEAL SCHOOL SUPPLY COMPANY	<5
RP	ACTCRD	SAME OR DIFFERENT PROPORTION CARDS	DEVELOPMENTAL LEARNING MATERIALS	<5
RP	ACTCRD	SAME OR DIFFERENT SIZE CARDS	DEVELOPMENTAL LEARNING MATERIALS	<5
RP	A/VKIT	STARTER SET: SHAPES, COLORS, SIZES, LETTERS, NUMBERS	EYE GATE MEDIA	76-100
RP	DITTO	READINESS: SIZE DISCRIMINATION & CLASSIFICATION	INSTRUCTIONAL FAIR	<5
RP	DITTO	WHAT'S NEXT?	IDEAL SCHOOL SUPPLY COMPANY	6-10
RP	DITTO	VISUAL PERCEPTION	ACTIVITY RESOURCES COMPANY, INC.	<5
RP	DITTO	LOOK SHARP	ACTIVITY RESOURCES COMPANY, INC.	<5
RP	FLNLBD	SIZE DISCRIMINATION CIRCUS	INSTRUCTO/MCGRAW-HILL	6-10

LEVEL	FORMAT	TITLE	PUBLISHER	NT	$PRICE

11 - SKILL: VISUAL DISCRIMINATION - SIZE

LEVEL	FORMAT	TITLE	PUBLISHER	$PRICE
RP	MANIPU	FIT-A-SIZE	CONSTRUCTIVE PLAYTHINGS	6-10
RP	MANIPU	SHAPES, COLORS & FORMS	CONSTRUCTIVE PLAYTHINGS	6-10
RP	MANIPU	GRADED CYLINDER BLOCKS WITH KNOBS	CONSTRUCTIVE PLAYTHINGS	11-20
RP	MANIPU	SMALL/LARGE MATCH PUZZLES	CONSTRUCTIVE PLAYTHINGS	<5
RP	MANIPU	SIZE & SHAPE PUZZLES WITH KNOBS: TWO LADYBUGS	CHILDCRAFT EDUCATION CORPORATION	11-20
RP	MANIPU	SIZE & SHAPE PUZZLES WITH KNOBS: SNOWMAN	CHILDCRAFT EDUCATION CORPORATION	11-20
RP	MANIPU	SIZE & SHAPE PUZZLES WITH KNOBS: FLOWER POT	CHILDCRAFT EDUCATION CORPORATION	11-20
RP	MANIPU	SIZE & SHAPE PUZZLES WITH KNOBS: KITES	CHILDCRAFT EDUCATION CORPORATION	11-20
RP	MANIPU	SIZE & SHAPE PUZZLES WITH KNOBS: THREE FISH	CHILDCRAFT EDUCATION CORPORATION	11-20
RP	MANIPU	SIZE & SHAPE PUZZLES WITH KNOBS: TOAD STOOL	CHILDCRAFT EDUCATION CORPORATION	11-20
RP	MANIPU	SIZE & SHAPE PUZZLES WITH KNOBS: FOUR DUCKS	CHILDCRAFT EDUCATION CORPORATION	11-20
RP	MANIPU	SIZE & SHAPE PUZZLES WITH KNOBS: BIRDS IN A FRUIT TREE	CHILDCRAFT EDUCATION CORPORATION	11-20
RP	MANIPU	ETA DISCOVERY BLOCKS	EDUCATIONAL TEACHING AIDS	21-30
RP	MANIPU	SIZE & SHAPE PUZZLE	DEVELOPMENTAL LEARNING MATERIALS	6-10
RP	MANIPU	LACING BOARDS	DEVELOPMENTAL LEARNING MATERIALS	<5
RP	MANIPU	SHAPES SORTING BOX	DEVELOPMENTAL LEARNING MATERIALS	11-20
RP	MANIPU	MIX 'N' MATCH PUZZLES: SMALL, MEDIUM, LARGE	TREND ENTERPRISES, INC.	6-10
RP	PUPILB	I CAN DO IT	BOWMAR/NOBLE PUBLISHERS, INC.	51-75
RP	SND FS	BASIC CONCEPTS	EDUCATIONAL ENRICHMENT MATERIALS	76-100
RP	SP EQT	PERCEPTUAL TRAINING, SET 6: BEGINNING ADDITIONS	INSTRUCTIONAL INDUSTRIES (G.E.)	51-75
P	AUDKIT	VISUAL DISCRIMINATION	EBSCO CURRICULUM MATERIALS	51-75
P	MANIPU	MATCH-N-FIT: CIRCLES	LITTLE KENNY PUBLICATIONS, INC.	11-20
P	MANIPU	MATCH-N-FIT: TRIANGLES	LITTLE KENNY PUBLICATIONS, INC.	11-20
P	MANIPU	MATCH-N-FIT: SQUARES	LITTLE KENNY PUBLICATIONS, INC.	11-20
P	MANIPU	MATCH-N-FIT: MIXED	LITTLE KENNY PUBLICATIONS, INC.	11-20
P	MULTIM	OBSERVING & DESCRIBING SIZE	ENCYCLOPEDIA BRITANNICA	31-50

12 - SKILL: VISUAL DISCRIMINATION - SHAPE

LEVEL	FORMAT	TITLE	PUBLISHER	$PRICE
R	ACTCRD	TUTORGRAM: PUZZLES I	ENRICHMENT READING CORP OF AMER.	11-20
R	AUDCAS	LOOKING FOR ROUND SHAPES	ASSOCIATED EDUCATIONAL MATERIALS	11-20
R	AUDCAS	LOOKING FOR SQUARE SHAPES	ASSOCIATED EDUCATIONAL MATERIALS	11-20
R	AUDKIT	VISUAL DISCRIMINATION	MEDIA MATERIALS, INC.	6-10
R	MANIPU	FIT-A-SQUARE, FIT-A-CIRCLE	CHILDCRAFT EDUCATION CORPORATION	6-10
R	MANIPU	VARI-SHAPE BEADS	CHILDCRAFT EDUCATION CORPORATION	11-20
R	MANIPU	SIZE FIT-INS	EDUCATIONAL TEACHING AIDS	6-10
R	MANIPU	COLOR & SHAPE BOARD	EDUCATIONAL TEACHING AIDS	6-10
R	MANIPU	MIXED SHAPE-FINDING	EDUCATIONAL TEACHING AIDS	6-10
R	MANIPU	ETA JUMBO FORM BOARD	EDUCATIONAL TEACHING AIDS	6-10
R	MANIPU	SHAPE SORTING CUBES	EDUCATIONAL TEACHING AIDS	6-10
R	MULTIU	EXPERIENCES WITH PERCEPTION	MILTON BRADLEY/PLAYSKOOL	76-100
R	PUPILB	CIRCLES, TRIANGLES, SQUARES	CHILDCRAFT EDUCATION CORPORATION	6-10
R	SKLKIT	THREE-DIMENSIONAL SHAPES	DELTA EDUCATION, INC.	21-30
R	WKBOOK	LESSONS TO GROW ON, BOOK 1	PRESCHOOL LEARNING CORPORATION	<5
RP	ACTCRD	CURVES & CORNERS	IDEAL SCHOOL SUPPLY COMPANY	11-20
RP	ACTCRD	SHAPE DOMINOES	DEVELOPMENTAL LEARNING MATERIALS	<5
RP	ACTCRD	MULTIMOES	DEVELOPMENTAL LEARNING MATERIALS	<5
RP	ACTCRD	PARQUETRY DESIGN BLOCK PATTERNS	MILTON BRADLEY/PLAYSKOOL	<5
RP	AUDCAS	DOODLE DOLLY & HER DAN DISCOVER SHAPES	EDUCATIONAL DIMENSIONS CORP.	31-50
RP	AUDKIT	HOWDY PARTNER, AGAIN	MEDIA MATERIALS, INC.	6-10
RP	A/VKIT	STARTER SET: SHAPES, COLORS, SIZES, LETTERS, NUMBERS	EYE GATE MEDIA	76-100
RP	A/VKIT	BASIC SHAPES	SVE	76-100
RP	CHART	PUZZLE POSTERS: DINOSAURS & SHAPES	TREND ENTERPRISES, INC.	<5
RP	CHART	COLORS & SHAPES	CHILD'S WORLD	6-10
RP	CL SET	FIVE SENSE STORE	COMENIUS, INC.	6 >450
RP	CL SET	SHAPES	COMENIUS, INC.	76-100
RP	CL SET	SHAPE RELATIONSHIPS	COMENIUS, INC.	76-100
RP	CL SET	SHAPE & PATTERNS	COMENIUS, INC.	76-100
RP	CL SET	STAR BOOKS	ARISTA CORPORATION	51-75
RP	DITTO	BASIC SHAPES DUPLICATING MASTERS	CLEARVUE, INC.	<5
RP	DITTO	VISUAL PERCEPTION	ACTIVITY RESOURCES COMPANY, INC.	<5
RP	DITTO	LOOK SHARP	ACTIVITY RESOURCES COMPANY, INC.	<5
RP	GAME	GAMEBOARD KIT F	READING JOY, INC.	6-10
RP	MANIPU	FORM BLOCKS	COMMUNITY PLAYTHINGS	151-200
RP	MANIPU	SEQUENTIAL SORTING BOX	CONSTRUCTIVE PLAYTHINGS	11-20
RP	MANIPU	SHAPES BOARD	CONSTRUCTIVE PLAYTHINGS	6-10
RP	MANIPU	SHAPES, COLORS & FORMS	CONSTRUCTIVE PLAYTHINGS	6-10
RP	MANIPU	FIT-A-SHAPE	CONSTRUCTIVE PLAYTHINGS	6-10
RP	MANIPU	FAMILIAR THINGS PUZZLE	CONSTRUCTIVE PLAYTHINGS	6-10
RP	MANIPU	SIZE & SHAPE PUZZLES WITH KNOBS: TWO LADYBUGS	CHILDCRAFT EDUCATION CORPORATION	11-20
RP	MANIPU	SIZE & SHAPE PUZZLES WITH KNOBS: SNOWMAN	CHILDCRAFT EDUCATION CORPORATION	11-20
RP	MANIPU	SIZE & SHAPE PUZZLES WITH KNOBS: FLOWER POT	CHILDCRAFT EDUCATION CORPORATION	11-20
RP	MANIPU	SIZE & SHAPE PUZZLES WITH KNOBS: KITES	CHILDCRAFT EDUCATION CORPORATION	11-20
RP	MANIPU	SIZE & SHAPE PUZZLES WITH KNOBS: THREE FISH	CHILDCRAFT EDUCATION CORPORATION	11-20
RP	MANIPU	SIZE & SHAPE PUZZLES WITH KNOBS: TOAD STOOL	CHILDCRAFT EDUCATION CORPORATION	11-20
RP	MANIPU	SIZE & SHAPE PUZZLES WITH KNOBS: FOUR DUCKS	CHILDCRAFT EDUCATION CORPORATION	11-20
RP	MANIPU	SIZE & SHAPE PUZZLES WITH KNOBS: BIRDS IN A FRUIT TREE	CHILDCRAFT EDUCATION CORPORATION	11-20
RP	MANIPU	DOTS & COLOR	CHILDCRAFT EDUCATION CORPORATION	11-20
RP	MANIPU	SEQUENTIAL SORTING BOX	CHILDCRAFT EDUCATION CORPORATION	11-20
RP	MANIPU	PARQUETRY PLUS	INCENTIVES FOR LEARNING, INC.	6-10

LEVEL	FORMAT	TITLE	PUBLISHER	NT	$PRICE

---

12 - SKILL: VISUAL DISCRIMINATION - SHAPE

LEVEL	FORMAT	TITLE	PUBLISHER	NT	$PRICE
RP	MANIPU	PARQUETRY PLUS DESIGNS	INCENTIVES FOR LEARNING, INC.		<5
RP	MANIPU	SEQUENCING BEADS & DESIGN CARDS	INCENTIVES FOR LEARNING, INC.		11-20
RP	MANIPU	ETA PICTURE & SHAPE SORTING CARDS	EDUCATIONAL TEACHING AIDS		11-20
RP	MANIPU	ETA PRE-READING VISUAL DISCRIMINATION BOARDS	EDUCATIONAL TEACHING AIDS		11-20
RP	MANIPU	ETA DISCOVERY BLOCKS	EDUCATIONAL TEACHING AIDS		21-30
RP	MANIPU	SHIFTING SHAPES, SET 1	IDEAL SCHOOL SUPPLY COMPANY		6-10
RP	MANIPU	SHAPE IN A SHAPE	LAURI, INC.		6-10
RP	MANIPU	FORM PUZZLE	DEVELOPMENTAL LEARNING MATERIALS		<5
RP	MANIPU	SIZE & SHAPE PUZZLE	DEVELOPMENTAL LEARNING MATERIALS		6-10
RP	MANIPU	LACING BOARDS	DEVELOPMENTAL LEARNING MATERIALS		<5
RP	MANIPU	SHAPES SORTING BOX	DEVELOPMENTAL LEARNING MATERIALS		11-20
RP	MANIPU	SHAPE PUZZLES	DEVELOPMENTAL LEARNING MATERIALS		6-10
RP	MANIPU	COLOR & SHAPE SET	DEVELOPMENTAL LEARNING MATERIALS		31-50
RP	MANIPU	LOCKING SHAPES	LITTLE KENNY PUBLICATIONS, INC.		11-20
RP	MANIPU	PARQUETRY DESIGN BLOCKS	MILTON BRADLEY/PLAYSKOOL		6-10
RP	MULTIM	WHAT'S YOUR STORY?	HARCOURT BRACE JOVANOVICH, INC.		101-150
RP	PUPILB	PARADE OF SHAPES	CHILDREN'S PRESS, INC.		6-10
RP	PUPILB	CALICO CAT LOOKS AROUND	CHILDREN'S PRESS, INC.		6-10
RP	PUPILB	VISUAL DISCRIMINATION, BOOK 1: PICTURES	EDUCATIONAL TEACHING AIDS		<5
RP	PUPILB	VISUAL DISCRIMINATION, BOOK 2: SHAPES	EDUCATIONAL TEACHING AIDS		<5
RP	PUPILB	VISUAL DISCRIMINATION, BOOK 3: LINES & SHAPES	EDUCATIONAL TEACHING AIDS		<5
RP	PUPILB	PARADE OF SHAPES	CHILD'S WORLD		<5
RP	PUPILB	MAGIC MONSTERS LOOK FOR SHAPES	CHILD'S WORLD		6-10
RP	SND FS	BASIC SHAPES	CLEARVUE, INC.	6	76-100
RP	SND FS	BASIC SHAPES: FALLING STAR & THE CLEVER CLOWNS	CLEARVUE, INC.		11-20
RP	SND FS	BASIC SHAPES: SAM SHAPE & THE CLUMSY CAR	CLEARVUE, INC.		11-20
RP	SND FS	BASIC SHAPES: SHAPELESSVILLE "SHAPES" UP	CLEARVUE, INC.		11-20
RP	SND FS	BASIC SHAPES: STAR OF TRIANGLE TRAPEZE	CLEARVUE, INC.		11-20
RP	SND FS	BASIC SHAPES: SAM SHAPE MEETS MAGIC MAN	CLEARVUE, INC.		11-20
RP	SND FS	BASIC SHAPES: CIRCULAR CIRCUS ON PARADE	CLEARVUE, INC.		11-20
RP	SND FS	BASIC CONCEPTS	EDUCATIONAL ENRICHMENT MATERIALS		76-100
RP	SND FS	STORIES ABOUT SHAPES	CORONET MULTI MEDIA		76-100
RP	SP EQT	PERCEPTUAL TRAINING, SET 6: BEGINNING ADDITIONS	INSTRUCTIONAL INDUSTRIES (G.E.)		51-75
RP	WKBOOK	MATCH & MEMORY, BOOK 2: VISUAL DISCRIMINATION & PERCEPTION	EDUCATIONAL PROGRAMMERS, INC.		6-10
P	ACTCRD	VISUAL PERCEPTION CARDS	ACADEMIC THERAPY PUBLICATIONS		6-10
P	ACTCRD	SHAPES IN THINGS	IDEAL SCHOOL SUPPLY COMPANY		11-20
P	AUDKIT	VISUAL DISCRIMINATION	EBSCO CURRICULUM MATERIALS		51-75
P	DITTO	SKILL BUILDING SERIES: CODE BOOK	ACADEMIC THERAPY PUBLICATIONS		6-10
P	DITTO	CONFIGURATIONS, BOOK 1	ACADEMIC THERAPY PUBLICATIONS		6-10
P	DITTO	CONFIGURATIONS, BOOK 2	ACADEMIC THERAPY PUBLICATIONS		6-10
P	DITTO	CONFIGURATIONS, BOOK 3	ACADEMIC THERAPY PUBLICATIONS		6-10
P	FLASH	COLORS & SHAPES: FLIP & LEARN FLASHBOOK	MILTON BRADLEY/PLAYSKOOL		<5
P	MANIPU	ETA LETTER DISCRIMINATION INSET BOARDS	EDUCATIONAL TEACHING AIDS		11-20
P	MANIPU	SHAPE BOARD: FARM SHAPES	INVICTA PLASTICS LTD.		6-10
P	MANIPU	SHAPE BOARD: SEA SHAPES	INVICTA PLASTICS LTD.		6-10
P	MANIPU	MIX & MATCH MONSTER PUZZLES	DEVELOPMENTAL LEARNING MATERIALS		6-10
P	MANIPU	MATCH-N-STAMP	LITTLE KENNY PUBLICATIONS, INC.		11-20
P	MANIPU	MATCH-N-FIT: CIRCLES	LITTLE KENNY PUBLICATIONS, INC.		11-20
P	MANIPU	MATCH-N-FIT: TRIANGLES	LITTLE KENNY PUBLICATIONS, INC.		11-20
P	MANIPU	MATCH-N-FIT: SQUARES	LITTLE KENNY PUBLICATIONS, INC.		11-20
P	MANIPU	MATCH-N-FIT: MIXED	LITTLE KENNY PUBLICATIONS, INC.		11-20
P	MULTIU	PERCEPTION TASK CARDS	MILTON BRADLEY/PLAYSKOOL		21-30
P	MULTIM	OBSERVING & DESCRIBING SHAPE	ENCYCLOPEDIA BRITANNICA		31-50
PI	ACTCRD	SEQUENTIAL CARDS, BY SIZE	INCENTIVES FOR LEARNING, INC.		<5
PI	MANIPU	PATTERN BLOCKS TASK CARDS	CREATIVE TEACHING ASSOCIATES		6-10
PI	MULTIM	LISTEN, SPEAK, READ, & SPELL	DEVELOPMENTAL LEARNING MATERIALS		76-100

---

13 - SKILL: VISUAL IDENTIFICATION

LEVEL	FORMAT	TITLE	PUBLISHER	NT	$PRICE
R	AUDCAS	WHAT IS BIG? WHAT IS SMALL?	ASSOCIATED EDUCATIONAL MATERIALS		11-20
R	AUDCAS	MUCH & LITTLE	ASSOCIATED EDUCATIONAL MATERIALS		11-20
R	DITTO	SOUND, WRITE, READ, SPELL	HAYES SCHOOL PUBLISHING COMPANY		<5
R	MANIPU	JUMBO HUNDRED PEGBOARD	CHILDCRAFT EDUCATION CORPORATION		21-30
R	MULTIU	EXPERIENCES WITH PERCEPTION	MILTON BRADLEY/PLAYSKOOL		76-100
R	VISKIT	VERSA-TILES, EARLY CHILDHOOD SET	EDUCATIONAL TEACHING AIDS		11-20
RP	ACTCRD	READINESS: SHAPES & DESIGN REPRODUCTION	INSTRUCTIONAL FAIR		<5
RP	ACTCRD	TUTORGRAM: LANGUAGE ARTS READINESS	ENRICHMENT READING CORP OF AMER.		11-20
RP	ACTCRD	TUTORGRAM: LANGUAGE ARTS READINESS	ENRICHMENT READING CORP OF AMER.		11-20
RP	ACTCRD	TUTORGRAM: BASIC WORD RECOGNITION	ENRICHMENT READING CORP OF AMER.		11-20
RP	ACTCRD	TUTORGRAM: MORE BASIC WORDS	ENRICHMENT READING CORP OF AMER.		11-20
RP	ACTCRD	SAME OR DIFFERENT DESIGN CARDS	DEVELOPMENTAL LEARNING MATERIALS		<5
RP	ACTCRD	SAME OR DIFFERENT PROPORTION CARDS	DEVELOPMENTAL LEARNING MATERIALS		<5
RP	ACTCRD	SAME OR DIFFERENT SIZE CARDS	DEVELOPMENTAL LEARNING MATERIALS		<5
RP	ACTCRD	SYMMETRICAL MATCH-UP	DEVELOPMENTAL LEARNING MATERIALS		<5
RP	ACTCRD	STORY CARDS TELL WHAT PART IS MISSING	MILTON BRADLEY/PLAYSKOOL		<5
RP	AUDKIT	MINISYSTEMS: ORIENTATION TO SHAPES	CORONET MULTI MEDIA		11-20
RP	AUDKIT	MINISYSTEMS: ORIENTATION TO LETTERS	CORONET MULTI MEDIA		11-20
RP	AUDKIT	MINISYSTEMS: LETTER RECOGNITION	CORONET MULTI MEDIA		11-20
RP	AUDKIT	MINISYSTEMS: LETTERS B,M,S,H	CORONET MULTI MEDIA		11-20

LEVEL	FORMAT	TITLE	PUBLISHER	NT	$PRICE

13 - SKILL: VISUAL IDENTIFICATION

LEVEL	FORMAT	TITLE	PUBLISHER	NT	$PRICE
RP	AUDKIT	MINISYSTEMS: LETTERS N,P,F,R	CORONET MULTI MEDIA		11-20
RP	AUDKIT	MINISYSTEMS: LETTERS D,A,E,C	CORONET MULTI MEDIA		11-20
RP	AUDKIT	MINISYSTEMS: LETTERS Y,G,J,K	CORONET MULTI MEDIA		11-20
RP	AUDKIT	MINISYSTEMS: LETTERS L,T,O,W,U,V	CORONET MULTI MEDIA		11-20
RP	A/VKIT	BASIC COLORS	SVE		76-100
RP	CHART	FUN WITH SUPER SHAPES	CREATIVE TEACHING ASSOCIATES		<5
RP	CHART	COLOR CATS	TREND ENTERPRISES, INC.		<5
RP	CHART	LEARNING COLORS	TREND ENTERPRISES, INC.		<5
RP	CHART	PUZZLE POSTERS: ALPHABET VILLAGE	TREND ENTERPRISES, INC.		<5
RP	CL SET	STAR BOOKS	ARISTA CORPORATION		51-75
RP	DITTO	READINESS: SHAPES & DESIGN REPRODUCTION	INSTRUCTIONAL FAIR		<5
RP	DITTO	BASIC COLOS DUPLICATING MASTERS	CLEARVUE, INC.		<5
RP	DITTO	LETTER KNOWLEDGE DUPLICATING MASTERS	SCOTT, FORESMAN & CO.		11-20
RP	DITTO	READING READINESS	GEL-STEN, INC.		<5
RP	DITTO	LETTER RECOGNITION	INSTRUCTO/MCGRAW-HILL		<5
RP	DITTO	LOOK SHARP	ACTIVITY RESOURCES COMPANY, INC.		<5
RP	FILMST	READING READINESS	ENCYCLOPEDIA BRITANNICA		76-100
RP	FLASH	COLOR CARDS	IDEAL SCHOOL SUPPLY COMPANY		<5
RP	GAME	CONNECT	CONSTRUCTIVE PLAYTHINGS		6-10
RP	GAME	GAMEBOARD KIT F	READING JOY, INC.		6-10
RP	GAME	COLOR & SHAPE BINGO	TREND ENTERPRISES, INC.		6-10
RP	GAME	TEDDY BEAR BINGO	MILTON BRADLEY/PLAYSKOOL		6-10
RP	MANIPU	COLOR WORMS	CHILDCRAFT EDUCATION CORPORATION		6-10
RP	MANIPU	MIX 'N' MATCH PUZZLES: COLORS	TREND ENTERPRISES, INC.		6-10
RP	PICTUR	RHYMING PICTURES	INSTRUCTO/MCGRAW-HILL		6-10
RP	PUPILB	ALPHABET CARDS	SCOTT, FORESMAN & CO.		6-10
RP	PUPILB	COLORS FLIP BOOK	TREND ENTERPRISES, INC.		<5
RP	SND FS	BASIC COLORS	CLEARVUE, INC.	6	76-100
RP	SND FS	BASIC COLORS: TRAVELLER, GREEN	CLEARVUE, INC.		11-20
RP	SND FS	BASIC COLORS: MAGICAL FOREST, YELLOW	CLEARVUE, INC.		11-20
RP	SND FS	BASIC COLORS: MR. BLUE JEANS, ORANGE	CLEARVUE, INC.		11-20
RP	SND FS	BASIC COLORS: MAGICIAN, RED	CLEARVUE, INC.		11-20
RP	SND FS	BASIC COLORS: THREE WISHES, BLUE	CLEARVUE, INC.		11-20
RP	SND FS	BASIC COLOS: COLOR FULL WORLD	CLEARVUE, INC.		11-20
RP	SND FS	PERCEPTUAL TRAINING FILMSTRIPS	TROLL ASSOCIATES		101-150
RP	WKBOOK	COLOR-CUT-CREATE	ACADIA PRESS, INC.		<5
RP	WKBOOK	BEGINNING READINESS	JENN PUBLICATIONS		<5
P	ACTCRD	VISUAL PERCEPTION CARDS	ACADEMIC THERAPY PUBLICATIONS		6-10
P	ACTCRD	LITTLE PICTURE CARDS	SCOTT, FORESMAN & CO.		<5
P	ACTCRD	VOCAB-TRACKS	DEVELOPMENTAL LEARNING MATERIALS		<5
P	ACTCRD	VEGETABLES & FRUITS POSTER CARDS	MILTON BRADLEY/PLAYSKOOL		6-10
P	AUDKIT	VISUAL DISCRIMINATION	EBSCO CURRICULUM MATERIALS		51-75
P	AUDKIT	HAPPY WORLD OF COLOR	EDUCATIONAL ACTIVITIES, INC.		11-20
P	CHART	PICTURE COMPOSITE CHART	SOUND MATERIALS		<5
P	DITTO	PRE-READING EXERCISES & PERCEPTUAL SKILLS	BOOK-LAB, INC.		6-10
P	DITTO	WORD SPY, GRADE 1	CONTINENTAL PRESS, INC.		<5
P	DITTO	SKILL BUILDING SERIES: CODE BOOK	ACADEMIC THERAPY PUBLICATIONS		6-10
P	DITTO	SKILL BUILDING SERIES: WORD SHAPES	ACADEMIC THERAPY PUBLICATIONS		6-10
P	DITTO	CONFIGURATIONS, BOOK 1	ACADEMIC THERAPY PUBLICATIONS		6-10
P	DITTO	CONFIGURATIONS, BOOK 2	ACADEMIC THERAPY PUBLICATIONS		6-10
P	DITTO	CONFIGURATIONS, BOOK 3	ACADEMIC THERAPY PUBLICATIONS		6-10
P	DITTO	READING READINESS	MILTON BRADLEY/PLAYSKOOL		<5
P	FILMST	DEVELOPING BASIC SKILLS: WHERE IS IT?	ENCYCLOPEDIA BRITANNICA		31-50
P	FLASH	PICTURE FLASHCARD SET	SOUND MATERIALS		<5
P	GAME	SEQUENCE BINGO	TREND ENTERPRISES, INC.		6-10
P	MANIPU	MAKE-A-WORD CARDS	DEVELOPMENTAL LEARNING MATERIALS		<5
P	MANIPU	SAME OR DIFFERENT WORD CARDS	DEVELOPMENTAL LEARNING MATERIALS		<5
P	MULTIU	READY GO ALPHABET	EDUCATIONAL ACTIVITIES, INC.		51-75
P	MULTIU	PERCEPTION TASK CARDS	MILTON BRADLEY/PLAYSKOOL		21-30
P	PICTUR	WHAT'S WRONG HERE?, LEVEL 1	TEACHING RESOURCES CORPORATION		6-10
P	PICTUR	PICTURE COMPOSITE	SOUND MATERIALS		6-10
P	PUPILB	ORANGE IS A COLOR	LERNER PUBLICATIONS COMPANY		<5
P	SND FS	SEEING CLEARLY: VISUAL READINESS	TROLL ASSOCIATES		51-75
P	SP EQT	LANGUAGE SKILLS PROGRAM: READINESS SKILLS (YY)	SPELLBINDER, INC.		51-75
P	WKBOOK	CUES & SIGNALS I	ANN ARBOR PUBLISHERS		<5
P	WKBOOK	CUES & SIGNALS II	ANN ARBOR PUBLISHERS		<5
P	WKBOOK	CUES & SIGNALS III	ANN ARBOR PUBLISHERS		<5
P	WKBOOK	CUES & SIGNALS IV	ANN ARBOR PUBLISHERS		<5
P	WKBOOK	WORD LISTS	SOUND MATERIALS		6-10
PI	ACTCRD	TUTORGRAM: WORD COMPLETION I	ENRICHMENT READING CORP OF AMER.		11-20
PI	ACTCRD	TUTORGRAM: WORD COMPLETION II	ENRICHMENT READING CORP OF AMER.		11-20
PI	CHART	COLOR WHEEL	MILTON BRADLEY/PLAYSKOOL		<5
PI	DITTO	WORD PERCEPTION	MILTON BRADLEY/PLAYSKOOL		<5
PI	SP EQT	TAC-MATES PROGRAMS: SEEING & WRITING WORDS	AV CONCEPTS CORPORATION		11-20
PI	TRANSP	LANGUAGE DEVELOPMENT & READING SKILLS	UNITED TRANSPARENCIES, INC.		201-300
IJ	PICTUR	WHAT'S WRONG HERE?, LEVEL 2	TEACHING RESOURCES CORPORATION		6-10

14 - SKILL: VISUAL MATCHING - GENERAL

LEVEL	FORMAT	TITLE	PUBLISHER	NT	$PRICE
R	ACTCRD	INTRODUCING ATTRIBUTES, TASK CARDS WITH BLOCKS	CREATIVE TEACHING ASSOCIATES		21-30

LEVEL	FORMAT	TITLE	PUBLISHER	NT	$PRICE

14 - SKILL: VISUAL MATCHING - GENERAL

LEVEL	FORMAT	TITLE	PUBLISHER	$PRICE
R	ACTCRD	WIPE-OFF CARDS: FINDING PAIRS	TREND ENTERPRISES, INC.	<5
R	AUDKIT	STORIES ABOUT LETTERS	CORONET MULTI MEDIA	76-100
R	EQUIPM	PLAY PLANKS	CHILDCRAFT EDUCATION CORPORATION	201-300
R	MANIPU	ANIMAL DOMINOES	DICK BLICK COMPANY	6-10
R	MANIPU	GEOMETRIC SORTING BOARD	CHILDCRAFT EDUCATION CORPORATION	6-10
R	MANIPU	MIX 'N' MATCH PUZZLES: GO-TOGETHERS	TREND ENTERPRISES, INC.	6-10
R	MANIPU	MIX 'N' MATCH PUZZLES: MONEY	TREND ENTERPRISES, INC.	6-10
R	MANIPU	FIRST PUZZLES: MY HOUSE	PLAYSKOOL, INC.	<5
R	MULTIU	PEABODY EARLY EXPERIENCES KIT	AMERICAN GUIDANCE SERVICE, INC.	201-300
R	MULTIU	EXPERIENCES WITH PERCEPTION	MILTON BRADLEY/PLAYSKOOL	76-100
R	SKLKIT	COLOR, SHAPE, TEXTURE, SIZE	DELTA EDUCATION, INC.	21-30
R	VISKIT	VERSA-TILES, EARLY CHILDHOOD SET	EDUCATIONAL TEACHING AIDS	11-20
RP	ACTCRD	MATCHING LETTERS, A	BARNELL LOFT, LTD.	6-10
RP	ACTCRD	MATCHING LETTERS & WORDS, A	BARNELL LOFT, LTD.	6-10
RP	ACTCRD	MATCHING WORDS, A	BARNELL LOFT, LTD.	6-10
RP	ACTCRD	MATCHING UPPER & LOWER CASE LETTERS, A	BARNELL LOFT, LTD.	6-10
RP	ACTCRD	TUTORGRAM: MATCHING	ENRICHMENT READING CORP OF AMER.	11-20
RP	ACTCRD	TUTORGRAM: MATCHING UPPER & LOWER CASE LETTERS	ENRICHMENT READING CORP OF AMER.	11-20
RP	ACTCRD	TUTORGRAM: LANGUAGE ARTS READINESS	ENRICHMENT READING CORP OF AMER.	11-20
RP	ACTCRD	TUTORGRAM: COMMON NOUNS	ENRICHMENT READING CORP OF AMER.	11-20
RP	ACTCRD	SYMMETRICAL MATCH-UP	DEVELOPMENTAL LEARNING MATERIALS	<5
RP	ACTCRD	DESIGN DOMINOES	DEVELOPMENTAL LEARNING MATERIALS	<5
RP	ACTCRD	PICTURES THAT RHYME	MILTON BRADLEY/PLAYSKOOL	<5
RP	AUDKIT	MINISYSTEMS: MATCHING LETTERS, UNLIKE PAIRS Bb,Mm,Rr,Ff	CORONET MULTI MEDIA	11-20
RP	AUDKIT	MINISYSTEMS: MATCHING LETTERS PAIRS Aa,Ee,Hh,Nn	CORONET MULTI MEDIA	11-20
RP	AUDKIT	MINISYSTEMS: MATCHING LETTERS, UNLIKE PAIRS Dd,Gg,Qq	CORONET MULTI MEDIA	11-20
RP	AUDKIT	MINISYSTEMS: MATCHING LETTERS, LIKE PAIRS Cc,Ii,Kk,Pp,Tt	CORONET MULTI MEDIA	11-20
RP	AUDKIT	MINISYSTEMS: MATCHING LETTERS, LIKE PAIRS Ll,Jj,Oo,Ss,Ww	CORONET MULTI MEDIA	11-20
RP	AUDKIT	MINISYSTEMS: LETTER MATCHING GAMES	CORONET MULTI MEDIA	11-20
RP	A/VKIT	STARTER SET: SHAPES, COLORS, SIZES, LETTERS, NUMBERS	EYE GATE MEDIA	76-100
RP	DITTO	I CAN DO IT, PART ONE	GEL-STEN, INC.	<5
RP	FILMST	READING READINESS	ENCYCLOPEDIA BRITANNICA	76-100
RP	FILMST	BEGINNING TO LEARN: PICTURES & LETTERS	URBAN MEDIA MATERIALS, INC.	31-50
RP	GAME	MATCH GAMES, SET 1	GARRARD PUBLISHING COMPANY	<5
RP	GAME	MATCH GAMES, SET 2	GARRARD PUBLISHING COMPANY	<5
RP	GAME	PICTURE CARD GAMES, SET I	MILTON BRADLEY/PLAYSKOOL	6-10
RP	GAME	PICTURE CARD GAMES, SET II	MILTON BRADLEY/PLAYSKOOL	6-10
RP	GAME	PICK-PAIRS CARD GAME	MILTON BRADLEY/PLAYSKOOL	<5
RP	MANIPU	RUBBER DIFFERENCES PUZZLES	CHILDCRAFT EDUCATION CORPORATION	11-20
RP	MANIPU	CHILDCRAFT INTERLOCKING RUBBER ANIMALS	CHILDCRAFT EDUCATION CORPORATION	6-10
RP	MANIPU	VISUAL CLOSURE & DISCRIMINATION PUZZLE KIT	EDUCATIONAL TEACHING AIDS	31-50
RP	MANIPU	PAIRS	EDUCATIONAL TEACHING AIDS	6-10
RP	MANIPU	COMPLEMENTARY OBJECT LOTTO	EDUCATIONAL TEACHING AIDS	6-10
RP	MANIPU	VERSA-TILES	LAURI, INC.	21-30
RP	MANIPU	FORM PUZZLE	DEVELOPMENTAL LEARNING MATERIALS	<5
RP	MANIPU	MIX 'N' MATCH PUZZLES: MAKING PAIRS	TREND ENTERPRISES, INC.	6-10
RP	MANIPU	MIX 'N' MATCH PUZZLES: MATCHING THINGS	TREND ENTERPRISES, INC.	6-10
RP	MANIPU	MIX 'N' MATCH PUZZLES: WHAT'S MISSING?	TREND ENTERPRISES, INC.	6-10
RP	MANIPU	MIX 'N' MATCH PUZZLES: BEFORE & AFTER	TREND ENTERPRISES, INC.	6-10
RP	MANIPU	MIX 'N' MATCH PUZZLES: ANIMALS & THEIR YOUNG	TREND ENTERPRISES, INC.	6-10
RP	MULTIU	GO-TOGETHER: CLASSIFYING & MATCHING	GEL-STEN, INC.	<5
RP	MULTIM	WHAT'S YOUR STORY?	HARCOURT BRACE JOVANOVICH, INC.	101-150
RP	SND FS	PERCEPTUAL TRAINING FILMSTRIPS	TROLL ASSOCIATES	101-150
RP	SP EQT	CHARLIE: ALPHABET, UPPER & LOWER CASE	EDUCATIONAL INSIGHTS, INC.	6-10
RP	WKBOOK	MATCH & MEMORY, BOOK 1: MATCHING OBJECTS & SHAPES	EDUCATIONAL PROGRAMMERS, INC.	6-10
P	ACTCRD	WORD CONFIGURATIONS	TEACHING RESOURCES CORPORATION	11-20
P	ACTCRD	SPREAD I	INCENTIVES FOR LEARNING, INC.	21-30
P	ACTCRD	MARK ON-WIPE OFF CARDS: LOOK ALIKES	IDEAL SCHOOL SUPPLY COMPANY	<5
P	ACTCRD	MARK ON-WIPE OFF CARDS: WHAT GOES TOGETHER?	IDEAL SCHOOL SUPPLY COMPANY	<5
P	ACTCRD	VISUAL DISCRIMINATION LEARNING- MATCHING LETTERS N	EDUCATIONAL PERFORMANCE ASSOC.	31-50
P	ACTCRD	VISUAL DISCRIMINATION LEARNING- MATCHING CAPITALS	EDUCATIONAL PERFORMANCE ASSOC.	31-50
P	ACTCRD	VISUAL DISCRIMINATION LEARNING-BEG. LETTER WORDS	EDUCATIONAL PERFORMANCE ASSOC.	31-50
P	ACTCRD	CAR MATCH-UPS	DEVELOPMENTAL LEARNING MATERIALS	<5
P	ACTCRD	SIZE SEQUENCING CARDS	DEVELOPMENTAL LEARNING MATERIALS	<5
P	ACTCRD	SOUND FOUNDATION, PROGRAM 1	DEVELOPMENTAL LEARNING MATERIALS	11-20
P	ACTCRD	WORD MATCHING FLIP BOOKS	DEVELOPMENTAL LEARNING MATERIALS	11-20
P	ACTCRD	LANGUAGE ARTS-SKILL DRILLS WITH MOTIVATORS	SVE	31-50
P	CHART	CLASSIFICATIONS-OPPOSITES-SEQUENCE	IDEAL SCHOOL SUPPLY COMPANY	11-20
P	DITTO	PRE-READING EXERCISES & PERCEPTUAL SKILLS	BOOK-LAB, INC.	6-10
P	GAME	PHONICS WHEEL	TEACHING RESOURCES CORPORATION	11-20
P	GAME	MISSING MATCH-UPS	DEVELOPMENTAL LEARNING MATERIALS	<5
P	GAME	SPIN-N-MATCH	JUDY COMPANY	11-20
P	GAME	ALPHABET MATCH DOMINOES	JUDY COMPANY	11-20
P	GAME	PAIRS WORD GAME	MILTON BRADLEY/PLAYSKOOL	<5
P	GAME	SPIN & SEE GAMES	MILTON BRADLEY/PLAYSKOOL	6-10
P	MANIPU	FACE & FIGURE PUZZLES	TEACHING RESOURCES CORPORATION	11-20
P	MANIPU	3-D PUZZLE: PIRATE	TEACHING RESOURCES CORPORATION	6-10
P	MANIPU	ANIMAL BODY BLOCKS	TEACHING RESOURCES CORPORATION	11-20
P	MANIPU	THINKER PUZZLES, SET 4	ACADEMIC THERAPY PUBLICATIONS	6-10

LEVEL	FORMAT	TITLE	PUBLISHER	NT	$PRICE

---

14 - SKILL: VISUAL MATCHING - GENERAL

LEVEL	FORMAT	TITLE	PUBLISHER	NT	$PRICE
P	MANIPU	THINKER PUZZLES, SET 5	ACADEMIC THERAPY PUBLICATIONS		6-10
P	MANIPU	THINKER PUZZLES, SET 6	ACADEMIC THERAPY PUBLICATIONS		6-10
P	MANIPU	ROYAL ROAD READING APPARATUS	EDUCATIONAL TEACHING AIDS		21-30
P	MULTIU	PERCEPTION TASK CARDS	MILTON BRADLEY/PLAYSKOOL		21-30
P	RECORD	BUILDING VERBAL POWER, VOLUME 1	CLASSROOM MATERIALS CO.		6-10
P	SP EQT	LANGUAGE SKILLS PROGRAM: READINESS SKILLS (YY)	SPELLBINDER, INC.		51-75
PI	DITTO	WORD PERCEPTION	MILTON BRADLEY/PLAYSKOOL		<5
PI	GAME	ATTRIBUTE DOMINOES	CREATIVE TEACHING ASSOCIATES		6-10
PI	MANIPU	INTRODUCING ATTRIBUTES, SPINNERS WITH BLOCKS	CREATIVE TEACHING ASSOCIATES		21-30
PI	MANIPU	ACTION VERB BOARDS	DEVELOPMENTAL LEARNING MATERIALS		6-10
PI	MANIPU	AERO VISUAL DISCRIMINATION LAB	AERO PUBLISHERS, INC.		76-100
PIJS	GAME	DOUBLE TAKE	CADACO		6-10

---

15 - SKILL: VISUAL MATCHING - COLORS

LEVEL	FORMAT	TITLE	PUBLISHER	NT	$PRICE
R	AUDCAS	COLORS WE SEE	ASSOCIATED EDUCATIONAL MATERIALS		11-20
R	AUDCAS	COLORS AT A PARTY	ASSOCIATED EDUCATIONAL MATERIALS		11-20
R	MANIPU	PRIMARY COLOR BOX	DICK BLICK COMPANY		11-20
R	MANIPU	JUMBO HUNDRED PEGBOARD	CHILDCRAFT EDUCATION CORPORATION		21-30
R	MANIPU	CIRCLE-SQUARE FIT-INS	EDUCATIONAL TEACHING AIDS		6-10
R	MANIPU	COLOR & SHAPE BOARD	EDUCATIONAL TEACHING AIDS		6-10
R	MANIPU	JUMBO ANIMAL DOMINOES	PLAYSKOOL, INC.		11-20
R	SKLKIT	PERCEPTION OF COLOR	DELTA EDUCATION, INC.		11-20
R	WKBOOK	FROM COLOR TO WORDS	CREATIVE TEACHING ASSOCIATES		<5
RP	ACTCRD	COLORCOLOR	COLORCO		6-10
RP	ACTCRD	CUBES IN COLOR	INCENTIVES FOR LEARNING, INC.		6-10
RP	ACTCRD	TUTORGRAM: LANGUAGE ARTS READINESS	ENRICHMENT READING CORP OF AMER.		11-20
RP	AUDKIT	VISUAL, MATCHING, MEMORY & SEQUENCING, BOOKS 4, 5, 6	DEVELOPMENTAL LEARNING MATERIALS		21-30
RP	A/VKIT	BASIC COLORS	SVE		76-100
RP	CHART	FUN WITH COLORS	ENRICH, INC.		<5
RP	CHART	LEARNING COLORS	TREND ENTERPRISES, INC.		<5
RP	CHART	COLORS & SHAPES	CHILD'S WORLD		6-10
RP	DITTO	BASIC COLOS DUPLICATING MASTERS	CLEARVUE, INC.		<5
RP	DITTO	VISUAL PERCEPTION	ACTIVITY RESOURCES COMPANY, INC.		<5
RP	GAME	COLOR & SHAPE BINGO	CONSTRUCTIVE PLAYTHINGS		<5
RP	GAME	SHAPES GAME	CONSTRUCTIVE PLAYTHINGS		6-10
RP	GAME	TEDDY BEAR BINGO	MILTON BRADLEY/PLAYSKOOL		6-10
RP	MANIPU	SHAPES, COLORS & FORMS	CONSTRUCTIVE PLAYTHINGS		6-10
RP	MANIPU	FIT-A-SHAPE	CONSTRUCTIVE PLAYTHINGS		6-10
RP	MANIPU	COLOR TABLETS: SECOND BOX	CONSTRUCTIVE PLAYTHINGS		11-20
RP	MANIPU	COLOR TABLETS: THIRD BOX	CONSTRUCTIVE PLAYTHINGS		31-50
RP	MANIPU	DOTS & COLOR	CHILDCRAFT EDUCATION CORPORATION		11-20
RP	MANIPU	CUBES IN COLOR DESIGN CARDS	INCENTIVES FOR LEARNING, INC.		6-10
RP	MANIPU	SEQUENCING BEADS & DESIGN CARDS	INCENTIVES FOR LEARNING, INC.		11-20
RP	MANIPU	ETA WHAT-IS-MY-COLOR? MATCHING CARDS	EDUCATIONAL TEACHING AIDS		<5
RP	MANIPU	WHAT'S IN THE SQUARE?	EDUCATIONAL TEACHING AIDS		21-30
RP	MANIPU	FIRST BOX OF COLORS	NIENHUIS MONTESSORI, INC.		6-10
RP	MANIPU	SECOND BOX OF COLORS	NIENHUIS MONTESSORI, INC.		11-20
RP	MANIPU	THIRD BOX OF COLORS	NIENHUIS MONTESSORI, INC.		31-50
RP	MANIPU	COLOR MATCHING PUZZLE	DEVELOPMENTAL LEARNING MATERIALS		<5
RP	MANIPU	COLOR & SHAPE SET	DEVELOPMENTAL LEARNING MATERIALS		31-50
RP	MULTIU	DOODLE DOLLY & HER DAO GAN DISCOVER COLORS	EDUCATIONAL DIMENSIONS CORP.		31-50
RP	MULTIM	COLORS EVERYWHERE	SPOKEN ARTS, INC.		151-200
RP	PICTUR	SAME OR DIFFERENT COLOR CARDS	DEVELOPMENTAL LEARNING MATERIALS		<5
RP	PICTUR	COLOR ASSOCIATION PICTURE CARDS	DEVELOPMENTAL LEARNING MATERIALS		<5
RP	PICTUR	COLOR DISCOVERY CARDS	DEVELOPMENTAL LEARNING MATERIALS		<5
RP	PUPILB	COLORS	BRADBURY PRESS, INC.		6-10
RP	PUPILB	I CAN DO IT	BOWMAR/NOBLE PUBLISHERS, INC.		51-75
RP	PUPILB	A WORLD OF COLOR	CHILD'S WORLD		6-10
RP	PUPILB	MAGIC MONSTERS LOOK FOR COLORS	CHILD'S WORLD		6-10
RP	SKLKIT	MULTI-CONCEPT SQUARES	CONSTRUCTIVE PLAYTHINGS		76-100
RP	SND FS	BASIC COLORS	CLEARVUE, INC.	6	76-100
RP	SND FS	BASIC COLORS: TRAVELLER, GREEN	CLEARVUE, INC.		11-20
RP	SND FS	BASIC COLORS: MAGICAL FOREST, YELLOW	CLEARVUE, INC.		11-20
RP	SND FS	BASIC COLORS: MR. BLUE JEANS, ORANGE	CLEARVUE, INC.		11-20
RP	SND FS	BASIC COLORS: MAGICIAN, RED	CLEARVUE, INC.		11-20
RP	SND FS	BASIC COLORS: THREE WISHES, BLUE	CLEARVUE, INC.		11-20
RP	SND FS	COLOR CONCEPTS	EDUCATIONAL ENRICHMENT MATERIALS		101-150
RP	SND FS	STORIES ABOUT COLORS	CORONET MULTI MEDIA		101-150
RP	WKBOOK	VISUAL, MATHING, MEMORY & SEQUENCING, BOOKS 1, 2, 3	DEVELOPMENTAL LEARNING MATERIALS		21-30
RPI	MANIPU	COLOR TABLETS: FIRST BOX	CONSTRUCTIVE PLAYTHINGS		6-10
P	ACTCRD	MARK ON-WIPE OFF CARDS: MATCHING COLORS	IDEAL SCHOOL SUPPLY COMPANY		<5
P	ACTCRD	COLOR MIX & MATCH	IDEAL SCHOOL SUPPLY COMPANY		11-20
P	ACTCRD	PEG PADS	DEVELOPMENTAL LEARNING MATERIALS		<5
P	ACTCRD	PEGBOARD DESIGNS	DEVELOPMENTAL LEARNING MATERIALS		11-20
P	ACTCRD	LARGE PARQUETRY DESIGNS CARDS	DEVELOPMENTAL LEARNING MATERIALS		<5
P	AUDKIT	ICE CREAM COLOR-CONES	MEDIA MATERIALS, INC.		6-10
P	AUDKIT	HAPPY WORLD OF COLOR	EDUCATIONAL ACTIVITIES, INC.		11-20
P	CHART	COLOR RECOGNITION CHART	IDEAL SCHOOL SUPPLY COMPANY		<5

LEVEL	FORMAT	TITLE	PUBLISHER	NT	$PRICE

15 - SKILL: VISUAL MATCHING - COLORS

LEVEL	FORMAT	TITLE	PUBLISHER	NT	$PRICE
P	CHART	COLOR TRAIN	IDEAL SCHOOL SUPPLY COMPANY		<5
P	CL SET	VISUAL MATCHING, MEMORY & SEQUENCING EXERCISES	DEVELOPMENTAL LEARNING MATERIALS	6	31-50
P	FLASH	COLOR NAME CARDS	IDEAL SCHOOL SUPPLY COMPANY		<5
P	FLASH	COLOR GRADATION CARDS	IDEAL SCHOOL SUPPLY COMPANY		<5
P	FLASH	COLORS & SHAPES: FLIP & LEARN FLASHBOOK	MILTON BRADLEY/PLAYSKOOL		<5
P	GAME	COLOR RECOGNITION	FRANK SCHAFFER PUBLICATIONS, INC		<5
P	GAME	ETA COLOR BINGO	EDUCATIONAL TEACHING AIDS		6-10
P	GAME	COLOR & SHAPE MEMORY GAME	DEVELOPMENTAL LEARNING MATERIALS		11-20
P	MANIPU	PEGBOARD	DEVELOPMENTAL LEARNING MATERIALS		<5
P	MANIPU	PEGS	DEVELOPMENTAL LEARNING MATERIALS		<5
P	MANIPU	LARGE PARQUETRY BLOCKS, WOOD	DEVELOPMENTAL LEARNING MATERIALS		6-10
P	MANIPU	SMALL PARQUETRY BLOCKS	DEVELOPMENTAL LEARNING MATERIALS		6-10
P	MANIPU	SMALL PARQUETRY, DESIGN I	DEVELOPMENTAL LEARNING MATERIALS		<5
P	MANIPU	SMALL PARQUETRY, DESIGN II	DEVELOPMENTAL LEARNING MATERIALS		<5
P	MANIPU	SMALL PARQUETRY, DESIGN III	DEVELOPMENTAL LEARNING MATERIALS		<5
P	MANIPU	SORTING BOX & ACCESSORIES	DEVELOPMENTAL LEARNING MATERIALS		21-30
P	MANIPU	COLOR LOTTO	JUDY COMPANY		6-10
P	MULTIU	COLOR	EDUCATIONAL DIMENSIONS CORP.		76-100
P	PUPILB	ORANGE IS A COLOR	LERNER PUBLICATIONS COMPANY		<5
P	VISKIT	COLOR CHARTS	INSTRUCTOR PUBLICATIONS, INC.		6-10
PI	CHART	COLOR WHEEL	MILTON BRADLEY/PLAYSKOOL		<5
PI	MANIPU	POPEYE'S SPECIAL LANGUAGE BUILDER: MATCHING DOMINOES(SP.ED.)	KING FEATURES		11-20

16 - SKILL: VISUAL MATCHING - SIZE

LEVEL	FORMAT	TITLE	PUBLISHER	NT	$PRICE
R	MANIPU	CIRCLE-SQUARE FIT-INS	EDUCATIONAL TEACHING AIDS		6-10
R	SKLKIT	RECOGNIZING & USING SHAPES	DELTA EDUCATION, INC.		31-50
RP	DITTO	WHAT'S NEXT?	IDEAL SCHOOL SUPPLY COMPANY		6-10
RP	DITTO	VISUAL PERCEPTION	ACTIVITY RESOURCES COMPANY, INC.		<5
RP	GAME	FROGGIE	IDEAL SCHOOL SUPPLY COMPANY		6-10
RP	MANIPU	FIT-A-SIZE	CONSTRUCTIVE PLAYTHINGS		6-10
RP	MANIPU	SHAPES, COLORS & FORMS	CONSTRUCTIVE PLAYTHINGS		6-10
RP	MANIPU	WHAT SIZE LOTTO	CONSTRUCTIVE PLAYTHINGS		6-10
RP	MANIPU	SIZE & SHAPE PUZZLES WITH KNOBS: TWO LADYBUGS	CHILDCRAFT EDUCATION CORPORATION		11-20
RP	MANIPU	SIZE & SHAPE PUZZLES WITH KNOBS: SNOWMAN	CHILDCRAFT EDUCATION CORPORATION		11-20
RP	MANIPU	SIZE & SHAPE PUZZLES WITH KNOBS: FLOWER POT	CHILDCRAFT EDUCATION CORPORATION		11-20
RP	MANIPU	SIZE & SHAPE PUZZLES WITH KNOBS: KITES	CHILDCRAFT EDUCATION CORPORATION		11-20
RP	MANIPU	SIZE & SHAPE PUZZLES WITH KNOBS: THREE FISH	CHILDCRAFT EDUCATION CORPORATION		11-20
RP	MANIPU	SIZE & SHAPE PUZZLES WITH KNOBS: TOAD STOOL	CHILDCRAFT EDUCATION CORPORATION		11-20
RP	MANIPU	SIZE & SHAPE PUZZLES WITH KNOBS: FOUR DUCKS	CHILDCRAFT EDUCATION CORPORATION		11-20
RP	MANIPU	SIZE & SHAPE PUZZLES WITH KNOBS: BIRDS IN A FRUIT TREE	CHILDCRAFT EDUCATION CORPORATION		11-20
RP	MANIPU	WHAT'S IN THE SQUARE?	EDUCATIONAL TEACHING AIDS		21-30
RP	MANIPU	ETA DISCOVERY BLOCKS	EDUCATIONAL TEACHING AIDS		21-30
RP	PUPILB	I CAN DO IT	BOWMAR/NOBLE PUBLISHERS, INC.		51-75
RP	SKLKIT	MULTI-CONCEPT SQUARES	CONSTRUCTIVE PLAYTHINGS		76-100
P	MANIPU	SIZE INSERT PUZZLES	TEACHING RESOURCES CORPORATION		21-30
P	MANIPU	FRUIT & VEGETABLE INSERT PUZZLES	TEACHING RESOURCES CORPORATION		21-30
P	MANIPU	ANIMAL INSERT PUZZLES	TEACHING RESOURCES CORPORATION		21-30
I	DITTO	VOCABULARY BUILDING, INTERMEDIATE	HAYES SCHOOL PUBLISHING COMPANY		<5

17 - SKILL: VISUAL MATCHING - SHAPE

LEVEL	FORMAT	TITLE	PUBLISHER	NT	$PRICE
R	AUDCAS	LOOKING FOR ROUND SHAPES	ASSOCIATED EDUCATIONAL MATERIALS		11-20
R	AUDCAS	LOOKING FOR SQUARE SHAPES	ASSOCIATED EDUCATIONAL MATERIALS		11-20
R	AUDCAS	WHAT IS BIG? WHAT IS SMALL?	ASSOCIATED EDUCATIONAL MATERIALS		11-20
R	MANIPU	FIT-A-SQUARE, FIT-A-CIRCLE	CHILDCRAFT EDUCATION CORPORATION		6-10
R	MANIPU	JUMBO HUNDRED PEGBOARD	CHILDCRAFT EDUCATION CORPORATION		21-30
R	MANIPU	VARI-SHAPE BEADS	CHILDCRAFT EDUCATION CORPORATION		11-20
R	MANIPU	SIZE FIT-INS	EDUCATIONAL TEACHING AIDS		6-10
R	MANIPU	COLOR & SHAPE BOARD	EDUCATIONAL TEACHING AIDS		6-10
R	MANIPU	MIXED SHAPE-FINDING	EDUCATIONAL TEACHING AIDS		6-10
R	MANIPU	ETA JUMBO FORM BOARD	EDUCATIONAL TEACHING AIDS		6-10
R	MANIPU	SHAPE SORTING CUBES	EDUCATIONAL TEACHING AIDS		6-10
R	PUPILB	CIRCLES, TRIANGLES, SQUARES	CHILDCRAFT EDUCATION CORPORATION		6-10
R	SKLKIT	THREE-DIMENSIONAL SHAPES	DELTA EDUCATION, INC.		21-30
RP	ACTCRD	TUTORGRAM: LANGUAGE ARTS READINESS	ENRICHMENT READING CORP OF AMER.		11-20
RP	ACTCRD	CURVES & CORNERS	IDEAL SCHOOL SUPPLY COMPANY		11-20
RP	ACTCRD	SHAPE DOMINOES	DEVELOPMENTAL LEARNING MATERIALS		<5
RP	ACTCRD	MULTIMOES	DEVELOPMENTAL LEARNING MATERIALS		<5
RP	AUDCAS	DOODLE DOLLY & HER DAN DISCOVER SHAPES	EDUCATIONAL DIMENSIONS CORP.		31-50
RP	AUDKIT	HOWDY PARTNER	MEDIA MATERIALS, INC.		6-10
RP	A/VKIT	BASIC SHAPES	SVE		76-100
RP	CHART	COLORS & SHAPES	CHILD'S WORLD		6-10
RP	CL SET	FIVE SENSE STORE	COMENIUS, INC.	6	>450
RP	CL SET	SHAPES	COMENIUS, INC.		76-100
RP	CL SET	SHAPE RELATIONSHIPS	COMENIUS, INC.		76-100
RP	CL SET	SHAPE & PATTERNS	COMENIUS, INC.		76-100
RP	DITTO	BASIC SHAPES DUPLICATING MASTERS	CLEARVUE, INC.		<5
RP	DITTO	VISUAL PERCEPTION	ACTIVITY RESOURCES COMPANY, INC.		<5
RP	GAME	COLOR & SHAPE BINGO	CONSTRUCTIVE PLAYTHINGS		<5

LEVEL	FORMAT	TITLE	PUBLISHER	NT	$PRICE

17 - SKILL: VISUAL MATCHING - SHAPE

LEVEL	FORMAT	TITLE	PUBLISHER	NT	$PRICE
RP	GAME	SHAPES GAME	CONSTRUCTIVE PLAYTHINGS		6-10
RP	MANIPU	DESIGN FORM BOARD	DICK BLICK COMPANY		11-20
RP	MANIPU	COORDINATION BOARD	DICK BLICK COMPANY		<5
RP	MANIPU	SEQUENTIAL SORTING BOX	CONSTRUCTIVE PLAYTHINGS		11-20
RP	MANIPU	SHAPES BOARD	CONSTRUCTIVE PLAYTHINGS		6-10
RP	MANIPU	SHAPES, COLORS & FORMS	CONSTRUCTIVE PLAYTHINGS		6-10
RP	MANIPU	FIT-A-SHAPE	CONSTRUCTIVE PLAYTHINGS		6-10
RP	MANIPU	FAMILIAR THINGS PUZZLE	CONSTRUCTIVE PLAYTHINGS		6-10
RP	MANIPU	SIZE & SHAPE PUZZLES WITH KNOBS: TWO LADYBUGS	CHILDCRAFT EDUCATION CORPORATION		11-20
RP	MANIPU	SIZE & SHAPE PUZZLES WITH KNOBS: SNOWMAN	CHILDCRAFT EDUCATION CORPORATION		11-20
RP	MANIPU	SIZE & SHAPE PUZZLES WITH KNOBS: FLOWER POT	CHILDCRAFT EDUCATION CORPORATION		11-20
RP	MANIPU	SIZE & SHAPE PUZZLES WITH KNOBS: KITES	CHILDCRAFT EDUCATION CORPORATION		11-20
RP	MANIPU	SIZE & SHAPE PUZZLES WITH KNOBS: THREE FISH	CHILDCRAFT EDUCATION CORPORATION		11-20
RP	MANIPU	SIZE & SHAPE PUZZLES WITH KNOBS: TOAD STOOL	CHILDCRAFT EDUCATION CORPORATION		11-20
RP	MANIPU	SIZE & SHAPE PUZZLES WITH KNOBS: FOUR DUCKS	CHILDCRAFT EDUCATION CORPORATION		11-20
RP	MANIPU	SIZE & SHAPE PUZZLES WITH KNOBS: BIRDS IN A FRUIT TREE	CHILDCRAFT EDUCATION CORPORATION		11-20
RP	MANIPU	SHAPERINO	CHILDCRAFT EDUCATION CORPORATION		<5
RP	MANIPU	GEO-SHAPE BOARD	CHILDCRAFT EDUCATION CORPORATION		21-30
RP	MANIPU	PARQUETRY PLUS	INCENTIVES FOR LEARNING, INC.		6-10
RP	MANIPU	PARQUETRY PLUS DESIGNS	INCENTIVES FOR LEARNING, INC.		<5
RP	MANIPU	SEQUENCING BEADS & DESIGN CARDS	INCENTIVES FOR LEARNING, INC.		11-20
RP	MANIPU	WHAT'S IN THE SQUARE?	EDUCATIONAL TEACHING AIDS		21-30
RP	MANIPU	ETA DISCOVERY BLOCKS	EDUCATIONAL TEACHING AIDS		21-30
RP	MANIPU	SHIFTING SHAPES, SET 1	IDEAL SCHOOL SUPPLY COMPANY		6-10
RP	MANIPU	SHAPE IN A SHAPE	LAURI, INC.		6-10
RP	MANIPU	SHAPES SORTING BOX	DEVELOPMENTAL LEARNING MATERIALS		11-20
RP	MANIPU	SHAPE PUZZLES	DEVELOPMENTAL LEARNING MATERIALS		6-10
RP	MANIPU	COLOR & SHAPE SET	DEVELOPMENTAL LEARNING MATERIALS		31-50
RP	MANIPU	LOCKING SHAPES	LITTLE KENNY PUBLICATIONS, INC.		11-20
RP	PUPILB	I CAN DO IT	BOWMAR/NOBLE PUBLISHERS, INC.		51-75
RP	PUPILB	PARADE OF SHAPES	CHILD'S WORLD		<5
RP	PUPILB	MAGIC MONSTERS LOOK FOR SHAPES	CHILD'S WORLD		6-10
RP	SKLKIT	MULTI-CONCEPT SQUARES	CONSTRUCTIVE PLAYTHINGS		76-100
RP	SND FS	BASIC SHAPES	CLEARVUE, INC.	6	76-100
RP	SND FS	BASIC SHAPES: FALLING STAR & THE CLEVER CLOWNS	CLEARVUE, INC.		11-20
RP	SND FS	BASIC SHAPES: SAM SHAPE & THE CLUMSY CAR	CLEARVUE, INC.		11-20
RP	SND FS	BASIC SHAPES: SHAPELESSVILLE "SHAPES" UP	CLEARVUE, INC.		11-20
RP	SND FS	BASIC SHAPES: STAR OF TRIANGLE TRAPEZE	CLEARVUE, INC.		11-20
RP	SND FS	BASIC SHAPES: SAM SHAPE MEETS MAGIC MAN	CLEARVUE, INC.		11-20
RP	SND FS	BASIC SHAPES: CIRCULAR CIRCUS ON PARADE	CLEARVUE, INC.		11-20
RP	SND FS	STORIES ABOUT SHAPES	CORONET MULTI MEDIA		76-100
RP	WKBOOK	MATCH THE ANIMALS, TELL & DRAW WORKBOOK	CREATIVE STORYTIME PRESS		<5
RP	WKBOOK	MATCH & MEMORY, BOOK 1: MATCHING OBJECTS & SHAPES	EDUCATIONAL PROGRAMMERS, INC.		6-10
P	ACTCRD	VISUAL PERCEPTION CARDS	ACADEMIC THERAPY PUBLICATIONS		6-10
P	ACTCRD	SHAPES IN THINGS	IDEAL SCHOOL SUPPLY COMPANY		11-20
P	DITTO	CONFIGURATIONS, BOOK 1	ACADEMIC THERAPY PUBLICATIONS		6-10
P	DITTO	CONFIGURATIONS, BOOK 2	ACADEMIC THERAPY PUBLICATIONS		6-10
P	DITTO	CONFIGURATIONS, BOOK 3	ACADEMIC THERAPY PUBLICATIONS		6-10
P	FILMST	DEVELOPING TECHNIQUES IN CONCENTRATION	CLASSROOM MATERIALS CO.		51-75
P	FLASH	COLORS & SHAPES: FLIP & LEARN FLASHBOOK	MILTON BRADLEY/PLAYSKOOL		<5
P	GAME	BUILD A SHAPE GAME	EDUCATIONAL TEACHING AIDS		11-20
P	GAME	COLOR & SHAPE MEMORY GAME	DEVELOPMENTAL LEARNING MATERIALS		11-20
P	MANIPU	THINKER PUZZLES, SET 1	ACADEMIC THERAPY PUBLICATIONS		6-10
P	MANIPU	THINKER PUZZLES, SET 2	ACADEMIC THERAPY PUBLICATIONS		6-10
P	MANIPU	THINKER PUZZLES, SET 3	ACADEMIC THERAPY PUBLICATIONS		6-10
P	MANIPU	SHAPE BOARD: FARM SHAPES	INVICTA PLASTICS LTD.		6-10
P	MANIPU	SHAPE BOARD: SEA SHAPES	INVICTA PLASTICS LTD.		6-10
P	MANIPU	LARGE PARQUETRY INSET BOARDS	DEVELOPMENTAL LEARNING MATERIALS		<5
P	MANIPU	SORTING BOX & ACCESSORIES	DEVELOPMENTAL LEARNING MATERIALS		21-30
PI	ACTCRD	SEQUENTIAL CARDS, BY SIZE	INCENTIVES FOR LEARNING, INC.		<5
PI	MANIPU	PATTERN BLOCKS TASK CARDS	CREATIVE TEACHING ASSOCIATES		6-10
IJ	AUDCAS	PRIMARY PATTERN BLOCKS TASK CARDS	CREATIVE TEACHING ASSOCIATES		6-10

18 - SKILL: VISUAL SORTING

LEVEL	FORMAT	TITLE	PUBLISHER	NT	$PRICE
R	EQUIPM	PLAY-ALL	CHILDCRAFT EDUCATION CORPORATION		51-75
R	MANIPU	GEOMETRIC SORTING BOARD	CHILDCRAFT EDUCATION CORPORATION		6-10
R	MANIPU	SEQUENTIAL SORTING BOX	IDEAL SCHOOL SUPPLY COMPANY		11-20
R	MULTIU	PEABODY EARLY EXPERIENCES KIT	AMERICAN GUIDANCE SERVICE, INC.		201-300
RP	DITTO	WHAT'S NEXT?	IDEAL SCHOOL SUPPLY COMPANY		6-10
RP	DITTO	I CAN DO IT, PART ONE	GEL-STEN, INC.		<5
RP	GAME	PICTURE CARD GAMES, SET I	MILTON BRADLEY/PLAYSKOOL		6-10
RP	GAME	PICTURE CARD GAMES, SET II	MILTON BRADLEY/PLAYSKOOL		6-10
RP	MANIPU	COLOR/SHAPE ABACUS	CHILDCRAFT EDUCATION CORPORATION		11-20
RP	MANIPU	SEQUENTIAL SORTING BOX	CHILDCRAFT EDUCATION CORPORATION		11-20
RP	MANIPU	SHAPES SORTING BOX	DEVELOPMENTAL LEARNING MATERIALS		11-20
RP	MANIPU	COLOR & SHAPE SET	DEVELOPMENTAL LEARNING MATERIALS		31-50
RP	MULTIU	GO-TOGETHER: CLASSIFYING & MATCHING	GEL-STEN, INC.		<5
P	ACTCRD	PICTURE CARDS	MILTON BRADLEY/PLAYSKOOL		6-10
P	GAME	CONCEPTO-SORT	EDUCATIONAL PERFORMANCE ASSOC.		6-10

LEVEL	FORMAT	TITLE	PUBLISHER	NT	$PRICE

18 - SKILL: VISUAL SORTING

LEVEL	FORMAT	TITLE	PUBLISHER		$PRICE
P	GAME	ANIMAL SORTING GAME, FARM ANIMALS	DEVELOPMENTAL LEARNING MATERIALS		<5
P	GAME	ANIMAL SORTING GAME, FOREST ANIMALS	DEVELOPMENTAL LEARNING MATERIALS		<5
P	GAME	ANIMAL SORTING GAME, WILD ANIMALS	DEVELOPMENTAL LEARNING MATERIALS		<5
P	MANIPU	COUNTING & SORTING TRAY	INVICTA PLASTICS LTD.		6-10
P	MANIPU	COUNTING & SORTING: ANIMAL SHAPES	INVICTA PLASTICS LTD.		11-20
P	MANIPU	COUNTING & SORTING: TRANSPORT SHAPES	INVICTA PLASTICS LTD.		6-10
P	MANIPU	COUNTING & SORTING: MIXED SHAPES	INVICTA PLASTICS LTD.		6-10
P	MANIPU	COUNTING & SORTING: COUNTERS	INVICTA PLASTICS LTD.		6-10
P	MANIPU	SAME OR DIFFERENT WORD CARDS	DEVELOPMENTAL LEARNING MATERIALS		<5
P	MANIPU	SORTING BOX & ACCESSORIES	DEVELOPMENTAL LEARNING MATERIALS		21-30
P	MANIPU	SORTING & GROUPING SET	DEVELOPMENTAL LEARNING MATERIALS		<5
P	PUPILB	SORTING FLIP BOOK	TREND ENTERPRISES, INC.		<5
P	WKBOOK	FITZHUGH PLUS PROGRAM, BOOK 104: SHAPE ANALYSIS & SEQUENC.	ALLIED EDUCATION COUNCIL		<5

19 - SKILL: VISUAL ASSOCIATION

LEVEL	FORMAT	TITLE	PUBLISHER		$PRICE
R	MULTIU	EXPERIENCES IN READING READINESS	MILTON BRADLEY/PLAYSKOOL		76-100
RP	ACTCRD	TUTORGRAM: BODY PARTS & EVERYDAY THINGS	ENRICHMENT READING CORP OF AMER.		11-20
RP	ACTCRD	PICTURE WORD CARDS	GARRARD PUBLISHING COMPANY		<5
RP	ACTCRD	STORY CARDS TELL WHAT PART IS MISSING	MILTON BRADLEY/PLAYSKOOL		<5
RP	AUDKIT	MINISYSTEMS: ORIENTATION TO SHAPES	CORONET MULTI MEDIA		11-20
RP	AUDKIT	MINISYSTEMS: ORIENTATION TO LETTERS	CORONET MULTI MEDIA		11-20
RP	DITTO	I CAN DO IT, PART TWO	GEL-STEN, INC.		<5
RP	GAME	MATCH GAMES, SET 1	GARRARD PUBLISHING COMPANY		<5
RP	GAME	MATCH GAMES, SET 2	GARRARD PUBLISHING COMPANY		<5
RP	GAME	CLASSIFICATION GAME	EDUCATIONAL TEACHING AIDS		11-20
RP	MANIPU	PARQUETRY PLUS	INCENTIVES FOR LEARNING, INC.		6-10
RP	MANIPU	PARQUETRY PLUS DESIGNS	INCENTIVES FOR LEARNING, INC.		<5
RP	MANIPU	BASIC-CUT, PUZZLE 1	DEVELOPMENTAL LEARNING MATERIALS		6-10
RP	MANIPU	BASIC-CUT, PUZZLE 2	DEVELOPMENTAL LEARNING MATERIALS		6-10
RP	MANIPU	BASIC-CUT PEOPLE PUZZLES	DEVELOPMENTAL LEARNING MATERIALS		6-10
RP	MANIPU	ANIMAL PUZZLES	DEVELOPMENTAL LEARNING MATERIALS		6-10
RP	MULTIM	HELP: PATTERN DETECTION	CENTER FOR EARLY LEARNING		6-10
RP	PICTUR	PEOPLE, PLACES & THINGS: OCCUPATIONS	TEACHING RESOURCES CORPORATION		6-10
RP	PICTUR	PEOPLE, PLACES & THINGS: STORIES	TEACHING RESOURCES CORPORATION		6-10
RP	PUPILB	I CAN DO IT	BOWMAR/NOBLE PUBLISHERS, INC.		51-75
RP	SKLKIT	MULTI-CONCEPT SQUARES	CONSTRUCTIVE PLAYTHINGS		76-100
P	ACTCRD	MARK ON-WIPE OFF CARDS: MATCHING COLORS	IDEAL SCHOOL SUPPLY COMPANY		<5
P	ACTCRD	MARK ON-WIPE OFF CARDS: LOOK ALIKES	IDEAL SCHOOL SUPPLY COMPANY		<5
P	ACTCRD	MARK ON-WIPE OFF CARDS: WHAT GOES TOGETHER?	IDEAL SCHOOL SUPPLY COMPANY		<5
P	ACTCRD	MARK ON-WIPE OFF CARDS: MATCHING MOTHERS & BABIES	IDEAL SCHOOL SUPPLY COMPANY		<5
P	ACTCRD	LARGE PARQUETRY DESIGNS CARDS	DEVELOPMENTAL LEARNING MATERIALS		<5
P	ACTCRD	ASSOCIATION PICTURE CARDS 1	DEVELOPMENTAL LEARNING MATERIALS		<5
P	ACTCRD	ASSOCIATION PICTURE CARDS 2	DEVELOPMENTAL LEARNING MATERIALS		<5
P	ACTCRD	ASSOCIATION PICTURE CARDS 3	DEVELOPMENTAL LEARNING MATERIALS		<5
P	ACTCRD	ASSOCIATION PICTURE CARDS 4	DEVELOPMENTAL LEARNING MATERIALS		<5
P	ACTCRD	PART/WHOLE LOTTO	MILTON BRADLEY/PLAYSKOOL		<5
P	AUDKIT	ANIMAL CRACKERS	MEDIA MATERIALS, INC.		6-10
P	DITTO	SKILL BUILDING SERIES: WORD SHAPES	ACADEMIC THERAPY PUBLICATIONS		6-10
P	DITTO	PHONICS & READING	HAYES SCHOOL PUBLISHING COMPANY		<5
P	FLASH	PICTURE FLASH WORDS FOR BEGINNERS	MILTON BRADLEY/PLAYSKOOL		<5
P	GAME	COLOR RECOGNITION	FRANK SCHAFFER PUBLICATIONS, INC		<5
P	GAME	EDUCATIONAL PASSWORD	MILTON BRADLEY/PLAYSKOOL		<5
P	GAME	PAIRS WORD GAME	MILTON BRADLEY/PLAYSKOOL		<5
P	GAME	SPIN & SEE GAMES	MILTON BRADLEY/PLAYSKOOL		6-10
P	MANIPU	GO TOGETHER LOTTO	NIENHUIS MONTESSORI, INC.		21-30
P	MANIPU	LARGE PARQUETRY BLOCKS, WOOD	DEVELOPMENTAL LEARNING MATERIALS		6-10
P	MANIPU	SMALL PARQUETRY BLOCKS	DEVELOPMENTAL LEARNING MATERIALS		6-10
P	MANIPU	SMALL PARQUETRY, DESIGN I	DEVELOPMENTAL LEARNING MATERIALS		<5
P	MANIPU	SMALL PARQUETRY, DESIGN II	DEVELOPMENTAL LEARNING MATERIALS		<5
P	MANIPU	SMALL PARQUETRY, DESIGN III	DEVELOPMENTAL LEARNING MATERIALS		<5
P	PICTUR	PEOPLE, PLACES & THINGS: RECREATION	TEACHING RESOURCES CORPORATION		6-10
P	PICTUR	PEOPLE, PLACES & THINGS: SPORTS	TEACHING RESOURCES CORPORATION		6-10
P	VISKIT	COLOR CHARTS	INSTRUCTOR PUBLICATIONS, INC.		6-10
P	VISKIT	PICTURE/WORD CONCEPTS: CLOTHING	INSTRUCTOR PUBLICATIONS, INC.		<5
P	VISKIT	PICTURE/WORD CONCEPTS: HOUSEHOLD ITEMS	INSTRUCTOR PUBLICATIONS, INC.		<5
P	VISKIT	PICTURE/WORD CONCEPTS: CLOTHING ACCESSORIES	INSTRUCTOR PUBLICATIONS, INC.		<5
P	VISKIT	PICTURE/WORD CONCEPTS: DISHES & UTENSILS	INSTRUCTOR PUBLICATIONS, INC.		<5
P	VISKIT	PICTURE/WORD CONCEPTS: SCHOOL ITEMS	INSTRUCTOR PUBLICATIONS, INC.		<5
P	WKBOOK	SOUND WE USE, BOOK 1	HAYES SCHOOL PUBLISHING COMPANY		<5
PI	MANIPU	AERO VISUAL DISCRIMINATION LAB	AERO PUBLISHERS, INC.		76-100
PI	SP EQT	TAC-MATES PROGRAMS: SEEING & WRITING WORDS	AV CONCEPTS CORPORATION		11-20

20 - SKILL: VISUAL FIGURE-GROUND

LEVEL	FORMAT	TITLE	PUBLISHER		$PRICE
R	MULTIU	EXPERIENCES WITH PERCEPTION	MILTON BRADLEY/PLAYSKOOL		76-100
RP	ACTCRD	STRING ALONG ADVANCED PATTERNS	DEVELOPMENTAL LEARNING MATERIALS		6-10
RP	ACTCRD	FIGURE-GROUND ACTIVITY CARDS	DEVELOPMENTAL LEARNING MATERIALS		6-10
RP	GAME	FIND IT LOTTO	CONSTRUCTIVE PLAYTHINGS		6-10
RP	MANIPU	STRING ALONG	DEVELOPMENTAL LEARNING MATERIALS		11-20

LEVEL	FORMAT	TITLE	PUBLISHER	NT	$PRICE

20 - SKILL: VISUAL FIGURE-GROUND

LEVEL	FORMAT	TITLE	PUBLISHER	$PRICE
RP	PICTUR	CAMOUFLAGED ANIMAL CARDS	DEVELOPMENTAL LEARNING MATERIALS	6-10
RP	SND FS	PERCEPTUAL TRAINING FILMSTRIPS	TROLL ASSOCIATES	101-150
P	DITTO	CATEGORY WORD HUNT I	DEVELOPMENTAL LEARNING MATERIALS	<5
P	DITTO	CATEGORY WORD HUNT II	DEVELOPMENTAL LEARNING MATERIALS	<5
P	DITTO	BEGINNING SOUND WORD HUNT I	DEVELOPMENTAL LEARNING MATERIALS	<5
P	DITTO	BEGINNING SOUND WORD HUNT II	DEVELOPMENTAL LEARNING MATERIALS	<5
P	DITTO	READING READINESS	MILTON BRADLEY/PLAYSKOOL	<5
P	FILMST	DEVELOPING TECHNIQUES IN CONCENTRATION	CLASSROOM MATERIALS CO.	51-75
PI	DITTO	PERCEPTUAL ENHANCEMENT: FIGURE-GROUND	MODERN EDUCATION CORPORATION	6-10

21 - SKILL: VISUAL SPATIAL RELATIONSHIPS

LEVEL	FORMAT	TITLE	PUBLISHER	$PRICE
R	AUDKIT	VISUAL DISCRIMINATION	MEDIA MATERIALS, INC.	6-10
R	MANIPU	JUMBO HUNDRED PEGBOARD	CHILDCRAFT EDUCATION CORPORATION	21-30
R	WKBOOK	LESSONS TO GROW ON, BOOK 1	PRESCHOOL LEARNING CORPORATION	<5
RP	ACTCRD	WHAT IS IT? SPATIAL RELATIONSHIP CARDS	IDEAL SCHOOL SUPPLY COMPANY	<5
RP	CHART	PUZZLE POSTERS: DONKEY TRAIL	TREND ENTERPRISES, INC.	<5
RP	CHART	DINOSAURS & SPATIAL RELATIONSHIPS	ACTIVITY RESOURCES COMPANY, INC.	<5
RP	DITTO	MAZES	MILTON BRADLEY/PLAYSKOOL	<5
RP	PUPILB	I CAN DO IT	BOWMAR/NOBLE PUBLISHERS, INC.	51-75
RP	SND FS	PERCEPTUAL TRAINING FILMSTRIPS	TROLL ASSOCIATES	101-150
RP	WKBOOK	COLOR WORDS, LEFT & RIGHT: PROBLEM SOLVING, PHONICS, OPPOS.	JENN PUBLICATIONS	<5
P	ACTCRD	LARGE PARQUETRY DESIGNS CARDS	DEVELOPMENTAL LEARNING MATERIALS	<5
P	AUDKIT	ANIMAL CRACKERS	MEDIA MATERIALS, INC.	6-10
P	GAME	ANIMAL SORTING GAME, FARM ANIMALS	DEVELOPMENTAL LEARNING MATERIALS	<5
P	GAME	ANIMAL SORTING GAME, FOREST ANIMALS	DEVELOPMENTAL LEARNING MATERIALS	<5
P	GAME	ANIMAL SORTING GAME, WILD ANIMALS	DEVELOPMENTAL LEARNING MATERIALS	<5
P	MANIPU	PROGRESSION LOTTO	NIENHUIS MONTESSORI, INC.	21-30
P	MANIPU	LARGE PARQUETRY BLOCKS, WOOD	DEVELOPMENTAL LEARNING MATERIALS	6-10
P	MANIPU	SMALL PARQUETRY BLOCKS	DEVELOPMENTAL LEARNING MATERIALS	6-10
P	MANIPU	SMALL PARQUETRY, DESIGN I	DEVELOPMENTAL LEARNING MATERIALS	<5
P	MANIPU	SMALL PARQUETRY, DESIGN II	DEVELOPMENTAL LEARNING MATERIALS	<5
P	MANIPU	SMALL PARQUETRY, DESIGN III	DEVELOPMENTAL LEARNING MATERIALS	<5
PI	DITTO	PERCEPTUAL ENHANCEMENT: SPATIAL RELATIONS	MODERN EDUCATION CORPORATION	6-10
PI	DITTO	PERCEPTUAL ENHANCEMENT: DIRECTIONALITY & LATERALITY	MODERN EDUCATION CORPORATION	6-10

22 - SKILL: VISUAL CLOSURE

LEVEL	FORMAT	TITLE	PUBLISHER	$PRICE
R	MULTIU	GOAL, LEVEL I: LANGUAGE DEVELOPMENT	MILTON BRADLEY/PLAYSKOOL	151-200
RP	ACTCRD	WIPE-OFF CARDS: DRAW WHAT'S MISSING	TREND ENTERPRISES, INC.	<5
RP	ACTCRD	STORY CARDS TELL WHAT PART IS MISSING	MILTON BRADLEY/PLAYSKOOL	<5
RP	CHART	ALPHABET MURAL	IDEAL SCHOOL SUPPLY COMPANY	6-10
RP	MANIPU	CHILDCRAFT INTERLOCKING RUBBER ANIMALS	CHILDCRAFT EDUCATION CORPORATION	6-10
RP	MANIPU	VISUAL CLOSURE & DISCRIMINATION PUZZLE KIT	EDUCATIONAL TEACHING AIDS	31-50
RP	MANIPU	WHAT'S IN THE SQUARE?	EDUCATIONAL TEACHING AIDS	21-30
RPI	FLASH	VISUAL CLOSURE CARDS	MODERN EDUCATION CORPORATION	11-20
P	ACTCRD	MARK ON-WIPE OFF CARDS: WHAT'S MISSING?	IDEAL SCHOOL SUPPLY COMPANY	<5
P	ACTCRD	PART/WHOLE LOTTO	MILTON BRADLEY/PLAYSKOOL	<5
P	DITTO	SKILL BUILDING SERIES: WORD SHAPES	ACADEMIC THERAPY PUBLICATIONS	6-10
P	DITTO	READING READINESS	MILTON BRADLEY/PLAYSKOOL	<5
P	MANIPU	CONCEPTO-PUZZLES	EDUCATIONAL PERFORMANCE ASSOC.	6-10
P	MANIPU	SKETCH-A-PUZZLE	EDUCATIONAL PERFORMANCE ASSOC.	6-10
P	SP EQT	LANGUAGE SKILLS PROGRAM: READINESS SKILLS (YY)	SPELLBINDER, INC.	51-75
P	WKBOOK	FITZHUGH PLUS PROGRAM, BOOK 102: SHAPE COMPLETION	ALLIED EDUCATION COUNCIL	<5
PI	DITTO	PERCEPTUAL ENHANCEMENT: VISUAL CLOSURE	MODERN EDUCATION CORPORATION	6-10

23 - SKILL: VISUAL SEQUENCING

LEVEL	FORMAT	TITLE	PUBLISHER	NT	$PRICE
R	AUDKIT	GETTING READY TO READ	MEDIA MATERIALS, INC.		6-10
R	MANIPU	SEQUENCE PUZZLES: SEQUENCE 3	PLAYSKOOL, INC.		6-10
R	MANIPU	SEQUENCE PUZZLES: SEQUENCE 4	PLAYSKOOL, INC.		6-10
R	VISKIT	READY STEPS	HOUGHTON MIFFLIN COMPANY		151-200
RP	ACTCRD	READINESS: SEQUENCING	INSTRUCTIONAL FAIR		<5
RP	ACTCRD	READINESS TASK CARDS: SEQUENCING	CONSTRUCTIVE PLAYTHINGS		<5
RP	ACTCRD	SEQUENTIAL CARDS, LEVEL I	INCENTIVES FOR LEARNING, INC.		<5
RP	ACTCRD	CUBES IN COLOR	INCENTIVES FOR LEARNING, INC.		6-10
RP	ACTCRD	A DAY AT SCHOOL, LOGIC SEQUENCE CARDS	IDEAL SCHOOL SUPPLY COMPANY		<5
RP	ACTCRD	WHAT FOLLOWS NEXT? SEQUENCE PICTURE CARDS	IDEAL SCHOOL SUPPLY COMPANY		6-10
RP	ACTCRD	VISUAL MEMORY CARDS, SET I, COLORS	DEVELOPMENTAL LEARNING MATERIALS		<5
RP	ACTCRD	VISUAL MEMORY CARDS, SET II, OBJECTS	DEVELOPMENTAL LEARNING MATERIALS		<5
RP	ACTCRD	VISUAL MEMORY CARDS, SET III, SHAPES	DEVELOPMENTAL LEARNING MATERIALS		<5
RP	ACTCRD	VISUAL MEMORY CARDS, SET IV, LETTERS	DEVELOPMENTAL LEARNING MATERIALS		<5
RP	ACTCRD	BEADS & LACES PATERN CARDS	MILTON BRADLEY/PLAYSKOOL		<5
RP	AUDKIT	VISUAL, MATCHING, MEMORY & SEQUENCING, BOOKS 4, 5, 6	DEVELOPMENTAL LEARNING MATERIALS		21-30
RP	CHART	ALPHABET MURAL	IDEAL SCHOOL SUPPLY COMPANY		6-10
RP	CHART	SEQUENCE CHARTS	CHILD'S WORLD	8	51-75
RP	CHART	TAKE A WALK IN SPRING	CHILD'S WORLD		6-10
RP	CHART	TAKE A WALK IN SUMMER	CHILD'S WORLD		6-10
RP	CHART	TAKE A WALK IN FALL	CHILD'S WORLD		6-10
RP	CHART	TAKE A WALK IN WINTER	CHILD'S WORLD		6-10
RP	CHART	LIFE CYCLE OF A FROG	CHILD'S WORLD		6-10

LEVEL	FORMAT	TITLE	PUBLISHER	NT	$PRICE

23 - SKILL: VISUAL SEQUENCING

LEVEL	FORMAT	TITLE	PUBLISHER	NT	$PRICE
RP	CHART	LIFE CYCLE OF A ROBIN	CHILD'S WORLD		6-10
RP	CHART	LIFE CYCLE OF A MONARCH BUTTERFLY	CHILD'S WORLD		6-10
RP	CHART	STORY OF CORN	CHILD'S WORLD		6-10
RP	DITTO	SEQUENCING	CHILDREN'S LEARNING CENTER, INC.		<5
RP	DITTO	READINESS: SEQUENCING	INSTRUCTIONAL FAIR		<5
RP	DITTO	I CAN DO IT, PART TWO	GEL-STEN, INC.		<5
RP	DITTO	RETELLING FAVORITE STORIES	INSTRUCTO/MCGRAW-HILL		<5
RP	DITTO	WHAT COMES FIRST? NEXT? LAST?	INSTRUCTO/MCGRAW-HILL		<5
RP	GAME	READINESS DISCOVERY	DISCOVERY LEARNING		<5
RP	GAME	ETA LET'S LEARN SEQUENCE	EDUCATIONAL TEACHING AIDS		11-20
RP	MANIPU	SEQUENTIAL SORTING BOX	CONSTRUCTIVE PLAYTHINGS		11-20
RP	MANIPU	CUBES IN COLOR DESIGN CARDS	INCENTIVES FOR LEARNING, INC.		6-10
RP	MANIPU	SEQUENCE PUZZLES	EDUCATIONAL TEACHING AIDS		11-20
RP	MANIPU	SEQUENCE CARDS	EDUCATIONAL TEACHING AIDS		6-10
RP	MANIPU	PARADE LOTTO	NIENHUIS MONTESSORI, INC.		31-50
RP	MANIPU	MIX 'N' MATCH PUZZLES: SEQUENCE, LEVEL 1	TREND ENTERPRISES, INC.		6-10
RP	MANIPU	LET'S LEARN SEQUENCE	INSTRUCTO/MCGRAW-HILL		6-10
RP	MULTIM	HELP: TIME SEQUENCES	CENTER FOR EARLY LEARNING		6-10
RP	MULTIM	HELP: PATTERN DETECTION	CENTER FOR EARLY LEARNING		6-10
RP	PICTUR	TELL AGAIN NURSERY RHYMES CARDS	AEVAC, INC.		11-20
RP	PUPILB	ROXY THE ROBIN	ANN ARBOR PUBLISHERS		<5
RP	WKBOOK	MATCH & MEMORY, BOOK 4: VISUAL MEMORY SEQUENTIAL, LEVEL I	EDUCATIONAL PROGRAMMERS, INC.		6-10
RP	WKBOOK	MATCH & MEMORY, BOOK 5: VISUAL MEMORY SEQUENTIAL, LEVEL II	EDUCATIONAL PROGRAMMERS, INC.		6-10
RP	WKBOOK	VISUAL, MATHING, MEMORY & SEQUENCING, BOOKS 1, 2, 3	DEVELOPMENTAL LEARNING MATERIALS		21-30
P	ACTCRD	SEQUENTIAL CARDS, LEVEL II	INCENTIVES FOR LEARNING, INC.		<5
P	ACTCRD	DESIGN SEQUENCE CARDS	ACADEMIC THERAPY PUBLICATIONS		6-10
P	ACTCRD	TUTORGRAM: ALPHABET RECOGNITION & SEQUENCING	ENRICHMENT READING CORP OF AMER.		11-20
P	ACTCRD	MARK ON-WIPE OFF CARDS: SEQUENCING PICTURE STORIES	IDEAL SCHOOL SUPPLY COMPANY		<5
P	ACTCRD	MAGIC CARDS: CLASSIFICATION, OPPOSITES, SEQUENCE	IDEAL SCHOOL SUPPLY COMPANY		6-10
P	ACTCRD	VISUAL DISCRIMINATIN LEARNING- SEQUENCING M	EDUCATIONAL PERFORMANCE ASSOC.		31-50
P	ACTCRD	LARGE PARQUETRY DESIGNS CARDS	DEVELOPMENTAL LEARNING MATERIALS		<5
P	ACTCRD	BEFORE-AFTER SEQUENTIAL CARDS	DEVELOPMENTAL LEARNING MATERIALS		<5
P	ACTCRD	SENTENCE-BUILDING SEQUENTIAL CARDS	DEVELOPMENTAL LEARNING MATERIALS		<5
P	ACTCRD	ANIMAL-GROWTH SEQUENTIAL CARDS	DEVELOPMENTAL LEARNING MATERIALS		<5
P	ACTCRD	SELF-CARE SEQUENTIAL CARDS	DEVELOPMENTAL LEARNING MATERIALS		<5
P	ACTCRD	SEQUENTIAL CARDS, HEALTH & SAFETY	DEVELOPMENTAL LEARNING MATERIALS		<5
P	ACTCRD	SEQUENTIAL STRIPS	DEVELOPMENTAL LEARNING MATERIALS		<5
P	AUDKIT	CLASSIFICATION-OPPOSITES-SEQUENCE	EDUCATIONAL MEDIA, INC.		31-50
P	CL SET	VISUAL MATCHING, MEMORY & SEQUENCING EXERCISES	DEVELOPMENTAL LEARNING MATERIALS	6	31-50
P	DITTO	READING READINESS	MILTON BRADLEY/PLAYSKOOL		<5
P	GAME	HALF ANIMAL LOTTO	NIENHUIS MONTESSORI, INC.		31-50
P	GAME	SEQUENCE BINGO	TREND ENTERPRISES, INC.		6-10
P	MANIPU	CRONIN LETTER BOX	ACADEMIC THERAPY PUBLICATIONS		6-10
P	MANIPU	TRANSPORTATION PUZZLE	NIENHUIS MONTESSORI, INC.		31-50
P	MANIPU	FLOOR PUZZLES, FARM	NIENHUIS MONTESSORI, INC.		51-75
P	MANIPU	FLOOR PUZZLES, ZOO	NIENHUIS MONTESSORI, INC.		51-75
P	MANIPU	LARGE PARQUETRY BLOCKS, WOOD	DEVELOPMENTAL LEARNING MATERIALS		6-10
P	MANIPU	SMALL PARQUETRY BLOCKS	DEVELOPMENTAL LEARNING MATERIALS		6-10
P	MANIPU	SMALL PARQUETRY, DESIGN I	DEVELOPMENTAL LEARNING MATERIALS		<5
P	MANIPU	SMALL PARQUETRY, DESIGN II	DEVELOPMENTAL LEARNING MATERIALS		<5
P	MANIPU	SMALL PARQUETRY, DESIGN III	DEVELOPMENTAL LEARNING MATERIALS		<5
P	MANIPU	ANIMALS IN PLACE	DEVELOPMENTAL LEARNING MATERIALS		6-10
P	MULTIM	SOUND CLOSURE	MILTON BRADLEY/PLAYSKOOL		11-20
PI	ACTCRD	SEQUENTIAL CARDS, LEVEL III	INCENTIVES FOR LEARNING, INC.		<5
PI	ACTCRD	SEQUENTIAL CARDS, FROM-TO SERIES	INCENTIVES FOR LEARNING, INC.		<5
PI	ACTCRD	SEQUENTIAL CARDS, A FAMILY'S DAY	INCENTIVES FOR LEARNING, INC.		<5
PI	ACTCRD	SEQUENTIAL CARDS, BY SIZE	INCENTIVES FOR LEARNING, INC.		<5
PI	GAME	SPIDER CRAWL	IDEAL SCHOOL SUPPLY COMPANY		6-10
PI	GUIDE	A MANUAL FOR THE TRAINING OF SEQUENTIAL MEMORY & ATTENTION	ACADEMIC THERAPY PUBLICATIONS		<5
PI	MANIPU	GENERAL SEQUENCING CARDS	MODERN EDUCATION CORPORATION		11-20
PI	MANIPU	DIMENSIONAL SEQUENCING CARDS	MODERN EDUCATION CORPORATION		11-20
PI	MANIPU	COLOR SEQUENCING CARDS	MODERN EDUCATION CORPORATION		11-20
PI	MANIPU	PICTURE SEQUENCE CARDS, SET 1	MODERN EDUCATION CORPORATION		11-20
PI	MANIPU	PICTURE SEQUENCE CARDS, SET 2	MODERN EDUCATION CORPORATION		11-20
PI	MANIPU	AERO VISUAL DISCRIMINATION LAB	AERO PUBLISHERS, INC.		76-100
PI	MANIPU	SEQUENCING STORIES	CHILD'S WORLD	5	31-50
PI	MANIPU	GOING PLACES BY AIR	CHILD'S WORLD		6-10
PI	MANIPU	GOING PLACES BY LAND	CHILD'S WORLD		6-10
PI	MANIPU	GOING PLACES BY WATER	CHILD'S WORLD		6-10
PI	MANIPU	COMMUNICATIONS	CHILD'S WORLD		6-10
PI	MANIPU	REPTILES, FROM DINOSAURS TO ALLIGATORS	CHILD'S WORLD		6-10
IJS	PICTUR	CONSUMER SEQUENTIAL CARDS	DEVELOPMENTAL LEARNING MATERIALS		<5

24 - SKILL: VISUAL MEMORY

LEVEL	FORMAT	TITLE	PUBLISHER	NT	$PRICE
R	RECORD	LISTENING SKILLS FOR PRE-READERS, VOLUME 3	CLASSROOM MATERIALS CO.		6-10
RP	ACTCRD	VISUAL MEMORY CARDS, SET I, COLORS	DEVELOPMENTAL LEARNING MATERIALS		<5
RP	ACTCRD	VISUAL MEMORY CARDS, SET II, OBJECTS	DEVELOPMENTAL LEARNING MATERIALS		<5
RP	ACTCRD	VISUAL MEMORY CARDS, SET III, SHAPES	DEVELOPMENTAL LEARNING MATERIALS		<5

LEVEL	FORMAT	TITLE	PUBLISHER	NT	$PRICE

24 - SKILL: VISUAL MEMORY

LEVEL	FORMAT	TITLE	PUBLISHER	NT	$PRICE
RP	ACTCRD	VISUAL MEMORY CARDS, SET IV, LETTERS	DEVELOPMENTAL LEARNING MATERIALS		<5
RP	ACTCRD	BEADS & LACES PATERN CARDS	MILTON BRADLEY/PLAYSKOOL		<5
RP	AUDKIT	VISUAL, MATCHING, MEMORY & SEQUENCING, BOOKS 4, 5, 6	DEVELOPMENTAL LEARNING MATERIALS		21-30
RP	DITTO	VISUAL DISCRIMINATION GAMES	CHILDREN'S LEARNING CENTER, INC.		<5
RP	GAME	CONNECT	CONSTRUCTIVE PLAYTHINGS		6-10
RP	MANIPU	SEQUENCING BEADS & DESIGN CARDS	INCENTIVES FOR LEARNING, INC.		11-20
RP	PUPILB	ROXY THE ROBIN	ANN ARBOR PUBLISHERS		<5
RP	WKBOOK	MATCH & MEMORY, BOOK 3: VISUAL MEMORY, POSITION IN SPACE	EDUCATIONAL PROGRAMMERS, INC.		6-10
RP	WKBOOK	VISUAL, MATHING, MEMORY & SEQUENCING, BOOKS 1, 2, 3	DEVELOPMENTAL LEARNING MATERIALS		21-30
P	ACTCRD	DESIGN SEQUENCE CARDS	ACADEMIC THERAPY PUBLICATIONS		6-10
P	AUDKIT	SOUND IT!	EDUCATIONAL TEACHING AIDS		101-150
P	CL SET	VISUAL MATCHING, MEMORY & SEQUENCING EXERCISES	DEVELOPMENTAL LEARNING MATERIALS	6	31-50
P	DITTO	READING READINESS	MILTON BRADLEY/PLAYSKOOL		<5
P	FILMST	DEVELOPING TECHNIQUES IN CONCENTRATION	CLASSROOM MATERIALS CO.		51-75
P	FLASH	PICTURE FLASH WORDS FOR BEGINNERS	MILTON BRADLEY/PLAYSKOOL		<5
P	GAME	COLOR & SHAPE MEMORY GAME	DEVELOPMENTAL LEARNING MATERIALS		11-20
P	GAME	ANIMAL SORTING GAME, FARM ANIMALS	DEVELOPMENTAL LEARNING MATERIALS		<5
P	GAME	ANIMAL SORTING GAME, FOREST ANIMALS	DEVELOPMENTAL LEARNING MATERIALS		<5
P	GAME	ANIMAL SORTING GAME, WILD ANIMALS	DEVELOPMENTAL LEARNING MATERIALS		<5
P	GAME	SPLICE	STANWIX HOUSE, INC.		6-10
P	MANIPU	ANIMALS IN PLACE	DEVELOPMENTAL LEARNING MATERIALS		6-10
P	MULTIM	SOUND CLOSURE	MILTON BRADLEY/PLAYSKOOL		11-20
PI	GAME	WORD RECOGNITION	PAUL S. AMIDON & ASSOC., INC.		<5
PI	GUIDE	LEARNING ACTIVITIES FOR THE LEARNING DISABLED	FEARON PITMAN PUBLISHERS, INC.		<5
PI	GUIDE	A MANUAL FOR THE TRAINING OF SEQUENTIAL MEMORY & ATTENTION	ACADEMIC THERAPY PUBLICATIONS		<5
PI	MULTIU	GOAL, LEVEL II: LANGUAGE DEVELOPMENT	MILTON BRADLEY/PLAYSKOOL		151-200
PI	SP EQT	TAC-MATES PROGRAMS: SEEING & WRITING WORDS	AV CONCEPTS CORPORATION		11-20
PIJS	GAME	JACK & THE BEANSTALK MEMORY GAME	CADACO		6-10
PIJS	GAME	MUG SHOTS	CADACO		6-10
IJ	VISKIT	VERSA-TILES, BEGINNING READING SET	EDUCATIONAL TEACHING AIDS		11-20

25 - SKILL: VISUAL MOTOR INTEGRATION

LEVEL	FORMAT	TITLE	PUBLISHER	NT	$PRICE
R	AUDKIT	GETTING READY TO READ	MEDIA MATERIALS, INC.		6-10
R	EQUIPM	PLAY PLANKS	CHILDCRAFT EDUCATION CORPORATION		201-300
R	GUIDE	AUDITORY VISUAL MOTOR SKILLS: STARTING OFF W/PHONICS, BOOK 1	MODERN CURRICULUM PRESS		<5
R	MANIPU	FARM PEGS	CHILDCRAFT EDUCATION CORPORATION		11-20
R	MANIPU	FIRST JIGSAWS	CHILDCRAFT EDUCATION CORPORATION		11-20
R	MANIPU	GEOMETRIC SORTING BOARD	CHILDCRAFT EDUCATION CORPORATION		6-10
R	MANIPU	KEYS & LOCKS KNOB PUZZLE	CHILDCRAFT EDUCATION CORPORATION		6-10
R	MANIPU	KNOB PUZZLES: CITY TRAFFIC	CHILDCRAFT EDUCATION CORPORATION		6-10
R	MANIPU	KNOB PUZZLES: FARM LIFE	CHILDCRAFT EDUCATION CORPORATION		6-10
R	MANIPU	KNOB PUZZLES: FAMILIAR SUBJECTS	CHILDCRAFT EDUCATION CORPORATION		6-10
R	MANIPU	KNOB PUZZLES: TOYS 'N' STUFF	CHILDCRAFT EDUCATION CORPORATION		6-10
R	MANIPU	KNOB PUZZLES: FRIENDLY ANIMALS	CHILDCRAFT EDUCATION CORPORATION		6-10
R	MANIPU	KNOB PUZZLES: CLASSROOM	CHILDCRAFT EDUCATION CORPORATION		6-10
R	MANIPU	KNOB PUZZLES: GARAGE	CHILDCRAFT EDUCATION CORPORATION		6-10
R	MANIPU	KNOB PUZZLES: CIRCUS TIME	CHILDCRAFT EDUCATION CORPORATION		6-10
R	MANIPU	KNOB PUZZLES: TRANSPORTATION VEHICLES	CHILDCRAFT EDUCATION CORPORATION		6-10
R	MANIPU	KNOB PUZZLES: ACTIVITIES	CHILDCRAFT EDUCATION CORPORATION		6-10
R	MANIPU	KNOB PUZZLES: WILDLIFE	CHILDCRAFT EDUCATION CORPORATION		6-10
R	MANIPU	POCKET PUZZLES	CHILDCRAFT EDUCATION CORPORATION		11-20
R	MANIPU	PLAYBOARD PUZZLES	CHILDCRAFT EDUCATION CORPORATION		11-20
R	MANIPU	VARI-SHAPE BEADS	CHILDCRAFT EDUCATION CORPORATION		11-20
R	MANIPU	ETA JUMBO POUND AWAY	EDUCATIONAL TEACHING AIDS		11-20
R	MANIPU	TRY: EXPERIENCES FOR YOUNG CHILDREN	BOWMAR/NOBLE PUBLISHERS, INC.		31-50
R	WKBOOK	LESSONS TO GROW ON, BOOK 1	PRESCHOOL LEARNING CORPORATION		<5
R	WKBOOK	LESSONS TO GROW ON, BOOK 3	PRESCHOOL LEARNING CORPORATION		<5
R	WKBOOK	AUDITORY VISUAL MOTOR SKILLS: STARTING OFF W/PHONICS, BOOK 1	MODERN CURRICULUM PRESS		<5
RP	ACTCRD	READINESS: SHAPES & DESIGN REPRODUCTION	INSTRUCTIONAL FAIR		<5
RP	ACTCRD	SAME OR DIFFERENT DESIGN CARDS	DEVELOPMENTAL LEARNING MATERIALS		<5
RP	ACTCRD	SAME OR DIFFERENT PROPORTION CARDS	DEVELOPMENTAL LEARNING MATERIALS		<5
RP	ACTCRD	SAME OR DIFFERENT SIZE CARDS	DEVELOPMENTAL LEARNING MATERIALS		<5
RP	ACTCRD	BEADS & LACES PATERN CARDS	MILTON BRADLEY/PLAYSKOOL		<5
RP	ACTCRD	PARQUETRY DESIGN BLOCK PATTERNS	MILTON BRADLEY/PLAYSKOOL		<5
RP	AUDKIT	EARLY PRIMARY SKILLS SERIES	MEDIA MATERIALS, INC.	7	51-75
RP	DITTO	READINESS: SHAPES & DESIGN REPRODUCTION	INSTRUCTIONAL FAIR		<5
RP	GAME	CHIP MATES	MILTON BRADLEY/PLAYSKOOL		6-10
RP	MANIPU	ANIMAL PUZZLES WITH KNOBS: SEA HORSE	CHILDCRAFT EDUCATION CORPORATION		11-20
RP	MANIPU	ANIMAL PUZZLES WITH KNOBS: SNAIL	CHILDCRAFT EDUCATION CORPORATION		11-20
RP	MANIPU	RHYMING PUZZLE	CHILDCRAFT EDUCATION CORPORATION		<5
RP	MANIPU	RUBBER DIFFERENCES PUZZLES	CHILDCRAFT EDUCATION CORPORATION		11-20
RP	MANIPU	CHILDCRAFT INTERLOCKING RUBBER ANIMALS	CHILDCRAFT EDUCATION CORPORATION		6-10
RP	MANIPU	PUZZLE CUBES	CHILDCRAFT EDUCATION CORPORATION		6-10
RP	MANIPU	SEQUENTIAL SORTING BOX	CHILDCRAFT EDUCATION CORPORATION		11-20
RP	MANIPU	FOAM LETTERS	IDEAL SCHOOL SUPPLY COMPANY		6-10
RP	MANIPU	SHIFTING SHAPES, SET 1	IDEAL SCHOOL SUPPLY COMPANY		6-10
RP	MANIPU	PRE-ALPHABET PUZZLE	DEVELOPMENTAL LEARNING MATERIALS		<5
RP	MANIPU	BASIC-CUT, PUZZLE 1	DEVELOPMENTAL LEARNING MATERIALS		6-10

LEVEL	FORMAT	TITLE	PUBLISHER	NT	$PRICE

---

25 - SKILL: VISUAL MOTOR INTEGRATION

LEVEL	FORMAT	TITLE	PUBLISHER	$PRICE
RP	MANIPU	BASIC-CUT, PUZZLE 2	DEVELOPMENTAL LEARNING MATERIALS	6-10
RP	MANIPU	BASIC-CUT PEOPLE PUZZLES	DEVELOPMENTAL LEARNING MATERIALS	6-10
RP	MANIPU	ANIMAL PUZZLES	DEVELOPMENTAL LEARNING MATERIALS	6-10
RP	MANIPU	STEPPING STONES, WALK-ON ALPHABET CAPITALS	INSTRUCTO/MCGRAW-HILL	21-30
RP	MANIPU	STEPPING STONES, WALK-ON ALPHABET LOWERCASE	INSTRUCTO/MCGRAW-HILL	21-30
RP	MANIPU	WALK-ON ALPHABET	INSTRUCTO/MCGRAW-HILL	11-20
RP	MULTIU	ALPHA PHONICS PROGRAM	ARISTA CORPORATION	201-300
RP	WKBOOK	COLOR-CUT-CREATE	ACADIA PRESS, INC.	<5
P	ACTCRD	MARK ON-WIPE OFF CARDS: TRACING SHAPES	IDEAL SCHOOL SUPPLY COMPANY	<5
P	DITTO	PRE-READING EXERCISES & PERCEPTUAL SKILLS	BOOK-LAB, INC.	6-10
P	DITTO	RHYMING: CUT & PASTE	FRANK SCHAFFER PUBLICATIONS, INC	<5
P	FILMST	DEVELOPING TECHNIQUES IN CONCENTRATION	CLASSROOM MATERIALS CO.	51-75
P	GAME	SPLICE	STANWIX HOUSE, INC.	6-10
P	MANIPU	FACE & FIGURE PUZZLES	TEACHING RESOURCES CORPORATION	11-20
P	MANIPU	SIZE INSERT PUZZLES	TEACHING RESOURCES CORPORATION	21-30
P	MANIPU	FRUIT & VEGETABLE INSERT PUZZLES	TEACHING RESOURCES CORPORATION	21-30
P	MANIPU	ANIMAL INSERT PUZZLES	TEACHING RESOURCES CORPORATION	21-30
P	MANIPU	3-D PUZZLE: PIRATE	TEACHING RESOURCES CORPORATION	6-10
P	MANIPU	ANIMAL BODY BLOCKS	TEACHING RESOURCES CORPORATION	11-20
P	MANIPU	SKETCH-A-PUZZLE	EDUCATIONAL PERFORMANCE ASSOC.	6-10
P	MANIPU	LARGE PEGBOARD	DEVELOPMENTAL LEARNING MATERIALS	31-50
P	MANIPU	LARGE PARQUETRY INSET BOARDS	DEVELOPMENTAL LEARNING MATERIALS	<5
P	MANIPU	PEOPLE PUPPETS & SCRIPTS, BLACK	DEVELOPMENTAL LEARNING MATERIALS	21-30
P	MANIPU	PEOPLE PUPPETS & SCRIPTS, WHITE	DEVELOPMENTAL LEARNING MATERIALS	21-30
P	MANIPU	HOUND DOG PUPPET	DEVELOPMENTAL LEARNING MATERIALS	11-20
P	MANIPU	TURTLE PUPPET	DEVELOPMENTAL LEARNING MATERIALS	11-20
P	MANIPU	ANIMAL PUPPETS & TAPE	DEVELOPMENTAL LEARNING MATERIALS	21-30
P	WKBOOK	SYMBOL DISCRIMINATION & SEQUENCING	ANN ARBOR PUBLISHERS	<5
PI	ACTCRD	READING FUN FACTORY	KIDS & COMPANY	<5
PI	AUDKIT	SOUND-SIGHT SKILLS	CHILDREN'S BOOK & MUSIC CENTER	51-75
PI	DITTO	PERCEPTUAL ENHANCEMENT: EYE-MOTOR COORDINATION	MODERN EDUCATION CORPORATION	6-10
I	ACTCRD	WRITTEN LANGUAGE CARDS, GENERAL	DEVELOPMENTAL LEARNING MATERIALS	6-10

26 - SKILL: AUDITORY SKILLS - GENERAL

LEVEL	FORMAT	TITLE	PUBLISHER	$PRICE
R	AUDCAS	SUPER EARS	BARNELL LOFT, LTD.	11-20
R	MULTIU	PEABODY EARLY EXPERIENCES KIT	AMERICAN GUIDANCE SERVICE, INC.	201-300
R	MULTIM	CONCEPTS & LANGUAGE	NATIONAL EDUCATIONAL LABORATORY	301-400
R	RECORD	SOUND GAMES THROUGH THE GRADES, VOLUME 1	CLASSROOM MATERIALS CO.	6-10
RP	AUDCAS	BASIC TRAINING IN AUDITORY PERCEPTION: SPEECH ELEMENTS	CONCEPT RECORDS	6-10
RP	AUDKIT	SOUND MATCHING	INCENTIVES FOR LEARNING, INC.	11-20
RP	A/VKIT	SIGHTS & SOUNDS, SET 1	EDL/MCGRAW-HILL	101-150
RP	A/VKIT	SIGHTS & SOUNDS, SET 2	EDL/MCGRAW-HILL	76-100
RP	CL SET	LEARNING LANGUAGE SKILLS 1	AEVAC, INC.	51-75
RP	CL SET	LEARNING LANGUAGE SKILLS 2	AEVAC, INC.	51-75
RP	CL SET	SHARPEN THEIR EARS!	MAFEX ASSOCIATES, INC.	51-75
RP	GAME	GAMEBOARD KIT F	READING JOY, INC.	6-10
RP	MULTIU	LISTENING TO THE WORLD	AMERICAN GUIDANCE SERVICE, INC.	101-150
RP	MULTIM	ALPHABET MOTOR ACTIVITIES, BOOK & TAPE	DEVELOPMENTAL LEARNING MATERIALS	11-20
RP	REFBK	BEGINNING DISCOVERY	DISCOVERY LEARNING	<5
RP	SKLKIT	MWM PROGRAM FOR DEVELOPING LANGUAGE ABILITIES	EDUCATIONAL PERFORMANCE ASSOC.	201-300
RP	SKLKIT	GOLDMAN-LYNCH SOUNDS & SYMBOLS DEVELOPMENT KIT	AMERICAN GUIDANCE SERVICE, INC.	151-200
RP	WKBOOK	BEGINNING READINESS	JENN PUBLICATIONS	<5
P	ACTCRD	LEARNING LANGUAGE AT HOME, LEVEL II	COUNCIL FOR EXCEPTIONAL CHILDREN	31-50
P	ACTCRD	SOUND, PICTURE MATCH-UP	DEVELOPMENTAL LEARNING MATERIALS	6-10
P	AUDKIT	AUDITORY DISCRIMINATION	EBSCO CURRICULUM MATERIALS	51-75
P	CL SET	LEARNING LANGUAGE SKILLS 3	AEVAC, INC.	51-75
P	CL SET	LEARNING LANGUAGE SKILLS 4	AEVAC, INC.	51-75
P	CL SET	SEMEL AUDITORY PROCESSING PROGRAM (BEGINNING BASE)	FOLLETT PUBLISHING COMPANY	21-30
P	CL SET	SEMEL AUDITORY PROCESSING PROGRAM (INTERMEDIATE BASE)	FOLLETT PUBLISHING COMPANY	21-30
P	CL SET	SEMEL AUDITORY PROCESSING PROGRAM (ADVANCED BASE)	FOLLETT PUBLISHING COMPANY	21-30
P	CL SET	AUDITORY STIMULATOR CLASS KIT	EDUCATIONAL PERFORMANCE ASSOC.	51-75
P	CL SET	SOUND LOTTO 1	LAKESHORE CURRICULUM MATERIALS	11-20
P	CL SET	SOUND LOTTO 2	LAKESHORE CURRICULUM MATERIALS	21-30
P	MANIPU	BLOCK BASICS	WORD MAKING PRODUCTIONS, INC.	6-10
P	MANIPU	TOK-BACK	DEVELOPMENTAL LEARNING MATERIALS	N/A
P	MULTIU	LANGUAGE PATTERNS/SELF-INSTRUCTIONAL MODALITIES APPROACH	MILTON BRADLEY/PLAYSKOOL	76-100
P	MULTIM	LISTENING YOUR WAY TO BETTER READING	ASSOCIATED EDUCATIONAL MATERIALS	301-400
P	MULTIM	PRS: THE PRE-READING SKILLS PROGRAM	ENCYCLOPEDIA BRITANNICA	>450
P	MULTIM	APT (AUDITORY PERCEPTION TRAINING): MOTOR	DEVELOPMENTAL LEARNING MATERIALS	76-100
P	MULTIM	APT (AUDITORY PERCEPTION TRAINING) IMAGERY	DEVELOPMENTAL LEARNING MATERIALS	31-50
P	MULTIM	BLENDING SOUNDS WITH COCO & CHARLIE	EDUCATIONAL ACTIVITIES, INC.	31-50
P	RECORD	SOUND GAMES THROUGH THE GRADES, VOLUME 2	CLASSROOM MATERIALS CO.	6-10
PI	ACTCRD	BUILDING AUDITORY & VISUAL PERCEPTION SKILLS	B. L. WINCH & ASSOCIATES	6-10
PI	GUIDE	100 INDIVIDUALIZED ACTIVITIES FOR READING	FEARON PITMAN PUBLISHERS, INC.	<5
PI	MULTIU	GOAL, LEVEL II: LANGUAGE DEVELOPMENT	MILTON BRADLEY/PLAYSKOOL	151-200
PI	SND FS	INDEPENDENT WORD PERCEPTION	ASSOCIATED EDUCATIONAL MATERIALS	151-200
I	MULTIM	LISTENING SKILLS, INTERMEDIATE LEVEL	EDUCATIONAL PROGRESS CORPORATION	301-400
I	RECORD	SOUND GAMES THROUGH THE GRADES, VOLUME 3	CLASSROOM MATERIALS CO.	6-10
IJ	GUIDE	DEVELOPING THE LISTENING SKILLS	EDUCATIONAL ACTIVITIES, INC.	<5

LEVEL	FORMAT	TITLE	PUBLISHER	NT $PRICE

26 - SKILL: AUDITORY SKILLS - GENERAL

LEVEL	FORMAT	TITLE	PUBLISHER	NT $PRICE
J	MULTIM	LISTENING SKILLS, SERIES 7/8/9 LEVEL	EDUCATIONAL PROGRESS CORPORATION	151-200
JS	RECORD	SOUND GAMES THROUGH THE GRADES, VOLUME 4	CLASSROOM MATERIALS CO.	6-10
S	MULTIM	LISTENING SKILLS, ADVANCED LEVEL	EDUCATIONAL PROGRESS CORPORATION	151-200

27 - SKILL: AUDITORY DISCRIMINATION

LEVEL	FORMAT	TITLE	PUBLISHER	NT $PRICE
R	AUDCAS	LISTENING SKILLS FOR PRE-READERS, VOLUME 2	CLASSROOM MATERIALS CO.	6-10
R	GUIDE	AUDITORY VISUAL MOTOR SKILLS: STARTING OFF W/PHONICS, BOOK 1	MODERN CURRICULUM PRESS	<5
R	MANIPU	SOUND DISCRIMINATION SET: FIRST SET	DICK BLICK COMPANY	11-20
R	MANIPU	SOUND DISCRIMINATION SET: SECOND SET	DICK BLICK COMPANY	11-20
R	MULTIU	EXPERIENCES IN READING READINESS	MILTON BRADLEY/PLAYSKOOL	76-100
R	VISKIT	READY STEPS	HOUGHTON MIFFLIN COMPANY	151-200
R	WKBOOK	AUDITORY VISUAL MOTOR SKILLS: STARTING OFF W/PHONICS, BOOK 1	MODERN CURRICULUM PRESS	<5
RP	ACTCRD	BUZZER BOARD PATTERN CARDS	DEVELOPMENTAL LEARNING MATERIALS	<5
RP	AUDCAS	BASIC TRAINING IN AUDITORY PERCEPTION: SOUND DISCRIMINATION	CONCEPT RECORDS	6-10
RP	AUDKIT	SOUND MATCHING	INCENTIVES FOR LEARNING, INC.	11-20
RP	AUDKIT	PERCEIVE & RESPOND, VOLUME I	MODERN EDUCATION CORPORATION	51-75
RP	AUDKIT	PERCEIVE & RESPOND, VOLUME II	MODERN EDUCATION CORPORATION	76-100
RP	A/VKIT	READING READINESS	EYE GATE MEDIA	101-150
RP	CL SET	SHARPEN THEIR EARS!	MAFEX ASSOCIATES, INC.	51-75
RP	DITTO	READING READINESS	GEL-STEN, INC.	<5
RP	GAME	ETA CARNIVAL OF BEGINNING SOUNDS	EDUCATIONAL TEACHING AIDS	11-20
RP	GAME	GAMEBOARD KIT F	READING JOY, INC.	6-10
RP	MANIPU	SOUND BOXES	CONSTRUCTIVE PLAYTHINGS	31-50
RP	MANIPU	SOUND BOXES	NIENHUIS MONTESSORI, INC.	31-50
RP	MANIPU	BUZZER BOARDS	DEVELOPMENTAL LEARNING MATERIALS	11-20
RP	MULTIU	ALPHA TIME PRE-READING PROGRAM	ARISTA CORPORATION	201-300
RP	MULTIU	READING READINESS: PARTS I, II, III, IV, V, VI	EDUCATIONAL DIMENSIONS CORP.	101-150
RP	MULTIM	AUDITORY FAMILIAR SOUNDS	DEVELOPMENTAL LEARNING MATERIALS	<5
RP	MULTIM	WHAT'S YOUR STORY?	HARCOURT BRACE JOVANOVICH, INC.	101-150
RP	PICTUR	TOY CHEST OF BEGINNING SOUNDS	INSTRUCTO/MCGRAW-HILL	6-10
RP	PUPILB	KINDERGARTEN KEYS: THE CATERPILLAR CAPER	ECONOMY COMPANY	<5
RP	SKLKIT	AIMS: INITIAL CONSONANTS KIT	CONTINENTAL PRESS, INC.	51-75
RP	SKLKIT	JUNIOR LISTEN-HEAR PROGRAM	FOLLETT PUBLISHING COMPANY	51-75
RP	SND FS	SIGNS & SOUNDS	TROLL ASSOCIATES	76-100
RP	WKBOOK	TELL & DRAW STORIES	CREATIVE STORYTIME PRESS	6-10
RP	WKBOOK	MORE TELL & DRAW STORIES	CREATIVE STORYTIME PRESS	6-10
RP	WKBOOK	LOTS MORE TELL & DRAW STORIES	CREATIVE STORYTIME PRESS	6-10
RP	WKBOOK	BEGINNING READINESS	JENN PUBLICATIONS	<5
RPI	GAME	AUDITORY DISCRIMINATION GAME	MODERN EDUCATION CORPORATION	21-30
RPI	MULTIU	B T M P D R H S F KIT	LESWING PRESS	31-50
P	ACTCRD	CONSONANT SOUNDS	MILTON BRADLEY/PLAYSKOOL	<5
P	AUDKIT	AUDITORY DISCRIMINATION	EBSCO CURRICULUM MATERIALS	51-75
P	AUDKIT	SOUND IT!	EDUCATIONAL TEACHING AIDS	101-150
P	AUDKIT	READING CASSETTES: READING READINESS	IDEAL SCHOOL SUPPLY COMPANY	51-75
P	AUDKIT	SOUNDS IN MY WORLD	IDEAL SCHOOL SUPPLY COMPANY	21-30
P	DITTO	READING STEP BY STEP, KIT A	CONTINENTAL PRESS, INC.	51-75
P	DITTO	BEGINNING SOUND WORD HUNT I	DEVELOPMENTAL LEARNING MATERIALS	<5
P	DITTO	BEGINNING SOUND WORD HUNT II	DEVELOPMENTAL LEARNING MATERIALS	<5
P	GAME	AUDITORY DISCRIMINATION	FRANK SCHAFFER PUBLICATIONS, INC	<5
P	GAME	PHONICS WHEEL	TEACHING RESOURCES CORPORATION	11-20
P	GAME	PHONICS PUZZLES & GAMES	TEACHING RESOURCES CORPORATION	11-20
P	GAME	BALLOON GAME	JUDY COMPANY	6-10
P	GAME	ALPHA, MATCH	JUDY COMPANY	6-10
P	MANIPU	SOUND PUZZLES	TEACHING RESOURCES CORPORATION	11-20
P	MULTIM	DEVELOPING READING SKILLS, PART I: WORD RECOGNITION	EDUCATIONAL ENRICHMENT MATERIALS	101-150
P	MULTIM	APT (AUDITORY PERCEPTION TRAINING) DISCRIMINATION	DEVELOPMENTAL LEARNING MATERIALS	76-100
P	SKLKIT	LISTEN-HEAR PROGRAM	FOLLETT PUBLISHING COMPANY	51-75
P	SP EQT	AUDITORY SKILLS: CONSONANT DISCRIMINATION A	INSTRUCTIONAL INDUSTRIES (G.E.)	101-150
P	SP EQT	AUDITORY SKILLS: CONSONANT DISCRIMINATION B	INSTRUCTIONAL INDUSTRIES (G.E.)	101-150
P	SP EQT	AUDITORY SKILLS: VOWEL DISCRIMINATION	INSTRUCTIONAL INDUSTRIES (G.E.)	101-150
PI	AUDKIT	PEP, VOLUME III	MODERN EDUCATION CORPORATION	76-100
PI	GAME	ARE YOU LISTENING?	JUDY COMPANY	6-10
PI	GAME	SOUND DOMINO GAME	JUDY COMPANY	6-10
PI	GAME	SPIN-A-WORD	JUDY COMPANY	6-10
PI	GAME	APPLE TREE	XEROX EDUCATION PUBLICATIONS	51-75
PI	GAME	PLUM TREE	XEROX EDUCATION PUBLICATIONS	51-75
PI	RECORD	SINGING ABOUT COLOR	CLASSROOM MATERIALS CO.	6-10
PIJ	MULTIM	VISUAL AURAL DISCRIMINATIONS, BOOK I	ANN ARBOR PUBLISHERS	<5
PIJ	MULTIM	AUDITORY DISCRIMINATION IN DEPTH	TEACHING RESOURCES CORPORATION	76-100
JS	AUDKIT	PRE- READING SKILLS SERIES	MEDIA MATERIALS, INC.	21-30

28 - SKILL: AUDITORY ASSOCIATION

LEVEL	FORMAT	TITLE	PUBLISHER	NT $PRICE
R	PUPILB	INTERSENSORY READING PROGRAM, BLEND - IT	BOOK-LAB, INC.	<5
RP	AUDKIT	SOUND MATCHING	INCENTIVES FOR LEARNING, INC.	11-20
RP	AUDKIT	PERCEIVE & RESPOND, VOLUME I	MODERN EDUCATION CORPORATION	51-75
RP	DITTO	READING READINESS	GEL-STEN, INC.	<5
RP	MANIPU	SOUND BOXES	CONSTRUCTIVE PLAYTHINGS	31-50
RP	MULTIM	AUDITORY FAMILIAR SOUNDS	DEVELOPMENTAL LEARNING MATERIALS	<5

LEVEL	FORMAT	TITLE	PUBLISHER	NT	$PRICE

28 - SKILL: AUDITORY ASSOCIATION

LEVEL	FORMAT	TITLE	PUBLISHER	NT	$PRICE
RP	VISKIT	VISUAL MOTOR & CLOSURE DUPLICATING KIT	EDUCATIONAL TEACHING AIDS		21-30
P	GAME	GET SET: GAMES FOR BEGINNING READERS	HOUGHTON MIFFLIN COMPANY	8	101-150
P	GAME	GET SET: SILLY SENTENCES	HOUGHTON MIFFLIN COMPANY		11-20
P	GAME	GET SET: TREASURE CAPTURE	HOUGHTON MIFFLIN COMPANY		11-20
P	MANIPU	PALS: PERCEPTUAL AUDITORY LEARNING SERIES	ACADEMIC THERAPY PUBLICATIONS		31-50
P	SND FS	DEVELOPING ALPHABET SKILLS	LEARNING TREE FILMSTRIPS		51-75

29 - SKILL: AUDITORY ATTENTION

LEVEL	FORMAT	TITLE	PUBLISHER	NT	$PRICE
R	GAME	PICTURE READINESS GAME	GARRARD PUBLISHING COMPANY		<5
R	PUPILB	LADYBIRD BOOK: PLAYBOOK 1	IDEAL SCHOOL SUPPLY COMPANY		<5
R	PUPILB	LADYBIRD BOOK: PLAYBOOK 2	IDEAL SCHOOL SUPPLY COMPANY		<5
R	PUPILB	LADYBIRD BOOK: PLAYBOOK 3	IDEAL SCHOOL SUPPLY COMPANY		<5
R	PUPILB	LADYBIRD BOOK: PLAYBOOK 4	IDEAL SCHOOL SUPPLY COMPANY		<5
R	VISKIT	READY STEPS	HOUGHTON MIFFLIN COMPANY		151-200
RP	AUDCAS	BASIC ACTION POEMS & STORIES FOR EXCEPTIONAL CHILDREN, VOL 1	CONCEPT RECORDS		11-20
RP	AUDCAS	BASIC ACTION POEMS & STORIES FOR EXCEPTIONAL CHILDREN, VOL 2	CONCEPT RECORDS		11-20
RP	AUDKIT	LISTENING SKILLS PROGRAM, GRADES 1-3 (RL 1-3)	BENEFIC PRESS		51-75
RP	AUDKIT	EARS	ECONOMY COMPANY		76-100
RP	AUDKIT	LEARN TO LISTEN	IDEAL SCHOOL SUPPLY COMPANY		11-20
RP	AUDKIT	LISTENING SKILLS	WEBER COSTELLO COMPANY		11-20
RP	AUDKIT	CAN YOU FIND MY MOTHER?	MEDIA MATERIALS, INC.		6-10
RP	AUDKIT	HEAR HOW, SET 1	MEDIA MATERIALS, INC.		6-10
RP	AUDKIT	HEAR HOW, SET 2	MEDIA MATERIALS, INC.		6-10
RP	AUDKIT	RED HEN & SLY FOX	MEDIA MATERIALS, INC.		6-10
RP	AUDKIT	SUE GOES TO THE ZOO	MEDIA MATERIALS, INC.		6-10
RP	AUDKIT	SHELLY HELPS MOTHER SHOP	MEDIA MATERIALS, INC.		6-10
RP	AUDKIT	BOY WHO DIDN'T LISTEN	MEDIA MATERIALS, INC.		6-10
RP	AUDKIT	WHAT CAN YOU DO WITH A PENNY?	MEDIA MATERIALS, INC.		6-10
RP	AUDKIT	LISTENING & LEARNING	HOUGHTON MIFFLIN COMPANY		51-75
RP	CHART	EASEL LISTENING GAMES	ACADIA PRESS, INC.		6-10
RP	DITTO	MANUSCRIPT LETTERS, UPPER & LOWER CASE	CHILDREN'S LEARNING CENTER, INC.		<5
RP	FLASH	LISTENING EARS CARD SET	STANWIX HOUSE, INC.		11-20
RP	GAME	GAMEBOARDS FOR SPEECH & LANGUAGE DEVELOPMENT	COMMUNICATION SKILL BUILDERS,INC		31-50
RP	GAME	GAMEBOARDS FOR EARLY CHILDHOOD EDUCATION	COMMUNICATION SKILL BUILDERS,INC		31-50
RP	GAME	INDIVIDUAL LISTENING GAMES	ACADIA PRESS, INC.		<5
RP	GUIDE	PAY ATTENTION	P.S. ASSOCIATES		<5
RP	GUIDE	LISTENING EARS	STANWIX HOUSE, INC.		11-20
RP	GUIDE	LISTENING ACTIVITIES: A MANUAL OF LISTENING ACTIVITIES	PAUL S. AMIDON & ASSOC., INC.		<5
RP	GUIDE	101 LANGUAGE ARTS ACTIVITIES	COMMUNICATION SKILL BUILDERS,INC		6-10
RP	MANIPU	SOUND BOXES	CONSTRUCTIVE PLAYTHINGS		31-50
RP	MULTIM	AUDITORY FAMILIAR SOUNDS	DEVELOPMENTAL LEARNING MATERIALS		<5
RP	RECORD	ACTION SONGS FOR RHYTHMIC ACTIVITIES: SING A SONG OF ACTION	KIMBO EDUCATIONAL		11-20
RP	RECORD	NURSERY RHYMES FOR LITTLE PEOPLE	KIMBO EDUCATIONAL		6-10
RP	RECORD	SIMPLIFIED LUMMI STICK ACTIVITIES	KIMBO EDUCATIONAL		11-20
RP	RECORD	LISTENING ACTIVITIES RECORD ALBUM	SCOTT, FORESMAN & CO.		6-10
RP	RECORD	LISTENING SKILLS FOR PRE-READERS	CHILDREN'S BOOK & MUSIC CENTER		21-30
RP	SND FS	LISTENING GAMES	CORONET MULTI MEDIA		76-100
RP	SND FS	ADVENTURES IN LISTENING	CORONET MULTI MEDIA		101-150
RP	TUTORL	DEVELOPMENTAL STORY BOOKS	DEVELOPMENTAL LEARNING MATERIALS		6-10
RP	VISKIT	VISUAL MOTOR & CLOSURE DUPLICATING KIT	EDUCATIONAL TEACHING AIDS		21-30
RPI	GAME	GAMES & MORE GAMES KIDS LIKE	COMMUNICATION SKILL BUILDERS,INC		11-20
P	AUDCAS	WHO SAID IT?	EDUCATIONAL ACTIVITIES, INC.		11-20
P	AUDCAS	MEET MR. MIX-UP	EDUCATIONAL ACTIVITIES, INC.		6-10
P	AUDKIT	LISTENING SKILLS	EBSCO CURRICULUM MATERIALS		51-75
P	AUDKIT	SRA LISTENING LANGUAGE LABORATORY: PRIMARY KIT 1A	SRA		301-400
P	AUDKIT	SRA LISTENING LANGUAGE LABORATORY: PRIMARY KIT 1B	SRA		301-400
P	AUDKIT	SRA LISTENING LANGUAGE LABORATORY: PRIMARY KIT 1C	SRA		301-400
P	AUDKIT	READING CASSETTES: LEARN TO LISTEN	IDEAL SCHOOL SUPPLY COMPANY		6-10
P	CL SET	LISTEN HERE	LAKESHORE CURRICULUM MATERIALS		11-20
P	DITTO	LISTEN & SPEAK TO READ	HAYES SCHOOL PUBLISHING COMPANY		<5
P	GUIDE	LISTENING & LEARNING	FEARON PITMAN PUBLISHERS, INC.		<5
P	MANIPU	DEVELOPING LISTENING SKILLS WITH "THREE BILLY GOATS GRUFF"	LESWING PRESS		11-20
P	MULTIU	LISTENING SKILLS PROGRAM, UNIT I: EASY EARS	SCHOLASTIC BOOK SERVICE		101-150
P	MULTIM	CONCEPTS FOR COMMUNICATION, UNIT 1: LISTEN. W/UNDERSTANDING	DEVELOPMENTAL LEARNING MATERIALS		31-50
P	RECORD	COMPREHENSION THROUGH LISTENING, VOLUME 1	CLASSROOM MATERIALS CO.		6-10
P	RECORD	COMPREHENSION THROUGH LISTENING, VOLUME 3	CLASSROOM MATERIALS CO.		6-10
P	RECORD	COMPREHENSION THROUGH LISTENING, VOLUME 4	CLASSROOM MATERIALS CO.		6-10
P	RECORD	LET'S LISTEN	CLASSROOM MATERIALS CO.		6-10
P	RECORD	ACTION SONGS FOR RHYTHMIC ACTIVITIES: HOLIDAY ACTION SONGS	KIMBO EDUCATIONAL		11-20
P	RECORD	WHO SAID IT?	EDUCATIONAL ACTIVITIES, INC.		11-20
P	RECORD	MEET MR. MIX-UP	EDUCATIONAL ACTIVITIES, INC.		6-10
P	SKLKIT	COMMUNICATION SKILLS IN ACTION	MCCORMICK-MATHERS PUBLISHING CO.		151-200
P	SND FS	LEARNING SPEECH SOUNDS, SET 1	AEVAC, INC.		51-75
P	SND FS	LEARNING SPEECH SOUNDS, SET 2	AEVAC, INC.		51-75
P	SND FS	LEARNING SPEECH SOUNDS, SET 3	AEVAC, INC.		51-75
P	SND FS	LET'S LISTEN	CORONET MULTI MEDIA		76-100
PI	ACTCRD	SOUNDS, WORDS & ACTIONS	PEEK PUBLICATIONS		<5
PI	AUDCAS	I HEARD IT WITH MY OWN TWO EARS	SPOKEN ARTS, INC.		101-150
PI	AUDKIT	PEP, VOLUME IV	MODERN EDUCATION CORPORATION		31-50

LEVEL	FORMAT	TITLE	PUBLISHER	NT	$PRICE

29 - SKILL: AUDITORY ATTENTION

LEVEL	FORMAT	TITLE	PUBLISHER	$PRICE
PI	DITTO	ASSIST ONE & TWO & THREE	COMMUNICATION SKILL BUILDERS,INC	11-20
PI	MULTIM	TEACHING READING THROUGH CREATIVE MOVEMENT	KIMBO EDUCATIONAL	31-50
PIJS	WKBOOK	SPACE ADVENTURES READING SERIES	COMMUNICATION SKILL BUILDERS,INC	11-20
I	AUDCAS	COUNTDOWN FOR LISTENING	STANWIX HOUSE, INC.	31-50
I	GUIDE	LISTENING ACTIVITY BOOK	FEARON PITMAN PUBLISHERS, INC.	<5
I	MULTIU	LISTENING SKILLS PROGRAM, UNIT II: EAR POWER	SCHOLASTIC BOOK SERVICE	101-150
I	RECORD	EAR TRAINING FOR MIDDLE GRADES	CLASSROOM MATERIALS CO.	6-10
IJ	AUDKIT	LISTENING SKILLS PROGRAM, GRADES 4-8 (RL 4-9)	BENEFIC PRESS	51-75
IJ	GUIDE	BASIC PRACTICE IN LISTENING	LOVE PUBLISHING COMPANY	<5
IJ	MULTIM	LISTEN, HEAR	PAUL S. AMIDON & ASSOC., INC.	76-100
J	AUDKIT	SRA LISTENING LANGUAGE LABORATORY: INTERMEDIATE KIT 2A	SRA	301-400
J	AUDKIT	SRA LISTENING LANGUAGE LABORATORY: INTERMEDIATE KIT 2B	SRA	301-400
J	AUDKIT	SRA LISTENING LANGUAGE LABORATORY: INTERMEDIATE KIT 2C	SRA	301-400
S	MULTIM	SKITS FOR SKILLS: THE ADULT SCENE, KIT A	JABBERWOCKY	101-150
S	MULTIM	SKITS FOR SKILLS: FRIENDS INDEED, KIT B	JABBERWOCKY	101-150
S	MULTIM	SKITS FOR SKILLS: SCRIPTS ON SOCIETY, KIT C	JABBERWOCKY	101-150
S	MULTIM	SKITS FOR SKILLS: FUN WITH FANTASY, KIT D	JABBERWOCKY	101-150

30 - SKILL: AUDITORY CLOSURE

LEVEL	FORMAT	TITLE	PUBLISHER	$PRICE
R	MULTIU	GOAL, LEVEL I: LANGUAGE DEVELOPMENT	MILTON BRADLEY/PLAYSKOOL	151-200
RP	VISKIT	VISUAL MOTOR & CLOSURE DUPLICATING KIT	EDUCATIONAL TEACHING AIDS	21-30
P	MULTIM	SOUND CLOSURE	MILTON BRADLEY/PLAYSKOOL	11-20
P	SP EQT	AUDITORY SKILLS: SYNTHESIS	INSTRUCTIONAL INDUSTRIES (G.E.)	51-75
P	SP EQT	AUDITORY SKILLS: SYNTAX A	INSTRUCTIONAL INDUSTRIES (G.E.)	101-150
P	SP EQT	AUDITORY SKILLS: SYNTAX B	INSTRUCTIONAL INDUSTRIES (G.E.)	101-150
P	SP EQT	AUDITORY SKILLS: MORPHOLOGY & CLOSURE	INSTRUCTIONAL INDUSTRIES (G.E.)	101-150
PI	MULTIU	GOAL, LEVEL II: LANGUAGE DEVELOPMENT	MILTON BRADLEY/PLAYSKOOL	151-200

31 - SKILL: AUDITORY SEQUENCING

LEVEL	FORMAT	TITLE	PUBLISHER	$PRICE
R	VISKIT	READY STEPS	HOUGHTON MIFFLIN COMPANY	151-200
RP	AUDKIT	SHELLY HELPS MOTHER SHOP	MEDIA MATERIALS, INC.	6-10
RP	AUDKIT	WHAT CAN YOU DO WITH A PENNY?	MEDIA MATERIALS, INC.	6-10
RP	AUDKIT	PERCEIVE & RESPOND, VOLUME III	MODERN EDUCATION CORPORATION	31-50
RP	DITTO	RETELLING FAVORITE STORIES	INSTRUCTO/MCGRAW-HILL	<5
RP	MULTIM	HELP: TIME SEQUENCES	CENTER FOR EARLY LEARNING	6-10
P	ACTCRD	SOUND STORIES CARDS	LAKESHORE CURRICULUM MATERIALS	6-10
P	AUDCAS	SOUND ABSURDITIES	LAKESHORE CURRICULUM MATERIALS	6-10
P	AUDCAS	SOUND STORIES	LAKESHORE CURRICULUM MATERIALS	6-10
P	MANIPU	CRONIN LETTER BOX	ACADEMIC THERAPY PUBLICATIONS	6-10
P	MANIPU	PALS: PERCEPTUAL AUDITORY LEARNING SERIES	ACADEMIC THERAPY PUBLICATIONS	31-50
P	RECORD	MAINSTREAMING CHILDREN'S GAMES	KIMBO EDUCATIONAL	6-10
PI	GUIDE	A MANUAL FOR THE TRAINING OF SEQUENTIAL MEMORY & ATTENTION	ACADEMIC THERAPY PUBLICATIONS	<5
PI	GUIDE	CONCEPT TOWN	DEVELOPMENTAL LEARNING MATERIALS	11-20
PIJS	MANIPU	PHOTO SEQUENCE CARDS, SET 1: OCCUPATIONS	MODERN EDUCATION CORPORATION	11-20
PIJS	MANIPU	PHOTO SEQUENCE CARDS, SET 2: RECREATION	MODERN EDUCATION CORPORATION	11-20
PIJS	MANIPU	PHOTO SEQUENCE CARDS, SET 3: DAILY LIVING ACTIVITIES	MODERN EDUCATION CORPORATION	11-20

32 - SKILL: AUDITORY FIGURE-GROUND

LEVEL	FORMAT	TITLE	PUBLISHER	$PRICE
RP	AUDCAS	BASIC TRAINING IN AUDITORY PERCEPTION: FIGURE-GROUND	CONCEPT RECORDS	6-10
RP	AUDKIT	PERCEIVE & RESPOND, VOLUME II	MODERN EDUCATION CORPORATION	76-100
RP	TRANSP	FIGURE-GROUND TRANSPARENCIES	MODERN EDUCATION CORPORATION	11-20
P	MULTIM	APT (AUDITORY PERCEPTION TRAINING) FIGURE GROUND	DEVELOPMENTAL LEARNING MATERIALS	51-75
PI	GUIDE	A MANUAL FOR THE TRAINING OF SEQUENTIAL MEMORY & ATTENTION	ACADEMIC THERAPY PUBLICATIONS	<5

33 - SKILL: AUDITORY MEMORY

LEVEL	FORMAT	TITLE	PUBLISHER	$PRICE
R	MULTIU	EXPERIENCES IN READING READINESS	MILTON BRADLEY/PLAYSKOOL	76-100
R	MULTIU	GOAL, LEVEL I: LANGUAGE DEVELOPMENT	MILTON BRADLEY/PLAYSKOOL	151-200
RP	ACTCRD	BUZZER BOARD PATTERN CARDS	DEVELOPMENTAL LEARNING MATERIALS	<5
RP	AUDKIT	RED HEN & SLY FOX	MEDIA MATERIALS, INC.	6-10
RP	AUDKIT	SUE GOES TO THE ZOO	MEDIA MATERIALS, INC.	6-10
RP	AUDKIT	SHELLY HELPS MOTHER SHOP	MEDIA MATERIALS, INC.	6-10
RP	AUDKIT	WHAT CAN YOU DO WITH A PENNY?	MEDIA MATERIALS, INC.	6-10
RP	AUDKIT	PERCEIVE & RESPOND, VOLUME III	MODERN EDUCATION CORPORATION	31-50
RP	A/VKIT	RIDDLE-A-RHYME	EYE GATE MEDIA	101-150
RP	CL SET	SHARPEN THEIR EARS!	MAFEX ASSOCIATES, INC.	51-75
RP	MANIPU	SOUND BOXES	CONSTRUCTIVE PLAYTHINGS	31-50
RP	MANIPU	BUZZER BOARDS	DEVELOPMENTAL LEARNING MATERIALS	11-20
RP	RECORD	SING A SONG OF SOUND	KIMBO EDUCATIONAL	11-20
P	AUDKIT	SOUND IT!	EDUCATIONAL TEACHING AIDS	101-150
P	AUDKIT	SOUNDS IN MY WORLD	IDEAL SCHOOL SUPPLY COMPANY	21-30
P	CL SET	AUDITORY STIMULATOR CLASS KIT	EDUCATIONAL PERFORMANCE ASSOC.	51-75
P	DITTO	READING READINESS	MILTON BRADLEY/PLAYSKOOL	<5
P	MANIPU	DEVELOPING LISTENING SKILLS WITH "THREE BILLY GOATS GRUFF"	LESWING PRESS	11-20
P	MANIPU	DEVELOPING LISTENING SKILLS WITH "THE GINGERBREAD BOY"	LESWING PRESS	6-10
P	MULTIM	APT (AUDITORY PERCEPTION TRAINING) MEMORY	DEVELOPMENTAL LEARNING MATERIALS	51-75
P	SP EQT	AUDITORY SKILLS: AUDITORY MEMORY	INSTRUCTIONAL INDUSTRIES (G.E.)	51-75
PI	AUDKIT	PEP, VOLUME I	MODERN EDUCATION CORPORATION	51-75
PI	AUDKIT	PEP, VOLUME II	MODERN EDUCATION CORPORATION	76-100
PI	GAME	SPIDER CRAWL	IDEAL SCHOOL SUPPLY COMPANY	6-10

LEVEL	FORMAT	TITLE	PUBLISHER	NT	$PRICE

33 - SKILL: AUDITORY MEMORY

LEVEL	FORMAT	TITLE	PUBLISHER	NT	$PRICE
PI	GUIDE	CONCEPT TOWN	DEVELOPMENTAL LEARNING MATERIALS		11-20
PI	MULTIU	GOAL, LEVEL II: LANGUAGE DEVELOPMENT	MILTON BRADLEY/PLAYSKOOL		151-200
I	ACTCRD	LEARNING CENTER PAK (GRADES 3 - 5)	WISE OWL PUBLICATIONS		31-50
IJS	AUDKIT	HITS, LEVEL 3: HARRY CHAPIN, CIRCLE	MODULEARN, INC.		11-20

34 - SKILL: AUDITORY VISUAL SKILLS - GENERAL

LEVEL	FORMAT	TITLE	PUBLISHER	NT	$PRICE
R	DITTO	ALPHABET	EBSCO CURRICULUM MATERIALS		<5
R	MANIPU	STRUCTO BRICKS	CHILDCRAFT EDUCATION CORPORATION		31-50
RP	AUDKIT	MINISYSTEMS: LEFT TO RIGHT PROGRESSION	CORONET MULTI MEDIA		11-20
RP	CL SET	SHARPEN THEIR EARS!	MAFEX ASSOCIATES, INC.		51-75
RP	DITTO	BEGINNING PHONICS, UPPER CASE	CHILDREN'S LEARNING CENTER, INC.		<5
RP	DITTO	BEGINNING PHONICS, LOWER CASE	CHILDREN'S LEARNING CENTER, INC.		<5
RP	MULTIM	SIGHT & SOUND DISCOVERY TRIPS: LISTENING & SIGHT EXPERIENCE	EYE GATE MEDIA		76-100
RP	WKBOOK	TELL & DRAW STORIES	CREATIVE STORYTIME PRESS		6-10
RP	WKBOOK	MORE TELL & DRAW STORIES	CREATIVE STORYTIME PRESS		6-10
RP	WKBOOK	LOTS MORE TELL & DRAW STORIES	CREATIVE STORYTIME PRESS		6-10
P	SKLKIT	TARGET RED: AUDITORY-VISUAL DISCRIMINATION KIT	ADDISON-WESLEY PUBLISHING CO.		151-200

35 - SKILL: LISTENING SKILLS - GENERAL

LEVEL	FORMAT	TITLE	PUBLISHER	NT	$PRICE
R	ACTCRD	LEARNING LANGUAGE AT HOME, LEVEL I	COUNCIL FOR EXCEPTIONAL CHILDREN		31-50
R	AUDCAS	SUPER EARS	BARNELL LOFT, LTD.		11-20
R	MULTIM	BEGINNING TO READ, WRITE & LISTEN	HARPER & ROW PUBLISHERS, INC.		101-150
R	PUPILB	LADYBIRD BOOK: PLAYBOOK 1	IDEAL SCHOOL SUPPLY COMPANY		<5
R	PUPILB	LADYBIRD BOOK: PLAYBOOK 2	IDEAL SCHOOL SUPPLY COMPANY		<5
R	PUPILB	LADYBIRD BOOK: PLAYBOOK 3	IDEAL SCHOOL SUPPLY COMPANY		<5
R	PUPILB	LADYBIRD BOOK: PLAYBOOK 4	IDEAL SCHOOL SUPPLY COMPANY		<5
RP	ACTCRD	TUTORGRAM: MATCHING UPPER & LOWER CASE LETTERS	ENRICHMENT READING CORP OF AMER.		11-20
RP	AUDCAS	PROGRAMMED ENRICHMENT SONGS FOR EXCEPTIONAL CHILDREN	CONCEPT RECORDS		21-30
RP	AUDCRD	SOUNDS AROUND US	AUDIOTRONICS CORPORATION		21-30
RP	AUDKIT	LISTENING SKILLS PROGRAM, GRADES 1-3 (RL 1-3)	BENEFIC PRESS		51-75
RP	AUDKIT	LITTLE TROLLY BOOKS & TAPES	ECONOMY COMPANY		101-150
RP	AUDKIT	EARS	ECONOMY COMPANY		76-100
RP	AUDKIT	LISTENING SKILLS	WEBER COSTELLO COMPANY		11-20
RP	AUDKIT	CAN YOU FIND MY MOTHER?	MEDIA MATERIALS, INC.		6-10
RP	AUDKIT	HEAR HOW, SET 1	MEDIA MATERIALS, INC.		6-10
RP	AUDKIT	HEAR HOW, SET 2	MEDIA MATERIALS, INC.		6-10
RP	AUDKIT	RED HEN & SLY FOX	MEDIA MATERIALS, INC.		6-10
RP	AUDKIT	SUE GOES TO THE ZOO	MEDIA MATERIALS, INC.		6-10
RP	AUDKIT	SHELLY HELPS MOTHER SHOP	MEDIA MATERIALS, INC.		6-10
RP	AUDKIT	BOY WHO DIDN'T LISTEN	MEDIA MATERIALS, INC.		6-10
RP	AUDKIT	WHAT CAN YOU DO WITH A PENNY?	MEDIA MATERIALS, INC.		6-10
RP	AUDKIT	LISTENING & LEARNING	HOUGHTON MIFFLIN COMPANY		51-75
RP	AUDTAP	LISTENING-DOING-LEARNING TAPES	SRA		21-30
RP	A/VKIT	SIGHTS & SOUNDS, SET 1	EDL/MCGRAW-HILL		101-150
RP	A/VKIT	SIGHTS & SOUNDS, SET 2	EDL/MCGRAW-HILL		76-100
RP	CL SET	CROSSTIES PROGRAM	ECONOMY COMPANY	11	76-100
RP	CL SET	CROSSTIES PROGRAM: GRAND CENTRAL BOOKS, SEPTEMBER	ECONOMY COMPANY		201-300
RP	CL SET	CROSSTIES PROGRAM: GRAND CENTRAL BOOKS, OCTOBER	ECONOMY COMPANY		31-50
RP	CL SET	CROSSTIES PROGRAM: GRAND CENTRAL BOOKS, NOVEMBER	ECONOMY COMPANY		31-50
RP	CL SET	CROSSTIES PROGRAM: GRAND CENTRAL BOOKS, DECEMBER	ECONOMY COMPANY		31-50
RP	CL SET	CROSSTIES PROGRAM: GRAND CENTRAL BOOKS, JANUARY	ECONOMY COMPANY		31-50
RP	CL SET	CROSSTIES PROGRAM: GRAND CENTRAL BOOKS, FEBRUARY	ECONOMY COMPANY		31-50
RP	CL SET	CROSSTIES PROGRAM: GRAND CENTRAL BOOKS, MARCH	ECONOMY COMPANY		31-50
RP	CL SET	CROSSTIES PROGRAM: GRAND CENTRAL BOOKS, APRIL	ECONOMY COMPANY		31-50
RP	CL SET	CROSSTIES PROGRAM: GRAND CENTRAL BOOKS, MAY	ECONOMY COMPANY		31-50
RP	CL SET	CROSSTIES PROGRAM: GRAND CENTRAL BOOKS, SUMMER	ECONOMY COMPANY		31-50
RP	CL SET	LEARNING LANGUAGE SKILLS 1	AEVAC, INC.		51-75
RP	CL SET	LEARNING LANGUAGE SKILLS 2	AEVAC, INC.		51-75
RP	CL SET	SHARPEN THEIR EARS!	MAFEX ASSOCIATES, INC.		51-75
RP	GAME	GAMEBOARD KIT F	READING JOY, INC.		6-10
RP	GAME	PICK-PAIRS CARD GAME	MILTON BRADLEY/PLAYSKOOL		<5
RP	GUIDE	TIME FOR PHONICS, BOOK R, T.E.	WEBSTER DIVISION/MCGRAW-HILL		<5
RP	MANIPU	FAT CAT & EBENEZER GEESER, THE TEENY TINY MOUSE	CREATIVE STORYTIME PRESS		<5
RP	MANIPU	ALOYSIOUS ALLIGATOR	CREATIVE STORYTIME PRESS		<5
RP	MANIPU	TELL & DRAW PAPER BAG PUPPET BOOK 1	CREATIVE STORYTIME PRESS		<5
RP	MANIPU	TELL & DRAW PAPER BAG PUPPET BOOK 2	CREATIVE STORYTIME PRESS		<5
RP	MULTIU	BASIC LANGUAGE STIMULATOR	EDUCATIONAL PERFORMANCE ASSOC.		76-100
RP	MULTIU	PEABODY LANGUAGE DEVELOPMENT KIT, LEVEL #P	AMERICAN GUIDANCE SERVICE, INC.		201-300
RP	MULTIU	LISTENING TO THE WORLD	AMERICAN GUIDANCE SERVICE, INC.		101-150
RP	MULTIM	SIGHT & SOUND DISCOVERY TRIPS: LISTENING & SIGHT EXPERIENCE	EYE GATE MEDIA		76-100
RP	PUPILB	WHAT I HEAR	CHILDREN'S PRESS, INC.		6-10
RP	PUPILB	FUN SOUNDS (RL K-3)	BENEFIC PRESS		<5
RP	PUPILB	GAY SOUNDS (RL K-3)	BENEFIC PRESS		<5
RP	RECORD	SING A SONG OF SOUND	KIMBO EDUCATIONAL		11-20
RP	RECORD	ADVENTURES IN SOUND	MELODY HOUSE PUBLISHING COMPANY		6-10
RP	RECORD	LISTENING TIME	BOWMAR/NOBLE PUBLISHERS, INC.		<5
RP	SKLKIT	MAKE & TELL: LIVING THINGS KIT	SRA		51-75
RP	SKLKIT	MAKE & TELL: TOWN THINGS KIT	SRA		51-75

LEVEL	FORMAT	TITLE	PUBLISHER	NT	$PRICE

35 - SKILL: LISTENING SKILLS - GENERAL

LEVEL	FORMAT	TITLE	PUBLISHER	NT	$PRICE
RP	SKLKIT	MAKE & TELL: COUNTRY THINGS KIT	SRA		51-75
RP	SKLKIT	GOLDMAN-LYNCH SOUNDS & SYMBOLS DEVELOPMENT KIT	AMERICAN GUIDANCE SERVICE, INC.		151-200
RP	WKBOOK	TIME FOR PHONICS, BOOK R	WEBSTER DIVISION/MCGRAW-HILL		<5
RPI	SKLKIT	PEEL & PUT READING PROGRAM	COMMUNICATION SKILL BUILDERS, INC		51-75
RPIJS	GUIDE	PLANNING INDIVIDUALIZED SPEECH & LANGUAGE INTERVENTION PROG.	COMMUNICATION SKILL BUILDERS, INC		11-20
RPIJS	GUIDE	SCHOOL & HOME PROGRAM	COMMUNICATION SKILL BUILDERS, INC		11-20
P	AUDCAS	HAPPY TIME LISTENING	EDUCATIONAL ACTIVITIES, INC.		6-10
P	AUDKIT	LISTENING SKILLS	EBSCO CURRICULUM MATERIALS		51-75
P	AUDKIT	SRA LISTENING LANGUAGE LABORATORY: PRIMARY KIT 1A	SRA		301-400
P	AUDKIT	SRA LISTENING LANGUAGE LABORATORY: PRIMARY KIT 1B	SRA		301-400
P	AUDKIT	SRA LISTENING LANGUAGE LABORATORY: PRIMARY KIT 1C	SRA		301-400
P	AUDKIT	LANGUAGE CENTER 1	EDUCATIONAL PROGRESS CORPORATION		151-200
P	AUDKIT	LISTENING SKILLS	EDUCATIONAL TEACHING AIDS		21-30
P	CL SET	LEARNING LANGUAGE SKILLS 3	AEVAC, INC.		51-75
P	CL SET	LEARNING LANGUAGE SKILLS 4	AEVAC, INC.		51-75
P	CL SET	LISTEN HERE	LAKESHORE CURRICULUM MATERIALS		11-20
P	DITTO	LISTENING SKILLS, LEVEL 1	FRANK SCHAFFER PUBLICATIONS, INC		<5
P	DITTO	LISTENING SKILLS, LEVEL 2	FRANK SCHAFFER PUBLICATIONS, INC		<5
P	DITTO	LISTENING SKILLS, LEVEL 3	FRANK SCHAFFER PUBLICATIONS, INC		<5
P	GAME	ANIMALS CAN TEACH	COMMUNICATION SKILL BUILDERS, INC		6-10
P	GAME	THREE LANGUAGE GAMES	CHILD FOCUS COMPANY		<5
P	GUIDE	LISTENING & LEARNING	FEARON PITMAN PUBLISHERS, INC.		<5
P	GUIDE	TIME FOR PHONICS, BOOK A, T.E.	WEBSTER DIVISION/MCGRAW-HILL		<5
P	GUIDE	TIME FOR PHONICS, BOOK B, T.E.	WEBSTER DIVISION/MCGRAW-HILL		<5
P	GUIDE	TIME FOR PHONICS, BOOK C, T.E.	WEBSTER DIVISION/MCGRAW-HILL		<5
P	MULTIU	DISTAR ACTIVITY KIT: READING	SRA		101-150
P	MULTIU	PEABODY LANGUAGE DEVELOPMENT KIT, LEVEL #3	AMERICAN GUIDANCE SERVICE, INC.		76-100
P	MULTIU	SEE-LISTEN-THINK	MCCORMICK-MATHERS PUBLISHING CO.		51-75
P	MULTIM	LISTENING YOUR WAY TO BETTER READING	ASSOCIATED EDUCATIONAL MATERIALS		301-400
P	MULTIM	SOUND IT, UNIT 1	IMPERIAL INTERNATIONAL LEARNING		51-75
P	MULTIM	SOUND IT, UNIT 2	IMPERIAL INTERNATIONAL LEARNING		51-75
P	MULTIM	LISTENING SKILLS, PRIMARY LEVEL	EDUCATIONAL PROGRESS CORPORATION		301-400
P	MULTIM	LANGUAGE EXPERIENCES IN READING (LEIR), LEVEL I	ENCYCLOPEDIA BRITANNICA		201-300
P	MULTIM	LANGUAGE EXPERIENCES IN READING (LEIR), LEVEL II	ENCYCLOPEDIA BRITANNICA		201-300
P	MULTIM	LANGUAGE EXPERIENCES IN READIN (LEIR), LEVEL III	ENCYCLOPEDIA BRITANNICA		201-300
P	PUPILB	HAPPY SOUNDS (RL 1-3)	BENEFIC PRESS		<5
P	PUPILB	GLAD SOUNDS (RL 1-3)	BENEFIC PRESS		<5
P	PUPILB	SAY & HEAR (RL 1-3)	BENEFIC PRESS		<5
P	RECORD	MAINSTREAMING CHILDREN'S GAMES	KIMBO EDUCATIONAL		6-10
P	RECORD	HAPPY TIME LISTENING	EDUCATIONAL ACTIVITIES, INC.		6-10
P	SND FS	LEARNING SPEECH SOUNDS, SET 1	AEVAC, INC.		51-75
P	SND FS	LEARNING SPEECH SOUNDS, SET 2	AEVAC, INC.		51-75
P	SND FS	LEARNING SPEECH SOUNDS, SET 3	AEVAC, INC.		51-75
P	WKBOOK	SOUND OUT: LISTENING SKILLS PROGRAM	ACADEMIC THERAPY PUBLICATIONS		<5
P	WKBOOK	TIME FOR PHONICS, BOOK A	WEBSTER DIVISION/MCGRAW-HILL		<5
P	WKBOOK	TIME FOR PHONICS, BOOK B	WEBSTER DIVISION/MCGRAW-HILL		<5
P	WKBOOK	TIME FOR PHONICS, BOOK C	WEBSTER DIVISION/MCGRAW-HILL		<5
PI	ACTCRD	GOT TO BE ME, 48 CARDS	DEVELOPMENTAL LEARNING MATERIALS		11-20
PI	ACTCRD	READING BOX	EDUCATIONAL INSIGHTS, INC.		6-10
PI	AUDCAS	I HEARD IT WITH MY OWN TWO EARS	SPOKEN ARTS, INC.		101-150
PI	CL SET	ORAL READING & LINGUISTICS PROGRAM (RL 1-6)	BENEFIC PRESS	8	11-20
PI	DITTO	ASSIST ONE & TWO & THREE	COMMUNICATION SKILL BUILDERS, INC		11-20
PI	MULTIU	LISTENING YOUR WAY TO UNDERSTANDING WORD PROBLEMS	ASSOCIATED EDUCATIONAL MATERIALS		31-50
PI	MULTIU	SOUND-SIGHT SKILLS, SET I	EDUCATIONAL ACTIVITIES, INC.		51-75
PI	MULTIM	WORLD OF WORK	ASSOCIATED EDUCATIONAL MATERIALS		76-100
PI	MULTIM	LISTEN, SPEAK, READ, & SPELL	DEVELOPMENTAL LEARNING MATERIALS		76-100
PI	MULTIM	LOOK & LISTEN	UNITED LEARNING		51-75
PI	RECORD	SINGING ABOUT COLOR	CLASSROOM MATERIALS CO.		6-10
PI	REFBK	SPECIAL NEEDS: SPECIAL ANSWERS	BOOK-LAB, INC.		11-20
PI	SKLKIT	READER IN THE KITCHEN	EDUCATIONAL PERFORMANCE ASSOC.		<5
PI	WKBOOK	GOT TO BE ME, WORKBOOK	DEVELOPMENTAL LEARNING MATERIALS		6-10
PIJS	REFBK	LANGUAGE REMEDIATION & EXPANSION	COMMUNICATION SKILL BUILDERS, INC		11-20
PIJS	SKLKIT	SYNTAX TWO	COMMUNICATION SKILL BUILDERS, INC		51-75
I	AUDKIT	LISTENING WITH A PURPOSE	CORONET MULTI MEDIA		101-150
I	MULTIM	LISTENING SKILLS, INTERMEDIATE LEVEL	EDUCATIONAL PROGRESS CORPORATION		301-400
I	MULTIM	LANGUAGE EXPERIENCES IN READING (LEIR), LEVEL IV	ENCYCLOPEDIA BRITANNICA		201-300
I	PUPILB	LOUD & CLEAR (RL 4-6)	BENEFIC PRESS		<5
I	PUPILB	HEAR YE! HEAR YE! (RL 4-6)	BENEFIC PRESS		<5
I	PUPILB	NOW HEAR THIS (RL 4-6)	BENEFIC PRESS		<5
IJ	AUDKIT	LEARNING TO LISTEN	EBSCO CURRICULUM MATERIALS		51-75
IJ	AUDKIT	LISTENING SKILLS PROGRAM, GRADES 4-8 (RL 4-9)	BENEFIC PRESS		51-75
IJ	AUDKIT	LISTENING	NATIONAL BOOK COMPANY		51-75
IJ	GUIDE	DEVELOPING THE LISTENING SKILLS	EDUCATIONAL ACTIVITIES, INC.		<5
IJ	SKLKIT	+10 VOCABULARY BOOSTER, LEVEL A	WEBSTER DIVISION/MCGRAW-HILL		151-200
IJ	SKLKIT	+10 VOCABULARY BOOSTER, LEVEL B	WEBSTER DIVISION/MCGRAW-HILL		151-200
IJ	SKLKIT	+10 VOCABULARY BOOSTER, LEVEL C	WEBSTER DIVISION/MCGRAW-HILL		151-200
IJ	SKLKIT	+10 VOCABULARY BOOSTER, LEVEL D	WEBSTER DIVISION/MCGRAW-HILL		151-200
IJ	SKLKIT	+10 VOCABULARY BOOSTER, LEVEL E	WEBSTER DIVISION/MCGRAW-HILL		151-200
IJS	MULTIU	SOUND-SIGHT SKILLS, SET II	EDUCATIONAL ACTIVITIES, INC.		51-75

LEVEL	FORMAT	TITLE	PUBLISHER	NT	$PRICE

---

35 - SKILL: LISTENING SKILLS - GENERAL

LEVEL	FORMAT	TITLE	PUBLISHER	NT	$PRICE
IJS	WKBOOK	ACQUIRING LANGUAGE SKILLS, BOOK A	WEBSTER DIVISION/MCGRAW-HILL		<5
IJS	WKBOOK	BUILDING LANGUAGE SKILLS, BOOK B	WEBSTER DIVISION/MCGRAW-HILL		<5
IJS	WKBOOK	CONTINUING LANGUAGE SKILLS, BOOK C	WEBSTER DIVISION/MCGRAW-HILL		<5
IJS	WKBOOK	DIRECTING LANGUAGE SKILLS, BOOK D	WEBSTER DIVISION/MCGRAW-HILL		<5
J	AUDKIT	SRA LISTENING LANGUAGE LABORATORY: INTERMEDIATE KIT 2A	SRA		301-400
J	AUDKIT	SRA LISTENING LANGUAGE LABORATORY: INTERMEDIATE KIT 2B	SRA		301-400
J	AUDKIT	SRA LISTENING LANGUAGE LABORATORY: INTERMEDIATE KIT 2C	SRA		301-400
J	AUDKIT	LANGUAGE CENTER 2	EDUCATIONAL PROGRESS CORPORATION		151-200
J	MULTIM	LISTENING SKILLS, SERIES 7/8/9 LEVEL	EDUCATIONAL PROGRESS CORPORATION		151-200
JS	AUDKIT	PRE- READING SKILLS SERIES	MEDIA MATERIALS, INC.		21-30
JS	CL SET	PLAN: LITERATURE, LANGUAGE & COMMUNICATION	WESTINGHOUSE LEARNING CORP.		101-150
JS	PUPILB	SPEAKING BY DOING	NATIONAL TEXTBOOK COMPANY		<5
S	AUDCAS	COMMUNICATIONS: THE BUSINESS OF ORAL COMMUNICATIN	SOUTH-WESTERN PUBLISHING CO.		201-300
S	MULTIM	RELEVANCE SERIES	CAMBRIDGE BOOK CO.	5	>450
S	MULTIM	RELEVANCE SERIES: RELEVANCE OF LISTENING	CAMBRIDGE BOOK CO.		201-300
S	MULTIM	LISTENING SKILLS, ADVANCED LEVEL	EDUCATIONAL PROGRESS CORPORATION		151-200
S	TRANSP	EFFECTIVE LISTENING	LANSFORD PUBLISHING COMPANY		101-150

---

36 - SKILL: LISTENING COMPREHENSION

LEVEL	FORMAT	TITLE	PUBLISHER	NT	$PRICE
R	GAME	BODY PARTS CARDS & GAMEBOARD	COMMUNICATION SKILL BUILDERS, INC		11-20
R	PUPILB	LADYBIRD BOOK: PLAYBOOK 1	IDEAL SCHOOL SUPPLY COMPANY		<5
R	PUPILB	LADYBIRD BOOK: PLAYBOOK 2	IDEAL SCHOOL SUPPLY COMPANY		<5
R	PUPILB	LADYBIRD BOOK: PLAYBOOK 3	IDEAL SCHOOL SUPPLY COMPANY		<5
R	PUPILB	LADYBIRD BOOK: PLAYBOOK 4	IDEAL SCHOOL SUPPLY COMPANY		<5
RP	AUDKIT	LISTENING SKILLS PROGRAM, GRADES 1-3 (RL 1-3)	BENEFIC PRESS		51-75
RP	AUDKIT	EARS	ECONOMY COMPANY		76-100
RP	AUDKIT	LEARN TO LISTEN	IDEAL SCHOOL SUPPLY COMPANY		11-20
RP	AUDKIT	LISTENING SKILLS	WEBER COSTELLO COMPANY		11-20
RP	AUDKIT	CAN YOU FIND MY MOTHER?	MEDIA MATERIALS, INC.		6-10
RP	AUDKIT	HEAR HOW, SET 1	MEDIA MATERIALS, INC.		6-10
RP	AUDKIT	HEAR HOW, SET 2	MEDIA MATERIALS, INC.		6-10
RP	AUDKIT	RED HEN & SLY FOX	MEDIA MATERIALS, INC.		6-10
RP	AUDKIT	SUE GOES TO THE ZOO	MEDIA MATERIALS, INC.		6-10
RP	AUDKIT	SHELLY HELPS MOTHER SHOP	MEDIA MATERIALS, INC.		6-10
RP	AUDKIT	BOY WHO DIDN'T LISTEN	MEDIA MATERIALS, INC.		6-10
RP	AUDKIT	WHAT CAN YOU DO WITH A PENNY?	MEDIA MATERIALS, INC.		6-10
RP	AUDKIT	LISTENING & LEARNING	HOUGHTON MIFFLIN COMPANY		51-75
RP	CHART	EASEL LISTENING GAMES	ACADIA PRESS, INC.		6-10
RP	FLASH	LISTENING EARS CARD SET	STANWIX HOUSE, INC.		11-20
RP	FLNLBD	ANIMAL CUT-OUTS	CREATIVE STORYTIME PRESS		<5
RP	FLNLBD	OLIVE THE OSTRICH	CREATIVE STORYTIME PRESS		<5
RP	GAME	INDIVIDUAL LISTENING GAMES	ACADIA PRESS, INC.		<5
RP	GUIDE	LISTENING EARS	STANWIX HOUSE, INC.		11-20
RP	GUIDE	LISTENING ACTIVITIES: A MANUAL OF LISTENING ACTIVITIES	PAUL S. AMIDON & ASSOC., INC.		<5
RP	MULTIU	ALPHA TIME WITH LARGE HUGGABLES	ARISTA CORPORATION		>450
RP	MULTIU	ALPHA TIME WITH SMALL HUGGABLES	ARISTA CORPORATION		301-400
RP	MULTIU	ALPHA TIME PRE-READING PROGRAM	ARISTA CORPORATION		201-300
RP	RECORD	ACTION SONGS FOR RHYTHMIC ACTIVITIES: SING A SONG OF ACTION	KIMBO EDUCATIONAL		11-20
RP	RECORD	NURSERY RHYMES FOR LITTLE PEOPLE	KIMBO EDUCATIONAL		6-10
RP	RECORD	SIMPLIFIED LUMMI STICK ACTIVITIES	KIMBO EDUCATIONAL		11-20
RP	RECORD	LISTENING ACTIVITIES RECORD ALBUM	SCOTT, FORESMAN & CO.		6-10
RP	RECORD	LISTENING SKILLS FOR PRE-READERS	CHILDREN'S BOOK & MUSIC CENTER		21-30
RP	SND FS	LISTENING GAMES	CORONET MULTI MEDIA		76-100
RP	SND FS	ADVENTURES IN LISTENING	CORONET MULTI MEDIA		101-150
RP	TUTORL	DEVELOPMENTAL STORY BOOKS	DEVELOPMENTAL LEARNING MATERIALS		6-10
P	AUDCAS	WHO SAID IT?	EDUCATIONAL ACTIVITIES, INC.		11-20
P	AUDCAS	MEET MR. MIX-UP	EDUCATIONAL ACTIVITIES, INC.		6-10
P	AUDKIT	LISTENING SKILLS	EBSCO CURRICULUM MATERIALS		51-75
P	AUDKIT	SRA LISTENING LANGUAGE LABORATORY: PRIMARY KIT 1A	SRA		301-400
P	AUDKIT	SRA LISTENING LANGUAGE LABORATORY: PRIMARY KIT 1B	SRA		301-400
P	AUDKIT	SRA LISTENING LANGUAGE LABORATORY: PRIMARY KIT 1C	SRA		301-400
P	AUDKIT	READING CASSETTES: LEARN TO LISTEN	IDEAL SCHOOL SUPPLY COMPANY		6-10
P	CL SET	LISTEN HERE	LAKESHORE CURRICULUM MATERIALS		11-20
P	GUIDE	LISTENING & LEARNING	FEARON PITMAN PUBLISHERS, INC.		<5
P	GUIDE	ORAL LANGUAGE CONTINUUM CHECKLIST	CHILD FOCUS COMPANY		11-20
P	MANIPU	DEVELOPING LISTENING SKILLS WITH "THREE BILLY GOATS GRUFF"	LESWING PRESS		11-20
P	MULTIU	DISTAR ACTIVITY KIT: LANGUAGE	SRA		101-150
P	MULTIU	LISTENING SKILLS PROGRAM, UNIT I: EASY EARS	SCHOLASTIC BOOK SERVICE		101-150
P	MULTIM	CONCEPTS FOR COMMUNICATION, UNIT 1: LISTEN. W/UNDERSTANDING	DEVELOPMENTAL LEARNING MATERIALS		31-50
P	MULTIM	CONCEPTS FOR COMMUNICATION, UNIT 3, COMMUNICATION	DEVELOPMENTAL LEARNING MATERIALS		51-75
P	RECORD	COMPREHENSION THROUGH LISTENING, VOLUME 1	CLASSROOM MATERIALS CO.		6-10
P	RECORD	COMPREHENSION THROUGH LISTENING, VOLUME 3	CLASSROOM MATERIALS CO.		6-10
P	RECORD	COMPREHENSION THROUGH LISTENING, VOLUME 4	CLASSROOM MATERIALS CO.		6-10
P	RECORD	LET'S LISTEN	CLASSROOM MATERIALS CO.		6-10
P	RECORD	ACTION SONGS FOR RHYTHMIC ACTIVITIES: HOLIDAY ACTION SONGS	KIMBO EDUCATIONAL		11-20
P	RECORD	WHO SAID IT?	EDUCATIONAL ACTIVITIES, INC.		11-20
P	RECORD	MEET MR. MIX-UP	EDUCATIONAL ACTIVITIES, INC.		6-10
P	SKLKIT	COMMUNICATION SKILLS IN ACTION	MCCORMICK-MATHERS PUBLISHING CO.		151-200
P	SND FS	LEARNING SPEECH SOUNDS, SET 1	AEVAC, INC.		51-75

LEVEL	FORMAT	TITLE	PUBLISHER	NT	$PRICE

36 - SKILL: LISTENING COMPREHENSION

LEVEL	FORMAT	TITLE	PUBLISHER	$PRICE
P	SND FS	LEARNING SPEECH SOUNDS, SET 2	AEVAC, INC.	51-75
P	SND FS	LEARNING SPEECH SOUNDS, SET 3	AEVAC, INC.	51-75
P	SND FS	LET'S LISTEN	CORONET MULTI MEDIA	76-100
PI	ACTCRD	SOUNDS, WORDS & ACTIONS	PEEK PUBLICATIONS	<5
PI	AUDCAS	I HEARD IT WITH MY OWN TWO EARS	SPOKEN ARTS, INC.	101-150
PI	AUDKIT	PEP, VOLUME IV	MODERN EDUCATION CORPORATION	31-50
PI	MULTIU	LISTENING YOUR WAY TO UNDERSTANDING WORD PROBLEMS	ASSOCIATED EDUCATIONAL MATERIALS	31-50
PI	MULTIU	LARC: MODULE W: WORD SKILLS	ARISTA CORPORATION	151-200
PI	MULTIM	TEACHING READING THROUGH CREATIVE MOVEMENT	KIMBO EDUCATIONAL	31-50
PI	MULTIM	UNDERSTANDING WHAT WE READ, LEVEL A	NYSTROM	151-200
I	AUDCAS	COUNTDOWN FOR LISTENING	STANWIX HOUSE, INC.	31-50
I	GUIDE	LISTENING ACTIVITY BOOK	FEARON PITMAN PUBLISHERS, INC.	<5
I	MULTIU	LISTENING SKILLS PROGRAM, UNIT II: EAR POWER	SCHOLASTIC BOOK SERVICE	101-150
I	RECORD	EAR TRAINING FOR MIDDLE GRADES	CLASSROOM MATERIALS CO.	6-10
IJ	AUDKIT	LEARNING TO LISTEN	EBSCO CURRICULUM MATERIALS	51-75
IJ	AUDKIT	LISTENING SKILLS PROGRAM, GRADES 4-8 (RL 4-9)	BENEFIC PRESS	51-75
IJ	GUIDE	BASIC PRACTICE IN LISTENING	LOVE PUBLISHING COMPANY	<5
IJ	MULTIM	LISTEN, HEAR	PAUL S. AMIDON & ASSOC., INC.	76-100
J	AUDKIT	SRA LISTENING LANGUAGE LABORATORY: INTERMEDIATE KIT 2A	SRA	301-400
J	AUDKIT	SRA LISTENING LANGUAGE LABORATORY: INTERMEDIATE KIT 2B	SRA	301-400
J	AUDKIT	SRA LISTENING LANGUAGE LABORATORY: INTERMEDIATE KIT 2C	SRA	301-400

37 - SKILL: LISTENING RESPONSE

LEVEL	FORMAT	TITLE	PUBLISHER	$PRICE
R	DITTO	SOUND, WRITE, READ, SPELL	HAYES SCHOOL PUBLISHING COMPANY	<5
R	PUPILB	LADYBIRD BOOK: PLAYBOOK 1	IDEAL SCHOOL SUPPLY COMPANY	<5
R	PUPILB	LADYBIRD BOOK: PLAYBOOK 2	IDEAL SCHOOL SUPPLY COMPANY	<5
R	PUPILB	LADYBIRD BOOK: PLAYBOOK 3	IDEAL SCHOOL SUPPLY COMPANY	<5
R	PUPILB	LADYBIRD BOOK: PLAYBOOK 4	IDEAL SCHOOL SUPPLY COMPANY	<5
RP	ACTCRD	LEARNING ACTIVITY CARDS FOR CHILDREN	LOVE PUBLISHING COMPANY	6-10
RP	AUDCAS	BASIC ACTION POEMS & STORIES FOR EXCEPTIONAL CHILDREN, VOL 1	CONCEPT RECORDS	11-20
RP	AUDCAS	BASIC ACTION POEMS & STORIES FOR EXCEPTIONAL CHILDREN, VOL 2	CONCEPT RECORDS	11-20
RP	AUDKIT	LISTENING SKILLS PROGRAM, GRADES 1-3 (RL 1-3)	BENEFIC PRESS	51-75
RP	AUDKIT	EARS	ECONOMY COMPANY	76-100
RP	AUDKIT	LEARN TO LISTEN	IDEAL SCHOOL SUPPLY COMPANY	11-20
RP	AUDKIT	CAN YOU FIND MY MOTHER?	MEDIA MATERIALS, INC.	6-10
RP	AUDKIT	HEAR HOW, SET 1	MEDIA MATERIALS, INC.	6-10
RP	AUDKIT	HEAR HOW, SET 2	MEDIA MATERIALS, INC.	6-10
RP	AUDKIT	RED HEN & SLY FOX	MEDIA MATERIALS, INC.	6-10
RP	AUDKIT	SUE GOES TO THE ZOO	MEDIA MATERIALS, INC.	6-10
RP	AUDKIT	SHELLY HELPS MOTHER SHOP	MEDIA MATERIALS, INC.	6-10
RP	AUDKIT	BOY WHO DIDN'T LISTEN	MEDIA MATERIALS, INC.	6-10
RP	AUDKIT	WHAT CAN YOU DO WITH A PENNY?	MEDIA MATERIALS, INC.	6-10
RP	AUDKIT	PERCEIVE & RESPOND, VOLUME III	MODERN EDUCATION CORPORATION	31-50
RP	AUDKIT	LISTENING & LEARNING	HOUGHTON MIFFLIN COMPANY	51-75
RP	FLNLBD	ANIMAL CUT-OUTS	CREATIVE STORYTIME PRESS	<5
RP	FLNLBD	OLIVE THE OSTRICH	CREATIVE STORYTIME PRESS	<5
RP	GAME	TEDDY BEAR BINGO	MILTON BRADLEY/PLAYSKOOL	6-10
RP	GUIDE	PAY ATTENTION	P.S. ASSOCIATES	<5
RP	RECORD	LISTENING SKILLS FOR PRE-READERS	CHILDREN'S BOOK & MUSIC CENTER	21-30
P	AUDCAS	WHO SAID IT?	EDUCATIONAL ACTIVITIES, INC.	11-20
P	AUDCAS	MEET MR. MIX-UP	EDUCATIONAL ACTIVITIES, INC.	6-10
P	AUDKIT	LISTENING SKILLS	EBSCO CURRICULUM MATERIALS	51-75
P	AUDKIT	SRA LISTENING LANGUAGE LABORATORY: PRIMARY KIT 1A	SRA	301-400
P	AUDKIT	SRA LISTENING LANGUAGE LABORATORY: PRIMARY KIT 1B	SRA	301-400
P	AUDKIT	SRA LISTENING LANGUAGE LABORATORY: PRIMARY KIT 1C	SRA	301-400
P	AUDKIT	READING CASSETTES: LEARN TO LISTEN	IDEAL SCHOOL SUPPLY COMPANY	6-10
P	CL SET	LISTEN HERE	LAKESHORE CURRICULUM MATERIALS	11-20
P	DITTO	LISTENING SKILLS, LEVEL 3	FRANK SCHAFFER PUBLICATIONS, INC	<5
P	GAME	THREE LANGUAGE GAMES	CHILD FOCUS COMPANY	<5
P	MULTIU	PEABODY LANGUAGE DEVELOPMENT KIT, LEVEL #3	AMERICAN GUIDANCE SERVICE, INC.	76-100
P	MULTIU	LISTENING SKILLS PROGRAM, UNIT I: EASY EARS	SCHOLASTIC BOOK SERVICE	101-150
P	MULTIM	CONCEPTS FOR COMMUNICATION, UNIT 1: LISTEN. W/UNDERSTANDING	DEVELOPMENTAL LEARNING MATERIALS	31-50
P	MULTIM	CONCEPTS FOR COMMUNICATION, UNIT 3, COMMUNICATION	DEVELOPMENTAL LEARNING MATERIALS	51-75
P	RECORD	WHO SAID IT?	EDUCATIONAL ACTIVITIES, INC.	11-20
P	RECORD	MEET MR. MIX-UP	EDUCATIONAL ACTIVITIES, INC.	6-10
P	SND FS	LEARNING SPEECH SOUNDS, SET 1	AEVAC, INC.	51-75
P	SND FS	LEARNING SPEECH SOUNDS, SET 2	AEVAC, INC.	51-75
P	SND FS	LEARNING SPEECH SOUNDS, SET 3	AEVAC, INC.	51-75
P	SP EQT	AUDITORY SKILLS: FOLLOWING DIRECTIONS	INSTRUCTIONAL INDUSTRIES (G.E.)	101-150
PI	AUDCAS	I HEARD IT WITH MY OWN TWO EARS	SPOKEN ARTS, INC.	101-150
PI	AUDKIT	PEP, VOLUME II	MODERN EDUCATION CORPORATION	76-100
PI	AUDKIT	PEP, VOLUME IV	MODERN EDUCATION CORPORATION	31-50
PI	MULTIU	LARC: MODULE O: ORDER & SEQUENCE SKILLS	ARISTA CORPORATION	151-200
I	AUDCAS	COUNTDOWN FOR LISTENING	STANWIX HOUSE, INC.	31-50
I	AUDKIT	KIT 22: BASIC SKILLS IN FOLLOWING DIRECTIONS	EDUCATIONAL RESEARCH, INC.	101-150
I	DITTO	PRACTICAL LANGUAGE SKILLS	MILTON BRADLEY/PLAYSKOOL	<5
I	MULTIU	LISTENING SKILLS PROGRAM, UNIT II: EAR POWER	SCHOLASTIC BOOK SERVICE	101-150
IJ	AUDKIT	LEARNING TO LISTEN	EBSCO CURRICULUM MATERIALS	51-75

LEVEL	FORMAT	TITLE	PUBLISHER	NT	$PRICE

37 - SKILL: LISTENING RESPONSE

LEVEL	FORMAT	TITLE	PUBLISHER	NT	$PRICE
IJ	AUDKIT	LISTENING SKILLS PROGRAM, GRADES 4-8 (RL 4-9)	BENEFIC PRESS		51-75
IJ	GUIDE	BASIC PRACTICE IN LISTENING	LOVE PUBLISHING COMPANY		<5
J	AUDKIT	SRA LISTENING LANGUAGE LABORATORY: INTERMEDIATE KIT 2A	SRA		301-400
J	AUDKIT	SRA LISTENING LANGUAGE LABORATORY: INTERMEDIATE KIT 2B	SRA		301-400
J	AUDKIT	SRA LISTENING LANGUAGE LABORATORY: INTERMEDIATE KIT 2C	SRA		301-400

38 - SKILL: LISTENING CRITICALLY

LEVEL	FORMAT	TITLE	PUBLISHER	NT	$PRICE
RP	AUDKIT	LISTENING SKILLS PROGRAM, GRADES 1-3 (RL 1-3)	BENEFIC PRESS		51-75
RP	AUDKIT	LEARN TO LISTEN	IDEAL SCHOOL SUPPLY COMPANY		11-20
RP	AUDKIT	LISTENING SKILLS	WEBER COSTELLO COMPANY		11-20
RP	CHART	EASEL LISTENING GAMES	ACADIA PRESS, INC.		6-10
RP	FLASH	LISTENING EARS CARD SET	STANWIX HOUSE, INC.		11-20
RP	GAME	INDIVIDUAL LISTENING GAMES	ACADIA PRESS, INC.		<5
RP	GUIDE	LISTENING EARS	STANWIX HOUSE, INC.		11-20
RP	GUIDE	LISTENING ACTIVITIES: A MANUAL OF LISTENING ACTIVITIES	PAUL S. AMIDON & ASSOC., INC.		<5
RP	MULTIU	BASIC LANGUAGE STIMULATOR	EDUCATIONAL PERFORMANCE ASSOC.		76-100
RP	RECORD	ACTION SONGS FOR RHYTHMIC ACTIVITIES: SING A SONG OF ACTION	KIMBO EDUCATIONAL		11-20
RP	RECORD	NURSERY RHYMES FOR LITTLE PEOPLE	KIMBO EDUCATIONAL		6-10
RP	RECORD	SIMPLIFIED LUMMI STICK ACTIVITIES	KIMBO EDUCATIONAL		11-20
RP	RECORD	LISTENING ACTIVITIES RECORD ALBUM	SCOTT, FORESMAN & CO.		6-10
RP	SND FS	LISTENING GAMES	CORONET MULTI MEDIA		76-100
P	AUDKIT	SRA LISTENING LANGUAGE LABORATORY: PRIMARY KIT 1A	SRA		301-400
P	AUDKIT	SRA LISTENING LANGUAGE LABORATORY: PRIMARY KIT 1B	SRA		301-400
P	AUDKIT	SRA LISTENING LANGUAGE LABORATORY: PRIMARY KIT 1C	SRA		301-400
P	GUIDE	LISTENING & LEARNING	FEARON PITMAN PUBLISHERS, INC.		<5
P	MULTIU	LISTENING SKILLS PROGRAM, UNIT I: EASY EARS	SCHOLASTIC BOOK SERVICE		101-150
P	MULTIM	CONCEPTS FOR COMMUNICATION, UNIT 1: LISTEN. W/UNDERSTANDING	DEVELOPMENTAL LEARNING MATERIALS		31-50
P	MULTIM	CONCEPTS FOR COMMUNICATION, UNIT 3, COMMUNICATION	DEVELOPMENTAL LEARNING MATERIALS		51-75
P	RECORD	COMPREHENSION THROUGH LISTENING, VOLUME 1	CLASSROOM MATERIALS CO.		6-10
P	RECORD	COMPREHENSION THROUGH LISTENING, VOLUME 3	CLASSROOM MATERIALS CO.		6-10
P	RECORD	LET'S LISTEN	CLASSROOM MATERIALS CO.		6-10
P	RECORD	ACTION SONGS FOR RHYTHMIC ACTIVITIES: HOLIDAY ACTION SONGS	KIMBO EDUCATIONAL		11-20
P	SKLKIT	COMMUNICATION SKILLS IN ACTION	MCCORMICK-MATHERS PUBLISHING CO.		151-200
PI	ACTCRD	SOUNDS, WORDS & ACTIONS	PEEK PUBLICATIONS		<5
PI	AUDKIT	PEP, VOLUME IV	MODERN EDUCATION CORPORATION		31-50
PI	MULTIM	TEACHING READING THROUGH CREATIVE MOVEMENT	KIMBO EDUCATIONAL		31-50
I	GUIDE	LISTENING ACTIVITY BOOK	FEARON PITMAN PUBLISHERS, INC.		<5
I	MULTIU	LISTENING SKILLS PROGRAM, UNIT II: EAR POWER	SCHOLASTIC BOOK SERVICE		101-150
I	RECORD	EAR TRAINING FOR MIDDLE GRADES	CLASSROOM MATERIALS CO.		6-10
IJ	AUDKIT	LEARNING TO LISTEN	EBSCO CURRICULUM MATERIALS		51-75
IJ	AUDKIT	LISTENING SKILLS PROGRAM, GRADES 4-8 (RL 4-9)	BENEFIC PRESS		51-75
IJ	A/VKIT	LEARNING COMMUNICATION SKILLS	BARR FILMS	5	201-300
IJ	A/VKIT	LET'S TALK ABOUT FAMILIES	BARR FILMS		51-75
IJ	A/VKIT	LET'S TALK ABOUT RULES	BARR FILMS		51-75
IJ	A/VKIT	LET'S TALK ABOUT LEARNING	BARR FILMS		51-75
IJ	A/VKIT	LET'S TALK ABOUT MAKING FRIENDS	BARR FILMS		51-75
IJ	GUIDE	BASIC PRACTICE IN LISTENING	LOVE PUBLISHING COMPANY		<5
IJ	MULTIM	LISTEN, HEAR	PAUL S. AMIDON & ASSOC., INC.		76-100
J	AUDKIT	SRA LISTENING LANGUAGE LABORATORY: INTERMEDIATE KIT 2A	SRA		301-400
J	AUDKIT	SRA LISTENING LANGUAGE LABORATORY: INTERMEDIATE KIT 2B	SRA		301-400
J	AUDKIT	SRA LISTENING LANGUAGE LABORATORY: INTERMEDIATE KIT 2C	SRA		301-400

39 - SKILL: ATTENTION

LEVEL	FORMAT	TITLE	PUBLISHER	NT	$PRICE
R	AUDCAS	LISTENING SKILLS FOR PRE-READERS, VOLUME 1	CLASSROOM MATERIALS CO.		6-10
R	AUDCAS	LISTENING SKILLS FOR PRE-READERS, VOLUME 4	CLASSROOM MATERIALS CO.		6-10
R	AUDCAS	LISTENING SKILLS FOR PRE-READERS, VOLUME 5	CLASSROOM MATERIALS CO.		6-10
R	RECORD	LISTENING SKILLS FOR PRE-READERS, VOLUME 1	CLASSROOM MATERIALS CO.		6-10
R	RECORD	LISTENING SKILLS FOR PRE-READERS, VOLUME 2	CLASSROOM MATERIALS CO.		6-10
R	RECORD	LISTENING SKILLS FOR PRE-READERS, VOLUME 3	CLASSROOM MATERIALS CO.		6-10
R	RECORD	LISTENING SKILLS FOR PRE-READERS, VOLUME 5	CLASSROOM MATERIALS CO.		6-10
RP	AUDKIT	LEARN TO LISTEN	IDEAL SCHOOL SUPPLY COMPANY		11-20
RP	AUDKIT	LISTENING SKILLS	WEBER COSTELLO COMPANY		11-20
RP	AUDTAP	LISTENING-DOING-LEARNING TAPES	SRA		21-30
RP	CHART	EASEL LISTENING GAMES	ACADIA PRESS, INC.		6-10
RP	FLASH	LISTENING EARS CARD SET	STANWIX HOUSE, INC.		11-20
RP	GAME	INDIVIDUAL LISTENING GAMES	ACADIA PRESS, INC.		<5
RP	GUIDE	PAY ATTENTION	P.S. ASSOCIATES		<5
RP	GUIDE	LISTENING EARS	STANWIX HOUSE, INC.		11-20
RP	GUIDE	LISTENING ACTIVITIES: A MANUAL OF LISTENING ACTIVITIES	PAUL S. AMIDON & ASSOC., INC.		<5
RP	RECORD	LISTENING ACTIVITIES RECORD ALBUM	SCOTT, FORESMAN & CO.		6-10
RP	RECORD	LISTENING SKILLS FOR PRE-READERS	CHILDREN'S BOOK & MUSIC CENTER		21-30
RP	SND FS	LISTENING GAMES	CORONET MULTI MEDIA		76-100
RP	SND FS	ADVENTURES IN LISTENING	CORONET MULTI MEDIA		101-150
P	AUDCAS	SOUND ABSURDITIES	LAKESHORE CURRICULUM MATERIALS		6-10
P	AUDCAS	SOUND STORIES	LAKESHORE CURRICULUM MATERIALS		6-10
P	AUDCAS	HAPPY TIME LISTENING	EDUCATIONAL ACTIVITIES, INC.		6-10
P	AUDCAS	WHO SAID IT?	EDUCATIONAL ACTIVITIES, INC.		11-20
P	AUDCAS	MEET MR. MIX-UP	EDUCATIONAL ACTIVITIES, INC.		6-10
P	AUDKIT	LISTENING SKILLS	EBSCO CURRICULUM MATERIALS		51-75

LEVEL	FORMAT	TITLE	PUBLISHER	NT	$PRICE

39 - SKILL: ATTENTION

LEVEL	FORMAT	TITLE	PUBLISHER	NT	$PRICE
P	AUDKIT	READING CASSETTES: LEARN TO LISTEN	IDEAL SCHOOL SUPPLY COMPANY		6-10
P	CL SET	AUDITORY STIMULATOR CLASS KIT	EDUCATIONAL PERFORMANCE ASSOC.		51-75
P	FILMST	LEARNING ABOUT OUR LANGUAGE, SET 1	AEVAC, INC.		31-50
P	MULTIM	NEW GOALS IN LISTENING, GRADES 1-3	TROLL ASSOCIATES		76-100
P	RECORD	COMPREHENSION THROUGH LISTENING, VOLUME 1	CLASSROOM MATERIALS CO.		6-10
P	RECORD	COMPREHENSION THROUGH LISTENING, VOLUME 3	CLASSROOM MATERIALS CO.		6-10
P	RECORD	COMPREHENSION THROUGH LISTENING, VOLUME 4	CLASSROOM MATERIALS CO.		6-10
P	RECORD	LISTENING SKILLS FOR PRE-READERS, VOLUME 4	CLASSROOM MATERIALS CO.		6-10
P	RECORD	MAINSTREAMING CHILDREN'S GAMES	KIMBO EDUCATIONAL		6-10
P	RECORD	HAPPY TIME LISTENING	EDUCATIONAL ACTIVITIES, INC.		6-10
P	RECORD	WHO SAID IT?	EDUCATIONAL ACTIVITIES, INC.		11-20
P	RECORD	MEET MR. MIX-UP	EDUCATIONAL ACTIVITIES, INC.		6-10
P	SND FS	LET'S LISTEN	CORONET MULTI MEDIA		76-100
PI	ACTCRD	SOUNDS, WORDS & ACTIONS	PEEK PUBLICATIONS		<5
PI	AUDKIT	READING-LISTENING COMPREHENSION SKILLS, LEVEL 3	EDUCATIONAL ACTIVITIES, INC.		31-50
PI	AUDKIT	PEP, VOLUME IV	MODERN EDUCATION CORPORATION		31-50
PI	MULTIM	NEW GOALS IN LISTENING, GRADES 2-4	TROLL ASSOCIATES		76-100
PIJ	AUDKIT	READING-LISTENING COMPREHENSION SKILLS, LEVEL 4	EDUCATIONAL ACTIVITIES, INC.		31-50
I	AUDCAS	COUNTDOWN FOR LISTENING	STANWIX HOUSE, INC.		31-50
I	GUIDE	LISTENING ACTIVITY BOOK	FEARON PITMAN PUBLISHERS, INC.		<5
IJ	AUDKIT	LEARNING TO LISTEN	EBSCO CURRICULUM MATERIALS		51-75
IJ	GUIDE	BASIC PRACTICE IN LISTENING	LOVE PUBLISHING COMPANY		<5
IJ	MULTIM	LISTEN, HEAR	PAUL S. AMIDON & ASSOC., INC.		76-100

40 - SKILL: EXPRESSION

LEVEL	FORMAT	TITLE	PUBLISHER	NT	$PRICE
R	AUDCAS	LISTENING SKILLS FOR PRE-READERS, VOLUME 1	CLASSROOM MATERIALS CO.		6-10
R	AUDCAS	LISTENING SKILLS FOR PRE-READERS, VOLUME 2	CLASSROOM MATERIALS CO.		6-10
R	AUDCAS	LISTENING SKILLS FOR PRE-READERS, VOLUME 4	CLASSROOM MATERIALS CO.		6-10
R	AUDCAS	LISTENING SKILLS FOR PRE-READERS, VOLUME 5	CLASSROOM MATERIALS CO.		6-10
R	RECORD	LISTENING SKILLS FOR PRE-READERS, VOLUME 1	CLASSROOM MATERIALS CO.		6-10
R	RECORD	LISTENING SKILLS FOR PRE-READERS, VOLUME 2	CLASSROOM MATERIALS CO.		6-10
R	RECORD	LISTENING SKILLS FOR PRE-READERS, VOLUME 3	CLASSROOM MATERIALS CO.		6-10
R	RECORD	LISTENING SKILLS FOR PRE-READERS, VOLUME 5	CLASSROOM MATERIALS CO.		6-10
RP	AUDKIT	LEARN TO LISTEN	IDEAL SCHOOL SUPPLY COMPANY		11-20
RP	AUDKIT	LISTENING SKILLS	WEBER COSTELLO COMPANY		11-20
RP	CHART	EASEL LISTENING GAMES	ACADIA PRESS, INC.		6-10
RP	CL SET	FIVE SENSE STORE	COMENIUS, INC.	6	>450
RP	CL SET	ARRANGING SOUNDS WITH MAGNETIC TAPES	COMENIUS, INC.		76-100
RP	DITTO	RETELLING FAVORITE STORIES	INSTRUCTO/MCGRAW-HILL		<5
RP	FLASH	LISTENING EARS CARD SET	STANWIX HOUSE, INC.		11-20
RP	GAME	INDIVIDUAL LISTENING GAMES	ACADIA PRESS, INC.		<5
RP	GUIDE	LISTENING EARS	STANWIX HOUSE, INC.		11-20
RP	GUIDE	LISTENING ACTIVITIES: A MANUAL OF LISTENING ACTIVITIES	PAUL S. AMIDON & ASSOC., INC.		<5
RP	RECORD	SING A SONG OF SOUND	KIMBO EDUCATIONAL		11-20
RP	RECORD	LISTENING ACTIVITIES RECORD ALBUM	SCOTT, FORESMAN & CO.		6-10
RP	RECORD	LISTENING SKILLS FOR PRE-READERS	CHILDREN'S BOOK & MUSIC CENTER		21-30
RP	SKLKIT	MAKE & TELL: LIVING THINGS KIT	SRA		51-75
RP	SKLKIT	MAKE & TELL: TOWN THINGS KIT	SRA		51-75
RP	SKLKIT	MAKE & TELL: COUNTRY THINGS KIT	SRA		51-75
RP	SND FS	LISTENING GAMES	CORONET MULTI MEDIA		76-100
RP	SND FS	ADVENTURES IN LISTENING	CORONET MULTI MEDIA		101-150
RP	WKBOOK	TELL & DRAW STORIES	CREATIVE STORYTIME PRESS		6-10
RP	WKBOOK	MORE TELL & DRAW STORIES	CREATIVE STORYTIME PRESS		6-10
RP	WKBOOK	LOTS MORE TELL & DRAW STORIES	CREATIVE STORYTIME PRESS		6-10
P	AUDCAS	SOUND ABSURDITIES	LAKESHORE CURRICULUM MATERIALS		6-10
P	AUDCAS	SOUND STORIES	LAKESHORE CURRICULUM MATERIALS		6-10
P	AUDCAS	HAPPY TIME LISTENING	EDUCATIONAL ACTIVITIES, INC.		6-10
P	AUDCAS	WHO SAID IT?	EDUCATIONAL ACTIVITIES, INC.		11-20
P	AUDCAS	MEET MR. MIX-UP	EDUCATIONAL ACTIVITIES, INC.		6-10
P	AUDKIT	LISTENING SKILLS	EBSCO CURRICULUM MATERIALS		51-75
P	AUDKIT	READING CASSETTES: LEARN TO LISTEN	IDEAL SCHOOL SUPPLY COMPANY		6-10
P	AUDKIT	READING CASSETTES: READING READINESS	IDEAL SCHOOL SUPPLY COMPANY		51-75
P	MULTIM	CONCEPTS FOR COMMUNICATION, UNIT 1: LISTEN. W/UNDERSTANDING	DEVELOPMENTAL LEARNING MATERIALS		31-50
P	MULTIM	NEW GOALS IN LISTENING, GRADES 1-3	TROLL ASSOCIATES		76-100
P	RECORD	COMPREHENSION THROUGH LISTENING, VOLUME 1	CLASSROOM MATERIALS CO.		6-10
P	RECORD	COMPREHENSION THROUGH LISTENING, VOLUME 3	CLASSROOM MATERIALS CO.		6-10
P	RECORD	COMPREHENSION THROUGH LISTENING, VOLUME 4	CLASSROOM MATERIALS CO.		6-10
P	RECORD	LISTENING SKILLS FOR PRE-READERS, VOLUME 4	CLASSROOM MATERIALS CO.		6-10
P	RECORD	HAPPY TIME LISTENING	EDUCATIONAL ACTIVITIES, INC.		6-10
P	RECORD	WHO SAID IT?	EDUCATIONAL ACTIVITIES, INC.		11-20
P	RECORD	MEET MR. MIX-UP	EDUCATIONAL ACTIVITIES, INC.		6-10
P	SND FS	LET'S LISTEN	CORONET MULTI MEDIA		76-100
P	SP EQT	AUDITORY SKILLS: FOLLOWING DIRECTIONS	INSTRUCTIONAL INDUSTRIES (G.E.)		101-150
P	WKBOOK	TALK TALK TALK	ST. JOHN SCHOOL FOR THE DEAF		<5
PI	ACTCRD	SOUNDS, WORDS & ACTIONS	PEEK PUBLICATIONS		<5
PI	AUDKIT	PEP, VOLUME IV	MODERN EDUCATION CORPORATION		31-50
PI	MULTIM	NEW GOALS IN LISTENING, GRADES 2-4	TROLL ASSOCIATES		76-100
PI	SND FS	STORY STARTERS	CLEARVUE, INC.	12	76-100
PI	SND FS	STORY STARTERS: FIREHOUSE	CLEARVUE, INC.		11-20

LEVEL	FORMAT	TITLE	PUBLISHER	NT	$PRICE

40 - SKILL: EXPRESSION

LEVEL	FORMAT	TITLE	PUBLISHER	NT	$PRICE
PI	SND FS	STORY STARTERS: IT'S MAGIC	CLEARVUE, INC.		11-20
PI	SND FS	STORY STARTERS: BIRTHDAY PARTY	CLEARVUE, INC.		11-20
PI	SND FS	STORY STARTERS: MYSTERY HAT	CLEARVUE, INC.		11-20
PI	SND FS	STORY STARTERS: UP, UP, UP	CLEARVUE, INC.		11-20
PI	SND FS	STORY STARTERS: SECRET MESSAGE	CLEARVUE, INC.		11-20
PI	SND FS	STORY STARTERS: LOST DOG	CLEARVUE, INC.		11-20
PI	SND FS	STORY STARTERS: WAITING	CLEARVUE, INC.		11-20
PI	SND FS	STORY STARTERS: PLAYGROUND	CLEARVUE, INC.		11-20
PI	SND FS	STORY STARTERS: CARNIVAL	CLEARVUE, INC.		11-20
PI	SND FS	STORY STARTERS: WINTER HIKE	CLEARVUE, INC.		11-20
I	AUDCAS	COUNTDOWN FOR LISTENING	STANWIX HOUSE, INC.		31-50
I	GUIDE	LISTENING ACTIVITY BOOK	FEARON PITMAN PUBLISHERS, INC.		<5
IJ	AUDKIT	LEARNING TO LISTEN	EBSCO CURRICULUM MATERIALS		51-75
IJ	MULTIM	LISTEN, HEAR	PAUL S. AMIDON & ASSOC., INC.		76-100
JS	SND FS	STRUCTURE WORDS	CORONET MULTI MEDIA		101-150

41 - SKILL: THINKING SKILLS - GENERAL

LEVEL	FORMAT	TITLE	PUBLISHER	NT	$PRICE
RP	GUIDE	101 LANGUAGE ARTS ACTIVITIES	COMMUNICATION SKILL BUILDERS,INC		6-10
RPI	SKLKIT	PEEL & PUT READING PROGRAM	COMMUNICATION SKILL BUILDERS,INC		51-75
RPIJS	GUIDE	SCHOOL & HOME PROGRAM	COMMUNICATION SKILL BUILDERS,INC		11-20
P	MULTIU	DISTAR ACTIVITY KIT: LANGUAGE	SRA		101-150
P	MULTIU	SEE-LISTEN-THINK	MCCORMICK-MATHERS PUBLISHING CO.		51-75
P	MULTIM	PRIMARY THINKING BOX (RL 1-3)	BENEFIC PRESS		151-200
P	MULTIM	LANGUAGE EXPERIENCES IN READING (LEIR), LEVEL I	ENCYCLOPEDIA BRITANNICA		201-300
P	MULTIM	LANGUAGE EXPERIENCES IN READING (LEIR), LEVEL II	ENCYCLOPEDIA BRITANNICA		201-300
P	MULTIM	LANGUAGE EXPERIENCES IN READIN (LEIR), LEVEL III	ENCYCLOPEDIA BRITANNICA		201-300
PI	ACTCRD	COMMUNICARDS	COMMUNICATION SKILL BUILDERS,INC		11-20
PI	ACTCRD	SEE HOW YOU FEEL	LAKESHORE CURRICULUM MATERIALS		11-20
PI	SND FS	THINKING SKILLS	TROLL ASSOCIATES		101-150
PIJS	MULTIU	COMMUNICATIVE COMPETENCE	COMMUNICATION SKILL BUILDERS,INC		201-300
PIJS	REFBK	LANGUAGE REMEDIATION & EXPANSION	COMMUNICATION SKILL BUILDERS,INC		11-20
PIJS	WKBOOK	SPACE ADVENTURES READING SERIES	COMMUNICATION SKILL BUILDERS,INC		11-20
I	MULTIM	LANGUAGE EXPERIENCES IN READING (LEIR), LEVEL IV	ENCYCLOPEDIA BRITANNICA		201-300
IJS	PICTUR	WHAT'S HAPPENING?	TEACHING RESOURCES CORPORATION		6-10

42 - SKILL: ASSOCIATION

LEVEL	FORMAT	TITLE	PUBLISHER	NT	$PRICE
R	GAME	BODY PARTS CARDS & GAMEBOARD	COMMUNICATION SKILL BUILDERS,INC		11-20
R	GUIDE	COLOR RECOGNITION	COMMUNICATION SKILL BUILDERS,INC		6-10
R	MULTIU	PEABODY EARLY EXPERIENCES KIT	AMERICAN GUIDANCE SERVICE, INC.		201-300
R	MULTIU	GOAL, LEVEL I: LANGUAGE DEVELOPMENT	MILTON BRADLEY/PLAYSKOOL		151-200
RP	ACTCRD	TUTORGRAM: CONCEPTUAL DISCRIMINATION	ENRICHMENT READING CORP OF AMER.		11-20
RP	CHART	ALPHABET POSTER CARDS	MILTON BRADLEY/PLAYSKOOL		6-10
RP	GAME	GAMEBOARDS FOR SPEECH & LANGUAGE DEVELOPMENT	COMMUNICATION SKILL BUILDERS,INC		31-50
RP	GAME	GAMEBOARDS FOR EARLY CHILDHOOD EDUCATION	COMMUNICATION SKILL BUILDERS,INC		31-50
RP	GAME	GUESS WHOSE FEET	CHILD'S WORLD		<5
RP	GAME	GUESS WHOSE EARS	CHILD'S WORLD		<5
RP	GAME	GUESS WHOSE TAIL	CHILD'S WORLD		<5
RP	GAME	WHAT GOES WITH WHAT?	CHILD'S WORLD		<5
RP	GAME	WHAT'S PART OF WHAT?	CHILD'S WORLD		<5
RP	GAME	WHAT BELONGS WHERE?	CHILD'S WORLD		<5
RP	GAME	WHICH PIECE FITS?	CHILD'S WORLD		<5
RP	GAME	WHAT'S THE OPPOSITE?	CHILD'S WORLD		<5
RP	GAME	WHAT DO THEY BECOME?	CHILD'S WORLD		<5
RP	GAME	WHAT'S GOING THROUGH THE TUNNEL?	CHILD'S WORLD		<5
RP	GUIDE	CONCEPT FORMATION: STEPS UP TO LANG. FOR LEARNING IMPAIRED	COMMUNICATION SKILL BUILDERS,INC		6-10
RP	MANIPU	BELONGING	CHILDCRAFT EDUCATION CORPORATION		6-10
RP	MULTIU	PEABODY LANGUAGE DEVELOPMENT KIT, LEVEL #P	AMERICAN GUIDANCE SERVICE, INC.		201-300
RP	MULTIU	PEABODY LANGUAGE DEVELOPMENT KIT, LEVEL #1	AMERICAN GUIDANCE SERVICE, INC.		76-100
RP	PICTUR	PEOPLE, PLACES & THINGS: OCCUPATIONS	TEACHING RESOURCES CORPORATION		6-10
RP	PICTUR	PEOPLE, PLACES & THINGS: STORIES	TEACHING RESOURCES CORPORATION		6-10
RP	SKLKIT	MULTI-CONCEPT SQUARES	CONSTRUCTIVE PLAYTHINGS		76-100
RP	SND FS	BASIC RELATIONSHIPS	CLEARVUE, INC.	6	76-100
RP	SND FS	BASIC RELATIONSHIPS: SAGE & TRIP'S FOREST GAMES	CLEARVUE, INC.		11-20
RP	SND FS	BASIC RELATIONSHIPS: PICNIC SITE	CLEARVUE, INC.		11-20
RP	SND FS	BASIC RELATIONSHIPS: ANIMAL CARNIVAL	CLEARVUE, INC.		11-20
RP	SND FS	BASIC RELATIONSHIPS: FOREST JOB BOARD	CLEARVUE, INC.		11-20
RP	SND FS	BASIC RELATIONSHIPS: ANDY'S NEW HOME	CLEARVUE, INC.		11-20
RP	SND FS	BASIC RELATIONSHIPS: PLAYING THE DAY AWAY	CLEARVUE, INC.		11-20
RP	WKBOOK	TELL & DRAW STORIES	CREATIVE STORYTIME PRESS		6-10
RP	WKBOOK	MORE TELL & DRAW STORIES	CREATIVE STORYTIME PRESS		6-10
RP	WKBOOK	LOTS MORE TELL & DRAW STORIES	CREATIVE STORYTIME PRESS		6-10
RP	WKBOOK	BEGINNING READINESS	JENN PUBLICATIONS		<5
RP	WKBOOK	COLOR WORDS, LEFT & RIGHT: PROBLEM SOLVING, PHONICS, OPPOS.	JENN PUBLICATIONS		<5
RP	WKBOOK	ALPHABET: STARTING OFF WITH PHONICS: BOOK 2	MODERN CURRICULUM PRESS		<5
RPI	MULTIU	B T M P D R H S F KIT	LESWING PRESS		31-50
RPI	VISKIT	STEP	C.C. PUBLICATIONS, INC.		101-150
RPIJS	PICTUR	PICTURES, PLEASE!	COMMUNICATION SKILL BUILDERS,INC		31-50
P	ACTCRD	LITTLE PICTURE CARDS	SCOTT, FORESMAN & CO.		<5
P	AUDKIT	READING CASSETTES: READING READINESS	IDEAL SCHOOL SUPPLY COMPANY		51-75

LEVEL	FORMAT	TITLE	PUBLISHER	NT	$PRICE

42 - SKILL: ASSOCIATION

LEVEL	FORMAT	TITLE	PUBLISHER	NT	$PRICE
P	CHART	VOWEL POSTER CARDS	MILTON BRADLEY/PLAYSKOOL		6-10
P	CL SET	SOUND LOTTO 1	LAKESHORE CURRICULUM MATERIALS		11-20
P	CL SET	SOUND LOTTO 2	LAKESHORE CURRICULUM MATERIALS		21-30
P	DITTO	READING STEP BY STEP, KIT A	CONTINENTAL PRESS, INC.		51-75
P	DITTO	COMPREHENSION SKILLS 2	ACTIVITY RESOURCES COMPANY, INC.		<5
P	GAME	EVERYBODY WINS!	ACADEMIC THERAPY PUBLICATIONS		<5
P	MANIPU	CONCEPT MATCH	CHILDCRAFT EDUCATION CORPORATION		<5
P	MANIPU	MATCH & CHECK, LEVEL 2	SCOTT, FORESMAN & CO.		6-10
P	MANIPU	MATCH & CHECK, LEVEL 3	SCOTT, FORESMAN & CO.		6-10
P	MANIPU	MATCH & CHECK, LEVEL 4	SCOTT, FORESMAN & CO.		6-10
P	MULTIU	PEABODY LANGUAGE DEVELOPMENT KIT, LEVEL #2	AMERICAN GUIDANCE SERVICE, INC.		101-150
P	PICTUR	PEOPLE, PLACES & THINGS: RECREATION	TEACHING RESOURCES CORPORATION		6-10
P	PICTUR	PEOPLE, PLACES & THINGS: SPORTS	TEACHING RESOURCES CORPORATION		6-10
P	SKLKIT	COMMUNICATION SKILLS IN ACTION	MCCORMICK-MATHERS PUBLISHING CO.		151-200
PI	MULTIU	GOAL, LEVEL II: LANGUAGE DEVELOPMENT	MILTON BRADLEY/PLAYSKOOL		151-200
PI	SND FS	THINKING SKILLS	TROLL ASSOCIATES		101-150
PI	TRANSP	LANGUAGE DEVELOPMENT & READING SKILLS	UNITED TRANSPARENCIES, INC.		201-300
PIJS	FLASH	LINES 'N DOTS CARD GAME	COMMUNICATION SKILL BUILDERS,INC		11-20
PIJS	MULTIU	COMMUNICATIVE COMPETENCE	COMMUNICATION SKILL BUILDERS,INC		201-300
IJS	GAME	SCARECROW CARD GAME	COMMUNICATION SKILL BUILDERS,INC		11-20

43 - SKILL: COMPARING

LEVEL	FORMAT	TITLE	PUBLISHER	NT	$PRICE
R	AUDCAS	WHAT IS BIG? WHAT IS SMALL?	ASSOCIATED EDUCATIONAL MATERIALS		11-20
R	MULTIU	PEABODY EARLY EXPERIENCES KIT	AMERICAN GUIDANCE SERVICE, INC.		201-300
RP	ACTCRD	TUTORGRAM: CONCEPTUAL DISCRIMINATION	ENRICHMENT READING CORP OF AMER.		11-20
RP	GUIDE	CONCEPT FORMATION: STEPS UP TO LANG. FOR LEARNING IMPAIRED	COMMUNICATION SKILL BUILDERS,INC		6-10
RP	MULTIU	PEABODY LANGUAGE DEVELOPMENT KIT, LEVEL #1	AMERICAN GUIDANCE SERVICE, INC.		76-100
RP	SKLKIT	MULTI-CONCEPT SQUARES	CONSTRUCTIVE PLAYTHINGS		76-100
RP	SND FS	BASIC RELATIONSHIPS	CLEARVUE, INC.	6	76-100
RP	SND FS	BASIC RELATIONSHIPS: SAGE & TRIP'S FOREST GAMES	CLEARVUE, INC.		11-20
RP	SND FS	BASIC RELATIONSHIPS: PICNIC SITE	CLEARVUE, INC.		11-20
RP	SND FS	BASIC RELATIONSHIPS: ANIMAL CARNIVAL	CLEARVUE, INC.		11-20
RP	SND FS	BASIC RELATIONSHIPS: FOREST JOB BOARD	CLEARVUE, INC.		11-20
RP	SND FS	BASIC RELATIONSHIPS: ANDY'S NEW HOME	CLEARVUE, INC.		11-20
RP	SND FS	BASIC RELATIONSHIPS: PLAYING THE DAY AWAY	CLEARVUE, INC.		11-20
RPI	VISKIT	STEP	C.C. PUBLICATIONS, INC.		101-150
RPIJS	PICTUR	PICTURES, PLEASE!	COMMUNICATION SKILL BUILDERS,INC		31-50
P	MULTIU	PEABODY LANGUAGE DEVELOPMENT KIT, LEVEL #2	AMERICAN GUIDANCE SERVICE, INC.		101-150
P	MULTIM	PRIMARY THINKING BOX (RL 1-3)	BENEFIC PRESS		151-200
P	SKLKIT	COMMUNICATION SKILLS IN ACTION	MCCORMICK-MATHERS PUBLISHING CO.		151-200
PIJS	FLASH	LINES 'N DOTS CARD GAME	COMMUNICATION SKILL BUILDERS,INC		11-20
PIJS	MULTIU	COMMUNICATIVE COMPETENCE	COMMUNICATION SKILL BUILDERS,INC		201-300
IJS	GAME	SCARECROW CARD GAME	COMMUNICATION SKILL BUILDERS,INC		11-20

44 - SKILL: CONVERGENT/DIVERGENT

LEVEL	FORMAT	TITLE	PUBLISHER	NT	$PRICE
RP	MULTIU	PEABODY LANGUAGE DEVELOPMENT KIT, LEVEL #P	AMERICAN GUIDANCE SERVICE, INC.		201-300
RP	WKBOOK	COLOR WORDS, LEFT & RIGHT: PROBLEM SOLVING, PHONICS, OPPOS.	JENN PUBLICATIONS		<5
P	MULTIU	PEABODY LANGUAGE DEVELOPMENT KIT, LEVEL #3	AMERICAN GUIDANCE SERVICE, INC.		76-100

45 - SKILL: SYNTHESIS/ANALYSIS

LEVEL	FORMAT	TITLE	PUBLISHER	NT	$PRICE
R	MULTIU	PEABODY EARLY EXPERIENCES KIT	AMERICAN GUIDANCE SERVICE, INC.		201-300
RP	DITTO	MAZES	MILTON BRADLEY/PLAYSKOOL		<5
RP	GAME	GUESS WHOSE FEET	CHILD'S WORLD		<5
RP	GAME	GUESS WHOSE EARS	CHILD'S WORLD		<5
RP	GAME	GUESS WHOSE TAIL	CHILD'S WORLD		<5
RP	GAME	WHAT GOES WITH WHAT?	CHILD'S WORLD		<5
RP	GAME	WHAT'S PART OF WHAT?	CHILD'S WORLD		<5
RP	GAME	WHAT BELONGS WHERE?	CHILD'S WORLD		<5
RP	GAME	WHICH PIECE FITS?	CHILD'S WORLD		<5
RP	GAME	WHAT'S THE OPPOSITE?	CHILD'S WORLD		<5
RP	GAME	WHAT DO THEY BECOME?	CHILD'S WORLD		<5
RP	GAME	WHAT'S GOING THROUGH THE TUNNEL?	CHILD'S WORLD		<5
RP	MULTIU	PEABODY LANGUAGE DEVELOPMENT KIT, LEVEL #1	AMERICAN GUIDANCE SERVICE, INC.		76-100
RPI	VISKIT	STEP	C.C. PUBLICATIONS, INC.		101-150
P	MANIPU	SMALL PARQUETRY BLOCKS	DEVELOPMENTAL LEARNING MATERIALS		6-10
P	MULTIU	PEABODY LANGUAGE DEVELOPMENT KIT, LEVEL #3	AMERICAN GUIDANCE SERVICE, INC.		76-100
P	MULTIM	PRIMARY THINKING BOX (RL 1-3)	BENEFIC PRESS		151-200
P	PICTUR	WHAT'S WRONG HERE?, LEVEL 1	TEACHING RESOURCES CORPORATION		6-10
P	PICTUR	TELL-A-STORY CARDS	AEVAC, INC.		11-20
P	SKLKIT	COMMUNICATION SKILLS IN ACTION	MCCORMICK-MATHERS PUBLISHING CO.		151-200
PI	ACTCRD	COGNITIVE CHALLENGE CARDS	ACADEMIC THERAPY PUBLICATIONS		6-10
PI	ACTCRD	LOGIC CARDS	DEVELOPMENTAL LEARNING MATERIALS		<5
IJ	PICTUR	WHAT'S WRONG HERE?, LEVEL 2	TEACHING RESOURCES CORPORATION		6-10

46 - SKILL: INDUCTIVE/DEDUCTIVE

LEVEL	FORMAT	TITLE	PUBLISHER	NT	$PRICE
R	MULTIM	CONCEPTS & LANGUAGE	NATIONAL EDUCATIONAL LABORATORY		301-400
RP	MANIPU	BELONGING	CHILDCRAFT EDUCATION CORPORATION		6-10

LEVEL	FORMAT	TITLE	PUBLISHER	NT	$PRICE

---

46 - SKILL: INDUCTIVE/DEDUCTIVE

LEVEL	FORMAT	TITLE	PUBLISHER	$PRICE
RP	MULTIU	PEABODY LANGUAGE DEVELOPMENT KIT, LEVEL #1	AMERICAN GUIDANCE SERVICE, INC.	76-100
RP	MULTIM	HELP: CASUAL RELATIONSHIPS	CENTER FOR EARLY LEARNING	6-10
RP	WKBOOK	COLOR WORDS, LEFT & RIGHT: PROBLEM SOLVING, PHONICS, OPPOS.	JENN PUBLICATIONS	<5
RPI	VISKIT	STEP	C.C. PUBLICATIONS, INC.	101-150
P	ACTCRD	PERCEPTION CARDS: COGITO	INVICTA PLASTICS LTD.	6-10
P	ACTCRD	PERCEPTION CARDS: TOM TURNIP	INVICTA PLASTICS LTD.	6-10
P	ACTCRD	PERCEPTION CARDS: CLOWNS	INVICTA PLASTICS LTD.	6-10
P	ACTCRD	PERCEPTION CARDS: BUSES	INVICTA PLASTICS LTD.	6-10
P	ACTCRD	PERCEPTION CARDS: TRUCKS	INVICTA PLASTICS LTD.	6-10
P	ACTCRD	ACTION CARDS, SET 1	LAKESHORE CURRICULUM MATERIALS	6-10
P	ACTCRD	ACTION CARDS, SET 2	LAKESHORE CURRICULUM MATERIALS	6-10
P	ACTCRD	ACTION CARDS, SET 3	LAKESHORE CURRICULUM MATERIALS	6-10
P	GUIDE	ORAL LANGUAGE CONTINUUM CHECKLIST	CHILD FOCUS COMPANY	11-20
P	MANIPU	CONCEPT MATCH	CHILDCRAFT EDUCATION CORPORATION	<5
P	MULTIU	PEABODY LANGUAGE DEVELOPMENT KIT, LEVEL #2	AMERICAN GUIDANCE SERVICE, INC.	101-150
P	MULTIU	PEABODY LANGUAGE DEVELOPMENT KIT, LEVEL #3	AMERICAN GUIDANCE SERVICE, INC.	76-100
P	MULTIM	PRIMARY THINKING BOX (RL 1-3)	BENEFIC PRESS	151-200
P	PICTUR	THINK AWHILE STORY CARDS	AEVAC, INC.	11-20
P	RECORD	BUILDING VERBAL POWER, VOLUME 3	CLASSROOM MATERIALS CO.	6-10
P	RECORD	BEGINNING EXPERIENCES IN LOGICAL THINKING	CLASSROOM MATERIALS CO.	6-10
P	SP EQT	FLASH-X-SET 1: READING PICTURES	EDL/MCGRAW-HILL	<5
PI	ACTCRD	COGNITIVE CHALLENGE CARDS	ACADEMIC THERAPY PUBLICATIONS	6-10
PI	ACTCRD	LOGIC CARDS	DEVELOPMENTAL LEARNING MATERIALS	<5
PI	SND FS	THINKING SKILLS	TROLL ASSOCIATES	101-150
PI	WKBOOK	READING SKILLS: DRAWING CONCLUSIONS	FRANK SCHAFFER PUBLICATIONS, INC	<5

---

47 - SKILL: CLASSIFYING/CATEGORIZING

LEVEL	FORMAT	TITLE	PUBLISHER	$PRICE
R	AUDCAS	LISTENING SKILLS FOR PRE-READERS, VOLUME 2	CLASSROOM MATERIALS CO.	6-10
R	RECORD	LISTENING SKILLS FOR PRE-READERS, VOLUME 2	CLASSROOM MATERIALS CO.	6-10
RP	ACTCRD	BEADS & LACES PATTERN CARDS	MILTON BRADLEY/PLAYSKOOL	<5
RP	ACTCRD	HOW ARE THEY ALIKE?	MILTON BRADLEY/PLAYSKOOL	<5
RP	A/VKIT	READING READINESS	EYE GATE MEDIA	101-150
RP	CL SET	STAR BOOKS	ARISTA CORPORATION	51-75
RP	DITTO	BOLD BEGINNING: DISCOVER & DO	IDEAL SCHOOL SUPPLY COMPANY	6-10
RP	GAME	GAMEBOARDS FOR EARLY CHILDHOOD EDUCATION	COMMUNICATION SKILL BUILDERS,INC	31-50
RP	GAME	CLASSIFICATION GAME	CHILDCRAFT EDUCATION CORPORATION	6-10
RP	GAME	CLASSIFICATION GAME	EDUCATIONAL TEACHING AIDS	11-20
RP	GAME	PICTURE CARD GAMES, SET I	MILTON BRADLEY/PLAYSKOOL	6-10
RP	GAME	PICTURE CARD GAMES, SET II	MILTON BRADLEY/PLAYSKOOL	6-10
RP	MANIPU	ATTRIBUTE BLOCKS	CHILDCRAFT EDUCATION CORPORATION	21-30
RP	MANIPU	COLOR/SHAPE ABACUS	CHILDCRAFT EDUCATION CORPORATION	11-20
RP	MANIPU	BELONGING	CHILDCRAFT EDUCATION CORPORATION	6-10
RP	MANIPU	COLOR & SHAPE SET	DEVELOPMENTAL LEARNING MATERIALS	31-50
RP	MANIPU	MIX 'N' MATCH PUZZLES: THINGS OF A KIND	TREND ENTERPRISES, INC.	6-10
RP	MULTIU	PEABODY LANGUAGE DEVELOPMENT KIT, LEVEL #P	AMERICAN GUIDANCE SERVICE, INC.	201-300
RP	MULTIU	PEABODY LANGUAGE DEVELOPMENT KIT, LEVEL #1	AMERICAN GUIDANCE SERVICE, INC.	76-100
RP	MULTIU	GO-TOGETHER: CLASSIFYING & MATCHING	GEL-STEN, INC.	<5
RP	OLFACT	USE YOUR SENSES	COMMUNICATION SKILL BUILDERS,INC	31-50
RP	PICTUR	TR LARGE PICTURE CARDS, SET 1	TEACHING RESOURCES CORPORATION	31-50
RP	PICTUR	TR LARGE PICTURE CARDS, SET 2	TEACHING RESOURCES CORPORATION	31-50
RP	SP EQT	CONCEPT DEVELOPMENT: BEGINNING LANGUAGE CONCEPTS, KIT I	BORG-WARNER EDUCATIONAL SYSTEMS	101-150
RPIJS	PICTUR	PICTURES, PLEASE!	COMMUNICATION SKILL BUILDERS,INC	31-50
P	ACTCRD	MAGIC CARDS: CLASSIFICATION, OPPOSITES, SEQUENCE	IDEAL SCHOOL SUPPLY COMPANY	6-10
P	ACTCRD	LITTLE PICTURE CARDS	SCOTT, FORESMAN & CO.	<5
P	ACTCRD	ASSOCIATION PICTURE CARDS 1	DEVELOPMENTAL LEARNING MATERIALS	<5
P	ACTCRD	ASSOCIATION PICTURE CARDS 2	DEVELOPMENTAL LEARNING MATERIALS	<5
P	ACTCRD	ASSOCIATION PICTURE CARDS 3	DEVELOPMENTAL LEARNING MATERIALS	<5
P	ACTCRD	ASSOCIATION PICTURE CARDS 4	DEVELOPMENTAL LEARNING MATERIALS	<5
P	ACTCRD	CLASSIFICATION CARDS, PEOPLE & THINGS	DEVELOPMENTAL LEARNING MATERIALS	<5
P	ACTCRD	CATEGORY CARDS	DEVELOPMENTAL LEARNING MATERIALS	<5
P	ACTCRD	PICTURE CARDS	MILTON BRADLEY/PLAYSKOOL	6-10
P	AUDKIT	CLASSIFICATION-OPPOSITES-SEQUENCE	EDUCATIONAL MEDIA, INC.	31-50
P	CHART	CLASSIFICATIONS-OPPOSITES-SEQUENCE	IDEAL SCHOOL SUPPLY COMPANY	11-20
P	DITTO	READING ESSENTIALS: CONTEXT CLUES, GRADE 1	CONTINENTAL PRESS, INC.	<5
P	DITTO	READING ESSENTIALS: VOCABULARY DEVELOPMENT, GRADE 1	CONTINENTAL PRESS, INC.	<5
P	DITTO	READING ESSENTIALS: VOCABULARY DEVELOPMENT, GRADE 3, BOOK 2	CONTINENTAL PRESS, INC.	<5
P	DITTO	INDIVIDUALIZED READING DEVELOPMENT ACTIVITIES	LOVE PUBLISHING COMPANY	6-10
P	DITTO	GENERAL CLASSIFICATION	INSTRUCTOR PUBLICATIONS, INC.	<5
P	DITTO	COMPREHENSION SKILLS 1	ACTIVITY RESOURCES COMPANY, INC.	<5
P	FLASH	CLASSIFICATION-OPPOSITES PICTURES FOR PEGBOARD	IDEAL SCHOOL SUPPLY COMPANY	6-10
P	GAME	EVERYBODY WINS!	ACADEMIC THERAPY PUBLICATIONS	<5
P	GAME	CONCEPTO-SORT	EDUCATIONAL PERFORMANCE ASSOC.	6-10
P	GAME	CAR-RALLY GAME	DEVELOPMENTAL LEARNING MATERIALS	6-10
P	GAME	ANIMAL SORTING GAME, FARM ANIMALS	DEVELOPMENTAL LEARNING MATERIALS	<5
P	GAME	ANIMAL SORTING GAME, FOREST ANIMALS	DEVELOPMENTAL LEARNING MATERIALS	<5
P	GAME	ANIMAL SORTING GAME, WILD ANIMALS	DEVELOPMENTAL LEARNING MATERIALS	<5
P	MANIPU	CONCEPT MATCH	CHILDCRAFT EDUCATION CORPORATION	<5
P	MANIPU	WORD CONSERVATION GROUPING CARDS	EDUCATIONAL TEACHING AIDS	11-20
P	MANIPU	COUNTING & SORTING TRAY	INVICTA PLASTICS LTD.	6-10

LEVEL	FORMAT	TITLE	PUBLISHER	NT	$PRICE

47 - SKILL: CLASSIFYING/CATEGORIZING

LEVEL	FORMAT	TITLE	PUBLISHER	$PRICE
P	MANIPU	COUNTING & SORTING: ANIMAL SHAPES	INVICTA PLASTICS LTD.	11-20
P	MANIPU	COUNTING & SORTING: TRANSPORT SHAPES	INVICTA PLASTICS LTD.	6-10
P	MANIPU	COUNTING & SORTING: MIXED SHAPES	INVICTA PLASTICS LTD.	6-10
P	MANIPU	COUNTING & SORTING: COUNTERS	INVICTA PLASTICS LTD.	6-10
P	MANIPU	SHAPE BOARD: FARM SHAPES	INVICTA PLASTICS LTD.	6-10
P	MANIPU	SHAPE BOARD: SEA SHAPES	INVICTA PLASTICS LTD.	6-10
P	MANIPU	SHAPE-UPS: CLASSIFICATION	READING JOY, INC.	<5
P	MANIPU	SORTING & GROUPING SET	DEVELOPMENTAL LEARNING MATERIALS	<5
P	MULTIU	PEABODY LANGUAGE DEVELOPMENT KIT, LEVEL #2	AMERICAN GUIDANCE SERVICE, INC.	101-150
P	MULTIU	LANGUAGE PATTERNS/SELF-INSTRUCTIONAL MODALITIES APPROACH	MILTON BRADLEY/PLAYSKOOL	76-100
P	MULTIM	PRIMARY THINKING BOX (RL 1-3)	BENEFIC PRESS	151-200
P	MULTIM	OBSERVING & DESCRIBING SHAPE	ENCYCLOPEDIA BRITANNICA	31-50
P	MULTIM	CONCEPTS FOR COMMUNICATION, UNIT 2, CONCEPT BUILDING	DEVELOPMENTAL LEARNING MATERIALS	51-75
P	SP EQT	LANGUAGE SKILLS PROGRAM: READINESS SKILLS (YY)	SPELLBINDER, INC.	51-75
P	SP EQT	FLASH-X-SET 1: READING PICTURES	EDL/MCGRAW-HILL	<5
PI	ACTCRD	COMMUNICARDS	COMMUNICATION SKILL BUILDERS,INC	11-20
PI	ACTCRD	CLASSIFYING WORD PACER	DM EDUCATIONAL PUBLICATIONS	<5
PI	GAME	GAMEBOARD KIT C	READING JOY, INC.	6-10
PI	GUIDE	LEARNING THROUGH SONG	TEACHING RESOURCES CORPORATION	21-30
PI	SND FS	THINKING SKILLS	TROLL ASSOCIATES	101-150
PIJS	MULTIU	COMMUNICATIVE COMPETENCE	COMMUNICATION SKILL BUILDERS,INC	201-300
I	DITTO	READING ESSENTIALS: VOCABULARY DEVELOPMENT, GRADE 3	CONTINENTAL PRESS, INC.	<5
I	DITTO	WORD SPY, GRADE 5	CONTINENTAL PRESS, INC.	<5
I	GAME	LANGUAGE CATEGORY GAMES	MILTON BRADLEY/PLAYSKOOL	6-10
I	RECORD	BUILDING VERBAL POWER IN THE UPPER GRADES, VOLUME 2	CLASSROOM MATERIALS CO.	6-10
I	RECORD	BUILDING VERBAL POWER IN THE UPPER GRADES, VOLUME 3	CLASSROOM MATERIALS CO.	6-10

48 - SKILL: PHONETIC ANALYSIS - GENERAL

LEVEL	FORMAT	TITLE	PUBLISHER	$PRICE
R	RECORD	SOUND GAMES THROUGH THE GRADES, VOLUME 1	CLASSROOM MATERIALS CO.	6-10
R	WKBOOK	WORDS WE USE, BOOK I (RL K-3)	BENEFIC PRESS	<5
RP	DITTO	DECODING & COMPREHENSION SKILLS 1	CHILDREN'S LEARNING CENTER, INC.	<5
RP	DITTO	DECODING & COMPREHENSION SKILLS 2	CHILDREN'S LEARNING CENTER, INC.	<5
RP	DITTO	DECODING & COMPREHENSION SKILLS 3	CHILDREN'S LEARNING CENTER, INC.	<5
RP	GAME	PHONIC RUMMY CARD GAMES, READINESS	KENWORTHY EDUCATIONAL SERVICE	<5
RP	GAME	GAMEBOARD KIT G	READING JOY, INC.	6-10
RP	GAME	PHONETIC QUIZMO	MILTON BRADLEY/PLAYSKOOL	<5
RP	GUIDE	TIME FOR PHONICS, BOOK R, T.E.	WEBSTER DIVISION/MCGRAW-HILL	<5
RP	MULTIU	ALPHA TIME WITH LARGE HUGGABLES	ARISTA CORPORATION	>450
RP	MULTIU	ALPHA TIME WITH SMALL HUGGABLES	ARISTA CORPORATION	301-400
RP	MULTIU	ALPHA PHONICS PROGRAM	ARISTA CORPORATION	201-300
RP	MULTIM	ALPHA-SOUND PROGRAM, GROUP 1	CLEARVUE, INC.	201-300
RP	MULTIM	HEAR-SEE-SAY, PHONICS READING COURSE	MELODY HOUSE PUBLISHING COMPANY	11-20
RP	MULTIM	PHONICS FOR FUN	ARISTA CORPORATION	201-300
RP	PUPILB	TIGER CUB READERS	LESWING PRESS	21-30
RP	WKBOOK	DELL HOME ACTIVITY: PHONICS	DELL PUBLISHING COMPANY, INC.	<5
RP	WKBOOK	TIME FOR PHONICS, BOOK R	WEBSTER DIVISION/MCGRAW-HILL	<5
RPI	GAME	SULLIVAN READING GAMES	BEHAVIORAL RESEARCH LABORATORIES	51-75
RPI	GUIDE	WORD ATTACK JOY	READING JOY, INC.	6-10
P	ACTCRD	ONE TOO MANY, KIT B	BARNELL LOFT, LTD.	6-10
P	ACTCRD	FUN WITH WORDS, A	BARNELL LOFT, LTD.	6-10
P	ACTCRD	FUN WITH WORDS, B	BARNELL LOFT, LTD.	6-10
P	ACTCRD	FUN WITH WORDS, C	BARNELL LOFT, LTD.	6-10
P	ACTCRD	WORD CONFIGURATIONS	TEACHING RESOURCES CORPORATION	11-20
P	ACTCRD	VISUAL DISCRIMINATION LEARNING-BEG. LETTER WORDS	EDUCATIONAL PERFORMANCE ASSOC.	31-50
P	ACTCRD	PRIMARY PHONICS-SKILL DRILLS WITH MOTIVATORS	SVE	31-50
P	ACTCRD	PHONETIC DRILL CARDS	MILTON BRADLEY/PLAYSKOOL	<5
P	ACTCRD	LIGHT & LEARN CARDS: BEGINNING & ENDING SOUNDS	MILTON BRADLEY/PLAYSKOOL	<5
P	AUDCAS	FROM PHONICS TO READING	UNITED LEARNING	31-50
P	AUDCRD	PHONOGRAMS	AUDIOTRONICS CORPORATION	21-30
P	AUDKIT	CREATURE TEACHERS	ECONOMY COMPANY	151-200
P	AUDKIT	KIT 1: BUILDING READING SKILLS, LEVEL 2	EDUCATIONAL RESEARCH, INC.	101-150
P	AUDKIT	KIT 2: BUILDING READING SKILLS, LEVEL 3	EDUCATIONAL RESEARCH, INC.	101-150
P	AUDKIT	KIT 31: BUILDING PHONICS SKILLS	EDUCATIONAL RESEARCH, INC.	101-150
P	AUDKIT	SIGHT & SOUND PHONICS	WEBER COSTELLO COMPANY	21-30
P	A/VKIT	PHONICS-VOWEL SOUNDS (INITIAL & MEDIAL)	SVE	151-200
P	CL SET	CHEST OF FUN (RL 1-3)	BENEFIC PRESS	76-100
P	DITTO	NEW PHONICS & WORD ANALYSIS SKILLS: GRADE 1, PART 1	CONTINENTAL PRESS, INC.	<5
P	DITTO	NEW PHONICS & WORD ANALYSIS SKILLS: GRADE 3, PART 3	CONTINENTAL PRESS, INC.	<5
P	DITTO	SPICE, VOLUME I	EDUCATIONAL SERVICE, INC.	6-10
P	DITTO	BEGINNING PHONICS	EBSCO CURRICULUM MATERIALS	<5
P	DITTO	PHONICS PROGRAM	FRANK SCHAFFER PUBLICATIONS, INC	12 51-75
P	DITTO	WORD ATTACK SKILLS: READINESS, BOOK 1	EDL/MCGRAW-HILL	6-10
P	DITTO	WORD ATTACK SKILLS: READINESS, BOOK 2	EDL/MCGRAW-HILL	6-10
P	DITTO	PHONICS IIIA	HAYES SCHOOL PUBLISHING COMPANY	<5
P	DITTO	PHONICS IVB	HAYES SCHOOL PUBLISHING COMPANY	<5
P	DITTO	PHONICS & READING	HAYES SCHOOL PUBLISHING COMPANY	<5
P	FILMST	DEVELOPMENTAL READING SKILLS: DECODING	CLASSROOM MATERIALS CO.	51-75
P	FLASH	PHONIC WORD DRILL CARDS, PRIMARY	KENWORTHY EDUCATIONAL SERVICE	<5
P	FLASH	PICTURE FLASH WORDS FOR BEGINNERS	MILTON BRADLEY/PLAYSKOOL	<5

LEVEL	FORMAT	TITLE	PUBLISHER	NT	$PRICE

48 - SKILL: PHONETIC ANALYSIS - GENERAL

LEVEL	FORMAT	TITLE	PUBLISHER	NT	$PRICE
P	GAME	SPLIT WORDS	CONSTRUCTIVE PLAYTHINGS		<5
P	GAME	PHONOGAMES SERIES: THE READINESS STAGE	SRA		101-150
P	GAME	PHONOGAMES SERIES: THE PHONICS EXPLORER	SRA		101-150
P	GAME	PHONOGAMES SERIES: THE PHONICS EXPRESS	SRA		101-150
P	GAME	PHONIC RUMMY CARD GAMES, PRIMARY	KENWORTHY EDUCATIONAL SERVICE		<5
P	GAME	BALLOON GAME	JUDY COMPANY		6-10
P	GUIDE	TIME FOR PHONICS, BOOK A, T.E.	WEBSTER DIVISION/MCGRAW-HILL		<5
P	GUIDE	TIME FOR PHONICS, BOOK B, T.E.	WEBSTER DIVISION/MCGRAW-HILL		<5
P	GUIDE	TIME FOR PHONICS, BOOK C, T.E.	WEBSTER DIVISION/MCGRAW-HILL		<5
P	MANIPU	PHONICS E-Z LANGUAGE LEARNING SLIDE RULES, WORD-BUILDING	E-Z GRADER COMPANY		<5
P	MANIPU	ETA PHONOGRAM PICTURE & WORD GROUPING CARDS	EDUCATIONAL TEACHING AIDS		6-10
P	MANIPU	WORD PICTURE DOMINOES, PHONICS	DEVELOPMENTAL LEARNING MATERIALS		<5
P	MULTIU	DISTAR ACTIVITY KIT: READING	SRA		101-150
P	MULTIU	ALPHA ONE	ARISTA CORPORATION		>450
P	MULTIU	ALPHA TIME PLUS	ARISTA CORPORATION		151-200
P	MULTIU	SPEECH-TO-PRINT PHONICS: A PHONICS FOUNDATION FOR READING	HARCOURT BRACE JOVANOVICH, INC.		51-75
P	MULTIU	EPIC: EMPHASIZING PHONICS IN CONTEXT	MCCORMICK-MATHERS PUBLISHING CO.		151-200
P	MULTIU	LANGUAGE PATTERNS/SELF-INSTRUCTIONAL MODALITIES APPROACH	MILTON BRADLEY/PLAYSKOOL		76-100
P	MULTIM	LISTENING YOUR WAY TO BETTER READING	ASSOCIATED EDUCATIONAL MATERIALS		301-400
P	MULTIM	PRS: THE PRE-READING SKILLS PROGRAM	ENCYCLOPEDIA BRITANNICA		>450
P	MULTIM	PHONICS FOR READING & SPELLING, GRADE 2	MEDIA MARKETING, INC.		101-150
P	MULTIM	PHONICS FOR READING & SPELLING, GRADE 3	MEDIA MARKETING, INC.		101-150
P	MULTIM	MR. PHUN PHONICS	MEDIA MARKETING, INC.		51-75
P	PI/PRT	INDIVIDUAL LANGUAGE ARTS, GRADE 2	CREATIVE TEACHING ASSOCIATES		6-10
P	PI/PRT	INDIVIDUAL LANGUAGE ARTS, GRADE 3	CREATIVE TEACHING ASSOCIATES		6-10
P	PUPILB	MY OWN READING BOOK, VOLUME 2	BOOK-LAB, INC.		<5
P	PUPILB	JOHNNY LEARNS TO READ FOR FUN & QUICKLY	WENKART		<5
P	RECORD	SOUND GAMES THROUGH THE GRADES, VOLUME 2	CLASSROOM MATERIALS CO.		6-10
P	REFBK	DISCOVER NEW WAYS	DISCOVERY LEARNING		<5
P	SKLKIT	READING BRIDGE	BFA EDUCATIONAL MEDIA		101-150
P	SKLKIT	SRA SKILLS SERIES: PHONICS	SRA		<5
P	SKLKIT	SCHOOLHOUSE: WORD ATTACK SKILLS KIT	SRA		101-150
P	SKLKIT	LOGOS 1A	IDEAL SCHOOL SUPPLY COMPANY		101-150
P	SKLKIT	READ-ALONG BEGINNING PHONICS, SET 1	MODERN CURRICULUM PRESS		101-150
P	SKLKIT	READ-ALONG BEGINNING PHONICS, SET 2	MODERN CURRICULUM PRESS		101-150
P	SND FS	FIRST CONCEPTS FILMSTRIP LIBRARY	TROLL ASSOCIATES		101-150
P	TUTORL	MACMILLAN TUTORIAL SYSTEM KIT, GRADE 1	MACMILLAN PUBLISHING CO., INC.		51-75
P	TUTORL	MACMILLAN TUTORIAL SYSTEM KIT, GRADE 2	MACMILLAN PUBLISHING CO., INC.		51-75
P	TUTORL	MACMILLAN TUTORIAL SYSTEM KIT, GRADE 3	MACMILLAN PUBLISHING CO., INC.		51-75
P	VISKIT	TASK CARDS: PRIMARY LANGUAGE ARTS	DIVERSIFIED PRODUCTION RESOURCES		6-10
P	VISKIT	VERSA-TILES, LANGUAGE ARTS LAB 1	EDUCATIONAL TEACHING AIDS		51-75
P	VISKIT	ACTION READING: THE PARTICIPATORY APPROACH	ALLYN AND BACON, INC.		201-300
P	WKBOOK	WORDS WE USE, BOOK II (RL 1-3)	BENEFIC PRESS		<5
P	WKBOOK	WORDS WE USE, BOOK III (RL 1-3)	BENEFIC PRESS		<5
P	WKBOOK	WORDS WE USE, BOOK IV (RL 1-3)	BENEFIC PRESS		<5
P	WKBOOK	WORDS WE USE, BOOK V (RL 1-3)	BENEFIC PRESS		<5
P	WKBOOK	NEW SPECIFIC SKILL SERIES: WORKING WITH SOUNDS, BOOK A	BARNELL LOFT, LTD.		<5
P	WKBOOK	NEW SPECIFIC SKILL SERIES: WORKING WITH SOUNDS, BOOK B	BARNELL LOFT, LTD.		<5
P	WKBOOK	NEW SPECIFIC SKILL SERIES: WORKING WITH SOUNDS, BOOK C	BARNELL LOFT, LTD.		<5
P	WKBOOK	AEVAC PHONICS PROGRAM	AEVAC, INC.	6	11-20
P	WKBOOK	AEVAC PHONICS PROGRAM, BOOK A	AEVAC, INC.		<5
P	WKBOOK	AEVAC PHONICS PROGRAM, BOOK B	AEVAC, INC.		<5
P	WKBOOK	AEVAC PHONICS PROGRAM, BOOK C	AEVAC, INC.		<5
P	WKBOOK	AEVAC PHONICS PROGRAM, BOOK E	AEVAC, INC.		<5
P	WKBOOK	AEVAC PHONICS PROGRAM, BOOK F	AEVAC, INC.		<5
P	WKBOOK	LEARNING PREDICTABLE LANGUAGE	ACADEMIC THERAPY PUBLICATIONS		6-10
P	WKBOOK	DELL HOME ACTIVITY: PHONICS BOOK 2	DELL PUBLISHING COMPANY, INC.		<5
P	WKBOOK	DELL HOME ACTIVITY: PHONICS BOOK 3	DELL PUBLISHING COMPANY, INC.		<5
P	WKBOOK	TALK ABOUT IT	ST. JOHN SCHOOL FOR THE DEAF		<5
P	WKBOOK	SOUNDS & SIGNALS A	HARPER & ROW PUBLISHERS, INC.		<5
P	WKBOOK	SOUNDS & SIGNALS B	HARPER & ROW PUBLISHERS, INC.		<5
P	WKBOOK	SOUNDS & SIGNALS C	HARPER & ROW PUBLISHERS, INC.		<5
P	WKBOOK	SOUNDS & SIGNALS D	HARPER & ROW PUBLISHERS, INC.		<5
P	WKBOOK	SOUNDS & SIGNALS E	HARPER & ROW PUBLISHERS, INC.		<5
P	WKBOOK	READING WITH PHONICS A	HARPER & ROW PUBLISHERS, INC.		<5
P	WKBOOK	READING WITH PHONICS B	HARPER & ROW PUBLISHERS, INC.		<5
P	WKBOOK	READING WITH PHONICS C	HARPER & ROW PUBLISHERS, INC.		<5
P	WKBOOK	COVE SCHOOL READING PROGRAM	DEVELOPMENTAL LEARNING MATERIALS		76-100
P	WKBOOK	NEW PHONICS WORKBOOK, BOOK A	MODERN CURRICULUM PRESS		<5
P	WKBOOK	NEW PHONICS WORKBOOK, BOOK B	MODERN CURRICULUM PRESS		<5
P	WKBOOK	NEW PHONICS WORKBOOK, BOOK C	MODERN CURRICULUM PRESS		<5
P	WKBOOK	TIME FOR PHONICS, BOOK A	WEBSTER DIVISION/MCGRAW-HILL		<5
P	WKBOOK	TIME FOR PHONICS, BOOK B	WEBSTER DIVISION/MCGRAW-HILL		<5
P	WKBOOK	TIME FOR PHONICS, BOOK C	WEBSTER DIVISION/MCGRAW-HILL		<5
P	WKBOOK	PHONICS & WORD POWER, BOOK 1	XEROX EDUCATION PUBLICATIONS		<5
P	WKBOOK	PHONICS & WORD POWER, BOOK 2	XEROX EDUCATION PUBLICATIONS		<5
P	WKBOOK	PHONICS & WORD POWER, BOOK 3	XEROX EDUCATION PUBLICATIONS		<5
P	WKBOOK	SOUND WE USE, BOOK 1	HAYES SCHOOL PUBLISHING COMPANY		<5
P	WKBOOK	SOUNDS WE USE, BOOK 3	HAYES SCHOOL PUBLISHING COMPANY		<5

LEVEL	FORMAT	TITLE	PUBLISHER	NT	$PRICE

48 - SKILL: PHONETIC ANALYSIS - GENERAL

LEVEL	FORMAT	TITLE	PUBLISHER	NT	$PRICE
PI	ACTCRD	LEARNING CENTER PAK (GRADES 2 - 4)	WISE OWL PUBLICATIONS		31-50
PI	ACTCRD	READING BOX	EDUCATIONAL INSIGHTS, INC.		6-10
PI	AUDKIT	TOTAL BUILDING READING SKILLS (KITS 1 - 5)	EDUCATIONAL RESEARCH, INC.	5	>450
PI	AUDKIT	BLENDS & SIGHT WORDS AUDIO LESSONS	SVE		101-150
PI	A/VKIT	BLENDS & SIGHT WORDS, GROUP 1	SVE		76-100
PI	A/VKIT	BLENDS & SIGHT WORDS, GROUP 2	SVE		76-100
PI	CL SET	CHEST OF ACTION (RL 1-6)	BENEFIC PRESS		76-100
PI	CL SET	SOUNDER CLASSROOM SET	EDMARK ASSOCIATES		301-400
PI	CL SET	AEVAC STARTER 101 (NON-READERS)	AEVAC, INC.	10	11-20
PI	DITTO	SPICE, VOLUME II	EDUCATIONAL SERVICE, INC.		6-10
PI	DITTO	SPECIAL KIDS' STUFF, PART IV: WORK STUDY SKILLS (SP. ED.)	INCENTIVE PUBLICATIONS, INC.		6-10
PI	FILMST	I READ & I UNDERSTAND, LEVEL TWO	EDUCATIONAL ACTIVITIES, INC.		31-50
PI	FILMST	I READ & I UNDERSTAND, LEVELS THREE & FOUR	EDUCATIONAL ACTIVITIES, INC.		51-75
PI	GAME	SUPER STOCK	ALLIED EDUCATION COUNCIL		51-75
PI	GAME	MONSTER HUNT	ALLIED EDUCATION COUNCIL		51-75
PI	GAME	PHONIC DOMINO GAME	WEBER COSTELLO COMPANY		<5
PI	GAME	PHONO SENIOR GAME	T.S. DENISON & COMPANY		6-10
PI	GAME	ARE YOU LISTENING?	JUDY COMPANY		6-10
PI	GAME	WORD RECOGNITION	PAUL S. AMIDON & ASSOC., INC.		<5
PI	MULTIM	LISTEN, SPEAK, READ, & SPELL	DEVELOPMENTAL LEARNING MATERIALS		76-100
PI	MULTIM	TALKING PICTURE DICTIONARY	TROLL ASSOCIATES		151-200
PI	MULTIM	WORKING WITH PHONICS	TROLL ASSOCIATES		301-400
PI	MULTIM	MORE NEW WORDS	TROLL ASSOCIATES		151-200
PI	PUPILB	FUNNY-FACE PHONICS	CREATIVE TEACHING ASSOCIATES		6-10
PI	PUPILB	GILLIGAN MILLIGAN	SRA		<5
PI	REFBK	SPECIAL NEEDS: SPECIAL ANSWERS	BOOK-LAB, INC.		11-20
PI	REFBK	SPICE SERIES: SPICE	EDUCATIONAL SERVICE, INC.	8	6-10
PI	SKLKIT	TARGET YELLOW: PHONIC ANALYSIS KIT	ADDISON-WESLEY PUBLISHING CO.		151-200
PI	SND FS	WORKING WTH BLENDS & DIGRAPHS	TROLL ASSOCIATES		101-150
PI	TEXTBK	WORDS, FROM PRINT TO MEANING	ADDISON-WESLEY PUBLISHING CO.		6-10
PI	TRANSP	LANGUAGE DEVELOPMENT & READING SKILLS	UNITED TRANSPARENCIES, INC.		201-300
PI	TUTORL	SOUNDER RESOURCE SET	EDMARK ASSOCIATES		51-75
PI	VISKIT	VERSA-TILES, LANGUAGE ARTS LAB 2	EDUCATIONAL TEACHING AIDS		51-75
PI	VISKIT	READING & LANG. ARTS COMPLETE SET OF 50 JOY ACT. CARDS KITS	INSTRUCTO/MCGRAW-HILL		201-300
PI	WKBOOK	SOUND PUZZLES	ACADEMIC THERAPY PUBLICATIONS		<5
PI	WKBOOK	SPECTRUM OF SKILLS: WORD ANALYSIS, LEVEL 1	MACMILLAN PUBLISHING CO., INC.		<5
PI	WKBOOK	SPECTRUM OF SKILLS: WORD ANALYSIS, LEVEL 2	MACMILLAN PUBLISHING CO., INC.		<5
PI	WKBOOK	SPECTRUM OF SKILLS: WORD ANALYSIS, LEVEL 3	MACMILLAN PUBLISHING CO., INC.		<5
PI	WKBOOK	SPECTRUM OF SKILLS: WORD ANALYSIS, LEVEL 4	MACMILLAN PUBLISHING CO., INC.		<5
PI	WKBOOK	SPECTRUM OF SKILLS: WORD ANALYSIS, LEVEL 5	MACMILLAN PUBLISHING CO., INC.		<5
PI	WKBOOK	SPECTRUM OF SKILLS: WORD ANALYSIS, LEVEL 6	MACMILLAN PUBLISHING CO., INC.		<5
PIJ	ACTCRD	REBUS GLOSSARY CARDS	AMERICAN GUIDANCE SERVICE, INC.		51-75
PIJ	CL SET	CHESTS OF BOOKS (RL 1-9)	BENEFIC PRESS	4	301-400
PIJ	DITTO	RESCUE, VOLUME I	EDUCATIONAL SERVICE, INC.		6-10
PIJ	DITTO	PORTFOLIO OF RUB-ON REBUSES	AMERICAN GUIDANCE SERVICE, INC.		11-20
PIJ	MULTIM	RIGHT-TO-READ PROGRAM, LEVEL I	ACADEMIC THERAPY PUBLICATIONS		151-200
PIJ	REFBK	SPICE SERIES: RESCUE	EDUCATIONAL SERVICE, INC.		6-10
PIJ	REFBK	STANDARD REBUS GLOSSARY	AMERICAN GUIDANCE SERVICE, INC.		<5
I	ACTCRD	FUN WITH WORDS, D	BARNELL LOFT, LTD.		6-10
I	ACTCRD	FUN WITH WORDS, E	BARNELL LOFT, LTD.		6-10
I	ACTCRD	FUN WITH WORDS, F	BARNELL LOFT, LTD.		6-10
I	ACTCRD	LEARNING CENTER PAK (GRADES 3 - 5)	WISE OWL PUBLICATIONS		31-50
I	AUDKIT	PHONICS ANALYSIS	EDUCATIONAL MEDIA, INC.		51-75
I	AUDKIT	WORDS IN MOTION, KIT A	MACMILLAN PUBLISHING CO., INC.		76-100
I	AUDKIT	WORDS IN MOTION, KIT B	MACMILLAN PUBLISHING CO., INC.		76-100
I	AUDKIT	WORDS IN MOTION, KIT C	MACMILLAN PUBLISHING CO., INC.		76-100
I	AUDKIT	KIT 3: BUILDING READING SKILLS, LEVEL 4	EDUCATIONAL RESEARCH, INC.		101-150
I	AUDKIT	KIT 4: BUILDING READING SKILLS, LEVEL 5	EDUCATIONAL RESEARCH, INC.		101-150
I	AUDKIT	KIT 5: BUILDING READING SKILLS, LEVEL 6	EDUCATIONAL RESEARCH, INC.		101-150
I	DITTO	ANCHOR, VOLUME I	EDUCATIONAL SERVICE, INC.		6-10
I	DITTO	BIRDS-EYE VIEW OF LANGUAGE ARTS	FEARON PITMAN PUBLISHERS, INC.		6-10
I	FLASH	PHONIC WORD DRILL CARDS, INTERMEDIATE	KENWORTHY EDUCATIONAL SERVICE		<5
I	GAME	PHONIC RUMMY CARD GAMES, INTERMEDIATE	KENWORTHY EDUCATIONAL SERVICE		<5
I	GAME	TAKE	GARRARD PUBLISHING COMPANY		<5
I	MULTIM	PHONICS FOR READING & SPELLING, GRADE 4	MEDIA MARKETING, INC.		101-150
I	PI/PRT	INDIVIDUAL LANGUAGE ARTS, GRADE 4	CREATIVE TEACHING ASSOCIATES		6-10
I	PI/PRT	INDIVIDUAL LANGUAGE ARTS, GRADE 5	CREATIVE TEACHING ASSOCIATES		6-10
I	PI/PRT	INDIVIDUAL LANGUAGE ARTS, GRADE 6	CREATIVE TEACHING ASSOCIATES		6-10
I	PUPILB	SLY SPY & OTHER STORIES	ANN ARBOR PUBLISHERS		<5
I	RECORD	SOUND GAMES THROUGH THE GRADES, VOLUME 3	CLASSROOM MATERIALS CO.		6-10
I	SKLKIT	SCHOOLHOUSE: WORD ATTACK 1C	SRA		101-150
I	SKLKIT	SOUND FOUNDATION PROGRAM III	DEVELOPMENTAL LEARNING MATERIALS		21-30
I	VISKIT	VERSA-TILES, LANGUAGE ARTS LAB 3	EDUCATIONAL TEACHING AIDS		51-75
I	WKBOOK	WORDS WE USE, BOOK VI (RL 4-6)	BENEFIC PRESS		<5
I	WKBOOK	WORDS WE USE, BOOK VII (RL 4-6)	BENEFIC PRESS		<5
I	WKBOOK	WORDS WE USE, BOOK VIII (RL 4-6)	BENEFIC PRESS		<5
I	WKBOOK	NEW SPECIFIC SKILL SERIES: WORKING WITH SOUNDS, BOOK D	BARNELL LOFT, LTD.		<5
I	WKBOOK	NEW SPECIFIC SKILL SERIES: WORKING WITH SOUNDS, BOOK E	BARNELL LOFT, LTD.		<5
I	WKBOOK	NEW SPECIFIC SKILL SERIES: WORKING WITH SOUNDS, BOOK F	BARNELL LOFT, LTD.		<5

LEVEL	FORMAT	TITLE	PUBLISHER	NT	$PRICE

48 - SKILL: PHONETIC ANALYSIS - GENERAL

LEVEL	FORMAT	TITLE	PUBLISHER	NT	$PRICE
I	WKBOOK	CLUES TO WORDS	MACMILLAN PUBLISHING CO., INC.		<5
IJ	ACTCRD	LANGUAGE SCOOP	KIDS & COMPANY		<5
IJ	CL SET	CHEST OF SUCCESS (RL 4-9)	BENEFIC PRESS		76-100
IJ	CL SET	BIG ADVENTURE BOX	XEROX EDUCATION PUBLICATIONS		101-150
IJ	DITTO	ANCHOR, VOLUME II	EDUCATIONAL SERVICE, INC.		6-10
IJ	FLASH	PHONIC WORD DRILL CARDS, ADVANCED	KENWORTHY EDUCATIONAL SERVICE		<5
IJ	GUIDE	CRACKING THE CODE: TEACHER HANDBOOK	SRA		<5
IJ	GUIDE	RR (REMEDIAL READING), T.M.	MODERN CURRICULUM PRESS		<5
IJ	PUPILB	CRACKING THE CODE: STUDENT READER (CLOTH)	SRA		6-10
IJ	REFBK	SPICE SERIES: ANCHOR	EDUCATIONAL SERVICE, INC.		6-10
IJ	SKLKIT	WORD CLUES	CHARLES E. MERRILL PUBLISHING CO		76-100
IJ	SKLKIT	+4 READING BOOSTER	WEBSTER DIVISION/MCGRAW-HILL		301-400
IJ	VISKIT	PHONICS PROGRAM	EDUCATIONAL TEACHING AIDS		11-20
IJ	WKBOOK	CRACKING THE CODE: STUDENT WORKBOOK	SRA		<5
IJ	WKBOOK	SEQUENTIAL SKILLS DEVELOPMENT ACTIVITIES FOR READING	T.S. DENISON & COMPANY	4	6-10
IJ	WKBOOK	RR (REMEDIAL READING)	MODERN CURRICULUM PRESS		<5
IJS	AUDKIT	HITS SKILLBOOK SERIES, BOOK A (RL 1 - 2)	MODULEARN, INC.		<5
IJS	AUDKIT	HITS SKILLBOOK SERIES, BOOK B (RL 2 - 3)	MODULEARN, INC.		<5
IJS	AUDKIT	HITS SKILLBOOK SERIES, BOOK C (RL 3 - 4)	MODULEARN, INC.		<5
IJS	GAME	AUTO PHONICS: PHONETIC ALPHABET	EDUCATIONAL ACTIVITIES, INC.		<5
IJS	GAME	PAL READING SKILL GAME, RALLY 1	XEROX EDUCATION PUBLICATIONS		51-75
IJS	GAME	PAL READING SKILLS GAME, RALLY 2	XEROX EDUCATION PUBLICATIONS		51-75
IJS	WKBOOK	SOUND WAY, BOOK 1	HAYES SCHOOL PUBLISHING COMPANY		<5
IJS	WKBOOK	SOUND WAY, BOOK 2	HAYES SCHOOL PUBLISHING COMPANY		<5
J	WKBOOK	NEW SPECIFIC SKILL SERIES: WORKING WITH SOUNDS, BOOK G	BARNELL LOFT, LTD.		<5
J	WKBOOK	TROUBLESHOOTER I	HOUGHTON MIFFLIN COMPANY	8	11-20
JS	CHART	RIGHT-TO-READ PROGRAM, LEVEL II	ACADEMIC THERAPY PUBLICATIONS		101-150
JS	CL SET	PLAN: READING IN THE CONTENT AREAS	WESTINGHOUSE LEARNING CORP.		101-150
JS	RECORD	SOUND GAMES THROUGH THE GRADES, VOLUME 4	CLASSROOM MATERIALS CO.		6-10
S	MULTIM	RELEVANCE SERIES	CAMBRIDGE BOOK CO.	5	>450
S	MULTIM	RELEVANCE SERIES: RELEVANCE OF SOUND	CAMBRIDGE BOOK CO.		201-300
S	WKBOOK	NEW SPECIFIC SKILL SERIES: WORKING WITH SOUNDS, BOOK I	BARNELL LOFT, LTD.		<5
S	WKBOOK	NEW SPECIFIC SKILL SERIES: WORKING WITH SOUNDS, BOOK J	BARNELL LOFT, LTD.		<5
S	WKBOOK	NEW SPECIFIC SKILL SERIES: WORKING WITH SOUNDS, BOOK K	BARNELL LOFT, LTD.		<5
S	WKBOOK	NEW SPECIFIC SKILL SERIES: WORKING WITH SOUNDS, BOOK L	BARNELL LOFT, LTD.		<5

49 - SKILL: ALPHABET

LEVEL	FORMAT	TITLE	PUBLISHER	NT	$PRICE
R	AUDKIT	GETTING READY TO READ	MEDIA MATERIALS, INC.		6-10
R	AUDKIT	TRAVELING WITH THE ALPHABET	MEDIA MATERIALS, INC.		6-10
R	AUDKIT	SOUNDS & SYMBOLS	EDUCATORS PUBLISHING SERVICE		101-150
R	AUDKIT	STORIES ABOUT LETTERS	CORONET MULTI MEDIA		76-100
R	MANIPU	TRY: EXPERIENCES FOR YOUNG CHILDREN	BOWMAR/NOBLE PUBLISHERS, INC.		31-50
R	MANIPU	DISNEY WOOD BLOCKS	PLAYSKOOL, INC.		<5
R	MANIPU	SESAME STREET MATCH-UPS	PLAYSKOOL, INC.		11-20
R	MULTIM	BEGINNING TO READ, WRITE & LISTEN	HARPER & ROW PUBLISHERS, INC.		101-150
R	PUPILB	CURIOUS GEORGE LEARNS THE ALPHABET	CHILDCRAFT EDUCATION CORPORATION		<5
R	PUPILB	ABC	GROSSET & DUNLAP, INC.		<5
R	PUPILB	MY ABC BOOK	GROSSET & DUNLAP, INC.		<5
R	VISKIT	READY STEPS	HOUGHTON MIFFLIN COMPANY		151-200
R	WKBOOK	LESSONS TO GROW ON, BOOK 1	PRESCHOOL LEARNING CORPORATION		<5
R	WKBOOK	LESSONS TO GROW ON, BOOK 3	PRESCHOOL LEARNING CORPORATION		<5
R	WKBOOK	ALPHABET FUN	GROSSET & DUNLAP, INC.		<5
R	WKBOOK	I LEARN MY ABC'S	GROSSET & DUNLAP, INC.		<5
RP	ACTCRD	READINESS: ALPHABET	INSTRUCTIONAL FAIR		<5
RP	ACTCRD	READINESS TASK CARDS: ALPHABET	CONSTRUCTIVE PLAYTHINGS		<5
RP	ACTCRD	MATCHING LETTERS, A	BARNELL LOFT, LTD.		6-10
RP	ACTCRD	MATCHING UPPER & LOWER CASE LETTERS, A	BARNELL LOFT, LTD.		6-10
RP	ACTCRD	KINDERGARTEN KEYS: LANGUAGE DEVELOPMENT CARDS, GROUP B	ECONOMY COMPANY		31-50
RP	ACTCRD	ALPHABET CLUE PICTURES	IDEAL SCHOOL SUPPLY COMPANY		6-10
RP	ACTCRD	PLAYMATES	IDEAL SCHOOL SUPPLY COMPANY		6-10
RP	ACTCRD	CREEPING RUG CARD PROGRAMS: ALPHABET-LANGUAGE DEVELOPMENT	MOSIER MATERIALS		21-30
RP	ACTCRD	LEARNING CENTER PAK (GRADES K - 3)	WISE OWL PUBLICATIONS		31-50
RP	ACTCRD	ALPHABET RHYMES	WISE OWL PUBLICATIONS		<5
RP	ACTCRD	ALPHABET CARDS	MODERN CURRICULUM PRESS		<5
RP	AUDCRD	ALPHABET ZOO	AUDIOTRONICS CORPORATION		11-20
RP	AUDKIT	LETTER SOUNDS ALL AROUND	BOWMAR/NOBLE PUBLISHERS, INC.		301-400
RP	AUDKIT	EARLY PRIMARY SKILLS SERIES	MEDIA MATERIALS, INC.	7	51-75
RP	AUDKIT	CONSONANTS	HAMPDEN PUBLICATIONS, INC.		101-150
RP	AUDKIT	ALPHABET ACTIVITIES	HAMPDEN PUBLICATIONS, INC.		21-30
RP	AUDKIT	ALPHABET IN ACTION	CHILDREN'S BOOK & MUSIC CENTER		21-30
RP	AUDKIT	MINISYSTEMS: LETTER RECOGNITION	CORONET MULTI MEDIA		11-20
RP	AUDKIT	MINISYSTEMS: LETTERS B,M,S,H	CORONET MULTI MEDIA		11-20
RP	AUDKIT	MINISYSTEMS: LETTERS N,P,F,R	CORONET MULTI MEDIA		11-20
RP	AUDKIT	MINISYSTEMS: LETTERS D,A,E,C	CORONET MULTI MEDIA		11-20
RP	AUDKIT	MINISYSTEMS: LETTERS Y,G,J,K	CORONET MULTI MEDIA		11-20
RP	AUDKIT	MINISYSTEMS: LETTERS L,T,O,W,U,V	CORONET MULTI MEDIA		11-20
RP	AUDKIT	MINISYSTEMS: MATCHING LETTERS, UNLIKE PAIRS Bb,Mm,Rr,Ff	CORONET MULTI MEDIA		11-20
RP	AUDKIT	MINISYSTEMS: MATCHING LETTERS PAIRS Aa,Ee,Hh,Nn	CORONET MULTI MEDIA		11-20
RP	AUDKIT	MINISYSTEMS: MATCHING LETTERS, UNLIKE PAIRS Dd,Gg,Qq	CORONET MULTI MEDIA		11-20

LEVEL	FORMAT	TITLE	PUBLISHER	NT	$PRICE

49 – SKILL: ALPHABET

LEVEL	FORMAT	TITLE	PUBLISHER	$PRICE
RP	AUDKIT	MINISYSTEMS: MATCHING LETTERS, LIKE PAIRS Cc,Ii,Kk,Pp,Tt	CORONET MULTI MEDIA	11-20
RP	AUDKIT	MINISYSTEMS: MATCHING LETTERS, LIKE PAIRS Ll,Jj,Oo,Ss,Ww	CORONET MULTI MEDIA	11-20
RP	AUDKIT	MINISYSTEMS: LETTER MATCHING GAMES	CORONET MULTI MEDIA	11-20
RP	A/VKIT	STARTER SET: SHAPES, COLORS, SIZES, LETTERS, NUMBERS	EYE GATE MEDIA	76-100
RP	A/VKIT	READING READINESS	EYE GATE MEDIA	101-150
RP	CHART	ALPHABET FLIP CHART	KENWORTHY EDUCATIONAL SERVICE	11-20
RP	CHART	ALPHABET MURAL	IDEAL SCHOOL SUPPLY COMPANY	6-10
RP	CHART	PUZZLE POSTERS: ALPHABET VILLAGE	TREND ENTERPRISES, INC.	<5
RP	CHART	PUZZLE POSTERS: ALPHABET BOATING	TREND ENTERPRISES, INC.	<5
RP	CHART	COUNTING & ABC'S	CHILD'S WORLD	6-10
RP	CHART	ALPHABET EXPRESS	INSTRUCTO/MCGRAW-HILL	<5
RP	CHART	GIANT ALPHABET TAPE	INSTRUCTO/MCGRAW-HILL	<5
RP	CHART	ALPHABET STORYLAND	INSTRUCTO/MCGRAW-HILL	<5
RP	CHART	ALPHABET POSTER CARDS	MILTON BRADLEY/PLAYSKOOL	6-10
RP	DITTO	ALPHABET ADVENTURES	CREATIVE TEACHING ASSOCIATES	<5
RP	DITTO	ABC BOOK, GRADE 1	CONTINENTAL PRESS, INC.	<5
RP	DITTO	VISUAL DISCRIMINATION GAMES	CHILDREN'S LEARNING CENTER, INC.	<5
RP	DITTO	ALPHABET MANUSCRIPT BOOKS, UPPER CASE	CHILDREN'S LEARNING CENTER, INC.	<5
RP	DITTO	ALPHABET MANUSCRIPT BOOKS, LOWER CASE	CHILDREN'S LEARNING CENTER, INC.	<5
RP	DITTO	NAME-A-LETTER: MATCH-A-SOUND	CHILDREN'S LEARNING CENTER, INC.	<5
RP	DITTO	VISUAL DISCRIMINATION	CHILDREN'S LEARNING CENTER, INC.	<5
RP	DITTO	ALPHABET BOOK	CHILDREN'S LEARNING CENTER, INC.	<5
RP	DITTO	READINESS: ALPHABET	INSTRUCTIONAL FAIR	<5
RP	DITTO	LETTER KNOWLEDGE DUPLICATING MASTERS	SCOTT, FORESMAN & CO.	11-20
RP	DITTO	ALPHABET ADVENTURE	ENRICH, INC.	<5
RP	DITTO	READING READINESS	GEL-STEN, INC.	<5
RP	DITTO	LETTER RECOGNITION	INSTRUCTO/MCGRAW-HILL	<5
RP	DITTO	ALPHABET ADVENTURES	ACTIVITY RESOURCES COMPANY, INC.	<5
RP	DITTO	DECODING SKILLS 1	ACTIVITY RESOURCES COMPANY, INC.	<5
RP	FILMST	BEGINNING TO LEARN: ALPHABET ZOO	URBAN MEDIA MATERIALS, INC.	31-50
RP	FILMST	BEGINNING TO LEARN: THE ALPHABET CITY	URBAN MEDIA MATERIALS, INC.	31-50
RP	FILMST	BEGINNING TO LEARN: ALPHABET HOUSE	URBAN MEDIA MATERIALS, INC.	31-50
RP	FILMST	BEGINNING TO LEARN: PICTURES & LETTERS	URBAN MEDIA MATERIALS, INC.	31-50
RP	FILMST	ALPHABET CITY	MILLER-BRODY PRODUCTIONS, INC.	31-50
RP	FILMST	ALPHABET ZOO	MILLER-BRODY PRODUCTIONS, INC.	31-50
RP	FLASH	LETTER CARDS	BOOK-LAB, INC.	<5
RP	FLASH	ALPHABET FLASH CARDS	KENWORTHY EDUCATIONAL SERVICE	<5
RP	FLASH	MANUSCRIPT ABC CARDS	MODERN CURRICULUM PRESS	<5
RP	FLASH	LEARN THE ALPHABET	MILTON BRADLEY/PLAYSKOOL	<5
RP	FLNLBD	FLANNEL BOARD MANUSCRIPT LETTERS, LOWER CASE	MILTON BRADLEY/PLAYSKOOL	<5
RP	FLNLBD	FLANNEL BOARD MANUSCRIPT LETTERS, CAPITALS	MILTON BRADLEY/PLAYSKOOL	<5
RP	GAME	ALPHADART	CONSTRUCTIVE PLAYTHINGS	6-10
RP	GAME	FROGGIE	IDEAL SCHOOL SUPPLY COMPANY	6-10
RP	GUIDE	ALPHABET PUPPETS	FEARON PITMAN PUBLISHERS, INC.	<5
RP	GUIDE	LETTER NAMES & SOUNDS	EDUCATIONAL PROGRAMMERS, INC.	6-10
RP	GUIDE	MY PHONICS PRACTICE BOOK, T.E.	GINN & COMPANY	<5
RP	GUIDE	ALPHABET: STARTING OFF WITH PHONICS, BOOK 2	MODERN CURRICULUM PRESS	<5
RP	GUIDE	PHONICS IS FUN, BOOK 1	MODERN CURRICULUM PRESS	<5
RP	MANIPU	RAISED ALPHABET PUZZLE	CONSTRUCTIVE PLAYTHINGS	6-10
RP	MANIPU	ALPHABET MATCHMATES	CONSTRUCTIVE PLAYTHINGS	6-10
RP	MANIPU	A TO Z PANEL – CAPITAL LETTERS	CHILDCRAFT EDUCATION CORPORATION	<5
RP	MANIPU	A TO Z PANEL – LOWER CASE LETTERS	CHILDCRAFT EDUCATION CORPORATION	<5
RP	MANIPU	KNOBBED ALPHA WORM PUZZLE	CHILDCRAFT EDUCATION CORPORATION	<5
RP	MANIPU	ALPHABET INSET BOARD	EDUCATIONAL TEACHING AIDS	11-20
RP	MANIPU	ALPHABET DOG	EDUCATIONAL TEACHING AIDS	11-20
RP	MANIPU	BOLD BEGINNING: CUT & PASTE ALPHABET BOOK	IDEAL SCHOOL SUPPLY COMPANY	6-10
RP	MANIPU	BOLD BEGINNING: DRAW-A-SOUND	IDEAL SCHOOL SUPPLY COMPANY	6-10
RP	MANIPU	FOAM LETTERS	IDEAL SCHOOL SUPPLY COMPANY	6-10
RP	MANIPU	ALPHABLOCKS	IDEAL SCHOOL SUPPLY COMPANY	6-10
RP	MANIPU	SKANEATELES ALPHABET BLOCKS	IDEAL SCHOOL SUPPLY COMPANY	11-20
RP	MANIPU	PRE-ALPHABET PUZZLE	DEVELOPMENTAL LEARNING MATERIALS	<5
RP	MANIPU	ALPHABET FORMS	DEVELOPMENTAL LEARNING MATERIALS	6-10
RP	MANIPU	ALPHABET TEMPLATE	DEVELOPMENTAL LEARNING MATERIALS	<5
RP	MANIPU	ALPHABET INLAY PUZZLES: AIRPLANE	JUDY COMPANY	<5
RP	MANIPU	ALPHABET INLAY PUZZLES: BARN	JUDY COMPANY	<5
RP	MANIPU	ALPHABET INLAY PUZZLES: BUS	JUDY COMPANY	<5
RP	MANIPU	ALPHABET INLAY PUZZLES: COW	JUDY COMPANY	<5
RP	MANIPU	ALPHABET INLAY PUZZLES: DOG, TERRIER	JUDY COMPANY	<5
RP	MANIPU	ALPHABET INLAY PUZZLES: FROG	JUDY COMPANY	<5
RP	MANIPU	ALPHABET INLAY PUZZLES: HOUSE	JUDY COMPANY	<5
RP	MANIPU	ALPHABET INLAY PUZZLES: TRACTOR	JUDY COMPANY	<5
RP	MANIPU	ALPHABET INLAY PUZZLES: TRAIN	JUDY COMPANY	<5
RP	MANIPU	ALPHABET INLAY PUZZLES: TRUCK	JUDY COMPANY	<5
RP	MANIPU	STEPPING STONES, WALK-ON ALPHABET CAPITALS	INSTRUCTO/MCGRAW-HILL	21-30
RP	MANIPU	STEPPING STONES, WALK-ON ALPHABET LOWERCASE	INSTRUCTO/MCGRAW-HILL	21-30
RP	MANIPU	WALK-ON ALPHABET	INSTRUCTO/MCGRAW-HILL	11-20
RP	MANIPU	ALPHA WORM	INSTRUCTO/MCGRAW-HILL	11-20
RP	MANIPU	WOODEN LETTERS	INSTRUCTO/MCGRAW-HILL	11-20
RP	MULTIM	ALPHABET ACROBATICS	BEHAVIORAL RESEARCH LABORATORIES	76-100

LEVEL	FORMAT	TITLE	PUBLISHER	NT	$PRICE

49 - SKILL: ALPHABET

LEVEL	FORMAT	TITLE	PUBLISHER	$PRICE
RP	MULTIM	ALPHA-SOUND PROGRAM, GROUP 1	CLEARVUE, INC.	201-300
RP	MULTIM	CURIOUS GEORGE LEARNS THE ALPHABET	EDUCATIONAL ENRICHMENT MATERIALS	51-75
RP	MULTIM	LEARNING THE ALPHABET WITH AMOS & HIS FRIENDS	IMPERIAL INTERNATIONAL LEARNING	11-20
RP	MULTIM	HEAR-SEE-SAY, PHONICS READING COURSE	MELODY HOUSE PUBLISHING COMPANY	11-20
RP	MULTIM	ALPHABET MOTOR ACTIVITIES, BOOK & TAPE	DEVELOPMENTAL LEARNING MATERIALS	11-20
RP	PICTUR	ABC LOTTO	CHILDCRAFT EDUCATION CORPORATION	<5
RP	PUPILB	HEY, LOOK AT ME!	BRADBURY PRESS, INC.	6-10
RP	PUPILB	LETTERS FROM CALICO CAT	CHILDREN'S PRESS, INC.	6-10
RP	PUPILB	AGATHA'S ALPHABET	CHILDCRAFT EDUCATION CORPORATION	6-10
RP	PUPILB	ALPHABET ZOO	ODDO PUBLISHING, INC.	6-10
RP	PUPILB	ABC: AN ALPHABET OF MANY THINGS	WESTERN PUBLISHING EDUC. SERVICE	6-10
RP	PUPILB	LITTLE MONSTER'S ALPHABET BOOK	WESTERN PUBLISHING EDUC. SERVICE	<5
RP	PUPILB	ABC RHYMES	WESTERN PUBLISHING EDUC. SERVICE	<5
RP	PUPILB	A-APPLE PIE	FREDERICK WARNE & CO., INC.	6-10
RP	PUPILB	ALPHABET CARDS	SCOTT, FORESMAN & CO.	6-10
RP	PUPILB	GREAT BIG ALPHABET PICTURE BOOK	GROSSET & DUNLAP, INC.	<5
RP	PUPILB	AN ANIMAL ALPHABET	GROSSET & DUNLAP, INC.	<5
RP	PUPILB	ADVENTURES OF A, APPLE PIE	DOVER PUBLICATIONS	<5
RP	PUPILB	MOTHER'S PICTURE ALPHABET	DOVER PUBLICATIONS	<5
RP	PUPILB	CHAPBOOK ABC'S	DOVER PUBLICATIONS	<5
RP	PUPILB	NOAH'S ARK ABC & 8 OTHER ALPHABET BOOKS	DOVER PUBLICATIONS	<5
RP	PUPILB	3-D ALPHABET COLORING BOOK	DOVER PUBLICATIONS	<5
RP	PUPILB	ABC COLORING BOOK	DOVER PUBLICATIONS	<5
RP	PUPILB	HILLTOP SERIES, BOOK 1 & THE HILLTOP SERIES COLORING BOOK	ALLYN AND BACON, INC.	21-30
RP	PUPILB	HILLTOP SERIES, BOOK 2 & GOGO	ALLYN AND BACON, INC.	21-30
RP	PUPILB	ALPHABET FLIP BOOK	TREND ENTERPRISES, INC.	<5
RP	PUPILB	HAYES PHONETIC ALPHABET	HAYES SCHOOL PUBLISHING COMPANY	<5
RP	RECORD	ALPHABET SOUP	MELODY HOUSE PUBLISHING COMPANY	6-10
RP	SKLKIT	ALPHABET SHOW	BFA EDUCATIONAL MEDIA	76-100
RP	SKLKIT	SWEET PICKLES READING READINESS PROGRAM	BFA EDUCATIONAL MEDIA	101-150
RP	SKLKIT	LETTERS OF THE ALPHABET, KIT I	WEBSTER DIVISION/MCGRAW-HILL	101-150
RP	SKLKIT	SOUNDS & LETTERS, KIT II	WEBSTER DIVISION/MCGRAW-HILL	101-150
RP	SND FS	ALPHABET: MAGIC MAN MAKES LETTERS TALK	CLEARVUE, INC.	11-20
RP	SND FS	BASIC CONCEPTS	EDUCATIONAL ENRICHMENT MATERIALS	76-100
RP	SND FS	ALPHABET FUN	CORONET MULTI MEDIA	76-100
RP	SP EQT	CONCEPT DEVELOPMENT: LETTER NAMES THROUGH SOUNDS, KIT F	BORG-WARNER EDUCATIONAL SYSTEMS	101-150
RP	SP EQT	CONCEPT DEVELOPMENT: LETTER NAMES THROUGH SOUNDS, KIT G	BORG-WARNER EDUCATIONAL SYSTEMS	151-200
RP	SP EQT	CHARLIE: ALPHABET, UPPER & LOWER CASE	EDUCATIONAL INSIGHTS, INC.	6-10
RP	TRANSP	ALPHABET	UNITED TRANSPARENCIES, INC.	201-300
RP	VISKIT	ALPHABET SERIES	WALKER EDUCATIONAL BOOK CORP.	31-50
RP	WKBOOK	DELL HOME ACTIVITY: MAKE ZOUP, AN ALPHABET BOOK	DELL PUBLISHING COMPANY, INC.	<5
RP	WKBOOK	MY PHONICS PRACTICE BOOK	GINN & COMPANY	<5
RP	WKBOOK	COLOR WORDS, LEFT & RIGHT: PROBLEM SOLVING, PHONICS, OPPOS.	JENN PUBLICATIONS	<5
RP	WKBOOK	ALPHABET	JENN PUBLICATIONS	<5
RP	WKBOOK	ALPHABET: STARTING OFF WITH PHONICS: BOOK 2	MODERN CURRICULUM PRESS	<5
RP	WKBOOK	PHONICS IS FUN, BOOK 1	MODERN CURRICULUM PRESS	<5
RP	WKBOOK	ALPHAGRAMS	ACTIVITY RESOURCES COMPANY, INC.	<5
P	ACTCRD	TUTORGRAM: ALPHABET RECOGNITION & SEQUENCING	ENRICHMENT READING CORP OF AMER.	11-20
P	ACTCRD	PHONIC TALKING LETTERS	IDEAL SCHOOL SUPPLY COMPANY	<5
P	ACTCRD	LANGUAGE ACTIVITY CARDS: KNOW YOUR ALPHABET	WEBER COSTELLO COMPANY	6-10
P	ACTCRD	VISUAL DISCRIMINATION LEARNING- MATCHING CAPITALS	EDUCATIONAL PERFORMANCE ASSOC.	31-50
P	ACTCRD	ALPHABET CARDS	DEVELOPMENTAL LEARNING MATERIALS	6-10
P	ACTCRD	KNOW 'N' SHOW ALPHABET	GEL-STEN, INC.	6-10
P	ACTCRD	LANGUAGE ARTS-SKILL DRILLS WITH MOTIVATORS	SVE	31-50
P	AUDCAS	CLUES TO CONSONANTS, WORKTAPES	ALLYN AND BACON, INC.	101-150
P	AUDCAS	ALPHABET ACTIVITIES	UNITED LEARNING	31-50
P	AUDKIT	EARLY PRIMARY LANG. ARTS: TRAVELING WITH THE ALPHABET	EYE GATE MEDIA	6-10
P	AUDKIT	KIT 80: BASIC PHONICS, READINESS LEVEL	EDUCATIONAL RESEARCH, INC.	101-150
P	AUDKIT	KIT 81: BASIC PHONICS, LEVEL 1	EDUCATIONAL RESEARCH, INC.	101-150
P	AUDKIT	LEARNING LETTERS FROM A TO Z	MEDIA MATERIALS, INC.	6-10
P	A/VKIT	BEGINNING PHONICS	MEDIA MARKETING, INC.	51-75
P	CHART	ALPHABET, CONSONANTS, VOWELS	BEMISS-JASON CORPORATION	6-10
P	CHART	ETA PICTORIAL ALPHABET FRIEZE	EDUCATIONAL TEACHING AIDS	11-20
P	CHART	PICTURE COMPOSITE CHART	SOUND MATERIALS	<5
P	CHART	A-Z POSTERS: ALLIGATORS TO ZOMBIES	DEVELOPMENTAL LEARNING MATERIALS	6-10
P	CHART	MS. GOOD-BODY: ALPHABET	LITTLE KENNY PUBLICATIONS, INC.	<5
P	DITTO	MY ALPHABET BOOK	FRANK SCHAFFER PUBLICATIONS, INC	<5
P	DITTO	SKILL BUILDING SERIES: CODE BOOK	ACADEMIC THERAPY PUBLICATIONS	6-10
P	DITTO	ALPHABET	INSTRUCTOR PUBLICATIONS, INC.	<5
P	FLASH	PICTURE FLASHCARD SET	SOUND MATERIALS	<5
P	FLASH	ALPHABET FLASH CARDS FOR STUDENTS	LESWING PRESS	<5
P	FLASH	ALPHABET: FLIP & LEARN FLASHBOOK	MILTON BRADLEY/PLAYSKOOL	<5
P	GAME	ALPHABET BINGO	CONSTRUCTIVE PLAYTHINGS	<5
P	GAME	ABC SKILL BUILDER	KENWORTHY EDUCATIONAL SERVICE	<5
P	GAME	NEW PHONICS WE USE LEARNING GAMES KITS, KIT ONE	RAND MCNALLY & COMPANY	76-100
P	GAME	CHECKMATE: THE ALPHABET	DM EDUCATIONAL PUBLICATIONS	<5
P	GAME	SPIN-N-MATCH	JUDY COMPANY	11-20
P	GAME	ALPHA, MATCH	JUDY COMPANY	6-10
P	GAME	ALPHABET MATCH DOMINOES	JUDY COMPANY	11-20

LEVEL	FORMAT	TITLE	PUBLISHER	NT	$PRICE

---
49 - SKILL: ALPHABET

LEVEL	FORMAT	TITLE	PUBLISHER	NT	$PRICE
P	GAME	LETTO	HOUGHTON MIFFLIN COMPANY		<5
P	GAME	GET SET: GAMES FOR BEGINNING READERS	HOUGHTON MIFFLIN COMPANY	8	101-150
P	GAME	GET SET: BROKEN LETTERS	HOUGHTON MIFFLIN COMPANY		11-20
P	GAME	ALPHABET BINGO	TREND ENTERPRISES, INC.		6-10
P	GUIDE	MERRILL PHONICS SKILL TEXT: COSTUME BOOK, LEVEL R	CHARLES E. MERRILL PUBLISHING CO		<5
P	MANIPU	LACE-A-SHAPE, ANIMAL FRIENDS & PETS	CREATIVE TEACHING ASSOCIATES		<5
P	MANIPU	LACE-A-SHAPE, TOYS & FAVORITE THINGS	CREATIVE TEACHING ASSOCIATES		<5
P	MANIPU	WORD BUILDERS: LARGE LETTER CARDS	KENWORTHY EDUCATIONAL SERVICE		<5
P	MANIPU	WORD BUILDERS: SMALL LETTER CARDS	KENWORTHY EDUCATIONAL SERVICE		<5
P	MANIPU	THINKER PUZZLES, SET 1	ACADEMIC THERAPY PUBLICATIONS		6-10
P	MANIPU	THINKER PUZZLES, SET 2	ACADEMIC THERAPY PUBLICATIONS		6-10
P	MANIPU	THINKER PUZZLES, SET 3	ACADEMIC THERAPY PUBLICATIONS		6-10
P	MANIPU	ETA SEE & SOUND ALPHABET CARDS	EDUCATIONAL TEACHING AIDS		11-20
P	MANIPU	ETA LETTER DISCRIMINATION INSET BOARDS	EDUCATIONAL TEACHING AIDS		11-20
P	MANIPU	ALPHABET PATTERN PLAQUES	EDUCATIONAL TEACHING AIDS		6-10
P	MANIPU	LARRY THE LEARNING LION	IDEAL SCHOOL SUPPLY COMPANY		6-10
P	MANIPU	ALPHABET MATCHING FLIP BOOK	DEVELOPMENTAL LEARNING MATERIALS		<5
P	MANIPU	ALPHABET ZOO ACIVITIES	DEVELOPMENTAL LEARNING MATERIALS		6-10
P	MANIPU	SOUND & SYMBOL PUZZLES	DEVELOPMENTAL LEARNING MATERIALS		6-10
P	MANIPU	LINK LETTERS	MILTON BRADLEY/PLAYSKOOL		<5
P	MULTIU	READY GO ALPHABET	EDUCATIONAL ACTIVITIES, INC.		51-75
P	MULTIU	ALPHA SET	PAUL S. AMIDON & ASSOC., INC.		51-75
P	MULTIM	LEARNING PHONICS	MEDIA MARKETING, INC.		51-75
P	MULTIM	ALPHABET	SVE		76-100
P	MULTIM	OLD FASHIONED ALPHABETS	SVE		76-100
P	PICTUR	PICTURE COMPOSITE	SOUND MATERIALS		6-10
P	PICTUR	BLACK ABC'S STUDY PRINTS	SVE		31-50
P	PUPILB	LETTERS, SOUNDS & WORDS	GROSSET & DUNLAP, INC.		<5
P	PUPILB	HILLTOP SERIES, BOOK 3 & JO JO	ALLYN AND BACON, INC.		21-30
P	PUPILB	HILLTOP SERIES, BOOK 4 & FLO	ALLYN AND BACON, INC.		21-30
P	PUPILB	HILLTOP SERIES, BOOK 5 & SALTY	ALLYN AND BACON, INC.		21-30
P	PUPILB	LEARNING THE LETTERS, BOOK I	EDUCATORS PUBLISHING SERVICE		<5
P	SKLKIT	READING BRIDGE	BFA EDUCATIONAL MEDIA		101-150
P	SND FS	DEVELOPING ALPHABET SKILLS	LEARNING TREE FILMSTRIPS		51-75
P	SND FS	SOLVING THE PHONICS MYSTERY: CLUE OF THE COMBINING LETTERS	LEARNING TREE FILMSTRIPS		76-100
P	SND FS	ALPHABET SOUP FACTORY & OTHER STORIES	CHILDREN'S BOOK & MUSIC CENTER		51-75
P	SND FS	OLD FASHIONED ALPHABETS	CHILDREN'S BOOK & MUSIC CENTER		76-100
P	SND FS	LET'S LEARN THE ALPHABET	TROLL ASSOCIATES		101-150
P	SND FS	FIRST CONCEPTS FILMSTRIP LIBRARY	TROLL ASSOCIATES		101-150
P	WKBOOK	ALPHABET ACTIVITIES	CREATIVE TEACHING ASSOCIATES		<5
P	WKBOOK	A MAFEX PROGRAM TO DEVELOP BASIC SKILLS	MAFEX ASSOCIATES, INC.	9	31-50
P	WKBOOK	A MAFEX PROGRAM TO DEVELOP BASIC SKILLS: ALPHA-BITS	MAFEX ASSOCIATES, INC.		<5
P	WKBOOK	CONSONANT SOUNDS & SYMBOLS, BOOK B	GINN & COMPANY		<5
P	WKBOOK	LANGUAGE ARTS, GRADE 2	JENN PUBLICATIONS		<5
P	WKBOOK	LANGUAGE ARTS, GRADE 3	JENN PUBLICATIONS		<5
P	WKBOOK	MERRILL PHONICS SKILL TEXT: COSTUME BOOK, LEVEL R	CHARLES E. MERRILL PUBLISHING CO		<5
P	WKBOOK	ALPHABET BOOK	EDUCATORS PUBLISHING SERVICE		<5
P	WKBOOK	MCP PHONICS WORKBOOKS: LEVEL A	MODERN CURRICULUM PRESS		<5
P	WKBOOK	PHONICS & WORD POWER, BOOK 1	XEROX EDUCATION PUBLICATIONS		<5
P	WKBOOK	PHONICS & WORD POWER, BOOK 3	XEROX EDUCATION PUBLICATIONS		<5
P	WKBOOK	PHONICS COME FIRST	ACTIVITY RESOURCES COMPANY, INC.		6-10
PI	ACTCRD	EGGHEAD JAZZ	LESWING PRESS		11-20
PI	AUDKIT	USING PHONICS	EBSCO CURRICULUM MATERIALS		51-75
PI	CHART	ALPHABET ROBOTS	CREATIVE TEACHING ASSOCIATES		<5
PI	CL SET	AEVAC STARTER 101 (NON-READERS)	AEVAC, INC.	10	11-20
PI	DITTO	ALPHABETIZING ACTIVITIES	ENRICH, INC.		<5
PI	DITTO	PROJECT ALPHABETIZING	ENRICH, INC.		<5
PI	GAME	SPIDER CRAWL	IDEAL SCHOOL SUPPLY COMPANY		6-10
PI	GUIDE	PHONICS IS FUN, BOOK 3	MODERN CURRICULUM PRESS		<5
PI	SP EQT	LEARNING LETTER NAMES, KIT A	BORG-WARNER EDUCATIONAL SYSTEMS		101-150
PI	SP EQT	LEARNING LETTER NAMES, KIT B	BORG-WARNER EDUCATIONAL SYSTEMS		101-150
PI	WKBOOK	AEVAC STARTER 101, BOOK 1 (NON-READERS)	AEVAC, INC.		<5
PI	WKBOOK	AEVAC STARTER 101, BOOK 2 (NON-READERS)	AEVAC, INC.		<5
PI	WKBOOK	AEVAC STARTER 101, BOOK 3 (NON-READERS)	AEVAC, INC.		<5
PI	WKBOOK	AEVAC STARTER 101, BOOK 4 (NON-READERS)	AEVAC, INC.		<5
PI	WKBOOK	AEVAC STARTER 101, BOOK 5 (NON-READERS)	AEVAC, INC.		<5
PI	WKBOOK	AEVAC STARTER 101, BOOK 6 (NON-READERS)	AEVAC, INC.		<5
PI	WKBOOK	AEVAC STARTER 101, BOOK 7 (NON-READERS)	AEVAC, INC.		<5
PI	WKBOOK	AEVAC STARTER 101, BOOK 8 (NON-READERS)	AEVAC, INC.		<5
PI	WKBOOK	AEVAC STARTER 101, BOOK 9 (NON-READERS)	AEVAC, INC.		<5
PI	WKBOOK	PHONICS IS FUN, BOOK 3	MODERN CURRICULUM PRESS		<5
IJ	DITTO	THINKERTHINGS: A STUDENT GENERATED APPROACH TO LANGUAGE EXP.	ADDISON-WESLEY PUBLISHING CO.		11-20
JS	FLASH	NEW STREAMLINED ENGLISH SERIES: PHONICS CARDS	NEW READERS PRESS		<5
JS	WKBOOK	NEW STREAMLINED ENGLISH SERIES: SKILL BOOK 1	NEW READERS PRESS		<5

---
50 - SKILL: SOUND-SYMBOL

LEVEL	FORMAT	TITLE	PUBLISHER	NT	$PRICE
R	AUDKIT	SOUNDS & SYMBOLS	EDUCATORS PUBLISHING SERVICE		101-150
R	GAME	ONE TWO THREE & AWAY PHONIC CARD GAME	INDIVIDUALIZED LEARNING MATERIAL		21-30

LEVEL	FORMAT	TITLE	PUBLISHER	NT	$PRICE

---

50 - SKILL: SOUND-SYMBOL

LEVEL	FORMAT	TITLE	PUBLISHER	NT	$PRICE
R	MULTIM	BEGINNING TO READ, WRITE & LISTEN	HARPER & ROW PUBLISHERS, INC.		101-150
R	PI/PRT	INDIVIDUAL LANGUAGE ARTS, PHONICS	CREATIVE TEACHING ASSOCIATES		<5
R	SKLKIT	INTERSENSORY PHONICS READINESS KIT	BOOK-LAB, INC.		11-20
R	WKBOOK	LESSONS TO GROW ON, BOOK 1	PRESCHOOL LEARNING CORPORATION		<5
R	WKBOOK	LESSONS TO GROW ON, BOOK 3	PRESCHOOL LEARNING CORPORATION		<5
RP	ACTCRD	MATCHING LETTERS & WORDS, A	BARNELL LOFT, LTD.		6-10
RP	ACTCRD	ALPHABET CLUE PICTURES	IDEAL SCHOOL SUPPLY COMPANY		6-10
RP	ACTCRD	BEGINNING SOUNDS	MILTON BRADLEY/PLAYSKOOL		<5
RP	AUDKIT	SOUNDS I SAY	CHRONICLE GUIDANCE PUBLICATIONS		11-20
RP	AUDKIT	LETTER SOUNDS ALL AROUND	BOWMAR/NOBLE PUBLISHERS, INC.		301-400
RP	CHART	ALPHABET FLIP CHART	KENWORTHY EDUCATIONAL SERVICE		11-20
RP	DITTO	BEGINNING PHONICS, UPPER CASE	CHILDREN'S LEARNING CENTER, INC.		<5
RP	DITTO	BEGINNING PHONICS, LOWER CASE	CHILDREN'S LEARNING CENTER, INC.		<5
RP	DITTO	MANUSCRIPT LETTERS, UPPER & LOWER CASE	CHILDREN'S LEARNING CENTER, INC.		<5
RP	DITTO	LETTER SOUND ASSOCIATION, PART I	CHILDREN'S LEARNING CENTER, INC.		<5
RP	DITTO	TRACE-A-LETTER: SAY-A-SOUND	CHILDREN'S LEARNING CENTER, INC.		<5
RP	DITTO	NAME-A-LETTER: MATCH-A-SOUND	CHILDREN'S LEARNING CENTER, INC.		<5
RP	DITTO	LETTER SOUND ASSOCIATION, PART II	CHILDREN'S LEARNING CENTER, INC.		<5
RP	DITTO	TRACE-A-LETTER: MATCH-A-SOUND	CHILDREN'S LEARNING CENTER, INC.		<5
RP	DITTO	PHONICS: MANUSCRIPT	CHILDREN'S LEARNING CENTER, INC.		<5
RP	DITTO	BOLD BEGINNING: IDENTIFYING SOUNDS OF THE ALPHABET	IDEAL SCHOOL SUPPLY COMPANY		6-10
RP	DITTO	READING READINESS	GEL-STEN, INC.		<5
RP	FLASH	LETTER CARDS	BOOK-LAB, INC.		<5
RP	GAME	GAMEBOARDS FOR SPEECH & LANGUAGE DEVELOPMENT	COMMUNICATION SKILL BUILDERS,INC		31-50
RP	GAME	GAMEBOARD KIT A	READING JOY, INC.		6-10
RP	GAME	GAMEBOARD KIT G	READING JOY, INC.		6-10
RP	GUIDE	ALPHABET PUPPETS	FEARON PITMAN PUBLISHERS, INC.		<5
RP	GUIDE	LETTER NAMES & SOUNDS	EDUCATIONAL PROGRAMMERS, INC.		6-10
RP	GUIDE	MY PHONICS PRACTICE BOOK, T.E.	GINN & COMPANY		<5
RP	MANIPU	RAISED ALPHABET PUZZLE	CONSTRUCTIVE PLAYTHINGS		6-10
RP	MANIPU	BOLD BEGINNING: CUT & PASTE ALPHABET BOOK	IDEAL SCHOOL SUPPLY COMPANY		6-10
RP	MANIPU	BOLD BEGINNING: DRAW-A-SOUND	IDEAL SCHOOL SUPPLY COMPANY		6-10
RP	MULTIM	ALPHA-SOUND PROGRAM, GROUP 1	CLEARVUE, INC.		201-300
RP	MULTIM	HEAR-SEE-SAY, PHONICS READING COURSE	MELODY HOUSE PUBLISHING COMPANY		11-20
RP	PUPILB	READING READINESS	BEHAVIORAL RESEARCH LABORATORIES	4	6-10
RP	PUPILB	READING READINESS, TEXTBOOK A	BEHAVIORAL RESEARCH LABORATORIES		<5
RP	PUPILB	READING READINESS, TEXTBOOK B	BEHAVIORAL RESEARCH LABORATORIES		<5
RP	PUPILB	READING READINESS, TEXTBOOK C	BEHAVIORAL RESEARCH LABORATORIES		<5
RP	PUPILB	READING READINESS, TEXTBOOK D	BEHAVIORAL RESEARCH LABORATORIES		<5
RP	PUPILB	I CAN READ	BEHAVIORAL RESEARCH LABORATORIES	8	51-75
RP	PUPILB	I CAN READ, BOOK 1	BEHAVIORAL RESEARCH LABORATORIES		<5
RP	PUPILB	I CAN READ, BOOK 2	BEHAVIORAL RESEARCH LABORATORIES		<5
RP	PUPILB	I CAN READ, BOOK 3	BEHAVIORAL RESEARCH LABORATORIES		<5
RP	PUPILB	I CAN READ, BOOK 4	BEHAVIORAL RESEARCH LABORATORIES		<5
RP	PUPILB	I CAN READ, BOOK 5	BEHAVIORAL RESEARCH LABORATORIES		<5
RP	PUPILB	I CAN READ, BOOK 6	BEHAVIORAL RESEARCH LABORATORIES		<5
RP	PUPILB	I CAN READ, BOOK 7	BEHAVIORAL RESEARCH LABORATORIES		<5
RP	PUPILB	I CAN READ, BOOK 8	BEHAVIORAL RESEARCH LABORATORIES		<5
RP	PUPILB	HILLTOP SERIES, BOOK 1 & THE HILLTOP SERIES COLORING BOOK	ALLYN AND BACON, INC.		21-30
RP	PUPILB	HILLTOP SERIES, BOOK 2 & GOGO	ALLYN AND BACON, INC.		21-30
RP	PUPILB	HAYES PHONETIC ALPHABET	HAYES SCHOOL PUBLISHING COMPANY		<5
RP	RECORD	SINGING SOUNDS	BOWMAR/NOBLE PUBLISHERS, INC.		<5
RP	SKLKIT	ALPHABET SHOW	BFA EDUCATIONAL MEDIA		76-100
RP	SKLKIT	GOLDMAN-LYNCH SOUNDS & SYMBOLS DEVELOPMENT KIT	AMERICAN GUIDANCE SERVICE, INC.		151-200
RP	SKLKIT	SOUNDS & LETTERS, KIT II	WEBSTER DIVISION/MCGRAW-HILL		101-150
RP	SND FS	ALPHABET: MAGIC MAN MAKES LETTERS TALK	CLEARVUE, INC.		11-20
RP	VISKIT	SINGLE SOUNDS	EDUCATIONAL TEACHING AIDS	3	31-50
RP	VISKIT	SINGLE SOUNDS: INFANT PROGRAM	EDUCATIONAL TEACHING AIDS		11-20
RP	WKBOOK	MY OWN READING BOOK, VOLUME 1	BOOK-LAB, INC.		<5
RP	WKBOOK	MY PHONICS PRACTICE BOOK	GINN & COMPANY		<5
RP	WKBOOK	READINESS BOOK: COME TO MY PARTY	PHONOVISUAL PRODUCTS, INC.		<5
RPI	WKBOOK	COLOR WORDS, LEFT & RIGHT: PROBLEM SOLVING, PHONICS, OPPOS.	JENN PUBLICATIONS		<5
RPI	WKBOOK	LADYBIRD: WORKBOOKS	IDEAL SCHOOL SUPPLY COMPANY	6	6-10
P	ACTCRD	WIPE-OFF CARDS: BEGINNING SOUNDS	CONSTRUCTIVE PLAYTHINGS		<5
P	ACTCRD	ETA SORT & SOUND WORD-MAKING CARDS	EDUCATIONAL TEACHING AIDS		11-20
P	ACTCRD	PHONIC TALKING LETTERS	IDEAL SCHOOL SUPPLY COMPANY		<5
P	ACTCRD	BASIC SKILLS KIT- PHONICS H	EDUCATIONAL PERFORMANCE ASSOC.		31-50
P	ACTCRD	LINQUISTIC PACER	DM EDUCATIONAL PUBLICATIONS		6-10
P	ACTCRD	ANIMATED KEY CARDS	HOUGHTON MIFFLIN COMPANY		11-20
P	ACTCRD	LANGUAGE ARTS-SKILL DRILLS WITH MOTIVATORS	SVE		31-50
P	AUDCAS	SOUNDS FOR YOUNG READERS, VOLUME 1	CLASSROOM MATERIALS CO.		6-10
P	AUDCAS	LISTENING FOR SOUNDS	MEDIA MARKETING, INC.		51-75
P	AUDCAS	CLUES TO CONSONANTS, WORKTAPES	ALLYN AND BACON, INC.		101-150
P	AUDKIT	KIT 80: BASIC PHONICS, READINESS LEVEL	EDUCATIONAL RESEARCH, INC.		101-150
P	AUDKIT	KIT 81: BASIC PHONICS, LEVEL 1	EDUCATIONAL RESEARCH, INC.		101-150
P	AUDKIT	SIGHT & SOUND PHONICS	WEBER COSTELLO COMPANY		21-30
P	A/VKIT	BEGINNING PHONICS	MEDIA MARKETING, INC.		51-75
P	A/VKIT	PHONICS SOUND & SYMBOL	MEDIA MARKETING, INC.		101-150
P	CHART	ETA PICTORIAL ALPHABET FRIEZE	EDUCATIONAL TEACHING AIDS		11-20

LEVEL	FORMAT	TITLE	PUBLISHER	NT	$PRICE

50 - SKILL: SOUND-SYMBOL

LEVEL	FORMAT	TITLE	PUBLISHER	NT	$PRICE
P	CL SET	SOUND LOTTO 1	LAKESHORE CURRICULUM MATERIALS		11-20
P	CL SET	SOUND LOTTO 2	LAKESHORE CURRICULUM MATERIALS		21-30
P	DITTO	UNDERSTANDING CONSONANTS	CREATIVE TEACHING ASSOCIATES		<5
P	DITTO	UNDERSTANDING CONSONANTS	ENRICH, INC.		<5
P	DITTO	SOUNDS IN WORDS, BOOK 1	GEL-STEN, INC.		<5
P	DITTO	SOUNDS IN WORDS, BOOK 2	GEL-STEN, INC.		<5
P	DITTO	PASTING PARTY	CREATIVE TEACHING PRESS, INC.		<5
P	DITTO	DECODING SKILLS 2	ACTIVITY RESOURCES COMPANY, INC.		<5
P	FILMST	LEARNING ABOUT OUR LANGUAGE, SET 1	AEVAC, INC.		31-50
P	GAME	PHONICS PUZZLES & GAMES	TEACHING RESOURCES CORPORATION		11-20
P	GAME	PHONO JUNIOR GAME	T.S. DENISON & COMPANY		6-10
P	GAME	GET SET: GAMES FOR BEGINNING READERS	HOUGHTON MIFFLIN COMPANY	8	101-150
P	GAME	GET SET: PICK A FIT	HOUGHTON MIFFLIN COMPANY		11-20
P	GUIDE	INTEGRATED TOTAL LANGUAGE	ACADEMIC THERAPY PUBLICATIONS		31-50
P	GUIDE	MERRILL PHONICS SKILL TEXT: COSTUME BOOK, LEVEL R	CHARLES E. MERRILL PUBLISHING CO		<5
P	MANIPU	SOUND PUZZLES	TEACHING RESOURCES CORPORATION		11-20
P	MANIPU	CRONIN LETTER BOX	ACADEMIC THERAPY PUBLICATIONS		6-10
P	MANIPU	PALS: PERCEPTUAL AUDITORY LEARNING SERIES	ACADEMIC THERAPY PUBLICATIONS		31-50
P	MANIPU	ETA SEE & SOUND ALPHABET CARDS	EDUCATIONAL TEACHING AIDS		11-20
P	MANIPU	ETA PHONOGRAM PICTURE & WORD GROUPING CARDS	EDUCATIONAL TEACHING AIDS		6-10
P	MANIPU	ETA PHONICS COUPLETS	EDUCATIONAL TEACHING AIDS		<5
P	MANIPU	ETA ALPHABET PICTURE & SOUND MATCHING CARDS	EDUCATIONAL TEACHING AIDS		<5
P	MANIPU	ALPHABET PATTERN PLAQUES	EDUCATIONAL TEACHING AIDS		6-10
P	MANIPU	ETA APPROACH PICTURE & WORD-BUILDING CARDS	EDUCATIONAL TEACHING AIDS		31-50
P	MANIPU	SOUND & SYMBOL PUZZLES	DEVELOPMENTAL LEARNING MATERIALS		6-10
P	MANIPU	LETTER-PICTURE SOLITAIRE	HOUGHTON MIFFLIN COMPANY		21-30
P	MANIPU	PLASTIC OBJECTS, SET 1	HOUGHTON MIFFLIN COMPANY		6-10
P	MANIPU	PLASTIC OBJECTS, SET 2	HOUGHTON MIFFLIN COMPANY		6-10
P	MANIPU	PLASTIC OBJECTS, SET 3	HOUGHTON MIFFLIN COMPANY		6-10
P	MULTIU	SULLIVAN DECODING KIT	BEHAVIORAL RESEARCH LABORATORIES	4	31-50
P	MULTIU	ALPHA SET	PAUL S. AMIDON & ASSOC., INC.		51-75
P	MULTIM	MR. PHUN PHONICS	MEDIA MARKETING, INC.		51-75
P	MULTIM	STOP THAT WORM!	MEDIA MATERIALS, INC.		6-10
P	MULTIM	ALPHABET	SVE		76-100
P	MULTIM	OLD FASHIONED ALPHABETS	SVE		76-100
P	PUPILB	PICTURES & SOUNDS ALPHABET BOOK	EDUCATIONAL TEACHING AIDS		11-20
P	PUPILB	LADYBIRD BOOK: 4C, SAY THE SOUND	IDEAL SCHOOL SUPPLY COMPANY		<5
P	PUPILB	LADYBIRD BOOK: 5C, MORE SOUNDS TO SAY	IDEAL SCHOOL SUPPLY COMPANY		<5
P	PUPILB	LADYBIRD BOOK: 6C, READING WITH SOUNDS	IDEAL SCHOOL SUPPLY COMPANY		<5
P	PUPILB	LADYBIRD BOOK: 7C, EASY TO SOUND	IDEAL SCHOOL SUPPLY COMPANY		<5
P	PUPILB	LADYBIRD BOOK: 8C, FUN WITH SOUNDS	IDEAL SCHOOL SUPPLY COMPANY		<5
P	PUPILB	LETTERS, SOUNDS & WORDS	GROSSET & DUNLAP, INC.		<5
P	PUPILB	HILLTOP SERIES, BOOK 3 & JO JO	ALLYN AND BACON, INC.		21-30
P	PUPILB	HILLTOP SERIES, BOOK 4 & FLO	ALLYN AND BACON, INC.		21-30
P	PUPILB	HILLTOP SERIES, BOOK 5 & SALTY	ALLYN AND BACON, INC.		21-30
P	PUPILB	LEARNING THE LETTERS, BOOK I	EDUCATORS PUBLISHING SERVICE		<5
P	RECORD	SOUNDS FOR YOUNG READERS, VOLUME 1	CLASSROOM MATERIALS CO.		6-10
P	SKLKIT	READING BRIDGE	BFA EDUCATIONAL MEDIA		101-150
P	SND FS	DEVELOPING ALPHABET SKILLS	LEARNING TREE FILMSTRIPS		51-75
P	SND FS	SOLVING THE PHONICS MYSTERY: CLUE OF THE COMBINING LETTERS	LEARNING TREE FILMSTRIPS		76-100
P	SND FS	CONSONANTS: HOW THEY LOOK & SOUND	UNITED LEARNING		201-300
P	SP EQT	AUDITORY SKILLS: SYNTHESIS	INSTRUCTIONAL INDUSTRIES (G.E.)		51-75
P	SP EQT	FLASH-X-SET 1: READING PICTURES	EDL/MCGRAW-HILL		<5
P	VISKIT	SINGLE SOUNDS: SECOND PROGRAM	EDUCATIONAL TEACHING AIDS		11-20
P	WKBOOK	MOTT BASIC LANG. SKILLS: BOOK 1301	ALLIED EDUCATION COUNCIL		<5
P	WKBOOK	AEVAC PHONICS PROGRAM, BOOK C	AEVAC, INC.		<5
P	WKBOOK	A MAFEX PROGRAM TO DEVELOP BASIC SKILLS: LET'S WRITE & SPELL	MAFEX ASSOCIATES, INC.		<5
P	WKBOOK	LADYBIRD: WORKBOOK 4	IDEAL SCHOOL SUPPLY COMPANY		<5
P	WKBOOK	LADYBIRD: WORKBOOK 5	IDEAL SCHOOL SUPPLY COMPANY		<5
P	WKBOOK	LADYBIRD: WORKBOOK 6	IDEAL SCHOOL SUPPLY COMPANY		<5
P	WKBOOK	CONSONANT SOUNDS & SYMBOLS, BOOK B	GINN & COMPANY		<5
P	WKBOOK	TRANSITION BOOK: I CAN & NOW I CAN READ	PHONOVISUAL PRODUCTS, INC.		<5
P	WKBOOK	FUN PHONIC JINGLES, BOOK I	WORD MAKING PRODUCTIONS, INC.		<5
P	WKBOOK	HIDDEN PICTURE PUZZLES, BOOK I	WORD MAKING PRODUCTIONS, INC.		<5
P	WKBOOK	HIDDEN PICTURE PUZZLES, BOOK II	WORD MAKING PRODUCTIONS, INC.		<5
P	WKBOOK	LETTERS & SOUNDS, PRIMARY	SCOTT, FORESMAN & CO.		<5
P	WKBOOK	ABC OF PHONICS	T.S. DENISON & COMPANY		6-10
P	WKBOOK	MERRILL PHONICS SKILL TEXT: COSTUME BOOK, LEVEL R	CHARLES E. MERRILL PUBLISHING CO		<5
P	WKBOOK	PHONICS COME FIRST	ACTIVITY RESOURCES COMPANY, INC.		6-10
PI	ACTCRD	PHONIC WIPE OFF CARDS	WEBER COSTELLO COMPANY		<5
PI	ACTCRD	SOUNDS MAKE WORDS	LESWING PRESS		6-10
PI	CL SET	SOUND OFF & READ	MAFEX ASSOCIATES, INC.		31-50
PI	DITTO	RUFUS RABBIT'S RHYME TIME	FRANK SCHAFFER PUBLICATIONS, INC		<5
PI	GAME	PHONIC DOMINO GAME	WEBER COSTELLO COMPANY		<5
PI	GAME	SPIN-A-WORD	JUDY COMPANY		6-10
PI	GAME	APPLE TREE	XEROX EDUCATION PUBLICATIONS		51-75
PI	GUIDE	FOCUS ON PHONICS 1: TEACHER'S EDITION	NEW READERS PRESS		<5
PI	MULTIM	PHONICS: THE F.I.R.S.T. APPROACH TO READING	WEBER COSTELLO COMPANY		101-150
PI	WKBOOK	AEVAC STARTER 101, BOOK 1 (NON-READERS)	AEVAC, INC.		<5

LEVEL	FORMAT	TITLE	PUBLISHER	NT	$PRICE

50 - SKILL: SOUND-SYMBOL

LEVEL	FORMAT	TITLE	PUBLISHER	$PRICE
PI	WKBOOK	AEVAC STARTER 101, BOOK 2 (NON-READERS)	AEVAC, INC.	<5
PI	WKBOOK	AEVAC STARTER 101, BOOK 3 (NON-READERS)	AEVAC, INC.	<5
PI	WKBOOK	AEVAC STARTER 101, BOOK 4 (NON-READERS)	AEVAC, INC.	<5
PI	WKBOOK	AEVAC STARTER 101, BOOK 5 (NON-READERS)	AEVAC, INC.	<5
PI	WKBOOK	AEVAC STARTER 101, BOOK 6 (NON-READERS)	AEVAC, INC.	<5
PI	WKBOOK	AEVAC STARTER 101, BOOK 7 (NON-READERS)	AEVAC, INC.	<5
PI	WKBOOK	AEVAC STARTER 101, BOOK 8 (NON-READERS)	AEVAC, INC.	<5
PI	WKBOOK	AEVAC STARTER 101, BOOK 10 (NON-READERS)	AEVAC, INC.	<5
PI	WKBOOK	FOCUS ON PHONICS 1: SOUNDS & NAMES OF LETTERS	NEW READERS PRESS	<5
PI	WKBOOK	PHONICS FAST & EASY	ACTIVITY RESOURCES COMPANY, INC.	<5
PIJ	MULTIM	RIGHT-TO-READ PROGRAM, LEVEL I	ACADEMIC THERAPY PUBLICATIONS	151-200
PIJ	PICTUR	PICTURES FOR SOUNDS	TEACHING RESOURCES CORPORATION	31-50
PIJ	REFBK	STANDARD REBUS GLOSSARY	AMERICAN GUIDANCE SERVICE, INC.	<5
I	CHART	PREPOSTEROUS PHONICS POSTERS	SCOTT RESOURCES, INC.	11-20
I	FILMST	PRONUNCIATION SKILLS	EDUCATIONAL PROJECTIONS COMPANY	21-30
I	GUIDE	MERRILL PHONICS SKILL TEXT: WHIZ KID, LEVEL F	CHARLES E. MERRILL PUBLISHING CO	<5
I	WKBOOK	MERRILL PHONICS SKILL TEXT: WHIZ KID, LEVEL F	CHARLES E. MERRILL PUBLISHING CO	<5
IJ	SKLKIT	+4 READING BOOSTER	WEBSTER DIVISION/MCGRAW-HILL	301-400
JS	CHART	RIGHT-TO-READ PROGRAM, LEVEL II	ACADEMIC THERAPY PUBLICATIONS	101-150
JS	FLASH	NEW STREAMLINED ENGLISH SERIES: PHONICS CARDS	NEW READERS PRESS	<5
JS	WKBOOK	NEW STREAMLINED ENGLISH SERIES: SKILL BOOK 1	NEW READERS PRESS	<5

51 - SKILL: RHYMING

LEVEL	FORMAT	TITLE	PUBLISHER	$PRICE
R	AUDKIT	GETTING READY TO READ	MEDIA MATERIALS, INC.	6-10
R	GAME	ONE TWO THREE & AWAY PHONIC CARD GAME	INDIVIDUALIZED LEARNING MATERIAL	21-30
R	MANIPU	SESAME STREET MATCH-UPS	PLAYSKOOL, INC.	11-20
R	PUPILB	LADYBIRD BOOK: FINGER RHYMES	IDEAL SCHOOL SUPPLY COMPANY	<5
R	PUPILB	LADYBIRD BOOK: NUMBER RHYMES	IDEAL SCHOOL SUPPLY COMPANY	<5
R	PUPILB	LADYBIRD BOOK: MEMORY RHYMES	IDEAL SCHOOL SUPPLY COMPANY	<5
R	PUPILB	LADYBIRD BOOK: TALKING RHYMES	IDEAL SCHOOL SUPPLY COMPANY	<5
R	PUPILB	LADYBIRD BOOK: ACTION RHYMES	IDEAL SCHOOL SUPPLY COMPANY	<5
R	PUPILB	LADYBIRD BOOK: DANCING RHYMES	IDEAL SCHOOL SUPPLY COMPANY	<5
R	WKBOOK	RHYMING READER, BOOK A	HAYES SCHOOL PUBLISHING COMPANY	<5
RP	ACTCRD	WIPE-OFF CARDS: RHYMING WORDS	TREND ENTERPRISES, INC.	<5
RP	ACTCRD	WIPE-OFF CARDS: RHYMING WORDS, LEVEL 2	TREND ENTERPRISES, INC.	<5
RP	ACTCRD	PICTURES THAT RHYME	MILTON BRADLEY/PLAYSKOOL	<5
RP	AUDKIT	RHYTHMS TO READING	BOWMAR/NOBLE PUBLISHERS, INC.	151-200
RP	AUDKIT	WANTED EARS... FOR RHYMING	MEDIA MATERIALS, INC.	6-10
RP	AUDKIT	MINISYSTEMS: PARTICIPATING IN RHYMES	CORONET MULTI MEDIA	11-20
RP	AUDKIT	MINISYSTEMS: RHYMING WORDS WITH PICTURES I	CORONET MULTI MEDIA	11-20
RP	AUDKIT	MINISYSTEMS: RHYMING WORDS WITH PICTURES II	CORONET MULTI MEDIA	11-20
RP	AUDKIT	MINISYSTEMS: RHYMING REVIEW	CORONET MULTI MEDIA	11-20
RP	AUDKIT	MINISYSTEMS: LISTENING TO RHYMES	CORONET MULTI MEDIA	11-20
RP	A/VKIT	I HEAR A RHYME	EYE GATE MEDIA	101-150
RP	A/VKIT	EXPLORING WITH RIDDLES & RHYMES	EYE GATE MEDIA	151-200
RP	A/VKIT	RIDDLE-A-RHYME	EYE GATE MEDIA	101-150
RP	DITTO	TIME TO RHYME	CREATIVE TEACHING ASSOCIATES	<5
RP	DITTO	RHYMING, LEVEL A	CONTINENTAL PRESS, INC.	<5
RP	DITTO	TIME TO RHYME	ENRICH, INC.	<5
RP	DITTO	RHYMING KITTENS	INSTRUCTO/MCGRAW-HILL	<5
RP	DITTO	TIME TO RHYME	ACTIVITY RESOURCES COMPANY, INC.	<5
RP	FILMST	EARLY READING RECOGNITION SKILLS	CLASSROOM MATERIALS CO.	51-75
RP	GAME	READINESS DISCOVERY	DISCOVERY LEARNING	<5
RP	GAME	ETA FUN WITH RHYMES	EDUCATIONAL TEACHING AIDS	11-20
RP	GAME	GAMEBOARD KIT A	READING JOY, INC.	6-10
RP	GAME	GAMEBOARD KIT F	READING JOY, INC.	6-10
RP	GAME	SOLO GAMES: RHYMING	WISE OWL PUBLICATIONS	<5
RP	GAME	FUN WITH RHYMES	INSTRUCTO/MCGRAW-HILL	6-10
RP	MANIPU	RHYMING PUZZLE	CHILDCRAFT EDUCATION CORPORATION	<5
RP	MANIPU	CHEVES PROGRAM, PART 4: PHONICS PUZZLES & GAMES	TEACHING RESOURCES CORPORATION	11-20
RP	MANIPU	MIX 'N' MATCH PUZZLES: RHYMING WORDS, LEVEL 1	TREND ENTERPRISES, INC.	6-10
RP	MULTIU	READING READINESS: PARTS I, II, III, IV, V, VI	EDUCATIONAL DIMENSIONS CORP.	101-150
RP	MULTIM	HELP: RHYMING WORDS	CENTER FOR EARLY LEARNING	6-10
RP	MULTIM	RHYMING WORDS	ENRICH, INC.	21-30
RP	MULTIM	WHAT'S YOUR STORY?	HARCOURT BRACE JOVANOVICH, INC.	101-150
RP	PICTUR	TELL AGAIN NURSERY RHYMES CARDS	AEVAC, INC.	11-20
RP	PICTUR	SILLY SOUNDING RHYMES, SET 1	IDEAL SCHOOL SUPPLY COMPANY	6-10
RP	PICTUR	SILLY SOUNDING RHYMES, SET 2	IDEAL SCHOOL SUPPLY COMPANY	6-10
RP	PICTUR	SILLY SOUNDING RHYMES, SET 3	IDEAL SCHOOL SUPPLY COMPANY	6-10
RP	PICTUR	SILLY SOUNDING RHYMES, SET 4	IDEAL SCHOOL SUPPLY COMPANY	6-10
RP	PICTUR	RHYMING PICTURES	INSTRUCTO/MCGRAW-HILL	6-10
RP	PUPILB	TIME TO RHYME WITH CALICO CAT	CHILDREN'S PRESS, INC.	6-10
RP	PUPILB	KINDERGARTEN KEYS: THE CATERPILLAR CAPER	ECONOMY COMPANY	<5
RP	PUPILB	KINDERGARTEN KEYS: MOCKINGBIRD FLIGHT	ECONOMY COMPANY	11-20
RP	PUPILB	ABC RHYMES	WESTERN PUBLISHING EDUC. SERVICE	<5
RP	PUPILB	RHYME ME A RHYME	CHILD'S WORLD	<5
RP	RECORD	NURSERY RHYMES FOR LITTLE PEOPLE	KIMBO EDUCATIONAL	6-10
RP	WKBOOK	DELL HOME ACTIVITY: RHYMING ROOTS	DELL PUBLISHING COMPANY, INC.	<5

LEVEL	FORMAT	TITLE	PUBLISHER	NT	$PRICE

51 - SKILL: RHYMING

LEVEL	FORMAT	TITLE	PUBLISHER	NT	$PRICE
RP	WKBOOK	READINESS BOOK: COME TO MY PARTY	PHONOVISUAL PRODUCTS, INC.		<5
RP	WKBOOK	CATCH A CONSONANT	WISE OWL PUBLICATIONS		<5
RPI	GAME	AUDITORY DISCRIMINATION GAME	MODERN EDUCATION CORPORATION		21-30
P	ACTCRD	BASIC PHONICS: BASIC RHYMING FAMILIES	INSTRUCTIONAL FAIR		<5
P	ACTCRD	WIPE-OFF CARDS: RHYMING WORDS	CONSTRUCTIVE PLAYTHINGS		<5
P	ACTCRD	RIDDLE RIDDLE RHYME TIME, KIT A: INITIAL CONSONANTS	BARNELL LOFT, LTD.		6-10
P	ACTCRD	RIDDLE RIDDLE RHYME TIME, KIT B: INITIAL BLENDS & DIGRAPHS	BARNELL LOFT, LTD.		6-10
P	ACTCRD	WORD FAMILY FUN	KENWORTHY EDUCATIONAL SERVICE		<5
P	ACTCRD	RHYME-O BOX II	ACADEMIC THERAPY PUBLICATIONS		6-10
P	ACTCRD	TUTORGRAM: RHYMING ELEMENTS	ENRICHMENT READING CORP OF AMER.		11-20
P	ACTCRD	RHYMING ALPHABET	IDEAL SCHOOL SUPPLY COMPANY		6-10
P	ACTCRD	SOUND FOUNDATION, PROGRAM 1	DEVELOPMENTAL LEARNING MATERIALS		11-20
P	ACTCRD	RHYMING WORDS	CREATIVE TEACHING PRESS, INC.		<5
P	ACTCRD	PUNCH-THRU CARDS: RHYMING WORDS	TREND ENTERPRISES, INC.		<5
P	AUDCAS	SOUNDS FOR YOUNG READERS, VOLUME 1	CLASSROOM MATERIALS CO.		6-10
P	AUDKIT	KIT 80: BASIC PHONICS, READINESS LEVEL	EDUCATIONAL RESEARCH, INC.		101-150
P	AUDKIT	KIT 81: BASIC PHONICS, LEVEL 1	EDUCATIONAL RESEARCH, INC.		101-150
P	AUDKIT	READING CASSETTES: READING READINESS	IDEAL SCHOOL SUPPLY COMPANY		51-75
P	AUDKIT	FAT CAT'S DISH WISH	MEDIA MATERIALS, INC.		6-10
P	AUDKIT	MINISYSTEMS: RHYMING, ALL,AT,AY	CORONET MULTI MEDIA		11-20
P	AUDKIT	MINISYSTEMS: RHYMING, OW,OY,OI	CORONET MULTI MEDIA		11-20
P	CL SET	SUPPORTIVE READING SKILLS: RHYME TIME (MULTI COPIES)	BARNELL LOFT, LTD.	10	11-20
P	DITTO	RHYMING, LEVEL B	CONTINENTAL PRESS, INC.		<5
P	DITTO	RHYMING, LEVEL C	CONTINENTAL PRESS, INC.		<5
P	DITTO	WORD SPY, GRADE 1	CONTINENTAL PRESS, INC.		<5
P	DITTO	WORD SPY, GRADE 2	CONTINENTAL PRESS, INC.		<5
P	DITTO	WORD SPY, GRADE 3	CONTINENTAL PRESS, INC.		<5
P	DITTO	BASIC PHONICS: BASIC RHYMING FAMILIES	INSTRUCTIONAL FAIR		<5
P	DITTO	RHYMING: CUT & PASTE	FRANK SCHAFFER PUBLICATIONS, INC		<5
P	DITTO	READ, THINK, COLOR	FRANK SCHAFFER PUBLICATIONS, INC		<5
P	DITTO	SPELLING PROGRAM, BOOK G	FRANK SCHAFFER PUBLICATIONS, INC		<5
P	DITTO	RHYMING SOUNDS	INSTRUCTOR PUBLICATIONS, INC.		<5
P	DITTO	CIRCUS DAYS READING ACTIVITIES	CREATIVE TEACHING PRESS, INC.		<5
P	DITTO	READING STAND UPS RHYMING	CREATIVE TEACHING PRESS, INC.		<5
P	DITTO	READING ENRICHMENT ACTIVITIES	XEROX EDUCATION PUBLICATIONS		<5
P	DITTO	DECODING SKILLS 2	ACTIVITY RESOURCES COMPANY, INC.		<5
P	DITTO	BASIC RHYMING WORDS	ACTIVITY RESOURCES COMPANY, INC.		<5
P	FILMST	LEARNING ABOUT OUR LANGUAGE, SET 1	AEVAC, INC.		31-50
P	FLNLBD	INITIAL CONSONANT SUBSTITUTION	INSTRUCTO/MCGRAW-HILL		6-10
P	GAME	MATCH ME CARDS	CREATIVE TEACHING ASSOCIATES	4	11-20
P	GAME	MATCH ME CARDS, RHYMING WORDS	CREATIVE TEACHING ASSOCIATES		<5
P	GAME	RHYMING	FRANK SCHAFFER PUBLICATIONS, INC		<5
P	GAME	AUDITORY DISCRIMINATION	FRANK SCHAFFER PUBLICATIONS, INC		<5
P	GAME	RHYMES I KNOW CAN MAKE DOGS GROW	CONSTRUCTIVE PLAYTHINGS		6-10
P	GAME	RHYMING BINGO	CONSTRUCTIVE PLAYTHINGS		<5
P	GAME	RHYMING WHEEL	TEACHING RESOURCES CORPORATION		11-20
P	GAME	PHONICS PUZZLES & GAMES	TEACHING RESOURCES CORPORATION		11-20
P	GAME	RHYMING GAME	IDEAL SCHOOL SUPPLY COMPANY		6-10
P	GAME	SPELLING/LANGUAGE LEARNING GAMES KITS, KIT ONE	RAND MCNALLY & COMPANY		76-100
P	GAME	MATCH ME CARDS: RHYMING WORDS	TREND ENTERPRISES, INC.		<5
P	GAME	RHYMING WORDS & VARIANT CONSONANTS	ACTIVITY RESOURCES COMPANY, INC.		<5
P	GAME	PAIRS WORD GAME	MILTON BRADLEY/PLAYSKOOL		<5
P	GUIDE	MERRILL PHONICS SKILL TEXT: COSTUME BOOK, LEVEL R	CHARLES E. MERRILL PUBLISHING CO		<5
P	MANIPU	RHYMING WORDS	CONSTRUCTIVE PLAYTHINGS		<5
P	MANIPU	RHYMING PAIRS	EDUCATIONAL TEACHING AIDS		<5
P	MANIPU	OBJECTS THAT RHYME	IDEAL SCHOOL SUPPLY COMPANY		<5
P	MANIPU	RHYMING PUZZLES	IDEAL SCHOOL SUPPLY COMPANY		<5
P	MANIPU	ALADDIN CHART: RHYMING	IDEAL SCHOOL SUPPLY COMPANY		<5
P	MANIPU	RHYMING CARDS	DEVELOPMENTAL LEARNING MATERIALS		<5
P	MANIPU	RHYMING WORD PUZZLES	DEVELOPMENTAL LEARNING MATERIALS		<5
P	MULTIM	DEVELOPING READING SKILLS, PART I: WORD RECOGNITION	EDUCATIONAL ENRICHMENT MATERIALS		101-150
P	MULTIM	READING SKILLS SUPPORT SYSTEM, BOX 1	EDL/MCGRAW-HILL		301-400
P	MULTIM	NEW GOALS IN LISTENING, GRADES 1-3	TROLL ASSOCIATES		76-100
P	PICTUR	RHYMING PICTURES FOR PEGBOARD	IDEAL SCHOOL SUPPLY COMPANY		<5
P	PI/PRT	INDIVIDUAL LANGUAGE ARTS, GRADE 1	CREATIVE TEACHING ASSOCIATES		6-10
P	PUPILB	SUPPORTIVE READING SKILLS: RHYME TIME, A1-A4	BARNELL LOFT, LTD.		11-20
P	PUPILB	SUPPORTIVE READING SKILLS: RHYME TIME, B	BARNELL LOFT, LTD.		11-20
P	RECORD	SOUNDS FOR YOUNG READERS, VOLUME 1	CLASSROOM MATERIALS CO.		6-10
P	RECORD	SOUNDS, VOL. 1	CHILDREN'S BOOK & MUSIC CENTER		6-10
P	SND FS	I HEAR A RHYME	EYE GATE MEDIA		101-150
P	SP EQT	FLASH-X-SET 1: READING PICTURES	EDL/MCGRAW-HILL		<5
P	VISKIT	WORD FAMILY FABLES	INSTRUCTOR PUBLICATIONS, INC.		6-10
P	WKBOOK	READ, THINK, COLOR	FRANK SCHAFFER PUBLICATIONS, INC		<5
P	WKBOOK	MORE READ, THINK, COLOR	FRANK SCHAFFER PUBLICATIONS, INC		<5
P	WKBOOK	AEVAC PHONICS PROGRAM, BOOK B	AEVAC, INC.		<5
P	WKBOOK	AEVAC PHONICS PROGRAM, BOOK C	AEVAC, INC.		<5
P	WKBOOK	AEVAC PHONICS PROGRAM, BOOK D	AEVAC, INC.		<5
P	WKBOOK	TRANSITION BOOK: I CAN & NOW I CAN READ	PHONOVISUAL PRODUCTS, INC.		<5
P	WKBOOK	FUN PHONIC JINGLES, BOOK I	WORD MAKING PRODUCTIONS, INC.		<5

LEVEL	FORMAT	TITLE	PUBLISHER	NT	$PRICE

51 - SKILL: RHYMING

LEVEL	FORMAT	TITLE	PUBLISHER	NT	$PRICE
P	WKBOOK	FUN PHONIC JINGLES, BOOK II	WORD MAKING PRODUCTIONS, INC.		<5
P	WKBOOK	HIDDEN PICTURE PUZZLES, BOOK I	WORD MAKING PRODUCTIONS, INC.		<5
P	WKBOOK	HIDDEN PICTURE PUZZLES, BOOK II	WORD MAKING PRODUCTIONS, INC.		<5
P	WKBOOK	MERRILL PHONICS SKILL TEXT: COSTUME BOOK, LEVEL R	CHARLES E. MERRILL PUBLISHING CO		<5
P	WKBOOK	PHONICS & WORD POWER, BOOK 1	XEROX EDUCATION PUBLICATIONS		<5
P	WKBOOK	PHONICS COME FIRST	ACTIVITY RESOURCES COMPANY, INC.		6-10
PI	ACTCRD	ADVANCED PHONICS: ADVANCED RHYMING FAMILIES	INSTRUCTIONAL FAIR		<5
PI	ACTCRD	ADVANCED PHONICS PAK	INSTRUCTIONAL FAIR		21-30
PI	ACTCRD	TUTORGRAM: RHYMING	ENRICHMENT READING CORP OF AMER.		11-20
PI	ACTCRD	WORD DEVILS SKILL CARDS	MILTON BRADLEY/PLAYSKOOL		<5
PI	DITTO	ADVANCED PHONICS: ADVANCED RHYMING FAMILIES	INSTRUCTIONAL FAIR		<5
PI	DITTO	ADVANCED PHONICS PAK	INSTRUCTIONAL FAIR		21-30
PI	DITTO	RUFUS RABBIT'S RHYME TIME	FRANK SCHAFFER PUBLICATIONS, INC		<5
PI	GAME	PHONICS SOUP, RHYMING GAMES SET A	CREATIVE TEACHING ASSOCIATES		6-10
PI	GAME	PHONICS SOUP, RHYMING GAMES SET B	CREATIVE TEACHING ASSOCIATES		6-10
PI	GAME	RHYMING ZIG ZAG	IDEAL SCHOOL SUPPLY COMPANY		6-10
PI	GAME	RHYMING WORD GAME	JUDY COMPANY		6-10
PI	GAME	PHONICS SOUP GAME PACKAGES: RHYMING, SET A	SCOTT RESOURCES, INC.		6-10
PI	GAME	PHONICS SOUP GAME PACKAGES: RHYMING, SET B	SCOTT RESOURCES, INC.		6-10
PI	MANIPU	RHYMING PUZZLES	INCENTIVES FOR LEARNING, INC.		6-10
PI	MULTIU	PHONICS SOUP	CREATIVE TEACHING ASSOCIATES	5	31-50
PI	SP EQT	LANGUAGE SKILLS PROGRAM: WORD GAMES & PUZZLES	SPELLBINDER, INC.		51-75
PI	TRANSP	LANGUAGE DEVELOPMENT & READING SKILLS	UNITED TRANSPARENCIES, INC.		201-300
PI	WKBOOK	RHYMING & READING	GOOD APPLE, INC.		6-10
PI	WKBOOK	CHUMPY'S WORD GAMES	XEROX EDUCATION PUBLICATIONS		<5
I	AUDKIT	WORDPLAY	CORONET MULTI MEDIA		76-100
I	DITTO	WORD SPY, GRADE 4	CONTINENTAL PRESS, INC.		<5

52 - SKILL: CONSONANTS - GENERAL

LEVEL	FORMAT	TITLE	PUBLISHER	NT	$PRICE
R	MULTIU	EXPERIENCES IN READING READINESS	MILTON BRADLEY/PLAYSKOOL		76-100
R	MULTIM	BEGINNING TO READ, WRITE & LISTEN	HARPER & ROW PUBLISHERS, INC.		101-150
RP	ACTCRD	WIPE-OFF CARDS: BEGINNING SOUNDS	TREND ENTERPRISES, INC.		<5
RP	A/VKIT	RIDDLE-A-RHYME	EYE GATE MEDIA		101-150
RP	DITTO	BEGINNING SOUNDS, LEVEL A	CONTINENTAL PRESS, INC.		<5
RP	DITTO	BEGINNING SOUNDS, LEVEL B	CONTINENTAL PRESS, INC.		<5
RP	FILMST	EARLY READING RECOGNITION SKILLS	CLASSROOM MATERIALS CO.		51-75
RP	FLASH	LEARN THE ALPHABET	MILTON BRADLEY/PLAYSKOOL		<5
RP	GAME	GAMEBOARD KIT G	READING JOY, INC.		6-10
RP	GUIDE	PHONICS IS FUN, BOOK 1	MODERN CURRICULUM PRESS		<5
RP	MANIPU	FLOOR PUZZLES: INNER CITY CONSONANTS	TREND ENTERPRISES, INC.		6-10
RP	MANIPU	MIX 'N' MATCH PUZZLES: CONSONANTS	TREND ENTERPRISES, INC.		6-10
RP	MANIPU	MIX 'N' MATCH PUZZLES: INITIAL CONSONANTS, LEVEL 2	TREND ENTERPRISES, INC.		6-10
RP	MULTIU	READING READINESS: PARTS I, II, III, IV, V, VI	EDUCATIONAL DIMENSIONS CORP.		101-150
RP	MULTIM	WORDS & SOUND SERIES, SET 1	EDL/MCGRAW-HILL		101-150
RP	MULTIM	WORDS & SOUND SERIES, SET 2	EDL/MCGRAW-HILL		101-150
RP	MULTIM	WORDS & SOUND SERIES, SET 3	EDL/MCGRAW-HILL		101-150
RP	MULTIM	WORDS & SOUND SERIES, SET 4	EDL/MCGRAW-HILL		101-150
RP	SKLKIT	AIMS: INITIAL CONSONANTS KIT	CONTINENTAL PRESS, INC.		51-75
RP	WKBOOK	PHONICS IS FUN, BOOK 1	MODERN CURRICULUM PRESS		<5
RPI	GUIDE	WORD ATTACK JOY	READING JOY, INC.		6-10
P	ACTCRD	BASIC PHONICS PAK	INSTRUCTIONAL FAIR		21-30
P	ACTCRD	RAINBOW WORD BUILDERS	KENWORTHY EDUCATIONAL SERVICE		<5
P	ACTCRD	SAY THE SOUNDS	KENWORTHY EDUCATIONAL SERVICE		<5
P	ACTCRD	SPREAD I	INCENTIVES FOR LEARNING, INC.		21-30
P	ACTCRD	GROUP-SIZE CONSONANT CARDS	GARRARD PUBLISHING COMPANY		<5
P	ACTCRD	CONSONANT FLIPSTRIPS	PHONOVISUAL PRODUCTS, INC.		<5
P	ACTCRD	SKILLBUILDERS	PHONOVISUAL PRODUCTS, INC.		<5
P	ACTCRD	LANGUAGE ACTIVITY CARDS: VOWELS & CONSONANTS	WEBER COSTELLO COMPANY		6-10
P	ACTCRD	PRIMARY PHONICS-SKILL DRILLS WITH MOTIVATORS	SVE		31-50
P	ACTCRD	PUNCH-THRU CARDS: FINAL CONSONANTS	TREND ENTERPRISES, INC.		<5
P	ACTCRD	PUNCH-THRU CARDS: INITIAL CONSONANTS	TREND ENTERPRISES, INC.		<5
P	ACTCRD	WIPE-OFF CARDS: INITIAL CONSONANTS	TREND ENTERPRISES, INC.		<5
P	ACTCRD	WIPE-OFF CARDS: BEGINNING SOUNDS, LEVEL 2	TREND ENTERPRISES, INC.		<5
P	AUDCAS	SOUNDS FOR YOUNG READERS, VOLUME 2	CLASSROOM MATERIALS CO.		6-10
P	AUDCAS	LISTENING FOR SOUNDS	MEDIA MARKETING, INC.		51-75
P	AUDCAS	FUN WITH CONSONANTS	UNITED LEARNING		31-50
P	AUDCRD	INITIAL CONSONANTS, PART 1	AUDIOTRONICS CORPORATION		11-20
P	AUDCRD	INITIAL CONSONANTS, PART 2	AUDIOTRONICS CORPORATION		11-20
P	AUDKIT	PRIMARY WORK RECOGNITION	EYE GATE MEDIA	5	31-50
P	AUDKIT	MIGHTY CONSONANTS	EYE GATE MEDIA		6-10
P	AUDKIT	CREATURE TEACHERS	ECONOMY COMPANY		151-200
P	AUDKIT	KIT 82: BASIC PHONICS, LEVEL 2	EDUCATIONAL RESEARCH, INC.		101-150
P	AUDKIT	KIT 83: BASIC PHONICS, LEVEL 3	EDUCATIONAL RESEARCH, INC.		101-150
P	AUDKIT	KIT 84: BASIC PHONICS, LEVEL 4	EDUCATIONAL RESEARCH, INC.		101-150
P	AUDKIT	ABC'S OF PHONICS PROGRAM 1: CONSONANT LETTERS B-L W/CASSETTE	Q-ED PRODUCTIONS		51-75
P	AUDKIT	ABC'S OF PHONICS PROGRAM 1: CONSONANT LETTERS B-L W/RECORDS	Q-ED PRODUCTIONS		76-100
P	AUDKIT	ABC'S OF PHONICS PROGRAM 2: CONSONANT LETTERS M-Z W/CASSETTE	Q-ED PRODUCTIONS		76-100
P	AUDKIT	ABC'S OF PHONICS PROGRAM 2: CONSONANT LETTERS M-Z W/RECORDS	Q-ED PRODUCTIONS		76-100

LEVEL	FORMAT	TITLE	PUBLISHER	NT	$PRICE

52 - SKILL: CONSONANTS - GENERAL

LEVEL	FORMAT	TITLE	PUBLISHER	NT	$PRICE
P	AUDKIT	ABC'S OF PHONICS PROGRAMS 1 - 3 W/RECORDS	Q-ED PRODUCTIONS		201-300
P	AUDKIT	MINISYSTEMS: BUILDING VOCABULARY, BLENDS, VOWELS, CONSONANTS	CORONET MULTI MEDIA		11-20
P	A/VKIT	PHONICS-VOWEL SOUNDS (INITIAL & MEDIAL)	SVE		151-200
P	DITTO	BEGINNING SOUNDS, LEVEL C	CONTINENTAL PRESS, INC.		<5
P	DITTO	CROSSWORD PUZZLES FOR PHONICS: PICTURE CLUES	CONTINENTAL PRESS, INC.		<5
P	DITTO	CROSSWORD PUZZLES FOR PHONICS: WORD/PICTURE CLUES	CONTINENTAL PRESS, INC.		<5
P	DITTO	NEW PHONICS & WORD ANALYSIS SKILLS: GRADE 1, PART 1	CONTINENTAL PRESS, INC.		<5
P	DITTO	NEW PHONICS & WORD ANALYSIS SKILLS: GRADE 1, PART 2	CONTINENTAL PRESS, INC.		<5
P	DITTO	NEW PHONICS & WORD ANALYSIS SKILLS: GRADE 2, PART 1	CONTINENTAL PRESS, INC.		<5
P	DITTO	NEW PHONICS & WORD ANALYSIS SKILLS: GRADE 3, PART 1	CONTINENTAL PRESS, INC.		<5
P	DITTO	PHONICS FUN, GRADE 1	CONTINENTAL PRESS, INC.		<5
P	DITTO	READING STEP BY STEP, KIT A	CONTINENTAL PRESS, INC.		51-75
P	DITTO	READING ESSENTIALS: CONTEXT CLUES, GRADE 1	CONTINENTAL PRESS, INC.		<5
P	DITTO	BASIC PHONICS PAK	INSTRUCTIONAL FAIR		21-30
P	DITTO	READ, THINK, COLOR	FRANK SCHAFFER PUBLICATIONS, INC		<5
P	DITTO	CONSONANT BOOK	FRANK SCHAFFER PUBLICATIONS, INC		<5
P	DITTO	INDIVIDUALIZED READING DEVELOPMENT ACTIVITIES	LOVE PUBLISHING COMPANY		6-10
P	DITTO	PHONICS FUN: CONSONANT	PHONOVISUAL PRODUCTS, INC.		6-10
P	DITTO	BEGINNING PHONICS, BOOK 1	GEL-STEN, INC.		<5
P	DITTO	BEGINNING PHONICS, BOOK 2	GEL-STEN, INC.		<5
P	DITTO	PHONICS IA	HAYES SCHOOL PUBLISHING COMPANY		<5
P	DITTO	PHONICS IB	HAYES SCHOOL PUBLISHING COMPANY		<5
P	DITTO	PHONICS IIA	HAYES SCHOOL PUBLISHING COMPANY		<5
P	DITTO	PHONICS & READING	HAYES SCHOOL PUBLISHING COMPANY		<5
P	GAME	CONSONANT BINGO	CONSTRUCTIVE PLAYTHINGS		<5
P	GAME	PHONICS DISCOVERY	DISCOVERY LEARNING		<5
P	GAME	PHONOVISUAL LEARNING GAMES 1	PHONOVISUAL PRODUCTS, INC.		11-20
P	GAME	PHONOVISUAL LEARNING GAMES 2	PHONOVISUAL PRODUCTS, INC.		31-50
P	GAME	NEW PHONICS WE USE LEARNING GAMES KITS, KIT ONE	RAND MCNALLY & COMPANY		76-100
P	GAME	MATCH ME CARDS: BEGINNING SOUNDS	TREND ENTERPRISES, INC.		<5
P	GAME	TABLET GAMES: BEGINNING CONSONANTS	TREND ENTERPRISES, INC.		<5
P	GUIDE	PHONICS WORKTEXT: ANSWER KEY (6)	HAMMOND, INC.		<5
P	GUIDE	MERRILL PHONICS SKILL TEXT: COSTUME SHOP, LEVEL A	CHARLES E. MERRILL PUBLISHING CO		<5
P	GUIDE	CONSONANT SOUNDS: STARTING OFF WITH PHONICS, BOOK 3	MODERN CURRICULUM PRESS		<5
P	GUIDE	MORE CONSONANT SOUNDS: STARTING OFF WITH PHONICS, BOOK 4	MODERN CURRICULUM PRESS		<5
P	MANIPU	MIX 'N' MATCH PUZZLES: CONSONANTS	CONSTRUCTIVE PLAYTHINGS		<5
P	MANIPU	PHONICS E-Z LANGUAGE LEARNING SLIDE RULES	E-Z GRADER COMPANY	5	6-10
P	MANIPU	PHONICS E-Z LANGUAGE LEARNING SLIDE RULES, 1ST & 2ND	E-Z GRADER COMPANY		<5
P	MANIPU	FINAL CONSONANT DISCS	TREND ENTERPRISES, INC.		<5
P	MANIPU	INITIAL CONSONANT DISCS	TREND ENTERPRISES, INC.		<5
P	MANIPU	MAGIC TEACHER PUZZLE-PLANS: PHONICS (CONSONANT SOUNDS)	HAYES SCHOOL PUBLISHING COMPANY		<5
P	MULTIU	VOWEL SOUNDS/SELF-INSTRUCTIONAL MODALITIES APPROACH	MILTON BRADLEY/PLAYSKOOL		76-100
P	MULTIM	LISTENING YOUR WAY TO BETTER READING	ASSOCIATED EDUCATIONAL MATERIALS		301-400
P	MULTIM	SOUND IT, UNIT 1	IMPERIAL INTERNATIONAL LEARNING		51-75
P	MULTIM	FIRST TALKING ALPHABET: PART 1, CONSONANTS	SCOTT, FORESMAN & CO.		76-100
P	MULTIM	BLENDING SOUNDS WITH COCO & CHARLIE	EDUCATIONAL ACTIVITIES, INC.		31-50
P	PUPILB	ANIMAL PUZZLERS PHONICS ACTIVITIES	CREATIVE TEACHING ASSOCIATES		<5
P	RECORD	SOUNDS FOR YOUNG READERS, VOLUME 2	CLASSROOM MATERIALS CO.		6-10
P	SND FS	VOWELS & CONSONANTS	HERBERT M. ELKINS COMPANY		11-20
P	SP EQT	LANGUAGE SKILLS PROGRAM: READINESS SKILLS (YY)	SPELLBINDER, INC.		51-75
P	SP EQT	LANGUAGE SKILLS PROGRAM: INTRODUCTION TO SPELLING	SPELLBINDER, INC.		51-75
P	TRANSP	BASIC PHONETIC SKILL DRILLS	PAUL S. AMIDON & ASSOC., INC.		21-30
P	WKBOOK	CUES & SIGNALS III	ANN ARBOR PUBLISHERS		<5
P	WKBOOK	READ, THINK, COLOR	FRANK SCHAFFER PUBLICATIONS, INC		<5
P	WKBOOK	MORE READ, THINK, COLOR	FRANK SCHAFFER PUBLICATIONS, INC		<5
P	WKBOOK	AEVAC PHONICS PROGRAM	AEVAC, INC.	6	11-20
P	WKBOOK	AEVAC PHONICS PROGRAM, BOOK A	AEVAC, INC.		<5
P	WKBOOK	AEVAC PHONICS PROGRAM, BOOK B	AEVAC, INC.		<5
P	WKBOOK	AEVAC PHONICS PROGRAM, BOOK C	AEVAC, INC.		<5
P	WKBOOK	AEVAC PHONICS PROGRAM, BOOK E	AEVAC, INC.		<5
P	WKBOOK	CONSONANT WORKBOOK: SEE, HEAR, SAY, DO	PHONOVISUAL PRODUCTS, INC.		<5
P	WKBOOK	WINDOWS TO READING, BOOK A	FOLLETT PUBLISHING COMPANY		<5
P	WKBOOK	WINDOWS TO READING, BOOK B	FOLLETT PUBLISHING COMPANY		<5
P	WKBOOK	WINDOWS TO READING, BOOK C	FOLLETT PUBLISHING COMPANY		<5
P	WKBOOK	PHONICS WORKTEXT: CONSONANTS 1	HAMMOND, INC.		<5
P	WKBOOK	PHONICS WORKTEXT: CONSONANTS 2	HAMMOND, INC.		<5
P	WKBOOK	LETTERS & SOUNDS, PRIMARY	SCOTT, FORESMAN & CO.		<5
P	WKBOOK	COVE SCHOOL READING PROGRAM	DEVELOPMENTAL LEARNING MATERIALS		76-100
P	WKBOOK	CONSONANT FLIP BOOKS	DEVELOPMENTAL LEARNING MATERIALS		6-10
P	WKBOOK	MERRILL PHONICS SKILL TEXT: COSTUME SHOP, LEVEL A	CHARLES E. MERRILL PUBLISHING CO		<5
P	WKBOOK	CONSONANT CAPERS	HOUGHTON MIFFLIN COMPANY		6-10
P	WKBOOK	CONSONANT SOUNDS: STARTING OFF WITH PHONICS, BOOK 3	MODERN CURRICULUM PRESS		<5
P	WKBOOK	MORE CONSONANT SOUNDS: STARTING OFF WITH PHONICS, BOOK 4	MODERN CURRICULUM PRESS		<5
P	WKBOOK	MCP PHONICS WORKBOOKS: LEVEL A	MODERN CURRICULUM PRESS		<5
P	WKBOOK	NEW PHONICS WORKBOOK, BOOK B	MODERN CURRICULUM PRESS		<5
P	WKBOOK	NEW PHONICS WORKBOOK, BOOK C	MODERN CURRICULUM PRESS		<5
P	WKBOOK	NEW PHONICS WORKBOOK, BOOK D	MODERN CURRICULUM PRESS		<5
P	WKBOOK	PHONICS WORKBOOK, BOOK D	MODERN CURRICULUM PRESS		<5
P	WKBOOK	SOUND WE USE, BOOK 1	HAYES SCHOOL PUBLISHING COMPANY		<5

LEVEL	FORMAT	TITLE	PUBLISHER	NT	$PRICE

52 - SKILL: CONSONANTS - GENERAL

LEVEL	FORMAT	TITLE	PUBLISHER	NT	$PRICE
P	WKBOOK	SOUNDS WE USE, BOOK 2	HAYES SCHOOL PUBLISHING COMPANY		<5
P	WKBOOK	BIG LOOK AT BEGINNING CONSONANTS	MILTON BRADLEY/PLAYSKOOL		<5
PI	ACTCRD	ADVANCED PHONICS PAK	INSTRUCTIONAL FAIR		21-30
PI	AUDKIT	USING PHONICS	EBSCO CURRICULUM MATERIALS		51-75
PI	AUDKIT	POWERPAC I	IMPERIAL INTERNATIONAL LEARNING		101-150
PI	AUDKIT	POWERPAC II	IMPERIAL INTERNATIONAL LEARNING		101-150
PI	AUDKIT	POWERPAC PROGRAM	IMPERIAL INTERNATIONAL LEARNING	4	>450
PI	DITTO	ADVANCED PHONICS PAK	INSTRUCTIONAL FAIR		21-30
PI	DITTO	BASIC READING SKILLS	EDUCATIONAL INSIGHTS, INC.		51-75
PI	DITTO	WORD PERCEPTION	MILTON BRADLEY/PLAYSKOOL		<5
PI	GAME	SILLY SOUNDS	IDEAL SCHOOL SUPPLY COMPANY		6-10
PI	MULTIM	WORKING WITH PHONICS	TROLL ASSOCIATES		301-400
PI	SND FS	INDEPENDENT WORD PERCEPTION	ASSOCIATED EDUCATIONAL MATERIALS		151-200
PI	SND FS	WORKING WITH CONSONANTS	TROLL ASSOCIATES		101-150
PI	SP EQT	LANGUAGE SKILLS PROGRAM: WORD GAMES & PUZZLES	SPELLBINDER, INC.		51-75
PI	TRANSP	LANGUAGE DEVELOPMENT & READING SKILLS	UNITED TRANSPARENCIES, INC.		201-300
I	CHART	PREPOSTEROUS PHONICS POSTERS	SCOTT RESOURCES, INC.		11-20
I	GUIDE	MERRILL PHONICS SKILL TEXT: WHIZ KID, LEVEL F	CHARLES E. MERRILL PUBLISHING CO		<5
I	MULTIM	GAMES 'N' FRAMES: COOKING WITH CONSONANTS	IMPERIAL INTERNATIONAL LEARNING		21-30
I	MULTIM	SELECT-A-SKILL KIT, UNIT 1: MYSTERY ADVENTURE	IMPERIAL INTERNATIONAL LEARNING		51-75
I	MULTIM	SELECT-A-SKILL KIT, UNIT 1: MYSTERY ADVENTURE	IMPERIAL INTERNATIONAL LEARNING		51-75
I	SP EQT	LANGUAGE SKILLS PROGRAM: READING-SPELLING COMPREHENSION	SPELLBINDER, INC.		51-75
I	WKBOOK	LETTERS & SOUNDS, INTERMEDIATE	SCOTT, FORESMAN & CO.		<5
I	WKBOOK	MERRILL PHONICS SKILL TEXT: WHIZ KID, LEVEL F	CHARLES E. MERRILL PUBLISHING CO		<5
IJS	AUDCRD	CONFUSING CONSONANTS	AUDIOTRONICS CORPORATION		11-20
IJS	GAME	AUTO PHONICS: ALL ABOUT CONSONANTS	EDUCATIONAL ACTIVITIES, INC.		<5
JS	AUDKIT	READING CASSETTES: CONSONANTS & DIGRAPHS	IDEAL SCHOOL SUPPLY COMPANY		51-75
S	AUDKIT	CONSONANTS & DIGRAPHS	EDUCATIONAL MEDIA, INC.		51-75

53 - SKILL: CONSONANT BLENDS & DIGRAPHS

LEVEL	FORMAT	TITLE	PUBLISHER	NT	$PRICE
R	AUDKIT	SOUNDS & SYMBOLS	EDUCATORS PUBLISHING SERVICE		101-150
RP	ACTCRD	FORM-A-SOUND	IDEAL SCHOOL SUPPLY COMPANY		11-20
RP	AUDKIT	PERCEIVE & RESPOND, VOLUME II	MODERN EDUCATION CORPORATION		76-100
RP	DITTO	FUN WITH BLENDS & DIGRAPHS	CONTINENTAL PRESS, INC.		<5
RP	DITTO	CONSONANT DIGRAPH GAMES	CHILDREN'S LEARNING CENTER, INC.		<5
RP	DITTO	CONSONANT DIGRAPHS	CHILDREN'S LEARNING CENTER, INC.		<5
RP	FILMST	EARLY READING RECOGNITION SKILLS	CLASSROOM MATERIALS CO.		51-75
RP	GUIDE	PHONICS IS FUN, BOOK 1	MODERN CURRICULUM PRESS		<5
RP	MULTIU	READING STEP BY STEP, UNIT 2	IMPERIAL INTERNATIONAL LEARNING		51-75
RP	MULTIU	READING READINESS: PARTS I, II, III, IV, V, VI	EDUCATIONAL DIMENSIONS CORP.		101-150
RP	MULTIM	LEARNING THE CONSONANT BLENDS WITH AMOS & HIS FRIENDS	IMPERIAL INTERNATIONAL LEARNING		11-20
RP	MULTIM	HELP: BLENDS & DIGRAPHS	CENTER FOR EARLY LEARNING		6-10
RP	MULTIM	HEAR-SEE-SAY, PHONICS READING COURSE	MELODY HOUSE PUBLISHING COMPANY		11-20
RP	SP EQT	LEARNING LETTER SOUNDS, KIT E	BORG-WARNER EDUCATIONAL SYSTEMS		101-150
RP	SP EQT	LEARNING LETTER SOUNDS, KIT F	BORG-WARNER EDUCATIONAL SYSTEMS		101-150
RP	SP EQT	LEARNING LETTER SOUNDS, KIT EE	BORG-WARNER EDUCATIONAL SYSTEMS		101-150
RP	SP EQT	LEARNING LETTER SOUNDS, KIT FF	BORG-WARNER EDUCATIONAL SYSTEMS		101-150
RP	VISKIT	ALPHABET SERIES	WALKER EDUCATIONAL BOOK CORP.		31-50
RP	WKBOOK	PHONICS IS FUN, BOOK 1	MODERN CURRICULUM PRESS		<5
RPI	AUDKIT	PHONICS SERIES	MEDIA MATERIALS, INC.	10	76-100
P	ACTCRD	THINK PATTERNS, BLENDS TASK CARDS	CREATIVE TEACHING ASSOCIATES		11-20
P	ACTCRD	BASIC PHONICS PAK	INSTRUCTIONAL FAIR		21-30
P	ACTCRD	RIDDLE RIDDLE RHYME TIME, KIT B: INITIAL BLENDS & DIGRAPHS	BARNELL LOFT, LTD.		6-10
P	ACTCRD	TIME FOR SOUNDS, KIT B: INITIAL BLENDS & DIGRAPHS	BARNELL LOFT, LTD.		6-10
P	ACTCRD	INITIAL CONSONANT BLENDS, B	BARNELL LOFT, LTD.		6-10
P	ACTCRD	DIGRAPHS & FINAL BLENDS, B	BARNELL LOFT, LTD.		6-10
P	ACTCRD	RAINBOW WORD BUILDERS	KENWORTHY EDUCATIONAL SERVICE		<5
P	ACTCRD	SAY THE SOUNDS	KENWORTHY EDUCATIONAL SERVICE		<5
P	ACTCRD	SPEECH SOUNDS PICTURE CARDS: INITIAL CONSONANT BLENDS	TEACHING RESOURCES CORPORATION		6-10
P	ACTCRD	PHONIC HELPERS	EDUCATIONAL PROGRAMMERS, INC.		11-20
P	ACTCRD	GROUP-SIZE CONSONANT CARDS	GARRARD PUBLISHING COMPANY		<5
P	ACTCRD	MAGIC CARDS: BLENDS & DIGRAPHS	IDEAL SCHOOL SUPPLY COMPANY		6-10
P	ACTCRD	CONSONANT PICTURE PACK	PHONOVISUAL PRODUCTS, INC.		<5
P	ACTCRD	SOUND FOUNDATION, PROGRAM 1	DEVELOPMENTAL LEARNING MATERIALS		11-20
P	ACTCRD	FINAL CONSONANT BLENDS	GEL-STEN, INC.		6-10
P	ACTCRD	BEGINNING BLENDS	CREATIVE TEACHING PRESS, INC.		<5
P	ACTCRD	PUNCH-THRU CARDS: CONSONANT BLENDS	TREND ENTERPRISES, INC.		<5
P	ACTCRD	WIPE-OFF CARDS: BLENDS, LEVEL 1	TREND ENTERPRISES, INC.		<5
P	ACTCRD	CONSONANT SOUNDS	MILTON BRADLEY/PLAYSKOOL		<5
P	AUDCAS	SOUNDS FOR YOUNG READERS, VOLUME 2	CLASSROOM MATERIALS CO.		6-10
P	AUDCAS	SOUNDS FOR YOUNG READERS, VOLUME 4	CLASSROOM MATERIALS CO.		6-10
P	AUDCAS	SIGHT & SOUND PHONICS	EDUCATIONAL TEACHING AIDS		21-30
P	AUDCAS	FUN WITH CONSONANT BLENDS	UNITED LEARNING		31-50
P	AUDCRD	CONSONANT BLENDS	AUDIOTRONICS CORPORATION		21-30
P	AUDCRD	CONSONANT DIGRAPHS	AUDIOTRONICS CORPORATION		11-20
P	AUDCRD	THREE-LETTER CONSONANT BLENDS	AUDIOTRONICS CORPORATION		11-20
P	AUDKIT	PRIMARY WORK RECOGNITION	EYE GATE MEDIA	5	31-50
P	AUDKIT	CONSONANT BLEND JUNGLE	EYE GATE MEDIA		6-10

LEVEL	FORMAT	TITLE	PUBLISHER	NT	$PRICE

53 – SKILL: CONSONANT BLENDS & DIGRAPHS

LEVEL	FORMAT	TITLE	PUBLISHER	NT	$PRICE
P	AUDKIT	PHONICS	EYE GATE MEDIA	10	76-100
P	AUDKIT	PHONICS: CONSONANT CLUSTER FUN	EYE GATE MEDIA		6-10
P	AUDKIT	BLENDS & DIGRAPHS	EDUCATIONAL MEDIA, INC.		31-50
P	AUDKIT	KIT 7: BASIC WORD ATTACH – BEG., END. CONSONANT BLENDS	EDUCATIONAL RESEARCH, INC.		101-150
P	AUDKIT	READING CASSETTES: BLENDS & DIGRAPHS	IDEAL SCHOOL SUPPLY COMPANY		31-50
P	AUDKIT	ABC'S OF PHONICS PROGRAM 3: CONSONANT DIGRAPHS W/CASSETTES	Q-ED PRODUCTIONS		76-100
P	AUDKIT	ABC'S OF PHONICS PROGRAM 3: CONSONANT DIGRAPHS W/RECORDS	Q-ED PRODUCTIONS		76-100
P	AUDKIT	ABC'S OF PHONICS PROGRAMS 1 – 3 W/CASSETTES	Q-ED PRODUCTIONS		201-300
P	AUDKIT	ABC'S OF PHONICS PROGRAMS 1 – 3 W/RECORDS	Q-ED PRODUCTIONS		201-300
P	AUDKIT	INITIAL CONSONANT BLENDS, PART 1	MEDIA MATERIALS, INC.		6-10
P	AUDKIT	INITIAL CONSONANT BLENDS, PART 2	MEDIA MATERIALS, INC.		6-10
P	AUDKIT	INITIAL CONSONANT BLENDS, PART 3	MEDIA MATERIALS, INC.		6-10
P	AUDKIT	TWOS COMPANY	MEDIA MATERIALS, INC.		6-10
P	AUDKIT	LISTEN & DO: CONSONANTS	HOUGHTON MIFFLIN COMPANY		101-150
P	AUDKIT	MINISYSTEMS: LISTENING, SEEING, WRITING D,N,L,P,T,CH	CORONET MULTI MEDIA		11-20
P	AUDKIT	MINISYSTEMS: LISTENING, SEEING, SRITING M,B,K,S,G,SH	CORONET MULTI MEDIA		11-20
P	AUDKIT	MINISYSTEMS: THE BLENDS OF S	CORONET MULTI MEDIA		11-20
P	AUDKIT	MINISYSTEMS: THREE-LETTER BLENDS	CORONET MULTI MEDIA		11-20
P	AUDKIT	MINISYSTEMS: REVIEW OF BLENDS	CORONET MULTI MEDIA		11-20
P	AUDKIT	MINISYSTEMS: CONSONANT DIGRAPHS	CORONET MULTI MEDIA		11-20
P	AUDKIT	MINISYSTEMS: REVIEW OF CONSONANT DIGRAPHS	CORONET MULTI MEDIA		11-20
P	AUDKIT	MINISYSTEMS: BUILDING VOCABULARY, BLENDS, VOWELS, CONSONANTS	CORONET MULTI MEDIA		11-20
P	CHART	BLENDS & DIGRAPHS PICTURES FOR PEGBOARD	IDEAL SCHOOL SUPPLY COMPANY		6-10
P	CHART	BLENDS & DIGRAPHS	IDEAL SCHOOL SUPPLY COMPANY		11-20
P	CL SET	REBUS SOUND-CENTERED PICTURE PUZZLES	WORD MAKING PRODUCTIONS, INC.		11-20
P	DITTO	CROSSWORD PUZZLES FOR PHONICS: BLENDS I	CONTINENTAL PRESS, INC.		<5
P	DITTO	NEW PHONICS & WORD ANALYSIS SKILLS: GRADE 1, PART 3	CONTINENTAL PRESS, INC.		<5
P	DITTO	NEW PHONICS & WORD ANALYSIS SKILLS: GRADE 2, PART 1	CONTINENTAL PRESS, INC.		<5
P	DITTO	NEW PHONICS & WORD ANALYSIS SKILLS: GRADE 2, PART 2	CONTINENTAL PRESS, INC.		<5
P	DITTO	NEW PHONICS & WORD ANALYSIS SKILLS: GRADE 3, PART 1	CONTINENTAL PRESS, INC.		<5
P	DITTO	BASIC PHONICS PAK	INSTRUCTIONAL FAIR		21-30
P	DITTO	LEARNING CENTER ACTIVITIES GRADES 2-3	INSTRUCTIONAL FAIR		<5
P	DITTO	CONSONANT BOOK	FRANK SCHAFFER PUBLICATIONS, INC		<5
P	DITTO	SPELLING PROGRAM, BOOK I	FRANK SCHAFFER PUBLICATIONS, INC		<5
P	DITTO	PHONICS PROGRAM, BOOK 11	FRANK SCHAFFER PUBLICATIONS, INC		<5
P	DITTO	PHONICS PROGRAM, BOOK 12	FRANK SCHAFFER PUBLICATIONS, INC		<5
P	DITTO	MIGHT "L" BLENDS	LITTLE KENNY PUBLICATIONS, INC.		<5
P	DITTO	INCREDIBLE "R" BLENDS	LITTLE KENNY PUBLICATIONS, INC.		<5
P	DITTO	SUPER "S" BLENDS	LITTLE KENNY PUBLICATIONS, INC.		<5
P	DITTO	DIGRAPH DISCO	LITTLE KENNY PUBLICATIONS, INC.		<5
P	DITTO	WORD ATTACK SKILLS: CONSONANT BLENDS & DIGRAPHS	EDL/MCGRAW-HILL		6-10
P	DITTO	BEGINNING PHONICS, BOOK 2	GEL-STEN, INC.		<5
P	DITTO	SOUNDS IN WORDS, BOOK 4	GEL-STEN, INC.		<5
P	DITTO	SOUNDS IN WORDS, BOOK 5	GEL-STEN, INC.		<5
P	DITTO	SOUNDS IN WORDS, BOOK 6	GEL-STEN, INC.		<5
P	DITTO	SOUNDS IN WORDS, BOOK 7	GEL-STEN, INC.		<5
P	DITTO	INITIAL CONSONANTS DIGRAPHS/CLUSTERS (GRADES 1 – 2)	INSTRUCTOR PUBLICATIONS, INC.		<5
P	DITTO	SOUND-OFF 3	EDUCATORS PUBLISHING SERVICE		6-10
P	DITTO	PASTING TIME	CREATIVE TEACHING PRESS, INC.		<5
P	DITTO	CONSONANT BLENDS, PART I	INSTRUCTO/MCGRAW-HILL		<5
P	DITTO	CONSONANT BLENDS & DIGRAPHS, PART II	INSTRUCTO/MCGRAW-HILL		<5
P	DITTO	PHONICS IB	HAYES SCHOOL PUBLISHING COMPANY		<5
P	DITTO	PHONICS IIA	HAYES SCHOOL PUBLISHING COMPANY		<5
P	DITTO	PHONICS IIB	HAYES SCHOOL PUBLISHING COMPANY		<5
P	DITTO	PHONICS IIIA	HAYES SCHOOL PUBLISHING COMPANY		<5
P	DITTO	DECODING SKILLS 3	ACTIVITY RESOURCES COMPANY, INC.		<5
P	FILMST	LEARNING ABOUT OUR LANGUAGE, SET 2	AEVAC, INC.		31-50
P	FILMST	BREAK THROUGH FILM STRIPS: CONSONANT SOUND ASSOCIATION	HOUGHTON MIFFLIN COMPANY		76-100
P	FLNLBD	FINAL CONSONANT BLENDS	INSTRUCTO/MCGRAW-HILL		6-10
P	GAME	NEW WORD GAME SAFARI	BFA EDUCATIONAL MEDIA		101-150
P	GAME	CONSONANT BLENDS	FRANK SCHAFFER PUBLICATIONS, INC		<5
P	GAME	PHONICS GAMES	FRANK SCHAFFER PUBLICATIONS, INC		<5
P	GAME	PUNCH-THRU CRDS: CONSONANT BLENDS	CONSTRUCTIVE PLAYTHINGS		<5
P	GAME	PHONICS DISCOVERY	DISCOVERY LEARNING		<5
P	GAME	PHONICS WHEEL	TEACHING RESOURCES CORPORATION		11-20
P	GAME	PHONICS PUZZLES & GAMES	TEACHING RESOURCES CORPORATION		11-20
P	GAME	CONSONANT BLENDS PEEK-A-BOO	READING JOY, INC.		6-10
P	GAME	NEW PHONICS WE USE LEARNING GAMES KITS, KIT ONE	RAND MCNALLY & COMPANY		76-100
P	GAME	SPELLING/LANGUAGE LEARNING GAMES KITS, KIT ONE	RAND MCNALLY & COMPANY		76-100
P	GAME	WORD TREK, BLENDS & DIGRAPHS	DEVELOPMENTAL LEARNING MATERIALS		6-10
P	GAME	CHECKMATE: BLENDS	DM EDUCATIONAL PUBLICATIONS		<5
P	GAME	BLENDS & DIGRAPHS	CREATIVE TEACHING PRESS, INC.		<5
P	GAME	INITIAL CONSONANT BINGO	TREND ENTERPRISES, INC.		6-10
P	GAME	CONSONANT BLENDS & DIGRAPHS PLAYING CARDS	INSTRUCTO/MCGRAW-HILL		6-10
P	GAME	BLENDS & DIGRAPHS	ACTIVITY RESOURCES COMPANY, INC.		<5
P	GUIDE	MERRILL PHONICS SKILL TEXT: COSTUME KIDS, LEVEL B	CHARLES E. MERRILL PUBLISHING CO		<5
P	GUIDE	MERRILL PHONICS SKILL TEXT: SPACE VISITORS, LEVEL C	CHARLES E. MERRILL PUBLISHING CO		<5
P	MANIPU	BLENDS PUZZLES	INCENTIVES FOR LEARNING, INC.		<5
P	MANIPU	PHONICS E-Z LANGUAGE LEARNING SLIDE RULES	E-Z GRADER COMPANY	5	6-10

LEVEL	FORMAT	TITLE	PUBLISHER	NT	$PRICE

53 - SKILL: CONSONANT BLENDS & DIGRAPHS

LEVEL	FORMAT	TITLE	PUBLISHER	NT	$PRICE
P	MANIPU	INITIAL BLENDS	EDUCATIONAL TEACHING AIDS		<5
P	MANIPU	TRAY PUZZLES: PHONICS	IDEAL SCHOOL SUPPLY COMPANY		11-20
P	MANIPU	PHONICS SLENT INITIAL CONSONANTS-FINAL CONSONANTS CLUSTERS	AERO PUBLISHERS, INC.		6-10
P	MANIPU	PHONICS INITIAL CONSONANT BLENDS	AERO PUBLISHERS, INC.		6-10
P	MANIPU	PHONICS CONSONANT DIGRAHS, 2 SOUNDS OF C & G	AERO PUBLISHERS, INC.		6-10
P	MANIPU	PLASTIC OBJECTS, SET 3	HOUGHTON MIFFLIN COMPANY		6-10
P	MANIPU	CONSONANTS	INSTRUCTO/MCGRAW-HILL		11-20
P	MANIPU	ROLLING PHONICS	INSTRUCTO/MCGRAW-HILL		6-10
P	MANIPU	MAGIC TEACHER PUZZLE-PLANS: PHONICS (CONSONANT BLENDS)	HAYES SCHOOL PUBLISHING COMPANY		<5
P	MANIPU	CONSONANT WHEELS	MILTON BRADLEY/PLAYSKOOL		6-10
P	MULTIU	EYE-EAR-HAND PHONICS, SET B: CONSONANT DIGRAPHS & BLENDS	EDUCATIONAL ACTIVITIES, INC.		31-50
P	MULTIM	SOUND IT, UNIT 1	IMPERIAL INTERNATIONAL LEARNING		51-75
P	MULTIM	CONSONANT & VOWEL LAB	ENRICH, INC.		>450
P	MULTIM	READING SKILLS SUPPORT SYSTEM, BOX 2	EDL/MCGRAW-HILL		301-400
P	MULTIM	NEW GOALS IN LISTENING, GRADES 1-3	TROLL ASSOCIATES		76-100
P	MULTIM	SOUND CLOSURE	MILTON BRADLEY/PLAYSKOOL		11-20
P	PI/PRT	LEARNING SLATE: PHONICS	IDEAL SCHOOL SUPPLY COMPANY		<5
P	PUPILB	READ-THE-PICTURE STORYBOOKS	WORD MAKING PRODUCTIONS, INC.		21-30
P	PUPILB	WOG'S LOG BOOK IV	EDUCATORS PUBLISHING SERVICE		<5
P	PUPILB	STORIES FROM SOUND, LEVEL A	EDUCATORS PUBLISHING SERVICE		<5
P	PUPILB	STORIES FROM SOUNDS, LEVEL B	EDUCATORS PUBLISHING SERVICE		<5
P	PUPILB	STORIES FROM SOUNDS, LEVEL C	EDUCATORS PUBLISHING SERVICE		<5
P	PUPILB	STORIES FROM SOUNDS, LEVEL D	EDUCATORS PUBLISHING SERVICE		<5
P	PUPILB	STORIES FROM SOUNDS, LEVEL E	EDUCATORS PUBLISHING SERVICE		<5
P	PUPILB	FIRST PHONICS, PART 1	EDUCATORS PUBLISHING SERVICE		<5
P	PUPILB	FIRST PHONICS, PART 2	EDUCATORS PUBLISHING SERVICE		<5
P	PUPILB	ALPHABET SERIES	EDUCATORS PUBLISHING SERVICE		11-20
P	PUPILB	LEARNING THE LETTERS, BOOK IV	EDUCATORS PUBLISHING SERVICE		<5
P	PUPILB	LEARNING THE LETTERS, BOOK V	EDUCATORS PUBLISHING SERVICE		<5
P	PUPILB	LEARNING THE LETTERS, BOOK VI	EDUCATORS PUBLISHING SERVICE		<5
P	PUPILB	PRIMARY READER, SET 3: BLENDS	MODERN CURRICULUM PRESS		<5
P	PUPILB	PRIMARY READER, SET 4: DIGRAPHS	MODERN CURRICULUM PRESS		<5
P	RECORD	SOUNDS FOR YOUNG READERS, VOLUME 2	CLASSROOM MATERIALS CO.		6-10
P	RECORD	SOUNDS FOR YOUNG READERS, VOLUME 4	CLASSROOM MATERIALS CO.		6-10
P	RECORD	SOUNDS, VOL. 2	CHILDREN'S BOOK & MUSIC CENTER		6-10
P	SKLKIT	SWEET PICKLES PHONICS PROGRAM	BFA EDUCATIONAL MEDIA		101-150
P	SND FS	SOLVING THE PHONICS MYSTERY: CLUE OF THE COMBINING LETTERS	LEARNING TREE FILMSTRIPS		76-100
P	SND FS	STORY OF CH & SCH	HERBERT M. ELKINS COMPANY		11-20
P	SND FS	STORY OF H & WH	HERBERT M. ELKINS COMPANY		11-20
P	SND FS	STORY OF NG	HERBERT M. ELKINS COMPANY		11-20
P	SND FS	STORY OF SH	HERBERT M. ELKINS COMPANY		11-20
P	SND FS	STORY OF TH	HERBERT M. ELKINS COMPANY		11-20
P	SP EQT	LANGUAGE SKILLS PROGRAM: READING-SPELLING COMPREHENSION	SPELLBINDER, INC.		51-75
P	SP EQT	CHARLIE: PHONICS, BEGINNING & ENDING CONSONANT BLENDS	EDUCATIONAL INSIGHTS, INC.		6-10
P	VISKIT	RECIPE FOR READING	EDUCATORS PUBLISHING SERVICE		11-20
P	WKBOOK	CUES & SIGNALS I	ANN ARBOR PUBLISHERS		<5
P	WKBOOK	CUES & SIGNALS II	ANN ARBOR PUBLISHERS		<5
P	WKBOOK	THINK PATTERNS, CONSONANTS & BLENDS	CREATIVE TEACHING ASSOCIATES		6-10
P	WKBOOK	PHONIC PICTURE CARDS	KENWORTHY EDUCATIONAL SERVICE		<5
P	WKBOOK	MOTT BASIC LANG. SKILLS: BOOK 1303	ALLIED EDUCATION COUNCIL		<5
P	WKBOOK	AEVAC PHONICS PROGRAM	AEVAC, INC.	6	11-20
P	WKBOOK	AEVAC PHONICS PROGRAM, BOOK A	AEVAC, INC.		<5
P	WKBOOK	AEVAC PHONICS PROGRAM, BOOK B	AEVAC, INC.		<5
P	WKBOOK	AEVAC PHONICS PROGRAM, BOOK D	AEVAC, INC.		<5
P	WKBOOK	AEVAC PHONICS PROGRAM, BOOK E	AEVAC, INC.		<5
P	WKBOOK	S.T.A.R.T., BOOK 3	EMC CORPORATION		<5
P	WKBOOK	S.T.A.R.T, BOOK 4	EMC CORPORATION		<5
P	WKBOOK	FUN PHONIC JINGLES, BOOK II	WORD MAKING PRODUCTIONS, INC.		<5
P	WKBOOK	HIDDEN PICTURE PUZZLES, BOOK II	WORD MAKING PRODUCTIONS, INC.		<5
P	WKBOOK	PHONICS: VOWELS-BLENDS READING REVIEW	JENN PUBLICATIONS		<5
P	WKBOOK	PHONICS: INITIAL & FINAL BLENDS, GRADE 2	JENN PUBLICATIONS		<5
P	WKBOOK	PHONICS, GRADE 3	JENN PUBLICATIONS		<5
P	WKBOOK	COVE SCHOOL READING PROGRAM	DEVELOPMENTAL LEARNING MATERIALS		76-100
P	WKBOOK	CONSONANT FLIP BOOKS	DEVELOPMENTAL LEARNING MATERIALS		6-10
P	WKBOOK	MERRILL PHONICS SKILL TEXT: COSTUME KIDS, LEVEL B	CHARLES E. MERRILL PUBLISHING CO		<5
P	WKBOOK	MERRILL PHONICS SKILL TEXT: SPACE VISITORS, LEVEL C	CHARLES E. MERRILL PUBLISHING CO		<5
P	WKBOOK	PHONICS BOOK E: CONSONANT BLENDS	SCHOLASTIC BOOK SERVICE		<5
P	WKBOOK	THIRD CONSONANT BOOK	EDUCATORS PUBLISHING SERVICE		<5
P	WKBOOK	PRIMARY PHONICS WORKBOOK 2	EDUCATORS PUBLISHING SERVICE		<5
P	WKBOOK	PRIMARY PHONICS WORKBOOK 3	EDUCATORS PUBLISHING SERVICE		<5
P	WKBOOK	MCP PHONICS WORKBOOKS: LEVEL B	MODERN CURRICULUM PRESS		<5
P	WKBOOK	MCP PHONICS WORKBOOKS: LEVEL C	MODERN CURRICULUM PRESS		<5
P	WKBOOK	SOUNDS WE USE, BOOK 2	HAYES SCHOOL PUBLISHING COMPANY		<5
PI	ACTCRD	ADVANCED PHONICS: CONSONANT DIGRAPHS	INSTRUCTIONAL FAIR		<5
PI	ACTCRD	ADVANCED PHONICS: ADVANCED INITIAL & FINAL BLENDS	INSTRUCTIONAL FAIR		<5
PI	ACTCRD	ADVANCED PHONICS PAK	INSTRUCTIONAL FAIR		21-30
PI	ACTCRD	SOUND SODA	KIDS & COMPANY		<5
PI	AUDKIT	BASIC WORD ATTACK SKILLS	EDUCATIONAL RESEARCH, INC.	4	>450
PI	AUDKIT	CONSONANT CLUSTER FUN	MEDIA MATERIALS, INC.		6-10

LEVEL	FORMAT	TITLE	PUBLISHER	NT	$PRICE

53 - SKILL: CONSONANT BLENDS & DIGRAPHS

LEVEL	FORMAT	TITLE	PUBLISHER	NT	$PRICE
PI	AUDKIT	CONSONANT BLEND JUNGLE	MEDIA MATERIALS, INC.		6-10
PI	AUDKIT	MORE PHONICS	HAMPDEN PUBLICATIONS, INC.		101-150
PI	AUDKIT	FUN WITH CONSONANT BLENDS	HAMPDEN PUBLICATIONS, INC.		21-30
PI	AUDTAP	SPACE FLIGHT	IDEAL SCHOOL SUPPLY COMPANY		6-10
PI	CHART	CONSONANT BLENDS & DIGRAPHS	BEMISS-JASON CORPORATION		6-10
PI	CL SET	SOUND OFF & READ	MAFEX ASSOCIATES, INC.		31-50
PI	DITTO	ADVANCED PHONICS: CONSONANT DIGRAPHS	INSTRUCTIONAL FAIR		<5
PI	DITTO	ADVANCED PHONICS: ADVANCED INITIAL & FINAL BLENDS	INSTRUCTIONAL FAIR		<5
PI	DITTO	ADVANCED PHONICS PAK	INSTRUCTIONAL FAIR		21-30
PI	DITTO	SPELLING PROGRAM, BOOK L	FRANK SCHAFFER PUBLICATIONS, INC		<5
PI	DITTO	DECODING SKILLS A	ACTIVITY RESOURCES COMPANY, INC.		<5
PI	DITTO	DECODING SKILLS B	ACTIVITY RESOURCES COMPANY, INC.		<5
PI	FILMST	PHONICS FILM STRIP SERIES 2	MEDIA MATERIALS, INC.	5	76-100
PI	FILMST	USING CONSONANT BLENDS	MEDIA MATERIALS, INC.		11-20
PI	GAME	PHONICS SOUP, BLEND GAMES	CREATIVE TEACHING ASSOCIATES		6-10
PI	GAME	PHONICS SOUP, DIGRAPH GAMES	CREATIVE TEACHING ASSOCIATES		6-10
PI	GAME	BLEND DOMINOES	IDEAL SCHOOL SUPPLY COMPANY		11-20
PI	GAME	READING ZINGO	BOWMAR/NOBLE PUBLISHERS, INC.		51-75
PI	GAME	PHONICS SOUP GAME PACKAGES: BLENDS	SCOTT RESOURCES, INC.		6-10
PI	GAME	PHONICS SOUP GAME PACKAGES: DIGRAPHS	SCOTT RESOURCES, INC.		6-10
PI	GAME	APPLE TREE	XEROX EDUCATION PUBLICATIONS		51-75
PI	GAME	PLUM TREE	XEROX EDUCATION PUBLICATIONS		51-75
PI	GUIDE	PHONICS IS FUN, BOOK 3	MODERN CURRICULUM PRESS		<5
PI	MANIPU	PHONICS E-Z LANGUAGE LEARNING SLIDE RULES, 3RD & 4TH	E-Z GRADER COMPANY		<5
PI	MANIPU	AERO PHONICS LAB	AERO PUBLISHERS, INC.		76-100
PI	MULTIU	PHONICS SOUP	CREATIVE TEACHING ASSOCIATES	5	31-50
PI	MULTIU	PHONICS IN CONTEXT, SET I	EDUCATIONAL ACTIVITIES, INC.		76-100
PI	MULTIM	WORKING WITH PHONICS	TROLL ASSOCIATES		301-400
PI	PUPILB	EXPLODE THE CODE, BOOK 2	EDUCATORS PUBLISHING SERVICE		<5
PI	PUPILB	EXPLODE THE CODE, BOOK 5	EDUCATORS PUBLISHING SERVICE		<5
PI	SND FS	PHONICS SERIES 2	HAMPDEN PUBLICATIONS, INC.		76-100
PI	SND FS	BASIC WORD ATTACK	EDL/MCGRAW-HILL		301-400
PI	SND FS	WORKING WTH BLENDS & DIGRAPHS	TROLL ASSOCIATES		101-150
PI	SP EQT	LANGUAGE SKILLS PROGRAM: WORD GAMES & PUZZLES	SPELLBINDER, INC.		51-75
PI	TRANSP	LANGUAGE DEVELOPMENT & READING SKILLS	UNITED TRANSPARENCIES, INC.		201-300
PI	WKBOOK	SOUND SODA	CREATIVE TEACHING ASSOCIATES		<5
PI	WKBOOK	SOUND SEARCH	CREATIVE TEACHING ASSOCIATES		6-10
PI	WKBOOK	PREFIXES, SUFFIXES, SYLLABLES	FRANK SCHAFFER PUBLICATIONS, INC		<5
PI	WKBOOK	AEVAC STARTER 101, BOOK 4 (NON-READERS)	AEVAC, INC.		<5
PI	WKBOOK	AEVAC STARTER 101, BOOK 6 (NON-READERS)	AEVAC, INC.		<5
PI	WKBOOK	AEVAC STARTER 101, BOOK 7 (NON-READERS)	AEVAC, INC.		<5
PI	WKBOOK	AEVAC STARTER 101, BOOK 8 (NON-READERS)	AEVAC, INC.		<5
PI	WKBOOK	PRIMARY PHONICS WORKBOOK 4	EDUCATORS PUBLISHING SERVICE		<5
PI	WKBOOK	PHONICS IS FUN, BOOK 3	MODERN CURRICULUM PRESS		<5
PI	WKBOOK	PHONICS FAST & EASY	ACTIVITY RESOURCES COMPANY, INC.		<5
PIJ	CL SET	WEBSTER WORD WHEELS	WEBSTER DIVISION/MCGRAW-HILL		31-50
PIJ	MULTIM	VISUAL AURAL DISCRIMINATIONS, BOOK I	ANN ARBOR PUBLISHERS		<5
PIJ	MULTIM	VISUAL AURAL DISCRIMINATIONS, BOOK II	ANN ARBOR PUBLISHERS		<5
PIJ	MULTIM	VISUAL AURAL DISCRIMINATIONS, BOOK III	ANN ARBOR PUBLISHERS		<5
PIJ	MULTIM	VISUAL AURAL DISCRIMINATIONS, BOOK V	ANN ARBOR PUBLISHERS		<5
I	DITTO	CROSSWORD PUZZLES FOR PHONICS: BLENDS II	CONTINENTAL PRESS, INC.		<5
I	DITTO	SOUNDS IN WORDS, BOOK 10	GEL-STEN, INC.		<5
I	DITTO	SOUNDS IN WORDS, BOOK 11	GEL-STEN, INC.		<5
I	DITTO	SOUNDS IN WORDS, BOOK 16	GEL-STEN, INC.		<5
I	DITTO	CONSONANTS	MILTON BRADLEY/PLAYSKOOL		<5
I	GAME	NEW PHONICS WE USE LEARNING GAMES KITS, KIT TWO	RAND MCNALLY & COMPANY		76-100
I	GUIDE	MERRILL PHONICS SKILL TEXT: SIGN MAKERS, LEVEL D	CHARLES E. MERRILL PUBLISHING CO		<5
I	GUIDE	MERRILL PHONICS SKILL TEXT: DETECTIVE CLUB, LEVEL E	CHARLES E. MERRILL PUBLISHING CO		<5
I	MULTIM	GAMES 'N' FRAMES: VINCENT VAN BLEEP	IMPERIAL INTERNATIONAL LEARNING		21-30
I	MULTIM	SELECT-A-SKILL KIT, UNIT 1: MYSTERY ADVENTURE	IMPERIAL INTERNATIONAL LEARNING		51-75
I	MULTIM	SELECT-A-SKILL KIT, UNIT 1: MYSTERY ADVENTURE	IMPERIAL INTERNATIONAL LEARNING		51-75
I	RECORD	SOUND SKILLS FOR UPPER GRADES	CLASSROOM MATERIALS CO.	3	21-30
I	RECORD	SOUND SKILLS FOR UPPER GRADES, VOLUME 1	CLASSROOM MATERIALS CO.		6-10
I	SP EQT	LANGUAGE SKILLS PROGRAM: READING-SPELLING COMPREHENSION (RP)	SPELLBINDER, INC.		51-75
I	WKBOOK	TALES FOR TRANSFER SKILL SERIES	ANN ARBOR PUBLISHERS		<5
I	WKBOOK	MERRILL PHONICS SKILL TEXT: SIGN MAKERS, LEVEL D	CHARLES E. MERRILL PUBLISHING CO		<5
I	WKBOOK	MERRILL PHONICS SKILL TEXT: DETETIVE CLUB, LEVEL E	CHARLES E. MERRILL PUBLISHING CO		<5
IJ	ACTCRD	WORD CIRCUS	LESWING PRESS		6-10
IJ	MULTIM	CREEPY CREATURES (RL 2)	INSTRUCTO/MCGRAW-HILL		11-20
IJ	MULTIM	FLIGHT TIME (RL 2)	INSTRUCTO/MCGRAW-HILL		11-20
IJ	MULTIM	STAR TRIP (RL 2)	INSTRUCTO/MCGRAW-HILL		11-20
IJ	MULTIM	SPORT SCRAMBLE (RL 3)	INSTRUCTO/MCGRAW-HILL		11-20
IJ	WKBOOK	BOOK ONE, PART ONE: PHONIC ANALYSIS ACTIVITIES	T.S. DENISON & COMPANY		6-10
IJS	ACTCRD	CANTANKEROUS CONSONANTS	LESWING PRESS		6-10
IJS	ACTCRD	WORD KALEIDOSCOPE	LESWING PRESS		6-10
IJS	ACTCRD	DOUBLE TROUBLE	LESWING PRESS		6-10
IJS	ACTCRD	CONSONANT CAPERS	LESWING PRESS		6-10
IJS	AUDKIT	HITS, LEVEL 1: AMERICA, TODAY'S THE DAY	MODULEARN, INC.		11-20
IJS	AUDKIT	HITS, LEVEL 1: AMERICA, LONELY PEOPLE	MODULEARN, INC.		11-20

LEVEL	FORMAT	TITLE	PUBLISHER	NT	$PRICE

---

53 - SKILL: CONSONANT BLENDS & DIGRAPHS

LEVEL	FORMAT	TITLE	PUBLISHER	NT	$PRICE
IJS	AUDKIT	HITS, LEVEL 1: SANTANA, LET IT SHINE	MODULEARN, INC.		11-20
IJS	AUDKIT	HITS, LEVEL 1: AMERICA, TIN MAN	MODULEARN, INC.		11-20
IJS	AUDKIT	HITS, LEVEL 1: AMERICA, VENTURA HIGHWAY	MODULEARN, INC.		11-20
IJS	AUDKIT	HITS, LEVEL 1: JAMES TAYLOR, SWEET BABY JAMES	MODULEARN, INC.		11-20
IJS	AUDKIT	HITS, LEVEL 1: PAUL SIMON, EL CONDOR PASA	MODULEARN, INC.		11-20
IJS	AUDKIT	HITS, LEVEL 1: BLACKBYRDS, YOU'VE GOT THAT SOMETHING	MODULEARN, INC.		11-20
IJS	AUDKIT	HITS, LEVEL 2: SPINNERS, GAMES PEOPLE PLAY	MODULEARN, INC.		11-20
IJS	AUDKIT	HITS, LEVEL 2: BELLAMY BROTHERS, LET YOUR LOVE FLOW	MODULEARN, INC.		11-20
IJS	AUDKIT	HITS, LEVEL 2: JOHN SEBASTIAN, WELCOME BACK	MODULEARN, INC.		11-20
IJS	AUDKIT	HITS, LEVEL 2: DONNIE & MARIE OSMOND, IT TAKES TWO	MODULEARN, INC.		11-20
IJS	AUDKIT	HITS, LEVEL 3: JOHNNY NASH, I CAN SEE CLEARLY NOW	MODULEARN, INC.		11-20
IJS	AUDKIT	HITS, LEVEL 3: JAMES TAYLOR, SHOWER THE PEOPLE	MODULEARN, INC.		11-20
IJS	AUDKIT	HITS, LEVEL 3: FIREFALL, LIVIN' AIN'T LIVIN'	MODULEARN, INC.		11-20
IJS	MULTIU	PHONICS IN CONTEXT, SET II	EDUCATIONAL ACTIVITIES, INC.		51-75
IJS	PICTUR	CUC PICTURE-WORD PROGRAM	PAUL S. AMIDON & ASSOC., INC.		11-20
JS	AUDKIT	READING CASSETTES: CONSONANTS & DIGRAPHS	IDEAL SCHOOL SUPPLY COMPANY		51-75
JS	AUDKIT	READING CASSETTES: BLENDS	IDEAL SCHOOL SUPPLY COMPANY		31-50
JS	AUDKIT	USING PHONICS SERIES	MEDIA MATERIALS, INC.		101-150
JS	AUDKIT	LEARNING PHONICS	HAMPDEN PUBLICATIONS, INC.		101-150
JS	PICTUR	40-FOURS, SET 1: S SOUND	MODERN EDUCATION CORPORATION		11-20
JS	PICTUR	40-FOURS, SET 2: R SOUND	MODERN EDUCATION CORPORATION		11-20
JS	SND FS	ADVANCED WORD ATTACK	EDL/MCGRAW-HILL		301-400
JS	WKBOOK	NEW STREAMLINED ENGLISH SERIES: SKILL BOOK 2	NEW READERS PRESS		<5
S	AUDKIT	CONSONANTS & DIGRAPHS	EDUCATIONAL MEDIA, INC.		51-75
S	AUDKIT	PHONICS SERIES 2	HAMPDEN PUBLICATIONS, INC.		76-100
S	SND FS	USING CONSONANT BLENDS	MEDIA MATERIALS, INC.		11-20

---

54 - SKILL: CONSONANTS - HARD & SOFT

LEVEL	FORMAT	TITLE	PUBLISHER	NT	$PRICE
P	ACTCRD	READING SELF-CHECK: SPECIAL VOWELS & CONSONANTS	FRANK SCHAFFER PUBLICATIONS, INC		<5
P	AUDKIT	ABC'S OF PHONICS PROGRAMS 1 - 3 W/RECORDS	Q-ED PRODUCTIONS		201-300
P	AUDKIT	ROAD TO READING, PHONICS PROGRAM, LANGUAGE SKILLS	SPOKEN ARTS, INC.		301-400
P	AUDKIT	MINISYSTEMS: HARD & SOFT C & G	CORONET MULTI MEDIA		11-20
P	DITTO	SOUNDS IN WORDS, BOOK 7	GEL-STEN, INC.		<5
P	DITTO	DECODING SKILLS 3	ACTIVITY RESOURCES COMPANY, INC.		<5
P	GAME	RHYMING WORDS & VARIANT CONSONANTS	ACTIVITY RESOURCES COMPANY, INC.		<5
P	MANIPU	PHONICS CONSONANT DIGRAHS, 2 SOUNDS OF C & G	AERO PUBLISHERS, INC.		6-10
P	MULTIM	SOUND IT, UNIT 1	IMPERIAL INTERNATIONAL LEARNING		51-75
P	MULTIM	READING SKILLS SUPPORT SYSTEM, BOX 2	EDL/MCGRAW-HILL		301-400
P	PUPILB	WOG'S LOG BOOK III	EDUCATORS PUBLISHING SERVICE		<5
P	PUPILB	WOG'S LOG BOOK VII	EDUCATORS PUBLISHING SERVICE		<5
P	PUPILB	WOG'S LOG BOOK VIII	EDUCATORS PUBLISHING SERVICE		<5
P	SND FS	STORY OF C	HERBERT M. ELKINS COMPANY		11-20
P	SND FS	STORY OF G	HERBERT M. ELKINS COMPANY		11-20
P	SND FS	TICK TOCK TIME & OTHER STORIES	CHILDREN'S BOOK & MUSIC CENTER		51-75
P	SND FS	JELLY JAR BLUES & OTHER STORIES	CHILDREN'S BOOK & MUSIC CENTER		51-75
P	WKBOOK	PHONICS, GRADE 3	JENN PUBLICATIONS		<5
PI	AUDKIT	CHANGEABLE CONSONANTS	MEDIA MATERIALS, INC.		6-10
PI	AUDKIT	HARD & SOFT C & G	MEDIA MATERIALS, INC.		6-10
PI	AUDKIT	CONSONANTS COUNT	MEDIA MATERIALS, INC.		6-10
PI	AUDKIT	MORE PHONICS	HAMPDEN PUBLICATIONS, INC.		101-150
PI	DITTO	DECODING SKILLS A	ACTIVITY RESOURCES COMPANY, INC.		<5
PI	DITTO	FUNNY FACE PHONICS	ACTIVITY RESOURCES COMPANY, INC.		<5
PI	MANIPU	AERO PHONICS LAB	AERO PUBLISHERS, INC.		76-100
PI	WKBOOK	AEVAC STARTER 101, BOOK 9 (NON-READERS)	AEVAC, INC.		<5
PI	WKBOOK	AFVAC STARTER 101, BOOK 10 (NON-READERS)	AEVAC, INC.		<5
PIJ	MULTIU	C & G TRIO	LESWING PRESS		6-10
I	DITTO	SOUNDS IN WORDS, BOOK 10	GEL-STEN, INC.		<5
I	DITTO	SOUNDS IN WORDS, BOOK 16	GEL-STEN, INC.		<5
I	GAME	NEW PHONICS WE USE LEARNING GAMES KITS, KIT TWO	RAND MCNALLY & COMPANY		76-100
I	GUIDE	MERRILL PHONICS SKILL TEXT: SIGN MAKERS, LEVEL D	CHARLES E. MERRILL PUBLISHING CO		<5
I	RECORD	SOUND SKILLS FOR UPPER GRADES	CLASSROOM MATERIALS CO.	3	21-30
I	RECORD	SOUND SKILLS FOR UPPER GRADES, VOLUME 1	CLASSROOM MATERIALS CO.		6-10
I	WKBOOK	MERRILL PHONICS SKILL TEXT: SIGN MAKERS, LEVEL D	CHARLES E. MERRILL PUBLISHING CO		<5
IJ	ACTCRD	WORD FUN	LESWING PRESS		6-10
IJS	ACTCRD	CANTANKEROUS CONSONANTS	LESWING PRESS		6-10
IJS	AUDCRD	CONFUSING CONSONANTS	AUDIOTRONICS CORPORATION		11-20
J	WKBOOK	MOTT BASIC LANG. SKILLS: BOOK 1306	ALLIED EDUCATION COUNCIL		<5
JS	AUDKIT	READING CASSETTES: CONSONANTS & DIGRAPHS	IDEAL SCHOOL SUPPLY COMPANY		51-75
JS	AUDKIT	USING PHONICS SERIES	MEDIA MATERIALS, INC.		101-150
JS	SND FS	ADVANCED WORD ATTACK	EDL/MCGRAW-HILL		301-400
JS	WKBOOK	NEW STREAMLINED ENGLISH SERIES: SKILL BOOK 5	NEW READERS PRESS		<5

---

55 - SKILL: CONSONANTS - SILENT

LEVEL	FORMAT	TITLE	PUBLISHER	NT	$PRICE
RP	FLASH	LEARN THE ALPHABET	MILTON BRADLEY/PLAYSKOOL		<5
RPI	AUDKIT	PHONICS SERIES	MEDIA MATERIALS, INC.	10	76-100
P	ACTCRD	READING SELF-CHECK: SPECIAL VOWELS & CONSONANTS	FRANK SCHAFFER PUBLICATIONS, INC		<5
P	ACTCRD	BASIC SKILLS KIT- PHONICS H	EDUCATIONAL PERFORMANCE ASSOC.		31-50
P	AUDCRD	SILENT CONSONANTS	AUDIOTRONICS CORPORATION		11-20
P	AUDKIT	PHONICS	EYE GATE MEDIA	10	76-100

LEVEL	FORMAT	TITLE	PUBLISHER	NT	$PRICE

55 - SKILL: CONSONANTS - SILENT

LEVEL	FORMAT	TITLE	PUBLISHER	NT	$PRICE
P	AUDKIT	PHONICS: VARIANTS & SILENT LETTERS	EYE GATE MEDIA		6-10
P	AUDKIT	ROAD TO READING, PHONICS PROGRAM, LANGUAGE SKILLS	SPOKEN ARTS, INC.		301-400
P	AUDKIT	MINISYSTEMS: B WITH L & R	CORONET MULTI MEDIA		11-20
P	AUDKIT	MINISYSTEMS: C WITH L & R	CORONET MULTI MEDIA		11-20
P	AUDKIT	MINISYSTEMS: G WITH L & R	CORONET MULTI MEDIA		11-20
P	AUDKIT	MINISYSTEMS: F WITH L & R	CORONET MULTI MEDIA		11-20
P	AUDKIT	MINISYSTEMS: P WITH L & R	CORONET MULTI MEDIA		11-20
P	AUDKIT	MINISYSTEMS: D WITH L & R	CORONET MULTI MEDIA		11-20
P	DITTO	SOUNDS IN WORDS, BOOK 7	GEL-STEN, INC.		<5
P	GAME	RHYMING WORDS & VARIANT CONSONANTS	ACTIVITY RESOURCES COMPANY, INC.		<5
P	MANIPU	PHONICS SILENT INITIAL CONSONANTS-FINAL CONSONANTS CLUSTERS	AERO PUBLISHERS, INC.		6-10
P	MULTIM	SOUND IT, UNIT 1	IMPERIAL INTERNATIONAL LEARNING		51-75
P	MULTIM	LEARNING PHONICS	MEDIA MARKETING, INC.		51-75
P	PUPILB	WOG'S LOG BOOK VII	EDUCATORS PUBLISHING SERVICE		<5
P	PUPILB	WOG'S LOG BOOK VIII	EDUCATORS PUBLISHING SERVICE		<5
P	PUPILB	LEARNING THE LETTERS, BOOK V	EDUCATORS PUBLISHING SERVICE		<5
P	PUPILB	LEARNING THE LETTERS, BOOK VI	EDUCATORS PUBLISHING SERVICE		<5
P	SND FS	STORY OF F & PH	HERBERT M. ELKINS COMPANY		11-20
P	SND FS	STORY OF GH	HERBERT M. ELKINS COMPANY		11-20
P	SND FS	STORY OF NG	HERBERT M. ELKINS COMPANY		11-20
P	SND FS	STORY OF Q	HERBERT M. ELKINS COMPANY		11-20
P	SND FS	STORY OF X	HERBERT M. ELKINS COMPANY		11-20
P	WKBOOK	AEVAC PHONICS PROGRAM, BOOK E	AEVAC, INC.		<5
P	WKBOOK	PHONICS, GRADE 3	JENN PUBLICATIONS		<5
P	WKBOOK	THIRD CONSONANT BOOK	EDUCATORS PUBLISHING SERVICE		<5
PI	AUDKIT	USING PHONICS	EBSCO CURRICULUM MATERIALS		51-75
PI	AUDKIT	VOWEL SOUNDS & SILENT LETTERS	NATIONAL BOOK COMPANY		21-30
PI	AUDKIT	CHANGEABLE CONSONANTS	MEDIA MATERIALS, INC.		6-10
PI	AUDKIT	SILENT LETTERS	MEDIA MATERIALS, INC.		6-10
PI	AUDKIT	VARIANTS AND SILENT LETTERS	MEDIA MATERIALS, INC.		6-10
PI	AUDKIT	CONSONANTS COUNT	MEDIA MATERIALS, INC.		6-10
PI	AUDKIT	MORE PHONICS	HAMPDEN PUBLICATIONS, INC.		101-150
PI	MANIPU	AERO PHONICS LAB	AERO PUBLISHERS, INC.		76-100
PI	PUPILB	EXPLODE THE CODE, BOOK 5	EDUCATORS PUBLISHING SERVICE		<5
PIJ	MULTIM	VISUAL AURAL DISCRIMINATIONS, BOOK V	ANN ARBOR PUBLISHERS		<5
I	DITTO	SOUNDS IN WORDS, BOOK 10	GEL-STEN, INC.		<5
I	DITTO	SOUNDS IN WORDS, BOOK 16	GEL-STEN, INC.		<5
I	GAME	WORDFACTS GAMES	MILTON BRADLEY/PLAYSKOOL		21-30
I	GUIDE	MERRILL PHONICS SKILL TEXT: SIGN MAKERS, LEVEL D	CHARLES E. MERRILL PUBLISHING CO		<5
I	GUIDE	MERRILL PHONICS SKILL TEXT: DETECTIVE CLUB, LEVEL E	CHARLES E. MERRILL PUBLISHING CO		<5
I	MULTIM	GAMES 'N' FRAMES: GETTING TO KNOW THE UNKNOWN	IMPERIAL INTERNATIONAL LEARNING		21-30
I	WKBOOK	MERRILL PHONICS SKILL TEXT: SIGN MAKERS, LEVEL D	CHARLES E. MERRILL PUBLISHING CO		<5
I	WKBOOK	MERRILL PHONICS SKILL TEXT: DETECTIVE CLUB, LEVEL E	CHARLES E. MERRILL PUBLISHING CO		<5
IJS	ACTCRD	CANTANKEROUS CONSONANTS	LESWING PRESS		6-10
IJS	ACTCRD	CONSONANT CAPERS	LESWING PRESS		6-10
IJS	AUDCRD	CONFUSING CONSONANTS	AUDIOTRONICS CORPORATION		11-20
IJS	AUDCRD	LAZY LETTERS	AUDIOTRONICS CORPORATION		21-30
J	WKBOOK	MOTT BASIC LANG. SKILLS: BOOK 1306	ALLIED EDUCATION COUNCIL		<5
JS	AUDKIT	READING CASSETTES: CONSONANTS & DIGRAPHS	IDEAL SCHOOL SUPPLY COMPANY		51-75
JS	AUDKIT	LEARNING PHONICS	HAMPDEN PUBLICATIONS, INC.		101-150
JS	SND FS	ADVANCED WORD ATTACK	EDL/MCGRAW-HILL		301-400
JS	WKBOOK	NEW STREAMLINED ENGLISH SERIES: SKILL BOOK 5	NEW READERS PRESS		<5

56 - SKILL: VOWELS - GENERAL

LEVEL	FORMAT	TITLE	PUBLISHER	NT	$PRICE
RP	A/VKIT	RIDDLE-A-RHYME	EYE GATE MEDIA		101-150
RP	MULTIM	ALPHA-SOUND PROGRAM, GROUP 2	CLEARVUE, INC.		151-200
RP	SKLKIT	AIMS: VOWELS KIT	CONTINENTAL PRESS, INC.		51-75
P	ACTCRD	THINK PATTERNS, VOWELS TASK CARDS	CREATIVE TEACHING ASSOCIATES		11-20
P	ACTCRD	VOWELS, B	BARNELL LOFT, LTD.		6-10
P	ACTCRD	SPREAD I	INCENTIVES FOR LEARNING, INC.		21-30
P	ACTCRD	VOWEL FLIPSTRIPS	PHONOVISUAL PRODUCTS, INC.		<5
P	ACTCRD	SKILLBUILDERS	PHONOVISUAL PRODUCTS, INC.		<5
P	ACTCRD	VOWEL PICTURE PACK	PHONOVISUAL PRODUCTS, INC.		<5
P	ACTCRD	LANGUAGE ACTIVITY CARDS: VOWELS & CONSONANTS	WEBER COSTELLO COMPANY		6-10
P	ACTCRD	PRIMARY PHONICS-SKILL DRILLS WITH MOTIVATORS	SVE		31-50
P	ACTCRD	VOWEL SKILL CARDS	MILTON BRADLEY/PLAYSKOOL		<5
P	AUDCAS	LISTENING FOR SOUNDS	MEDIA MARKETING, INC.		51-75
P	AUDCAS	FUN WITH VOWEL SOUNDS	UNITED LEARNING		31-50
P	AUDKIT	PRIMARY WORK RECOGNITION	EYE GATE MEDIA	5	31-50
P	AUDKIT	VOWEL VACATION	EYE GATE MEDIA		6-10
P	AUDKIT	VOWELS	EDUCATIONAL MEDIA, INC.		51-75
P	AUDKIT	VOWEL ENRICHMENT	EDUCATIONAL MEDIA, INC.		51-75
P	AUDKIT	CREATURE TEACHERS	ECONOMY COMPANY		151-200
P	AUDKIT	KIT 82: BASIC PHONICS, LEVEL 2	EDUCATIONAL RESEARCH, INC.		101-150
P	AUDKIT	KIT 83: BASIC PHONICS, LEVEL 3	EDUCATIONAL RESEARCH, INC.		101-150
P	AUDKIT	KIT 84: BASIC PHONICS, LEVEL 4	EDUCATIONAL RESEARCH, INC.		101-150
P	AUDKIT	VOWEL SOUNDS AUDIO LESSONS	SVE		76-100
P	CHART	VOWELS	IDEAL SCHOOL SUPPLY COMPANY		11-20
P	CL SET	PHONETIC VOWELS	MAFEX ASSOCIATES, INC.		31-50

LEVEL	FORMAT	TITLE	PUBLISHER	NT	$PRICE

----
56 - SKILL: VOWELS - GENERAL

LEVEL	FORMAT	TITLE	PUBLISHER	NT	$PRICE
P	DITTO	READ, THINK, COLOR	FRANK SCHAFFER PUBLICATIONS, INC		<5
P	DITTO	PHONICS FUN: VOWEL	PHONOVISUAL PRODUCTS, INC.		6-10
P	DITTO	SOUNDS IN WORDS, BOOK 4	GEL-STEN, INC.		<5
P	DITTO	SOUNDS IN WORDS, BOOK 5	GEL-STEN, INC.		<5
P	DITTO	READING ENRICHMENT ACTIVITIES	XEROX EDUCATION PUBLICATIONS		<5
P	DITTO	VOWEL HOWL	MILTON BRADLEY/PLAYSKOOL		<5
P	FLASH	VOWELS: FLIP & LEARN FLASHBOOK	MILTON BRADLEY/PLAYSKOOL		<5
P	GAME	VOWEL BINGO	CONSTRUCTIVE PLAYTHINGS		<5
P	GAME	VOWEL LOTTO	GARRARD PUBLISHING COMPANY		<5
P	MULTIM	LISTENING YOUR WAY TO BETTER READING	ASSOCIATED EDUCATIONAL MATERIALS		301-400
P	MULTIM	SOUND IT, UNIT 2	IMPERIAL INTERNATIONAL LEARNING		51-75
P	MULTIM	LEARNING PHONICS	MEDIA MARKETING, INC.		51-75
P	MULTIM	BLENDING SOUNDS WITH COCO & CHARLIE	EDUCATIONAL ACTIVITIES, INC.		31-50
P	MULTIM	READING SKILLS SUPPORT SYSTEM, BOX 3	EDL/MCGRAW-HILL		301-400
P	PICTUR	PICTURE A VOWEL SOUND II	DEVELOPMENTAL LEARNING MATERIALS		11-20
P	PUPILB	ANIMAL PUZZLERS PHONICS ACTIVITIES	CREATIVE TEACHING ASSOCIATES		<5
P	SND FS	VOWELS & CONSONANTS	HERBERT M. ELKINS COMPANY		11-20
P	SP EQT	AUDITORY SKILLS: VOWEL DISCRIMINATION	INSTRUCTIONAL INDUSTRIES (G.E.)		101-150
P	WKBOOK	CUES & SIGNALS III	ANN ARBOR PUBLISHERS		<5
P	WKBOOK	THINK PATTERNS, VOWELS	CREATIVE TEACHING ASSOCIATES		6-10
P	WKBOOK	VOWEL OWL	CREATIVE TEACHING ASSOCIATES		<5
P	WKBOOK	READ, THINK, COLOR	FRANK SCHAFFER PUBLICATIONS, INC		<5
P	WKBOOK	MORE READ, THINK, COLOR	FRANK SCHAFFER PUBLICATIONS, INC		<5
P	WKBOOK	AEVAC PHONICS PROGRAM	AEVAC, INC.	6	11-20
P	WKBOOK	AEVAC PHONICS PROGRAM, BOOK F	AEVAC, INC.		<5
P	WKBOOK	S.T.A.R.T, BOOK 10	EMC CORPORATION		<5
P	WKBOOK	S.T.A.R.T., BOOK 11	EMC CORPORATION		<5
P	WKBOOK	S.T.A.R.T., BOOK 18	EMC CORPORATION		<5
P	WKBOOK	NEW PHONICS WORKBOOK, BOOK C	MODERN CURRICULUM PRESS		<5
P	WKBOOK	NEW PHONICS WORKBOOK, BOOK D	MODERN CURRICULUM PRESS		<5
P	WKBOOK	PHONICS WORKBOOK, BOOK D	MODERN CURRICULUM PRESS		<5
PI	ACTCRD	VOWEL OWL	KIDS & COMPANY		<5
PI	ACTCRD	WORD FAMILIES	TEACHING RESOURCES CORPORATION		31-50
PI	AUDKIT	BASIC WORD ATTACK SKILLS	EDUCATIONAL RESEARCH, INC.	4	>450
PI	DITTO	SPIRIT MASTER WORKBOOKS: VOWELS	IDEAL SCHOOL SUPPLY COMPANY		6-10
PI	DITTO	BASIC READING SKILLS	EDUCATIONAL INSIGHTS, INC.		51-75
PI	GAME	APPLE TREE	XEROX EDUCATION PUBLICATIONS		51-75
PI	GAME	PLUM TREE	XEROX EDUCATION PUBLICATIONS		51-75
PI	MULTIU	PHONICS SOUP	CREATIVE TEACHING ASSOCIATES	5	31-50
PI	MULTIU	CREATURE FEATURES: STRUCTURAL ANALYSIS	EDUCATIONAL ACTIVITIES, INC.		51-75
PI	RECORD	PHONICS & WORD DEVELOPMENT	EDUCATIONAL ACTIVITIES, INC.		31-50
PI	SND FS	INDEPENDENT WORD PERCEPTION	ASSOCIATED EDUCATIONAL MATERIALS		151-200
PIJ	ACTCRD	VOWEL QUARTET	LESWING PRESS		6-10
I	GUIDE	MERRILL PHONICS SKILL TEXT: WHIZ KID, LEVEL F	CHARLES E. MERRILL PUBLISHING CO		<5
I	SP EQT	LANGUAGE SKILLS PROGRAM: READING-SPELLING COMPREHENSION	SPELLBINDER, INC.		51-75
I	WKBOOK	MERRILL PHONICS SKILL TEXT: WHIZ KID, LEVEL F	CHARLES E. MERRILL PUBLISHING CO		<5
IJS	GAME	AUTO PHONICS: VOWEL REVIEW	EDUCATIONAL ACTIVITIES, INC.		<5
IJS	PICTUR	CUC PICTURE-WORD PROGRAM	PAUL S. AMIDON & ASSOC., INC.		11-20
JS	AUDKIT	READING CASSETTES: VOWELS	IDEAL SCHOOL SUPPLY COMPANY		51-75
S	AUDKIT	VOWELS (IMMEDIATE-SECONDARY)	EDUCATIONAL MEDIA, INC.		31-50

----
57 - SKILL: VOWELS - SHORT

LEVEL	FORMAT	TITLE	PUBLISHER	NT	$PRICE
R	AUDKIT	SOUNDS & SYMBOLS	EDUCATORS PUBLISHING SERVICE		101-150
RP	ACTCRD	FORM-A-SOUND	IDEAL SCHOOL SUPPLY COMPANY		11-20
RP	AUDKIT	PERCEIVE & RESPOND, VOLUME II	MODERN EDUCATION CORPORATION		76-100
RP	DITTO	LONG & SHORT VOWELS	CONTINENTAL PRESS, INC.		<5
RP	DITTO	SHORT VOWELS	CREATIVE TEACHING PRESS, INC.		<5
RP	FILMST	EARLY READING RECOGNITION SKILLS	CLASSROOM MATERIALS CO.		51-75
RP	GAME	GAMEBOARD KIT A	READING JOY, INC.		6-10
RP	GUIDE	PHONICS IS FUN, BOOK 1	MODERN CURRICULUM PRESS		<5
RP	MANIPU	MIX 'N' MATCH PUZZLES: SHORT VOWELS	TREND ENTERPRISES, INC.		6-10
RP	MULTIU	READING STEP BY STEP, UNIT 2	IMPERIAL INTERNATIONAL LEARNING		51-75
RP	MULTIU	READING READINESS: PARTS I, II, III, IV, V, VI	EDUCATIONAL DIMENSIONS CORP.		101-150
RP	MULTIM	ALPHA-SOUND PROGRAM, GROUP 2	CLEARVUE, INC.		151-200
RP	MULTIM	HELP: VOWELS	CENTER FOR EARLY LEARNING		6-10
RP	MULTIM	HEAR-SEE-SAY, PHONICS READING COURSE	MELODY HOUSE PUBLISHING COMPANY		11-20
RP	MULTIM	WORDS & SOUND SERIES, SET 1	EDL/MCGRAW-HILL		101-150
RP	MULTIM	WORDS & SOUND SERIES, SET 2	EDL/MCGRAW-HILL		101-150
RP	MULTIM	WORDS & SOUND SERIES, SET 3	EDL/MCGRAW-HILL		101-150
RP	MULTIM	WORDS & SOUND SERIES, SET 4	EDL/MCGRAW-HILL		101-150
RP	PUPILB	ALPHABET BOOKS	CHILD'S WORLD	5	21-30
RP	PUPILB	ALPHABET BOOKS: PLAY WITH "A" & "T"	CHILD'S WORLD		<5
RP	PUPILB	ALPHABET BOOKS: PLAY WITH "E" & "D"	CHILD'S WORLD		<5
RP	PUPILB	ALPHABET BOOKS: PLAY WITH "I" & "G"	CHILD'S WORLD		<5
RP	PUPILB	ALPHABET BOOKS: PLAY WITH "O" & "G"	CHILD'S WORLD		<5
RP	PUPILB	ALPHABET BOOKS: PLAY WITH "U" & "G"	CHILD'S WORLD		<5
RP	PUPILB	SHORT & LONG VOWELS PLAY A GAME	CHILD'S WORLD	5	21-30
RP	PUPILB	SHORT "A" & LONG "A" PLAY A GAME	CHILD'S WORLD		6-10
RP	PUPILB	SHORT "E" & LONG "E" PLAY A GAME	CHILD'S WORLD		6-10

LEVEL	FORMAT	TITLE	PUBLISHER	NT	$PRICE

57 - SKILL: VOWELS - SHORT

LEVEL	FORMAT	TITLE	PUBLISHER	NT	$PRICE
RP	PUPILB	SHORT "I" & LONG "I" PLAY A GAME	CHILD'S WORLD		6-10
RP	PUPILB	SHORT "O" & LONG "O" PLAY A GAME	CHILD'S WORLD		6-10
RP	PUPILB	SHORT "U" & LONG "U" PLAY A GAME	CHILD'S WORLD		6-10
RP	SKLKIT	AIMS: VOWELS KIT	CONTINENTAL PRESS, INC.		51-75
RP	SND FS	READ ALONG BEGINNING PHONICS, SET 1	CORONET MULTI MEDIA		101-150
RP	SP EQT	LEARNING LETTER SOUNDS, KIT H	BORG-WARNER EDUCATIONAL SYSTEMS		101-150
RP	SP EQT	LEARNING LETTER SOUNDS, KIT HH	BORG-WARNER EDUCATIONAL SYSTEMS		101-150
RP	VISKIT	ALPHABET SERIES	WALKER EDUCATIONAL BOOK CORP.		31-50
RP	WKBOOK	PRIMARY PHONICS WORKBOOK 1	EDUCATORS PUBLISHING SERVICE		<5
RP	WKBOOK	PHONICS IS FUN, BOOK 1	MODERN CURRICULUM PRESS		<5
RPI	AUDKIT	PHONICS SERIES	MEDIA MATERIALS, INC.	10	76-100
RPI	GUIDE	WORD ATTACK JOY	READING JOY, INC.		6-10
P	ACTCRD	BASIC PHONICS: SHORT VOWELS	INSTRUCTIONAL FAIR		<5
P	ACTCRD	BASIC PHONICS PAK	INSTRUCTIONAL FAIR		21-30
P	ACTCRD	READING SELF-CHECK: SHORT VOWELS, LONG VOWELS	FRANK SCHAFFER PUBLICATIONS, INC		<5
P	ACTCRD	WIPE-OFF CARDS: SHORT VOWELS	CONSTRUCTIVE PLAYTHINGS		<5
P	ACTCRD	RAINBOW WORD BUILDERS	KENWORTHY EDUCATIONAL SERVICE		<5
P	ACTCRD	SAY THE SOUNDS	KENWORTHY EDUCATIONAL SERVICE		<5
P	ACTCRD	SPEECH SOUNDS PICTURE CARDS: CONSONANTS & VOWELS	TEACHING RESOURCES CORPORATION		6-10
P	ACTCRD	PHONIC HELPERS	EDUCATIONAL PROGRAMMERS, INC.		11-20
P	ACTCRD	TUTORGRAM: VOWELS	ENRICHMENT READING CORP OF AMER.		11-20
P	ACTCRD	TUTORGRAM: MATCHING VOWEL SOUNDS	ENRICHMENT READING CORP OF AMER.		11-20
P	ACTCRD	GROUP-SIZE VOWEL CARDS	GARRARD PUBLISHING COMPANY		<5
P	ACTCRD	MARK ON-WIPE OFF CARDS: VOWEL SOUNDS	IDEAL SCHOOL SUPPLY COMPANY		<5
P	ACTCRD	MAGIC CARDS: VOWELS	IDEAL SCHOOL SUPPLY COMPANY		6-10
P	ACTCRD	SOUND FOUNDATION, PROGRAM 2	DEVELOPMENTAL LEARNING MATERIALS		11-20
P	ACTCRD	LINQUISTIC PACER	DM EDUCATIONAL PUBLICATIONS		6-10
P	ACTCRD	VOWEL PACER	DM EDUCATIONAL PUBLICATIONS		<5
P	ACTCRD	LONG & SHORT VOWELS	GEL-STEN, INC.		6-10
P	ACTCRD	SHORT & LONG VOWELS	CREATIVE TEACHING PRESS, INC.		<5
P	ACTCRD	PUNCH-THRU CARDS: SHORT VOWELS	TREND ENTERPRISES, INC.		<5
P	ACTCRD	WIPE-OFF CARDS: SHORT VOWELS	TREND ENTERPRISES, INC.		<5
P	ACTCRD	VOWEL SOUNDS	MILTON BRADLEY/PLAYSKOOL		<5
P	AUDCAS	SOUNDS FOR YOUNG READERS, VOLUME 2	CLASSROOM MATERIALS CO.		6-10
P	AUDCAS	SOUNDS FOR YOUNG READERS, VOLUME 3	CLASSROOM MATERIALS CO.		6-10
P	AUDCAS	VIEW ON VOWELS, WORKTAPES	ALLYN AND BACON, INC.		101-150
P	AUDCRD	LONG & SHORT OF IT	AUDIOTRONICS CORPORATION		21-30
P	AUDCRD	SHORT & LONG VOWELS	AUDIOTRONICS CORPORATION		11-20
P	AUDKIT	PHONICS	EYE GATE MEDIA	10	76-100
P	AUDKIT	PHONICS: SHORT VOWEL SOUND FUN	EYE GATE MEDIA		6-10
P	AUDKIT	VOWELS	EDUCATIONAL MEDIA, INC.		51-75
P	AUDKIT	VOWEL ENRICHMENT	EDUCATIONAL MEDIA, INC.		51-75
P	AUDKIT	KIT 8: BASIC WORD ATTACK - LONG, SHORT VOWELS	EDUCATIONAL RESEARCH, INC.		101-150
P	AUDKIT	PHONETICS FACTORY	IDEAL SCHOOL SUPPLY COMPANY		51-75
P	AUDKIT	READING CASSETTES: VOWELS	IDEAL SCHOOL SUPPLY COMPANY		51-75
P	AUDKIT	READING CASSETTES: VOWEL ENRICHMENT	IDEAL SCHOOL SUPPLY COMPANY		51-75
P	AUDKIT	ABC'S OF PHONICS PROGRAM 3: CONSONANT DIGRAPHS W/CASSETTES	Q-ED PRODUCTIONS		76-100
P	AUDKIT	ABC'S OF PHONICS PROGRAM 3: CONSONANT DIGRAPHS W/RECORDS	Q-ED PRODUCTIONS		76-100
P	AUDKIT	ABC'S OF PHONICS PROGRAMS 1 - 3 W/CASSETTES	Q-ED PRODUCTIONS		201-300
P	AUDKIT	ROAD TO READING, PHONICS PROGRAM, LANGUAGE SKILLS	SPOKEN ARTS, INC.		301-400
P	AUDKIT	VOWEL SOUNDS: SHORT A	MEDIA MATERIALS, INC.		6-10
P	AUDKIT	VOWEL SOUNDS: SHORT E	MEDIA MATERIALS, INC.		6-10
P	AUDKIT	VOWEL SOUNDS: SHORT I	MEDIA MATERIALS, INC.		6-10
P	AUDKIT	VOWEL SOUNDS: SHORT O	MEDIA MATERIALS, INC.		6-10
P	AUDKIT	VOWEL SOUNDS: SHORT U	MEDIA MATERIALS, INC.		6-10
P	AUDKIT	SHORT VOWEL SOUND FUN	MEDIA MATERIALS, INC.		6-10
P	AUDKIT	VOWEL IN THE MIDDLE	MEDIA MATERIALS, INC.		6-10
P	AUDKIT	SHORT VOWEL TAPE PROGRAM	DEVELOPMENTAL LEARNING MATERIALS		21-30
P	AUDKIT	LONG & SHORT VOWELS	HAMPDEN PUBLICATIONS, INC.		101-150
P	AUDKIT	FUN WITH VOWEL SOUNDS	HAMPDEN PUBLICATIONS, INC.		21-30
P	AUDKIT	LISTEN & DO: VOWELS	HOUGHTON MIFFLIN COMPANY		76-100
P	AUDKIT	MINISYSTEMS: SHORT a	CORONET MULTI MEDIA		11-20
P	AUDKIT	MINISYSTEMS: SPELLING WITH SHORT a	CORONET MULTI MEDIA		11-20
P	AUDKIT	MINISYSTEMS: SHORT i	CORONET MULTI MEDIA		11-20
P	AUDKIT	MINISYSTEMS: SPELLING WITH SHORT i	CORONET MULTI MEDIA		11-20
P	AUDKIT	MINISYSTEMS: CHANGING SHORT a TO SHORT i	CORONET MULTI MEDIA		11-20
P	AUDKIT	MINISYSTEMS: SHORT e	CORONET MULTI MEDIA		11-20
P	AUDKIT	MINISYSTEMS: SPELLING WITH SHORT e	CORONET MULTI MEDIA		11-20
P	AUDKIT	MINISYSTEMS: BUILDING POWER VOCABULARY A,E,I	CORONET MULTI MEDIA		11-20
P	AUDKIT	MINISYSTEMS: SHORT o	CORONET MULTI MEDIA		11-20
P	AUDKIT	MINISYSTEMS: SPELLING WITH SHORT o	CORONET MULTI MEDIA		11-20
P	AUDKIT	MINISYSTEMS: BUILDING POWER VOCABULARY A,E,I,O	CORONET MULTI MEDIA		11-20
P	AUDKIT	MINISYSTEMS: SHORT u	CORONET MULTI MEDIA		11-20
P	AUDKIT	MINISYSTEMS: SPELLING WITH SHORT u	CORONET MULTI MEDIA		11-20
P	AUDKIT	MINISYSTEMS: SPELLING WITH VOWELS & CONSONANTS	CORONET MULTI MEDIA		11-20
P	AUDKIT	MINISYSTEMS: BUILDING VOCABULARY, BLENDS, VOWELS, CONSONANTS	CORONET MULTI MEDIA		11-20
P	CHART	ALPHABET, CONSONANTS, VOWELS	BEMISS-JASON CORPORATION		6-10
P	CHART	VOWEL PICTURES FOR PEGBOARD	IDEAL SCHOOL SUPPLY COMPANY		6-10
P	CHART	PROSPECTING IN PHONICS	IDEAL SCHOOL SUPPLY COMPANY		6-10

LEVEL	FORMAT	TITLE	PUBLISHER	NT	$PRICE

57 - SKILL: VOWELS - SHORT

LEVEL	FORMAT	TITLE	PUBLISHER	NT	$PRICE
P	CHART	SHORT VOWELS POSTER	GOOD APPLE, INC.		<5
P	CHART	LONG & SHORT VOWELS	INSTRUCTO/MCGRAW-HILL		<5
P	CHART	VOWEL POSTER CARDS	MILTON BRADLEY/PLAYSKOOL		6-10
P	CL SET	LONG & SHORT VOWELS DESK TAPES	INSTRUCTO/MCGRAW-HILL		6-10
P	DITTO	SHORT & LONG VOWELS	CREATIVE TEACHING ASSOCIATES		<5
P	DITTO	PARADE OF VOWELS	CREATIVE TEACHING ASSOCIATES		<5
P	DITTO	CROSSWORD PUZZLES FOR PHONICS: PICTURE CLUES	CONTINENTAL PRESS, INC.		<5
P	DITTO	CROSSWORD PUZZLES FOR PHONICS: WORD/PICTURE CLUES	CONTINENTAL PRESS, INC.		<5
P	DITTO	CROSSWORD PUZZLES FOR PHONICS: VOWELS I	CONTINENTAL PRESS, INC.		<5
P	DITTO	FUN WITH VOWEL SOUNDS, GRADES 1 & 2	CONTINENTAL PRESS, INC.		<5
P	DITTO	LONG & SHORT VOWELS, GRADES 1 & 2	CONTINENTAL PRESS, INC.		<5
P	DITTO	NEW PHONICS & WORD ANALYSIS SKILLS: GRADE 2, PART 1	CONTINENTAL PRESS, INC.		<5
P	DITTO	NEW PHONICS & WORD ANALYSIS SKILLS: GRADE 2, PART 2	CONTINENTAL PRESS, INC.		<5
P	DITTO	NEW PHONICS & WORD ANALYSIS SKILLS: GRADE 3, PART 1	CONTINENTAL PRESS, INC.		<5
P	DITTO	VARIANT VOWEL SOUNDS, GRADES 2 & 3	CONTINENTAL PRESS, INC.		<5
P	DITTO	BASIC PHONICS: SHORT VOWELS	INSTRUCTIONAL FAIR		<5
P	DITTO	BASIC PHONICS PAK	INSTRUCTIONAL FAIR		21-30
P	DITTO	PHONICS STORIES	FRANK SCHAFFER PUBLICATIONS, INC		<5
P	DITTO	LEARNING SHORT VOWELS	FRANK SCHAFFER PUBLICATIONS, INC		<5
P	DITTO	SPELLING PROGRAM, BOOK A	FRANK SCHAFFER PUBLICATIONS, INC		<5
P	DITTO	SPELLING PROGRAM, BOOK B	FRANK SCHAFFER PUBLICATIONS, INC		<5
P	DITTO	SPELLING PROGRAM, BOOK C	FRANK SCHAFFER PUBLICATIONS, INC		<5
P	DITTO	SPELLING PROGRAM, BOOK D	FRANK SCHAFFER PUBLICATIONS, INC		<5
P	DITTO	SPELLING PROGRAM, BOOK E	FRANK SCHAFFER PUBLICATIONS, INC		<5
P	DITTO	SPELLING PROGRAM, BOOK F	FRANK SCHAFFER PUBLICATIONS, INC		<5
P	DITTO	PHONICS PROGRAM, BOOK 7	FRANK SCHAFFER PUBLICATIONS, INC		<5
P	DITTO	PHONICS PROGRAM, BOOK 8	FRANK SCHAFFER PUBLICATIONS, INC		<5
P	DITTO	NEWSPAPER TASKS SWING INTO LANGUAGE ARTS, PRIMARY	ORE PRESS, INC.		<5
P	DITTO	ENRICHMENT ROUSERS: SHORT VOWEL	IDEAL SCHOOL SUPPLY COMPANY		6-10
P	DITTO	INDIVIDUALIZED READING DEVELOPMENT ACTIVITIES	LOVE PUBLISHING COMPANY		6-10
P	DITTO	SHORT & LONG VOWELS	ENRICH, INC.		<5
P	DITTO	PARADE OF VOWELS	ENRICH, INC.		<5
P	DITTO	WORD ATTACK SKILLS: SHORT & LONG VOWEL SOUNDS	EDL/MCGRAW-HILL		6-10
P	DITTO	SOUNDS IN WORDS, BOOK 6	GEL-STEN, INC.		<5
P	DITTO	SHORT VOWEL SOUNDS	INSTRUCTOR PUBLICATIONS, INC.		<5
P	DITTO	LONG, SHORT & COMBINED VOWEL SOUNDS	INSTRUCTOR PUBLICATIONS, INC.		<5
P	DITTO	VOWELS I (GRADE 1)	INSTRUCTOR PUBLICATIONS, INC.		<5
P	DITTO	VOWELS II (GRADE 2)	INSTRUCTOR PUBLICATIONS, INC.		<5
P	DITTO	SOUND-OFF 2	EDUCATORS PUBLISHING SERVICE		6-10
P	DITTO	CIRCUS DAYS READING ACTIVITIES	CREATIVE TEACHING PRESS, INC.		<5
P	DITTO	PASTING PARADE	CREATIVE TEACHING PRESS, INC.		<5
P	DITTO	V2 VOWELS & VALUES, SET 1: SHORT VOWEL WORDS	MODERN CURRICULUM PRESS		11-20
P	DITTO	LONG & SHORT VOWELS, PART I	INSTRUCTO/MCGRAW-HILL		<5
P	DITTO	LONG & SHORT VOWELS, PART II	INSTRUCTO/MCGRAW-HILL		<5
P	DITTO	SPECIAL VOWEL PATTERNS, PART I	INSTRUCTO/MCGRAW-HILL		<5
P	DITTO	PHONICS IC	HAYES SCHOOL PUBLISHING COMPANY		<5
P	DITTO	PHONICS IIA	HAYES SCHOOL PUBLISHING COMPANY		<5
P	DITTO	PHONICS IIB	HAYES SCHOOL PUBLISHING COMPANY		<5
P	DITTO	PHONICS IIIB	HAYES SCHOOL PUBLISHING COMPANY		<5
P	DITTO	PHONICS & READING	HAYES SCHOOL PUBLISHING COMPANY		<5
P	DITTO	SHORT & LONG VOWELS	ACTIVITY RESOURCES COMPANY, INC.		<5
P	DITTO	DECODING SKILLS 4	ACTIVITY RESOURCES COMPANY, INC.		<5
P	DITTO	PARADE OF VOWELS	ACTIVITY RESOURCES COMPANY, INC.		<5
P	DITTO	VOWEL SOUNDS WORD SLIDES	ACTIVITY RESOURCES COMPANY, INC.		<5
P	DITTO	MASTERING THE SHORT VOWEL	ACTIVITY RESOURCES COMPANY, INC.		<5
P	FILMST	LEARNING ABOUT OUR LANGUAGE, SET 3	AEVAC, INC.		31-50
P	FILMST	PHONICS FILMSTRIP SERIES 1	MEDIA MATERIALS, INC.	5	76-100
P	FILMST	SHORT & LONG A	MEDIA MATERIALS, INC.		11-20
P	FILMST	SHORT & LONG E	MEDIA MATERIALS, INC.		11-20
P	FILMST	SHORT & LONG I	MEDIA MATERIALS, INC.		11-20
P	FILMST	SHORT & LONG O	MEDIA MATERIALS, INC.		11-20
P	FILMST	SHORT & LONG U	MEDIA MATERIALS, INC.		11-20
P	FLNLBD	LONG & SHORT VOWELS	INSTRUCTO/MCGRAW-HILL		6-10
P	GAME	NEW WORD GAME SAFARI	BFA EDUCATIONAL MEDIA		101-150
P	GAME	SHORT VOWELS	FRANK SCHAFFER PUBLICATIONS, INC		<5
P	GAME	PHONICS GAMES	FRANK SCHAFFER PUBLICATIONS, INC		<5
P	GAME	VOWEL BINGO	CONSTRUCTIVE PLAYTHINGS		<5
P	GAME	PUNCH-THRU CARDS: SHORT VOWELS	CONSTRUCTIVE PLAYTHINGS		<5
P	GAME	PHONICS DISCOVERY	DISCOVERY LEARNING		<5
P	GAME	SHORT & LONG VOWELS PEEK-A-BOO KID	READING JOY, INC.		6-10
P	GAME	VOWEL BEES	GOOD APPLE, INC.		6-10
P	GAME	NEW PHONICS WE USE LEARNING GAMES KITS, KIT ONE	RAND MCNALLY & COMPANY		76-100
P	GAME	SHORT VOWEL TIC TAC TOE	DEVELOPMENTAL LEARNING MATERIALS		11-20
P	GAME	MAGICAL SILENT E	DEVELOPMENTAL LEARNING MATERIALS		6-10
P	GAME	SPLICE	STANWIX HOUSE, INC.		6-10
P	GAME	LONG & SHORT VOWELS	CREATIVE TEACHING PRESS, INC.		<5
P	GAME	TABLET GAMES: SHORT VOWELS	TREND ENTERPRISES, INC.		<5
P	GAME	SHORT VOWELS	ACTIVITY RESOURCES COMPANY, INC.		<5
P	GUIDE	PHONICS WORKTEXT: ANSWER KEY (6)	HAMMOND, INC.		<5

LEVEL	FORMAT	TITLE	PUBLISHER	NT	$PRICE

57 - SKILL: VOWELS - SHORT

LEVEL	FORMAT	TITLE	PUBLISHER	NT	$PRICE
P	GUIDE	MERRILL PHONICS SKILL TEXT: COSTUME SHOP, LEVEL A	CHARLES E. MERRILL PUBLISHING CO		<5
P	GUIDE	MERRILL PHONICS SKILL TEXT: SPACE VISITORS, LEVEL C	CHARLES E. MERRILL PUBLISHING CO		<5
P	GUIDE	SHORT VOWELS: STARTING OFF WITH PHONICS, BOOK 5	MODERN CURRICULUM PRESS		<5
P	GUIDE	PHONICS IS FUN, BOOK 2	MODERN CURRICULUM PRESS		<5
P	MANIPU	MIX 'N' MATCH PUZZLES: SHORT VOWELS	CONSTRUCTIVE PLAYTHINGS		<5
P	MANIPU	PHONICS E-Z LANGUAGE LEARNING SLIDE RULES	E-Z GRADER COMPANY	5	6-10
P	MANIPU	PHONICS E-Z LANGUAGE LEARNING SLIDE RULES, 1ST & 2ND	E-Z GRADER COMPANY		<5
P	MANIPU	VOWEL SORTING & WORD CARDS	EDUCATIONAL TEACHING AIDS		6-10
P	MANIPU	ALADDIN CHART: VOWEL SOUNDS	IDEAL SCHOOL SUPPLY COMPANY		<5
P	MANIPU	LARRY THE LEARNING LION	IDEAL SCHOOL SUPPLY COMPANY		6-10
P	MANIPU	TRAY PUZZLES: PHONICS	IDEAL SCHOOL SUPPLY COMPANY		11-20
P	MANIPU	PHONICS SHORT VOWELS	AERO PUBLISHERS, INC.		6-10
P	MANIPU	PHONICS OTHER VOWEL SOUNDS, REVIEW LONG & SHORT VOWELS	AERO PUBLISHERS, INC.		6-10
P	MANIPU	VOWELS	INSTRUCTO/MCGRAW-HILL		11-20
P	MANIPU	ROLLING PHONICS	INSTRUCTO/MCGRAW-HILL		6-10
P	MANIPU	MAGIC TEACHER PUZZLE-PLANS: PHONICS (VOWEL SOUNDS)	HAYES SCHOOL PUBLISHING COMPANY		<5
P	MANIPU	VOWEL WHEELS	MILTON BRADLEY/PLAYSKOOL		6-10
P	MULTIU	EYE-EAR-HAND PHONICS SET C: LONG & SHORT VOWELS	EDUCATIONAL ACTIVITIES, INC.		31-50
P	MULTIU	VOWEL SOUNDS/SELF-INSTRUCTIONAL MODALITIES APPROACH	MILTON BRADLEY/PLAYSKOOL		76-100
P	MULTIM	LISTENING YOUR WAY TO BETTER READING	ASSOCIATED EDUCATIONAL MATERIALS		301-400
P	MULTIM	DEVELOPING READING SKILLS, PART II: PHONICS, VOWEL SOUNDS	EDUCATIONAL ENRICHMENT MATERIALS		101-150
P	MULTIM	SOUND IT, UNIT 2	IMPERIAL INTERNATIONAL LEARNING		51-75
P	MULTIM	FIRST TALKING ALPHABET: PART 2, VOWELS	SCOTT, FORESMAN & CO.		76-100
P	MULTIM	VOWEL SOUNDS KIT	ENRICH, INC.		76-100
P	MULTIM	CONSONANT & VOWEL LAB	ENRICH, INC.		>450
P	MULTIM	READING SKILLS SUPPORT SYSTEM, BOX 2	EDL/MCGRAW-HILL		301-400
P	MULTIM	NEW GOALS IN LISTENING, GRADES 1-3	TROLL ASSOCIATES		76-100
P	PI/PRT	LEARNING SLATE: PHONICS	IDEAL SCHOOL SUPPLY COMPANY		<5
P	PI/PRT	SHORT VOWEL DISCS	TREND ENTERPRISES, INC.		<5
P	PUPILB	MASTERING THE SHORT VOWELS	CREATIVE TEACHING ASSOCIATES		<5
P	PUPILB	WOG'S LOG BOOK I	EDUCATORS PUBLISHING SERVICE		<5
P	PUPILB	WOG'S LOG BOOK II	EDUCATORS PUBLISHING SERVICE		<5
P	PUPILB	WOG'S LOG BOOK III	EDUCATORS PUBLISHING SERVICE		<5
P	PUPILB	WOG'S LOG BOOK IV	EDUCATORS PUBLISHING SERVICE		<5
P	PUPILB	EXPLODE THE CODE, BOOK 1	EDUCATORS PUBLISHING SERVICE		<5
P	PUPILB	STORIES FROM SOUND, LEVEL A	EDUCATORS PUBLISHING SERVICE		<5
P	PUPILB	STORIES FROM SOUNDS, LEVEL B	EDUCATORS PUBLISHING SERVICE		<5
P	PUPILB	STORIES FROM SOUNDS, LEVEL C	EDUCATORS PUBLISHING SERVICE		<5
P	PUPILB	STORIES FROM SOUNDS, LEVEL D	EDUCATORS PUBLISHING SERVICE		<5
P	PUPILB	STORIES FROM SOUNDS, LEVEL E	EDUCATORS PUBLISHING SERVICE		<5
P	PUPILB	FIRST PHONICS, PART 1	EDUCATORS PUBLISHING SERVICE		<5
P	PUPILB	FIRST PHONICS, PART 2	EDUCATORS PUBLISHING SERVICE		<5
P	PUPILB	LEARNING THE LETTERS, BOOK II	EDUCATORS PUBLISHING SERVICE		<5
P	PUPILB	LEARNING THE LETTERS, BOOK III	EDUCATORS PUBLISHING SERVICE		<5
P	PUPILB	LEARNING THE LETTERS, BOOK IV	EDUCATORS PUBLISHING SERVICE		<5
P	PUPILB	LEARNING THE LETTERS, BOOK V	EDUCATORS PUBLISHING SERVICE		<5
P	PUPILB	LEARNING THE LETTERS, BOOK VI	EDUCATORS PUBLISHING SERVICE		<5
P	PUPILB	PRIMARY READERS: SET 1, SHORT VOWELS	MODERN CURRICULUM PRESS		<5
P	RECORD	SOUNDS FOR YOUNG READERS, VOLUME 2	CLASSROOM MATERIALS CO.		6-10
P	RECORD	SOUNDS FOR YOUNG READERS, VOLUME 3	CLASSROOM MATERIALS CO.		6-10
P	RECORD	SOUNDS, VOL. 2	CHILDREN'S BOOK & MUSIC CENTER		6-10
P	RECORD	SOUNDS, VOL. 3	CHILDREN'S BOOK & MUSIC CENTER		6-10
P	SKLKIT	SWEET PICKLES PHONICS PROGRAM	BFA EDUCATIONAL MEDIA		101-150
P	SND FS	SOLVING THE PHONICS MYSTERY: CASE OF THE LONG & SHORT VOWELS	LEARNING TREE FILMSTRIPS		76-100
P	SND FS	STORY OF A, E, O	HERBERT M. ELKINS COMPANY		11-20
P	SND FS	STORY OF I & Y	HERBERT M. ELKINS COMPANY		11-20
P	SND FS	STORY OF U, W & W CONTROLLER	HERBERT M. ELKINS COMPANY		11-20
P	SND FS	SHORT VOWELS	HERBERT M. ELKINS COMPANY		11-20
P	SND FS	TICK TOCK TIME & OTHER STORIES	CHILDREN'S BOOK & MUSIC CENTER		51-75
P	SND FS	VOWELS: HOW THEY LOOK & SOUND	UNITED LEARNING		101-150
P	SP EQT	LANGUAGE SKILLS PROGRAM: INTRODUCTION TO SPELLING	SPELLBINDER, INC.		51-75
P	SP EQT	CHARLIE: PHONICS, LONG & SHORT VOWELS	EDUCATIONAL INSIGHTS, INC.		6-10
P	TRANSP	BASIC PHONETIC SKILL DRILLS	PAUL S. AMIDON & ASSOC., INC.		21-30
P	VISKIT	PICTURE A VOWEL SOUND	DEVELOPMENTAL LEARNING MATERIALS		11-20
P	WKBOOK	PHONIC PICTURE CARDS	KENWORTHY EDUCATIONAL SERVICE		<5
P	WKBOOK	MOTT BASIC LANG. SKILLS: BOOK 1302	ALLIED EDUCATION COUNCIL		<5
P	WKBOOK	AEVAC PHONICS PROGRAM	AEVAC, INC.	6	11-20
P	WKBOOK	AEVAC PHONICS PROGRAM, BOOK A	AEVAC, INC.		<5
P	WKBOOK	AEVAC PHONICS PROGRAM, BOOK C	AEVAC, INC.		<5
P	WKBOOK	AEVAC PHONICS PROGRAM, BOOK D	AEVAC, INC.		<5
P	WKBOOK	AEVAC PHONICS PROGRAM, BOOK E	AEVAC, INC.		<5
P	WKBOOK	SPELL CHECK: LONG VOWELS, SET 1	ORE PRESS, INC.		6-10
P	WKBOOK	SPELL CHECK: LONG VOWELS, SET 2	ORE PRESS, INC.		6-10
P	WKBOOK	S.T.A.R.T., BOOK 1	EMC CORPORATION		<5
P	WKBOOK	S.T.A.R.T., BOOK 2	EMC CORPORATION		<5
P	WKBOOK	S.T.A.R.T., BOOK 3	EMC CORPORATION		<5
P	WKBOOK	S.T.A.R.T., BOOK 7	EMC CORPORATION		<5
P	WKBOOK	S.T.A.R.T., BOOK 12	EMC CORPORATION		<5
P	WKBOOK	S.T.A.R.T., BOOK 15	EMC CORPORATION		<5

LEVEL	FORMAT	TITLE	PUBLISHER	NT	$PRICE

57 - SKILL: VOWELS - SHORT

LEVEL	FORMAT	TITLE	PUBLISHER	NT	$PRICE
P	WKBOOK	S.T.A.R.T., BOOK 16	EMC CORPORATION		<5
P	WKBOOK	S.T.A.R.T., BOOK 17	EMC CORPORATION		<5
P	WKBOOK	VOWELS & VARIANTS, BOOK C	GINN & COMPANY		<5
P	WKBOOK	VOWEL WORKBOOK: SOUND, SPELL, READ	PHONOVISUAL PRODUCTS, INC.		<5
P	WKBOOK	WINDOWS TO READING, BOOK A	FOLLETT PUBLISHING COMPANY		<5
P	WKBOOK	PHONICS WORKTEXT: SHORT VOWELS 1	HAMMOND, INC.		<5
P	WKBOOK	PHONICS WORKTEXT: SHORT VOWELS 2	HAMMOND, INC.		<5
P	WKBOOK	PHONICS WORKTEXT: VARIANT VOWELS	HAMMOND, INC.		<5
P	WKBOOK	PHONICS: VOWELS-BLENDS READING REVIEW	JENN PUBLICATIONS		<5
P	WKBOOK	PHONICS: VOWELS, GRADE 2	JENN PUBLICATIONS		<5
P	WKBOOK	PHONICS, GRADE 3	JENN PUBLICATIONS		<5
P	WKBOOK	LETTERS & SOUNDS, PRIMARY	SCOTT, FORESMAN & CO.		<5
P	WKBOOK	COVE SCHOOL READING PROGRAM	DEVELOPMENTAL LEARNING MATERIALS		76-100
P	WKBOOK	MERRILL PHONICS SKILL TEXT: COSTUME SHOP, LEVEL A	CHARLES E. MERRILL PUBLISHING CO		<5
P	WKBOOK	MERRILL PHONICS SKILL TEXT: SPACE VISITORS, LEVEL C	CHARLES E. MERRILL PUBLISHING CO		<5
P	WKBOOK	PHONICS BOOK C: SHORT VOWEL SOUNDS	SCHOLASTIC BOOK SERVICE		<5
P	WKBOOK	VIEW ON VOWELS	ALLYN AND BACON, INC.		<5
P	WKBOOK	PRIMARY PHONICS WORKBOOK 3	EDUCATORS PUBLISHING SERVICE		<5
P	WKBOOK	WORKBOOK M1	EDUCATORS PUBLISHING SERVICE		<5
P	WKBOOK	SHORT VOWELS: STARTING OFF WITH PHONICS, BOOK 5	MODERN CURRICULUM PRESS		<5
P	WKBOOK	MCP PHONICS WORKBOOKS: LEVEL A	MODERN CURRICULUM PRESS		<5
P	WKBOOK	MCP PHONICS WORKBOOKS: LEVEL C	MODERN CURRICULUM PRESS		<5
P	WKBOOK	PHONICS IS FUN, BOOK 2	MODERN CURRICULUM PRESS		<5
P	WKBOOK	NEW PHONICS WORKBOOK, BOOK B	MODERN CURRICULUM PRESS		<5
P	WKBOOK	SOUND WE USE, BOOK 1	HAYES SCHOOL PUBLISHING COMPANY		<5
P	WKBOOK	SOUNDS WE USE, BOOK 3	HAYES SCHOOL PUBLISHING COMPANY		<5
P	WKBOOK	VOWEL OWL	ACTIVITY RESOURCES COMPANY, INC.		<5
P	WKBOOK	BIG LOOK AT LONG & SHORT VOWELS	MILTON BRADLEY/PLAYSKOOL		<5
PI	ACTCRD	VOWEL OWL	KIDS & COMPANY		<5
PI	ACTCRD	LONG & SHORT VOWEL PUZZLES	INCENTIVES FOR LEARNING, INC.		6-10
PI	ACTCRD	PHONIC WIPE OFF CARDS	WEBER COSTELLO COMPANY		<5
PI	AUDKIT	USING PHONICS	EBSCO CURRICULUM MATERIALS		51-75
PI	AUDKIT	POWERPAC III	IMPERIAL INTERNATIONAL LEARNING		101-150
PI	AUDKIT	POWERPAC IV	IMPERIAL INTERNATIONAL LEARNING		101-150
PI	AUDKIT	POWERPAC PROGRAM	IMPERIAL INTERNATIONAL LEARNING	4	>450
PI	AUDKIT	VOWEL SOUNDS & SILENT LETTERS	NATIONAL BOOK COMPANY		21-30
PI	CL SET	SOUND OFF & READ	MAFEX ASSOCIATES, INC.		31-50
PI	DITTO	POSITIVELY PHONICS: SHORT VOWELS	FRANK SCHAFFER PUBLICATIONS, INC		<5
PI	DITTO	COLOR, CUT & PASTE VOWEL	PAUL S. AMIDON & ASSOC., INC.		<5
PI	DITTO	SPECIAL VOWEL PATTERNS, PART II	INSTRUCTO/MCGRAW-HILL		<5
PI	DITTO	FUNNY FACE PHONICS	ACTIVITY RESOURCES COMPANY, INC.		<5
PI	DITTO	WORD PERCEPTION	MILTON BRADLEY/PLAYSKOOL		<5
PI	GAME	PHONICS SOUP, SHORT VOWEL GAMES	CREATIVE TEACHING ASSOCIATES		6-10
PI	GAME	SEA OF VOWELS	IDEAL SCHOOL SUPPLY COMPANY		6-10
PI	GAME	TEAM CHECKERS: SHORT VOWELS	LITTLE KENNY PUBLICATIONS, INC.		6-10
PI	GAME	PHONICS SOUP GAME PACKAGES: SHORT VOWELS	SCOTT RESOURCES, INC.		6-10
PI	MANIPU	SOUND 'N' SPELL ALPHABET PUZZLE	CREATIVE TEACHING ASSOCIATES		6-10
PI	MANIPU	PHONICS E-Z LANGUAGE LEARNING SLIDE RULES, 3RD & 4TH	E-Z GRADER COMPANY		<5
PI	MANIPU	AERO PHONICS LAB	AERO PUBLISHERS, INC.		76-100
PI	MULTIU	LONG & SHORT VOWEL SOUNDS KIT	LESWING PRESS		31-50
PI	MULTIU	PHONICS IN CONTEXT, SET I	EDUCATIONAL ACTIVITIES, INC.		76-100
PI	MULTIM	PHONICS: THE F.I.R.S.T. APPROACH TO READING	WEBER COSTELLO COMPANY		101-150
PI	MULTIM	WORKING WITH PHONICS	TROLL ASSOCIATES		301-400
PI	SND FS	PHONICS SERIES 1	HAMPDEN PUBLICATIONS, INC.		76-100
PI	SND FS	BASIC WORD ATTACK	EDL/MCGRAW-HILL		301-400
PI	SND FS	WORKING WITH VOWELS	TROLL ASSOCIATES		101-150
PI	WKBOOK	SHORT VOWELS	FRANK SCHAFFER PUBLICATIONS, INC		<5
PI	WKBOOK	AEVAC STARTER 101, BOOK 1 (NON-READERS)	AEVAC, INC.		<5
PI	WKBOOK	AEVAC STARTER 101, BOOK 2 (NON-READERS)	AEVAC, INC.		<5
PI	WKBOOK	AEVAC STARTER 101, BOOK 3 (NON-READERS)	AEVAC, INC.		<5
PI	WKBOOK	AEVAC STARTER 101, BOOK 4 (NON-READERS)	AEVAC, INC.		<5
PI	WKBOOK	AEVAC STARTER 101, BOOK 5 (NON-READERS)	AEVAC, INC.		<5
PI	WKBOOK	AEVAC STARTER 101, BOOK 6 (NON-READERS)	AEVAC, INC.		<5
PI	WKBOOK	AEVAC STARTER 101, BOOK 7 (NON-READERS)	AEVAC, INC.		<5
PI	WKBOOK	AEVAC STARTER 101, BOOK 8 (NON-READERS)	AEVAC, INC.		<5
PI	WKBOOK	FOCUS ON PHONICS 2A	NEW READERS PRESS		<5
PI	WKBOOK	PRIMARY PHONICS WORKBOOK 4	EDUCATORS PUBLISHING SERVICE		<5
PI	WKBOOK	PHONICS FAST & EASY	ACTIVITY RESOURCES COMPANY, INC.		<5
PIJ	GAME	SOUND OFF & READ GAMES	MAFEX ASSOCIATES, INC.		11-20
I	DITTO	CROSSWORD PUZZLES FOR PHONICS: VOWELS II	CONTINENTAL PRESS, INC.		<5
I	DITTO	SOUNDS IN WORDS, BOOK 8	GEL-STEN, INC.		<5
I	DITTO	SOUNDS IN WORDS, BOOK 10	GEL-STEN, INC.		<5
I	DITTO	SOUNDS IN WORDS, BOOK 11	GEL-STEN, INC.		<5
I	DITTO	SOUNDS IN WORDS, BOOK 14	GEL-STEN, INC.		<5
I	DITTO	SOUNDS IN WORDS, BOOK 16	GEL-STEN, INC.		<5
I	DITTO	SOUNDS IN WORDS, BOOK 17	GEL-STEN, INC.		<5
I	DITTO	DECODING SKILLS D	ACTIVITY RESOURCES COMPANY, INC.		<5
I	DITTO	VOWELS	MILTON BRADLEY/PLAYSKOOL		<5
I	GAME	NEW PHONICS WE USE LEARNING GAMES KITS, KIT TWO	RAND MCNALLY & COMPANY		76-100

LEVEL	FORMAT	TITLE	PUBLISHER	NT	$PRICE

---

57 - SKILL: VOWELS - SHORT

LEVEL	FORMAT	TITLE	PUBLISHER	NT	$PRICE
I	GAME	VOWEL SOLITAIRE	SCOTT, FORESMAN & CO.		6-10
I	MULTIM	GAMES 'N' FRAMES: THE STRANGE CASE OF THE VANISHING VOWELS	IMPERIAL INTERNATIONAL LEARNING		21-30
I	MULTIM	GAMES 'N' FRAMES: SOUL TRIP	IMPERIAL INTERNATIONAL LEARNING		21-30
I	MULTIM	SELECT-A-SKILL KIT, UNIT 2: PIONEER LIFE	IMPERIAL INTERNATIONAL LEARNING		51-75
I	MULTIM	SELECT-A-SKILL KIT, UNIT 2: PIONEER LIFE	IMPERIAL INTERNATIONAL LEARNING		51-75
I	MULTIM	SELECT-A-SKILL KIT, UNIT 8: LEGENDS, TALES & POETRY	IMPERIAL INTERNATIONAL LEARNING		51-75
I	RECORD	SOUND SKILLS FOR UPPER GRADES	CLASSROOM MATERIALS CO.	3	21-30
I	RECORD	SOUND SKILLS FOR UPPER GRADES, VOLUME 2	CLASSROOM MATERIALS CO.		6-10
I	WKBOOK	PHONICS FOR THE INTERMEDIATE GRADES (4, 5, 6)	JENN PUBLICATIONS		<5
I	WKBOOK	LETTERS & SOUNDS, INTERMEDIATE	SCOTT, FORESMAN & CO.		<5
IJ	ACTCRD	FICKLE VOWELS	LESWING PRESS		6-10
IJ	GAME	VOWEL BINGO	TREND ENTERPRISES, INC.		6-10
IJ	WKBOOK	BOOK ONE, PART ONE: PHONIC ANALYSIS ACTIVITIES	T.S. DENISON & COMPANY		6-10
IJS	ACTCRD	JOIN THE VOWEL QUINTET	LESWING PRESS		6-10
IJS	AUDKIT	HITS, LEVEL 1: THREE DOG NIGHT, ONE MAN BAND	MODULEARN, INC.		11-20
IJS	AUDKIT	HITS, LEVEL 1: AMERICA, LONELY PEOPLE	MODULEARN, INC.		11-20
IJS	AUDKIT	HITS, LEVEL 1: SANTANA, LET IT SHINE	MODULEARN, INC.		11-20
IJS	AUDKIT	HITS, LEVEL 1: DOOBIE BROTHERS, IT KEEPS YOU RUNNING	MODULEARN, INC.		11-20
IJS	AUDKIT	HITS, LEVEL 1: AMERICA, TIN MAN	MODULEARN, INC.		11-20
IJS	AUDKIT	HITS, LEVEL 1: AMERICA, VENTURA HIGHWAY	MODULEARN, INC.		11-20
IJS	AUDKIT	HITS, LEVEL 1: JAMES TAYLOR, SWEET BABY JAMES	MODULEARN, INC.		11-20
IJS	AUDKIT	HITS, LEVEL 1: PAUL SIMON, EL CONDOR PASA	MODULEARN, INC.		11-20
IJS	AUDKIT	HITS, LEVEL 1: BLACKBYRDS, YOU'VE GOT THAT SOMETHING	MODULEARN, INC.		11-20
IJS	AUDKIT	HITS, LEVEL 2: FLEETWOOD MAC, OVER MY HEAD	MODULEARN, INC.		11-20
IJS	AUDKIT	HITS, LEVEL 2: SPINNERS, GAMES PEOPLE PLAY	MODULEARN, INC.		11-20
IJS	AUDKIT	HITS, LEVEL 2: BELLAMY BROTHERS, LET YOUR LOVE FLOW	MODULEARN, INC.		11-20
IJS	AUDKIT	HITS, LEVEL 2: JOHN SEBASTIAN, WELCOME BACK	MODULEARN, INC.		11-20
IJS	AUDKIT	HITS, LEVEL 2: SPINNERS, COULD IT BE I'M FALLING IN LOVE	MODULEARN, INC.		11-20
IJS	AUDKIT	HITS, LEVEL 2: ABBA, KNOWING ME, KNOWING YOU	MODULEARN, INC.		11-20
IJS	AUDKIT	HITS, LEVEL 2: DONNIE & MARIE OSMOND, IT TAKES TWO	MODULEARN, INC.		11-20
IJS	AUDKIT	HITS, LEVEL 2: ABBA, S.O.S.	MODULEARN, INC.		11-20
IJS	AUDKIT	HITS, LEVEL 2: EARTH WIND & FIRE, SHINING STAR	MODULEARN, INC.		11-20
IJS	AUDKIT	HITS, LEVEL 2: PAUL SIMON, STILL CRAZY AFTER ALL THESE YEARS	MODULEARN, INC.		11-20
IJS	AUDKIT	HITS, LEVEL 2: SIDE EFFECT, S.O.S.	MODULEARN, INC.		11-20
IJS	AUDKIT	HITS, LEVEL 3: JOHNNY NASH, I CAN SEE CLEARLY NOW	MODULEARN, INC.		11-20
IJS	AUDKIT	HITS, LEVEL 3: JAMES TAYLOR, SHOWER THE PEOPLE	MODULEARN, INC.		11-20
IJS	AUDKIT	HITS, LEVEL 3: FIREFALL, LIVIN' AIN'T LIVIN'	MODULEARN, INC.		11-20
IJS	AUDKIT	HITS, LEVEL 3: DOOBIE BROTHERS, LISTEN TO THE MUSIC	MODULEARN, INC.		11-20
IJS	AUDKIT	HITS, LEVEL 3: PAUL SIMON, 50 WAYS TO LEAVE YOUR LOVER	MODULEARN, INC.		11-20
IJS	AUDKIT	HITS, LEVEL 3: EMOTION, BEST OF MY LOVE	MODULEARN, INC.		11-20
IJS	AUDKIT	HITS, LEVEL 3: THREE DOG NIGHT, THE FAMILY OF MAN	MODULEARN, INC.		11-20
IJS	AUDKIT	HITS, LEVEL 3: FLEETWOOD MAC, DON'T STOP	MODULEARN, INC.		11-20
IJS	AUDKIT	HITS, LEVEL 3: CARLY SIMON, GROWN UP	MODULEARN, INC.		11-20
IJS	AUDKIT	HITS, LEVEL 3: SPINNERS, ONE OF A KIND LOVE AFFAIR	MODULEARN, INC.		11-20
IJS	AUDKIT	HITS, LEVEL 3: SPINNERS, JUST CAN'T GET YOU OUT OF MY MIND	MODULEARN, INC.		11-20
IJS	MULTIU	LONG & SHORT OF IT	LESWING PRESS		11-20
IJS	MULTIU	PHONICS IN CONTEXT, SET II	EDUCATIONAL ACTIVITIES, INC.		51-75
JS	AUDKIT	READING CASSETTES: VOWELS	IDEAL SCHOOL SUPPLY COMPANY		51-75
JS	AUDKIT	USING PHONICS SERIES	MEDIA MATERIALS, INC.		101-150
JS	FLASH	NEW STREAMLINED ENGLISH SERIES: FLASH CARDS	NEW READERS PRESS		<5
JS	SND FS	ADVANCED WORD ATTACK	EDL/MCGRAW-HILL		301-400
JS	WKBOOK	NEW STREAMLINED ENGLISH SERIES: SKILL BOOK 2	NEW READERS PRESS		<5
S	AUDKIT	VOWELS (IMMEDIATE-SECONDARY)	EDUCATIONAL MEDIA, INC.		31-50
S	AUDKIT	PHONICS SERIES 1	HAMPDEN PUBLICATIONS, INC.		76-100
S	SND FS	SHORT & LONG A	MEDIA MATERIALS, INC.		11-20
S	SND FS	SHORT & LONG E	MEDIA MATERIALS, INC.		11-20
S	SND FS	SHORT & LONG I	MEDIA MATERIALS, INC.		11-20
S	SND FS	SHORT & LONG O	MEDIA MATERIALS, INC.		11-20
S	SND FS	SHORT & LONG U	MEDIA MATERIALS, INC.		11-20

---

58 - SKILL: VOWELS - LONG

LEVEL	FORMAT	TITLE	PUBLISHER	NT	$PRICE
R	AUDKIT	SOUNDS & SYMBOLS	EDUCATORS PUBLISHING SERVICE		101-150
RP	ACTCRD	FORM-A-SOUND	IDEAL SCHOOL SUPPLY COMPANY		11-20
RP	AUDKIT	PERCEIVE & RESPOND, VOLUME II	MODERN EDUCATION CORPORATION		76-100
RP	DITTO	LONG & SHORT VOWELS	CONTINENTAL PRESS, INC.		<5
RP	FILMST	EARLY READING RECOGNITION SKILLS	CLASSROOM MATERIALS CO.		51-75
RP	GUIDE	PHONICS IS FUN, BOOK 1	MODERN CURRICULUM PRESS		<5
RP	MANIPU	FLOOR PUZZLES: RURAL VOWELS	TREND ENTERPRISES, INC.		6-10
RP	MANIPU	MIX 'N' MATCH PUZZLES: LONG VOWELS	TREND ENTERPRISES, INC.		6-10
RP	MULTIU	READING STEP BY STEP, UNIT 2	IMPERIAL INTERNATIONAL LEARNING		51-75
RP	MULTIU	READING READINESS: PARTS I, II, III, IV, V, VI	EDUCATIONAL DIMENSIONS CORP.		101-150
RP	MULTIM	ALPHA-SOUND PROGRAM, GROUP 2	CLEARVUE, INC.		151-200
RP	MULTIM	HELP: VOWELS	CENTER FOR EARLY LEARNING		6-10
RP	MULTIM	HEAR-SEE-SAY, PHONICS READING COURSE	MELODY HOUSE PUBLISHING COMPANY		11-20
RP	MULTIM	WORDS & SOUND SERIES, SET 1	EDL/MCGRAW-HILL		101-150
RP	MULTIM	WORDS & SOUND SERIES, SET 2	EDL/MCGRAW-HILL		101-150
RP	MULTIM	WORDS & SOUND SERIES, SET 3	EDL/MCGRAW-HILL		101-150
RP	MULTIM	WORDS & SOUND SERIES, SET 4	EDL/MCGRAW-HILL		101-150
RP	PUPILB	SHORT & LONG VOWELS PLAY A GAME	CHILD'S WORLD	5	21-30

LEVEL	FORMAT	TITLE	PUBLISHER	NT	$PRICE

58 - SKILL: VOWELS - LONG

LEVEL	FORMAT	TITLE	PUBLISHER	NT	$PRICE
RP	PUPILB	SHORT "A" & LONG "A" PLAY A GAME	CHILD'S WORLD		6-10
RP	PUPILB	SHORT "E" & LONG "E" PLAY A GAME	CHILD'S WORLD		6-10
RP	PUPILB	SHORT "I" & LONG "I" PLAY A GAME	CHILD'S WORLD		6-10
RP	PUPILB	SHORT "O" & LONG "O" PLAY A GAME	CHILD'S WORLD		6-10
RP	PUPILB	SHORT "U" & LONG "U" PLAY A GAME	CHILD'S WORLD		6-10
RP	SKLKIT	AIMS: VOWELS KIT	CONTINENTAL PRESS, INC.		51-75
RP	SND FS	READ ALONG BEGINNING PHONICS, SET 2	CORONET MULTI MEDIA		101-150
RP	SP EQT	LEARNING LETTER SOUNDS, KIT G	BORG-WARNER EDUCATIONAL SYSTEMS		101-150
RP	SP EQT	LEARNING LETTER SOUNDS, KIT GG	BORG-WARNER EDUCATIONAL SYSTEMS		101-150
RP	WKBOOK	PHONICS IS FUN, BOOK 1	MODERN CURRICULUM PRESS		<5
RPI	AUDKIT	PHONICS SERIES	MEDIA MATERIALS, INC.	10	76-100
RPI	GUIDE	WORD ATTACK JOY	READING JOY, INC.		6-10
P	ACTCRD	BASIC PHONICS: LONG VOWELS	INSTRUCTIONAL FAIR		<5
P	ACTCRD	BASIC PHONICS PAK	INSTRUCTIONAL FAIR		21-30
P	ACTCRD	READING SELF-CHECK: SHORT VOWELS, LONG VOWELS	FRANK SCHAFFER PUBLICATIONS, INC		<5
P	ACTCRD	WIPE-OFF CARDS: LONG VOWELS	CONSTRUCTIVE PLAYTHINGS		<5
P	ACTCRD	RAINBOW WORD BUILDERS	KENWORTHY EDUCATIONAL SERVICE		<5
P	ACTCRD	SAY THE SOUNDS	KENWORTHY EDUCATIONAL SERVICE		<5
P	ACTCRD	SPEECH SOUNDS PICTURE CARDS: CONSONANTS & VOWELS	TEACHING RESOURCES CORPORATION		6-10
P	ACTCRD	TUTORGRAM: VOWELS	ENRICHMENT READING CORP OF AMER.		11-20
P	ACTCRD	TUTORGRAM: MATCHING VOWEL SOUNDS	ENRICHMENT READING CORP OF AMER.		11-20
P	ACTCRD	GROUP-SIZE VOWEL CARDS	GARRARD PUBLISHING COMPANY		<5
P	ACTCRD	MARK ON-WIPE OFF CARDS: VOWEL SOUNDS	IDEAL SCHOOL SUPPLY COMPANY		<5
P	ACTCRD	MAGIC CARDS: VOWELS	IDEAL SCHOOL SUPPLY COMPANY		6-10
P	ACTCRD	SOUND FOUNDATION, PROGRAM 1	DEVELOPMENTAL LEARNING MATERIALS		11-20
P	ACTCRD	SOUND FOUNDATION, PROGRAM 2	DEVELOPMENTAL LEARNING MATERIALS		11-20
P	ACTCRD	LINQUISTIC PACER	DM EDUCATIONAL PUBLICATIONS		6-10
P	ACTCRD	VOWEL PACER	DM EDUCATIONAL PUBLICATIONS		<5
P	ACTCRD	LONG & SHORT VOWELS	GEL-STEN, INC.		6-10
P	ACTCRD	SHORT & LONG VOWELS	CREATIVE TEACHING PRESS, INC.		<5
P	ACTCRD	PUNCH-THRU CARDS: LONG VOWELS	TREND ENTERPRISES, INC.		<5
P	ACTCRD	WIPE-OFF CARDS: LONG VOWELS	TREND ENTERPRISES, INC.		<5
P	ACTCRD	VOWEL SOUNDS	MILTON BRADLEY/PLAYSKOOL		<5
P	AUDCAS	SOUNDS FOR YOUNG READERS, VOLUME 2	CLASSROOM MATERIALS CO.		6-10
P	AUDCAS	SOUNDS FOR YOUNG READERS, VOLUME 3	CLASSROOM MATERIALS CO.		6-10
P	AUDCAS	VIEW ON VOWELS, WORKTAPES	ALLYN AND BACON, INC.		101-150
P	AUDCRD	LONG & SHORT OF IT	AUDIOTRONICS CORPORATION		21-30
P	AUDCRD	SHORT & LONG VOWELS	AUDIOTRONICS CORPORATION		11-20
P	AUDKIT	PHONICS	EYE GATE MEDIA	10	76-100
P	AUDKIT	PHONICS: LONG VOWEL SOUND FUN	EYE GATE MEDIA		6-10
P	AUDKIT	VOWELS	EDUCATIONAL MEDIA, INC.		51-75
P	AUDKIT	VOWEL ENRICHMENT	EDUCATIONAL MEDIA, INC.		51-75
P	AUDKIT	KIT 8: BASIC WORD ATTACK - LONG, SHORT VOWELS	EDUCATIONAL RESEARCH, INC.		101-150
P	AUDKIT	PHONETICS FACTORY	IDEAL SCHOOL SUPPLY COMPANY		51-75
P	AUDKIT	READING CASSETTES: VOWELS	IDEAL SCHOOL SUPPLY COMPANY		51-75
P	AUDKIT	READING CASSETTES: VOWEL ENRICHMENT	IDEAL SCHOOL SUPPLY COMPANY		51-75
P	AUDKIT	ABC'S OF PHONICS PROGRAMS 1 - 3 W/CASSETTES	Q-ED PRODUCTIONS		201-300
P	AUDKIT	ABC'S OF PHONICS PROGRAMS 1 - 3 W/RECORDS	Q-ED PRODUCTIONS		201-300
P	AUDKIT	ROAD TO READING, PHONICS PROGRAM, LANGUAGE SKILLS	SPOKEN ARTS, INC.		301-400
P	AUDKIT	VOWEL SOUNDS: LONG A	MEDIA MATERIALS, INC.		6-10
P	AUDKIT	VOWEL SOUNDS: LONG E	MEDIA MATERIALS, INC.		6-10
P	AUDKIT	VOWEL SOUNDS: LONG I	MEDIA MATERIALS, INC.		6-10
P	AUDKIT	VOWEL SOUNDS: LONG O	MEDIA MATERIALS, INC.		6-10
P	AUDKIT	VOWEL SOUNDS: LONG U	MEDIA MATERIALS, INC.		6-10
P	AUDKIT	VOWEL VACATION	MEDIA MATERIALS, INC.		6-10
P	AUDKIT	LONG VOWEL SOUND FUN	MEDIA MATERIALS, INC.		6-10
P	AUDKIT	SIMPLE LONG VOWEL SOUNDS	MEDIA MATERIALS, INC.		6-10
P	AUDKIT	LONG & SHORT VOWELS	HAMPDEN PUBLICATIONS, INC.		101-150
P	AUDKIT	FUN WITH VOWEL SOUNDS	HAMPDEN PUBLICATIONS, INC.		21-30
P	AUDKIT	LISTEN & DO: VOWELS	HOUGHTON MIFFLIN COMPANY		76-100
P	AUDKIT	MINISYSTEMS: LONG VOWELS A,E	CORONET MULTI MEDIA		11-20
P	AUDKIT	MINISYSTEMS: LONG VOWELS I,O,U	CORONET MULTI MEDIA		11-20
P	AUDKIT	MINISYSTEMS: SPELLING WITH VOWELS & CONSONANTS	CORONET MULTI MEDIA		11-20
P	AUDKIT	MINISYSTEMS: BUILDING VOCABULARY, BLENDS, VOWELS, CONSONANTS	CORONET MULTI MEDIA		11-20
P	CHART	ALPHABET, CONSONANTS, VOWELS	BEMISS-JASON CORPORATION		6-10
P	CHART	VOWEL PICTURES FOR PEGBOARD	IDEAL SCHOOL SUPPLY COMPANY		6-10
P	CHART	PROSPECTING IN PHONICS	IDEAL SCHOOL SUPPLY COMPANY		6-10
P	CHART	LONG & SHORT VOWELS	INSTRUCTO/MCGRAW-HILL		<5
P	CHART	VOWEL POSTER CARDS	MILTON BRADLEY/PLAYSKOOL		6-10
P	CL SET	LONG & SHORT VOWELS DESK TAPES	INSTRUCTO/MCGRAW-HILL		6-10
P	DITTO	SHORT & LONG VOWELS	CREATIVE TEACHING ASSOCIATES		<5
P	DITTO	PARADE OF VOWELS	CREATIVE TEACHING ASSOCIATES		<5
P	DITTO	CROSSWORD PUZZLES FOR PHONICS: PICTURE CLUES	CONTINENTAL PRESS, INC.		<5
P	DITTO	CROSSWORD PUZZLES FOR PHONICS: WORD/PICTURE CLUES	CONTINENTAL PRESS, INC.		<5
P	DITTO	CROSSWORD PUZZLES FOR PHONICS: VOWELS I	CONTINENTAL PRESS, INC.		<5
P	DITTO	FUN WITH VOWEL SOUNDS, GRADES 1 & 2	CONTINENTAL PRESS, INC.		<5
P	DITTO	LONG & SHORT VOWELS, GRADES 1 & 2	CONTINENTAL PRESS, INC.		<5
P	DITTO	NEW PHONICS & WORD ANALYSIS SKILLS: GRADE 2, PART 1	CONTINENTAL PRESS, INC.		<5
P	DITTO	NEW PHONICS & WORD ANALYSIS SKILLS: GRADE 2, PART 2	CONTINENTAL PRESS, INC.		<5

LEVEL	FORMAT	TITLE	PUBLISHER	NT	$PRICE

```
                    -----------------------------------------------------
                              58 - SKILL:    VOWELS - LONG
                    -----------------------------------------------------
```

LEVEL	FORMAT	TITLE	PUBLISHER	NT	$PRICE
P	DITTO	NEW PHONICS & WORD ANALYSIS SKILLS: GRADE 3, PART 1	CONTINENTAL PRESS, INC.		<5
P	DITTO	VARIANT VOWEL SOUNDS, GRADES 2 & 3	CONTINENTAL PRESS, INC.		<5
P	DITTO	BASIC PHONICS: LONG VOWELS	INSTRUCTIONAL FAIR		<5
P	DITTO	BASIC PHONICS PAK	INSTRUCTIONAL FAIR		21-30
P	DITTO	PHONICS STORIES	FRANK SCHAFFER PUBLICATIONS, INC		<5
P	DITTO	SPELLING PROGRAM, BOOK H	FRANK SCHAFFER PUBLICATIONS, INC		<5
P	DITTO	PHONICS PROGRAM, BOOK 9	FRANK SCHAFFER PUBLICATIONS, INC		<5
P	DITTO	NEWSPAPER TASKS SWING INTO LANGUAGE ARTS, PRIMARY	ORE PRESS, INC.		<5
P	DITTO	INDIVIDUALIZED READING DEVELOPMENT ACTIVITIES	LOVE PUBLISHING COMPANY		6-10
P	DITTO	SHORT & LONG VOWELS	ENRICH, INC.		<5
P	DITTO	PARADE OF VOWELS	ENRICH, INC.		<5
P	DITTO	WORD ATTACK SKILLS: SHORT & LONG VOWEL SOUNDS	EDL/MCGRAW-HILL		6-10
P	DITTO	SOUNDS IN WORDS, BOOK 6	GEL-STEN, INC.		<5
P	DITTO	LONG VOWEL SOUNDS	INSTRUCTOR PUBLICATIONS, INC.		<5
P	DITTO	LONG, SHORT & COMBINED VOWEL SOUNDS	INSTRUCTOR PUBLICATIONS, INC.		<5
P	DITTO	VOWELS I (GRADE 1)	INSTRUCTOR PUBLICATIONS, INC.		<5
P	DITTO	VOWELS II (GRADE 2)	INSTRUCTOR PUBLICATIONS, INC.		<5
P	DITTO	SOUND-OFF 5	EDUCATORS PUBLISHING SERVICE		6-10
P	DITTO	CIRCUS DAYS READING ACTIVITIES	CREATIVE TEACHING PRESS, INC.		<5
P	DITTO	PASTING PARADE	CREATIVE TEACHING PRESS, INC.		<5
P	DITTO	LONG VOWELS	TREND ENTERPRISES, INC.		<5
P	DITTO	V2 VOWELS & VALUES, SET 2: LONG VOWEL WORDS	MODERN CURRICULUM PRESS		11-20
P	DITTO	LONG & SHORT VOWELS, PART I	INSTRUCTO/MCGRAW-HILL		<5
P	DITTO	LONG & SHORT VOWELS, PART II	INSTRUCTO/MCGRAW-HILL		<5
P	DITTO	SPECIAL VOWEL PATTERNS, PART I	INSTRUCTO/MCGRAW-HILL		<5
P	DITTO	PHONICS IC	HAYES SCHOOL PUBLISHING COMPANY		<5
P	DITTO	PHONICS IIA	HAYES SCHOOL PUBLISHING COMPANY		<5
P	DITTO	PHONICS IIB	HAYES SCHOOL PUBLISHING COMPANY		<5
P	DITTO	PHONICS IIIB	HAYES SCHOOL PUBLISHING COMPANY		<5
P	DITTO	PHONICS & READING	HAYES SCHOOL PUBLISHING COMPANY		<5
P	DITTO	SHORT & LONG VOWELS	ACTIVITY RESOURCES COMPANY, INC.		<5
P	DITTO	DECODING SKILLS 4	ACTIVITY RESOURCES COMPANY, INC.		<5
P	DITTO	PARADE OF VOWELS	ACTIVITY RESOURCES COMPANY, INC.		<5
P	DITTO	VOWEL SOUNDS WORD SLIDES	ACTIVITY RESOURCES COMPANY, INC.		<5
P	FILMST	PHONICS FILMSTRIP SERIES 1	MEDIA MATERIALS, INC.	5	76-100
P	FILMST	SHORT & LONG A	MEDIA MATERIALS, INC.		11-20
P	FILMST	SHORT & LONG E	MEDIA MATERIALS, INC.		11-20
P	FILMST	SHORT & LONG I	MEDIA MATERIALS, INC.		11-20
P	FILMST	SHORT & LONG O	MEDIA MATERIALS, INC.		11-20
P	FILMST	SHORT & LONG U	MEDIA MATERIALS, INC.		11-20
P	FLNLBD	LONG & SHORT VOWELS	INSTRUCTO/MCGRAW-HILL		6-10
P	GAME	NEW WORD GAME SAFARI	BFA EDUCATIONAL MEDIA		101-150
P	GAME	PHONICS GAMES	FRANK SCHAFFER PUBLICATIONS, INC		<5
P	GAME	VOWEL BINGO	CONSTRUCTIVE PLAYTHINGS		<5
P	GAME	PUNCH-THRU CARDS: LONG VOWELS	CONSTRUCTIVE PLAYTHINGS		<5
P	GAME	PHONICS DISCOVERY	DISCOVERY LEARNING		<5
P	GAME	SHORT & LONG VOWELS PEEK-A-BOO KID	READING JOY, INC.		6-10
P	GAME	VOWEL BEES	GOOD APPLE, INC.		6-10
P	GAME	NEW PHONICS WE USE LEARNING GAMES KITS, KIT ONE	RAND MCNALLY & COMPANY		76-100
P	GAME	MAGICAL SILENT E	DEVELOPMENTAL LEARNING MATERIALS		6-10
P	GAME	LONG & SHORT VOWELS	CREATIVE TEACHING PRESS, INC.		<5
P	GAME	TABLET GAMES: LONG VOWELS	TREND ENTERPRISES, INC.		<5
P	GAME	LONG VOWELS	ACTIVITY RESOURCES COMPANY, INC.		<5
P	GUIDE	PHONICS WORKTEXT: ANSWER KEY (6)	HAMMOND, INC.		<5
P	GUIDE	MERRILL PHONICS SKILL TEXT: COSTUME KIDS, LEVEL B	CHARLES E. MERRILL PUBLISHING CO		<5
P	GUIDE	MERRILL PHONICS SKILL TEXT: SPACE VISITORS, LEVEL C	CHARLES E. MERRILL PUBLISHING CO		<5
P	GUIDE	SHORT VOWELS: STARTING OFF WITH PHONICS, BOOK 5	MODERN CURRICULUM PRESS		<5
P	GUIDE	LONG VOWELS: STARTING OFF WITH PHONICS, BOOK 6	MODERN CURRICULUM PRESS		<5
P	GUIDE	PHONICS IS FUN, BOOK 2	MODERN CURRICULUM PRESS		<5
P	MANIPU	MIX 'N' MATCH PUZZLES: LONG VOWELS	CONSTRUCTIVE PLAYTHINGS		<5
P	MANIPU	PHONICS E-Z LANGUAGE LEARNING SLIDE RULES	E-Z GRADER COMPANY	5	6-10
P	MANIPU	PHONICS E-Z LANGUAGE LEARNING SLIDE RULES, 1ST & 2ND	E-Z GRADER COMPANY		<5
P	MANIPU	VOWEL SORTING & WORD CARDS	EDUCATIONAL TEACHING AIDS		6-10
P	MANIPU	ALADDIN CHART: VOWEL SOUNDS	IDEAL SCHOOL SUPPLY COMPANY		<5
P	MANIPU	LARRY THE LEARNING LION	IDEAL SCHOOL SUPPLY COMPANY		6-10
P	MANIPU	TRAY PUZZLES: PHONICS	IDEAL SCHOOL SUPPLY COMPANY		11-20
P	MANIPU	PHONICS LONG VOWELS	AERO PUBLISHERS, INC.		6-10
P	MANIPU	PHONICS OTHER VOWEL SOUNDS, REVIEW LONG & SHORT VOWELS	AERO PUBLISHERS, INC.		6-10
P	MANIPU	LONG VOWEL DISCS	TREND ENTERPRISES, INC.		<5
P	MANIPU	VOWELS	INSTRUCTO/MCGRAW-HILL		11-20
P	MANIPU	ROLLING PHONICS	INSTRUCTO/MCGRAW-HILL		6-10
P	MANIPU	MAGIC TEACHER PUZZLE-PLANS: PHONICS (VOWEL SOUNDS)	HAYES SCHOOL PUBLISHING COMPANY		<5
P	MANIPU	VOWEL WHEELS	MILTON BRADLEY/PLAYSKOOL		6-10
P	MULTIU	EYE-EAR-HAND PHONIS, SET C: LONG & SHORT VOWELS	EDUCATIONAL ACTIVITIES, INC.		31-50
P	MULTIU	VOWEL SOUNDS/SELF-INSTRUCTIONAL MODALITIES APPROACH	MILTON BRADLEY/PLAYSKOOL		76-100
P	MULTIM	LISTENING YOUR WAY TO BETTER READING	ASSOCIATED EDUCATIONAL MATERIALS		301-400
P	MULTIM	DEVELOPING READING SKILLS, PART II: PHONICS, VOWEL SOUNDS	EDUCATIONAL ENRICHMENT MATERIALS		101-150
P	MULTIM	SOUND IT, UNIT 2	IMPERIAL INTERNATIONAL LEARNING		51-75
P	MULTIM	FIRST TALKING ALPHABET: PART 2, VOWELS	SCOTT, FORESMAN & CO.		76-100

LEVEL	FORMAT	TITLE	PUBLISHER	NT	$PRICE

58 - SKILL: VOWELS - LONG

LEVEL	FORMAT	TITLE	PUBLISHER	NT	$PRICE
P	MULTIM	VOWEL SOUNDS KIT	ENRICH, INC.		76-100
P	MULTIM	CONSONANT & VOWEL LAB	ENRICH, INC.		>450
P	MULTIM	READING SKILLS SUPPORT SYSTEM, BOX 2	EDL/MCGRAW-HILL		301-400
P	MULTIM	NEW GOALS IN LISTENING, GRADES 1-3	TROLL ASSOCIATES		76-100
P	PI/PRT	LEARNING SLATE: PHONICS	IDEAL SCHOOL SUPPLY COMPANY		<5
P	PUPILB	LEARNING THE LETTERS, BOOK II	EDUCATORS PUBLISHING SERVICE		<5
P	PUPILB	LEARNING THE LETTERS, BOOK III	EDUCATORS PUBLISHING SERVICE		<5
P	PUPILB	LEARNING THE LETTERS, BOOK IV	EDUCATORS PUBLISHING SERVICE		<5
P	PUPILB	LEARNING THE LETTERS, BOOK V	EDUCATORS PUBLISHING SERVICE		<5
P	PUPILB	LEARNING THE LETTERS, BOOK VI	EDUCATORS PUBLISHING SERVICE		<5
P	PUPILB	PRIMARY READERS, SET 2: LONG VOWELS	MODERN CURRICULUM PRESS		<5
P	RECORD	SOUNDS FOR YOUNG READERS, VOLUME 2	CLASSROOM MATERIALS CO.		6-10
P	RECORD	SOUNDS FOR YOUNG READERS, VOLUME 3	CLASSROOM MATERIALS CO.		6-10
P	RECORD	SOUNDS, VOL. 3	CHILDREN'S BOOK & MUSIC CENTER		6-10
P	SKLKIT	SWEET PICKLES PHONICS PROGRAM	BFA EDUCATIONAL MEDIA		101-150
P	SND FS	SOLVING THE PHONICS MYSTERY: CASE OF THE LONG & SHORT VOWELS	LEARNING TREE FILMSTRIPS		76-100
P	SND FS	STORY OF A, E, O	HERBERT M. ELKINS COMPANY		11-20
P	SND FS	STORY OF I & Y	HERBERT M. ELKINS COMPANY		11-20
P	SND FS	STORY OF U, W & W CONTROLLER	HERBERT M. ELKINS COMPANY		11-20
P	SND FS	LONG VOWELS	HERBERT M. ELKINS COMPANY		11-20
P	SND FS	VOWELS: HOW THEY LOOK & SOUND	UNITED LEARNING		101-150
P	SP EQT	LANGUAGE SKILLS PROGRAM: INTRODUCTION TO SPELLING	SPELLBINDER, INC.		51-75
P	SP EQT	CHARLIE: PHONICS, LONG & SHORT VOWELS	EDUCATIONAL INSIGHTS, INC.		6-10
P	TRANSP	BASIC PHONETIC SKILL DRILLS	PAUL S. AMIDON & ASSOC., INC.		21-30
P	VISKIT	PICTURE A VOWEL SOUND	DEVELOPMENTAL LEARNING MATERIALS		11-20
P	WKBOOK	PHONIC PICTURE CARDS	KENWORTHY EDUCATIONAL SERVICE		<5
P	WKBOOK	AEVAC PHONICS PROGRAM	AEVAC, INC.	6	11-20
P	WKBOOK	AEVAC PHONICS PROGRAM, BOOK A	AEVAC, INC.		<5
P	WKBOOK	AEVAC PHONICS PROGRAM, BOOK C	AEVAC, INC.		<5
P	WKBOOK	AEVAC PHONICS PROGRAM, BOOK D	AEVAC, INC.		<5
P	WKBOOK	AEVAC PHONICS PROGRAM, BOOK E	AEVAC, INC.		<5
P	WKBOOK	S.T.A.R.T., BOOK 7	EMC CORPORATION		<5
P	WKBOOK	S.T.A.R.T., BOOK 12	EMC CORPORATION		<5
P	WKBOOK	S.T.A.R.T., BOOK 15	EMC CORPORATION		<5
P	WKBOOK	S.T.A.R.T., BOOK 16	EMC CORPORATION		<5
P	WKBOOK	S.T.A.R.T., BOOK 17	EMC CORPORATION		<5
P	WKBOOK	VOWELS & VARIANTS, BOOK C	GINN & COMPANY		<5
P	WKBOOK	MORE VOWELS & VARIANTS, BOOK D	GINN & COMPANY		<5
P	WKBOOK	VOWEL WORKBOOK: SOUND, SPELL, READ	PHONOVISUAL PRODUCTS, INC.		<5
P	WKBOOK	PHONICS WORKTEXT: LONG VOWELS	HAMMOND, INC.		<5
P	WKBOOK	PHONICS WORKTEXT: VARIANT VOWELS	HAMMOND, INC.		<5
P	WKBOOK	PHONICS: VOWELS-BLENDS READING REVIEW	JENN PUBLICATIONS		<5
P	WKBOOK	PHONICS: VOWELS, GRADE 2	JENN PUBLICATIONS		<5
P	WKBOOK	PHONICS, GRADE 3	JENN PUBLICATIONS		<5
P	WKBOOK	LETTERS & SOUNDS, PRIMARY	SCOTT, FORESMAN & CO.		<5
P	WKBOOK	MERRILL PHONICS SKILL TEXT: COSTUME KIDS, LEVEL B	CHARLES E. MERRILL PUBLISHING CO		<5
P	WKBOOK	MERRILL PHONICS SKILL TEXT: SPACE VISITORS, LEVEL C	CHARLES E. MERRILL PUBLISHING CO		<5
P	WKBOOK	PHONICS BOOK D: LONG VOWEL SOUNDS, VOWEL DIGRAPHS	SCHOLASTIC BOOK SERVICE		<5
P	WKBOOK	VIEW ON VOWELS	ALLYN AND BACON, INC.		<5
P	WKBOOK	PRIMARY PHONICS WORKBOOK 2	EDUCATORS PUBLISHING SERVICE		<5
P	WKBOOK	PRIMARY PHONICS WORKBOOK 3	EDUCATORS PUBLISHING SERVICE		<5
P	WKBOOK	WORKBOOK M2	EDUCATORS PUBLISHING SERVICE		<5
P	WKBOOK	LONG VOWELS: STARTING OFF WITH PHONICS, BOOK 6	MODERN CURRICULUM PRESS		<5
P	WKBOOK	MCP PHONICS WORKBOOKS: LEVEL A	MODERN CURRICULUM PRESS		<5
P	WKBOOK	MCP PHONICS WORKBOOKS: LEVEL C	MODERN CURRICULUM PRESS		<5
P	WKBOOK	PHONICS IS FUN, BOOK 2	MODERN CURRICULUM PRESS		<5
P	WKBOOK	NEW PHONICS WORKBOOK, BOOK B	MODERN CURRICULUM PRESS		<5
P	WKBOOK	SOUNDS WE USE, BOOK 1	HAYES SCHOOL PUBLISHING COMPANY		<5
P	WKBOOK	SOUNDS WE USE, BOOK 3	HAYES SCHOOL PUBLISHING COMPANY		<5
P	WKBOOK	VOWEL OWL	ACTIVITY RESOURCES COMPANY, INC.		<5
P	WKBOOK	BIG LOOK AT LONG & SHORT VOWELS	MILTON BRADLEY/PLAYSKOOL		<5
PI	ACTCRD	VOWEL OWL	KIDS & COMPANY		<5
PI	ACTCRD	LONG & SHORT VOWEL PUZZLES	INCENTIVES FOR LEARNING, INC.		6-10
PI	ACTCRD	PHONIC WIPE OFF CARDS	WEBER COSTELLO COMPANY		<5
PI	AUDKIT	POWERPAC III	IMPERIAL INTERNATIONAL LEARNING		101-150
PI	AUDKIT	POWERPAC IV	IMPERIAL INTERNATIONAL LEARNING		101-150
PI	AUDKIT	POWERPAC PROGRAM	IMPERIAL INTERNATIONAL LEARNING	4	>450
PI	AUDKIT	VOWEL SOUNDS & SILENT LETTERS	NATIONAL BOOK COMPANY		21-30
PI	AUDKIT	WAY TO SPELL LONG VOWEL SOUNDS	MEDIA MATERIALS, INC.		6-10
PI	CL SET	SOUND OFF & READ	MAFEX ASSOCIATES, INC.		31-50
PI	DITTO	POSITIVELY PHONICS: LONG VOWELS	FRANK SCHAFFER PUBLICATIONS, INC		<5
PI	DITTO	COLOR, CUT & PASTE VOWEL	PAUL S. AMIDON & ASSOC., INC.		<5
PI	DITTO	SPECIAL VOWEL PATTERNS, PART II	INSTRUCTO/MCGRAW-HILL		<5
PI	DITTO	FUNNY FACE PHONICS	ACTIVITY RESOURCES COMPANY, INC.		<5
PI	DITTO	WORD PERCEPTION	MILTON BRADLEY/PLAYSKOOL		<5
PI	FILMST	LEARNING ABOUT OUR LANGUAGE, SET 4	AEVAC, INC.		31-50
PI	GAME	PHONICS SOUP, LONG VOWEL GAMES	CREATIVE TEACHING ASSOCIATES		6-10
PI	GAME	LONG VOWELS	FRANK SCHAFFER PUBLICATIONS, INC		<5
PI	GAME	SEA OF VOWELS	IDEAL SCHOOL SUPPLY COMPANY		6-10

LEVEL	FORMAT	TITLE	PUBLISHER	NT	$PRICE

58 - SKILL: VOWELS - LONG

LEVEL	FORMAT	TITLE	PUBLISHER	NT	$PRICE
PI	GAME	TEAM CHECKERS: LONG VOWELS	LITTLE KENNY PUBLICATIONS, INC.		6-10
PI	GAME	PHONICS SOUP GAME PACKAGES: LONG VOWELS	SCOTT RESOURCES, INC.		6-10
PI	MANIPU	SOUND 'N' SPELL ALPHABET PUZZLE	CREATIVE TEACHING ASSOCIATES		6-10
PI	MANIPU	PHONICS E-Z LANGUAGE LEARNING SLIDE RULES, 3RD & 4TH	E-Z GRADER COMPANY		<5
PI	MANIPU	AERO PHONICS LAB	AERO PUBLISHERS, INC.		76-100
PI	MULTIU	LONG & SHORT VOWEL SOUNDS KIT	LESWING PRESS		31-50
PI	MULTIU	PHONICS IN CONTEXT, SET I	EDUCATIONAL ACTIVITIES, INC.		76-100
PI	MULTIM	PHONICS: THE F.I.R.S.T. APPROACH TO READING	WEBER COSTELLO COMPANY		101-150
PI	MULTIM	WORKING WITH PHONICS	TROLL ASSOCIATES		301-400
PI	SND FS	PHONICS SERIES 1	HAMPDEN PUBLICATIONS, INC.		76-100
PI	SND FS	BASIC WORD ATTACK	EDL/MCGRAW-HILL		301-400
PI	SND FS	WORKING WITH VOWELS	TROLL ASSOCIATES		101-150
PI	SP EQT	LANGUAGE SKILLS PROGRAM: READING-SPELLING COMPREHENSION	SPELLBINDER, INC.		51-75
PI	WKBOOK	LONG VOWELS	FRANK SCHAFFER PUBLICATIONS, INC		<5
PI	WKBOOK	PRIMARY PHONICS WORKBOOK 4	EDUCATORS PUBLISHING SERVICE		<5
PI	WKBOOK	PHONICS FAST & EASY	ACTIVITY RESOURCES COMPANY, INC.		<5
PIJ	GAME	SOUND OFF & READ GAMES	MAFEX ASSOCIATES, INC.		11-20
I	DITTO	CROSSWORD PUZZLES FOR PHONICS: VOWELS II	CONTINENTAL PRESS, INC.		<5
I	DITTO	SOUNDS IN WORDS, BOOK 8	GEL-STEN, INC.		<5
I	DITTO	SOUNDS IN WORDS, BOOK 10	GEL-STEN, INC.		<5
I	DITTO	SOUNDS IN WORDS, BOOK 11	GEL-STEN, INC.		<5
I	DITTO	SOUNDS IN WORDS, BOOK 14	GEL-STEN, INC.		<5
I	DITTO	SOUNDS IN WORDS, BOOK 16	GEL-STEN, INC.		<5
I	DITTO	SOUNDS IN WORDS, BOOK 17	GEL-STEN, INC.		<5
I	DITTO	DECODING SKILLS D	ACTIVITY RESOURCES COMPANY, INC.		<5
I	DITTO	VOWELS	MILTON BRADLEY/PLAYSKOOL		<5
I	GAME	NEW PHONICS WE USE LEARNING GAMES KITS, KIT TWO	RAND MCNALLY & COMPANY		76-100
I	GAME	VOWEL SOLITAIRE	SCOTT, FORESMAN & CO.		6-10
I	GUIDE	MERRILL PHONICS SKILL TEXT: DETECTIVE CLUB, LEVEL E	CHARLES E. MERRILL PUBLISHING CO		<5
I	MULTIM	GAMES 'N' FRAMES: THE STRANGE CASE OF THE VANISHING VOWELS	IMPERIAL INTERNATIONAL LEARNING		21-30
I	MULTIM	GAMES 'N' FRAMES: SOUL TRIP	IMPERIAL INTERNATIONAL LEARNING		21-30
I	MULTIM	SELECT-A-SKILL KIT, UNIT 2: PIONEER LIFE	IMPERIAL INTERNATIONAL LEARNING		51-75
I	MULTIM	SELECT-A-SKILL KIT, UNIT 2: PIONEER LIFE	IMPERIAL INTERNATIONAL LEARNING		51-75
I	MULTIM	SELECT-A-SKILL KIT, UNIT 8: LEGENDS, TALES & POETRY	IMPERIAL INTERNATIONAL LEARNING		51-75
I	RECORD	SOUND SKILLS FOR UPPER GRADES	CLASSROOM MATERIALS CO.	3	21-30
I	RECORD	SOUND SKILLS FOR UPPER GRADES, VOLUME 2	CLASSROOM MATERIALS CO.		6-10
I	WKBOOK	MOTT BASIC LANG. SKILLS: BOOK 1304	ALLIED EDUCATION COUNCIL		<5
I	WKBOOK	PHONICS FOR THE INTERMEDIATE GRADES (4, 5, 6)	JENN PUBLICATIONS		<5
I	WKBOOK	LETTERS & SOUNDS, INTERMEDIATE	SCOTT, FORESMAN & CO.		<5
I	WKBOOK	MERRILL PHONICS SKILL TEXT: DETECTIVE CLUB, LEVEL E	CHARLES E. MERRILL PUBLISHING CO		<5
IJ	ACTCRD	FICKLE VOWELS	LESWING PRESS		6-10
IJ	GAME	VOWEL BINGO	TREND ENTERPRISES, INC.		6-10
IJ	WKBOOK	BOOK ONE, PART ONE: PHONIC ANALYSIS ACTIVITIES	T.S. DENISON & COMPANY		6-10
IJS	ACTCRD	JOIN THE VOWEL QUINTET	LESWING PRESS		6-10
IJS	AUDKIT	HITS, LEVEL 1: AMERICA, LONELY PEOPLE	MODULEARN, INC.		11-20
IJS	AUDKIT	HITS, LEVEL 1: SANTANA, LET IT SHINE	MODULEARN, INC.		11-20
IJS	AUDKIT	HITS, LEVEL 1: DOOBIE BROTHERS, IT KEEPS YOU RUNNING	MODULEARN, INC.		11-20
IJS	AUDKIT	HITS, LEVEL 1: AMERICA, TIN MAN	MODULEARN, INC.		11-20
IJS	AUDKIT	HITS, LEVEL 1: AMERICA, VENTURA HIGHWAY	MODULEARN, INC.		11-20
IJS	AUDKIT	HITS, LEVEL 1: JAMES TAYLOR, SWEET BABY JAMES	MODULEARN, INC.		11-20
IJS	AUDKIT	HITS, LEVEL 1: PAUL SIMON, EL CONDOR PASA	MODULEARN, INC.		11-20
IJS	AUDKIT	HITS, LEVEL 1: BLACKBYRDS, YOU'VE GOT THAT SOMETHING	MODULEARN, INC.		11-20
IJS	AUDKIT	HITS, LEVEL 2: FLEETWOOD MAC, OVER MY HEAD	MODULEARN, INC.		11-20
IJS	AUDKIT	HITS, LEVEL 2: SPINNERS, GAMES PEOPLE PLAY	MODULEARN, INC.		11-20
IJS	AUDKIT	HITS, LEVEL 2: BELLAMY BROTHERS, LET YOUR LOVE FLOW	MODULEARN, INC.		11-20
IJS	AUDKIT	HITS, LEVEL 2: JOHN SEBASTIAN, WELCOME BACK	MODULEARN, INC.		11-20
IJS	AUDKIT	HITS, LEVEL 2: SPINNERS, COULD IT BE I'M FALLING IN LOVE	MODULEARN, INC.		11-20
IJS	AUDKIT	HITS, LEVEL 2: ABBA, KNOWING ME, KNOWING YOU	MODULEARN, INC.		11-20
IJS	AUDKIT	HITS, LEVEL 2: DONNIE & MARIE OSMOND, IT TAKES TWO	MODULEARN, INC.		11-20
IJS	AUDKIT	HITS, LEVEL 2: ABBA, S.O.S.	MODULEARN, INC.		11-20
IJS	AUDKIT	HITS, LEVEL 2: EARTH WIND & FIRE, SHINING STAR	MODULEARN, INC.		11-20
IJS	AUDKIT	HITS, LEVEL 2: PAUL SIMON, STILL CRAZY AFTER ALL THESE YEARS	MODULEARN, INC.		11-20
IJS	AUDKIT	HITS, LEVEL 2: SIDE EFFECT, S.O.S.	MODULEARN, INC.		11-20
IJS	AUDKIT	HITS, LEVEL 3: JOHNNY NASH, I CAN SEE CLEARLY NOW	MODULEARN, INC.		11-20
IJS	AUDKIT	HITS, LEVEL 3: JAMES TAYLOR, SHOWER THE PEOPLE	MODULEARN, INC.		11-20
IJS	AUDKIT	HITS, LEVEL 3: FIREFALL, LIVIN' AIN'T LIVIN'	MODULEARN, INC.		11-20
IJS	AUDKIT	HITS, LEVEL 3: DOOBIE BROTHERS, LISTEN TO THE MUSIC	MODULEARN, INC.		11-20
IJS	AUDKIT	HITS, LEVEL 3: PAUL SIMON, 50 WAYS TO LEAVE YOUR LOVER	MODULEARN, INC.		11-20
IJS	AUDKIT	HITS, LEVEL 3: EMOTION, BEST OF MY LOVE	MODULEARN, INC.		11-20
IJS	AUDKIT	HITS, LEVEL 3: THREE DOG NIGHT, THE FAMILY OF MAN	MODULEARN, INC.		11-20
IJS	AUDKIT	HITS, LEVEL 3: FLEETWOOD MAC, DON'T STOP	MODULEARN, INC.		11-20
IJS	AUDKIT	HITS, LEVEL 3: CARLY SIMON, GROWN UP	MODULEARN, INC.		11-20
IJS	AUDKIT	HITS, LEVEL 3: SPINNERS, ONE OF A KIND LOVE AFFAIR	MODULEARN, INC.		11-20
IJS	AUDKIT	HITS, LEVEL 3: SPINNERS, JUST CAN'T GET YOU OUT OF MY MIND	MODULEARN, INC.		11-20
IJS	MULTIU	LONG & SHORT OF IT	LESWING PRESS		11-20
IJS	MULTIU	PHONICS IN CONTEXT, SET II	EDUCATIONAL ACTIVITIES, INC.		51-75
JS	AUDKIT	READING CASSETTES: VOWELS	IDEAL SCHOOL SUPPLY COMPANY		51-75
JS	AUDKIT	USING PHONICS SERIES	MEDIA MATERIALS, INC.		101-150
JS	HI INT	READING FOR RESULTS (RL 2 - 3)	CAMBRIDGE BOOK CO.		<5

LEVEL	FORMAT	TITLE	PUBLISHER	NT	$PRICE

```
                      ------------------------------------------------------
                      58 - SKILL:    VOWELS - LONG
                      ------------------------------------------------------
```

LEVEL	FORMAT	TITLE	PUBLISHER	NT	$PRICE
JS	SND FS	ADVANCED WORD ATTACK	EDL/MCGRAW-HILL		301-400
JS	WKBOOK	NEW STREAMLINED ENGLISH SERIES: SKILL BOOK 3	NEW READERS PRESS		<5
S	AUDKIT	VOWELS (IMMEDIATE-SECONDARY)	EDUCATIONAL MEDIA, INC.		31-50
S	AUDKIT	PHONICS SERIES 1	HAMPDEN PUBLICATIONS, INC.		76-100
S	SND FS	SHORT & LONG A	MEDIA MATERIALS, INC.		11-20
S	SND FS	SHORT & LONG E	MEDIA MATERIALS, INC.		11-20
S	SND FS	SHORT & LONG I	MEDIA MATERIALS, INC.		11-20
S	SND FS	SHORT & LONG O	MEDIA MATERIALS, INC.		11-20
S	SND FS	SHORT & LONG U	MEDIA MATERIALS, INC.		11-20

```
                      ------------------------------------------------------
                      59 - SKILL:    VOWEL DIGRAPHS
                      ------------------------------------------------------
```

LEVEL	FORMAT	TITLE	PUBLISHER	NT	$PRICE
RP	MULTIM	ALPHA-SOUND PROGRAM, GROUP 2	CLEARVUE, INC.		151-200
RPI	AUDKIT	PHONICS SERIES	MEDIA MATERIALS, INC.	10	76-100
P	ACTCRD	SPEECH SOUNDS PICTURE CARDS: DIGRAPHS & DIPHTHONGS	TEACHING RESOURCES CORPORATION		6-10
P	ACTCRD	GROUP-SIZE VOWEL CARDS	GARRARD PUBLISHING COMPANY		<5
P	ACTCRD	ETA SORT & SOUND VOWEL DIGRAPH CARDS	EDUCATIONAL TEACHING AIDS		6-10
P	ACTCRD	SOUND FOUNDATION, PROGRAM 1	DEVELOPMENTAL LEARNING MATERIALS		11-20
P	ACTCRD	VOWEL PACER	DM EDUCATIONAL PUBLICATIONS		<5
P	ACTCRD	VOWEL SOUNDS	MILTON BRADLEY/PLAYSKOOL		<5
P	AUDCAS	SIGHT & SOUND PHONICS	EDUCATIONAL TEACHING AIDS		21-30
P	AUDCAS	VIEW ON VOWELS, WORKTAPES	ALLYN AND BACON, INC.		101-150
P	AUDKIT	PRIMARY WORK RECOGNITION	EYE GATE MEDIA	5	31-50
P	AUDKIT	VOWEL DIGRAPHS & DIPHTHONGS	EYE GATE MEDIA		6-10
P	AUDKIT	PHONICS: VOWEL CLUSTER FUN	EYE GATE MEDIA		6-10
P	AUDKIT	PHONETICS FACTORY	IDEAL SCHOOL SUPPLY COMPANY		51-75
P	CHART	PROSPECTING IN PHONICS	IDEAL SCHOOL SUPPLY COMPANY		6-10
P	CHART	VOWEL POSTER CARDS	MILTON BRADLEY/PLAYSKOOL		6-10
P	DITTO	CROSSWORD PUZZLES FOR PHONICS: SPECIAL SOUNDS I	CONTINENTAL PRESS, INC.		<5
P	DITTO	LEARNING CENTER ACTIVITIS, GRADES 2-3	INSTRUCTIONAL FAIR		<5
P	DITTO	LONG, SHORT & COMBINED VOWEL SOUNDS	INSTRUCTOR PUBLICATIONS, INC.		<5
P	DITTO	SOUND-OFF 5	EDUCATORS PUBLISHING SERVICE		6-10
P	DITTO	SPECIAL VOWEL PATTERNS, PART I	INSTRUCTO/MCGRAW-HILL		<5
P	DITTO	VOWEL DIGRAPHS & DIPHTHONGS	INSTRUCTO/MCGRAW-HILL		<5
P	GAME	SPECIAL VOWELS	FRANK SCHAFFER PUBLICATIONS, INC		<5
P	GAME	PHONICS GAMES	FRANK SCHAFFER PUBLICATIONS, INC		<5
P	GAME	PHONICS DISCOVERY	DISCOVERY LEARNING		<5
P	GAME	VOWEL LOTTO	GARRARD PUBLISHING COMPANY		<5
P	GAME	CHECKMATE: DIGRAPHS	DM EDUCATIONAL PUBLICATIONS		<5
P	MANIPU	LARRY THE LEARNING LION	IDEAL SCHOOL SUPPLY COMPANY		6-10
P	MULTIM	SOUND IT, UNIT 2	IMPERIAL INTERNATIONAL LEARNING		51-75
P	PUPILB	WOG'S LOG BOOK V	EDUCATORS PUBLISHING SERVICE		<5
P	PUPILB	WOG'S LOG BOOK VI	EDUCATORS PUBLISHING SERVICE		<5
P	PUPILB	WOG'S LOG BOOK VII	EDUCATORS PUBLISHING SERVICE		<5
P	PUPILB	WOG'S LOG BOOK VIII	EDUCATORS PUBLISHING SERVICE		<5
P	PUPILB	FIRST PHONICS, PART 2	EDUCATORS PUBLISHING SERVICE		<5
P	PUPILB	ALPHABET SERIES	EDUCATORS PUBLISHING SERVICE		11-20
P	SKLKIT	SWEET PICKLES PHONICS PROGRAM	BFA EDUCATIONAL MEDIA		101-150
P	SND FS	SOLVING THE PHONICS MYSTERY: CLUE OF THE COMBINING LETTERS	LEARNING TREE FILMSTRIPS		76-100
P	VISKIT	RECIPE FOR READING	EDUCATORS PUBLISHING SERVICE		11-20
P	VISKIT	VOWEL COMBINATIONS: CITY SOUNDS	INSTRUCTO/MCGRAW-HILL		11-20
P	WKBOOK	S.T.A.R.T., BOOK 8	EMC CORPORATION		<5
P	WKBOOK	S.T.A.R.T., BOOK 13	EMC CORPORATION		<5
P	WKBOOK	S.T.A.R.T., BOOK 14	EMC CORPORATION		<5
P	WKBOOK	MORE VOWELS & VARIANTS, BOOK D	GINN & COMPANY		<5
P	WKBOOK	SOUNDS & SYLLABLES, BOOK E	GINN & COMPANY		<5
P	WKBOOK	WINDOWS TO READING, BOOK D	FOLLETT PUBLISHING COMPANY		<5
P	WKBOOK	PHONICS BOOK D: LONG VOWEL SOUNDS, VOWEL DIGRAPHS	SCHOLASTIC BOOK SERVICE		<5
P	WKBOOK	VIEW ON VOWELS	ALLYN AND BACON, INC.		<5
P	WKBOOK	PRIMARY PHONICS WORKBOOK 2	EDUCATORS PUBLISHING SERVICE		<5
P	WKBOOK	PRIMARY PHONICS WORKBOOK 3	EDUCATORS PUBLISHING SERVICE		<5
P	WKBOOK	SOUNDS WE USE, BOOK 2	HAYES SCHOOL PUBLISHING COMPANY		<5
PI	ACTCRD	ADVANCED PHONICS: DIPHTHONGS & VOWEL DIGRAPHS	INSTRUCTIONAL FAIR		<5
PI	ACTCRD	ADVANCED PHONICS PAK	INSTRUCTIONAL FAIR		21-30
PI	ACTCRD	VOWEL OWL	KIDS & COMPANY		<5
PI	ACTCRD	PHONIC WIPE OFF CARDS	WEBER COSTELLO COMPANY		<5
PI	AUDCRD	VOWEL COMBINATIONS	AUDIOTRONICS CORPORATION		11-20
PI	AUDKIT	POWERPAC III	IMPERIAL INTERNATIONAL LEARNING		101-150
PI	AUDKIT	POWERPAC IV	IMPERIAL INTERNATIONAL LEARNING		101-150
PI	AUDKIT	POWERPAC PROGRAM	IMPERIAL INTERNATIONAL LEARNING	4	>450
PI	AUDKIT	VOWEL SOUNDS: VOWEL DIGRAPHS	MEDIA MATERIALS, INC.		6-10
PI	AUDKIT	VOWEL CLUSTER FUN	MEDIA MATERIALS, INC.		6-10
PI	AUDKIT	VOWEL DIGRAPHS AND DIPHTHONGS	MEDIA MATERIALS, INC.		6-10
PI	AUDKIT	MORE PHONICS	HAMPDEN PUBLICATIONS, INC.		101-150
PI	CL SET	SOUND OFF & READ	MAFEX ASSOCIATES, INC.		31-50
PI	DITTO	ADVANCED PHONICS: DIPHTHONGS & VOWEL DIGRAPHS	INSTRUCTIONAL FAIR		<5
PI	DITTO	ADVANCED PHONICS PAK	INSTRUCTIONAL FAIR		21-30
PI	DITTO	SPELLING PROGRAM, BOOK J	FRANK SCHAFFER PUBLICATIONS, INC		<5
PI	DITTO	SPECIAL VOWEL PATTERNS, PART II	INSTRUCTO/MCGRAW-HILL		<5

LEVEL	FORMAT	TITLE	PUBLISHER	NT	$PRICE

59 - SKILL: VOWEL DIGRAPHS

LEVEL	FORMAT	TITLE	PUBLISHER	NT	$PRICE
PI	DITTO	FUNNY FACE PHONICS	ACTIVITY RESOURCES COMPANY, INC.		<5
PI	FILMST	LEARNING ABOUT OUR LANGUAGE, SET 4	AEVAC, INC.		31-50
PI	FILMST	PHONICS FILM STRIP SERIES 2	MEDIA MATERIALS, INC.	5	76-100
PI	FILMST	USING VOWEL DIGRAPHS	MEDIA MATERIALS, INC.		11-20
PI	GAME	SEA OF VOWELS	IDEAL SCHOOL SUPPLY COMPANY		6-10
PI	GAME	VOWEL COMBINATIONS PLAYING CARDS	INSTRUCTO/MCGRAW-HILL		6-10
PI	MANIPU	AERO PHONICS LAB	AERO PUBLISHERS, INC.		76-100
PI	MULTIU	PHONICS IN CONTEXT, SET I	EDUCATIONAL ACTIVITIES, INC.		76-100
PI	PUPILB	EXPLODE THE CODE, BOOK 3	EDUCATORS PUBLISHING SERVICE		<5
PI	SND FS	PHONICS SERIES 2	HAMPDEN PUBLICATIONS, INC.		76-100
PI	SND FS	BASIC WORD ATTACK	EDL/MCGRAW-HILL		301-400
PI	SND FS	WORKING WITH VOWELS	TROLL ASSOCIATES		101-150
PI	SP EQT	LANGUAGE SKILLS PROGRAM: WORD GAMES & PUZZLES	SPELLBINDER, INC.		51-75
PI	WKBOOK	AEVAC STARTER 101, BOOK 9 (NON-READERS)	AEVAC, INC.		<5
PI	WKBOOK	AEVAC STARTER 101, BOOK 10 (NON-READERS)	AEVAC, INC.		<5
PI	WKBOOK	PRIMARY PHONICS WORKBOOK 4	EDUCATORS PUBLISHING SERVICE		<5
PI	WKBOOK	PRIMARY PHONICS WORKBOOK 5	EDUCATORS PUBLISHING SERVICE		<5
I	AUDKIT	READING CASSETTES: PHONIC ANALYSIS	IDEAL SCHOOL SUPPLY COMPANY		51-75
I	DITTO	CROSSWORD PUZZLES FOR PHONICS: SPECIAL SOUNDS II	CONTINENTAL PRESS, INC.		<5
I	DITTO	SOUNDS IN WORDS, BOOK 8	GEL-STEN, INC.		<5
I	DITTO	SOUNDS IN WORDS, BOOK 11	GEL-STEN, INC.		<5
I	DITTO	SOUNDS IN WORDS, BOOK 14	GEL-STEN, INC.		<5
I	DITTO	SOUNDS IN WORDS, BOOK 16	GEL-STEN, INC.		<5
I	DITTO	SOUNDS IN WORDS, BOOK 17	GEL-STEN, INC.		<5
I	DITTO	DECODING SKILLS E	ACTIVITY RESOURCES COMPANY, INC.		<5
I	MULTIM	GAMES 'N' FRAMES: DR. DIGRAPH'S HOCUS-POCUS	IMPERIAL INTERNATIONAL LEARNING		21-30
I	WKBOOK	TALES FOR TRANSFER SKILL SERIES	ANN ARBOR PUBLISHERS		<5
I	WKBOOK	MOTT BASIC LANG. SKILLS: BOOK 1304	ALLIED EDUCATION COUNCIL		<5
I	WKBOOK	PHONICS FOR THE INTERMEDIATE GRADES (4, 5, 6)	JENN PUBLICATIONS		<5
IJ	ACTCRD	VENTURE IN VOWELS	LESWING PRESS		6-10
IJ	MULTIM	SADDLE UP (RL 3)	INSTRUCTO/MCGRAW-HILL		11-20
IJ	WKBOOK	BOOK ONE, PART ONE: PHONIC ANALYSIS ACTIVITIES	T.S. DENISON & COMPANY		6-10
IJS	AUDKIT	HITS, LEVEL 1: DOOBIE BROTHERS, IT KEEPS YOU RUNNING	MODULEARN, INC.		11-20
IJS	AUDKIT	HITS, LEVEL 1: AMERICA, TIN MAN	MODULEARN, INC.		11-20
IJS	AUDKIT	HITS, LEVEL 1: AMERICA, VENTURA HIGHWAY	MODULEARN, INC.		11-20
IJS	AUDKIT	HITS, LEVEL 1: JAMES TAYLOR, SWEET BABY JAMES	MODULEARN, INC.		11-20
IJS	AUDKIT	HITS, LEVEL 1: PAUL SIMON, EL CONDOR PASA	MODULEARN, INC.		11-20
IJS	AUDKIT	HITS, LEVEL 1: BLACKBYRDS, YOU'VE GOT THAT SOMETHING	MODULEARN, INC.		11-20
IJS	AUDKIT	HITS, LEVEL 2: SPINNERS, GAMES PEOPLE PLAY	MODULEARN, INC.		11-20
IJS	AUDKIT	HITS, LEVEL 2: BELLAMY BROTHERS, LET YOUR LOVE FLOW	MODULEARN, INC.		11-20
IJS	AUDKIT	HITS, LEVEL 2: JOHN SEBASTIAN, WELCOME BACK	MODULEARN, INC.		11-20
IJS	AUDKIT	HITS, LEVEL 2: SPINNERS, COULD IT BE I'M FALLING IN LOVE	MODULEARN, INC.		11-20
IJS	AUDKIT	HITS, LEVEL 2: DONNIE & MARIE OSMOND, IT TAKES TWO	MODULEARN, INC.		11-20
IJS	AUDKIT	HITS, LEVEL 2: ABBA, S.O.S.	MODULEARN, INC.		11-20
IJS	AUDKIT	HITS, LEVEL 2: EARTH WIND & FIRE, SHINING STAR	MODULEARN, INC.		11-20
IJS	AUDKIT	HITS, LEVEL 2: PAUL SIMON, STILL CRAZY AFTER ALL THESE YEARS	MODULEARN, INC.		11-20
IJS	AUDKIT	HITS, LEVEL 2: SIDE EFFECT, S.O.S.	MODULEARN, INC.		11-20
IJS	AUDKIT	HITS, LEVEL 3: JOHNNY NASH, I CAN SEE CLEARLY NOW	MODULEARN, INC.		11-20
IJS	AUDKIT	HITS, LEVEL 3: FIREFALL, LIVIN' AIN'T LIVIN'	MODULEARN, INC.		11-20
IJS	AUDKIT	HITS, LEVEL 3: DOOBIE BROTHERS, LISTEN TO THE MUSIC	MODULEARN, INC.		11-20
IJS	AUDKIT	HITS, LEVEL 3: PAUL SIMON, 50 WAYS TO LEAVE YOUR LOVER	MODULEARN, INC.		11-20
IJS	AUDKIT	HITS, LEVEL 3: EMOTION, BEST OF MY LOVE	MODULEARN, INC.		11-20
IJS	AUDKIT	HITS, LEVEL 3: THREE DOG NIGHT, THE FAMILY OF MAN	MODULEARN, INC.		11-20
IJS	AUDKIT	HITS, LEVEL 3: FLEETWOOD MAC, DON'T STOP	MODULEARN, INC.		11-20
IJS	AUDKIT	HITS, LEVEL 3: CARLY SIMON, GROWN UP	MODULEARN, INC.		11-20
IJS	AUDKIT	HITS, LEVEL 3: SPINNERS, ONE OF A KIND LOVE AFFAIR	MODULEARN, INC.		11-20
IJS	AUDKIT	HITS, LEVEL 3: SPINNERS, JUST CAN'T GET YOU OUT OF MY MIND	MODULEARN, INC.		11-20
IJS	GAME	AUTO PHONICS: VOWEL DIGRAPHS & DIPHTHONGS	EDUCATIONAL ACTIVITIES, INC.		<5
IJS	MULTIU	PHONICS IN CONTEXT, SET II	EDUCATIONAL ACTIVITIES, INC.		51-75
JS	AUDKIT	READING CASSETTES: VOWELS	IDEAL SCHOOL SUPPLY COMPANY		51-75
JS	AUDKIT	USING PHONICS SERIES	MEDIA MATERIALS, INC.		101-150
JS	AUDKIT	LEARNING PHONICS	HAMPDEN PUBLICATIONS, INC.		101-150
JS	HI INT	READING FOR RESULTS (RL 2 - 3)	CAMBRIDGE BOOK CO.		<5
JS	WKBOOK	NEW STREAMLIND ENGLISH SERIES: SKILL BOOK 4	NEW READERS PRESS		<5
S	AUDKIT	PHONICS SERIES 2	HAMPDEN PUBLICATIONS, INC.		76-100
S	SND FS	USING VOWEL DIGRAPHS	MEDIA MATERIALS, INC.		11-20
S	SND FS	USING VOWEL DIPHTHONGS	MEDIA MATERIALS, INC.		11-20

60 - SKILL: VOWEL DIPHTHONGS

LEVEL	FORMAT	TITLE	PUBLISHER	NT	$PRICE
RPI	AUDKIT	PHONICS SERIES	MEDIA MATERIALS, INC.	10	76-100
P	ACTCRD	SAY THE SOUNDS	KENWORTHY EDUCATIONAL SERVICE		<5
P	ACTCRD	SPEECH SOUNDS PICTURE CARDS: DIGRAPHS & DIPHTHONGS	TEACHING RESOURCES CORPORATION		6-10
P	ACTCRD	HOWL FOR OWL, LEVEL I	INCENTIVES FOR LEARNING, INC.		<5
P	ACTCRD	GROUP-SIZE VOWEL CARDS	GARRARD PUBLISHING COMPANY		<5
P	ACTCRD	VOWEL SOUNDS	MILTON BRADLEY/PLAYSKOOL		<5
P	AUDCAS	SOUNDS FOR YOUNG READERS, VOLUME 6	CLASSROOM MATERIALS CO.		6-10
P	AUDCAS	SIGHT & SOUND PHONICS	EDUCATIONAL TEACHING AIDS		21-30
P	AUDCAS	VIEW ON VOWELS, WORKTAPES	ALLYN AND BACON, INC.		101-150

LEVEL	FORMAT	TITLE	PUBLISHER	NT	$PRICE

60 - SKILL: VOWEL DIPHTHONGS

LEVEL	FORMAT	TITLE	PUBLISHER	NT	$PRICE
P	AUDKIT	PRIMARY WORK RECOGNITION	EYE GATE MEDIA	5	31-50
P	AUDKIT	VOWEL DIGRAPHS & DIPHTHONGS	EYE GATE MEDIA		6-10
P	AUDKIT	PHONICS: VOWEL CLUSTER FUN	EYE GATE MEDIA		6-10
P	AUDKIT	MINISYSTEMS: DIPHTHONGS, EA,AI,OA	CORONET MULTI MEDIA		11-20
P	AUDKIT	MINISYSTEMS: DIPHTHONGS, EA,OU,OO	CORONET MULTI MEDIA		11-20
P	CHART	PROSPECTING IN PHONICS	IDEAL SCHOOL SUPPLY COMPANY		6-10
P	DITTO	NEW PHONICS & WORD ANALYSIS SKILLS: GRADE 2, PART 2	CONTINENTAL PRESS, INC.		<5
P	DITTO	NEW PHONICS & WORD ANALYSIS SKILLS: GRADE 3, PART 1	CONTINENTAL PRESS, INC.		<5
P	DITTO	LONG, SHORT & COMBINED VOWEL SOUNDS	INSTRUCTOR PUBLICATIONS, INC.		<5
P	DITTO	SOUND-OFF 5	EDUCATORS PUBLISHING SERVICE		6-10
P	DITTO	VOWEL DIGRAPHS & DIPHTHONGS	INSTRUCTO/MCGRAW-HILL		<5
P	FLASH	FLASH CARDS, SET B	MODERN CURRICULUM PRESS		11-20
P	GAME	SPECIAL VOWELS	FRANK SCHAFFER PUBLICATIONS, INC		<5
P	GAME	PHONICS GAMES	FRANK SCHAFFER PUBLICATIONS, INC		<5
P	GAME	VOWEL LOTTO	GARRARD PUBLISHING COMPANY		<5
P	GAME	CHECKMATE: DIPHTHONGS	DM EDUCATIONAL PUBLICATIONS		<5
P	MULTIM	SOUND IT, UNIT 2	IMPERIAL INTERNATIONAL LEARNING		51-75
P	PUPILB	WOG'S LOG BOOK V	EDUCATORS PUBLISHING SERVICE		<5
P	PUPILB	WOG'S LOG BOOK VI	EDUCATORS PUBLISHING SERVICE		<5
P	PUPILB	WOG'S LOG BOOK VII	EDUCATORS PUBLISHING SERVICE		<5
P	PUPILB	WOG'S LOG BOOK VIII	EDUCATORS PUBLISHING SERVICE		<5
P	RECORD	SOUNDS FOR YOUNG READERS, VOLUME 6	CLASSROOM MATERIALS CO.		6-10
P	SND FS	SOLVING THE PHONICS MYSTERY: CLUE OF THE COMBINING LETTERS	LEARNING TREE FILMSTRIPS		76-100
P	VISKIT	VOWEL COMBINATIONS: CITY SOUNDS	INSTRUCTO/MCGRAW-HILL		11-20
P	WKBOOK	PHONIC PICTURE CARDS	KENWORTHY EDUCATIONAL SERVICE		<5
P	WKBOOK	S.T.A.R.T., BOOK 8	EMC CORPORATION		<5
P	WKBOOK	S.T.A.R.T., BOOK 13	EMC CORPORATION		<5
P	WKBOOK	S.T.A.R.T., BOOK 14	EMC CORPORATION		<5
P	WKBOOK	MORE VOWELS & VARIANTS, BOOK D	GINN & COMPANY		<5
P	WKBOOK	SOUNDS & SYLLABLES, BOOK E	GINN & COMPANY		<5
P	WKBOOK	WINDOWS TO READING, BOOK D	FOLLETT PUBLISHING COMPANY		<5
P	WKBOOK	VIEW ON VOWELS	ALLYN AND BACON, INC.		<5
P	WKBOOK	MCP PHONICS WORKBOOKS: LEVEL B	MODERN CURRICULUM PRESS		<5
PI	ACTCRD	ADVANCED PHONICS: DIPHTHONGS & VOWEL DIGRAPHS	INSTRUCTIONAL FAIR		<5
PI	ACTCRD	ADVANCED PHONICS PAK	INSTRUCTIONAL FAIR		21-30
PI	ACTCRD	VOWEL OWL	KIDS & COMPANY		<5
PI	ACTCRD	SOUND SODA	KIDS & COMPANY		<5
PI	ACTCRD	HOWL FOR OWL, LEVEL II	INCENTIVES FOR LEARNING, INC.		<5
PI	ACTCRD	PHONIC WIPE OFF CARDS	WEBER COSTELLO COMPANY		<5
PI	AUDKIT	VOWEL SOUNDS & SILENT LETTERS	NATIONAL BOOK COMPANY		21-30
PI	AUDKIT	VOWEL SOUNDS: VOWEL DIPHTHONGS	MEDIA MATERIALS, INC.		6-10
PI	AUDKIT	VOWEL CLUSTER FUN	MEDIA MATERIALS, INC.		6-10
PI	AUDKIT	VOWEL DIGRAPHS AND DIPHTHONGS	MEDIA MATERIALS, INC.		6-10
PI	AUDKIT	MORE PHONICS	HAMPDEN PUBLICATIONS, INC.		101-150
PI	DITTO	ADVANCED PHONICS: DIPHTHONGS & VOWEL DIGRAPHS	INSTRUCTIONAL FAIR		<5
PI	DITTO	ADVANCED PHONICS PAK	INSTRUCTIONAL FAIR		21-30
PI	DITTO	SPELLING PROGRAM, BOOK J	FRANK SCHAFFER PUBLICATIONS, INC		<5
PI	DITTO	FUNNY FACE PHONICS	ACTIVITY RESOURCES COMPANY, INC.		<5
PI	FILMST	LEARNING ABOUT OUR LANGUAGE, SET 4	AEVAC, INC.		31-50
PI	FILMST	PHONICS FILM STRIP SERIES 2	MEDIA MATERIALS, INC.	5	76-100
PI	FILMST	USING VOWEL DIPHTHONGS	MEDIA MATERIALS, INC.		11-20
PI	GAME	SEA OF VOWELS	IDEAL SCHOOL SUPPLY COMPANY		6-10
PI	GAME	VOWEL COMBINATIONS PLAYING CARDS	INSTRUCTO/MCGRAW-HILL		6-10
PI	MANIPU	PHONICS E-Z LANGUAGE LEARNING SLIDE RULES, 5TH	E-Z GRADER COMPANY		<5
PI	PUPILB	EXPLODE THE CODE, BOOK 3	EDUCATORS PUBLISHING SERVICE		<5
PI	PUPILB	EXPLODE THE CODE, BOOK 6	EDUCATORS PUBLISHING SERVICE		<5
PI	SND FS	PHONICS SERIES 2	HAMPDEN PUBLICATIONS, INC.		76-100
PI	SND FS	BASIC WORD ATTACK	EDL/MCGRAW-HILL		301-400
PI	SND FS	WORKING WITH VOWELS	TROLL ASSOCIATES		101-150
PI	WKBOOK	AEVAC STARTER 101, BOOK 10 (NON-READERS)	AEVAC, INC.		<5
PIJ	GAME	SOUND OFF & READ GAMES	MAFEX ASSOCIATES, INC.		11-20
PIJ	MULTIM	VISUAL AURAL DISCRIMINATIONS, BOOK IV	ANN ARBOR PUBLISHERS		<5
I	AUDKIT	READING CASSETTES: PHONIC ANALYSIS	IDEAL SCHOOL SUPPLY COMPANY		51-75
I	DITTO	SOUNDS IN WORDS, BOOK 14	GEL-STEN, INC.		<5
I	DITTO	SOUNDS IN WORDS, BOOK 16	GEL-STEN, INC.		<5
I	DITTO	SOUNDS IN WORDS, BOOK 17	GEL-STEN, INC.		<5
I	DITTO	DECODING SKILLS D	ACTIVITY RESOURCES COMPANY, INC.		<5
I	GUIDE	MERRILL PHONICS SKILL TEXT: SIGN MAKERS, LEVEL D	CHARLES E. MERRILL PUBLISHING CO		<5
I	MULTIM	GAMES 'N' FRAMES: DR. DIGRAPH'S HOCUS-POCUS	IMPERIAL INTERNATIONAL LEARNING		21-30
I	MULTIM	SELECT-A-SKILL KIT, UNIT 1: MYSTERY ADVENTURE	IMPERIAL INTERNATIONAL LEARNING		51-75
I	MULTIM	SELECT-A-SKILL KIT, UNIT 1: MYSTERY ADVENTURE	IMPERIAL INTERNATIONAL LEARNING		51-75
I	WKBOOK	TALES FOR TRANSFER SKILL SERIES	ANN ARBOR PUBLISHERS		<5
I	WKBOOK	MOTT BASIC LANG. SKILLS: BOOK 1304	ALLIED EDUCATION COUNCIL		<5
I	WKBOOK	PHONICS FOR THE INTERMEDIATE GRADES (4, 5, 6)	JENN PUBLICATIONS		<5
I	WKBOOK	MERRILL PHONICS SKILL TEXT: SIGN MAKERS, LEVEL D	CHARLES E. MERRILL PUBLISHING CO		<5
IJ	ACTCRD	VENTURE IN VOWELS	LESWING PRESS		6-10
IJ	MULTIM	SADDLE UP (RL 3)	INSTRUCTO/MCGRAW-HILL		11-20
IJS	AUDKIT	HITS, LEVEL 1: AMERICA, TIN MAN	MODULEARN, INC.		11-20
IJS	AUDKIT	HITS, LEVEL 1: AMERICA, VENTURA HIGHWAY	MODULEARN, INC.		11-20

LEVEL	FORMAT	TITLE	PUBLISHER	NT $PRICE

60 - SKILL: VOWEL DIPHTHONGS

LEVEL	FORMAT	TITLE	PUBLISHER	NT $PRICE
IJS	AUDKIT	HITS, LEVEL 1: JAMES TAYLOR, SWEET BABY JAMES	MODULEARN, INC.	11-20
IJS	AUDKIT	HITS, LEVEL 1: PAUL SIMON, EL CONDOR PASA	MODULEARN, INC.	11-20
IJS	AUDKIT	HITS, LEVEL 1: BLACKBYRDS, YOU'VE GOT THAT SOMETHING	MODULEARN, INC.	11-20
IJS	AUDKIT	HITS, LEVEL 2: JOHN SEBASTIAN, WELCOME BACK	MODULEARN, INC.	11-20
IJS	AUDKIT	HITS, LEVEL 2: SPINNERS, COULD IT BE I'M FALLING IN LOVE	MODULEARN, INC.	11-20
IJS	AUDKIT	HITS, LEVEL 2: ABBA, KNOWING ME, KNOWING YOU	MODULEARN, INC.	11-20
IJS	AUDKIT	HITS, LEVEL 2: DONNIE & MARIE OSMOND, IT TAKES TWO	MODULEARN, INC.	11-20
IJS	AUDKIT	HITS, LEVEL 2: ABBA, S.O.S.	MODULEARN, INC.	11-20
IJS	AUDKIT	HITS, LEVEL 2: EARTH WIND & FIRE, SHINING STAR	MODULEARN, INC.	11-20
IJS	AUDKIT	HITS, LEVEL 2: PAUL SIMON, STILL CRAZY AFTER ALL THESE YEARS	MODULEARN, INC.	11-20
IJS	AUDKIT	HITS, LEVEL 2: SIDE EFFECT, S.O.S.	MODULEARN, INC.	11-20
IJS	AUDKIT	HITS, LEVEL 3: JOHNNY NASH, I CAN SEE CLEARLY NOW	MODULEARN, INC.	11-20
IJS	AUDKIT	HITS, LEVEL 3: DOOBIE BROTHERS, LISTEN TO THE MUSIC	MODULEARN, INC.	11-20
IJS	AUDKIT	HITS, LEVEL 3: PAUL SIMON, 50 WAYS TO LEAVE YOUR LOVER	MODULEARN, INC.	11-20
IJS	AUDKIT	HITS, LEVEL 3: EMOTION, BEST OF MY LOVE	MODULEARN, INC.	11-20
IJS	AUDKIT	HITS, LEVEL 3: THREE DOG NIGHT, THE FAMILY OF MAN	MODULEARN, INC.	11-20
IJS	AUDKIT	HITS, LEVEL 3: FLEETWOOD MAC, DON'T STOP	MODULEARN, INC.	11-20
IJS	AUDKIT	HITS, LEVEL 3: CARLY SIMON, GROWN UP	MODULEARN, INC.	11-20
IJS	AUDKIT	HITS, LEVEL 3: SPINNERS, ONE OF A KIND LOVE AFFAIR	MODULEARN, INC.	11-20
IJS	AUDKIT	HITS, LEVEL 3: SPINNERS, JUST CAN'T GET YOU OUT OF MY MIND	MODULEARN, INC.	11-20
IJS	GAME	AUTO PHONICS: VOWEL DIGRAPHS & DIPHTHONGS	EDUCATIONAL ACTIVITIES, INC.	<5
JS	AUDKIT	READING CASSETTES: VOWELS	IDEAL SCHOOL SUPPLY COMPANY	51-75
JS	AUDKIT	LEARNING PHONICS	HAMPDEN PUBLICATIONS, INC.	101-150
JS	WKBOOK	NEW STREAMLIND ENGLISH SERIES: SKILL BOOK 4	NEW READERS PRESS	<5
S	AUDKIT	PHONICS SERIES 2	HAMPDEN PUBLICATIONS, INC.	76-100

61 - SKILL: VOWEL MODIFICATION BY R, L, W

LEVEL	FORMAT	TITLE	PUBLISHER	NT $PRICE
RP	GAME	GAMEBOARD KIT G	READING JOY, INC.	6-10
P	ACTCRD	SAY THE SOUNDS	KENWORTHY EDUCATIONAL SERVICE	<5
P	ACTCRD	SPEECH SOUNDS PICTURE CARDS: VOWEL-R BLENDS	TEACHING RESOURCES CORPORATION	6-10
P	ACTCRD	HOWL FOR OWL, LEVEL I	INCENTIVES FOR LEARNING, INC.	<5
P	ACTCRD	CONSONANT SOUNDS	MILTON BRADLEY/PLAYSKOOL	<5
P	AUDCAS	SOUNDS FOR YOUNG READERS, VOLUME 6	CLASSROOM MATERIALS CO.	6-10
P	AUDKIT	VOWELS	EDUCATIONAL MEDIA, INC.	51-75
P	AUDKIT	MINISYSTEMS: VOWELS CONTROLLED BY R	CORONET MULTI MEDIA	11-20
P	AUDKIT	MINISYSTEMS: VOWELS CONTROLLED BY W & L	CORONET MULTI MEDIA	11-20
P	AUDKIT	MINISYSTEMS: REVIEW, VOWELS CONTROLLED BY R,W,L	CORONET MULTI MEDIA	11-20
P	CHART	PROSPECTING IN PHONICS	IDEAL SCHOOL SUPPLY COMPANY	6-10
P	DITTO	WORD ATTACK SKILLS: MODIFIED VOWEL SOUNDS	EDL/MCGRAW-HILL	6-10
P	DITTO	SPECIAL VOWEL PATTERNS, PART I	INSTRUCTO/MCGRAW-HILL	<5
P	DITTO	PHONICS IIA	HAYES SCHOOL PUBLISHING COMPANY	<5
P	GAME	NEW WORD GAME SAFARI	BFA EDUCATIONAL MEDIA	101-150
P	GAME	SPECIAL VOWELS	FRANK SCHAFFER PUBLICATIONS, INC	<5
P	GAME	"R" CONTROLLED & VARIANT VOWELS PEEK-A-BOO	READING JOY, INC.	6-10
P	GAME	CHECKMATE: VOWELS FOLLOWED BY R	DM EDUCATIONAL PUBLICATIONS	<5
P	GUIDE	PHONICS IS FUN, BOOK 2	MODERN CURRICULUM PRESS	<5
P	MANIPU	PHONICS R CONTROLLED VOWELS & Y AS A VOWEL	AERO PUBLISHERS, INC.	6-10
P	MULTIM	DEVELOPING READING SKILLS, PART II: PHONICS, VOWEL SOUNDS	EDUCATIONAL ENRICHMENT MATERIALS	101-150
P	MULTIM	SOUND IT, UNIT 2	IMPERIAL INTERNATIONAL LEARNING	51-75
P	PUPILB	WOG'S LOG BOOK V	EDUCATORS PUBLISHING SERVICE	<5
P	PUPILB	WOG'S LOG BOOK VI	EDUCATORS PUBLISHING SERVICE	<5
P	RECORD	SOUNDS FOR YOUNG READERS, VOLUME 6	CLASSROOM MATERIALS CO.	6-10
P	SND FS	STORY OF R & R CONTROLLER	HERBERT M. ELKINS COMPANY	11-20
P	SND FS	STORY OF U, W & W CONTROLLER	HERBERT M. ELKINS COMPANY	11-20
P	TRANSP	BASIC PHONETIC SKILL DRILLS	PAUL S. AMIDON & ASSOC., INC.	21-30
P	WKBOOK	S.T.A.R.T., BOOK 9	EMC CORPORATION	<5
P	WKBOOK	VOWELS & VARIANTS, BOOK C	GINN & COMPANY	<5
P	WKBOOK	MORE VOWELS & VARIANTS, BOOK D	GINN & COMPANY	<5
P	WKBOOK	PHONICS IS FUN, BOOK 2	MODERN CURRICULUM PRESS	<5
P	WKBOOK	SOUNDS WE USE, BOOK 3	HAYES SCHOOL PUBLISHING COMPANY	<5
PI	ACTCRD	HOWL FOR OWL, LEVEL II	INCENTIVES FOR LEARNING, INC.	<5
PI	AUDKIT	VOWEL SOUNDS: R-CONTROLLED VOWELS	MEDIA MATERIALS, INC.	6-10
PI	AUDKIT	VOWEL CLUSTER FUN	MEDIA MATERIALS, INC.	6-10
PI	AUDKIT	MORE PHONICS	HAMPDEN PUBLICATIONS, INC.	101-150
PI	DITTO	SPELLING PROGRAM, BOOK K	FRANK SCHAFFER PUBLICATIONS, INC	<5
PI	DITTO	SPECIAL VOWEL PATTERNS, PART II	INSTRUCTO/MCGRAW-HILL	<5
PI	FILMST	LEARNING ABOUT OUR LANGUAGE, SET 4	AEVAC, INC.	31-50
PI	GAME	SEA OF VOWELS	IDEAL SCHOOL SUPPLY COMPANY	6-10
PI	MANIPU	PHONICS E-Z LANGUAGE LEARNING SLIDE RULES, 5TH	E-Z GRADER COMPANY	<5
PI	MULTIU	PHONICS IN CONTEXT, SET I	EDUCATIONAL ACTIVITIES, INC.	76-100
PI	PUPILB	EXPLODE THE CODE, BOOK 6	EDUCATORS PUBLISHING SERVICE	<5
PI	WKBOOK	PRIMARY PHONICS WORKBOOK 4	EDUCATORS PUBLISHING SERVICE	<5
PIJ	GAME	SOUND OFF & READ GAMES	MAFEX ASSOCIATES, INC.	11-20
I	AUDKIT	READING CASSETTES: PHONIC ANALYSIS	IDEAL SCHOOL SUPPLY COMPANY	51-75
I	AUDKIT	WHEN R CONTROLS THE VOWEL	MEDIA MATERIALS, INC.	6-10
I	DITTO	SOUNDS IN WORDS, BOOK 14	GEL-STEN, INC.	<5
I	DITTO	SOUNDS IN WORDS, BOOK 17	GEL-STEN, INC.	<5
I	DITTO	DECODING SKILLS D	ACTIVITY RESOURCES COMPANY, INC.	<5
I	GAME	NEW PHONICS WE USE LEARNING GAMES KITS, KIT TWO	RAND MCNALLY & COMPANY	76-100

LEVEL	FORMAT	TITLE	PUBLISHER	NT	$PRICE

61 - SKILL: VOWEL MODIFICATION BY R, L, W

LEVEL	FORMAT	TITLE	PUBLISHER	NT	$PRICE
I	MULTIM	GAMES 'N' FRAMES: THE STRANGE CASE OF THE VANISHING VOWELS	IMPERIAL INTERNATIONAL LEARNING		21-30
I	WKBOOK	PHONICS FOR THE INTERMEDIATE GRADES (4, 5, 6)	JENN PUBLICATIONS		<5
IJS	AUDKIT	HITS, LEVEL 1: AMERICA, VENTURA HIGHWAY	MODULEARN, INC.		11-20
IJS	AUDKIT	HITS, LEVEL 1: JAMES TAYLOR, SWEET BABY JAMES	MODULEARN, INC.		11-20
IJS	AUDKIT	HITS, LEVEL 1: PAUL SIMON, EL CONDOR PASA	MODULEARN, INC.		11-20
IJS	AUDKIT	HITS, LEVEL 1: BLACKBYRDS, YOU'VE GOT THAT SOMETHING	MODULEARN, INC.		11-20
IJS	AUDKIT	HITS, LEVEL 2: SPINNERS, COULD IT BE I'M FALLING IN LOVE	MODULEARN, INC.		11-20
IJS	AUDKIT	HITS, LEVEL 2: DONNIE & MARIE OSMOND, IT TAKES TWO	MODULEARN, INC.		11-20
IJS	AUDKIT	HITS, LEVEL 2: ABBA, S.O.S.	MODULEARN, INC.		11-20
IJS	AUDKIT	HITS, LEVEL 2: EARTH WIND & FIRE, SHINING STAR	MODULEARN, INC.		11-20
IJS	AUDKIT	HITS, LEVEL 2: PAUL SIMON, STILL CRAZY AFTER ALL THESE YEARS	MODULEARN, INC.		11-20
IJS	AUDKIT	HITS, LEVEL 2: SIDE EFFECT, S.O.S.	MODULEARN, INC.		11-20
IJS	AUDKIT	HITS, LEVEL 3: JOHNNY NASH, I CAN SEE CLEARLY NOW	MODULEARN, INC.		11-20
IJS	AUDKIT	HITS, LEVEL 3: FIREFALL, LIVIN' AIN'T LIVIN'	MODULEARN, INC.		11-20
IJS	AUDKIT	HITS, LEVEL 3: DOOBIE BROTHERS, LISTEN TO THE MUSIC	MODULEARN, INC.		11-20
IJS	AUDKIT	HITS, LEVEL 3: PAUL SIMON, 50 WAYS TO LEAVE YOUR LOVER	MODULEARN, INC.		11-20
IJS	AUDKIT	HITS, LEVEL 3: EMOTION, BEST OF MY LOVE	MODULEARN, INC.		11-20
IJS	AUDKIT	HITS, LEVEL 3: THREE DOG NIGHT, THE FAMILY OF MAN	MODULEARN, INC.		11-20
IJS	AUDKIT	HITS, LEVEL 3: FLEETWOOD MAC, DON'T STOP	MODULEARN, INC.		11-20
IJS	AUDKIT	HITS, LEVEL 3: SPINNERS, ONE OF A KIND LOVE AFFAIR	MODULEARN, INC.		11-20
IJS	AUDKIT	HITS, LEVEL 3: SPINNERS, JUST CAN'T GET YOU OUT OF MY MIND	MODULEARN, INC.		11-20
IJS	MULTIU	PHONICS IN CONTEXT, SET II	EDUCATIONAL ACTIVITIES, INC.		51-75
JS	AUDKIT	READING CASSETTES: VOWELS	IDEAL SCHOOL SUPPLY COMPANY		51-75
JS	AUDKIT	USING PHONICS SERIES	MEDIA MATERIALS, INC.		101-150
JS	AUDKIT	LEARNING PHONICS	HAMPDEN PUBLICATIONS, INC.		101-150
JS	HI INT	READING FOR RESULTS (RL 2 - 3)	CAMBRIDGE BOOK CO.		<5
JS	WKBOOK	NEW STREAMLIND ENGLISH SERIES: SKILL BOOK 4	NEW READERS PRESS		<5
S	AUDKIT	VOWELS (IMMEDIATE-SECONDARY)	EDUCATIONAL MEDIA, INC.		31-50

62 - SKILL: IRREGULAR VOWEL SOUNDS

LEVEL	FORMAT	TITLE	PUBLISHER	NT	$PRICE
P	ACTCRD	READING SELF-CHECK: SPECIAL VOWELS & CONSONANTS	FRANK SCHAFFER PUBLICATIONS, INC		<5
P	CHART	PROSPECTING IN PHONICS	IDEAL SCHOOL SUPPLY COMPANY		6-10
P	DITTO	PHONICS IIIB	HAYES SCHOOL PUBLISHING COMPANY		<5
P	DITTO	PHONICS IVA	HAYES SCHOOL PUBLISHING COMPANY		<5
P	DITTO	DECODING SKILLS 4	ACTIVITY RESOURCES COMPANY, INC.		<5
P	FLASH	FLASH CARDS, SET B	MODERN CURRICULUM PRESS		11-20
P	GAME	NEW WORD GAME SAFARI	BFA EDUCATIONAL MEDIA		101-150
P	GAME	SPECIAL VOWELS	FRANK SCHAFFER PUBLICATIONS, INC		<5
P	GAME	CHECKMATE: VARIANT VOWEL SOUNDS	DM EDUCATIONAL PUBLICATIONS		<5
P	MANIPU	PHONICS R CONTROLLED VOWELS & Y AS A VOWEL	AERO PUBLISHERS, INC.		6-10
P	PUPILB	WOG'S LOG BOOK VII	EDUCATORS PUBLISHING SERVICE		<5
P	PUPILB	WOG'S LOG BOOK VIII	EDUCATORS PUBLISHING SERVICE		<5
P	PUPILB	FIRST PHONICS, PART 2	EDUCATORS PUBLISHING SERVICE		<5
P	SND FS	VOWELS THAT ARE NEITHER LONG NOR SHORT	HERBERT M. ELKINS COMPANY		11-20
P	WKBOOK	S.T.A.R.T., BOOK 13	EMC CORPORATION		<5
P	WKBOOK	S.T.A.R.T., BOOK 14	EMC CORPORATION		<5
P	WKBOOK	PHONICS WORKTEXT: VARIANT VOWELS	HAMMOND, INC.		<5
P	WKBOOK	PHONICS, GRADE 3	JENN PUBLICATIONS		<5
P	WKBOOK	NEW PHONICS WORKBOOK, BOOK A	MODERN CURRICULUM PRESS		<5
PI	AUDKIT	VOWEL SOUNDS & SILENT LETTERS	NATIONAL BOOK COMPANY		21-30
PI	AUDKIT	NEITHER LONG NOR SHORT	MEDIA MATERIALS, INC.		6-10
PI	CL SET	SOUND OFF & READ	MAFEX ASSOCIATES, INC.		31-50
PI	FILMST	LEARNING ABOUT OUR LANGUAGE, SET 4	AEVAC, INC.		31-50
PI	MULTIU	PHONICS IN CONTEXT, SET I	EDUCATIONAL ACTIVITIES, INC.		76-100
PIJ	GAME	SOUND OFF & READ GAMES	MAFEX ASSOCIATES, INC.		11-20
I	AUDKIT	READING CASSETTES: PHONIC ANALYSIS	IDEAL SCHOOL SUPPLY COMPANY		51-75
I	DITTO	DECODING SKILLS D	ACTIVITY RESOURCES COMPANY, INC.		<5
I	DITTO	DECODING SKILLS E	ACTIVITY RESOURCES COMPANY, INC.		<5
I	GAME	CHECKMATE: VARIANT VOWEL SOUNDS	DM EDUCATIONAL PUBLICATIONS		<5
I	WKBOOK	PHONICS FOR THE INTERMEDIATE GRADES (4, 5, 6)	JENN PUBLICATIONS		<5
IJ	ACTCRD	FICKLE VOWELS	LESWING PRESS		6-10
IJ	MULTIM	SADDLE UP (RL 3)	INSTRUCTO/MCGRAW-HILL		11-20
IJS	MULTIU	PHONICS IN CONTEXT, SET II	EDUCATIONAL ACTIVITIES, INC.		51-75
J	WKBOOK	MOTT BASIC LANG. SKILLS: BOOK 1305	ALLIED EDUCATION COUNCIL		<5
JS	AUDKIT	READING CASSETTES: VOWELS	IDEAL SCHOOL SUPPLY COMPANY		51-75

63 - SKILL: PHONETIC RULES

LEVEL	FORMAT	TITLE	PUBLISHER	NT	$PRICE
P	ACTCRD	VOWEL PACER	DM EDUCATIONAL PUBLICATIONS		<5
P	AUDKIT	KIT 8: BASIC WORD ATTACK - LONG, SHORT VOWELS	EDUCATIONAL RESEARCH, INC.		101-150
P	AUDKIT	READING CASSETTES: VOWELS	IDEAL SCHOOL SUPPLY COMPANY		51-75
P	AUDKIT	READING CASSETTES: VOWEL ENRICHMENT	IDEAL SCHOOL SUPPLY COMPANY		51-75
P	AUDKIT	MINISYSTEMS: MEDIAL SHORT TO LONG VOWELS PLUS E	CORONET MULTI MEDIA		11-20
P	CHART	VOWEL PICTURES FOR PEGBOARD	IDEAL SCHOOL SUPPLY COMPANY		6-10
P	DITTO	SOUNDS IN WORDS, BOOK 3	GEL-STEN, INC.		<5
P	DITTO	SOUNDS IN WORDS, BOOK 4	GEL-STEN, INC.		<5
P	DITTO	SOUNDS IN WORDS, BOOK 5	GEL-STEN, INC.		<5
P	DITTO	SOUND-OFF 4	EDUCATORS PUBLISHING SERVICE		6-10
P	FLNLBD	LONG & SHORT VOWELS	INSTRUCTO/MCGRAW-HILL		6-10

LEVEL	FORMAT	TITLE	PUBLISHER	NT	$PRICE

63 - SKILL: PHONETIC RULES

LEVEL	FORMAT	TITLE	PUBLISHER	NT	$PRICE
P	GAME	MAGICAL SILENT E	DEVELOPMENTAL LEARNING MATERIALS		6-10
P	PUPILB	WOG'S LOG BOOK V	EDUCATORS PUBLISHING SERVICE		<5
P	PUPILB	WOG'S LOG BOOK VI	EDUCATORS PUBLISHING SERVICE		<5
P	SND FS	SILENT E ON THE END OF A WORD	HERBERT M. ELKINS COMPANY		11-20
P	WKBOOK	VOWELS & VARIANTS, BOOK C	GINN & COMPANY		<5
P	WKBOOK	MORE VOWELS & VARIANTS, BOOK D	GINN & COMPANY		<5
P	WKBOOK	PHONICS, GRADE 3	JENN PUBLICATIONS		<5
P	WKBOOK	WORKBOOK M2	EDUCATORS PUBLISHING SERVICE		<5
PI	DITTO	FUNNY FACE PHONICS	ACTIVITY RESOURCES COMPANY, INC.		<5
PI	PUPILB	EXPLODE THE CODE, BOOK 3	EDUCATORS PUBLISHING SERVICE		<5
PI	PUPILB	EXPLODE THE CODE, BOOK 4	EDUCATORS PUBLISHING SERVICE		<5
PI	SND FS	WORD BUILDERS	MILLER-BRODY PRODUCTIONS, INC.		31-50
PI	WKBOOK	AEVAC STARTER 101, BOOK 9 (NON-READERS)	AEVAC, INC.		<5
I	AUDKIT	READING CASSETTES: PHONIC ANALYSIS	IDEAL SCHOOL SUPPLY COMPANY		51-75
I	DITTO	SOUNDS IN WORDS, BOOK 10	GEL-STEN, INC.		<5
I	DITTO	SOUNDS IN WORDS, BOOK 11	GEL-STEN, INC.		<5
I	RECORD	SOUND SKILLS FOR UPPER GRADES, VOLUME 2	CLASSROOM MATERIALS CO.		6-10
J	WKBOOK	MOTT BASIC LANG. SKILLS: BOOK 1305	ALLIED EDUCATION COUNCIL		<5
J	WKBOOK	MOTT BASIC LANG. SKILLS: BOOK 1306	ALLIED EDUCATION COUNCIL		<5
JS	HI INT	READING FOR RESULTS (RL 2 - 3)	CAMBRIDGE BOOK CO.		<5

64 - SKILL: SPELLING - GENERAL

LEVEL	FORMAT	TITLE	PUBLISHER	NT	$PRICE
R	DITTO	SOUND, WRITE, READ, SPELL	HAYES SCHOOL PUBLISHING COMPANY		<5
RP	GAME	SPELL MASTER	MARLON CREATIONS, INC.		<5
RP	WKBOOK	DELL HOME ACTIVITY: COLOR & SPELL	DELL PUBLISHING COMPANY, INC.		<5
RP	WKBOOK	DELL HOME ACTIVITY: SPELLING BOOK 1	DELL PUBLISHING COMPANY, INC.		<5
P	ACTCRD	ALL ABOUT ME	FRANK SCHAFFER PUBLICATIONS, INC		<5
P	ACTCRD	WORD MATCHING FLIP BOOKS	DEVELOPMENTAL LEARNING MATERIALS		11-20
P	AUDKIT	PRIMARY BASIC READING COMPREHENSION	EYE GATE MEDIA	5	31-50
P	AUDKIT	SPELLING, CAPITALIZATION & PUNCTUATION	EYE GATE MEDIA		6-10
P	AUDKIT	KIT 17: SPELLING, LEVEL 1	EDUCATIONAL RESEARCH, INC.		101-150
P	AUDKIT	KIT 18: SPELLING, LEVEL 2	EDUCATIONAL RESEARCH, INC.		101-150
P	DITTO	CROSSWORD PUZZLES FOR PHONICS: SPECIAL SOUNDS I	CONTINENTAL PRESS, INC.		<5
P	DITTO	NEW PHONICS & WORD ANALYSIS SKILLS: GRADE 3, PART 1	CONTINENTAL PRESS, INC.		<5
P	DITTO	SPELLING: BASIC SPELLING	EBSCO CURRICULUM MATERIALS		<5
P	DITTO	JUMBO SPELLING YEARBOOK 3	EBSCO CURRICULUM MATERIALS		11-20
P	DITTO	JUMBO SPELLING YEARBOOK	EYE GATE MEDIA		11-20
P	DITTO	BASIC SPELLING 1	EYE GATE MEDIA		<5
P	DITTO	BASIC SPELLING 2	EYE GATE MEDIA		<5
P	DITTO	WORD PUZZLES, GRADE 1	INSTRUCTO/MCGRAW-HILL		<5
P	DITTO	WORD PUZZLES, GRADE 2	INSTRUCTO/MCGRAW-HILL		<5
P	DITTO	WORD PUZZLES, GRADE 3	INSTRUCTO/MCGRAW-HILL		<5
P	DITTO	READING ENRICHMENT ACTIVITIES	XEROX EDUCATION PUBLICATIONS		<5
P	GAME	SPELL POWER	KENWORTHY EDUCATIONAL SERVICE		<5
P	GAME	ETA DIAL & SPELL	EDUCATIONAL TEACHING AIDS		6-10
P	GAME	ETA SPELLING GAME	EDUCATIONAL TEACHING AIDS		6-10
P	GAME	SPELLING/LANGUAGE LEARNING GAMES KITS, KIT ONE	RAND MCNALLY & COMPANY		76-100
P	GAME	TREASURE SPELL	LITTLE KENNY PUBLICATIONS, INC.		6-10
P	MULTIM	LANGUAGE EXPERIENCES IN READING (LEIR), LEVEL I	ENCYCLOPEDIA BRITANNICA		201-300
P	MULTIM	LANGUAGE EXPERIENCES IN READING (LEIR), LEVEL II	ENCYCLOPEDIA BRITANNICA		201-300
P	MULTIM	LANGUAGE EXPERIENCES IN READIN (LEIR), LEVEL III	ENCYCLOPEDIA BRITANNICA		201-300
P	MULTIM	STEPS TO SPELLING BREAKTHROUGH, LEVEL 1	EMC CORPORATION		76-100
P	MULTIM	BASIC SPELLING, GRADE I	MEDIA MARKETING, INC.		51-75
P	MULTIM	BASIC SPELLING, GRADE II	MEDIA MARKETING, INC.		51-75
P	MULTIM	BASIC SPELLING, GRADE III	MEDIA MARKETING, INC.		51-75
P	SP EQT	LANGUAGE SKILLS PROGRAM: INTRODUCTION TO SPELLING	SPELLBINDER, INC.		51-75
P	SP EQT	LANGUAGE SKILLS PROGRAM: READING-SPELLING COMPREHENSION	SPELLBINDER, INC.		51-75
P	WKBOOK	MY SPELLING BOOK	KENWORTHY EDUCATIONAL SERVICE		<5
P	WKBOOK	DELL HOME ACTIVITY: SPELLING BOOK 2	DELL PUBLISHING COMPANY, INC.		<5
P	WKBOOK	SPELLING	GROSSET & DUNLAP, INC.		<5
P	WKBOOK	WORD MASTERY, BOOK A	SCHOLASTIC BOOK SERVICE		<5
PI	ACTCRD	SPELLING	FRANK SCHAFFER PUBLICATIONS, INC		<5
PI	ACTCRD	FOCUS ON SKILLS: THE SPELLING BOX, PRIMARY	EDUCATIONAL INSIGHTS, INC.		11-20
PI	ACTCRD	WORD POWER SKILL CARDS	MILTON BRADLEY/PLAYSKOOL		<5
PI	AUDKIT	TOTAL SPELLING (KITS 17 - 21)	EDUCATIONAL RESEARCH, INC.	5	>450
PI	DITTO	MYSTERY READING RIDDLES	FRANK SCHAFFER PUBLICATIONS, INC		<5
PI	DITTO	SPELLING MASTERY	INCENTIVE PUBLICATIONS, INC.		<5
PI	DITTO	SPELLING, INTERMEDIATE	MILTON BRADLEY/PLAYSKOOL		<5
PI	GAME	ETA MAKE-A-WORD SPELLING GAMES	EDUCATIONAL TEACHING AIDS		6-10
PI	GAME	SPELLO	IDEAL SCHOOL SUPPLY COMPANY		11-20
PI	GAME	SOUND DOMINO GAME	JUDY COMPANY		6-10
PI	GAME	SPIN-A-WORD	JUDY COMPANY		6-10
PI	GUIDE	SPELL IT WRITE	PEEK PUBLICATIONS		<5
PI	GUIDE	SPELLING MAGIC	INCENTIVE PUBLICATIONS, INC.		<5
PI	MULTIU	SPELLING MONSTERS, UNIT A	SCHOLASTIC BOOK SERVICE		301-400
PI	MULTIU	SPELLING MONSTERS, UNIT B	SCHOLASTIC BOOK SERVICE		101-150
PI	MULTIU	SPELLING MONSTERS, UNIT C	SCHOLASTIC BOOK SERVICE		101-150
PI	MULTIU	SPELLING MONSTERS, UNIT D	SCHOLASTIC BOOK SERVICE		101-150

LEVEL	FORMAT	TITLE	PUBLISHER	NT	$PRICE

64 - SKILL: SPELLING - GENERAL

LEVEL	FORMAT	TITLE	PUBLISHER	NT	$PRICE
PI	MULTIM	INDEPENDENT LANGUAGE ARTS ACTIVITIES: PRIMARY	FEARON PITMAN PUBLISHERS, INC.		<5
PI	MULTIM	INDEPENDENT DRILL FOR MASTERY, FUNDAMENTALS OF SPELLING	DEVELOPMENTAL LEARNING MATERIALS		76-100
PI	MULTIM	VOCABULARY SKILLS PROGRAM	TROLL ASSOCIATES		201-300
PI	REFBK	SPELLING REFERENCE BOOK	DEVELOPMENTAL LEARNING MATERIALS		<5
PI	SKLKIT	CONTINUOUS PROGRESS IN SPELLING, PRIMARY	ECONOMY COMPANY		101-150
PI	SKLKIT	CONTINUOUS PROGRESS IN SPELLING, VARIETY DAY KIT 1	ECONOMY COMPANY		151-200
PI	SP EQT	LANGUAGE SKILLS PROGRAM: READING-SPELLING COMPREHENSION	SPELLBINDER, INC.		51-75
PI	WKBOOK	READING ACTIVITIES FOR LEARNING CENTERS	FRANK SCHAFFER PUBLICATIONS, INC		<5
PI	WKBOOK	WORD HUNT	FRANK SCHAFFER PUBLICATIONS, INC		<5
PI	WKBOOK	WORD MASTERY, BOOK B	SCHOLASTIC BOOK SERVICE		<5
PIJ	AUDKIT	SPELLTAPES SERIES	EDUCATIONAL PROGRESS CORPORATION	8	>450
PIJ	AUDKIT	SPELLTAPES: DIAGNOSIS & IMPROVEMENT OF SPELLING SKILLS, TR 1	EDUCATIONAL PROGRESS CORPORATION		76-100
PIJ	DITTO	I CAN SPELL	LOVE PUBLISHING COMPANY		<5
PIJ	GUIDE	GOOD APPLE SPELLING BOOK	GOOD APPLE, INC.		6-10
PIJ	MULTIM	RIGHT-TO-READ PROGRAM, LEVEL I	ACADEMIC THERAPY PUBLICATIONS		151-200
PIJ	MULTIM	SPELLING BOX, LEVEL 3	EDUCATIONAL ACTIVITIES, INC.		76-100
PIJ	WKBOOK	LOOKING AT WORDS A	EDL/MCGRAW-HILL		<5
I	AUDKIT	SPELLING GENERALIZATIONS	EDUCATIONAL MEDIA, INC.		51-75
I	AUDKIT	KIT 19: SPELLING, LEVEL 3	EDUCATIONAL RESEARCH, INC.		101-150
I	AUDKIT	KIT 20: SPELLING, LEVEL 4A	EDUCATIONAL RESEARCH, INC.		101-150
I	AUDKIT	KIT 21: SPELLING, LEVEL 4B	EDUCATIONAL RESEARCH, INC.		101-150
I	DITTO	CROSSWORD PUZZLES FOR PHONICS: SPECIAL SOUNDS II	CONTINENTAL PRESS, INC.		<5
I	DITTO	WORD PUZZLES, GRADE 4	INSTRUCTO/MCGRAW-HILL		<5
I	DITTO	WORD PUZZLES, GRADE 5	INSTRUCTO/MCGRAW-HILL		<5
I	DITTO	WORD PUZZLES, GRADE 6	INSTRUCTO/MCGRAW-HILL		<5
I	GAME	SPELLING WITH SPORTS	CREATIVE TEACHING ASSOCIATES		<5
I	GAME	SPAR	IDEAL SCHOOL SUPPLY COMPANY		11-20
I	GAME	SPELLING/LANGUAGE LEARNING GAMES KITS, KIT TWO	RAND MCNALLY & COMPANY		76-100
I	GAME	SPELLING GAMES	MILTON BRADLEY/PLAYSKOOL		31-50
I	GUIDE	BETTER READING & SPELLING THROUGH PHONICS	FEARON PITMAN PUBLISHERS, INC.		<5
I	GUIDE	GAMES MAKE SPELLING FUN	FEARON PITMAN PUBLISHERS, INC.		<5
I	MULTIM	LANGUAGE EXPERIENCES IN READING (LEIR), LEVEL IV	ENCYCLOPEDIA BRITANNICA		201-300
I	MULTIM	STEPS TO SPELLING BREAKTHROUGH, LEVEL 2	EMC CORPORATION		76-100
I	SKLKIT	SPELLING WORD POWER LABORATORY KIT 2A	SRA		151-200
I	SKLKIT	SPELLING WORD POWER LABORATORY KIT 2B	SRA		151-200
I	SKLKIT	SPELLING WORD POWER LABORATORY KIT 2C	SRA		151-200
I	SP EQT	LANGUAGE SKILLS PROGRAM: READING-SPELLING COMPREHENSION	SPELLBINDER, INC.		51-75
I	SP EQT	LANGUAGE SKILLS PROGRAM: READING-SPELLING COMPREHENSION (RP)	SPELLBINDER, INC.		51-75
I	WKBOOK	WORD MASTERY, BOOK C	SCHOLASTIC BOOK SERVICE		<5
IJ	ACTCRD	FOCUS ON SKILLS: THE SPELLING BOX, INTERMEDIATE	EDUCATIONAL INSIGHTS, INC.		11-20
IJ	A/VKIT	SPEAKING OF SPELLING	GUIDANCE ASSOCIATES		51-75
IJ	CL SET	WORDS	CHANNING L. BETE COMPANY, INC.		76-100
IJ	DITTO	SPELLING, ADVANCED	MILTON BRADLEY/PLAYSKOOL		<5
IJ	GUIDE	DR. SPELLO, T.E.	WEBSTER DIVISION/MCGRAW-HILL		<5
IJ	SKLKIT	CONTINUOUS PROGRESS IN SPELLING, INTERMEDIATE	ECONOMY COMPANY		101-150
IJ	SKLKIT	CONTINUOUS PROGRESS IN SPELLING, VARIETY DAY KIT 2	ECONOMY COMPANY		151-200
IJ	SKLKIT	+10 VOCABULARY BOOSTER, LEVEL A	WEBSTER DIVISION/MCGRAW-HILL		151-200
IJ	SKLKIT	+10 VOCABULARY BOOSTER, LEVEL B	WEBSTER DIVISION/MCGRAW-HILL		151-200
IJ	SKLKIT	+10 VOCABULARY BOOSTER, LEVEL C	WEBSTER DIVISION/MCGRAW-HILL		151-200
IJ	SKLKIT	+10 VOCABULARY BOOSTER, LEVEL D	WEBSTER DIVISION/MCGRAW-HILL		151-200
IJ	SKLKIT	+10 VOCABULARY BOOSTER, LEVEL E	WEBSTER DIVISION/MCGRAW-HILL		151-200
IJ	WKBOOK	MOST USED WORDS FOR SPELLING	FERN TRIPP		<5
IJ	WKBOOK	WORDS	CHANNING L. BETE COMPANY, INC.		<5
IJ	WKBOOK	DR. SPELLO	WEBSTER DIVISION/MCGRAW-HILL		<5
IJS	AUDCRD	LAZY LETTERS	AUDIOTRONICS CORPORATION		21-30
IJS	DITTO	CORRECTIVE SPELLING THROUGH MORPHOGRAPHS, SPIRIT MASTERS	SRA		101-150
IJS	MULTIU	CORRECTIVE SPELLING THROUGH MORPHOGRAPHS, TEACHER'S BOOK	SRA		31-50
IJS	MULTIU	PUZZLERS	LESWING PRESS		11-20
IJS	MULTIM	SPELLING BOX, LEVEL 4	EDUCATIONAL ACTIVITIES, INC.		76-100
IJS	PUPILB	CORRECTIVE SPELLING THROUGH MORPHOGRAPHS, STUDENT BOOK	SRA		<5
IJS	PUPILB	CORRECT SPELLING MADE EASY	DELL PUBLISHING COMPANY, INC.		<5
IJS	SKLKIT	SPELLING MASTERY & DIAGNOSTIC REFERENCE KIT	SPECIAL CHILD PUBLICATIONS		31-50
IJS	WKBOOK	ACQUIRING LANGUAGE SKILLS, BOOK A	WEBSTER DIVISION/MCGRAW-HILL		<5
IJS	WKBOOK	BUILDING LANGUAGE SKILLS, BOOK B	WEBSTER DIVISION/MCGRAW-HILL		<5
IJS	WKBOOK	CONTINUING LANGUAGE SKILLS, BOOK C	WEBSTER DIVISION/MCGRAW-HILL		<5
IJS	WKBOOK	DIRECTING LANGUAGE SKILLS, BOOK D	WEBSTER DIVISION/MCGRAW-HILL		<5
J	DITTO	SPELLING GAMES & PUZZLES FOR JUNIOR HIGH	FEARON PITMAN PUBLISHERS, INC.		6-10
J	MULTIM	STEPS TO SPELLING BREAKTHROUGH, LEVEL 3	EMC CORPORATION		76-100
J	SKLKIT	SPELLING WORD POWER LABORATORY KIT	SRA		151-200
J	WKBOOK	TROUBLESHOOTER II: BOOK 3, SPELLING & PARTS OF SPEECH	HOUGHTON MIFFLIN COMPANY		<5
JS	A/VKIT	CORRECTING COMPOSITION ERRORS	EYE GATE MEDIA		151-200
JS	A/VKIT	LEARNING TO SPELL CORRECTLY	SVE		101-150
JS	CHART	RIGHT-TO-READ PROGRAM, LEVEL II	ACADEMIC THERAPY PUBLICATIONS		101-150
JS	FILMST	SPELLING FILMSTRIPS 1	PERFECTION FORM COMPANY		21-30
JS	FILMST	SPELLING FILMSTRIPS 2	PERFECTION FORM COMPANY		21-30
JS	GUIDE	3,140 IMPORTANT WORDS, T.E.	FOLLETT PUBLISHING COMPANY		<5
JS	GUIDE	1,620 POWER WORDS, T.E.	FOLLETT PUBLISHING COMPANY		<5
JS	PUPILB	3,140 IMPORTANT WORDS (HARDCOVER)	FOLLETT PUBLISHING COMPANY		<5
JS	PUPILB	1,620 POWER WORDS (HARDCOVER)	FOLLETT PUBLISHING COMPANY		<5

LEVEL	FORMAT	TITLE	PUBLISHER	NT	$PRICE

64 - SKILL: SPELLING - GENERAL

LEVEL	FORMAT	TITLE	PUBLISHER	NT	$PRICE
JS	PUPILB	SPELL IT OUT, BOOK 1 (RL 3 - 5)	GLOBE BOOK COMPANY, INC.		<5
JS	PUPILB	SPELL IT OUT, BOOK 2 (RL 3 - 5)	GLOBE BOOK COMPANY, INC.		<5
JS	PUPILB	GATEWAYS TO CORRECT SPELLING	STECK-VAUGHN COMPANY		<5
JS	SP EQT	WORD RECOGNITION & SPELLING DEFA-COMBO-8	EDL/MCGRAW-HILL		151-200
JS	SP EQT	WORD RECOGNITION & SPELLING DEFA-35MM TACH-X	EDL/MCGRAW-HILL		151-200
JS	TEXTBK	WORD BOOK	GLENCOE PUBLISHING COMPANY, INC.		<5
JS	WKBOOK	SPELLBOUND	EDUCATORS PUBLISHING SERVICE		<5
S	GUIDE	SPELLING	NATIONAL LEARNING CORPORATION		6-10
S	PUPILB	BARRON'S DEV. SKILLS FOR H.S. EQUIV. EXAM (GED) IN GRAMMAR	BARRON'S EDUCATIONAL SERIES, INC.		<5
S	PUPILB	HOW TO PREPARE FOR H.S. EQUIV. EXAM: WRITING SKILLS TEST	BARRON'S EDUCATIONAL SERIES, INC.		<5
S	PUPILB	SYSTEMATIC SPELLING	EDUCATORS PUBLISHING SERVICE		<5
S	TEXTBK	BUSINESS COMMUNICATIONS	SOUTH-WESTERN PUBLISHING CO.	2	6-10
S	TEXTBK	BUSINESS COMMUNICATIONS: ENGLISH THE EASY WAY	SOUTH-WESTERN PUBLISHING CO.		<5
S	TEXTBK	SPELLING	GLENCOE PUBLISHING COMPANY, INC.		6-10

65 - SKILL: SPELLING PATTERNS

LEVEL	FORMAT	TITLE	PUBLISHER	NT	$PRICE
RP	ACTCRD	PICTURE WORD CARDS	GARRARD PUBLISHING COMPANY		<5
RP	CL SET	BREAKTHROUGH TO LITERACY	BOWMAR/NOBLE PUBLISHERS, INC.		201-300
RPIJS	GUIDE	SCHOOL & HOME PROGRAM	COMMUNICATION SKILL BUILDERS, INC		11-20
P	ACTCRD	LADYBIRD: COMPREHENSION CARDS, SET 1	IDEAL SCHOOL SUPPLY COMPANY		6-10
P	ACTCRD	LADYBIRD: COMPREHENSION CARDS, SET 2	IDEAL SCHOOL SUPPLY COMPANY		6-10
P	ACTCRD	WIPE-OFF CARDS: WORD PATTERNS, LEVEL 2	TREND ENTERPRISES, INC.		<5
P	A/VKIT	SPELLING POWER	MEDIA MARKETING, INC.		101-150
P	DITTO	JUMBO SPELLING YEARBOOK 3	EBSCO CURRICULUM MATERIALS		11-20
P	DITTO	MARK ON-WIPE OFF: SCRAMBLED WORDS	IDEAL SCHOOL SUPPLY COMPANY		6-10
P	DITTO	WORD ATTACK SKILLS: SYLLABICATION & SPELLING PATTERNS, BK.1	EDL/MCGRAW-HILL		6-10
P	DITTO	WORD ATTACK SKILLS: SYLLABICATION & SPELLING PATTERNS, BK.2	EDL/MCGRAW-HILL		6-10
P	GAME	SPLIT WORDS	CONSTRUCTIVE PLAYTHINGS		<5
P	GUIDE	SPELLING & WRITING PATTERNS BOOK A, T.E.	FOLLETT PUBLISHING COMPANY		<5
P	GUIDE	SPELLING & WRITING PATTERNS BOOK B, T.E.	FOLLETT PUBLISHING COMPANY		<5
P	GUIDE	SPELLING & WRITING PATTERNS BOOK C, T.E.	FOLLETT PUBLISHING COMPANY		<5
P	SND FS	PATTERNS	HERBERT M. ELKINS COMPANY		11-20
P	WKBOOK	SPELLING & WRITING PATTERNS BOOK A	FOLLETT PUBLISHING COMPANY		<5
P	WKBOOK	SPELLING & WRITING PATTERNS BOOK B	FOLLETT PUBLISHING COMPANY		<5
P	WKBOOK	SPELLING & WRITING PATTERNS BOOK C	FOLLETT PUBLISHING COMPANY		<5
P	WKBOOK	TARGET 180, GRADES 1 - 2	STECK-VAUGHN COMPANY		<5
P	WKBOOK	TARGET 360, GRADES 2 - 3	STECK-VAUGHN COMPANY		<5
PI	AUDKIT	PRIMARY SPELLING	HAMPDEN PUBLICATIONS, INC.		101-150
PI	CHART	SPELLING GENERALIZATIONS	IDEAL SCHOOL SUPPLY COMPANY		11-20
PI	DITTO	SPIRIT MASTER WORKBOOKS: SPELLING GENERALIZATIONS	IDEAL SCHOOL SUPPLY COMPANY		6-10
PI	FILMST	NEW ADVENTRURES IN LANGUAGE	TROLL ASSOCIATES		101-150
PI	GAME	ETA SPIN-AND-SPELL	EDUCATIONAL TEACHING AIDS		6-10
PI	GUIDE	INDIVIDUALIZED INSTRUCTION IN SPELLING	T.S. DENISON & COMPANY		6-10
PI	MANIPU	SOUND 'N' SPELL ALPHABET PUZZLE	CREATIVE TEACHING ASSOCIATES		6-10
PI	SKLKIT	SCHOOLHOUSE: SPELLING PATTERNS A	SRA		101-150
PI	SKLKIT	SCHOOLHOUSE: SPELLING PATTERNS B	SRA		101-150
PI	SKLKIT	CONTINUOUS PROGRESS IN SPELLING, PRIMARY	ECONOMY COMPANY		101-150
PI	SKLKIT	CONTINUOUS PROGRESS IN SPELLING, VARIETY DAY KIT 1	ECONOMY COMPANY		151-200
PI	WKBOOK	SUPER SPELLING FUN	GOOD APPLE, INC.		6-10
PI	WKBOOK	TARGET 540, GRADES 3 - 4	STECK-VAUGHN COMPANY		<5
PI	WKBOOK	SPELLING EXPRESS	ACTIVITY RESOURCES COMPANY, INC.		<5
PIJ	AUDKIT	SPELLTAPES: WORD ENDINGS, TRAY 5	EDUCATIONAL PROGRESS CORPORATION		76-100
PIJ	AUDKIT	SPELLTAPES: PREFIXES, PLURALS & POSSESSIVES, TRAY 6	EDUCATIONAL PROGRESS CORPORATION		76-100
PIJS	WKBOOK	SPACE ADVENTURES READING SERIES	COMMUNICATION SKILL BUILDERS, INC		11-20
I	AUDKIT	SPELLING GENERALIZATIONS	EDUCATIONAL MEDIA, INC.		51-75
I	AUDKIT	READING CASSETTES: SPELLING GENERALIZATIONS	IDEAL SCHOOL SUPPLY COMPANY		51-75
I	FILMST	LANGUAGE ARTS: SPELLING AIDS	EDUCATIONAL PROJECTIONS COMPANY		31-50
I	GUIDE	BETTER READING & SPELLING THROUGH PHONICS	FEARON PITMAN PUBLISHERS, INC.		<5
I	GUIDE	SPELLING & WRITING PATTERNS BOOK D, T.E.	FOLLETT PUBLISHING COMPANY		<5
I	GUIDE	SPELLING & WRITING PATTERNS BOOK E, T.E.	FOLLETT PUBLISHING COMPANY		<5
I	GUIDE	SPELLING & WRITING PATTERNS BOOK F, T.E.	FOLLETT PUBLISHING COMPANY		<5
I	WKBOOK	SPELLING & WRITING PATTERNS BOOK D	FOLLETT PUBLISHING COMPANY		<5
I	WKBOOK	SPELLING & WRITING PATTERNS BOOK E	FOLLETT PUBLISHING COMPANY		<5
I	WKBOOK	SPELLING & WRITING PATTERNS BOOK F	FOLLETT PUBLISHING COMPANY		<5
IJ	DITTO	SPOTLIGHT ON SPELLING, BOOK ONE	CREATIVE TEACHING PRESS, INC.		<5
IJ	DITTO	SPOTLIGHT ON SPELLING, BOOK TWO	CREATIVE TEACHING PRESS, INC.		<5
IJ	PUPILB	SPELLING	LEARNING TREE FILMSTRIPS		51-75
IJ	SKLKIT	CONTINUOUS PROGRESS IN SPELLING, INTERMEDIATE	ECONOMY COMPANY		101-150
IJ	SKLKIT	CONTINUOUS PROGRESS IN SPELLING, VARIETY DAY KIT 2	ECONOMY COMPANY		151-200
IJS	AUDKIT	HITS, LEVEL 2: FLEETWOOD MAC, OVER MY HEAD	MODULEARN, INC.		11-20
IJS	AUDKIT	HITS, LEVEL 2: SPINNERS, GAMES PEOPLE PLAY	MODULEARN, INC.		11-20
IJS	AUDKIT	HITS, LEVEL 2: BELLAMY BROTHERS, LET YOUR LOVE FLOW	MODULEARN, INC.		11-20
IJS	AUDKIT	HITS, LEVEL 2: JOHN SEBASTIAN, WELCOME BACK	MODULEARN, INC.		11-20
IJS	AUDKIT	HITS, LEVEL 2: SPINNERS, COULD IT BE I'M FALLING IN LOVE	MODULEARN, INC.		11-20
IJS	AUDKIT	HITS, LEVEL 2: ABBA, KNOWING ME, KNOWING YOU	MODULEARN, INC.		11-20
IJS	AUDKIT	HITS, LEVEL 2: ABBA, S.O.S.	MODULEARN, INC.		11-20
IJS	AUDKIT	HITS, LEVEL 2: EARTH WIND & FIRE, SHINING STAR	MODULEARN, INC.		11-20
IJS	AUDKIT	HITS, LEVEL 2: PAUL SIMON, STILL CRAZY AFTER ALL THESE YEARS	MODULEARN, INC.		11-20
IJS	AUDKIT	HITS, LEVEL 2: SIDE EFFECT, S.O.S.	MODULEARN, INC.		11-20

LEVEL	FORMAT	TITLE	PUBLISHER	NT	$PRICE

65 - SKILL: SPELLING PATTERNS

LEVEL	FORMAT	TITLE	PUBLISHER	NT	$PRICE
IJS	AUDKIT	HITS, LEVEL 3: JOHNNY NASH, I CAN SEE CLEARLY NOW	MODULEARN, INC.		11-20
IJS	AUDKIT	HITS, LEVEL 3: JAMES TAYLOR, SHOWER THE PEOPLE	MODULEARN, INC.		11-20
IJS	AUDKIT	HITS, LEVEL 3: FIREFALL, LIVIN' AIN'T LIVIN'	MODULEARN, INC.		11-20
IJS	AUDKIT	HITS, LEVEL 3: DOOBIE BROTHERS, LISTEN TO THE MUSIC	MODULEARN, INC.		11-20
IJS	AUDKIT	HITS, LEVEL 3: PAUL SIMON, 50 WAYS TO LEAVE YOUR LOVER	MODULEARN, INC.		11-20
IJS	AUDKIT	HITS, LEVEL 3: EMOTION, BEST OF MY LOVE	MODULEARN, INC.		11-20
IJS	AUDKIT	HITS, LEVEL 3: THREE DOG NIGHT, THE FAMILY OF MAN	MODULEARN, INC.		11-20
IJS	AUDKIT	HITS, LEVEL 3: FLEETWOOD MAC, DON'T STOP	MODULEARN, INC.		11-20
IJS	AUDKIT	HITS, LEVEL 3: CARLY SIMON, GROWN UP	MODULEARN, INC.		11-20
IJS	AUDKIT	HITS, LEVEL 3: SPINNERS, ONE OF A KIND LOVE AFFAIR	MODULEARN, INC.		11-20
IJS	AUDKIT	HITS, LEVEL 3: SPINNERS, JUST CAN'T GET YOU OUT OF MY MIND	MODULEARN, INC.		11-20
IJS	AUDKIT	HITS, LEVEL 4: AMERICA, I NEED YOU	MODULEARN, INC.		11-20
IJS	AUDKIT	HITS, LEVEL 4: COVEN, ONE TIN SOLDIER	MODULEARN, INC.		11-20
IJS	AUDKIT	HITS, LEVEL 4: PAUL SIMON, HOMEWARD BOUND	MODULEARN, INC.		11-20
IJS	AUDKIT	HITS, LEVEL 4: PAUL SIMON, LEAVES THAT ARE GREEN	MODULEARN, INC.		11-20
IJS	AUDKIT	HITS, LEVEL 4: PAUL SIMON, FLOWERS NEVER BEND W/THE RAINFALL	MODULEARN, INC.		11-20
IJS	AUDKIT	HITS, LEVEL 4: PAUL SIMON, I AM A ROCK	MODULEARN, INC.		11-20
IJS	AUDKIT	HITS, LEVEL 4: DAVE LOGGINS, PLEASE COME TO BOSTON	MODULEARN, INC.		11-20
IJS	AUDKIT	HITS, LEVEL 4: FLEETWOOD MAC, DREAMS	MODULEARN, INC.		11-20
IJS	AUDKIT	HITS, LEVEL 4: PAUL SIMON, BRIDGE OVER TROUBLED WATERS	MODULEARN, INC.		11-20
IJS	AUDKIT	HITS, LEVEL 4: ARETHA FRANKLIN, BRIDGE OVER TROUBLED WATERS	MODULEARN, INC.		11-20
IJS	AUDKIT	HITS, LEVEL 4: FOUR TOPS, KEEPER OF THE CASTLE	MODULEARN, INC.		11-20
IJS	AUDKIT	HITS, LEVEL 4: PAUL SIMON, AMERICAN TUNE	MODULEARN, INC.		11-20
IJS	MULTIM	KNIGHT INDIVIDUALIZED SPELLING PROGRAM KIT	EDUCATORS PUBLISHING SERVICE		76-100
J	WKBOOK	TROUBLESHOOTER I	HOUGHTON MIFFLIN COMPANY	8	11-20
JS	A/VKIT	LEARNING TO SPELL CORRECTLY	SVE		101-150
JS	DITTO	SPELLING PATTERNS	J. WESTON WALCH PUBLISHING		11-20
JS	DITTO	WRITE-ON WORKSHEETS AA	EDL/MCGRAW-HILL		21-30
JS	DITTO	WRITE-ON WORKSHEETS BA	EDL/MCGRAW-HILL		21-30
JS	DITTO	WRITE-ON WORKSHEETS CA	EDL/MCGRAW-HILL		21-30
JS	DITTO	BETTER SPELLING	HAYES SCHOOL PUBLISHING COMPANY		<5
JS	REFBK	WHAT TO DO ABOUT BILL?	COMMUNICATION SKILL BUILDERS,INC		11-20
JS	WKBOOK	A SPELLING WORKBOOK	EDUCATORS PUBLISHING SERVICE		<5
S	GUIDE	WORD PATTERNS	PEEK PUBLICATIONS		<5
S	WKBOOK	STRUCTURE OF WORDS	EDUCATORS PUBLISHING SERVICE		<5

66 - SKILL: PHONETIC SPELLING

LEVEL	FORMAT	TITLE	PUBLISHER	NT	$PRICE
P	ACTCRD	CHECKLIST OF BASIC SOUNDS	LAKESHORE CURRICULUM MATERIALS		<5
P	AUDKIT	MINISYSTEMS: SPELLING WITH SHORT a	CORONET MULTI MEDIA		11-20
P	AUDKIT	MINISYSTEMS: SPELLING WITH SHORT i	CORONET MULTI MEDIA		11-20
P	AUDKIT	MINISYSTEMS: SPELLING WITH SHORT e	CORONET MULTI MEDIA		11-20
P	AUDKIT	MINISYSTEMS: SPELLING WITH SHORT o	CORONET MULTI MEDIA		11-20
P	AUDKIT	MINISYSTEMS: SPELLING WITH SHORT u	CORONET MULTI MEDIA		11-20
P	AUDKIT	MINISYSTEMS: SPELLING WITH VOWELS & CONSONANTS	EBSCO CURRICULUM MATERIALS		11-20
P	DITTO	JUMBO SPELLING YEARBOOK 3	FRANK SCHAFFER PUBLICATIONS, INC		<5
P	DITTO	SPELLING PROGRAM, BOOK A	FRANK SCHAFFER PUBLICATIONS, INC		<5
P	DITTO	SPELLING PROGRAM, BOOK B	FRANK SCHAFFER PUBLICATIONS, INC		<5
P	DITTO	SPELLING PROGRAM, BOOK C	FRANK SCHAFFER PUBLICATIONS, INC		<5
P	DITTO	SPELLING PROGRAM, BOOK D	FRANK SCHAFFER PUBLICATIONS, INC		<5
P	DITTO	SPELLING PROGRAM, BOOK E	FRANK SCHAFFER PUBLICATIONS, INC		<5
P	DITTO	SPELLING PROGRAM, BOOK F	FRANK SCHAFFER PUBLICATIONS, INC		<5
P	DITTO	SPELLING PROGRAM, BOOK G	FRANK SCHAFFER PUBLICATIONS, INC		<5
P	DITTO	SPELLING PROGRAM, BOOK H	FRANK SCHAFFER PUBLICATIONS, INC		<5
P	DITTO	SPELLING PROGRAM, BOOK I	FRANK SCHAFFER PUBLICATIONS, INC		<5
P	GUIDE	SPELLING: SOUND TO LETTER, BOOK A, T.E.	MACMILLAN PUBLISHING CO., INC.		<5
P	GUIDE	SPELLING: SOUND TO LETTER, BOOK B, T.E.	MACMILLAN PUBLISHING CO., INC.		<5
P	GUIDE	SPELLING: SOUND TO LETTER, BOOK C, T.E.	MACMILLAN PUBLISHING CO., INC.		<5
P	MULTIM	PHONICS FOR READING & SPELLING, GRADE 2	MEDIA MARKETING, INC.		101-150
P	MULTIM	PHONICS FOR READING & SPELLING, GRADE 3	MEDIA MARKETING, INC.		101-150
P	WKBOOK	SPELLING: SOUND TO LETTER, BOOK A	MACMILLAN PUBLISHING CO., INC.		<5
P	WKBOOK	SPELLING: SOUND TO LETTER, BOOK B	MACMILLAN PUBLISHING CO., INC.		<5
P	WKBOOK	SPELLING: SOUND TO LETTER, BOOK C	MACMILLAN PUBLISHING CO., INC.		<5
P	WKBOOK	SPELL CHECK: LONG VOWELS, SET 1	ORE PRESS, INC.		6-10
P	WKBOOK	SPELL CHECK: LONG VOWELS, SET 2	ORE PRESS, INC.		6-10
P	WKBOOK	A MAFEX PROGRAM TO DEVELOP BASIC SKILLS: LET'S WRITE & SPELL	MAFEX ASSOCIATES, INC.		<5
P	WKBOOK	TARGET 180, GRADES 1 - 2	STECK-VAUGHN COMPANY		<5
P	WKBOOK	TARGET 360, GRADES 2 - 3	STECK-VAUGHN COMPANY		<5
PI	ACTCRD	SPELLING	FRANK SCHAFFER PUBLICATIONS, INC		<5
PI	AUDKIT	PRIMARY SPELLING	HAMPDEN PUBLICATIONS, INC.		101-150
PI	DITTO	SPELLING PROGRAM, BOOK J	FRANK SCHAFFER PUBLICATIONS, INC		<5
PI	DITTO	SPELLING PROGRAM, BOOK K	FRANK SCHAFFER PUBLICATIONS, INC		<5
PI	DITTO	SPELLING PROGRAM, BOOK L	FRANK SCHAFFER PUBLICATIONS, INC		<5
PI	GAME	ETA SPIN-AND-SPELL	EDUCATIONAL TEACHING AIDS		6-10
PI	GAME	PS: PREFIX-SUFFIX LANGUAGE-BUILDING GAME	COMMUNICATION SKILL BUILDERS,INC		6-10
PI	GUIDE	SPELL IT WRITE	PEEK PUBLICATIONS		<5
PI	GUIDE	INDIVIDUALIZED INSTRUCTION IN SPELLING	T.S. DENISON & COMPANY		6-10
PI	RECORD	PHONICS & WORD DEVELOPMENT	EDUCATIONAL ACTIVITIES, INC.		31-50
PI	SKLKIT	CONTINUOUS PROGRESS IN SPELLING, PRIMARY	ECONOMY COMPANY		101-150
PI	SKLKIT	CONTINUOUS PROGRESS IN SPELLING, VARIETY DAY KIT 1	ECONOMY COMPANY		151-200

LEVEL	FORMAT	TITLE	PUBLISHER	NT	$PRICE

66 - SKILL: PHONETIC SPELLING

LEVEL	FORMAT	TITLE	PUBLISHER	NT	$PRICE
PI	WKBOOK	TARGET 540, GRADES 3 - 4	STECK-VAUGHN COMPANY		<5
PI	WKBOOK	SPELLING EXPRESS	ACTIVITY RESOURCES COMPANY, INC.		<5
PIJ	AUDKIT	SPELLTAPES: SHORT VOWELS & CONSONANTS, TRAY 2	EDUCATIONAL PROGRESS CORPORATION		76-100
PIJ	AUDKIT	SPELLTAPES: LONG VOWELS & VOWEL DIGRAPHS, TRAY 3	EDUCATIONAL PROGRESS CORPORATION		76-100
PIJ	AUDKIT	SPELLTAPES: OTHER VOWELS & OTHER SPELLING TOPICS, TRAY 4	EDUCATIONAL PROGRESS CORPORATION		76-100
I	AUDKIT	SPELLING GENERALIZATIONS	EDUCATIONAL MEDIA, INC.		51-75
I	FILMST	LANGUAGE ARTS: SPELLING AIDS	EDUCATIONAL PROJECTIONS COMPANY		31-50
I	GAME	SPELLING GAMES	MILTON BRADLEY/PLAYSKOOL		31-50
I	GUIDE	SPELLING: SOUND TO LETTER, BOOK D, T.E.	MACMILLAN PUBLISHING CO., INC.		<5
I	GUIDE	SPELLING: SOUND TO LETTER, BOOK E, T.E.	MACMILLAN PUBLISHING CO., INC.		<5
I	GUIDE	SPELLING: SOUND TO LETTER, BOOK F, T.E.	MACMILLAN PUBLISHING CO., INC.		<5
I	MULTIM	PHONICS FOR READING & SPELLING, GRADE 4	MEDIA MARKETING, INC.		101-150
I	WKBOOK	SPELLING: SOUND TO LETTER, BOOK D	MACMILLAN PUBLISHING CO., INC.		<5
I	WKBOOK	SPELLING: SOUND TO LETTER, BOOK E	MACMILLAN PUBLISHING CO., INC.		<5
I	WKBOOK	SPELLING: SOUND TO LETTER, BOOK F	MACMILLAN PUBLISHING CO., INC.		<5
IJ	DITTO	SPOTLIGHT ON SPELLING, BOOK ONE	CREATIVE TEACHING PRESS, INC.		<5
IJ	DITTO	SPOTLIGHT ON SPELLING, BOOK TWO	CREATIVE TEACHING PRESS, INC.		<5
IJ	PUPILB	SPELLING	LEARNING TREE FILMSTRIPS		51-75
IJ	SKLKIT	CONTINUOUS PROGRESS IN SPELLING, INTERMEDIATE	ECONOMY COMPANY		101-150
IJ	SKLKIT	CONTINUOUS PROGRESS IN SPELLING, VARIETY DAY KIT 2	ECONOMY COMPANY		151-200
IJS	MULTIM	KNIGHT INDIVIDUALIZED SPELLING PROGRAM KIT	EDUCATORS PUBLISHING SERVICE		76-100
J	WKBOOK	TROUBLESHOOTER I	HOUGHTON MIFFLIN COMPANY	8	11-20
JS	A/VKIT	LEARNING TO SPELL CORRECTLY	SVE		101-150
JS	DITTO	BETTER SPELLING	HAYES SCHOOL PUBLISHING COMPANY		<5
JS	WKBOOK	A SPELLING WORKBOOK	EDUCATORS PUBLISHING SERVICE		<5
S	MULTIM	RELEVANCE SERIES	CAMBRIDGE BOOK CO.	5	>450
S	MULTIM	RELEVANCE SERIES: RELEVANCE OF WORDS	CAMBRIDGE BOOK CO.		201-300
S	WKBOOK	STRUCTURE OF WORDS	EDUCATORS PUBLISHING SERVICE		<5
S	WKBOOK	SPELL OF WORDS	EDUCATORS PUBLISHING SERVICE		<5

67 - SKILL: SPELLING RULES

LEVEL	FORMAT	TITLE	PUBLISHER	NT	$PRICE
P	ACTCRD	CHECKLIST OF BASIC SOUNDS	LAKESHORE CURRICULUM MATERIALS		<5
P	DITTO	JUMBO SPELLING YEARBOOK 3	EBSCO CURRICULUM MATERIALS		11-20
P	GUIDE	SPELLING: SOUND TO LETTER, BOOK A, T.E.	MACMILLAN PUBLISHING CO., INC.		<5
P	GUIDE	SPELLING: SOUND TO LETTER, BOOK B, T.E.	MACMILLAN PUBLISHING CO., INC.		<5
P	GUIDE	SPELLING: SOUND TO LETTER, BOOK C, T.E.	MACMILLAN PUBLISHING CO., INC.		<5
P	PUPILB	ALPHABET SERIES	EDUCATORS PUBLISHING SERVICE		11-20
P	VISKIT	RECIPE FOR READING	EDUCATORS PUBLISHING SERVICE		11-20
P	WKBOOK	SPELLING: SOUND TO LETTER, BOOK A	MACMILLAN PUBLISHING CO., INC.		<5
P	WKBOOK	SPELLING: SOUND TO LETTER, BOOK B	MACMILLAN PUBLISHING CO., INC.		<5
P	WKBOOK	SPELLING: SOUND TO LETTER, BOOK C	MACMILLAN PUBLISHING CO., INC.		<5
PI	AUDKIT	INTERMEDIATE SPELLING	HAMPDEN PUBLICATIONS, INC.		101-150
PI	GUIDE	INDIVIDUALIZED INSTRUCTION IN SPELLING	T.S. DENISON & COMPANY		6-10
PI	SKLKIT	SPELLING WORDS IN USE	LEARNCO, INC.		11-20
PI	SKLKIT	SPELLING WORDS IN USE DEVELOPMENTAL	LEARNCO, INC.		11-20
PI	WKBOOK	SPELLING EXPRESS	ACTIVITY RESOURCES COMPANY, INC.		<5
PIJ	AUDKIT	SPELLTAPES: SPECIAL SPELLING TOPICS, TRAY 7	EDUCATIONAL PROGRESS CORPORATION		76-100
I	FILMST	LANGUAGE ARTS: SPELLING AIDS	EDUCATIONAL PROJECTIONS COMPANY		31-50
I	GUIDE	SPELLING: SOUND TO LETTER, BOOK D, T.E.	MACMILLAN PUBLISHING CO., INC.		<5
I	GUIDE	SPELLING: SOUND TO LETTER, BOOK E, T.E.	MACMILLAN PUBLISHING CO., INC.		<5
I	GUIDE	SPELLING: SOUND TO LETTER, BOOK F, T.E.	MACMILLAN PUBLISHING CO., INC.		<5
I	WKBOOK	SPELLING: SOUND TO LETTER, BOOK D	MACMILLAN PUBLISHING CO., INC.		<5
I	WKBOOK	SPELLING: SOUND TO LETTER, BOOK E	MACMILLAN PUBLISHING CO., INC.		<5
I	WKBOOK	SPELLING: SOUND TO LETTER, BOOK F	MACMILLAN PUBLISHING CO., INC.		<5
IJ	DITTO	SPOTLIGHT ON SPELLING, BOOK ONE	CREATIVE TEACHING PRESS, INC.		<5
IJ	DITTO	SPOTLIGHT ON SPELLING, BOOK TWO	CREATIVE TEACHING PRESS, INC.		<5
IJS	MULTIM	KNIGHT INDIVIDUALIZED SPELLING PROGRAM KIT	EDUCATORS PUBLISHING SERVICE		76-100
JS	A/VKIT	LEARNING TO SPELL CORRECTLY	SVE		101-150
JS	WKBOOK	A SPELLING WORKBOOK	EDUCATORS PUBLISHING SERVICE		<5
JS	WKBOOK	SPELLBINDING 1	EDUCATORS PUBLISHING SERVICE		<5
JS	WKBOOK	SPELLBINDING 2	EDUCATORS PUBLISHING SERVICE		<5
S	TEXTBK	SPELLING: A MNEMONICS APPROACH	SOUTH-WESTERN PUBLISHING CO.		<5
S	TEXTBK	WORD STUDIES	SOUTH-WESTERN PUBLISHING CO.		6-10
S	WKBOOK	STRUCTURE OF WORDS	EDUCATORS PUBLISHING SERVICE		<5

68 - SKILL: FUNCTIONAL SPELLING

LEVEL	FORMAT	TITLE	PUBLISHER	NT	$PRICE
P	WKBOOK	TARGET 180, GRADES 1 - 2	STECK-VAUGHN COMPANY		<5
P	WKBOOK	TARGET 360, GRADES 2 - 3	STECK-VAUGHN COMPANY		<5
PI	SKLKIT	CONTINUOUS PROGRESS IN SPELLING, PRIMARY	ECONOMY COMPANY		101-150
PI	SKLKIT	CONTINUOUS PROGRESS IN SPELLING, VARIETY DAY KIT 1	ECONOMY COMPANY		151-200
PI	SKLKIT	SPELLING WORDS IN USE	LEARNCO, INC.		11-20
PI	SKLKIT	SPELLING WORDS IN USE DEVELOPMENTAL	LEARNCO, INC.		11-20
PI	WKBOOK	TARGET 540, GRADES 3 - 4	STECK-VAUGHN COMPANY		<5
I	GAME	SPELLING GAMES	MILTON BRADLEY/PLAYSKOOL		31-50
IJ	SKLKIT	CONTINUOUS PROGRESS IN SPELLING, INTERMEDIATE	ECONOMY COMPANY		101-150
IJ	SKLKIT	CONTINUOUS PROGRESS IN SPELLING, VARIETY DAY KIT 2	ECONOMY COMPANY		151-200
JS	A/VKIT	LEARNING TO SPELL CORRECTLY	SVE		101-150
JS	DITTO	BETTER SPELLING	HAYES SCHOOL PUBLISHING COMPANY		<5

LEVEL	FORMAT	TITLE	PUBLISHER	NT	$PRICE

68 - SKILL: FUNCTIONAL SPELLING

LEVEL	FORMAT	TITLE	PUBLISHER	NT	$PRICE
JS	GUIDE	3,140 IMPORTANT WORDS, T.E.	FOLLETT PUBLISHING COMPANY		<5
JS	GUIDE	1,620 POWER WORDS, T.E.	FOLLETT PUBLISHING COMPANY		<5
JS	PUPILB	3,140 IMPORTANT WORDS (HARDCOVER)	FOLLETT PUBLISHING COMPANY		<5
JS	PUPILB	1,620 POWER WORDS (HARDCOVER)	FOLLETT PUBLISHING COMPANY		<5
JS	PUPILB	SUCCEED IN SPELLING	J. WESTON WALCH PUBLISHING		6-10
S	TEXTBK	SPELLING: A MNEMONICS APPROACH	SOUTH-WESTERN PUBLISHING CO.		<5

69 - SKILL: SPELLING TROUBLESPOTS

LEVEL	FORMAT	TITLE	PUBLISHER	NT	$PRICE
RPIJS	REFBK	30,000 SELECTED WORDS ORGANIZED BY LETTER, SOUND & SYLLABLE	COMMUNICATION SKILL BUILDERS, INC		11-20
P	ACTCRD	CHECKLIST OF BASIC SOUNDS	LAKESHORE CURRICULUM MATERIALS		<5
P	WKBOOK	TARGET 180, GRADES 1 - 2	STECK-VAUGHN COMPANY		<5
P	WKBOOK	TARGET 360, GRADES 2 - 3	STECK-VAUGHN COMPANY		<5
PI	AUDKIT	PRIMARY SPELLING	HAMPDEN PUBLICATIONS, INC.		101-150
PI	AUDKIT	INTERMEDIATE SPELLING	HAMPDEN PUBLICATIONS, INC.		101-150
PI	MULTIM	BASIC SPELLING: PROBLEM WORDS	XEROX EDUCATION PUBLICATIONS		201-300
PI	PUPILB	INDIVIDUALIZED SPELLING	EDUCATIONAL TEACHING AIDS		6-10
PI	SKLKIT	CONTINUOUS PROGRESS IN SPELLING, PRIMARY	ECONOMY COMPANY		101-150
PI	SKLKIT	CONTINUOUS PROGRESS IN SPELLING, VARIETY DAY KIT 1	ECONOMY COMPANY		151-200
PI	SKLKIT	SPELLING WORDS IN USE	LEARNCO, INC.		11-20
PI	SKLKIT	SPELLING WORDS IN USE DEVELOPMENTAL	LEARNCO, INC.		11-20
PI	WKBOOK	TARGET 540, GRADES 3 - 4	STECK-VAUGHN COMPANY		<5
PIJ	AUDKIT	SPELLTAPES: SPECIAL SPELLING TOPICS, TRAY 7	EDUCATIONAL PROGRESS CORPORATION		76-100
PIJ	AUDKIT	SPELLTAPES: HOMONYMS & BIG DEMONS, TRAY 8	EDUCATIONAL PROGRESS CORPORATION		76-100
PIJ	AUDKIT	COMPLETE BOOK OF SPELLING DEMONS	NATIONAL BOOK COMPANY		151-200
PIJ	RECORD	DEMON SPELLING WORDS	EDUCATIONAL ACTIVITIES, INC.		6-10
I	AUDKIT	SIXTY DEMONS	MEDIA MATERIALS, INC.		6-10
IJ	DITTO	ENRICHMENT ROUSERS: SPELL STUMPERS	IDEAL SCHOOL SUPPLY COMPANY		6-10
IJ	GAME	MATCH THREE	CREATIVE TEACHING ASSOCIATES		6-10
IJ	SKLKIT	CONTINUOUS PROGRESS IN SPELLING, INTERMEDIATE	ECONOMY COMPANY		101-150
IJ	SKLKIT	CONTINUOUS PROGRESS IN SPELLING, VARIETY DAY KIT 2	ECONOMY COMPANY		151-200
JS	DITTO	BETTER SPELLING	HAYES SCHOOL PUBLISHING COMPANY		<5
JS	HI INT	READING FOR PROGRESS (RL 1 - 2)	CAMBRIDGE BOOK CO.		<5
JS	WKBOOK	A SPELLING WORKBOOK	EDUCATORS PUBLISHING SERVICE		<5
JS	WKBOOK	SPELLBINDING 1	EDUCATORS PUBLISHING SERVICE		<5
JS	WKBOOK	SPELLBINDING 2	EDUCATORS PUBLISHING SERVICE		<5
S	PUPILB	SPELLING FOR THE MILLIONS	ELSEVIER/NELSON BOOKS		6-10
S	TEXTBK	SPELLING: A MNEMONICS APPROACH	SOUTH-WESTERN PUBLISHING CO.		<5

70 - SKILL: PARTS OF SPEECH

LEVEL	FORMAT	TITLE	PUBLISHER	NT	$PRICE
RP	CHART	LANGUAGE ASSOCIATION BOARD NO. 1	MODERN EDUCATION CORPORATION		11-20
RP	PUPILB	JOAN HANSON WORD BOOKS	CHILD'S WORLD	16	51-75
RP	PUPILB	POSSESSIVES	CHILD'S WORLD		<5
P	ACTCRD	BASIC SKILLS KIT- SIGHT READING K	EDUCATIONAL PERFORMANCE ASSOC.		31-50
P	ACTCRD	BASIC SKILLS KIT- SIGHT READING L	EDUCATIONAL PERFORMANCE ASSOC.		31-50
P	ACTCRD	ACTION CARDS, SET 3	LAKESHORE CURRICULUM MATERIALS		6-10
P	DITTO	PRACTICE IN BASIC LANGUAGE SKILLS, BOOK 1 (GRADE 1)	INSTRUCTOR PUBLICATIONS, INC.		<5
P	DITTO	PRACTICE IN BASIC LANGUAGE SKILLS, BOOK 2 (GRADE 2)	INSTRUCTOR PUBLICATIONS, INC.		<5
P	DITTO	PRACTICE IN BASIC LANGUAGE SKILLS, BOOK 3 (GRADE 3)	INSTRUCTOR PUBLICATIONS, INC.		<5
P	DITTO	BASIC READING SKILLS	XEROX EDUCATION PUBLICATIONS		<5
P	MANIPU	NES LINGUISTIC BLOCK SERIES, SET 1W	SCOTT, FORESMAN & CO.		11-20
P	RECORD	BILLY BUILDS A SENTENCE	CLASSROOM MATERIALS CO.		6-10
P	RECORD	BILLY THE LONELY WORD	CLASSROOM MATERIALS CO.		6-10
P	SKLKIT	FOKES SENTENCE BUILDER	TEACHING RESOURCES CORPORATION		51-75
P	SKLKIT	FOKES SENTENCE BUILDER EXPANSION	TEACHING RESOURCES CORPORATION		31-50
P	SP EQT	PROGRAMMED LANGUAGE/READING, LEVEL I	INSTRUCTIONAL INDUSTRIES (G.E.)	8	>450
P	SP EQT	PROGRAMMED LANGUAGE/READING, LEVEL I: SET 7, CLOTHING	INSTRUCTIONAL INDUSTRIES (G.E.)		76-100
P	SP EQT	PROGRAMMED LANGUAGE/READING, LEVEL I: SET 8, SHELTER	INSTRUCTIONAL INDUSTRIES (G.E.)		101-150
P	WKBOOK	DELL HOME ACTIVITY: PARTS OF SPEECH	DELL PUBLISHING COMPANY, INC.		<5
PI	ACTCRD	LANGUAGE	FRANK SCHAFFER PUBLICATIONS, INC		<5
PI	AUDKIT	WORDS THAT SHOW OWNERSHIP	MEDIA MATERIALS, INC.		6-10
PI	CHART	PARTS OF SPEECH MOBILE	LITTLE KENNY PUBLICATIONS, INC.		<5
PI	FILMST	NEW ADVENTRURES IN LANGUAGE	TROLL ASSOCIATES		101-150
PI	GAME	PARTS OF SPEECH	FRANK SCHAFFER PUBLICATIONS, INC		<5
PI	GAME	PARTS OF SPEECH RUMMY	JUDY COMPANY		6-10
PI	MULTIU	CREATURE FEATURES: STRUCTURAL ANALYSIS	EDUCATIONAL ACTIVITIES, INC.		51-75
PI	SKLKIT	DEVELOPMENTAL SYNTAX PROGRAM	TEACHING RESOURCES CORPORATION		51-75
PI	SKLKIT	IMAGINATIVE ADJECTIVES & PREPOSITIONS	DORMAC, INC.	14	76-100
PI	SKLKIT	IMAGINATIVE ADJECTIVES & PREPOSITIONS, SET 1	DORMAC, INC.		6-10
PI	SKLKIT	IMAGINATIVE ADJECTIVES & PREPOSITIONS, SET 2	DORMAC, INC.		6-10
PI	SKLKIT	IMAGINATIVE ADJECTIVES & PREPOSITIONS, SET 3	DORMAC, INC.		6-10
PI	SKLKIT	IMAGINATIVE ADJECTIVES & PREPOSITIONS, SET 4	DORMAC, INC.		6-10
PI	SKLKIT	IMAGINATIVE ADJECTIVES & PREPOSITIONS, SET 5	DORMAC, INC.		6-10
PI	SKLKIT	IMAGINATIVE ADJECTIVES & PREPOSITIONS, SET 6	DORMAC, INC.		6-10
PI	SKLKIT	IMAGINATIVE ADJECTIVES & PREPOSITIONS, SET 7	DORMAC, INC.		6-10
PI	SKLKIT	IMAGINATIVE ADJECTIVES & PREPOSITIONS, SET 8	DORMAC, INC.		6-10
PI	SKLKIT	IMAGINATIVE ADJECTIVES & PREPOSITIONS, SET 9	DORMAC, INC.		6-10
PI	SKLKIT	IMAGINATIVE ADJECTIVES & PREPOSITIONS, SET 10	DORMAC, INC.		6-10
PI	SKLKIT	IMAGINATIVE ADJECTIVES & PREPOSITIONS, SET 11	DORMAC, INC.		6-10

LEVEL	FORMAT	TITLE	PUBLISHER	NT	$PRICE

70 - SKILL: PARTS OF SPEECH

LEVEL	FORMAT	TITLE	PUBLISHER	NT	$PRICE
PI	SKLKIT	IMAGINATIVE ADJECTIVES & PREPOSITIONS, SET 12	DORMAC, INC.		6-10
PI	SKLKIT	IMAGINATIVE ADJECTIVES & PREPOSITIONS, SET 13	DORMAC, INC.		6-10
PI	SKLKIT	IMAGINATIVE ADJECTIVES & PREPOSITIONS, SET 14	DORMAC, INC.		6-10
PI	SND FS	PUTTING WORDS IN ORDER / SENTENCE STRUCTURE	TROLL ASSOCIATES		101-150
PI	SP EQT	PROGRAMMED LANGUAGE/READING, LEVEL II	INSTRUCTIONAL INDUSTRIES (G.E.)	8	>450
PI	SP EQT	PROGRAMMED LANGUAGE/READING, LEVEL II: SET 9, SCHOOL	INSTRUCTIONAL INDUSTRIES (G.E.)		101-150
PI	SP EQT	PROGRAMMED LANGUAGE/READING, LEVEL II: SET 10, SELF	INSTRUCTIONAL INDUSTRIES (G.E.)		101-150
PI	SP EQT	PROGRAMMED LANGUAGE/READING, LEVEL II: SET 11, SELF	INSTRUCTIONAL INDUSTRIES (G.E.)		101-150
PI	SP EQT	PROGRAMMED LANGUAGE/READING, LEVEL II: SET 12, COMMUNITY	INSTRUCTIONAL INDUSTRIES (G.E.)		151-200
PI	SP EQT	PROGRAMMED LANGUAGE/READING, LEVEL II: SET 13, FOODS	INSTRUCTIONAL INDUSTRIES (G.E.)		151-200
PI	SP EQT	PROGRAMMED LANGUAGE/READING, LEVEL II: SET 14, HOME	INSTRUCTIONAL INDUSTRIES (G.E.)		101-150
PI	SP EQT	LANGUAGE SKILLS PROGRAM: WORD GAMES & PUZZLES	SPELLBINDER, INC.		51-75
PI	VISKIT	IDENTIFYING PARTS OF SPEECH	INSTRUCTO/MCGRAW-HILL		11-20
PI	WKBOOK	FITZHUGH PLUS PROGRAM, BOOK 207: GRAMMAR & GENL. KNOWLEDGE	ALLIED EDUCATION COUNCIL		<5
PIJ	WKBOOK	LOOKING AT WORDS A	EDL/MCGRAW-HILL		<5
I	AUDKIT	PREPOSITION 500 SPACE RACE	MEDIA MATERIALS, INC.		6-10
I	CHART	PARTS OF SPEECH	BEMISS-JASON CORPORATION		6-10
I	DITTO	BIRDS-EYE VIEW OF LANGUAGE ARTS	FEARON PITMAN PUBLISHERS, INC.		6-10
I	DITTO	PRACTICE IN BASIC LANGUAGE SKILLS, BOOK 4 (GRADE 4)	INSTRUCTOR PUBLICATIONS, INC.		<5
I	DITTO	PRACTICE IN BASIC LANGUAGE SKILLS, BOOK 5 (GRADE 5)	INSTRUCTOR PUBLICATIONS, INC.		<5
I	DITTO	PRACTICE IN BASIC LANGUAGE SKILLS, BOOK 6 (GRADE 6)	INSTRUCTOR PUBLICATIONS, INC.		<5
I	GAME	WORDFACTS GAMES	MILTON BRADLEY/PLAYSKOOL		21-30
I	MULTIM	GAMES 'N' FRAMES: AL'S PIT STOP	IMPERIAL INTERNATIONAL LEARNING		21-30
I	RECORD	BUILDING LANGUAGE USAGE POWER, VOLUME 1	CLASSROOM MATERIALS CO.		6-10
I	RECORD	BUILDING LANGUAGE USAGE POWER, VOLUME 2	CLASSROOM MATERIALS CO.		6-10
I	RECORD	BUILDING LANGUAGE USAGE POWER, VOLUME 3	CLASSROOM MATERIALS CO.		6-10
I	RECORD	BUILDING LANGUAGE USAGE POWER, VOLUEM 6	CLASSROOM MATERIALS CO.		6-10
I	RECORD	BUILDING LANGUAGE USAGE POWER, VOLUME 8	CLASSROOM MATERIALS CO.		6-10
I	WKBOOK	MOTT BASIC SKILLS: LANG., GRAMMAR & SURVIVAL SKILLS, BK 1608	ALLIED EDUCATION COUNCIL		<5
I	WKBOOK	MOTT BASIC SKILLS: LANG., GRAMMAR & SURVIVAL SKILLS, BK 1609	ALLIED EDUCATION COUNCIL		<5
I	WKBOOK	MOTT BASIC SKILLS: LANG., GRAMMAR & SURVIVAL SKILLS, BK 604	ALLIED EDUCATION COUNCIL		<5
I	WKBOOK	LANGUAGE ARTS FOR THE INTERMEDIATE GRADES (4, 5, 6)	JENN PUBLICATIONS		<5
IJ	ACTCRD	GRAMMAR GRAB BAG	KIDS & COMPANY		<5
IJ	ACTCRD	LEARNING CENTER PAK (GRADES 4 - 7)	WISE OWL PUBLICATIONS		31-50
IJ	CL SET	GRAMMAR	CHANNING L. BETE COMPANY, INC.		76-100
IJ	CL SET	WORDS	CHANNING L. BETE COMPANY, INC.		76-100
IJ	DITTO	WORD SKILLS: THE POWER OF WORDS, BOOK I	T.S. DENISON & COMPANY		6-10
IJ	FILMST	ENGLISH COMES ALIVE: PARTS OF SPEECH	UNITED LEARNING		31-50
IJ	FILMST	ENGLISH COMES ALIVE SERIES	UNITED LEARNING	6	151-200
IJ	GAME	WHAT'S THE WORD? GAME	INCENTIVES FOR LEARNING, INC.		76-100
IJ	GAME	WIDE, WIDE WORLD OF GRAMMAR: BASKETWORD	HARCOURT BRACE JOVANOVICH, INC.		11-20
IJ	GAME	WIDE, WIDE WORLD OF GRAMMAR: GOAL WORD SOCCER	HARCOURT BRACE JOVANOVICH, INC.		21-30
IJ	GAME	WIDE, WIDE WORLD OF GRAMMAR: GREAT GRAMMATICAL GOLF TOURN.	HARCOURT BRACE JOVANOVICH, INC.		21-30
IJ	GAME	PARTS OF SPEECH BINGO	TREND ENTERPRISES, INC.		6-10
IJ	MULTIM	EIGHT PARTS OF SPEECH	MEDIA MARKETING, INC.		51-75
IJ	PI/PRT	SKILLS IN LANGUAGE, BOOK 1	CAMBRIDGE BOOK CO.		<5
IJ	RECORD	LANGUAGE USAGE SKILLS FOR UPPER GRADES, VOLUME 2	CLASSROOM MATERIALS CO.		6-10
IJ	RECORD	LANGUAGE USAGE SKILLS FOR UPPER GRADES, VOLUME 3	CLASSROOM MATERIALS CO.		6-10
IJ	RECORD	LANGUAGE USAGE SKILLS FOR UPPER GRADES, VOLUME 6	CLASSROOM MATERIALS CO.		6-10
IJ	RECORD	LANGUAGE USAGE SKILLS FOR UPPER GRADES, VOLUME 8	CLASSROOM MATERIALS CO.		6-10
IJ	SKLKIT	TARGET MECHANICS KIT: GUIDES FOR STANDARD ENGLISH	ADDISON-WESLEY PUBLISHING CO.		201-300
IJ	SKLKIT	PARTS OF SPEECH SKILL BOX	TROLL ASSOCIATES		101-150
IJ	SP EQT	PROGRAMMED LANGUAGE/READING, LEVEL IV	INSTRUCTIONAL INDUSTRIES (G.E.)	8	>450
IJ	TRANSP	COLORGRAM ENGLISH	UNITED TRANSPARENCIES, INC.		101-150
IJ	VISKIT	VERSA-TILES, LANGUAGE ARTS & GRAMMAR SETS	EDUCATIONAL TEACHING AIDS		11-20
IJ	WKBOOK	WORDS	CHANNING L. BETE COMPANY, INC.		<5
IJ	WKBOOK	LANGUAGE 830, GRADES 4 - 8	STECK-VAUGHN COMPANY		<5
IJ	WKBOOK	USAGE SLEUTH	ACTIVITY RESOURCES COMPANY, INC.		6-10
IJS	GAME	ON-WORDS	STANWIX HOUSE, INC.		6-10
IJS	SKLKIT	LANGUAGE REHABILITATION PROGRAM	TEACHING RESOURCES CORPORATION		31-50
IJS	WKBOOK	SOUND WAY, BOOK 1	HAYES SCHOOL PUBLISHING COMPANY		<5
IJS	WKBOOK	SOUND WAY, BOOK 2	HAYES SCHOOL PUBLISHING COMPANY		<5
J	GUIDE	MASTERING THE SENTENCE IN SEVEN STEPS	MCCORMICK-MATHERS PUBLISHING CO.		<5
J	GUIDE	SIMPLE SENTENCE IN SEVEN STEPS	MCCORMICK-MATHERS PUBLISHING CO.		<5
J	PUPILB	MASTERING THE SENTENCE IN SEVEN STEPS	MCCORMICK-MATHERS PUBLISHING CO.		<5
J	PUPILB	SIMPLE SENTENCE IN SEVEN STEPS	MCCORMICK-MATHERS PUBLISHING CO.		<5
J	TEXTBK	LANGUAGE PATTERNS	CAMBRIDGE BOOK CO.		<5
J	WKBOOK	MASTERING PARTS OF SPEECH	CONTINENTAL PRESS, INC.		<5
J	WKBOOK	MOTT BASIC LANG. SKILLS: ADV. LANG./GRAMMAR SKILLS, BK 1912	ALLIED EDUCATION COUNCIL		<5
J	WKBOOK	MOTT BASIC LANG. SKILLS: ADV. LANG./GRAMMAR SKILLS, BK 1913	ALLIED EDUCATION COUNCIL		<5
J	WKBOOK	TROUBLESHOOTER II: BOOK 3, SPELLING & PARTS OF SPEECH	HOUGHTON MIFFLIN COMPANY		<5
JS	A/VKIT	CORRECTING COMPOSITION ERRORS	EYE GATE MEDIA		151-200
JS	DITTO	WORD GAMES ON GRAMMAR	J. WESTON WALCH PUBLISHING		11-20
JS	FILMST	UNDERSTANDING THE SENTENCE	ENCYCLOPEDIA BRITANNICA		76-100
JS	PI/PRT	SKILLS IN LANGUAGE, BOOK 2	CAMBRIDGE BOOK CO.		<5
JS	PUPILB	LANGUAGE WORKSHOP (RL 4 - 5)	GLOBE BOOK COMPANY, INC.		<5
JS	WKBOOK	VOCABULARY BUILDING EXERCISES FOR YOUNG ADULTS, BOOK A	DORMAC, INC.		<5
JS	WKBOOK	VOCABULARY BUILDING EXERCISES FOR YOUNG ADULTS, BOOK B	DORMAC, INC.		<5
JS	WKBOOK	VOCABULARY BUILDING EXERCISES FOR YOUNG ADULTS, BOOK C	DORMAC, INC.		<5

LEVEL	FORMAT	TITLE	PUBLISHER	NT	$PRICE

70 - SKILL: PARTS OF SPEECH

LEVEL	FORMAT	TITLE	PUBLISHER	NT	$PRICE
JS	WKBOOK	IMPROVING COMPOSITION	EDUCATORS PUBLISHING SERVICE		<5
S	MULTIM	RELEVANCE SERIES	CAMBRIDGE BOOK CO.	5	>450
S	MULTIM	RELEVANCE SERIES: RELEVANCE OF PATTERNS	CAMBRIDGE BOOK CO.		201-300
S	TEXTBK	BUSINESS COMMUNICATIONS	SOUTH-WESTERN PUBLISHING CO.	2	6-10
S	TEXTBK	BUSINESS COMMUNICATIONS: ENGLISH THE EASY WAY	SOUTH-WESTERN PUBLISHING CO.		<5
S	WKBOOK	MOTT BASIC LANG. SKILLS: ADV. LANG./GRAMMAR SKILLS, BK 1914	ALLIED EDUCATION COUNCIL		<5

71 - SKILL: NOUNS

LEVEL	FORMAT	TITLE	PUBLISHER	NT	$PRICE
RP	ACTCRD	TUTORGRAM: COMMON NOUNS	ENRICHMENT READING CORP OF AMER.		11-20
RP	CHART	LANGUAGE ASSOCIATION BOARD NO. 3	MODERN EDUCATION CORPORATION		11-20
RP	DITTO	LANGUAGE STIMULATION: NOUNS, ANIMALS & INSECTS	MODERN EDUCATION CORPORATION		6-10
RP	DITTO	LANGUAGE STIMULATION: NOUNS, FOOD	MODERN EDUCATION CORPORATION		6-10
RP	DITTO	LANGUAGE STIMULATION: NOUNS, HOUSEHOLD ITEMS	MODERN EDUCATION CORPORATION		6-10
RP	GAME	MATCH GAMES, SET 1	GARRARD PUBLISHING COMPANY		<5
RP	GAME	MATCH GAMES, SET 2	GARRARD PUBLISHING COMPANY		<5
RP	MULTIM	USING PRONOUNS	LISTEN & LEARN CORPORATION		76-100
P	ACTCRD	PARTS OF SPEECH SERIES	TEACHING RESOURCES CORPORATION	4	21-30
P	ACTCRD	PARTS OF SPEECH: NOUN CONCEPTS	TEACHING RESOURCES CORPORATION		6-10
P	ACTCRD	GROUP-SIZE PICTURE WORD CARDS	GARRARD PUBLISHING COMPANY		<5
P	ACTCRD	BASIC SKILLS KIT- SIGHT READING K	EDUCATIONAL PERFORMANCE ASSOC.		31-50
P	ACTCRD	BASIC SKILLS KIT- SIGHT READING L	EDUCATIONAL PERFORMANCE ASSOC.		31-50
P	ACTCRD	ACTION CARDS, SET 2	LAKESHORE CURRICULUM MATERIALS		6-10
P	AUDKIT	MINISYSTEMS: FROM SPELLING TO WRITING I	CORONET MULTI MEDIA		11-20
P	AUDKIT	MINISYSTEMS: FROM SPELLING TO WRITING II	CORONET MULTI MEDIA		11-20
P	AUDKIT	WORDS ARE FUN	CORONET MULTI MEDIA		101-150
P	DITTO	PHONETIC READER	HAYES SCHOOL PUBLISHING COMPANY		<5
P	FILMST	DEVELOPING LANGUAGE SKILLS: CAN YOU NAME IT?	ENCYCLOPEDIA BRITANNICA		31-50
P	GAME	PRONOUN PINCH HITTER	DEVELOPMENTAL LEARNING MATERIALS		6-10
P	MANIPU	NES LINGUISTIC BLOCK SERIES, SET 1W	SCOTT, FORESMAN & CO.		11-20
P	MANIPU	NOUN BOARDS	DEVELOPMENTAL LEARNING MATERIALS		6-10
P	MANIPU	NOUN PUZZLES	DEVELOPMENTAL LEARNING MATERIALS		<5
P	MANIPU	SIGHT READING: NOUNS	AERO PUBLISHERS, INC.		6-10
P	MANIPU	MAGIC TEACHER PUZZLE-PLANS (NOUNS), LEVEL 1	HAYES SCHOOL PUBLISHING COMPANY		<5
P	PI/PRT	LEARNING SLATE: ANIMALS (NOUNS)	IDEAL SCHOOL SUPPLY COMPANY		<5
P	PI/PRT	LEARNING SLATE: AT HOME (NOUNS)	IDEAL SCHOOL SUPPLY COMPANY		<5
P	RECORD	BILLY THE LONELY WORD	CLASSROOM MATERIALS CO.		6-10
P	RECORD	BUILDING VERBAL POWER, VOLUME 4	CLASSROOM MATERIALS CO.		6-10
P	SP EQT	PROGRAMMED LANGUAGE/READING, LEVEL I	INSTRUCTIONAL INDUSTRIES (G.E.)	8	>450
P	SP EQT	PROGRAMMED LANGUAGE/READING, LEVEL I: SET 1, SELF	INSTRUCTIONAL INDUSTRIES (G.E.)		101-150
P	SP EQT	PROGRAMMED LANGUAGE/READING, LEVEL I: SET 2, ANIMALS	INSTRUCTIONAL INDUSTRIES (G.E.)		101-150
P	SP EQT	PROGRAMMED LANGUAGE/READING, LEVEL I: SET 3, FOODS	INSTRUCTIONAL INDUSTRIES (G.E.)		101-150
P	SP EQT	PROGRAMMED LANGUAGE/READING, LEVEL I: SET 4, PLAYTHINGS	INSTRUCTIONAL INDUSTRIES (G.E.)		101-150
P	SP EQT	PROGRAMMED LANGUAGE/READING, LEVEL I: SET 5, ACTIVITIES	INSTRUCTIONAL INDUSTRIES (G.E.)		76-100
P	SP EQT	FLASH-X-SET 1: READING PICTURES	EDL/MCGRAW-HILL		<5
P	WKBOOK	FITZHUGH PLUS PROGRAM, BOOK 201: COMMON NOUNS	ALLIED EDUCATION COUNCIL		<5
P	WKBOOK	MY SPEECH BOOK (SP. ED.)	ST. JOHN SCHOOL FOR THE DEAF		<5
PI	ACTCRD	PRONOUN PARADE, A	BARNELL LOFT, LTD.		6-10
PI	ACTCRD	PRONOUN PARADE, B	BARNELL LOFT, LTD.		6-10
PI	ACTCRD	PRONOUN PARADE, C	BARNELL LOFT, LTD.		6-10
PI	ACTCRD	PRONOUN PARADE, D	BARNELL LOFT, LTD.		6-10
PI	ACTCRD	PRONOUN PARADE, E	BARNELL LOFT, LTD.		6-10
PI	ACTCRD	TUTORGRAM: NOUNS, VERBS, ADJECTIVES, ADVERBS	ENRICHMENT READING CORP OF AMER.		11-20
PI	ACTCRD	TUTORGRAM: PRONOUN REFERENCE	ENRICHMENT READING CORP OF AMER.		11-20
PI	ACTCRD	PLURALS	C.C. PUBLICATIONS, INC.		21-30
PI	GAME	PARTS OF SPEECH	FRANK SCHAFFER PUBLICATIONS, INC		<5
PI	GAME	SILLY SOUNDS	IDEAL SCHOOL SUPPLY COMPANY		6-10
PI	GAME	BUILDING VOCABULARY	INSTRUCTO/MCGRAW-HILL		11-20
PI	MANIPU	AERO SIGHT READING LAB	AERO PUBLISHERS, INC.		76-100
PI	MANIPU	MAGIC TEACHER PUZZLE-PLANS: READING (NOUNS), LEVEL 2	HAYES SCHOOL PUBLISHING COMPANY		<5
PI	SKLKIT	DEVELOPMENTAL SYNTAX PROGRAM	TEACHING RESOURCES CORPORATION		51-75
PI	SND FS	PRESENTING...PARTS OF SPEECH	JANUARY PRODUCTIONS		51-75
PI	SP EQT	PROGRAMMED LANGUAGE/READING, LEVEL II: SET 14, HOME	INSTRUCTIONAL INDUSTRIES (G.E.)		101-150
PI	WKBOOK	PRONOUN PAGES	DORMAC, INC.		<5
PIJ	FLASH	SEE IT, SAY IT	ADDISON-WESLEY PUBLISHING CO.		31-50
PIJ	MULTIU	CREATURE FEATURES: VOCABULARY DEVELOPMENT	EDUCATIONAL ACTIVITIES, INC.		31-50
PIJ	SKLKIT	SYSTEMATIC SENTENCE BUILDER, LEVEL TWO	MODERN EDUCATION CORPORATION		51-75
PIJ	SKLKIT	SYSTEMATIC SENTENCE BUILDER, LEVEL THREE	MODERN EDUCATION CORPORATION		51-75
PIJ	VISKIT	SYNTAX CODES SINGULAR NOUN PRESENT TENSE VERB	C.C. PUBLICATIONS, INC.		21-30
PIJ	VISKIT	VIP NOUNS, BOX 1	C.C. PUBLICATIONS, INC.		31-50
I	AUDKIT	POSSESSIVES - TEN FINGERS & THEY'RE ALL MINE	MEDIA MATERIALS, INC.		6-10
I	AUDKIT	GREAT COSMIC TREATY AGREEMENT OF SUBJECT: VERB	MEDIA MATERIALS, INC.		6-10
I	AUDKIT	NOUN-SENSE IN FAR OFF SPACE	MEDIA MATERIALS, INC.		6-10
I	AUDKIT	PRONOUN SPACE SHUTTLE	MEDIA MATERIALS, INC.		6-10
I	DITTO	VOCABULARY BUILDING, INTERMEDIATE	HAYES SCHOOL PUBLISHING COMPANY		<5
I	DITTO	VOCABULARY BUILDING, UPPER INTERMEDIATE	HAYES SCHOOL PUBLISHING COMPANY		<5
I	DITTO	FOURTH GRADE LANGUAGE DRILLS	HAYES SCHOOL PUBLISHING COMPANY		<5
I	DITTO	FIFTH GRADE LANGUAGE DRILLS	HAYES SCHOOL PUBLISHING COMPANY		<5
I	DITTO	SIXTH GRADE LANGUAGE DRILLS	HAYES SCHOOL PUBLISHING COMPANY		<5
I	MANIPU	MAGIC TEACHER PUZZLE-PLANS: READING (NOUNS), LEVEL 3	HAYES SCHOOL PUBLISHING COMPANY		<5

LEVEL	FORMAT	TITLE	PUBLISHER	NT	$PRICE

71 - SKILL: NOUNS

LEVEL	FORMAT	TITLE	PUBLISHER	NT	$PRICE
I	RECORD	BUILDING LANGUAGE USAGE POWER, VOLUME 4	CLASSROOM MATERIALS CO.		6-10
I	RECORD	BUILDING LANGUAGE USAGE POWER, VOLUEM 6	CLASSROOM MATERIALS CO.		6-10
I	RECORD	BUILDING LANGUAGE USAGE POWER, VOLUME 7	CLASSROOM MATERIALS CO.		6-10
I	RECORD	BUILDING LANGUAGE USAGE POWER, VOLUME 8	CLASSROOM MATERIALS CO.		6-10
I	RECORD	BUILDING VERBAL POWER IN THE UPPER GRADES, VOLUME 2	CLASSROOM MATERIALS CO.		6-10
I	WKBOOK	WORDS THAT NAME	EDUCATORS PUBLISHING SERVICE		<5
IJ	AUDKIT	WORD SIGNALS	EBSCO CURRICULUM MATERIALS		51-75
IJ	AUDKIT	DEVELOPING ENGLISH SKILLS	EDUCATIONAL ACTIVITIES, INC.		51-75
IJ	DITTO	BASIC LANGUAGE SKILLS: NOUNS & PRONOUNS	EDUCATIONAL INSIGHTS, INC.		6-10
IJ	DITTO	WORD SKILLS: LIVING WITH WORDS, BOOK II	T.S. DENISON & COMPANY		6-10
IJ	GAME	WHAT'S THE WORD? GAME	INCENTIVES FOR LEARNING, INC.		76-100
IJ	MULTIM	EIGHT PARTS OF SPEECH	MEDIA MARKETING, INC.		51-75
IJ	RECORD	LANGUAGE USAGE SKILLS FOR UPPER GRADES, VOLUME 2	CLASSROOM MATERIALS CO.		6-10
IJ	RECORD	LANGUAGE USAGE SKILLS FOR UPPER GRADES, VOLUME 4	CLASSROOM MATERIALS CO.		6-10
IJ	RECORD	LANGUAGE USAGE SKILLS FOR UPPER GRADES, VOLUME 6	CLASSROOM MATERIALS CO.		6-10
IJ	SKLKIT	TARGET MECHANICS KIT: CAPITALIZATION & PUNCTUATION	ADDISON-WESLEY PUBLISHING CO.		201-300
IJ	SP EQT	PROGRAMMED LANGUAGE/READING, LEVEL IV: SET 25,NATURE/ECOLOGY	INSTRUCTIONAL INDUSTRIES (G.E.)		151-200
IJ	TRANSP	KERNEL SENTENCES	UNITED TRANSPARENCIES, INC.		76-100
IJ	WKBOOK	LANGUAGE 720, GRADES 4 - 8	STECK-VAUGHN COMPANY		<5
IJS	DITTO	WORD SKILLS: TIME ON YOUR HANDS, BOOK VI	T.S. DENISON & COMPANY		6-10
J	A/VKIT	NOUNS	GUIDANCE ASSOCIATES		51-75
J	A/VKIT	PRONOUNS	GUIDANCE ASSOCIATES		51-75
J	DITTO	JR. HI LANGUAGE DRILLS, BOOK 1	HAYES SCHOOL PUBLISHING COMPANY		<5
J	DITTO	JR. HI LANGUAGE DRILLS, BOOK 2	HAYES SCHOOL PUBLISHING COMPANY		<5
JS	AUDKIT	SENTENCE PATTERNS	CORONET MULTI MEDIA		101-150
JS	DITTO	NOUNS, ADJECTIVES & VERBS COLOR 'N' LEARN	ACTIVITY RESOURCES COMPANY, INC.		<5
JS	SND FS	WORDS! WORDS! WORDS!	ENCORE VISUAL EDUCATION, INC.		101-150

72 - SKILL: VERBS

LEVEL	FORMAT	TITLE	PUBLISHER	NT	$PRICE
RP	ACTCRD	EXPRESSIVE LANGUAGE CARDS	MAFEX ASSOCIATES, INC.		11-20
RP	CHART	LANGUAGE ASSOCIATION BOARD NO. 2	MODERN EDUCATION CORPORATION		11-20
RP	DITTO	LANGUAGE STIMULATION: VERBS	MODERN EDUCATION CORPORATION		6-10
RPIJS	PICTUR	PICTURES, PLEASE!	COMMUNICATION SKILL BUILDERS,INC		31-50
P	ACTCRD	PARTS OF SPEECH SERIES	TEACHING RESOURCES CORPORATION	4	21-30
P	ACTCRD	PARTS OF SPEECH: VERB CONCEPTS	TEACHING RESOURCES CORPORATION		6-10
P	ACTCRD	VERBS - VERBS - VERBS	DORMAC, INC.		21-30
P	ACTCRD	TUTORGRAM: PAST TENSE VERBS	ENRICHMENT READING CORP OF AMER.		11-20
P	ACTCRD	VEE'S VERBS	WORD MAKING PRODUCTIONS, INC.		31-50
P	ACTCRD	BASIC SKILLS KIT- SIGHT READING K	EDUCATIONAL PERFORMANCE ASSOC.		31-50
P	ACTCRD	ACTION CARDS, SET 1	LAKESHORE CURRICULUM MATERIALS		6-10
P	AUDKIT	WORDS ARE FUN	CORONET MULTI MEDIA		101-150
P	DITTO	THIRD GRADE LANGUAGE DRILLS	HAYES SCHOOL PUBLISHING COMPANY		<5
P	FILMST	DEVELOPING LANGUAGE SKILLS: CAN YOU DO IT?	ENCYCLOPEDIA BRITANNICA		31-50
P	GAME	VERB USAGE	FRANK SCHAFFER PUBLICATIONS, INC		<5
P	GAME	VERBS: PAST, PRESENT, FUTURE	ST. JOHN SCHOOL FOR THE DEAF		<5
P	MANIPU	BUILDING SENTENCES STEP-BY-STEP	DORMAC, INC.		31-50
P	MANIPU	NES LINGUISTIC BLOCK SERIES, SET 1W	SCOTT, FORESMAN & CO.		11-20
P	MANIPU	VERB PUZZLE	DEVELOPMENTAL LEARNING MATERIALS		<5
P	MANIPU	VERB TENSE BOARDS	DEVELOPMENTAL LEARNING MATERIALS		<5
P	MANIPU	SIGHT READING: VERBS	AERO PUBLISHERS, INC.		6-10
P	MANIPU	MAGIC TEACHER PUZZLE-PLANS: READING (VERBS)	HAYES SCHOOL PUBLISHING COMPANY		<5
P	MULTIM	USING VERB TENSES	LISTEN & LEARN CORPORATION		76-100
P	PI/PRT	LEARNING SLATE: CHILDREN (VERBS)	IDEAL SCHOOL SUPPLY COMPANY		<5
P	RECORD	BILLY THE LONELY WORD	CLASSROOM MATERIALS CO.		6-10
P	RECORD	DEVELOPING FUNDAMENTAL LANGUAGE PATTERNS, VOLUME 2: TO BE	CLASSROOM MATERIALS CO.		6-10
P	RECORD	DEVELOPING FUNDAMENTAL LANGUAGE PATTERNS, VOLUME 3: TO SEE	CLASSROOM MATERIALS CO.		6-10
P	RECORD	DEVELOPING FUNDAMENTAL LANGUAGE PATTERNS, VOLUME 4: TO GO	CLASSROOM MATERIALS CO.		6-10
P	RECORD	DEVELOPING FUNDAMENTAL LANGUAGE PATTERNS, VOLUME 5: TO SAY	CLASSROOM MATERIALS CO.		6-10
P	RECORD	DEVELOPING FUNDAMENTAL LANGUAGE PATTERNS, VOLUME 6: TO DO	CLASSROOM MATERIALS CO.		6-10
P	SP EQT	DEVELOPING LANGUAGE SKILLS, KIT B	BORG-WARNER EDUCATIONAL SYSTEMS		201-300
P	SP EQT	DEVELOPING LANGUAGE SKILLS, KIT C	BORG-WARNER EDUCATIONAL SYSTEMS		201-300
P	SP EQT	DEVELOPING LANGUAGE SKILLS, KIT D	BORG-WARNER EDUCATIONAL SYSTEMS		201-300
P	SP EQT	PROGRAMMED LANGUAGE/READING, LEVEL I	INSTRUCTIONAL INDUSTRIES (G.E.)	8	>450
P	SP EQT	PROGRAMMED LANGUAGE/READING, LEVEL I: SET 1, SELF	INSTRUCTIONAL INDUSTRIES (G.E.)		101-150
P	SP EQT	PROGRAMMED LANGUAGE/READING, LEVEL I: SET 3, FOODS	INSTRUCTIONAL INDUSTRIES (G.E.)		101-150
P	SP EQT	PROGRAMMED LANGUAGE/READING, LEVEL I: SET 4, PLAYTHINGS	INSTRUCTIONAL INDUSTRIES (G.E.)		101-150
P	WKBOOK	FITZHUGH PLUS PROGRAM, BOOK 202: ACTION VERBS	ALLIED EDUCATION COUNCIL		<5
P	WKBOOK	SAY & DO	ST. JOHN SCHOOL FOR THE DEAF		<5
P	WKBOOK	BASIC VOCABULARY WORKSHEETS, BOOK 3	ST. JOHN SCHOOL FOR THE DEAF		<5
PI	ACTCRD	TUTORGRAM: PAST TENSE IRREGULAR VERBS	ENRICHMENT READING CORP OF AMER.		11-20
PI	ACTCRD	TUTORGRAM: NOUNS, VERBS, ADJECTIVES, ADVERBS	ENRICHMENT READING CORP OF AMER.		11-20
PI	ACTCRD	LANGUAGE: VERB ACTION PICTURES	WHITEHAVEN PUBLISHING COMPANY		11-20
PI	ACTCRD	LANGUAGE: PLURAL ACTION PICTURES	WHITEHAVEN PUBLISHING COMPANY		11-20
PI	AUDKIT	LET'S LOOK FOR ACTION WORDS	MEDIA MATERIALS, INC.		6-10
PI	AUDKIT	LET'S LOOK FOR MORE ACTION WORDS	MEDIA MATERIALS, INC.		6-10
PI	AUDKIT	INTERMEDIATE STRUCTURAL ANALYSIS	HAMPDEN PUBLICATIONS, INC.		101-150
PI	GAME	PARTS OF SPEECH	FRANK SCHAFFER PUBLICATIONS, INC		<5
PI	GAME	ETA VERB LOTTO GAME	EDUCATIONAL TEACHING AIDS		6-10

LEVEL	FORMAT	TITLE	PUBLISHER	NT	$PRICE

72 - SKILL: VERBS

LEVEL	FORMAT	TITLE	PUBLISHER	$PRICE
PI	GAME	SILLY SOUNDS	IDEAL SCHOOL SUPPLY COMPANY	6-10
PI	GAME	SIGN CARD GAMES (SP. ED.)	ST. JOHN SCHOOL FOR THE DEAF	6-10
PI	GAME	BASIC VOCABULARY BINGO GAME	ST. JOHN SCHOOL FOR THE DEAF	6-10
PI	GAME	BUILDING VOCABULARY	INSTRUCTO/MCGRAW-HILL	11-20
PI	GUIDE	LEARNING ACTION WORDS	KENWORTHY EDUCATIONAL SERVICE	<5
PI	MANIPU	ACTION VERB BOARDS	DEVELOPMENTAL LEARNING MATERIALS	6-10
PI	MANIPU	AERO SIGHT READING LAB	AERO PUBLISHERS, INC.	76-100
PI	MULTIU	LARC: MODULE O: ORDER & SEQUENCE SKILLS	ARISTA CORPORATION	151-200
PI	PICTUR	LAC CARDS, SET 2: GENERAL VERBS	MODERN EDUCATION CORPORATION	11-20
PI	RECORD	DEVELOPING FUNDAMENTAL LANGUAGE PATTERNS, VOLUME 1: TO HAVE	CLASSROOM MATERIALS CO.	6-10
PI	SKLKIT	DEVELOPMENTAL SYNTAX PROGRAM	TEACHING RESOURCES CORPORATION	51-75
PI	SND FS	PRESENTING...PARTS OF SPEECH	JANUARY PRODUCTIONS	51-75
PI	SP EQT	PROGRAMMED LANGUAGE/READING, LEVEL II: SET 9, SCHOOL	INSTRUCTIONAL INDUSTRIES (G.E.)	101-150
PI	SP EQT	PROGRAMMED LANGUAGE/READING, LEVEL II: SET 11, SELF	INSTRUCTIONAL INDUSTRIES (G.E.)	101-150
PI	SP EQT	PROGRAMMED LANGUAGE/READING, LEVEL II: SET 12, COMMUNITY	INSTRUCTIONAL INDUSTRIES (G.E.)	151-200
PI	SP EQT	PROGRAMMED LANGUAGE/READING, LEVEL II: SET 13, FOODS	INSTRUCTIONAL INDUSTRIES (G.E.)	151-200
PI	SP EQT	PROGRAMMED LANGUAGE/READING, LEVEL II: SET 14, HOME	INSTRUCTIONAL INDUSTRIES (G.E.)	101-150
PI	SP EQT	PROGRAMMED LANGUAGE/READING, LEVEL II: SET 16, CLOTHING	INSTRUCTIONAL INDUSTRIES (G.E.)	101-150
PI	WKBOOK	TEACHING VERB TENSE THROUGH CREATIVE CALENDAR ACTIVITIES	ST. JOHN SCHOOL FOR THE DEAF	<5
PI	WKBOOK	BASIC VOCABULARY WORKSHEETS, BOOK 6	ST. JOHN SCHOOL FOR THE DEAF	<5
PIJ	FLASH	SEE IT, SAY IT	ADDISON-WESLEY PUBLISHING CO.	31-50
PIJ	MULTIU	CREATURE FEATURES: VOCABULARY DEVELOPMENT	EDUCATIONAL ACTIVITIES, INC.	31-50
PIJ	SKLKIT	SYSTEMATIC SENTENCE BUILDER, LEVEL ONE	MODERN EDUCATION CORPORATION	51-75
PIJ	SKLKIT	SYSTEMATIC SENTENCE BUILDER, LEVEL TWO	MODERN EDUCATION CORPORATION	51-75
PIJ	SKLKIT	SYSTEMATIC SENTENCE BUILDER, LEVEL THREE	MODERN EDUCATION CORPORATION	51-75
PIJ	VISKIT	SYNTAX CODES IS, IS VERBING	C.C. PUBLICATIONS, INC.	21-30
PIJ	VISKIT	SYNTAX CODES ARE, ARE VERBING	C.C. PUBLICATIONS, INC.	21-30
PIJ	VISKIT	SYNTAX CODES SINGULAR NOUN PRESENT TENSE VERB	C.C. PUBLICATIONS, INC.	21-30
PIJ	VISKIT	SYNTAX CODES REGULAR PAST TENSE VERBS	C.C. PUBLICATIONS, INC.	21-30
PIJ	VISKIT	SYNTAX CODES IRREGULAR PAST TENSE VERBS, I	C.C. PUBLICATIONS, INC.	21-30
PIJ	VISKIT	SYNTAX CODES IRREGULAR PAST TENSE VERBS, II	C.C. PUBLICATIONS, INC.	21-30
PIJ	VISKIT	SYNTAX CODES IRREGULAR PAST TENSE VERBS, III	C.C. PUBLICATIONS, INC.	21-30
PIJ	VISKIT	SYNTAX CODES IRREGULAR PAST TENSE VERBS, IV	C.C. PUBLICATIONS, INC.	21-30
PIJ	VISKIT	VIP VERBS, BOX 1	C.C. PUBLICATIONS, INC.	31-50
I	AUDKIT	VERBS, MUSCLES IN ACTION	MEDIA MATERIALS, INC.	6-10
I	AUDKIT	GREAT COSMIC TREATY AGREEMENT OF SUBJECT: VERB	MEDIA MATERIALS, INC.	6-10
I	AUDKIT	SOLAR SWAMP VERB	MEDIA MATERIALS, INC.	6-10
I	AUDKIT	SPACE FIREWORKS: REGULAR VERBS VS. IRREGULAR	MEDIA MATERIALS, INC.	6-10
I	DITTO	VOCABULARY BUILDING, INTERMEDIATE	HAYES SCHOOL PUBLISHING COMPANY	<5
I	DITTO	VOCABULARY BUILDING, UPPER INTERMEDIATE	HAYES SCHOOL PUBLISHING COMPANY	<5
I	DITTO	FOURTH GRADE LANGUAGE DRILLS	HAYES SCHOOL PUBLISHING COMPANY	<5
I	DITTO	FIFTH GRADE LANGUAGE DRILLS	HAYES SCHOOL PUBLISHING COMPANY	<5
I	DITTO	SIXTH GRADE LANGUAGE DRILLS	HAYES SCHOOL PUBLISHING COMPANY	<5
I	WKBOOK	WORDS THAT TELL ACTION	EDUCATORS PUBLISHING SERVICE	<5
IJ	AUDKIT	WORD SIGNALS	EBSCO CURRICULUM MATERIALS	51-75
IJ	AUDKIT	LOOK IN THE MIRROR	MEDIA MATERIALS, INC.	6-10
IJ	AUDKIT	DEVELOPING ENGLISH SKILLS	EDUCATIONAL ACTIVITIES, INC.	51-75
IJ	DITTO	BASIC LANGUAGE SKILLS: VERBS	EDUCATIONAL INSIGHTS, INC.	6-10
IJ	DITTO	WORD SKILLS: LIVING WITH WORDS, BOOK II	T.S. DENISON & COMPANY	6-10
IJ	GAME	WHAT'S THE WORD? GAME	INCENTIVES FOR LEARNING, INC.	76-100
IJ	GAME	WIDE, WIDE WORLD OF GRAMMAR: GREAT GRAMMATICAL GOLF TOURN.	HARCOURT BRACE JOVANOVICH, INC.	21-30
IJ	MULTIM	EIGHT PARTS OF SPEECH	MEDIA MARKETING, INC.	51-75
IJ	RECORD	LANGUAGE USAGE SKILLS FOR UPPER GRADES, VOLUME 3	CLASSROOM MATERIALS CO.	6-10
IJ	RECORD	LANGUAGE USAGE SKILLS FOR UPPER GRADES, VOLUME 6	CLASSROOM MATERIALS CO.	6-10
IJ	RECORD	LANGUAGE USAGE SKILLS FOR UPPER GRADES, VOLUME 8	CLASSROOM MATERIALS CO.	6-10
IJ	SKLKIT	TARGET MECHANICS KIT: GUIDES FOR STANDARD ENGLISH	ADDISON-WESLEY PUBLISHING CO.	201-300
IJ	TRANSP	KERNEL SENTENCES	UNITED TRANSPARENCIES, INC.	76-100
IJ	TRANSP	TRANSFORMATIONS	UNITED TRANSPARENCIES, INC.	76-100
IJ	WKBOOK	LANGUAGE 720, GRADES 4 - 8	STECK-VAUGHN COMPANY	<5
IJS	AUDCRD	ACTION WORDS	AUDIOTRONICS CORPORATION	11-20
IJS	DITTO	WORD SKILLS: THE TIME OF YOUR LIFE, BOOK III	T.S. DENISON & COMPANY	6-10
IJS	DITTO	WORD SKILLS: LOOKING INTO THE FUTURE, BOOK IV	T.S. DENISON & COMPANY	6-10
IJS	DITTO	WORD SKILLS: TIME ON YOUR HANDS, BOOK VI	T.S. DENISON & COMPANY	6-10
IJS	SKLKIT	LANGUAGE REHABILITATION PROGRAM	TEACHING RESOURCES CORPORATION	31-50
J	A/VKIT	VERBS	GUIDANCE ASSOCIATES	51-75
J	DITTO	JR. HI LANGUAGE DRILLS, BOOK 1	HAYES SCHOOL PUBLISHING COMPANY	<5
J	DITTO	JR. HI LANGUAGE DRILLS, BOOK 2	HAYES SCHOOL PUBLISHING COMPANY	<5
J	RECORD	LANGUAGE USAGE SKILLS FOR UPPER GRADES, VOLUME 1	CLASSROOM MATERIALS CO.	6-10
JS	AUDKIT	SENTENCE PATTERNS	CORONET MULTI MEDIA	101-150
JS	DITTO	NOUNS, ADJECTIVES & VERBS COLOR 'N' LEARN	ACTIVITY RESOURCES COMPANY, INC.	<5
JS	SND FS	WORDS! WORDS! WORDS!	ENCORE VISUAL EDUCATION, INC.	101-150
S	SND FS	HELPING VERB	MEDIA MATERIALS, INC.	11-20

73 - SKILL: ADJECTIVES/ADVERBS

LEVEL	FORMAT	TITLE	PUBLISHER	$PRICE
RP	ACTCRD	EXPRESSIVE LANGUAGE CARDS	MAFEX ASSOCIATES, INC.	11-20
RP	CHART	LANGUAGE ASSOCIATION BOARD NO. 3	MODERN EDUCATION CORPORATION	11-20
RP	DITTO	LANGUAGE STIMULATION: ADJECTIVES	MODERN EDUCATION CORPORATION	6-10
RPIJS	PICTUR	PICTURES, PLEASE!	COMMUNICATION SKILL BUILDERS, INC	31-50

LEVEL	FORMAT	TITLE	PUBLISHER	NT	$PRICE

73 - SKILL: ADJECTIVES/ADVERBS

LEVEL	FORMAT	TITLE	PUBLISHER	NT	$PRICE
P	ACTCRD	PARTS OF SPEECH SERIES	TEACHING RESOURCES CORPORATION	4	21-30
P	ACTCRD	PARTS OF SPEECH: ADJECTIVE CONCEPTS	TEACHING RESOURCES CORPORATION		6-10
P	ACTCRD	PARTS OF SPEECH: ADVERB CONCEPTS	TEACHING RESOURCES CORPORATION		6-10
P	ACTCRD	BASIC SKILLS KIT- SIGHT READING L	EDUCATIONAL PERFORMANCE ASSOC.		31-50
P	AUDKIT	WORDS ARE FUN	CORONET MULTI MEDIA		101-150
P	MANIPU	NES LINGUISTIC BLOCK SERIES, SET 1W	SCOTT, FORESMAN & CO.		11-20
P	MANIPU	SIGHT READING: ADJECTIVES	AERO PUBLISHERS, INC.		6-10
P	MANIPU	SIGHT READING: ADVERBS	AERO PUBLISHERS, INC.		6-10
P	RECORD	BILLY THE LONELY WORD	CLASSROOM MATERIALS CO.		6-10
P	SP EQT	PROGRAMMED LANGUAGE/READING, LEVEL I	INSTRUCTIONAL INDUSTRIES (G.E.)	8	>450
P	SP EQT	PROGRAMMED LANGUAGE/READING, LEVEL I: SET 2, ANIMALS	INSTRUCTIONAL INDUSTRIES (G.E.)		101-150
P	SP EQT	PROGRAMMED LANGUAGE/READING, LEVEL I: SET 6, SELF	INSTRUCTIONAL INDUSTRIES (G.E.)		101-150
P	WKBOOK	TALK TALK TALK	ST. JOHN SCHOOL FOR THE DEAF		<5
PI	ACTCRD	TUTORGRAM: NOUNS, VERBS, ADJECTIVES, ADVERBS	ENRICHMENT READING CORP OF AMER.		11-20
PI	AUDKIT	LOOK FOR WORDS THAT COMPARE	MEDIA MATERIALS, INC.		6-10
PI	GAME	PARTS OF SPEECH	FRANK SCHAFFER PUBLICATIONS, INC		<5
PI	GAME	ETA ADJECTIVE LOTTO GAME	EDUCATIONAL TEACHING AIDS		6-10
PI	GAME	SILLY SOUNDS	IDEAL SCHOOL SUPPLY COMPANY		6-10
PI	GAME	BUILDING VOCABULARY	INSTRUCTO/MCGRAW-HILL		11-20
PI	MANIPU	AERO SIGHT READING LAB	AERO PUBLISHERS, INC.		76-100
PI	SKLKIT	DEVELOPMENTAL SYNTAX PROGRAM	TEACHING RESOURCES CORPORATION		51-75
PI	SKLKIT	IMAGINATIVE ADJECTIVES & PREPOSITIONS	DORMAC, INC.	14	76-100
PI	SKLKIT	IMAGINATIVE ADJECTIVES & PREPOSITIONS, SET 1	DORMAC, INC.		6-10
PI	SKLKIT	IMAGINATIVE ADJECTIVES & PREPOSITIONS, SET 2	DORMAC, INC.		6-10
PI	SKLKIT	IMAGINATIVE ADJECTIVES & PREPOSITIONS, SET 3	DORMAC, INC.		6-10
PI	SKLKIT	IMAGINATIVE ADJECTIVES & PREPOSITIONS, SET 4	DORMAC, INC.		6-10
PI	SKLKIT	IMAGINATIVE ADJECTIVES & PREPOSITIONS, SET 5	DORMAC, INC.		6-10
PI	SKLKIT	IMAGINATIVE ADJECTIVES & PREPOSITIONS, SET 6	DORMAC, INC.		6-10
PI	SKLKIT	IMAGINATIVE ADJECTIVES & PREPOSITIONS, SET 7	DORMAC, INC.		6-10
PI	SKLKIT	IMAGINATIVE ADJECTIVES & PREPOSITIONS, SET 8	DORMAC, INC.		6-10
PI	SKLKIT	IMAGINATIVE ADJECTIVES & PREPOSITIONS, SET 9	DORMAC, INC.		6-10
PI	SKLKIT	IMAGINATIVE ADJECTIVES & PREPOSITIONS, SET 10	DORMAC, INC.		6-10
PI	SKLKIT	IMAGINATIVE ADJECTIVES & PREPOSITIONS, SET 11	DORMAC, INC.		6-10
PI	SKLKIT	IMAGINATIVE ADJECTIVES & PREPOSITIONS, SET 12	DORMAC, INC.		6-10
PI	SKLKIT	IMAGINATIVE ADJECTIVES & PREPOSITIONS, SET 13	DORMAC, INC.		6-10
PI	SKLKIT	IMAGINATIVE ADJECTIVES & PREPOSITIONS, SET 14	DORMAC, INC.		6-10
PI	SND FS	PRESENTING...PARTS OF SPEECH	JANUARY PRODUCTIONS		51-75
PI	SP EQT	PROGRAMMED LANGUAGE/READING, LEVEL II: SET 11, SELF	INSTRUCTIONAL INDUSTRIES (G.E.)		101-150
PI	SP EQT	PROGRAMMED LANGUAGE/READING, LEVEL II: SET 12, COMMUNITY	INSTRUCTIONAL INDUSTRIES (G.E.)		151-200
PI	SP EQT	PROGRAMMED LANGUAGE/READING, LEVEL II: SET 13, FOODS	INSTRUCTIONAL INDUSTRIES (G.E.)		151-200
PI	SP EQT	PROGRAMMED LANGUAGE/READING, LEVEL II: SET 16, CLOTHING	INSTRUCTIONAL INDUSTRIES (G.E.)		101-150
PIJ	MULTIU	CREATURE FEATURES: VOCABULARY DEVELOPMENT	EDUCATIONAL ACTIVITIES, INC.		31-50
PIJ	SKLKIT	SYSTEMATIC SENTENCE BUILDER, LEVEL TWO	MODERN EDUCATION CORPORATION		51-75
PIJ	VISKIT	VIP ADJECTIVES	C.C. PUBLICATIONS, INC.		31-50
I	AUDKIT	ADJECTIVE MOON BASE ALARM	MEDIA MATERIALS, INC.		6-10
I	AUDKIT	ASTRO ADVERB PIRATES	MEDIA MATERIALS, INC.		6-10
I	DITTO	VOCABULARY BUILDING, INTERMEDIATE	HAYES SCHOOL PUBLISHING COMPANY		<5
I	DITTO	VOCABULARY BUILDING, UPPER INTERMEDIATE	HAYES SCHOOL PUBLISHING COMPANY		<5
I	DITTO	SIXTH GRADE LANGUAGE DRILLS	HAYES SCHOOL PUBLISHING COMPANY		<5
I	RECORD	BUILDING VERBAL POWER IN THE UPPER GRADES, VOLUME 4	CLASSROOM MATERIALS CO.		6-10
I	WKBOOK	WORDS THAT DESCRIBE	EDUCATORS PUBLISHING SERVICE		<5
IJ	AUDCRD	DESCRIPTIVE WORDS	AUDIOTRONICS CORPORATION		11-20
IJ	AUDKIT	WORD SIGNALS	EBSCO CURRICULUM MATERIALS		51-75
IJ	AUDKIT	DEVELOPING ENGLISH SKILLS	EDUCATIONAL ACTIVITIES, INC.		51-75
IJ	DITTO	BASIC LANGUAGE SKILLS: ADJECTIVES & ADVERBS	EDUCATIONAL INSIGHTS, INC.		6-10
IJ	DITTO	WORD SKILLS: LIVING WITH WORDS, BOOK II	T.S. DENISON & COMPANY		6-10
IJ	GAME	WIDE, WIDE WORLD OF GRAMMAR: GREAT GRAMMATICAL GOLF TOURN.	HARCOURT BRACE JOVANOVICH, INC.		21-30
IJ	MULTIM	EIGHT PARTS OF SPEECH	MEDIA MARKETING, INC.		51-75
IJ	SKLKIT	TARGET MECHANICS KIT: CAPITALIZATION & PUNCTUATION	ADDISON-WESLEY PUBLISHING CO.		201-300
IJ	SP EQT	PROGRAMMED LANGUAGE/READING, LEVEL IV: SET 25, NATURE/ECOLOGY	INSTRUCTIONAL INDUSTRIES (G.E.)		151-200
IJ	SP EQT	PROGRAMMED LANGUAGE/READING, LEVEL IV: SET 26, SCHOOL PROJECT	INSTRUCTIONAL INDUSTRIES (G.E.)		151-200
IJ	SP EQT	PROGRAMMED LANGUAGE/READING, LEVEL IV: SET 27, LIFE IN U.S.	INSTRUCTIONAL INDUSTRIES (G.E.)		151-200
IJ	TRANSP	KERNEL SENTENCES	UNITED TRANSPARENCIES, INC.		76-100
IJ	TRANSP	TRANSFORMATIONS	UNITED TRANSPARENCIES, INC.		76-100
IJ	WKBOOK	LANGUAGE 940, GRADES 4 - 8	STECK-VAUGHN COMPANY		<5
IJS	DITTO	WORD SKILLS: THE TIME OF YOUR LIFE, BOOK III	T.S. DENISON & COMPANY		6-10
IJS	DITTO	WORD SKILLS: LOOKING INTO THE FUTURE, BOOK IV	T.S. DENISON & COMPANY		6-10
IJS	DITTO	WORD SKILLS: TIME ON YOUR HANDS, BOOK VI	T.S. DENISON & COMPANY		6-10
J	A/VKIT	ADJECTIVES & ADVERBS	GUIDANCE ASSOCIATES		51-75
J	DITTO	JR. HI LANGUAGE DRILLS, BOOK 1	HAYES SCHOOL PUBLISHING COMPANY		<5
J	DITTO	JR. HI LANGUAGE DRILLS, BOOK 2	HAYES SCHOOL PUBLISHING COMPANY		<5
JS	AUDKIT	SENTENCE PATTERNS	CORONET MULTI MEDIA		101-150
JS	DITTO	NOUNS, ADJECTIVES & VERBS COLOR 'N' LEARN	ACTIVITY RESOURCES COMPANY, INC.		<5
JS	SND FS	WORDS! WORDS! WORDS!	ENCORE VISUAL EDUCATION, INC.		101-150

74 - SKILL: SYNTAX SENTENCES

LEVEL	FORMAT	TITLE	PUBLISHER	NT	$PRICE
R	AUDCAS	DISCOVERING LETTERS	ASSOCIATED EDUCATIONAL MATERIALS		11-20
R	AUDCAS	USING LETTERS	ASSOCIATED EDUCATIONAL MATERIALS		11-20

LEVEL	FORMAT	TITLE	PUBLISHER	NT	$PRICE

74 - SKILL: SYNTAX SENTENCES

LEVEL	FORMAT	TITLE	PUBLISHER	$PRICE
RP	PICTUR	TR LARGE PICTURE CARDS, SET 1	TEACHING RESOURCES CORPORATION	31-50
RP	PICTUR	TR LARGE PICTURE CARDS, SET 2	TEACHING RESOURCES CORPORATION	31-50
P	ACTCRD	WE READ SENTENCES, A1	BARNELL LOFT, LTD.	6-10
P	ACTCRD	WE READ SENTENCES, A2	BARNELL LOFT, LTD.	6-10
P	ACTCRD	WE READ SENTENCES, A3	BARNELL LOFT, LTD.	6-10
P	ACTCRD	WE READ SENTENCES, A4	BARNELL LOFT, LTD.	6-10
P	ACTCRD	WE READ SENTENCES, A5	BARNELL LOFT, LTD.	6-10
P	ACTCRD	SENTENCES SWING	ORE PRESS, INC.	<5
P	ACTCRD	STRUCTURED SYNTAX PROGRAM FOR AUDIO CARD READER	OPPORTUNITIES FOR LEARNING, INC.	201-300
P	ACTCRD	LIGHT & LEARN CARDS: SENTENCE SENSE	MILTON BRADLEY/PLAYSKOOL	<5
P	DITTO	NEW LANGUAGE PATTERNS & USAGE: GRADE 2, PART 2	CONTINENTAL PRESS, INC.	<5
P	DITTO	NEW LANGUAGE PATTERNS & USAGE: GRADE 2, PART 3	CONTINENTAL PRESS, INC.	<5
P	DITTO	SENTENCE STRUCTURE	INSTRUCTOR PUBLICATIONS, INC.	<5
P	DITTO	PRACTICE IN BASIC LANGUAGE SKILLS, BOOK 1 (GRADE 1)	INSTRUCTOR PUBLICATIONS, INC.	<5
P	DITTO	PRACTICE IN BASIC LANGUAGE SKILLS, BOOK 2 (GRADE 2)	INSTRUCTOR PUBLICATIONS, INC.	<5
P	DITTO	PRACTICE IN BASIC LANGUAGE SKILLS, BOOK 3 (GRADE 3)	INSTRUCTOR PUBLICATIONS, INC.	<5
P	GAME	BACKPACK: A LANGUAGE DEVELOPMENT GAME	DEVELOPMENTAL LEARNING MATERIALS	6-10
P	MANIPU	SENTENCE BUILDER	KENWORTHY EDUCATIONAL SERVICE	<5
P	MANIPU	BUILDING SENTENCES STEP-BY-STEP	DORMAC, INC.	31-50
P	MANIPU	SENTENCE-BUILDING WORD CARDS	EDUCATIONAL TEACHING AIDS	<5
P	MANIPU	ETA PICTURE SENTENCE-MAKING CARDS	EDUCATIONAL TEACHING AIDS	<5
P	MANIPU	ROLLING READER	INSTRUCTO/MCGRAW-HILL	6-10
P	MANIPU	ECONOMO SENTENCE BUILDER	MILTON BRADLEY/PLAYSKOOL	<5
P	MANIPU	LINK LETTERS	MILTON BRADLEY/PLAYSKOOL	<5
P	MANIPU	SENTENCE BUILDER	MILTON BRADLEY/PLAYSKOOL	<5
P	RECORD	BILLY BUILDS A SENTENCE	CLASSROOM MATERIALS CO.	6-10
P	SKLKIT	FOKES SENTENCE BUILDER	TEACHING RESOURCES CORPORATION	51-75
P	WKBOOK	WORKING WITH WORDS, BOOK G	GINN & COMPANY	<5
P	WKBOOK	LANGUAGE ARTS, GRADE 2	JENN PUBLICATIONS	<5
PI	ACTCRD	READING	FRANK SCHAFFER PUBLICATIONS, INC	<5
PI	ACTCRD	SENTENCE SHARPIES, LEVEL 1	TEACHING RESOURCES CORPORATION	11-20
PI	ACTCRD	BUILDING STORIES WITH JULIE & JACK	ST. JOHN SCHOOL FOR THE DEAF	<5
PI	ACTCRD	WORD POWER PACER	DM EDUCATIONAL PUBLICATIONS	6-10
PI	ACTCRD	STANDARD BASIC WORD POWER PACER	DM EDUCATIONAL PUBLICATIONS	6-10
PI	AUDCRD	SENTENCE BUILDING KIT	AUDIOTRONICS CORPORATION	31-50
PI	AUDCRD	STRUCTURED SYNTAX	B. L. WINCH & ASSOCIATES	201-300
PI	A/VKIT	USING GOOD ENGLISH	SVE	51-75
PI	FILMST	NEW ADVENTRURES IN LANGUAGE	TROLL ASSOCIATES	101-150
PI	GAME	BUILD A SENTENCE	CREATIVE TEACHING ASSOCIATES	6-10
PI	GAME	SENTENCE GAME FOR JUNIORS	CONSTRUCTIVE PLAYTHINGS	6-10
PI	GAME	SENTENCE GAME A	HARCOURT BRACE JOVANOVICH, INC.	11-20
PI	GAME	SENTENCE GAME B	HARCOURT BRACE JOVANOVICH, INC.	21-30
PI	GAME	POLY-STRIP SENTENCES	JUDY COMPANY	6-10
PI	MANIPU	POPEYE'S SPECIAL LANGUAGE BUILDER: STORY BUILDERS (SP.ED.)	KING FEATURES	21-30
PI	MANIPU	ETA POSITIONAL WORD & PICTURE MATCHING CARDS	EDUCATIONAL TEACHING AIDS	11-20
PI	MULTIU	LARC: MODULE O: ORDER & SEQUENCE SKILLS	ARISTA CORPORATION	151-200
PI	PUPILB	MONSTER BOOKS, SERIES I	BOWMAR/NOBLE PUBLISHERS, INC.	101-150
PI	PUPILB	MONSTER BOOKS, SERIES II	BOWMAR/NOBLE PUBLISHERS, INC.	151-200
PI	SKLKIT	DEVELOPMENTAL SYNTAX PROGRAM	TEACHING RESOURCES CORPORATION	51-75
PI	SND FS	SENTENCE STRUCTURE	ASSOCIATED EDUCATIONAL MATERIALS	51-75
PI	SND FS	EARLY LANGUAGE SKILLS	JANUARY PRODUCTIONS	51-75
PI	SND FS	PUTTING WORDS IN ORDER / SENTENCE STRUCTURE	TROLL ASSOCIATES	101-150
PI	SND FS	BUILDING SENTENCES	UNITED LEARNING	51-75
PI	WKBOOK	READING ACTIVITIES FOR LEARNING CENTERS	FRANK SCHAFFER PUBLICATIONS, INC	<5
PI	WKBOOK	SENTENCE SENSE	FRANK SCHAFFER PUBLICATIONS, INC	<5
PI	WKBOOK	BUILDING STORIES WITH JULIE & JACK	ST. JOHN SCHOOL FOR THE DEAF	<5
PIJ	SKLKIT	SYSTEMATIC SENTENCE BUILDER, LEVEL ONE	MODERN EDUCATION CORPORATION	51-75
PIJ	SKLKIT	SYSTEMATIC SENTENCE BUILDER, LEVEL TWO	MODERN EDUCATION CORPORATION	51-75
PIJ	SKLKIT	SYSTEMATIC SENTENCE BUILDER, LEVEL THREE	MODERN EDUCATION CORPORATION	51-75
PIJ	VISKIT	SYNTAX CODES IS, IS VERBING	C.C. PUBLICATIONS, INC.	21-30
PIJ	VISKIT	SYNTAX CODES ARE, ARE VERBING	C.C. PUBLICATIONS, INC.	21-30
PIJ	VISKIT	SYNTAX CODES SINGULAR NOUN PRESENT TENSE VERB	C.C. PUBLICATIONS, INC.	21-30
PIJ	VISKIT	SYNTAX CODES REGULAR PAST TENSE VERBS	C.C. PUBLICATIONS, INC.	21-30
PIJ	VISKIT	SYNTAX CODES IRREGULAR PAST TENSE VERBS, I	C.C. PUBLICATIONS, INC.	21-30
PIJ	VISKIT	SYNTAX CODES IRREGULAR PAST TENSE VERBS, II	C.C. PUBLICATIONS, INC.	21-30
PIJ	VISKIT	SYNTAX CODES IRREGULAR PAST TENSE VERBS, III	C.C. PUBLICATIONS, INC.	21-30
PIJ	VISKIT	SYNTAX CODES IRREGULAR PAST TENSE VERBS, IV	C.C. PUBLICATIONS, INC.	21-30
PIJS	REFBK	LANGUAGE REMEDIATION & EXPANSION	COMMUNICATION SKILL BUILDERS, INC	11-20
I	AUDKIT	SENTENCE SENSE	MEDIA MATERIALS, INC.	6-10
I	AUDKIT	SENTENCE SATELLITE	MEDIA MATERIALS, INC.	6-10
I	AUDKIT	GREAT COSMIC TREATY AGREEMENT OF SUBJECT: VERB	MEDIA MATERIALS, INC.	6-10
I	A/VKIT	MAKING ENGLISH WORK FOR YOU	SVE	76-100
I	A/VKIT	BASIC ENGLISH USAGE, THE SENTENCE	SVE	76-100
I	A/VKIT	SENTENCE STRUCTURE	SVE	101-150
I	DITTO	NEW LANGUAGE PATTERNS & USAGE: GRADE 5, PART 2	CONTINENTAL PRESS, INC.	<5
I	DITTO	PRACTICE IN BASIC LANGUAGE SKILLS, BOOK 4 (GRADE 4)	INSTRUCTOR PUBLICATIONS, INC.	<5
I	DITTO	PRACTICE IN BASIC LANGUAGE SKILLS, BOOK 5 (GRADE 5)	INSTRUCTOR PUBLICATIONS, INC.	<5
I	DITTO	PRACTICE IN BASIC LANGUAGE SKILLS, BOOK 6 (GRADE 6)	INSTRUCTOR PUBLICATIONS, INC.	<5
I	DITTO	FIFTH GRADE LANGUAGE DRILLS	HAYES SCHOOL PUBLISHING COMPANY	<5

LEVEL	FORMAT	TITLE	PUBLISHER	NT $PRICE

74 - SKILL: SYNTAX SENTENCES

LEVEL	FORMAT	TITLE	PUBLISHER	NT	$PRICE
I	DITTO	SIXTH GRADE LANGUAGE DRILLS	HAYES SCHOOL PUBLISHING COMPANY		<5
I	GAME	BUILDING BETTER SENTENCES	GEL-STEN, INC.		6-10
I	RECORD	BUILDING LANGUAGE USAGE POWER, VOLUME 1	CLASSROOM MATERIALS CO.		6-10
I	RECORD	BUILDING LANGUAGE USAGE POWER, VOLUME 5	CLASSROOM MATERIALS CO.		6-10
I	SKLKIT	WRITING SKILLS WORKSHOPS II	BFA EDUCATIONAL MEDIA		101-150
I	VISKIT	BUILDING BETTER SENTENCES	INSTRUCTO/MCGRAW-HILL		11-20
I	WKBOOK	LANGUAGE ARTS FOR THE INTERMEDIATE GRADES (4, 5, 6)	JENN PUBLICATIONS		<5
IJ	ACTCRD	GRAMMAR GRAB BAG	KIDS & COMPANY		<5
IJ	ACTCRD	SENTENCE SHARPIES, LEVEL 2	TEACHING RESOURCES CORPORATION		11-20
IJ	AUDKIT	ENGLISH TOPICS I & II: SIMPLE SENTENCES & COMPLEX SENTENCES	NATIONAL BOOK COMPANY		21-30
IJ	A/VKIT	SENTENCE FAMILY	TROLL ASSOCIATES		51-75
IJ	DITTO	THINKERTHINGS: A STUDENT GENERATED APPROACH TO LANGUAGE EXP.	ADDISON-WESLEY PUBLISHING CO.		11-20
IJ	DITTO	SPOTLIGHT ON SENTENCES, BOOK ONE	CREATIVE TEACHING PRESS, INC.		<5
IJ	DITTO	SPOTLIGHT ON SENTENCES, BOOK TWO	CREATIVE TEACHING PRESS, INC.		<5
IJ	GAME	SYNTAX GAME	TEACHING RESOURCES CORPORATION		31-50
IJ	GAME	WHAT'S THE WORD? GAME	INCENTIVES FOR LEARNING, INC.		76-100
IJ	GAME	WIDE, WIDE WORLD OF GRAMMAR: GREAT GRAMMATICAL GOLF TOURN.	HARCOURT BRACE JOVANOVICH, INC.		21-30
IJ	MULTIM	DEVELOPING SENTENCE SKILLS	MEDIA MARKETING, INC.		51-75
IJ	MULTIM	COMMUNICATION POWER SERIES	UNITED LEARNING	5	201-300
IJ	MULTIM	COMMUNICATION POWER SERIES: SENTENCE POWER	UNITED LEARNING		51-75
IJ	PUPILB	SENSE OF SENTENCES	AMSCO SCHOOL PUBLICATIONS, INC.		<5
IJ	SKLKIT	WRITING SKILLS WORKSHOPS III	BFA EDUCATIONAL MEDIA		101-150
IJ	SKLKIT	TARGET MECHANICS KIT: GUIDES FOR STANDARD ENGLISH	ADDISON-WESLEY PUBLISHING CO.		201-300
IJ	SKLKIT	LET'S WRITE A LETTER	TROLL ASSOCIATES		76-100
IJ	SP EQT	PROGRAMMED LANGUAGE/READING, LEVEL IV	INSTRUCTIONAL INDUSTRIES (G.E.)	8	>450
IJ	SP EQT	PROGRAMMED LANGUAGE/READING, LEVEL IV: SET 26,SCHOOL PROJECT	INSTRUCTIONAL INDUSTRIES (G.E.)		151-200
IJ	SP EQT	PROGRAMMED LANGUAGE/READING, LEVEL IV: SET 27, LIFE IN U.S.	INSTRUCTIONAL INDUSTRIES (G.E.)		151-200
IJ	SP EQT	PROGRAMMED LANGUAGE/READING, LEVEL IV: SET 28, NORTH AMERICA	INSTRUCTIONAL INDUSTRIES (G.E.)		151-200
IJ	SP EQT	PROGRAMMED LANGUAGE/READING, LEVEL IV: SET 29, SAFETY	INSTRUCTIONAL INDUSTRIES (G.E.)		151-200
IJ	TRANSP	COLORGRAM ENGLISH	UNITED TRANSPARENCIES, INC.		101-150
IJ	TRANSP	KERNEL SENTENCES	UNITED TRANSPARENCIES, INC.		76-100
IJ	TRANSP	TRANSFORMATIONS	UNITED TRANSPARENCIES, INC.		76-100
IJS	DITTO	WORD SKILLS: GOING PLACES, BOOK V	T.S. DENISON & COMPANY		6-10
IJS	PUPILB	ENGLISH GRAMMAR, VOLUME I	BEHAVIORAL RESEARCH LABORATORIES		6-10
IJS	PUPILB	ENGLISH GRAMMAR, VOLUME II	BEHAVIORAL RESEARCH LABORATORIES		6-10
IJS	SKLKIT	LANGUAGE REHABILITATION PROGRAM	TEACHING RESOURCES CORPORATION		31-50
IJS	SKLKIT	SPELLING MASTERY & DIAGNOSTIC REFERENCE KIT	SPECIAL CHILD PUBLICATIONS		31-50
J	AUDCAS	SENTENCE SKILLS	MEDIA MARKETING, INC.		11-20
J	GUIDE	MASTERING THE SENTENCE IN SEVEN STEPS	MCCORMICK-MATHERS PUBLISHING CO.		<5
J	GUIDE	SIMPLE SENTENCE IN SEVEN STEPS	MCCORMICK-MATHERS PUBLISHING CO.		<5
J	PUPILB	MASTERING THE SENTENCE IN SEVEN STEPS	MCCORMICK-MATHERS PUBLISHING CO.		<5
J	PUPILB	SIMPLE SENTENCE IN SEVEN STEPS	MCCORMICK-MATHERS PUBLISHING CO.		<5
J	TEXTBK	LANGUAGE PATTERNS	CAMBRIDGE BOOK CO.		<5
J	WKBOOK	MASTERING THE SENTENCE	CONTINENTAL PRESS, INC.		<5
J	WKBOOK	TROUBLESHOOTER I	HOUGHTON MIFFLIN COMPANY	8	11-20
J	WKBOOK	TROUBLESHOOTER I: BOOK 6, SENTENCE STRENGTH	HOUGHTON MIFFLIN COMPANY		<5
JS	AUDKIT	SENTENCE PATTERNS	CORONET MULTI MEDIA		101-150
JS	DITTO	SENTENCE STRUCTURE	J. WESTON WALCH PUBLISHING		11-20
JS	FILMST	UNDERSTANDING THE SENTENCE	ENCYCLOPEDIA BRITANNICA		76-100
JS	PROFMA	SPRINGBOARDS FOR WRITING	ACADEMIC THERAPY PUBLICATIONS		6-10
JS	PUPILB	LANGUAGE WORKSHOP (RL 4 - 5)	GLOBE BOOK COMPANY, INC.		<5
JS	SND FS	CONQUERING COMPOSITION SERIES	UNITED LEARNING	5	201-300
JS	SND FS	CONQUERING COMPOSITION SERIES: SENTENCE PROBLEMS I	UNITED LEARNING		51-75
JS	SND FS	CONQUERING COMPOSITION SERIES: SENTENCE PROBLEMS II	UNITED LEARNING		51-75
JS	WKBOOK	SENTENCE IMPROVEMENT SKILLS & DRILLS, LEVEL B	MCDOUGAL, LITTEL & COMPANY		<5
JS	WKBOOK	IMPROVING COMPOSITION	EDUCATORS PUBLISHING SERVICE		<5
S	PUPILB	HOW TO PREPARE FOR H.S. EQUIV. EXAM: WRITING SKILLS TEST	BARRON'S EDUCATIONAL SERIES,INC.		<5
S	SND FS	UNDERSTANDING SENTENCE	MEDIA MATERIALS, INC.		11-20
S	SND FS	SENTENCE PATTERNS	MEDIA MATERIALS, INC.		11-20
S	TEXTBK	BUSINESS COMMUNICATIONS	SOUTH-WESTERN PUBLISHING CO.	2	6-10
S	TEXTBK	BUSINESS COMMUNICATIONS: ENGLISH THE EASY WAY	SOUTH-WESTERN PUBLISHING CO.		<5
S	WKBOOK	SENTENCE IMPROVEMENT SKILLS & DRILLS, LEVEL C	MCDOUGAL, LITTEL & COMPANY		<5

75 - SKILL: STRUCTURAL ANALYSIS - GENERAL

LEVEL	FORMAT	TITLE	PUBLISHER	NT	$PRICE
R	WKBOOK	WORDS WE USE, BOOK I (RL K-3)	BENEFIC PRESS		<5
RP	MULTIM	WORDS & SOUND SERIES, SET 1	EDL/MCGRAW-HILL		101-150
RP	MULTIM	WORDS & SOUND SERIES, SET 2	EDL/MCGRAW-HILL		101-150
RP	MULTIM	WORDS & SOUND SERIES, SET 4	EDL/MCGRAW-HILL		101-150
RPI	GUIDE	WORD ATTACK JOY	READING JOY, INC.		6-10
P	ACTCRD	WORD ELEMENTS B3	BARNELL LOFT, LTD.		6-10
P	ACTCRD	WORD ELEMENTS CA	BARNELL LOFT, LTD.		6-10
P	ACTCRD	WORD ELEMENTS C2	BARNELL LOFT, LTD.		6-10
P	ACTCRD	SOUND FOUNDATION, PROGRAM 2	DEVELOPMENTAL LEARNING MATERIALS		11-20
P	ACTCRD	LINQUISTIC PACER	DM EDUCATIONAL PUBLICATIONS		6-10
P	ACTCRD	BUILD-A-WORD SKILL CARDS	MILTON BRADLEY/PLAYSKOOL		<5
P	AUDCAS	SOUNDS FOR YOUNG READERS, VOLUME 4	CLASSROOM MATERIALS CO.		6-10
P	AUDCAS	FROM PHONICS TO READING	UNITED LEARNING		31-50
P	AUDCAS	GETTING TO KNOW WORDS	UNITED LEARNING		31-50
P	AUDCRD	STRUCTURAL ANALYSIS FOR BEGINNING READERS	AUDIOTRONICS CORPORATION		21-30

LEVEL	FORMAT	TITLE	PUBLISHER	NT	$PRICE

75 - SKILL: STRUCTURAL ANALYSIS - GENERAL

LEVEL	FORMAT	TITLE	PUBLISHER	NT	$PRICE
P	AUDKIT	PRIMARY WORK RECOGNITION	EYE GATE MEDIA	5	31-50
P	AUDKIT	KIT 1: BUILDING READING SKILLS, LEVEL 2	EDUCATIONAL RESEARCH, INC.		101-150
P	AUDKIT	KIT 2: BUILDING READING SKILLS, LEVEL 3	EDUCATIONAL RESEARCH, INC.		101-150
P	CL SET	CHEST OF FUN (RL 1-3)	BENEFIC PRESS		76-100
P	DITTO	CROSSWORD PUZZLES FOR PHONICS: SPECIAL SOUNDS I	CONTINENTAL PRESS, INC.		<5
P	MANIPU	PHONICS E-Z LANGUAGE LEARNING SLIDE RULES	E-Z GRADER COMPANY	5	6-10
P	MANIPU	PHONICS E-Z LANGUAGE LEARNING SLIDE RULES, WORD-BUILDING	E-Z GRADER COMPANY		<5
P	MULTIU	DISTAR ACTIVITY KIT: READING	SRA		101-150
P	MULTIM	PRS: THE PRE-READING SKILLS PROGRAM	ENCYCLOPEDIA BRITANNICA		>450
P	RECORD	SOUNDS FOR YOUNG READERS, VOLUME 4	CLASSROOM MATERIALS CO.		6-10
P	SKLKIT	SCHOOLHOUSE: WORD ATTACK SKILLS KIT	SRA		101-150
P	SKLKIT	LOGOS 1A	IDEAL SCHOOL SUPPLY COMPANY		101-150
P	TUTORL	MACMILLAN TUTORIAL SYSTEM KIT, GRADE 1	MACMILLAN PUBLISHING CO., INC.		51-75
P	TUTORL	MACMILLAN TUTORIAL SYSTEM KIT, GRADE 2	MACMILLAN PUBLISHING CO., INC.		51-75
P	TUTORL	MACMILLAN TUTORIAL SYSTEM KIT, GRADE 3	MACMILLAN PUBLISHING CO., INC.		51-75
P	VISKIT	ACTION READING: THE PARTICIPATORY APPROACH	ALLYN AND BACON, INC.		201-300
P	WKBOOK	CUES & SIGNALS IV	ANN ARBOR PUBLISHERS		<5
P	WKBOOK	WORDS WE USE, BOOK II (RL 1-3)	BENEFIC PRESS		<5
P	WKBOOK	WORDS WE USE, BOOK III (RL 1-3)	BENEFIC PRESS		<5
P	WKBOOK	WORDS WE USE, BOOK IV (RL 1-3)	BENEFIC PRESS		<5
P	WKBOOK	WORDS WE USE, BOOK V (RL 1-3)	BENEFIC PRESS		<5
P	WKBOOK	TALK ABOUT IT	ST. JOHN SCHOOL FOR THE DEAF		<5
P	WKBOOK	MCP PHONICS WORKBOOKS: LEVEL A	MODERN CURRICULUM PRESS		<5
P	WKBOOK	NEW PHONICS WORKBOOK, BOOK B	MODERN CURRICULUM PRESS		<5
P	WKBOOK	NEW PHONICS WORKBOOK, BOOK D	MODERN CURRICULUM PRESS		<5
P	WKBOOK	PHONICS WORKBOOK, BOOK D	MODERN CURRICULUM PRESS		<5
P	WKBOOK	PHONICS & WORD POWER, BOOK 1	XEROX EDUCATION PUBLICATIONS		<5
P	WKBOOK	PHONICS & WORD POWER, BOOK 2	XEROX EDUCATION PUBLICATIONS		<5
P	WKBOOK	PHONICS & WORD POWER, BOOK 3	XEROX EDUCATION PUBLICATIONS		<5
PI	ACTCRD	WORD POWER PACER	DM EDUCATIONAL PUBLICATIONS		6-10
PI	AUDKIT	USING PHONICS	EBSCO CURRICULUM MATERIALS		51-75
PI	AUDKIT	TOTAL BUILDING READING SKILLS (KITS 1 - 5)	EDUCATIONAL RESEARCH, INC.	5	>450
PI	CL SET	CHEST OF ACTION (RL 1-6)	BENEFIC PRESS		76-100
PI	CL SET	SOUNDER CLASSROOM SET	EDMARK ASSOCIATES		301-400
PI	DITTO	SPICE, VOLUME II	EDUCATIONAL SERVICE, INC.		6-10
PI	DITTO	BASIC READING SKILLS	EDUCATIONAL INSIGHTS, INC.		51-75
PI	DITTO	SPECIAL KIDS' STUFF, PART IV: WORK STUDY SKILLS (SP. ED.)	INCENTIVE PUBLICATIONS, INC.		6-10
PI	FILMST	A WORD RECOGNITION SYSTEM	MEDIA MATERIALS, INC.		11-20
PI	FILMST	I READ & I UNDERSTAND, LEVEL TWO	EDUCATIONAL ACTIVITIES, INC.		31-50
PI	FILMST	I READ & I UNDERSTAND, LEVELS THREE & FOUR	EDUCATIONAL ACTIVITIES, INC.		51-75
PI	GAME	77 GAMES FOR READING GROUPS	FEARON PITMAN PUBLISHERS, INC.		<5
PI	GAME	ARE YOU LISTENING?	JUDY COMPANY		6-10
PI	GAME	WORD RECOGNITION	PAUL S. AMIDON & ASSOC., INC.		<5
PI	GAME	APPLE TREE	XEROX EDUCATION PUBLICATIONS		51-75
PI	GAME	PLUM TREE	XEROX EDUCATION PUBLICATIONS		51-75
PI	GUIDE	100 INDIVIDUALIZED ACTIVITIES FOR READING	FEARON PITMAN PUBLISHERS, INC.		<5
PI	MULTIU	LARC: MODULE W: WORD SKILLS	ARISTA CORPORATION		151-200
PI	MULTIU	CREATURE FEATURES: STRUCTURAL ANALYSIS	EDUCATIONAL ACTIVITIES, INC.		51-75
PI	MULTIM	TALKING PICTURE DICTIONARY	TROLL ASSOCIATES		151-200
PI	MULTIM	MORE NEW WORDS	TROLL ASSOCIATES		151-200
PI	PUPILB	GILLIGAN MILLIGAN	SRA		<5
PI	REFBK	SPICE SERIES: SPICE	EDUCATIONAL SERVICE, INC.	8	6-10
PI	SKLKIT	TARGET BLUE: STRUCTURAL ANALYSIS KIT	ADDISON-WESLEY PUBLISHING CO.		151-200
PI	TRANSP	LANGUAGE DEVELOPMENT & READING SKILLS	UNITED TRANSPARENCIES, INC.		201-300
PI	TUTORL	SOUNDER RESOURCE SET	EDMARK ASSOCIATES		51-75
PI	VISKIT	READING & LANG. ARTS COMPLETE SET OF 50 JOY ACT. CARDS KITS	INSTRUCTO/MCGRAW-HILL		201-300
PI	WKBOOK	SPECTRUM OF SKILLS: WORD ANALYSIS, LEVEL 1	MACMILLAN PUBLISHING CO., INC.		<5
PI	WKBOOK	SPECTRUM OF SKILLS: WORD ANALYSIS, LEVEL 2	MACMILLAN PUBLISHING CO., INC.		<5
PI	WKBOOK	SPECTRUM OF SKILLS: WORD ANALYSIS, LEVEL 3	MACMILLAN PUBLISHING CO., INC.		<5
PI	WKBOOK	SPECTRUM OF SKILLS: WORD ANALYSIS, LEVEL 4	MACMILLAN PUBLISHING CO., INC.		<5
PI	WKBOOK	SPECTRUM OF SKILLS: WORD ANALYSIS, LEVEL 5	MACMILLAN PUBLISHING CO., INC.		<5
PI	WKBOOK	SPECTRUM OF SKILLS: WORD ANALYSIS, LEVEL 6	MACMILLAN PUBLISHING CO., INC.		<5
PIJ	ACTCRD	REBUS GLOSSARY CARDS	AMERICAN GUIDANCE SERVICE, INC.		51-75
PIJ	CL SET	CHESTS OF BOOKS (RL 1-9)	BENEFIC PRESS	4	301-400
PIJ	DITTO	PORTFOLIO OF RUB-ON REBUSES	AMERICAN GUIDANCE SERVICE, INC.		11-20
PIJ	MULTIM	SPECTRUM SERIES	IMPERIAL INTERNATIONAL LEARNING	6	301-400
PIJ	REFBK	SPICE SERIES: RESCUE	EDUCATIONAL SERVICE, INC.		6-10
PIJ	REFBK	STANDARD REBUS GLOSSARY	AMERICAN GUIDANCE SERVICE, INC.		<5
PIJ	SKLKIT	SRA SKILLS SERIES: STRUCTURAL ANALYSIS	SRA		301-400
PIJ	SND FS	MORE ROADS TO MEANING	ENCYCLOPEDIA BRITANNICA		101-150
PIJ	WKBOOK	LOOKING AT WORDS A	EDL/MCGRAW-HILL		<5
I	AUDKIT	WORD BUILDING	EDUCATIONAL MEDIA, INC.		51-75
I	AUDKIT	WORDS IN MOTION, KIT A	MACMILLAN PUBLISHING CO., INC.		76-100
I	AUDKIT	WORDS IN MOTION, KIT B	MACMILLAN PUBLISHING CO., INC.		76-100
I	AUDKIT	KIT 3: BUILDING READING SKILLS, LEVEL 4	EDUCATIONAL RESEARCH, INC.		101-150
I	AUDKIT	KIT 4: BUILDING READING SKILLS, LEVEL 5	EDUCATIONAL RESEARCH, INC.		101-150
I	AUDKIT	KIT 5: BUILDING READING SKILLS, LEVEL 6	EDUCATIONAL RESEARCH, INC.		101-150
I	DITTO	CROSSWORD PUZZLES FOR PHONICS: SPECIAL SOUNDS II	CONTINENTAL PRESS, INC.		<5
I	DITTO	ANCHOR, VOLUME I	EDUCATIONAL SERVICE, INC.		6-10

LEVEL	FORMAT	TITLE	PUBLISHER	NT	$PRICE

75 - SKILL: STRUCTURAL ANALYSIS - GENERAL

LEVEL	FORMAT	TITLE	PUBLISHER	NT	$PRICE
I	GAME	TAKE	GARRARD PUBLISHING COMPANY		<5
I	GAME	LEMON TREE	XEROX EDUCATION PUBLICATIONS		51-75
I	GUIDE	BETTER READING & SPELLING THROUGH PHONICS	FEARON PITMAN PUBLISHERS, INC.		<5
I	GUIDE	WORDS ARE IMPORTANT: TAN LEVEL 4, KEY	HAMMOND, INC.		<5
I	GUIDE	WORDS ARE IMPORTANT: BLUE LEVEL 5, KEY	HAMMOND, INC.		<5
I	GUIDE	WORDS ARE IMPORTANT: RED LEVEL 6, KEY	HAMMOND, INC.		<5
I	SKLKIT	SCHOOLHOUSE: WORD ATTACK 1C	SRA		101-150
I	SKLKIT	SPELLING WORD POWER LABORATORY KIT 2A	SRA		151-200
I	SKLKIT	SPELLING WORD POWER LABORATORY KIT 2B	SRA		151-200
I	SKLKIT	SPELLING WORD POWER LABORATORY KIT 2C	SRA		151-200
I	SKLKIT	SOUND FOUNDATION PROGRAM III	DEVELOPMENTAL LEARNING MATERIALS		21-30
I	WKBOOK	WORDS WE USE, BOOK VI (RL 4-6)	BENEFIC PRESS		<5
I	WKBOOK	WORDS WE USE, BOOK VII (RL 4-6)	BENEFIC PRESS		<5
I	WKBOOK	WORDS WE USE, BOOK VIII (RL 4-6)	BENEFIC PRESS		<5
I	WKBOOK	WORDS ARE IMPORTANT: TAN LEVEL 4	HAMMOND, INC.		<5
I	WKBOOK	WORDS ARE IMPORTANT: BLUE LEVEL 5	HAMMOND, INC.		<5
I	WKBOOK	WORDS ARE IMPORTANT: RED LEVEL 6	HAMMOND, INC.		<5
IJ	ACTCRD	LANGUAGE SCOOP	KIDS & COMPANY		<5
IJ	CL SET	CHEST OF SUCCESS (RL 4-9)	BENEFIC PRESS		76-100
IJ	DITTO	ANCHOR, VOLUME II	EDUCATIONAL SERVICE, INC.		6-10
IJ	FILMST	ENGLISH COMES ALIVE: ADVENTURES IN WORDS	UNITED LEARNING		31-50
IJ	FILMST	ENGLISH COMES ALIVE SERIES	UNITED LEARNING	6	151-200
IJ	GUIDE	RR (REMEDIAL READING), T.M.	MODERN CURRICULUM PRESS		<5
IJ	MULTIU	TROLL JAM SESSIONS: JAZZ	TROLL ASSOCIATES		31-50
IJ	MULTIU	TROLL JAM SESSIONS: FOLK	TROLL ASSOCIATES		31-50
IJ	MULTIU	TROLL JAM SESSIONS: ROCK	TROLL ASSOCIATES		31-50
IJ	MULTIU	TROLL JAM SESSIONS: COUNTRY	TROLL ASSOCIATES		31-50
IJ	REFBK	SPICE SERIES: ANCHOR	EDUCATIONAL SERVICE, INC.		6-10
IJ	SKLKIT	WORD CLUES	CHARLES E. MERRILL PUBLISHING CO		76-100
IJ	SKLKIT	+4 READING BOOSTER	WEBSTER DIVISION/MCGRAW-HILL		301-400
IJ	WKBOOK	SEQUENTIAL SKILLS DEVELOPMENT ACTIVITIES FOR READING	T.S. DENISON & COMPANY	4	6-10
IJ	WKBOOK	RR (REMEDIAL READING)	MODERN CURRICULUM PRESS		<5
IJS	AUDCRD	WORD PARTS	AUDIOTRONICS CORPORATION		21-30
IJS	AUDKIT	HITS SKILLBOOK SERIES, BOOK A (RL 1 - 2)	MODULEARN, INC.		<5
IJS	AUDKIT	HITS SKILLBOOK SERIES, BOOK B (RL 2 - 3)	MODULEARN, INC.		<5
IJS	AUDKIT	HITS SKILLBOOK SERIES, BOOK C (RL 3 - 4)	MODULEARN, INC.		<5
IJS	DITTO	CORRECTIVE SPELLING THROUGH MORPHOGRAPHS, SPIRIT MASTERS	SRA		101-150
IJS	GAME	PAL READING SKILL GAME, RALLY 1	XEROX EDUCATION PUBLICATIONS		51-75
IJS	GAME	PAL READING SKILLS GAME, RALLY 2	XEROX EDUCATION PUBLICATIONS		51-75
IJS	MULTIU	CORRECTIVE SPELLING THROUGH MORPHOGRAPHS, TEACHER'S BOOK	SRA		31-50
IJS	PUPILB	CORRECTIVE SPELLING THROUGH MORPHOGRAPHS, STUDENT BOOK	SRA		<5
J	GUIDE	WORDS ARE IMPORTANT: GREEN LEVEL 7, KEY	HAMMOND, INC.		<5
J	GUIDE	WORDS ARE IMPORTANT: ORANGE LEVEL 8, KEY	HAMMOND, INC.		<5
J	GUIDE	WORDS ARE IMPORTANT: PURPLE LEVEL 9, KEY	HAMMOND, INC.		<5
J	SKLKIT	SPELLING WORD POWER LABORATORY KIT	SRA		151-200
J	WKBOOK	MOTT BASIC LANG. SKILLS: BOOK 1306	ALLIED EDUCATION COUNCIL		<5
J	WKBOOK	WORDS ARE IMPORTANT: GREEN LEVEL 7	HAMMOND, INC.		<5
J	WKBOOK	WORDS ARE IMPORTANT: ORANGE LEVEL 8	HAMMOND, INC.		<5
J	WKBOOK	WORDS ARE IMPORTANT: PURPLE LEVEL 9	HAMMOND, INC.		<5
J	WKBOOK	TROUBLESHOOTER I	HOUGHTON MIFFLIN COMPANY	8	11-20
JS	PUPILB	BASIC WORD LIST	BARRON'S EDUCATIONAL SERIES,INC.		<5
JS	SP EQT	WORD RECOGNITION & SPELLING DEFA-COMBO-8	EDL/MCGRAW-HILL		151-200
JS	SP EQT	WORD RECOGNITION & SPELLING DEFA-35MM TACH-X	EDL/MCGRAW-HILL		151-200
S	GUIDE	WORDS ARE IMPORTANT: BROWN LEVEL 10, KEY	HAMMOND, INC.		<5
S	GUIDE	WORDS ARE IMPORTANT: PINK LEVEL 11, KEY	HAMMOND, INC.		<5
S	GUIDE	WORDS ARE IMPORTANT: GRAY LEVEL 12, KEY	HAMMOND, INC.		<5
S	MULTIM	RELEVANCE SERIES	CAMBRIDGE BOOK CO.	5	>450
S	MULTIM	RELEVANCE SERIES: RELEVANCE OF SOUND	CAMBRIDGE BOOK CO.		201-300
S	WKBOOK	WORDS ARE IMPORTANT: BROWN LEVEL 10	HAMMOND, INC.		<5
S	WKBOOK	WORDS ARE IMPORTANT: PINK LEVEL 11	HAMMOND, INC.		<5
S	WKBOOK	WORDS ARE IMPORTANT: GRAY LEVEL 12	HAMMOND, INC.		<5

76 - SKILL: ROOT WORDS

LEVEL	FORMAT	TITLE	PUBLISHER	NT	$PRICE
RP	WKBOOK	DELL HOME ACTIVITY: RHYMING ROOTS	DELL PUBLISHING COMPANY, INC.		<5
P	ACTCRD	LINQUISTIC PACER	DM EDUCATIONAL PUBLICATIONS		6-10
P	ACTCRD	WORD PROBE SKILL CARDS	MILTON BRADLEY/PLAYSKOOL		<5
P	AUDCRD	STRUCTURAL ANALYSIS FOR BEGINNING READERS	AUDIOTRONICS CORPORATION		21-30
P	AUDKIT	KIT 84: BASIC PHONICS, LEVEL 4	EDUCATIONAL RESEARCH, INC.		101-150
P	AUDKIT	MINISYSTEMS: ROOTS, PREFIXES, SUFFIXES	CORONET MULTI MEDIA		11-20
P	DITTO	NEW PHONICS & WORD ANALYSIS SKILLS: GRADE 3, PART 2	CONTINENTAL PRESS, INC.		<5
P	DITTO	BASIC READING SKILLS	XEROX EDUCATION PUBLICATIONS		<5
P	DITTO	PHONICS IIB	HAYES SCHOOL PUBLISHING COMPANY		<5
P	DITTO	PHONICS IIIA	HAYES SCHOOL PUBLISHING COMPANY		<5
P	DITTO	PHONICS IVA	HAYES SCHOOL PUBLISHING COMPANY		<5
P	MULTIM	READING SKILLS SUPPORT SYSTEM, BOX 3	EDL/MCGRAW-HILL		301-400
P	SP EQT	AUDITORY SKILLS: MORPHOLOGY & CLOSURE	INSTRUCTIONAL INDUSTRIES (G.E.)		101-150
P	WKBOOK	LANGUAGE ARTS, GRADE 2	JENN PUBLICATIONS		<5
P	WKBOOK	NEW PHONICS WORKBOOK, BOOK C	MODERN CURRICULUM PRESS		<5
P	WKBOOK	NEW PHONICS WORKBOOK, BOOK D	MODERN CURRICULUM PRESS		<5

LEVEL	FORMAT	TITLE	PUBLISHER	NT	$PRICE

76 - SKILL: ROOT WORDS

LEVEL	FORMAT	TITLE	PUBLISHER	NT	$PRICE
P	WKBOOK	PHONICS WORKBOOK, BOOK D	MODERN CURRICULUM PRESS		<5
PI	ACTCRD	LANGUAGE LOLLIPOP	KIDS & COMPANY		<5
PI	AUDKIT	LET'S FIND SOME ROOT WORDS: INFLECTIONAL ENDINGS	MEDIA MATERIALS, INC.		6-10
PI	AUDKIT	LET'S FIND SOME ROOT WORDS: PREFIXES	MEDIA MATERIALS, INC.		6-10
PI	AUDKIT	LET'S FIND SOME ROOT WORDS: SUFFIXES	MEDIA MATERIALS, INC.		6-10
PI	DITTO	PRACTICE IN VOCABULARY BUILDING, BOOK A (GRADES 3 - 4)	INSTRUCTOR PUBLICATIONS, INC.		<5
PI	DITTO	DECODING SKILLS 5	ACTIVITY RESOURCES COMPANY, INC.		<5
PI	FILMST	STRUCTURAL ANALYSIS FILMSTRIP SERIES	MEDIA MATERIALS, INC.	5	76-100
PI	FILMST	ROOT WORDS	MEDIA MATERIALS, INC.		11-20
PI	MANIPU	E-Z PHONIC WORD-BUILDING SLIDE RULE	E-Z GRADER COMPANY		<5
PI	MULTIM	NEW GOALS IN LISTENING, GRADES 2-4	TROLL ASSOCIATES		76-100
PI	RECORD	PHONICS & WORD DEVELOPMENT	EDUCATIONAL ACTIVITIES, INC.		31-50
PI	SKLKIT	TARGET GREEN: VOCABULARY DEVELOPMENT KIT I	ADDISON-WESLEY PUBLISHING CO.		151-200
PI	SND FS	STRUCTURAL ANALYSIS SERIES	HAMPDEN PUBLICATIONS, INC.		76-100
PI	SND FS	WORD BUILDERS	MILLER-BRODY PRODUCTIONS, INC.		31-50
PI	SP EQT	DEVELOPING STRUCTURAL ANALYSIS SKILLS, KIT K	BORG-WARNER EDUCATIONAL SYSTEMS		101-150
PI	WKBOOK	WORD ENDINGS	FRANK SCHAFFER PUBLICATIONS, INC		<5
PIJ	CL SET	WHAT'S THE MEANING OF THIS?	MAFEX ASSOCIATES, INC.		51-75
I	ACTCRD	WORD ANALYSIS: ROOT WORDS	INSTRUCTIONAL FAIR		<5
I	ACTCRD	WORD ANALYSIS PAK	INSTRUCTIONAL FAIR		21-30
I	ACTCRD	ROOTS/STEMS, F1	BARNELL LOFT, LTD.		6-10
I	ACTCRD	ROOTS/STEMS, F2	BARNELL LOFT, LTD.		6-10
I	ACTCRD	AFFIXES PACER	DM EDUCATIONAL PUBLICATIONS		<5
I	AUDKIT	READING CASSETTES: WORD BUILDING	IDEAL SCHOOL SUPPLY COMPANY		51-75
I	AUDKIT	ROOT WORDS, THE HEART OF IT ALL	MEDIA MATERIALS, INC.		6-10
I	AUDKIT	EXPANDING VOCABULARY	HAMPDEN PUBLICATIONS, INC.		21-30
I	DITTO	WORD SPY, GRADE 5	CONTINENTAL PRESS, INC.		<5
I	DITTO	WORD ANALYSIS: ROOT WORDS	INSTRUCTIONAL FAIR		<5
I	DITTO	WORD ANALYSIS PAK	INSTRUCTIONAL FAIR		21-30
I	DITTO	SOUNDS IN WORDS, BOOK 9	GEL-STEN, INC.		<5
I	DITTO	SOUNDS IN WORDS, BOOK 12	GEL-STEN, INC.		<5
I	DITTO	SOUNDS IN WORDS, BOOK 13	GEL-STEN, INC.		<5
I	DITTO	SOUNDS IN WORDS, BOOK 15	GEL-STEN, INC.		<5
I	DITTO	SOUNDS IN WORDS, BOOK 18	GEL-STEN, INC.		<5
I	DITTO	PRACTICE IN VOCABULARY BUILDING, BOOK B (GRADES 4 - 5)	INSTRUCTOR PUBLICATIONS, INC.		<5
I	DITTO	DECODING SKILLS C	ACTIVITY RESOURCES COMPANY, INC.		<5
I	GAME	WORD COMPUTER	CREATIVE TEACHING ASSOCIATES		<5
I	GAME	SPELLING/LANGUAGE LEARNING GAMES KITS, KIT TWO	RAND MCNALLY & COMPANY		76-100
I	GAME	LEMON TREE	XEROX EDUCATION PUBLICATIONS		51-75
I	MULTIM	GAMES 'N' FRAMES: WORD NEWS ROUNDUP	IMPERIAL INTERNATIONAL LEARNING		21-30
I	MULTIM	GAMES 'N' FRAMES: STRENGTHENING SUFFIXES WITH GRIMN & BARRET	IMPERIAL INTERNATIONAL LEARNING		21-30
I	MULTIM	SELECT-A-SKILL KIT, UNIT 4: ANIMALS	IMPERIAL INTERNATIONAL LEARNING		51-75
I	MULTIM	SELECT-A-SKILL KIT, UNIT 4: ANIMALS	IMPERIAL INTERNATIONAL LEARNING		51-75
I	RECORD	SOUND SKILLS FOR UPPER GRADES, VOLUME 3	CLASSROOM MATERIALS CO.		6-10
I	WKBOOK	MORE EASY CROSSWORD PUZZLES	ENGLISH LANGUAGE SERVICES		<5
I	WKBOOK	EASY CROSSWORD PUZZLES	ENGLISH LANGUAGE SERVICES		<5
I	WKBOOK	LETTERS & SOUNDS, INTERMEDIATE	SCOTT, FORESMAN & CO.		<5
IJ	AUDKIT	VOCABULARY STUDY	EBSCO CURRICULUM MATERIALS		51-75
IJ	AUDKIT	DEVELOPMENTAL VOCABULARY	EBSCO CURRICULUM MATERIALS		51-75
IJ	DITTO	PRACTICE IN VOCABULARY BUILDING, BOOK C (GRADES 5 - 7)	INSTRUCTOR PUBLICATIONS, INC.		<5
IJ	GAME	TRIAD	CREATIVE TEACHING ASSOCIATES		6-10
IJ	GAME	GAMEBOARD KIT D	READING JOY, INC.		6-10
IJ	GAME	WIDE, WIDE WORLD OF GRAMMAR: BASKETWORD	HARCOURT BRACE JOVANOVICH, INC.		11-20
IJ	GAME	WIDE, WIDE WORLD OF GRAMMAR: GOAL WORD SOCCER	HARCOURT BRACE JOVANOVICH, INC.		21-30
IJ	MULTIM	SPECTRUM, UNIT 1 (RL 3.5 - 4.4)	IMPERIAL INTERNATIONAL LEARNING		51-75
IJ	MULTIM	COMMUNICATION POWER SERIES	UNITED LEARNING	5	201-300
IJ	MULTIM	COMMUNICATION POWER SERIES: BE A WORD DETECTIVE	UNITED LEARNING		51-75
IJ	WKBOOK	BOOK ONE, PART TWO: STRUCTURAL ANALYSIS ACTIVITIES	T.S. DENISON & COMPANY		6-10
IJS	AUDKIT	BASE	ECONOMY COMPANY		101-150
IJS	GAME	ON-WORDS	STANWIX HOUSE, INC.		6-10
IJS	MULTIM	KNIGHT INDIVIDUALIZED SPELLING PROGRAM KIT	EDUCATORS PUBLISHING SERVICE		76-100
J	ACTCRD	ROOTS/STEMS, ADVANCED 3	BARNELL LOFT, LTD.		6-10
J	ACTCRD	ROOTS/STEMS, ADVANCED 4	BARNELL LOFT, LTD.		6-10
J	ACTCRD	ROOTS/STEMS, ADVANCED 5	BARNELL LOFT, LTD.		6-10
J	ACTCRD	ROOTS/STEMS, ADVANCED 6	BARNELL LOFT, LTD.		6-10
J	ACTCRD	ROOTS/STEMS, ADVANCED 1	BARNELL LOFT, LTD.		6-10
J	ACTCRD	ROOTS/STEMS, ADVANCED 2	BARNELL LOFT, LTD.		6-10
J	AUDKIT	BUILDING WORD POWER	CORONET MULTI MEDIA		101-150
JS	AUDKIT	USING STRUCTURAL ANALYSIS SERIES	MEDIA MATERIALS, INC.		101-150
JS	AUDKIT	LEARNING STRUCTURAL ANALYSIS	HAMPDEN PUBLICATIONS, INC.		101-150
JS	HI INT	READING FOR PROGRESS (RL 1 - 2)	CAMBRIDGE BOOK CO.		<5
S	AUDKIT	STRUCTURAL ANALYSIS	HAMPDEN PUBLICATIONS, INC.		76-100
S	SND FS	ROOT WORDS	MEDIA MATERIALS, INC.		11-20
S	WKBOOK	STRUCTURE OF WORDS	EDUCATORS PUBLISHING SERVICE		<5

77 - SKILL: WORD ENDINGS

LEVEL	FORMAT	TITLE	PUBLISHER	NT	$PRICE
RP	PUPILB	PLURALS	CHILD'S WORLD		<5
RP	PUPILB	JOAN HANSON WORD BOOKS	CHILD'S WORLD	16	51-75

LEVEL	FORMAT	TITLE	PUBLISHER	NT	$PRICE

77 - SKILL: WORD ENDINGS

LEVEL	FORMAT	TITLE	PUBLISHER	NT	$PRICE
P	ACTCRD	ENDINGS/SUFFIXES, B	BARNELL LOFT, LTD.		6-10
P	ACTCRD	ENDINGS/SUFFIXES, C	BARNELL LOFT, LTD.		6-10
P	ACTCRD	LANGUAGE ACTIVITY CARDS: PLURALS & CONTRACTIONS	WEBER COSTELLO COMPANY		6-10
P	ACTCRD	INDIVIDUAL LETTER & WORD CARDS, SET 2	SCOTT, FORESMAN & CO.		<5
P	AUDCAS	LISTENING FOR SOUNDS	MEDIA MARKETING, INC.		51-75
P	AUDCRD	STRUCTURAL ANALYSIS FOR BEGINNING READERS	AUDIOTRONICS CORPORATION		21-30
P	AUDKIT	HAPPY ENDING	MEDIA MATERIALS, INC.		6-10
P	AUDKIT	MINISYSTEMS: FROM SPELLING TO WRITING I	CORONET MULTI MEDIA		11-20
P	AUDKIT	MINISYSTEMS: FROM SPELLING TO WRITING II	CORONET MULTI MEDIA		11-20
P	AUDKIT	MINISYSTEMS: ENDING S, 'S, ES, ING	CORONET MULTI MEDIA		11-20
P	AUDKIT	MINISYSTEMS: FINAL CONSONANTS PLUS ENDINGS	CORONET MULTI MEDIA		11-20
P	DITTO	NEW PHONICS & WORD ANALYSIS SKILLS: GRADE 1, PART 2	CONTINENTAL PRESS, INC.		<5
P	DITTO	NEW PHONICS & WORD ANALYSIS SKILLS: GRADE 1, PART 3	CONTINENTAL PRESS, INC.		<5
P	DITTO	NEW PHONICS & WORD ANALYSIS SKILLS: GRADE 2, PART 2	CONTINENTAL PRESS, INC.		<5
P	DITTO	NEW PHONICS & WORD ANALYSIS SKILLS: GRADE 3, PART 2	CONTINENTAL PRESS, INC.		<5
P	DITTO	PHONICS STORIES	FRANK SCHAFFER PUBLICATIONS, INC		<5
P	DITTO	NEWSPAPER TASKS SWING INTO LANGUAGE ARTS, PRIMARY	ORE PRESS, INC.		<5
P	DITTO	WORD ATTACK SKILLS: INFLECTIONAL ENDINGS	EDL/MCGRAW-HILL		6-10
P	DITTO	RIDING THE PLURALS TRAIN	INSTRUCTO/MCGRAW-HILL		<5
P	DITTO	PHONICS IB	HAYES SCHOOL PUBLISHING COMPANY		<5
P	DITTO	PHONICS IIIB	HAYES SCHOOL PUBLISHING COMPANY		<5
P	DITTO	DECODING SKILLS 4	ACTIVITY RESOURCES COMPANY, INC.		<5
P	FILMST	LEARNING ABOUT OUR LANGUAGE, SET 2	AEVAC, INC.		31-50
P	GAME	MATCH ME CARDS	CREATIVE TEACHING ASSOCIATES	4	11-20
P	GAME	MATCH ME CARDS, SINGULAR/PLURAL	CREATIVE TEACHING ASSOCIATES		<5
P	GAME	WORD TREK, BLENDS & DIGRAPHS	DEVELOPMENTAL LEARNING MATERIALS		6-10
P	GAME	CHECKMATE: WORD ENDINGS	DM EDUCATIONAL PUBLICATIONS		<5
P	GAME	MATCH ME CARDS: SINGULAR/PLURAL	TREND ENTERPRISES, INC.		<5
P	MANIPU	ETA MOTSPUR SINGULARS-AND-PLURALS CARDS	EDUCATIONAL TEACHING AIDS		6-10
P	MANIPU	QUIZZLE: PLURALS	IDEAL SCHOOL SUPPLY COMPANY		6-10
P	MANIPU	SINGULAR, PLURAL DOMINOES	DEVELOPMENTAL LEARNING MATERIALS		<5
P	MULTIM	READING SKILLS SUPPORT SYSTEM, BOX 1	EDL/MCGRAW-HILL		301-400
P	MULTIM	READING SKILLS SUPPORT SYSTEM, BOX 3	EDL/MCGRAW-HILL		301-400
P	SP EQT	PROGRAMMED LANGUAGE/READING, LEVEL I	INSTRUCTIONAL INDUSTRIES (G.E.)	8	>450
P	SP EQT	PROGRAMMED LANGUAGE/READING, LEVEL I: SET 1, SELF	INSTRUCTIONAL INDUSTRIES (G.E.)		101-150
P	SP EQT	PROGRAMMED LANGUAGE/READING, LEVEL I: SET 2, ANIMALS	INSTRUCTIONAL INDUSTRIES (G.E.)		101-150
P	SP EQT	PROGRAMMED LANGUAGE/READING, LEVEL I: SET 7, CLOTHING	INSTRUCTIONAL INDUSTRIES (G.E.)		76-100
P	WKBOOK	MOTT BASIC LANG. SKILLS: BOOK 1303	ALLIED EDUCATION COUNCIL		<5
P	WKBOOK	AEVAC PHONICS PROGRAM, BOOK F	AEVAC, INC.		<5
P	WKBOOK	CONSONANT SOUNDS & SYMBOLS, BOOK B	GINN & COMPANY		<5
P	WKBOOK	SOUNDS & SYLLABLES, BOOK E	GINN & COMPANY		<5
P	WKBOOK	SOUNDS WE USE, BOOK 3	HAYES SCHOOL PUBLISHING COMPANY		<5
PI	ACTCRD	PLURALS	C.C. PUBLICATIONS, INC.		21-30
PI	AUDCRD	MAKE IT MANY: IRREGULAR PLURALS	AUDIOTRONICS CORPORATION		11-20
PI	AUDKIT	BEGINNING VOCABULARY	EBSCO CURRICULUM MATERIALS		51-75
PI	AUDKIT	WORDS THAT MEAN MORE THAN ONE	MEDIA MATERIALS, INC.		6-10
PI	AUDKIT	PLEASANT PLURALS	MEDIA MATERIALS, INC.		6-10
PI	DITTO	SPELLING PROGRAM, BOOK L	FRANK SCHAFFER PUBLICATIONS, INC		<5
PI	MANIPU	SINGULAR - PLURAL PUZZLES	INCENTIVES FOR LEARNING, INC.		6-10
PI	MULTIU	CAVEMAN PLURALS	INSTRUCTO/MCGRAW-HILL		11-20
PI	SND FS	WORD ANALYSIS SKILLS: WORD FORMS II	LEARNING TREE FILMSTRIPS		51-75
PI	SND FS	WHAT'S THE GOOD WORD?	MILLER-BRODY PRODUCTIONS, INC.		51-75
PI	SP EQT	DEVELOPING STRUCTURAL ANALYSIS SKILLS, KIT I	BORG-WARNER EDUCATIONAL SYSTEMS		101-150
PI	SP EQT	DEVELOPING STRUCTURAL ANALYSIS SKILLS, KIT J	BORG-WARNER EDUCATIONAL SYSTEMS		101-150
PI	WKBOOK	WORD ENDINGS	CREATIVE TEACHING ASSOCIATES		<5
PI	WKBOOK	WORD ENDINGS	FRANK SCHAFFER PUBLICATIONS, INC		<5
PI	WKBOOK	PREFIXES, SUFFIXES, SYLLABLES	FRANK SCHAFFER PUBLICATIONS, INC		<5
PI	WKBOOK	RHYMING & READING	GOOD APPLE, INC.		6-10
PI	WKBOOK	PRIMARY PHONICS WORKBOOK 5	EDUCATORS PUBLISHING SERVICE		<5
I	ACTCRD	ENDINGS/SUFFIXES, D	BARNELL LOFT, LTD.		6-10
I	ACTCRD	ENDINGS/SUFFIXES, E	BARNELL LOFT, LTD.		6-10
I	ACTCRD	ENDINGS/SUFFIXES, F	BARNELL LOFT, LTD.		6-10
I	ACTCRD	ROOTS/STEMS, F1	BARNELL LOFT, LTD.		6-10
I	ACTCRD	ROOTS/STEMS, F2	BARNELL LOFT, LTD.		6-10
I	AUDKIT	EVERYDAY VOCABULARY	EBSCO CURRICULUM MATERIALS		51-75
I	AUDKIT	READING CASSETTES: WORD BUILDING	IDEAL SCHOOL SUPPLY COMPANY		51-75
I	AUDKIT	MORE-THAN-ONE, FUN FROM HEADQUARTERS	MEDIA MATERIALS, INC.		6-10
I	AUDKIT	POSSESSIVES - TEN FINGERS & THEY'RE ALL MINE	MEDIA MATERIALS, INC.		6-10
I	AUDKIT	DIFFICULT PLURALS	MEDIA MATERIALS, INC.		6-10
I	DITTO	READING ESSENTIALS: VOCABULARY DEVELOPMENT, GRADE 3	CONTINENTAL PRESS, INC.		<5
I	DITTO	NEWSPAPER TASKS SWING INTO LANGUAGE ARTS, INTERMEDIATE	ORE PRESS, INC.		<5
I	DITTO	DECODING SKILLS C	ACTIVITY RESOURCES COMPANY, INC.		<5
I	GAME	TAKE	GARRARD PUBLISHING COMPANY		<5
I	GAME	CHECKMATE: WORD ENDINGS	DM EDUCATIONAL PUBLICATIONS		<5
I	GAME	WORDFACTS GAMES	MILTON BRADLEY/PLAYSKOOL		21-30
I	MULTIM	GAMES 'N' FRAMES: AL'S PIT STOP	IMPERIAL INTERNATIONAL LEARNING		21-30
I	MULTIM	SELECT-A-SKILL KIT, UNIT 3: SPORTS	IMPERIAL INTERNATIONAL LEARNING		51-75
I	MULTIM	SELECT-A-SKILL KIT, UNIT 3: SPORTS	IMPERIAL INTERNATIONAL LEARNING		51-75
I	MULTIM	VOCABULARY DEVELOPMENT	MILTON BRADLEY/PLAYSKOOL		76-100

LEVEL	FORMAT	TITLE	PUBLISHER	NT	$PRICE

77 - SKILL: WORD ENDINGS

LEVEL	FORMAT	TITLE	PUBLISHER	NT	$PRICE
I	RECORD	BUILDING LANGUAGE USAGE POWER, VOLUME 2	CLASSROOM MATERIALS CO.		6-10
I	VISKIT	CAVEMAN PLURALS CENTER	INSTRUCTO/MCGRAW-HILL		11-20
I	WKBOOK	MORE EASY CROSSWORD PUZZLES	ENGLISH LANGUAGE SERVICES		<5
I	WKBOOK	EASY CROSSWORD PUZZLES	ENGLISH LANGUAGE SERVICES		<5
IJ	AUDKIT	VOCABULARY STUDY	EBSCO CURRICULUM MATERIALS		51-75
IJ	AUDKIT	DEVELOPMENTAL VOCABULARY	EBSCO CURRICULUM MATERIALS		51-75
IJ	A/VKIT	WORD BUILDERS	EYE GATE MEDIA		76-100
IJ	RECORD	LANGUAGE USAGE SKILLS FOR UPPER GRADES, VOLUME 2	CLASSROOM MATERIALS CO.		6-10
IJS	AUDKIT	BASE	ECONOMY COMPANY		101-150
IJS	GAME	ON-WORDS	STANWIX HOUSE, INC.		6-10
J	ACTCRD	ROOTS/STEMS, ADVANCED 3	BARNELL LOFT, LTD.		6-10
J	ACTCRD	ROOTS/STEMS, ADVANCED 4	BARNELL LOFT, LTD.		6-10
J	ACTCRD	ROOTS/STEMS, ADVANCED 5	BARNELL LOFT, LTD.		6-10
J	ACTCRD	ROOTS/STEMS, ADVANCED 6	BARNELL LOFT, LTD.		6-10
J	ACTCRD	ENDINGS/SUFFIXES, ADVANCED 1	BARNELL LOFT, LTD.		6-10
J	ACTCRD	ENDINGS/SUFFIXES, ADVANCED 2	BARNELL LOFT, LTD.		6-10
J	ACTCRD	ENDINGS/SUFFIXES, ADVANCED 3	BARNELL LOFT, LTD.		6-10
J	ACTCRD	ROOTS/STEMS, ADVANCED 1	BARNELL LOFT, LTD.		6-10
J	ACTCRD	ROOTS/STEMS, ADVANCED 2	BARNELL LOFT, LTD.		6-10
JS	AUDKIT	USING STRUCTURAL ANALYSIS SERIES	MEDIA MATERIALS, INC.		101-150
JS	AUDKIT	LEARNING STRUCTURAL ANALYSIS	HAMPDEN PUBLICATIONS, INC.		101-150
JS	HI INT	READING FOR PROGRESS (RL 1 - 2)	CAMBRIDGE BOOK CO.		<5
S	PUPILB	SYSTEMATIC SPELLING	EDUCATORS PUBLISHING SERVICE		<5

78 - SKILL: CONTRACTIONS

LEVEL	FORMAT	TITLE	PUBLISHER	NT	$PRICE
P	ACTCRD	TUTORGRAM: CONTRACTIONS	ENRICHMENT READING CORP OF AMER.		11-20
P	ACTCRD	LANGUAGE ACTIVITY CARDS: PLURALS & CONTRACTIONS	WEBER COSTELLO COMPANY		6-10
P	AUDCRD	STRUCTURAL ANALYSIS FOR BEGINNING READERS	AUDIOTRONICS CORPORATION		21-30
P	AUDKIT	MINISYSTEMS: CONTRACTIONS	CORONET MULTI MEDIA		11-20
P	DITTO	NEW PHONICS & WORD ANALYSIS SKILLS: GRADE 1, PART 2	CONTINENTAL PRESS, INC.		<5
P	DITTO	NEW PHONICS & WORD ANALYSIS SKILLS: GRADE 2, PART 3	CONTINENTAL PRESS, INC.		<5
P	DITTO	NEW PHONICS & WORD ANALYSIS SKILLS: GRADE 3, PART 3	CONTINENTAL PRESS, INC.		<5
P	DITTO	NEWSPAPER TASKS SWING INTO LANGUAGE ARTS, PRIMARY	ORE PRESS, INC.		<5
P	DITTO	CONTRACTIONS	INSTRUCTOR PUBLICATIONS, INC.		<5
P	DITTO	PASTING TIME	CREATIVE TEACHING PRESS, INC.		<5
P	DITTO	WORD WIZARDS, BOOK 1	HAYES SCHOOL PUBLISHING COMPANY		<5
P	DITTO	DECODING SKILLS 2	ACTIVITY RESOURCES COMPANY, INC.		<5
P	GUIDE	PHONICS IS FUN, BOOK 2	MODERN CURRICULUM PRESS		<5
P	MANIPU	QUIZZLE: CONTRACTIONS	IDEAL SCHOOL SUPPLY COMPANY		6-10
P	MANIPU	CONTRACTION BOARDS	DEVELOPMENTAL LEARNING MATERIALS		<5
P	MULTIM	LEARNING PHONICS	MEDIA MARKETING, INC.		51-75
P	MULTIM	READING SKILLS SUPPORT SYSTEM, BOX 1	EDL/MCGRAW-HILL		301-400
P	PUPILB	WOG'S LOG BOOK V	EDUCATORS PUBLISHING SERVICE		<5
P	PUPILB	WOG'S LOG BOOK VI	EDUCATORS PUBLISHING SERVICE		<5
P	WKBOOK	MCP PHONICS WORKBOOKS: LEVEL B	MODERN CURRICULUM PRESS		<5
P	WKBOOK	PHONICS IS FUN, BOOK 2	MODERN CURRICULUM PRESS		<5
P	WKBOOK	NEW PHONICS WORKBOOK, BOOK D	MODERN CURRICULUM PRESS		<5
P	WKBOOK	PHONICS WORKBOOK, BOOK D	MODERN CURRICULUM PRESS		<5
PI	AUDKIT	CONTRACTIONS: WHAT ARE THEY?	MEDIA MATERIALS, INC.		6-10
PI	AUDKIT	BEGINNING STRUCTURAL ANALYSIS	HAMPDEN PUBLICATIONS, INC.		101-150
PI	AUDKIT	INTERMEDIATE STRUCTURAL ANALYSIS	HAMPDEN PUBLICATIONS, INC.		101-150
PI	FILMST	STRUCTURAL ANALYSIS FILMSTRIP SERIES	MEDIA MATERIALS, INC.	5	76-100
PI	FILMST	CONTRACTIONS	MEDIA MATERIALS, INC.		11-20
PI	GAME	MEM-O-MATCH	CREATIVE TEACHING ASSOCIATES		6-10
PI	GAME	READING ZINGO	BOWMAR/NOBLE PUBLISHERS, INC.		51-75
PI	GAME	CHECKMATE: CONTRACTIONS	DM EDUCATIONAL PUBLICATIONS		<5
PI	MANIPU	CONTRACTION PUZZLES	INCENTIVES FOR LEARNING, INC.		6-10
PI	RECORD	PHONICS & WORD DEVELOPMENT	EDUCATIONAL ACTIVITIES, INC.		31-50
PI	SND FS	WORD ANALYSIS SKILLS: WORD FORMS II	LEARNING TREE FILMSTRIPS		51-75
PI	SND FS	STRUCTURAL ANALYSIS SERIES	HAMPDEN PUBLICATIONS, INC.		76-100
PI	SP EQT	DEVELOPING STRUCTURAL ANALYSIS SKILLS, KIT I	BORG-WARNER EDUCATIONAL SYSTEMS		101-150
PI	VISKIT	CONTRACTIONS MAGIC SHOW	INSTRUCTO/MCGRAW-HILL		11-20
PI	WKBOOK	WORD ENDINGS	FRANK SCHAFFER PUBLICATIONS, INC		<5
PI	WKBOOK	GOING BANANAS OVER LANGUAGE SKILLS	GOOD APPLE, INC.		6-10
PIJ	ACTCRD	READ & REASON	FRANK SCHAFFER PUBLICATIONS, INC		<5
PIJ	MULTIU	CREATURE FEATURES: VOCABULARY DEVELOPMENT	EDUCATIONAL ACTIVITIES, INC.		31-50
I	ACTCRD	WORD ANALYSIS: COMPOUND WORDS & CONTRACTIONS	INSTRUCTIONAL FAIR		<5
I	ACTCRD	WORD ANALYSIS PAK	INSTRUCTIONAL FAIR		21-30
I	AUDKIT	READING CASSETTES: WORD BUILDING	IDEAL SCHOOL SUPPLY COMPANY		51-75
I	AUDKIT	CUTTING CORNERS WITH CONTRACTIONS	MEDIA MATERIALS, INC.		6-10
I	AUDKIT	CONTRACTION SATISFACTION	MEDIA MATERIALS, INC.		6-10
I	DITTO	WORD ANALYSIS: COMPOUND WORDS & CONTRACTIONS	INSTRUCTIONAL FAIR		<5
I	DITTO	WORD ANALYSIS PAK	INSTRUCTIONAL FAIR		21-30
I	DITTO	WORD WIZARDS, BOOK 2	HAYES SCHOOL PUBLISHING COMPANY		<5
I	DITTO	WORD WIZARDS, BOOK 3	HAYES SCHOOL PUBLISHING COMPANY		<5
I	DITTO	FOURTH GRADE LANGUAGE DRILLS	HAYES SCHOOL PUBLISHING COMPANY		<5
I	DITTO	DECODING SKILLS C	ACTIVITY RESOURCES COMPANY, INC.		<5
I	GAME	PRESS & CHECK BINGO GAMES: ABBREVIATIONS & CONTRACTIONS	MILTON BRADLEY/PLAYSKOOL		6-10
I	MULTIM	GAMES 'N' FRAMES: AL'S PIT STOP	IMPERIAL INTERNATIONAL LEARNING		21-30

LEVEL	FORMAT	TITLE	PUBLISHER	NT	$PRICE

78 - SKILL: CONTRACTIONS

LEVEL	FORMAT	TITLE	PUBLISHER	NT	$PRICE
I	MULTIM	SELECT-A-SKILL KIT, UNIT 3: SPORTS	IMPERIAL INTERNATIONAL LEARNING		51-75
I	MULTIM	SELECT-A-SKILL KIT, UNIT 3: SPORTS	IMPERIAL INTERNATIONAL LEARNING		51-75
I	MULTIM	VOCABULARY DEVELOPMENT	MILTON BRADLEY/PLAYSKOOL		76-100
I	VISKIT	CONTRACTION CONCENTRATION	T.S. DENISON & COMPANY		<5
IJ	A/VKIT	WORD BUILDERS	EYE GATE MEDIA		76-100
IJ	WKBOOK	BOOK ONE, PART TWO: STRUCTURAL ANALYSIS ACTIVITIES	T.S. DENISON & COMPANY		6-10
IJS	AUDKIT	HITS, LEVEL 2: SPINNERS, COULD IT BE I'M FALLING IN LOVE	MODULEARN, INC.		11-20
IJS	AUDKIT	HITS, LEVEL 2: ABBA, KNOWING ME, KNOWING YOU	MODULEARN, INC.		11-20
IJS	AUDKIT	HITS, LEVEL 2: PAUL SIMON, STILL CRAZY AFTER ALL THESE YEARS	MODULEARN, INC.		11-20
IJS	AUDKIT	HITS, LEVEL 3: PAUL SIMON, 50 WAYS TO LEAVE YOUR LOVER	MODULEARN, INC.		11-20
IJS	AUDKIT	HITS, LEVEL 3: CARLY SIMON, GROWN UP	MODULEARN, INC.		11-20
JS	AUDKIT	USING STRUCTURAL ANALYSIS SERIES	MEDIA MATERIALS, INC.		101-150
JS	AUDKIT	LEARNING STRUCTURAL ANALYSIS	HAMPDEN PUBLICATIONS, INC.		101-150
JS	HI INT	READING FOR PROGRESS (RL 1 - 2)	CAMBRIDGE BOOK CO.		<5
S	AUDKIT	STRUCTURAL ANALYSIS	HAMPDEN PUBLICATIONS, INC.		76-100
S	SND FS	CONTRACTIONS	MEDIA MATERIALS, INC.		11-20

79 - SKILL: COMPOUND WORDS

LEVEL	FORMAT	TITLE	PUBLISHER	NT	$PRICE
RP	SND FS	STORIES ABOUT WORDS	CORONET MULTI MEDIA		101-150
P	ACTCRD	COMPOUNDS, A	BARNELL LOFT, LTD.		6-10
P	ACTCRD	COMPOUNDS, B	BARNELL LOFT, LTD.		6-10
P	ACTCRD	COMPOUNDS, C	BARNELL LOFT, LTD.		6-10
P	ACTCRD	COMPOUND WORDS	TEACHING RESOURCES CORPORATION		6-10
P	ACTCRD	LANGUAGE ACTIVITY CARDS: SYLLABLES & COMPOUND WORDS	WEBER COSTELLO COMPANY		6-10
P	ACTCRD	COMPOUND-A-WORD	DEVELOPMENTAL LEARNING MATERIALS		6-10
P	ACTCRD	COMPOUND WORD, PRELIMINARY	DEVELOPMENTAL LEARNING MATERIALS		<5
P	AUDCAS	SOUNDS FOR YOUNG READERS, VOLUME 5	CLASSROOM MATERIALS CO.		6-10
P	AUDCAS	LISTENING FOR SOUNDS	MEDIA MARKETING, INC.		51-75
P	AUDCRD	STRUCTURAL ANALYSIS FOR BEGINNING READERS	AUDIOTRONICS CORPORATION		21-30
P	AUDKIT	KIT 58: BUILDING WORD POWER, LEVEL 3	EDUCATIONAL RESEARCH, INC.		101-150
P	AUDKIT	MINISYSTEMS: COMPOUND WORDS	CORONET MULTI MEDIA		11-20
P	CHART	FILL THE CONE	IDEAL SCHOOL SUPPLY COMPANY		<5
P	DITTO	NEW PHONICS & WORD ANALYSIS SKILLS: GRADE 2, PART 3	CONTINENTAL PRESS, INC.		<5
P	DITTO	NEW PHONICS & WORD ANALYSIS SKILLS: GRADE 3, PART 3	CONTINENTAL PRESS, INC.		<5
P	DITTO	READING ESSENTIALS: VOCABULARY DEVELOPMENT, GRADE 1	CONTINENTAL PRESS, INC.		<5
P	DITTO	WORD SPY, GRADE 1	CONTINENTAL PRESS, INC.		<5
P	DITTO	COMPOUND WORDS	INSTRUCTOR PUBLICATIONS, INC.		<5
P	DITTO	PASTING TIME	CREATIVE TEACHING PRESS, INC.		<5
P	DITTO	PHONICS IIB	HAYES SCHOOL PUBLISHING COMPANY		<5
P	DITTO	WORD WIZARDS, BOOK 1	HAYES SCHOOL PUBLISHING COMPANY		<5
P	DITTO	DECODING SKILLS 3	ACTIVITY RESOURCES COMPANY, INC.		<5
P	GAME	COMPOUND WORD GAME	DEVELOPMENTAL LEARNING MATERIALS		<5
P	GAME	CHECKMATE: COMPOUND WORDS	DM EDUCATIONAL PUBLICATIONS		<5
P	MANIPU	COMPOUND-WORD PICTURE MATCHING CARDS	EDUCATIONAL TEACHING AIDS		6-10
P	MANIPU	COMPOUND WORD PUZZLES	IDEAL SCHOOL SUPPLY COMPANY		6-10
P	MANIPU	SHAPE-UPS: COMPOUND WORDS	READING JOY, INC.		<5
P	MULTIM	LEARNING PHONICS	MEDIA MARKETING, INC.		51-75
P	MULTIM	READING SKILLS SUPPORT SYSTEM, BOX 1	EDL/MCGRAW-HILL		301-400
P	MULTIM	READING SKILLS SUPPORT SYSTEM, BOX 3	EDL/MCGRAW-HILL		301-400
P	RECORD	SOUNDS FOR YOUNG READERS, VOLUME 5	CLASSROOM MATERIALS CO.		6-10
P	WKBOOK	SOUNDS & SYLLABLES, BOOK E	GINN & COMPANY		<5
P	WKBOOK	PRIMARY PHONICS WORKBOOK 3	EDUCATORS PUBLISHING SERVICE		<5
P	WKBOOK	MCP PHONICS WORKBOOKS: LEVEL B	MODERN CURRICULUM PRESS		<5
P	WKBOOK	NEW PHONICS WORKBOOK, BOOK A	MODERN CURRICULUM PRESS		<5
PI	ACTCRD	COMPOUND WORDS	KENWORTHY EDUCATIONAL SERVICE		<5
PI	ACTCRD	LANGUAGE LOLLIPOP	KIDS & COMPANY		<5
PI	ACTCRD	EGGHEAD JAZZ	LESWING PRESS		11-20
PI	AUDKIT	TOTAL BUILDING WORK POWER (KITS 58 - 61)	EDUCATIONAL RESEARCH, INC.	4	>450
PI	AUDKIT	LET'S LOOK FOR COMPOUND WORDS	MEDIA MATERIALS, INC.		6-10
PI	AUDKIT	BEGINNING STRUCTURAL ANALYSIS	HAMPDEN PUBLICATIONS, INC.		101-150
PI	DITTO	DECODING SKILLS B	ACTIVITY RESOURCES COMPANY, INC.		<5
PI	MANIPU	COMPOUND WORD PUZZLES	INCENTIVES FOR LEARNING, INC.		6-10
PI	MANIPU	POPEYE'S SPECIAL LANGUAGE BUILDER: BALLOON PUZZLES (SP.ED.)	KING FEATURES		11-20
PI	MANIPU	PHONICS E-Z LANGUAGE LEARNING SLIDE RULES, 5TH	E-Z GRADER COMPANY		<5
PI	SND FS	WORD ANALYSIS SKILLS: WORD FORMS II	LEARNING TREE FILMSTRIPS		51-75
PI	SND FS	WORKING WITH WORDS	TROLL ASSOCIATES		101-150
PI	SP EQT	DEVELOPING STRUCTURAL ANALYSIS SKILLS, KIT I	BORG-WARNER EDUCATIONAL SYSTEMS		101-150
PI	WKBOOK	PREFIXES, SUFFIXES, SYLLABLES	FRANK SCHAFFER PUBLICATIONS, INC		<5
PI	WKBOOK	PRIMARY PHONICS WORKBOOK 5	EDUCATORS PUBLISHING SERVICE		<5
I	ACTCRD	WORD ANALYSIS: COMPOUND WORDS & CONTRACTIONS	INSTRUCTIONAL FAIR		<5
I	ACTCRD	WORD ANALYSIS PAK	INSTRUCTIONAL FAIR		21-30
I	ACTCRD	COMPOUNDS, D	BARNELL LOFT, LTD.		6-10
I	ACTCRD	COMPOUNDS, E	BARNELL LOFT, LTD.		6-10
I	ACTCRD	COMPOUNDS, F	BARNELL LOFT, LTD.		6-10
I	AUDKIT	KIT 59: BUILDING WORD POWER, LEVEL 4	EDUCATIONAL RESEARCH, INC.		101-150
I	AUDKIT	KIT 60: BUILDING WORD POWER, LEVEL 5	EDUCATIONAL RESEARCH, INC.		101-150
I	AUDKIT	KIT 61: BUILDING WORD POWER, LEVEL 16	EDUCATIONAL RESEARCH, INC.		101-150
I	AUDKIT	READING CASSETTES: WORD BUILDING	IDEAL SCHOOL SUPPLY COMPANY		51-75
I	DITTO	READING ESSENTIALS: VOCABULARY DEVELOPMENT, GRADE 3	CONTINENTAL PRESS, INC.		<5

LEVEL	FORMAT	TITLE	PUBLISHER	NT	$PRICE

79 - SKILL: COMPOUND WORDS

LEVEL	FORMAT	TITLE	PUBLISHER	NT	$PRICE
I	DITTO	WORD ANALYSIS: COMPOUND WORDS & CONTRACTIONS	INSTRUCTIONAL FAIR		<5
I	DITTO	WORD ANALYSIS PAK	INSTRUCTIONAL FAIR		21-30
I	DITTO	SOUNDS IN WORDS, BOOK 9	GEL-STEN, INC.		<5
I	DITTO	SOUNDS IN WORDS, BOOK 12	GEL-STEN, INC.		<5
I	DITTO	SOUNDS IN WORDS, BOOK 18	GEL-STEN, INC.		<5
I	DITTO	WORD WIZARDS, BOOK 2	HAYES SCHOOL PUBLISHING COMPANY		<5
I	DITTO	WORD WIZARDS, BOOK 3	HAYES SCHOOL PUBLISHING COMPANY		<5
I	DITTO	DECODING SKILLS C	ACTIVITY RESOURCES COMPANY, INC.		<5
I	GAME	CHECKMATE: COMPOUND WORDS	DM EDUCATIONAL PUBLICATIONS		<5
I	MULTIM	SELECT-A-SKILL KIT, UNIT 3: SPORTS	IMPERIAL INTERNATIONAL LEARNING		51-75
I	MULTIM	SELECT-A-SKILL KIT, UNIT 3: SPORTS	IMPERIAL INTERNATIONAL LEARNING		51-75
I	RECORD	SOUND SKILLS FOR UPPER GRADES	CLASSROOM MATERIALS CO.	3	21-30
I	RECORD	SOUND SKILLS FOR UPPER GRADES, VOLUME 3	CLASSROOM MATERIALS CO.		6-10
I	WKBOOK	MOTT BASIC LANG. SKILLS: LANG./GRAMMAR SKILLS, BK 1607	ALLIED EDUCATION COUNCIL		<5
IJ	A/VKIT	WORD BUILDERS	EYE GATE MEDIA		76-100
IJ	WKBOOK	BOOK ONE, PART TWO: STRUCTURAL ANALYSIS ACTIVITIES	T.S. DENISON & COMPANY		6-10
J	ACTCRD	COMPOUNDS, ADVANCED	BARNELL LOFT, LTD.		6-10
JS	AUDKIT	USING STRUCTURAL ANALYSIS SERIES	MEDIA MATERIALS, INC.		101-150
JS	AUDKIT	LEARNING STRUCTURAL ANALYSIS	HAMPDEN PUBLICATIONS, INC.		101-150
S	PUPILB	SYSTEMATIC SPELLING	EDUCATORS PUBLISHING SERVICE		<5

80 - SKILL: PREFIXES

LEVEL	FORMAT	TITLE	PUBLISHER	NT	$PRICE
RP	MULTIM	WORDS & SOUND SERIES, SET 3	EDL/MCGRAW-HILL		101-150
RP	SND FS	STORIES ABOUT WORDS	CORONET MULTI MEDIA		101-150
P	ACTCRD	PREFIXES	KENWORTHY EDUCATIONAL SERVICE		<5
P	ACTCRD	LANGUAGE ACTIVITY CARDS: SUFFIXES & PREFIXES	WEBER COSTELLO COMPANY		6-10
P	ACTCRD	CHECKLIST OF BASIC SOUNDS	LAKESHORE CURRICULUM MATERIALS		<5
P	ACTCRD	WORD PROBE SKILL CARDS	MILTON BRADLEY/PLAYSKOOL		<5
P	AUDCAS	SOUNDS FOR YOUNG READERS, VOLUME 5	CLASSROOM MATERIALS CO.		6-10
P	AUDKIT	PHONICS	EYE GATE MEDIA	10	76-100
P	AUDKIT	PHONICS: FUN WITH AFFIXES	EYE GATE MEDIA		6-10
P	AUDKIT	KIT 58: BUILDING WORD POWER, LEVEL 3	EDUCATIONAL RESEARCH, INC.		101-150
P	AUDKIT	MINISYSTEMS: PREFIXES	CORONET MULTI MEDIA		11-20
P	AUDKIT	MINISYSTEMS: ROOTS, PREFIXES, SUFFIXES	CORONET MULTI MEDIA		11-20
P	CHART	PREFIX POW-WOW	IDEAL SCHOOL SUPPLY COMPANY		<5
P	DITTO	NEW PHONICS & WORD ANALYSIS SKILLS: GRADE 2, PART 3	CONTINENTAL PRESS, INC.		<5
P	DITTO	NEW PHONICS & WORD ANALYSIS SKILLS: GRADE 3, PART 2	CONTINENTAL PRESS, INC.		<5
P	DITTO	READING ESSENTIALS: VOCABULARY DEVELOPMENT, GRADE 3, BOOK 2	CONTINENTAL PRESS, INC.		<5
P	DITTO	BASIC READING SKILLS	XEROX EDUCATION PUBLICATIONS		<5
P	DITTO	PHONICS IIB	HAYES SCHOOL PUBLISHING COMPANY		<5
P	GAME	SPELL POWER	KENWORTHY EDUCATIONAL SERVICE		<5
P	GAME	CHECKMATE: AFFIXES	DM EDUCATIONAL PUBLICATIONS		<5
P	GUIDE	PHONICS IS FUN, BOOK 2	MODERN CURRICULUM PRESS		<5
P	MANIPU	ADVANCED PREFIX & SUFFIX PUZZLES	DEVELOPMENTAL LEARNING MATERIALS		6-10
P	MANIPU	PREFIX PUZZLES	DEVELOPMENTAL LEARNING MATERIALS		<5
P	MULTIM	READING SKILLS SUPPORT SYSTEM, BOX 3	EDL/MCGRAW-HILL		301-400
P	PUPILB	WOG'S LOG BOOK V	EDUCATORS PUBLISHING SERVICE		<5
P	PUPILB	WOG'S LOG BOOK VI	EDUCATORS PUBLISHING SERVICE		<5
P	RECORD	SOUNDS FOR YOUNG READERS, VOLUME 5	CLASSROOM MATERIALS CO.		6-10
P	SND FS	PREFIXES & SUFFIXES	HERBERT M. ELKINS COMPANY		11-20
P	SP EQT	AUDITORY SKILLS: MORPHOLOGY & CLOSURE	INSTRUCTIONAL INDUSTRIES (G.E.)		101-150
P	WKBOOK	MORE SOUNDS & SYMBOLS, BOOK F	GINN & COMPANY		<5
P	WKBOOK	MCP PHONICS WORKBOOKS: LEVEL B	MODERN CURRICULUM PRESS		<5
P	WKBOOK	MCP PHONICS WORKBOOKS: LEVEL C	MODERN CURRICULUM PRESS		<5
P	WKBOOK	PHONICS IS FUN, BOOK 2	MODERN CURRICULUM PRESS		<5
P	WKBOOK	NEW PHONICS WORKBOOK, BOOK C	MODERN CURRICULUM PRESS		<5
PI	ACTCRD	TUTORGRAM: PREFIX MEANINGS, INTERMEDIATE LEVEL	ENRICHMENT READING CORP OF AMER.		11-20
PI	AUDKIT	BASIC WORD ATTACK SKILLS	EDUCATIONAL RESEARCH, INC.	4	>450
PI	AUDKIT	TOTAL BUILDING WORK POWER (KITS 58 - 61)	EDUCATIONAL RESEARCH, INC.	4	>450
PI	AUDKIT	LET'S FIND SOME ROOT WORDS: PREFIXES	MEDIA MATERIALS, INC.		6-10
PI	AUDKIT	FUN WITH AFFIXES	MEDIA MATERIALS, INC.		6-10
PI	AUDKIT	BEGINNING STRUCTURAL ANALYSIS	HAMPDEN PUBLICATIONS, INC.		101-150
PI	AUDKIT	INTERMEDIATE STRUCTURAL ANALYSIS	HAMPDEN PUBLICATIONS, INC.		101-150
PI	DITTO	READING LANTERNS: AMUSEMENT PARK	EDUCATIONAL INSIGHTS, INC.		6-10
PI	DITTO	PRACTICE IN VOCABULARY BUILDING, BOOK A (GRADES 3 - 4)	INSTRUCTOR PUBLICATIONS, INC.		<5
PI	FILMST	STRUCTURAL ANALYSIS FILMSTRIP SERIES	MEDIA MATERIALS, INC.	5	76-100
PI	FILMST	PREFIXES	MEDIA MATERIALS, INC.		11-20
PI	GAME	PREFIXES	FRANK SCHAFFER PUBLICATIONS, INC		<5
PI	GAME	SUPER STOCK	ALLIED EDUCATION COUNCIL		51-75
PI	GAME	MONSTER HUNT	ALLIED EDUCATION COUNCIL		51-75
PI	GAME	BASE WORD RUMMY	JUDY COMPANY		6-10
PI	GUIDE	PHONICS IS FUN, BOOK 3	MODERN CURRICULUM PRESS		<5
PI	MANIPU	E-Z PHONIC WORD-BUILDING SLIDE RULE	E-Z GRADER COMPANY		<5
PI	MULTIM	NEW GOALS IN LISTENING, GRADES 2-4	TROLL ASSOCIATES		76-100
PI	SKLKIT	TARGET GREEN: VOCABULARY DEVELOPMENT KIT I	ADDISON-WESLEY PUBLISHING CO.		151-200
PI	SND FS	WORD ANALYSIS SKILLS: WORD PARTS I	LEARNING TREE FILMSTRIPS		51-75
PI	SND FS	STRUCTURAL ANALYSIS SERIES	HAMPDEN PUBLICATIONS, INC.		76-100
PI	SND FS	WORKING WITH WORDS	TROLL ASSOCIATES		101-150

LEVEL	FORMAT	TITLE	PUBLISHER	NT	$PRICE

80 - SKILL: PREFIXES

LEVEL	FORMAT	TITLE	PUBLISHER	NT	$PRICE
PI	SP EQT	DEVELOPING STRUCTURAL ANALYSIS SKILLS, KIT K	BORG-WARNER EDUCATIONAL SYSTEMS		101-150
PI	WKBOOK	PREFIXES, SUFFIXES, SYLLABLES	CREATIVE TEACHING ASSOCIATES		<5
PI	WKBOOK	WORD ENDINGS	FRANK SCHAFFER PUBLICATIONS, INC		<5
PI	WKBOOK	PREFIXES, SUFFIXES, SYLLABLES	FRANK SCHAFFER PUBLICATIONS, INC		<5
PI	WKBOOK	PHONICS IS FUN, BOOK 3	MODERN CURRICULUM PRESS		<5
PIJ	CL SET	WHAT'S THE MEANING OF THIS?	MAFEX ASSOCIATES, INC.		51-75
PIJ	CL SET	WEBSTER WORD WHEELS	WEBSTER DIVISION/MCGRAW-HILL		31-50
I	ACTCRD	WORD ANALYSIS: SUFFIXES & PREFIXES	INSTRUCTIONAL FAIR		<5
I	ACTCRD	PREFIXES, D	BARNELL LOFT, LTD.		6-10
I	ACTCRD	PREFIXES, E	BARNELL LOFT, LTD.		6-10
I	ACTCRD	PREFIXES, F	BARNELL LOFT, LTD.		6-10
I	ACTCRD	AFFIXES PACER	DM EDUCATIONAL PUBLICATIONS		<5
I	AUDKIT	EVERYDAY VOCABULARY	EBSCO CURRICULUM MATERIALS		51-75
I	AUDKIT	KIT 9: BASIC WORD ATTACK - STRUCTURAL ANALYSIS, PREFIXES	EDUCATIONAL RESEARCH, INC.		101-150
I	AUDKIT	KIT 59: BUILDING WORD POWER, LEVEL 4	EDUCATIONAL RESEARCH, INC.		101-150
I	AUDKIT	KIT 60: BUILDING WORD POWER, LEVEL 5	EDUCATIONAL RESEARCH, INC.		101-150
I	AUDKIT	KIT 61: BUILDING WORD POWER, LEVEL 16	EDUCATIONAL RESEARCH, INC.		101-150
I	AUDKIT	READING CASSETTES: WORD BUILDING	IDEAL SCHOOL SUPPLY COMPANY		51-75
I	AUDKIT	RED-BLOODED PREFIXES	MEDIA MATERIALS, INC.		6-10
I	AUDKIT	ADDING PREFIXES	MEDIA MATERIALS, INC.		6-10
I	AUDKIT	EXPANDING VOCABULARY	HAMPDEN PUBLICATIONS, INC.		21-30
I	DITTO	READING ESSENTIALS: VOCABULARY DEVELOPMENT, GRADE 4	CONTINENTAL PRESS, INC.		<5
I	DITTO	READING ESSENTIALS: VOCABULARY DEVELOPMENT, GRADE 5	CONTINENTAL PRESS, INC.		<5
I	DITTO	READING ESSENTIALS: VOCABULARY DEVELOPMENT, GRADE 6	CONTINENTAL PRESS, INC.		<5
I	DITTO	WORD ANALYSIS: SUFFIXES & PREFIXES	INSTRUCTIONAL FAIR		<5
I	DITTO	NEWSPAPER TASKS SWING INTO LANGUAGE ARTS, INTERMEDIATE	ORE PRESS, INC.		<5
I	DITTO	SOUNDS IN WORDS, BOOK 9	GEL-STEN, INC.		<5
I	DITTO	SOUNDS IN WORDS, BOOK 12	GEL-STEN, INC.		<5
I	DITTO	SOUNDS IN WORDS, BOOK 13	GEL-STEN, INC.		<5
I	DITTO	SOUNDS IN WORDS, BOOK 15	GEL-STEN, INC.		<5
I	DITTO	SOUNDS IN WORDS, BOOK 18	GEL-STEN, INC.		<5
I	DITTO	PRACTICE IN VOCABULARY BUILDING, BOOK B (GRADES 4 - 5)	INSTRUCTOR PUBLICATIONS, INC.		<5
I	DITTO	DECODING SKILLS E	ACTIVITY RESOURCES COMPANY, INC.		<5
I	FILMST	PREFIXES & SUFFIXES	EDUCATIONAL PROJECTIONS COMPANY		11-20
I	GAME	WORD COMPUTER	CREATIVE TEACHING ASSOCIATES		<5
I	GAME	CHECKMATE: AFFIXES	DM EDUCATIONAL PUBLICATIONS		<5
I	GAME	USING PREFIXES & SUFFIXES	GEL-STEN, INC.		6-10
I	GAME	PRESS & CHECK BINGO GAMES: PREFIXES & SUFFIXES	MILTON BRADLEY/PLAYSKOOL		6-10
I	GUIDE	MERRILL PHONICS SKILL TEXT: DETECTIVE CLUB, LEVEL E	CHARLES E. MERRILL PUBLISHING CO		<5
I	GUIDE	MERRILL PHONICS SKILL TEXT: WHIZ KID, LEVEL F	CHARLES E. MERRILL PUBLISHING CO		<5
I	MULTIM	GAMES 'N' FRAMES: WORD NEWS ROUNDUP	IMPERIAL INTERNATIONAL LEARNING		21-30
I	MULTIM	SELECT-A-SKILL KIT, UNIT 4: ANIMALS	IMPERIAL INTERNATIONAL LEARNING		51-75
I	MULTIM	SELECT-A-SKILL KIT, UNIT 5: FAMOUS PEOPLE	IMPERIAL INTERNATIONAL LEARNING		51-75
I	MULTIM	SELECT-A-SKILL KIT, UNIT 4: ANIMALS	IMPERIAL INTERNATIONAL LEARNING		51-75
I	MULTIM	SELECT-A-SKILL KIT, UNIT 5: FAMOUS PEOPLE	IMPERIAL INTERNATIONAL LEARNING		51-75
I	RECORD	SOUND SKILLS FOR UPPER GRADES	CLASSROOM MATERIALS CO.	3	21-30
I	RECORD	SOUND SKILLS FOR UPPER GRADES, VOLUME 3	CLASSROOM MATERIALS CO.		6-10
I	VISKIT	USING PREFIXES & SUFFIXES	INSTRUCTO/MCGRAW-HILL		11-20
I	WKBOOK	MORE EASY CROSSWORD PUZZLES	ENGLISH LANGUAGE SERVICES		<5
I	WKBOOK	EASY CROSSWORD PUZZLES	ENGLISH LANGUAGE SERVICES		<5
I	WKBOOK	MOTT BASIC LANG. SKILLS: LANG./GRAMMAR SKILLS, BK 1607	ALLIED EDUCATION COUNCIL		<5
I	WKBOOK	MERRILL PHONICS SKILL TEXT: DETETIVE CLUB, LEVEL E	CHARLES E. MERRILL PUBLISHING CO		<5
I	WKBOOK	MERRILL PHONICS SKILL TEXT: WHIZ KID, LEVEL F	CHARLES E. MERRILL PUBLISHING CO		<5
IJ	AUDKIT	DEVELOPMENTAL VOCABULARY	EBSCO CURRICULUM MATERIALS		51-75
IJ	AUDKIT	FORE & AFT	MEDIA MATERIALS, INC.		6-10
IJ	AUDKIT	VERSATILES	MEDIA MATERIALS, INC.		6-10
IJ	AUDKIT	INTERMEDIATE VOCABULARY	HAMPDEN PUBLICATIONS, INC.		101-150
IJ	A/VKIT	WORD BUILDERS	EYE GATE MEDIA		76-100
IJ	DITTO	PRACTICE IN VOCABULARY BUILDING, BOOK C (GRADES 5 - 7)	INSTRUCTOR PUBLICATIONS, INC.		<5
IJ	GAME	TRIAD	CREATIVE TEACHING ASSOCIATES		6-10
IJ	GAME	PURSUIT	CREATIVE TEACHING ASSOCIATES		6-10
IJ	GAME	GAMEBOARD KIT D	READING JOY, INC.		6-10
IJ	GAME	WIDE, WIDE WORLD OF GRAMMAR: BASKETWORD	HARCOURT BRACE JOVANOVICH, INC.		11-20
IJ	GAME	LIME TREE	XEROX EDUCATION PUBLICATIONS		51-75
IJ	MULTIM	SPECTRUM, UNIT 1 (RL 3.5 - 4.4)	IMPERIAL INTERNATIONAL LEARNING		51-75
IJS	ACTCRD	WORD PARADE	LESWING PRESS		6-10
IJS	AUDCRD	PERPLEXING PREFIXES	AUDIOTRONICS CORPORATION		21-30
IJS	AUDCRD	WORD PARTS	AUDIOTRONICS CORPORATION		21-30
IJS	AUDKIT	BASE	ECONOMY COMPANY		101-150
IJS	AUDKIT	HITS, LEVEL 4: COVEN, ONE TIN SOLDIER	MODULEARN, INC.		11-20
IJS	AUDKIT	HITS, LEVEL 4: PAUL SIMON, HOMEWARD BOUND	MODULEARN, INC.		11-20
IJS	AUDKIT	HITS, LEVEL 4: PAUL SIMON, FLOWERS NEVER BEND W/THE RAINFALL	MODULEARN, INC.		11-20
IJS	AUDKIT	HITS, LEVEL 4: PAUL SIMON, I AM A ROCK	MODULEARN, INC.		11-20
IJS	AUDKIT	HITS, LEVEL 4: FOUR TOPS, KEEPER OF THE CASTLE	MODULEARN, INC.		11-20
IJS	AUDKIT	HITS, LEVEL 4: PAUL SIMON, AMERICAN TUNE	MODULEARN, INC.		11-20
IJS	GAME	ON-WORDS	STANWIX HOUSE, INC.		6-10
IJS	MULTIM	KNIGHT INDIVIDUALIZED SPELLING PROGRAM KIT	EDUCATORS PUBLISHING SERVICE		76-100
J	ACTCRD	PREFIXES, ADVANCED 1	BARNELL LOFT, LTD.		6-10
J	ACTCRD	PREFIXES, ADVANCED 2	BARNELL LOFT, LTD.		6-10

LEVEL	FORMAT	TITLE	PUBLISHER	NT	$PRICE

80 - SKILL: PREFIXES

LEVEL	FORMAT	TITLE	PUBLISHER	NT	$PRICE
J	ACTCRD	PREFIXES, ADVANCED 3	BARNELL LOFT, LTD.		6-10
J	AUDKIT	BUILDING WORD POWER	CORONET MULTI MEDIA		101-150
JS	AUDKIT	USING STRUCTURAL ANALYSIS SERIES	MEDIA MATERIALS, INC.		101-150
JS	AUDKIT	LEARNING STRUCTURAL ANALYSIS	HAMPDEN PUBLICATIONS, INC.		101-150
JS	AUDKIT	LEARNING BASIC VOCABULARY	HAMPDEN PUBLICATIONS, INC.		101-150
JS	PUPILB	WORD ANALYSIS	J. WESTON WALCH PUBLISHING		<5
JS	SKLKIT	TARGET ORANGE: VOCABULARY DEVELOPMENT KIT II	ADDISON-WESLEY PUBLISHING CO.		151-200
JS	TEXTBK	READING PERFORMANCE	CAMBRIDGE BOOK CO.		<5
S	AUDKIT	STRUCTURAL ANALYSIS	HAMPDEN PUBLICATIONS, INC.		76-100
S	PUPILB	SYSTEMATIC SPELLING	EDUCATORS PUBLISHING SERVICE		<5
S	SND FS	PREFIXES	MEDIA MATERIALS, INC.		11-20
S	WKBOOK	STRUCTURE OF WORDS	EDUCATORS PUBLISHING SERVICE		<5

81 - SKILL: SUFFIXES

LEVEL	FORMAT	TITLE	PUBLISHER	NT	$PRICE
RP	SND FS	STORIES ABOUT WORDS	CORONET MULTI MEDIA		101-150
P	ACTCRD	ENDINGS/SUFFIXES, B	BARNELL LOFT, LTD.		6-10
P	ACTCRD	ENDINGS/SUFFIXES, C	BARNELL LOFT, LTD.		6-10
P	ACTCRD	SUFFIXES	KENWORTHY EDUCATIONAL SERVICE		<5
P	ACTCRD	TUTORGRAM: PRIMARY SUFFIXES	ENRICHMENT READING CORP OF AMER.		11-20
P	ACTCRD	LANGUAGE ACTIVITY CARDS: SUFFIXES & PREFIXES	WEBER COSTELLO COMPANY		6-10
P	ACTCRD	CHECKLIST OF BASIC SOUNDS	LAKESHORE CURRICULUM MATERIALS		<5
P	ACTCRD	WORD PROBE SKILL CARDS	MILTON BRADLEY/PLAYSKOOL		<5
P	AUDCAS	SOUNDS FOR YOUNG READERS, VOLUME 5	CLASSROOM MATERIALS CO.		6-10
P	AUDKIT	PHONICS: FUN WITH AFFIXES	EYE GATE MEDIA		6-10
P	AUDKIT	KIT 58: BUILDING WORD POWER, LEVEL 3	EDUCATIONAL RESEARCH, INC.		101-150
P	AUDKIT	MINISYSTEMS: SUFFIXES	CORONET MULTI MEDIA		11-20
P	AUDKIT	MINISYSTEMS: ROOTS, PREFIXES, SUFFIXES	CORONET MULTI MEDIA		11-20
P	CHART	SUFFIX PEDRO	IDEAL SCHOOL SUPPLY COMPANY		<5
P	DITTO	NEW PHONICS & WORD ANALYSIS SKILLS: GRADE 2, PART 3	CONTINENTAL PRESS, INC.		<5
P	DITTO	NEW PHONICS & WORD ANALYSIS SKILLS: GRADE 3, PART 2	CONTINENTAL PRESS, INC.		<5
P	DITTO	READING ESSENTIALS: VOCABULARY DEVELOPMENT, GRADE 3, BOOK 2	CONTINENTAL PRESS, INC.		<5
P	DITTO	BASIC READING SKILLS	XEROX EDUCATION PUBLICATIONS		<5
P	DITTO	PHONICS IIB	HAYES SCHOOL PUBLISHING COMPANY		<5
P	DITTO	PHONICS IVA	HAYES SCHOOL PUBLISHING COMPANY		<5
P	DITTO	PHONICS IVB	HAYES SCHOOL PUBLISHING COMPANY		<5
P	FLASH	FLASH CARDS, SET B	MODERN CURRICULUM PRESS		11-20
P	GAME	SPELL POWER	KENWORTHY EDUCATIONAL SERVICE		<5
P	GAME	CHECKMATE: AFFIXES	DM EDUCATIONAL PUBLICATIONS		<5
P	GUIDE	PHONICS IS FUN, BOOK 2	MODERN CURRICULUM PRESS		<5
P	MANIPU	ADVANCED PREFIX & SUFFIX PUZZLES	DEVELOPMENTAL LEARNING MATERIALS		6-10
P	MANIPU	SUFFIX PUZZLES	DEVELOPMENTAL LEARNING MATERIALS		<5
P	MULTIM	READING SKILLS SUPPORT SYSTEM, BOX 3	EDL/MCGRAW-HILL		301-400
P	PUPILB	WOG'S LOG BOOK V	EDUCATORS PUBLISHING SERVICE		<5
P	PUPILB	WOG'S LOG BOOK VI	EDUCATORS PUBLISHING SERVICE		<5
P	PUPILB	WOG'S LOG BOOK VII	EDUCATORS PUBLISHING SERVICE		<5
P	PUPILB	WOG'S LOG BOOK VIII	EDUCATORS PUBLISHING SERVICE		<5
P	RECORD	SOUNDS FOR YOUNG READERS, VOLUME 5	CLASSROOM MATERIALS CO.		6-10
P	SND FS	PREFIXES & SUFFIXES	HERBERT M. ELKINS COMPANY		11-20
P	SP EQT	AUDITORY SKILLS: MORPHOLOGY & CLOSURE	INSTRUCTIONAL INDUSTRIES (G.E.)		101-150
P	WKBOOK	MORE SOUNDS & SYMBOLS, BOOK F	GINN & COMPANY		<5
P	WKBOOK	MCP PHONICS WORKBOOKS: LEVEL A	MODERN CURRICULUM PRESS		<5
P	WKBOOK	MCP PHONICS WORKBOOKS: LEVEL B	MODERN CURRICULUM PRESS		<5
P	WKBOOK	MCP PHONICS WORKBOOKS: LEVEL C	MODERN CURRICULUM PRESS		<5
P	WKBOOK	PHONICS IS FUN, BOOK 2	MODERN CURRICULUM PRESS		<5
P	WKBOOK	NEW PHONICS WORKBOOK, BOOK C	MODERN CURRICULUM PRESS		<5
PI	ACTCRD	SUPER SUFFIXES	KIDS & COMPANY		<5
PI	ACTCRD	LANGUAGE LOLLIPOP	KIDS & COMPANY		<5
PI	AUDKIT	BEGINNING VOCABULARY	EBSCO CURRICULUM MATERIALS		51-75
PI	AUDKIT	BASIC WORD ATTACK SKILLS	EDUCATIONAL RESEARCH, INC.	4	>450
PI	AUDKIT	TOTAL BUILDING WORK POWER (KITS 58 - 61)	EDUCATIONAL RESEARCH, INC.	4	>450
PI	AUDKIT	LET'S FIND SOME ROOT WORDS: SUFFIXES	MEDIA MATERIALS, INC.		6-10
PI	AUDKIT	FUN WITH AFFIXES	MEDIA MATERIALS, INC.		6-10
PI	AUDKIT	BEGINNING STRUCTURAL ANALYSIS	HAMPDEN PUBLICATIONS, INC.		101-150
PI	AUDKIT	INTERMEDIATE STRUCTURAL ANALYSIS	HAMPDEN PUBLICATIONS, INC.		101-150
PI	DITTO	SUFFIXES	FRANK SCHAFFER PUBLICATIONS, INC		<5
PI	DITTO	READING LANTERNS: PLAY BALL!	EDUCATIONAL INSIGHTS, INC.		6-10
PI	DITTO	PRACTICE IN VOCABULARY BUILDING, BOOK A (GRADES 3 - 4)	INSTRUCTOR PUBLICATIONS, INC.		<5
PI	DITTO	DECODING SKILLS 5	ACTIVITY RESOURCES COMPANY, INC.		<5
PI	FILMST	A WORD RECOGNITION SYSTEM	MEDIA MATERIALS, INC.		11-20
PI	FILMST	STRUCTURAL ANALYSIS FILMSTRIP SERIES	MEDIA MATERIALS, INC.	5	76-100
PI	FILMST	SUFFIXES	MEDIA MATERIALS, INC.		11-20
PI	GAME	SUFFIXES	FRANK SCHAFFER PUBLICATIONS, INC		<5
PI	GAME	SUPER STOCK	ALLIED EDUCATION COUNCIL		51-75
PI	GAME	MONSTER HUNT	ALLIED EDUCATION COUNCIL		51-75
PI	GAME	ETA SUFFIX CHANGING CARDS	EDUCATIONAL TEACHING AIDS		11-20
PI	GAME	BASE WORD RUMMY	JUDY COMPANY		6-10
PI	GUIDE	PHONICS IS FUN, BOOK 3	MODERN CURRICULUM PRESS		<5
PI	MANIPU	E-Z PHONIC WORD-BUILDING SLIDE RULE	E-Z GRADER COMPANY		<5

LEVEL	FORMAT	TITLE	PUBLISHER	NT	$PRICE

81 - SKILL: SUFFIXES

LEVEL	FORMAT	TITLE	PUBLISHER	NT $PRICE
PI	MULTIM	NEW GOALS IN LISTENING, GRADES 2-4	TROLL ASSOCIATES	76-100
PI	SKLKIT	TARGET GREEN: VOCABULARY DEVELOPMENT KIT I	ADDISON-WESLEY PUBLISHING CO.	151-200
PI	SND FS	WORD ANALYSIS SKILLS: WORD PARTS I	LEARNING TREE FILMSTRIPS	51-75
PI	SND FS	STRUCTURAL ANALYSIS SERIES	HAMPDEN PUBLICATIONS, INC.	76-100
PI	SND FS	WORKING WITH WORDS	TROLL ASSOCIATES	101-150
PI	SP EQT	DEVELOPING STRUCTURAL ANALYSIS SKILLS, KIT K	BORG-WARNER EDUCATIONAL SYSTEMS	101-150
PI	WKBOOK	SUPER SUFFIXES	CREATIVE TEACHING ASSOCIATES	<5
PI	WKBOOK	PREFIXES, SUFFIXES, SYLLABLES	CREATIVE TEACHING ASSOCIATES	<5
PI	WKBOOK	WORD ENDINGS	FRANK SCHAFFER PUBLICATIONS, INC	<5
PI	WKBOOK	PREFIXES, SUFFIXES, SYLLABLES	FRANK SCHAFFER PUBLICATIONS, INC	<5
PI	WKBOOK	PHONICS IS FUN, BOOK 3	MODERN CURRICULUM PRESS	<5
PI	WKBOOK	SUPER SUFFIXES	ACTIVITY RESOURCES COMPANY, INC.	<5
PIJ	ACTCRD	READ & REASON	FRANK SCHAFFER PUBLICATIONS, INC	<5
PIJ	CL SET	WHAT'S THE MEANING OF THIS?	MAFEX ASSOCIATES, INC.	51-75
PIJ	CL SET	WEBSTER WORD WHEELS	WEBSTER DIVISION/MCGRAW-HILL	31-50
I	ACTCRD	WORD ANALYSIS: SUFFIXES & PREFIXES	INSTRUCTIONAL FAIR	<5
I	ACTCRD	WORD ANALYSIS PAK	INSTRUCTIONAL FAIR	21-30
I	ACTCRD	ENDINGS/SUFFIXES, D	BARNELL LOFT, LTD.	6-10
I	ACTCRD	ENDINGS/SUFFIXES, E	BARNELL LOFT, LTD.	6-10
I	ACTCRD	ENDINGS/SUFFIXES, F	BARNELL LOFT, LTD.	6-10
I	ACTCRD	AFFIXES PACER	DM EDUCATIONAL PUBLICATIONS	<5
I	AUDKIT	EVERYDAY VOCABULARY	EBSCO CURRICULUM MATERIALS	51-75
I	AUDKIT	KIT 9: BASIC WORD ATTACK - STRUCTURAL ANALYSIS, PREFIXES	EDUCATIONAL RESEARCH, INC.	101-150
I	AUDKIT	KIT 59: BUILDING WORD POWER, LEVEL 4	EDUCATIONAL RESEARCH, INC.	101-150
I	AUDKIT	KIT 60: BUILDING WORD POWER, LEVEL 5	EDUCATIONAL RESEARCH, INC.	101-150
I	AUDKIT	KIT 61: BUILDING WORD POWER, LEVEL 16	EDUCATIONAL RESEARCH, INC.	101-150
I	AUDKIT	READING CASSETTES: WORD BUILDING	IDEAL SCHOOL SUPPLY COMPANY	51-75
I	AUDKIT	BLUE-BLOODED SUFFIXES	MEDIA MATERIALS, INC.	6-10
I	AUDKIT	SUFFIXES TO WATCH	MEDIA MATERIALS, INC.	6-10
I	AUDKIT	SUFFIXES -ER -ENT AND FRIENDS	MEDIA MATERIALS, INC.	6-10
I	AUDKIT	SUFFIXES -ABLE -ION AND FRIENDS	MEDIA MATERIALS, INC.	6-10
I	AUDKIT	EXPANDING VOCABULARY	HAMPDEN PUBLICATIONS, INC.	21-30
I	DITTO	READING ESSENTIALS: VOCABULARY DEVELOPMENT, GRADE 3	CONTINENTAL PRESS, INC.	<5
I	DITTO	READING ESSENTIALS: VOCABULARY DEVELOPMENT, GRADE 4	CONTINENTAL PRESS, INC.	<5
I	DITTO	READING ESSENTIALS: VOCABULARY DEVELOPMENT, GRADE 5	CONTINENTAL PRESS, INC.	<5
I	DITTO	READING ESSENTIALS: VOCABULARY DEVELOPMENT, GRADE 6	CONTINENTAL PRESS, INC.	<5
I	DITTO	WORD ANALYSIS: SUFFIXES & PREFIXES	INSTRUCTIONAL FAIR	<5
I	DITTO	WORD ANALYSIS PAK	INSTRUCTIONAL FAIR	21-30
I	DITTO	NEWSPAPER TASKS SWING INTO LANGUAGE ARTS, INTERMEDIATE	ORE PRESS, INC.	<5
I	DITTO	SOUNDS IN WORDS, BOOK 9	GEL-STEN, INC.	<5
I	DITTO	SOUNDS IN WORDS, BOOK 13	GEL-STEN, INC.	<5
I	DITTO	SOUNDS IN WORDS, BOOK 15	GEL-STEN, INC.	<5
I	DITTO	SOUNDS IN WORDS, BOOK 18	GEL-STEN, INC.	<5
I	DITTO	PRACTICE IN VOCABULARY BUILDING, BOOK B (GRADES 4 - 5)	INSTRUCTOR PUBLICATIONS, INC.	<5
I	DITTO	DECODING SKILLS E	ACTIVITY RESOURCES COMPANY, INC.	<5
I	FILMST	PREFIXES & SUFFIXES	EDUCATIONAL PROJECTIONS COMPANY	11-20
I	GAME	WORD COMPUTER	CREATIVE TEACHING ASSOCIATES	<5
I	GAME	SPELLING/LANGUAGE LEARNING GAMES KITS, KIT TWO	RAND MCNALLY & COMPANY	76-100
I	GAME	CHECKMATE: AFFIXES	DM EDUCATIONAL PUBLICATIONS	<5
I	GAME	USING PREFIXES & SUFFIXES	GEL-STEN, INC.	6-10
I	GAME	PRESS & CHECK BINGO GAMES: PREFIXES & SUFFIXES	MILTON BRADLEY/PLAYSKOOL	6-10
I	GUIDE	MERRILL PHONICS SKILL TEXT: DETECTIVE CLUB, LEVEL E	CHARLES E. MERRILL PUBLISHING CO	<5
I	GUIDE	MERRILL PHONICS SKILL TEXT: WHIZ KID, LEVEL F	CHARLES E. MERRILL PUBLISHING CO	<5
I	MULTIM	GAMES 'N' FRAMES: STRENGTHENING SUFFIXES WITH GRIMN & BARRET	IMPERIAL INTERNATIONAL LEARNING	21-30
I	MULTIM	SELECT-A-SKILL KIT, UNIT 5: FAMOUS PEOPLE	IMPERIAL INTERNATIONAL LEARNING	51-75
I	MULTIM	SELECT-A-SKILL KIT, UNIT 5: FAMOUS PEOPLE	IMPERIAL INTERNATIONAL LEARNING	51-75
I	MULTIM	SELECT-A-SKILL KIT, UNIT 8: LEGENDS, TALES & POETRY	IMPERIAL INTERNATIONAL LEARNING	51-75
I	MULTIM	VOCABULARY DEVELOPMENT	MILTON BRADLEY/PLAYSKOOL	76-100
I	VISKIT	USING PREFIXES & SUFFIXES	INSTRUCTO/MCGRAW-HILL	11-20
I	WKBOOK	MORE EASY CROSSWORD PUZZLES	ENGLISH LANGUAGE SERVICES	<5
I	WKBOOK	EASY CROSSWORD PUZZLES	ENGLISH LANGUAGE SERVICES	<5
I	WKBOOK	MOTT BASIC LANG. SKILLS: LANG./GRAMMAR SKILLS, BK 1607	ALLIED EDUCATION COUNCIL	<5
I	WKBOOK	MERRILL PHONICS SKILL TEXT: DETETIVE CLUB, LEVEL E	CHARLES E. MERRILL PUBLISHING CO	<5
I	WKBOOK	MERRILL PHONICS SKILL TEXT: WHIZ KID, LEVEL F	CHARLES E. MERRILL PUBLISHING CO	<5
IJ	AUDKIT	DEVELOPMENTAL VOCABULARY	EBSCO CURRICULUM MATERIALS	51-75
IJ	AUDKIT	WORD SIGNALS	EBSCO CURRICULUM MATERIALS	51-75
IJ	AUDKIT	FORE & AFT	MEDIA MATERIALS, INC.	6-10
IJ	AUDKIT	PUT-ONS	MEDIA MATERIALS, INC.	6-10
IJ	AUDKIT	INTERMEDIATE VOCABULARY	HAMPDEN PUBLICATIONS, INC.	101-150
IJ	A/VKIT	WORD BUILDERS	EYE GATE MEDIA	76-100
IJ	DITTO	PRACTICE IN VOCABULARY BUILDING, BOOK C (GRADES 5 - 7)	INSTRUCTOR PUBLICATIONS, INC.	<5
IJ	GAME	TRIAD	CREATIVE TEACHING ASSOCIATES	6-10
IJ	GAME	GAMEBOARD KIT D	READING JOY, INC.	6-10
IJ	GAME	WIDE, WIDE WORLD OF GRAMMAR: GOAL WORD SOCCER	HARCOURT BRACE JOVANOVICH, INC.	21-30
IJ	GAME	LIME TREE	XEROX EDUCATION PUBLICATIONS	51-75
IJ	MULTIM	SPECTRUM, UNIT 1 (RL 3.5 - 4.4)	IMPERIAL INTERNATIONAL LEARNING	51-75
IJS	ACTCRD	WORD PARADE	LESWING PRESS	6-10
IJS	AUDCRD	SNEAKY SUFFIXES	AUDIOTRONICS CORPORATION	21-30
IJS	AUDCRD	WORD PARTS	AUDIOTRONICS CORPORATION	21-30

LEVEL	FORMAT	TITLE	PUBLISHER	NT	$PRICE

81 - SKILL: SUFFIXES

LEVEL	FORMAT	TITLE	PUBLISHER	NT	$PRICE
IJS	AUDKIT	BASE	ECONOMY COMPANY		101-150
IJS	AUDKIT	HITS, LEVEL 4: COVEN, ONE TIN SOLDIER	MODULEARN, INC.		11-20
IJS	GAME	ON-WORDS	STANWIX HOUSE, INC.		6-10
IJS	MULTIM	KNIGHT INDIVIDUALIZED SPELLING PROGRAM KIT	EDUCATORS PUBLISHING SERVICE		76-100
J	ACTCRD	ENDINGS/SUFFIXES, ADVANCED 1	BARNELL LOFT, LTD.		6-10
J	ACTCRD	ENDINGS/SUFFIXES, ADVANCED 2	BARNELL LOFT, LTD.		6-10
J	ACTCRD	ENDINGS/SUFFIXES, ADVANCED 3	BARNELL LOFT, LTD.		6-10
J	AUDKIT	BUILDING WORD POWER	CORONET MULTI MEDIA		101-150
JS	AUDKIT	USING STRUCTURAL ANALYSIS SERIES	MEDIA MATERIALS, INC.		101-150
JS	AUDKIT	LEARNING STRUCTURAL ANALYSIS	HAMPDEN PUBLICATIONS, INC.		101-150
JS	AUDKIT	LEARNING BASIC VOCABULARY	HAMPDEN PUBLICATIONS, INC.		101-150
JS	PUPILB	WORD ANALYSIS	J. WESTON WALCH PUBLISHING		<5
JS	SKLKIT	TARGET ORANGE: VOCABULARY DEVELOPMENT KIT II	ADDISON-WESLEY PUBLISHING CO.		151-200
JS	TEXTBK	READING PERFORMANCE	CAMBRIDGE BOOK CO.		<5
S	AUDKIT	STRUCTURAL ANALYSIS	HAMPDEN PUBLICATIONS, INC.		76-100
S	PUPILB	SYSTEMATIC SPELLING	EDUCATORS PUBLISHING SERVICE		<5
S	SND FS	SUFFIXES	MEDIA MATERIALS, INC.		11-20
S	WKBOOK	STRUCTURE OF WORDS	EDUCATORS PUBLISHING SERVICE		<5

82 - SKILL: SYLLABICATION

LEVEL	FORMAT	TITLE	PUBLISHER	NT	$PRICE
P	ACTCRD	SYLLABLES	KENWORTHY EDUCATIONAL SERVICE		<5
P	ACTCRD	TUTORGRAM: SYLLABICATION	ENRICHMENT READING CORP OF AMER.		11-20
P	ACTCRD	LANGUAGE ACTIVITY CARDS: SYLLABLES & COMPOUND WORDS	WEBER COSTELLO COMPANY		6-10
P	ACTCRD	WORD PROBE SKILL CARDS	MILTON BRADLEY/PLAYSKOOL		<5
P	AUDCAS	SOUNDS FOR YOUNG READERS, VOLUME 5	CLASSROOM MATERIALS CO.		6-10
P	AUDCAS	LISTENING FOR SOUNDS	MEDIA MARKETING, INC.		51-75
P	AUDCRD	SYLLABLES	AUDIOTRONICS CORPORATION		11-20
P	AUDKIT	PHONICS	EYE GATE MEDIA	10	76-100
P	AUDKIT	PHONICS: SYLLABLE FUN	EYE GATE MEDIA		6-10
P	AUDKIT	SYLLABLE RULES & ACCENT CLUE	EDUCATIONAL MEDIA, INC.		51-75
P	AUDKIT	READING CASSETTES: SYLLABLE RULE & ACCENT CLUE	IDEAL SCHOOL SUPPLY COMPANY		51-75
P	AUDKIT	BE SAFE WTIH SYLLABLES	MEDIA MATERIALS, INC.		6-10
P	DITTO	NEW PHONICS & WORD ANALYSIS SKILLS: GRADE 2, PART 3	CONTINENTAL PRESS, INC.		<5
P	DITTO	NEW PHONICS & WORD ANALYSIS SKILLS: GRADE 3, PART 2	CONTINENTAL PRESS, INC.		<5
P	DITTO	NEW PHONICS & WORD ANALYSIS SKILLS: GRADE 3, PART 3	CONTINENTAL PRESS, INC.		<5
P	DITTO	WORD ATTACK SKILLS: SYLLABICATION & SPELLING PATTERNS, BK.1	EDL/MCGRAW-HILL		6-10
P	DITTO	WORD ATTACK SKILLS: SYLLABICATION & SPELLING PATTERNS, BK.2	EDL/MCGRAW-HILL		6-10
P	DITTO	PHONICS IIIA	HAYES SCHOOL PUBLISHING COMPANY		<5
P	DITTO	PHONICS IIIB	HAYES SCHOOL PUBLISHING COMPANY		<5
P	DITTO	PHONICS IVA	HAYES SCHOOL PUBLISHING COMPANY		<5
P	DITTO	PHONICS IVB	HAYES SCHOOL PUBLISHING COMPANY		<5
P	GAME	SYLLABLE SCORE BOARD	DEVELOPMENTAL LEARNING MATERIALS		6-10
P	MANIPU	PHONICS E-Z LANGUAGE LEARNING SLIDE RULES	E-Z GRADER COMPANY	5	6-10
P	MANIPU	PHONICS E-Z LANGUAGE LEARNING SLIDE RULES, 1ST & 2ND	E-Z GRADER COMPANY		<5
P	MANIPU	SHAPE-UPS: SYLLABICATION, S - U	READING JOY, INC.		<5
P	MULTIM	LEARNING PHONICS	MEDIA MARKETING, INC.		51-75
P	MULTIM	READING SKILLS SUPPORT SYSTEM, BOX 2	EDL/MCGRAW-HILL		301-400
P	MULTIM	READING SKILLS SUPPORT SYSTEM, BOX 3	EDL/MCGRAW-HILL		301-400
P	PUPILB	SUPPORTIVE READING SKILLS: SYLLABICATION, B1-B2	BARNELL LOFT, LTD.		11-20
P	PUPILB	SUPPORTIVE READING SKILLS: SYLLABICATION, C1-C3	BARNELL LOFT, LTD.		11-20
P	RECORD	SOUNDS FOR YOUNG READERS, VOLUME 5	CLASSROOM MATERIALS CO.		6-10
P	SND FS	SYLLABLES	HERBERT M. ELKINS COMPANY		11-20
P	SP EQT	AUDITORY SKILLS: SYNTHESIS	INSTRUCTIONAL INDUSTRIES (G.E.)		51-75
P	WKBOOK	S.T.A.R.T., BOOK 14	EMC CORPORATION		<5
P	WKBOOK	SOUNDS & SYLLABLES, BOOK E	GINN & COMPANY		<5
P	WKBOOK	MORE SOUNDS & SYMBOLS, BOOK F	GINN & COMPANY		<5
P	WKBOOK	WORKING WITH WORDS, BOOK G	GINN & COMPANY		<5
P	WKBOOK	MCP PHONICS WORKBOOKS: LEVEL C	MODERN CURRICULUM PRESS		<5
P	WKBOOK	NEW PHONICS WORKBOOK, BOOK D	MODERN CURRICULUM PRESS		<5
P	WKBOOK	PHONICS WORKBOOK, BOOK D	MODERN CURRICULUM PRESS		<5
P	WKBOOK	SOUNDS WE USE, BOOK 3	HAYES SCHOOL PUBLISHING COMPANY		<5
PI	ACTCRD	ADVANCED PHONICS: MULTI-SYLLABLE WORDS	INSTRUCTIONAL FAIR		<5
PI	ACTCRD	LANGUAGE LOLLIPOP	KIDS & COMPANY		<5
PI	ACTCRD	EGGHEAD JAZZ	LESWING PRESS		11-20
PI	AUDCAS	LETTERS & SYLLABLES, WORKTAPES	ALLYN AND BACON, INC.		101-150
PI	AUDCAS	SYLLABLES & WORDS, WORKTAPES	ALLYN AND BACON, INC.		101-150
PI	AUDKIT	USING PHONICS	EBSCO CURRICULUM MATERIALS		51-75
PI	AUDKIT	LET'S FIND SYLLABLES IN WORDS	MEDIA MATERIALS, INC.		6-10
PI	AUDKIT	SYLLABLE FUN	MEDIA MATERIALS, INC.		6-10
PI	AUDKIT	FUN WITH WORDS	MEDIA MATERIALS, INC.		6-10
PI	AUDKIT	BEGINNING STRUCTURAL ANALYSIS	HAMPDEN PUBLICATIONS, INC.		101-150
PI	AUDKIT	INTERMEDIATE STRUCTURAL ANALYSIS	HAMPDEN PUBLICATIONS, INC.		101-150
PI	CHART	SYLLABLE RULE & ACCENT CLUE	IDEAL SCHOOL SUPPLY COMPANY		11-20
PI	DITTO	ADVANCED PHONICS: MULTI-SYLLABLE WORDS	INSTRUCTIONAL FAIR		<5
PI	DITTO	LEARNING CENTER ACTIVITIES, GRADES 3-4	INSTRUCTIONAL FAIR		<5
PI	DITTO	SPIRIT MASTER WORKBOOKS: SYLLABLE RULE & ACCENT CLUE	IDEAL SCHOOL SUPPLY COMPANY		6-10
PI	DITTO	DECODING SKILLS 5	ACTIVITY RESOURCES COMPANY, INC.		<5
PI	DITTO	LEARNING SYLLABLES	ACTIVITY RESOURCES COMPANY, INC.		<5

LEVEL	FORMAT	TITLE	PUBLISHER	NT	$PRICE

82 - SKILL: SYLLABICATION

LEVEL	FORMAT	TITLE	PUBLISHER	NT	$PRICE
PI	FILMST	A WORD RECOGNITION SYSTEM	MEDIA MATERIALS, INC.		11-20
PI	FILMST	STRUCTURAL ANALYSIS FILMSTRIP SERIES	MEDIA MATERIALS, INC.	5	76-100
PI	FILMST	SYLLABLES	MEDIA MATERIALS, INC.		11-20
PI	GAME	SUPER STOCK	ALLIED EDUCATION COUNCIL		51-75
PI	GAME	MONSTER HUNT	ALLIED EDUCATION COUNCIL		51-75
PI	GAME	SYLLABLE SAFARI	IDEAL SCHOOL SUPPLY COMPANY		6-10
PI	GAME	SYLLABLE SCRAMBLE	IDEAL SCHOOL SUPPLY COMPANY		11-20
PI	GAME	PLUM TREE	XEROX EDUCATION PUBLICATIONS		51-75
PI	GUIDE	PHONICS IS FUN, BOOK 3	MODERN CURRICULUM PRESS		<5
PI	MANIPU	SYLLABLE PUZZLES	INCENTIVES FOR LEARNING, INC.		6-10
PI	MANIPU	PHONICS E-Z LANGUAGE LEARNING SLIDE RULES, 5TH	E-Z GRADER COMPANY		<5
PI	PUPILB	EXPLODE THE CODE, BOOK 4	EDUCATORS PUBLISHING SERVICE		<5
PI	SND FS	WORD ANALYSIS SKILLS: WORD PARTS I	LEARNING TREE FILMSTRIPS		51-75
PI	SND FS	STRUCTURAL ANALYSIS SERIES	HAMPDEN PUBLICATIONS, INC.		76-100
PI	SND FS	WORD BUILDERS	MILLER-BRODY PRODUCTIONS, INC.		31-50
PI	SND FS	WORKING WITH WORDS	TROLL ASSOCIATES		101-150
PI	SP EQT	DEVELOPING STRUCTURAL ANALYSIS SKILLS, KIT K	BORG-WARNER EDUCATIONAL SYSTEMS		101-150
PI	WKBOOK	PREFIXES, SUFFIXES, SYLLABLES	CREATIVE TEACHING ASSOCIATES		<5
PI	WKBOOK	READING ACTIVITIES FOR LEARNING CENTERS	FRANK SCHAFFER PUBLICATIONS, INC		<5
PI	WKBOOK	PREFIXES, SUFFIXES, SYLLABLES	FRANK SCHAFFER PUBLICATIONS, INC		<5
PI	WKBOOK	LETTERS & SYLLABLES	ALLYN AND BACON, INC.		<5
PI	WKBOOK	PRIMARY PHONICS WORKBOOK 5	EDUCATORS PUBLISHING SERVICE		<5
PIJ	WKBOOK	PHONICS IS FUN, BOOK 3	MODERN CURRICULUM PRESS		<5
PIJ	CL SET	SUPPORTIVE READING SKILLS: SYLLABICATION (MULTI COPIES)	BARNELL LOFT, LTD.	7	21-30
I	ACTCRD	WORD ANALYSIS: SYLLABICATION	INSTRUCTIONAL FAIR		<5
I	ACTCRD	WORD ANALYSIS PAK	INSTRUCTIONAL FAIR		21-30
I	AUDKIT	EAR-ING THE ACCENT	MEDIA MATERIALS, INC.		6-10
I	AUDKIT	SYLLABLES, DIVIDE & CONQUER	MEDIA MATERIALS, INC.		6-10
I	AUDKIT	DECIDE WHERE TO DIVIDE	MEDIA MATERIALS, INC.		6-10
I	AUDKIT	MINISYSTEMS: SYLLABICATION	CORONET MULTI MEDIA		11-20
I	DITTO	WORD ANALYSIS: SYLLABICATION	INSTRUCTIONAL FAIR		<5
I	DITTO	WORD ANALYSIS PAK	INSTRUCTIONAL FAIR		21-30
I	DITTO	SOUNDS IN WORDS, BOOK 9	GEL-STEN, INC.		<5
I	DITTO	SOUNDS IN WORDS, BOOK 12	GEL-STEN, INC.		<5
I	DITTO	SOUNDS IN WORDS, BOOK 13	GEL-STEN, INC.		<5
I	DITTO	SOUNDS IN WORDS, BOOK 15	GEL-STEN, INC.		<5
I	DITTO	SOUNDS IN WORDS, BOOK 18	GEL-STEN, INC.		<5
I	DITTO	DECODING SKILLS E	ACTIVITY RESOURCES COMPANY, INC.		<5
I	GAME	NEW PHONICS WE USE LEARNING GAMES KITS, KIT TWO	RAND MCNALLY & COMPANY		76-100
I	GAME	LEMON TREE	XEROX EDUCATION PUBLICATIONS		51-75
I	GAME	WORDFACTS GAMES	MILTON BRADLEY/PLAYSKOOL		21-30
I	GUIDE	MERRILL PHONICS SKILL TEXT: DETECTIVE CLUB, LEVEL E	CHARLES E. MERRILL PUBLISHING CO		<5
I	GUIDE	MERRILL PHONICS SKILL TEXT: WHIZ KID, LEVEL F	CHARLES E. MERRILL PUBLISHING CO		<5
I	MULTIM	GAMES 'N' FRAMES: THE HOUSE OF FORTUNE	IMPERIAL INTERNATIONAL LEARNING		21-30
I	MULTIM	GAMES 'N' FRAMES: SOUL TRIP	IMPERIAL INTERNATIONAL LEARNING		21-30
I	MULTIM	SELECT-A-SKILL KIT, UNIT 4: ANIMALS	IMPERIAL INTERNATIONAL LEARNING		51-75
I	MULTIM	SELECT-A-SKILL KIT, UNIT 4: ANIMALS	IMPERIAL INTERNATIONAL LEARNING		51-75
I	MULTIM	SELECT-A-SKILL KIT, UNIT 8: LEGENDS, TALES & POETRY	IMPERIAL INTERNATIONAL LEARNING		51-75
I	PUPILB	SUPPORTIVE READING SKILLS: SYLLABICATION, D1-D3	BARNELL LOFT, LTD.		11-20
I	PUPILB	SUPPORTIVE READING SKILLS: SYLLABICATION, E1-E3	BARNELL LOFT, LTD.		11-20
I	PUPILB	SUPPORTIVE READING SKILLS: SYLLABICATION, F1-F3	BARNELL LOFT, LTD.		11-20
I	RECORD	SOUND SKILLS FOR UPPER GRADES	CLASSROOM MATERIALS CO.	3	21-30
I	RECORD	SOUND SKILLS FOR UPPER GRADES, VOLUME 3	CLASSROOM MATERIALS CO.		6-10
I	WKBOOK	CLUES TO WORDS	MACMILLAN PUBLISHING CO., INC.		<5
I	WKBOOK	PHONICS FOR THE INTERMEDIATE GRADES (4, 5, 6)	JENN PUBLICATIONS		<5
I	WKBOOK	MERRILL PHONICS SKILL TEXT: DETECTIVE CLUB, LEVEL E	CHARLES E. MERRILL PUBLISHING CO		<5
I	WKBOOK	MERRILL PHONICS SKILL TEXT: WHIZ KID, LEVEL F	CHARLES E. MERRILL PUBLISHING CO		<5
IJ	GAME	GROUP SOUNDING GAME	GARRARD PUBLISHING COMPANY		<5
IJ	GAME	GAMEBOARD KIT D	READING JOY, INC.		6-10
IJ	GAME	LIME TREE	XEROX EDUCATION PUBLICATIONS		51-75
IJ	MULTIM	COMMUNICATION POWER SERIES: BE A WORD DETECTIVE	UNITED LEARNING		51-75
IJ	SKLKIT	WORD CLUES	CHARLES E. MERRILL PUBLISHING CO		76-100
IJ	WKBOOK	BOOK ONE, PART TWO: STRUCTURAL ANALYSIS ACTIVITIES	T.S. DENISON & COMPANY		6-10
J	PUPILB	SUPPORTIVE READING SKILLS: SYLLABICATION, ADV. 1-ADV. 3	BARNELL LOFT, LTD.		11-20
JS	AUDKIT	USING STRUCTURAL ANALYSIS SERIES	MEDIA MATERIALS, INC.		101-150
JS	AUDKIT	LEARNING STRUCTURAL ANALYSIS	HAMPDEN PUBLICATIONS, INC.		101-150
JS	PUPILB	WORD ANALYSIS	J. WESTON WALCH PUBLISHING		<5
JS	WKBOOK	VOCABULARY BUILDING EXERCISES FOR YOUNG ADULTS, BOOK A	DORMAC, INC.		<5
JS	WKBOOK	VOCABULARY BUILDING EXERCISES FOR YOUNG ADULTS, BOOK B	DORMAC, INC.		<5
JS	WKBOOK	VOCABULARY BUILDING EXERCISES FOR YOUNG ADULTS, BOOK C	DORMAC, INC.		<5
S	AUDKIT	STRUCTURAL ANALYSIS	HAMPDEN PUBLICATIONS, INC.		76-100
S	SND FS	SYLLABLES	MEDIA MATERIALS, INC.		11-20

83 - SKILL: VOCABULARY - GENERAL

LEVEL	FORMAT	TITLE	PUBLISHER	NT	$PRICE
RP	ACTCRD	KINDERGARTEN KEYS: LANGUAGE DEVELOPMENT CARDS, GROUP A	ECONOMY COMPANY		76-100
RP	CL SET	LEARNING LANGUAGE SKILLS 1	AEVAC, INC.		51-75
RP	CL SET	LEARNING LANGUAGE SKILLS 2	AEVAC, INC.		51-75
RP	CL SET	STAR BOOKS	ARISTA CORPORATION		51-75

LEVEL	FORMAT	TITLE	PUBLISHER	NT	$PRICE

83 - SKILL: VOCABULARY - GENERAL

LEVEL	FORMAT	TITLE	PUBLISHER	$PRICE
RP	MULTIU	ALPHA TIME WITH LARGE HUGGABLES	ARISTA CORPORATION	>450
RP	MULTIU	ALPHA TIME WITH SMALL HUGGABLES	ARISTA CORPORATION	301-400
RP	MULTIU	READING READINESS: PARTS I, II, III, IV, V, VI	EDUCATIONAL DIMENSIONS CORP.	101-150
RP	MULTIM	WORDS & SOUND SERIES, SET 1	EDL/MCGRAW-HILL	101-150
RP	MULTIM	WORDS & SOUND SERIES, SET 2	EDL/MCGRAW-HILL	101-150
RP	MULTIM	WORDS & SOUND SERIES, SET 3	EDL/MCGRAW-HILL	101-150
RP	MULTIM	WORDS & SOUND SERIES, SET 4	EDL/MCGRAW-HILL	101-150
RP	PICTUR	TR LARGE PICTURE CARDS, SET 1	TEACHING RESOURCES CORPORATION	31-50
RP	PICTUR	TR LARGE PICTURE CARDS, SET 2	TEACHING RESOURCES CORPORATION	31-50
RP	PUPILB	MY EVERYTHING BOOK	EDUCATIONAL PERFORMANCE ASSOC.	<5
RP	SKLKIT	MAKE & TELL: LIVING THINGS KIT	SRA	51-75
RP	SKLKIT	MAKE & TELL: TOWN THINGS KIT	SRA	51-75
RP	SKLKIT	MAKE & TELL: COUNTRY THINGS KIT	SRA	51-75
RP	SKLKIT	MWM PROGRAM FOR DEVELOPING LANGUAGE ABILITIES	EDUCATIONAL PERFORMANCE ASSOC.	201-300
RP	WKBOOK	DELL HOME ACTIVITY: VOCABULARY BOOK 1	DELL PUBLISHING COMPANY, INC.	<5
RP	WKBOOK	MY EVERYTHING PRACTICE BOOK	EDUCATIONAL PERFORMANCE ASSOC.	<5
P	ACTCRD	SOUND FOUNDATION, PROGRAM 2	DEVELOPMENTAL LEARNING MATERIALS	11-20
P	ACTCRD	WORD MATCHING FLIP BOOKS	DEVELOPMENTAL LEARNING MATERIALS	11-20
P	ACTCRD	VOCABULARY BOX, PRIMARY	EDUCATIONAL INSIGHTS, INC.	6-10
P	ACTCRD	VOCABULARY-SKILL DRILLS WITH MOTIVATORS	SVE	21-30
P	AUDCAS	FROM PHONICS TO READING	UNITED LEARNING	31-50
P	AUDCAS	GETTING TO KNOW WORDS	UNITED LEARNING	31-50
P	AUDKIT	SRA LISTENING LANGUAGE LABORATORY: PRIMARY KIT 1A	SRA	301-400
P	AUDKIT	SRA LISTENING LANGUAGE LABORATORY: PRIMARY KIT 1B	SRA	301-400
P	AUDKIT	SRA LISTENING LANGUAGE LABORATORY: PRIMARY KIT 1C	SRA	301-400
P	AUDKIT	KIT 11: READ-ALONG	EDUCATIONAL RESEARCH, INC.	101-150
P	CL SET	LEARNING LANGUAGE SKILLS 3	AEVAC, INC.	51-75
P	CL SET	LEARNING LANGUAGE SKILLS 4	AEVAC, INC.	51-75
P	DITTO	READING ESSENTIALS: VOCABULARY DEVELOPMENT, GRADE 3, BOOK 2	CONTINENTAL PRESS, INC.	<5
P	DITTO	WORDSEARCH VOCABULARY BUILDERS, GRADE 2	INSTRUCTIONAL FAIR	<5
P	DITTO	WORDSEARCH VOCABULARY BUILDERS, GRADE 3	INSTRUCTIONAL FAIR	<5
P	DITTO	WORD RELATIONSHIPS: CUT & PASTE	FRANK SCHAFFER PUBLICATIONS, INC	<5
P	DITTO	CONFUSED WORDS	MILTON BRADLEY/PLAYSKOOL	<5
P	GAME	PHONOGAMES SERIES: THE READINESS STAGE	SRA	101-150
P	GAME	PHONOGAMES SERIES: THE PHONICS EXPLORER	SRA	101-150
P	GAME	PHONOGAMES SERIES: THE PHONICS EXPRESS	SRA	101-150
P	GAME	INSTRUCTIONAL AID PACKS: TACK ON! A	BARNELL LOFT, LTD.	6-10
P	GAME	INSTRUCTIONAL AID PACKS: TACK ON! B	BARNELL LOFT, LTD.	6-10
P	GAME	INSTRUCTIONAL AID PACKS: TACK ON! C	BARNELL LOFT, LTD.	6-10
P	GAME	INSTRUCTIONAL AID PACKS: TACK ON! D	BARNELL LOFT, LTD.	6-10
P	GAME	INSTRUCTIONAL AID PACKS: SWAP! A	BARNELL LOFT, LTD.	6-10
P	GAME	INSTRUCTIONAL AID PACKS: SWAP! B	BARNELL LOFT, LTD.	6-10
P	GAME	INSTRUCTIONAL AID PACKS: SWAP! C	BARNELL LOFT, LTD.	6-10
P	GAME	INSTRUCTIONAL AID PACKS: TURN ABOUT! A	BARNELL LOFT, LTD.	6-10
P	GAME	INSTRUCTIONAL AID PACKS: TURN ABOUT! B	BARNELL LOFT, LTD.	6-10
P	GAME	INSTRUCTIONAL AID PACKS: TURN ABOUT! C	BARNELL LOFT, LTD.	6-10
P	GAME	INSTRUCTIONAL AID PACKS: STRIKE OUT! A	BARNELL LOFT, LTD.	6-10
P	GAME	INSTRUCTIONAL AID PACKS: STRIKE OUT! B	BARNELL LOFT, LTD.	6-10
P	GAME	INSTRUCTIONAL AID PACKS: STRIKE OUT! C	BARNELL LOFT, LTD.	6-10
P	GAME	CONCEPTO-SORT	EDUCATIONAL PERFORMANCE ASSOC.	6-10
P	GAME	BALLOON GAME	JUDY COMPANY	6-10
P	GUIDE	PHONICS IS FUN, BOOK 2	MODERN CURRICULUM PRESS	<5
P	MANIPU	TRANSPORTATION PUZZLE	NIENHUIS MONTESSORI, INC.	31-50
P	MANIPU	MAKE-A-WORD CARDS	DEVELOPMENTAL LEARNING MATERIALS	<5
P	MANIPU	ECONOMO SENTENCE BUILDER	MILTON BRADLEY/PLAYSKOOL	<5
P	MOVIEL	TALK ABOUT IT SERIES	AEVAC, INC.	>450
P	MULTIU	DISTAR ACTIVITY KIT: READING	SRA	101-150
P	MULTIU	ALPHA ONE	ARISTA CORPORATION	>450
P	MULTIU	ALPHA TIME PLUS	ARISTA CORPORATION	151-200
P	MULTIM	PRS: VOCABULARY SEGMENT	ENCYCLOPEDIA BRITANNICA	76-100
P	PUPILB	CAN YOU DO THIS?	DEVELOPMENTAL LEARNING MATERIALS	<5
P	PUPILB	THIS IS THE WAY I GO	DEVELOPMENTAL LEARNING MATERIALS	<5
P	SKLKIT	READING VOCABULARY LABORATORIES C	BFA EDUCATIONAL MEDIA	101-150
P	SKLKIT	LOGOS 1A	IDEAL SCHOOL SUPPLY COMPANY	101-150
P	VISKIT	TASK CARDS: PRIMARY LANGUAGE ARTS	DIVERSIFIED PRODUCTION RESOURCES	6-10
P	VISKIT	VERSA-TILES, LANGUAGE ARTS LAB 1	EDUCATIONAL TEACHING AIDS	51-75
P	WKBOOK	AEVAC PHONICS PROGRAM, BOOK F	AEVAC, INC.	<5
P	WKBOOK	BASIC VOCABULARY WORKSHEETS, BOOK 1	ST. JOHN SCHOOL FOR THE DEAF	<5
P	WKBOOK	BASIC VOCABULARY WORKSHEETS, BOOK 2	ST. JOHN SCHOOL FOR THE DEAF	<5
P	WKBOOK	BASIC VOCABULARY WORKSHEETS, BOOK 3	ST. JOHN SCHOOL FOR THE DEAF	<5
P	WKBOOK	BASIC VOCABULARY WORKSHEETS, BOOK 4	ST. JOHN SCHOOL FOR THE DEAF	<5
P	WKBOOK	WORD MASTERY, BOOK A	SCHOLASTIC BOOK SERVICE	<5
P	WKBOOK	MCP PHONICS WORKBOOKS: LEVEL B	MODERN CURRICULUM PRESS	<5
P	WKBOOK	MCP PHONICS WORKBOOKS: LEVEL C	MODERN CURRICULUM PRESS	<5
P	WKBOOK	PHONICS IS FUN, BOOK 2	MODERN CURRICULUM PRESS	<5
P	WKBOOK	NEW PHONICS WORKBOOK, BOOK B	MODERN CURRICULUM PRESS	<5
P	WKBOOK	NEW PHONICS WORKBOOK, BOOK C	MODERN CURRICULUM PRESS	<5
P	WKBOOK	NEW PHONICS WORKBOOK, BOOK D	MODERN CURRICULUM PRESS	<5
P	WKBOOK	PHONICS WORKBOOK, BOOK D	MODERN CURRICULUM PRESS	<5

LEVEL	FORMAT	TITLE	PUBLISHER	NT	$PRICE

83 - SKILL: VOCABULARY - GENERAL

LEVEL	FORMAT	TITLE	PUBLISHER	NT	$PRICE
PI	ACTCRD	VOCABULARY	FRANK SCHAFFER PUBLICATIONS, INC		<5
PI	ACTCRD	FOCUS ON SKILLS: THE VOCABULARY BOX, PRIMARY	EDUCATIONAL INSIGHTS, INC.		11-20
PI	ACTCRD	WORD POWER PACER	DM EDUCATIONAL PUBLICATIONS		6-10
PI	ACTCRD	STANDARD BASIC WORD POWER PACER	DM EDUCATIONAL PUBLICATIONS		6-10
PI	ACTCRD	WORD POWER SKILL CARDS	MILTON BRADLEY/PLAYSKOOL		<5
PI	AUDKIT	BEGINNING VOCABULARY	EBSCO CURRICULUM MATERIALS		51-75
PI	AUDKIT	USING PHONICS	EBSCO CURRICULUM MATERIALS		51-75
PI	AUDKIT	KIT 32: BUILDING READING COMPREHENSION & VOCABULARY SKILLS	EDUCATIONAL RESEARCH, INC.		101-150
PI	CL SET	AEVAC STARTER 101 (NON-READERS)	AEVAC, INC.	10	11-20
PI	DITTO	FIND-A-WORD	FRANK SCHAFFER PUBLICATIONS, INC		<5
PI	DITTO	SPECIAL KIDS' STUFF, PART IV: WORK STUDY SKILLS (SP. ED.)	INCENTIVE PUBLICATIONS, INC.		6-10
PI	DITTO	READING ACTIVITIES & SKILLS	XEROX EDUCATION PUBLICATIONS		<5
PI	FILMST	I READ & I UNDERSTAND, LEVEL TWO	EDUCATIONAL ACTIVITIES, INC.		31-50
PI	FILMST	I READ & I UNDERSTAND, LEVELS THREE & FOUR	EDUCATIONAL ACTIVITIES, INC.		51-75
PI	GAME	INSTRUCTIONAL AID PACKS - VOCABULARY GAMES	BARNELL LOFT, LTD.	20	101-150
PI	GAME	BASIC VOCABULARY BINGO GAME	ST. JOHN SCHOOL FOR THE DEAF		6-10
PI	GAME	SOUND DOMINO GAME	JUDY COMPANY		6-10
PI	GAME	SPIN-A-WORD	JUDY COMPANY		6-10
PI	GUIDE	PHONICS IS FUN, BOOK 3	MODERN CURRICULUM PRESS		<5
PI	MULTIU	LARC: MODULE W: WORD SKILLS	ARISTA CORPORATION		151-200
PI	MULTIM	TALKING PICTURE DICTIONARY	TROLL ASSOCIATES		151-200
PI	MULTIM	MORE NEW WORDS	TROLL ASSOCIATES		151-200
PI	PUPILB	GILLIGAN MILLIGAN	SRA		<5
PI	PUPILB	MONSTER BOOKS, SERIES I	BOWMAR/NOBLE PUBLISHERS, INC.		101-150
PI	PUPILB	MONSTER BOOKS, SERIES II	BOWMAR/NOBLE PUBLISHERS, INC.		151-200
PI	SKLKIT	READER IN THE KITCHEN	EDUCATIONAL PERFORMANCE ASSOC.		<5
PI	SND FS	INDEPENDENT WORD PERCEPTION	ASSOCIATED EDUCATIONAL MATERIALS		151-200
PI	VISKIT	VERSA-TILES, LANGUAGE ARTS LAB 2	EDUCATIONAL TEACHING AIDS		51-75
PI	VISKIT	READING & LANG. ARTS COMPLETE SET OF 50 JOY ACT. CARDS KITS	INSTRUCTO/MCGRAW-HILL		201-300
PI	WKBOOK	READING ACTIVITIES FOR LEARNING CENTERS	FRANK SCHAFFER PUBLICATIONS, INC		<5
PI	WKBOOK	WORD HUNT	FRANK SCHAFFER PUBLICATIONS, INC		<5
PI	WKBOOK	READING RIDDLES	FRANK SCHAFFER PUBLICATIONS, INC		<5
PI	WKBOOK	AHOY! SAILING TO TREASURES THROUGH WORDS	CONSTRUCTIVE PLAYTHINGS		6-10
PI	WKBOOK	BASIC VOCABULARY WORKSHEETS, BOOK 5	ST. JOHN SCHOOL FOR THE DEAF		<5
PI	WKBOOK	BASIC VOCABULARY WORKSHEETS, BOOK 6	ST. JOHN SCHOOL FOR THE DEAF		<5
PI	WKBOOK	WORD MASTERY, BOOK B	SCHOLASTIC BOOK SERVICE		<5
PI	WKBOOK	PHONICS IS FUN, BOOK 3	MODERN CURRICULUM PRESS		<5
PI	WKBOOK	CHUMPY'S WORD GAMES	XEROX EDUCATION PUBLICATIONS		<5
PIJ	DITTO	VOCABULARY SCAVENGER HUNTS	PAUL S. AMIDON & ASSOC., INC.		11-20
PIJ	MULTIM	SPECTRUM SERIES	IMPERIAL INTERNATIONAL LEARNING	6	301-400
PIJ	SND FS	MORE ROADS TO MEANING	ENCYCLOPEDIA BRITANNICA		101-150
PIJ	WKBOOK	SPECTRUM OF SKILLS: VOCABULARY DEVELOPMENT, LEVEL 1	MACMILLAN PUBLISHING CO., INC.		<5
PIJ	WKBOOK	SPECTRUM OF SKILLS: VOCABULARY DEVELOPMENT, LEVEL 2	MACMILLAN PUBLISHING CO., INC.		<5
PIJ	WKBOOK	SPECTRUM OF SKILLS: VOCABULARY DEVELOPMENT, LEVEL 3	MACMILLAN PUBLISHING CO., INC.		<5
PIJ	WKBOOK	SPECTRUM OF SKILLS: VOCABULARY DEVELOPMENT, LEVEL 4	MACMILLAN PUBLISHING CO., INC.		<5
PIJ	WKBOOK	SPECTRUM OF SKILLS: VOCABULARY DEVELOPMENT, LEVEL 5	MACMILLAN PUBLISHING CO., INC.		<5
PIJ	WKBOOK	SPECTRUM OF SKILLS: VOCABULARY DEVELOPMENT, LEVEL 6	MACMILLAN PUBLISHING CO., INC.		<5
I	ACTCRD	VOCABULARY BOX, INTERMEDIATE	EDUCATIONAL INSIGHTS, INC.		6-10
I	AUDKIT	EVERYDAY VOCABULARY	EBSCO CURRICULUM MATERIALS		51-75
I	AUDKIT	WORDS IN MOTION, KIT A	MACMILLAN PUBLISHING CO., INC.		76-100
I	AUDKIT	WORDS IN MOTION, KIT B	MACMILLAN PUBLISHING CO., INC.		76-100
I	AUDKIT	WORDS IN MOTION, KIT C	MACMILLAN PUBLISHING CO., INC.		76-100
I	DITTO	READING ESSENTIALS: VOCABULARY DEVELOPMENT, GRADE 4	CONTINENTAL PRESS, INC.		<5
I	DITTO	WORDSEARCH VOCABULARY BUILDERS, GRADE 4	INSTRUCTIONAL FAIR		<5
I	DITTO	WORDSEARCH VOCABULARY BUILDERS, GRADE 5	INSTRUCTIONAL FAIR		<5
I	DITTO	WORDSEARCH VOCABULARY BUILDERS, GRADE 6	INSTRUCTIONAL FAIR		<5
I	FILMST	VOCABULARY BUILDING	EDUCATIONAL PROJECTIONS COMPANY		21-30
I	GAME	INSTRUCTIONAL AID PACKS: TACK ON! E	BARNELL LOFT, LTD.		6-10
I	GAME	INSTRUCTIONAL AID PACKS: SWAP! D	BARNELL LOFT, LTD.		6-10
I	GAME	INSTRUCTIONAL AID PACKS: SWAP! E	BARNELL LOFT, LTD.		6-10
I	GAME	INSTRUCTIONAL AID PACKS: TURN ABOUT! D	BARNELL LOFT, LTD.		6-10
I	GAME	INSTRUCTIONAL AID PACKS: TURN ABOUT! E	BARNELL LOFT, LTD.		6-10
I	GAME	INSTRUCTIONAL AID PACKS: STRIKE OUT! D	BARNELL LOFT, LTD.		6-10
I	GAME	INSTRUCTIONAL AID PACKS: STRIKE OUT! E	BARNELL LOFT, LTD.		6-10
I	GAME	WORDFACTS GAMES	MILTON BRADLEY/PLAYSKOOL		21-30
I	GAME	VOCABULARY QUIZMO	MILTON BRADLEY/PLAYSKOOL		<5
I	GUIDE	BETTER READING & SPELLING THROUGH PHONICS	FEARON PITMAN PUBLISHERS, INC.		<5
I	GUIDE	WORDS ARE IMPORTANT: TAN LEVEL 4, KEY	HAMMOND, INC.		<5
I	GUIDE	WORDS ARE IMPORTANT: BLUE LEVEL 5, KEY	HAMMOND, INC.		<5
I	GUIDE	WORDS ARE IMPORTANT: RED LEVEL 6, KEY	HAMMOND, INC.		<5
I	SKLKIT	READING VOCABULARY LABORATORIES D	BFA EDUCATIONAL MEDIA		101-150
I	SKLKIT	READING VOCABULARY LABORATORIES E	BFA EDUCATIONAL MEDIA		101-150
I	SKLKIT	READING VOCABULARY LABORATORIES F	BFA EDUCATIONAL MEDIA		101-150
I	SKLKIT	SPELLING WORD POWER LABORATORY KIT 2A	SRA		151-200
I	SKLKIT	SPELLING WORD POWER LABORATORY KIT 2B	SRA		151-200
I	SKLKIT	SPELLING WORD POWER LABORATORY KIT 2C	SRA		151-200
I	VISKIT	VERSA-TILES, LANGUAGE ARTS LAB 3	EDUCATIONAL TEACHING AIDS		51-75
I	WKBOOK	WORDS ARE IMPORTANT: TAN LEVEL 4	HAMMOND, INC.		<5
I	WKBOOK	WORDS ARE IMPORTANT: BLUE LEVEL 5	HAMMOND, INC.		<5

LEVEL	FORMAT	TITLE	PUBLISHER	NT	$PRICE

83 - SKILL: VOCABULARY - GENERAL

LEVEL	FORMAT	TITLE	PUBLISHER	NT	$PRICE
I	WKBOOK	WORDS ARE IMPORTANT: RED LEVEL 6	HAMMOND, INC.		<5
I	WKBOOK	WORD MASTERY, BOOK C	SCHOLASTIC BOOK SERVICE		<5
IJ	ACTCRD	FOCUS ON SKILLS: THE VOCABULARY BOX, INTERMEDIATE	EDUCATIONAL INSIGHTS, INC.		11-20
IJ	A/VKIT	PROBLEM WORDS MADE EASY	EYE GATE MEDIA		76-100
IJ	A/VKIT	VOCABULARY BUILDERS	EYE GATE MEDIA		51-75
IJ	CL SET	WORDS	CHANNING L. BETE COMPANY, INC.		76-100
IJ	CL SET	BIG ADVENTURE BOX	XEROX EDUCATION PUBLICATIONS		101-150
IJ	FILMST	ENGLISH COMES ALIVE: ADVENTURES IN WORDS	UNITED LEARNING		31-50
IJ	FILMST	ENGLISH COMES ALIVE SERIES	UNITED LEARNING	6	151-200
IJ	PI/PRT	SKILLS IN LANGUAGE, BOOK 1	CAMBRIDGE BOOK CO.		<5
IJ	SKLKIT	READING TO LEARN: FOCUS ON LEISURE TIME	DEVELOPMENTAL LEARNING MATERIALS		51-75
IJ	SKLKIT	+10 VOCABULARY BOOSTER, LEVEL A	WEBSTER DIVISION/MCGRAW-HILL		151-200
IJ	SKLKIT	+10 VOCABULARY BOOSTER, LEVEL B	WEBSTER DIVISION/MCGRAW-HILL		151-200
IJ	SKLKIT	+10 VOCABULARY BOOSTER, LEVEL C	WEBSTER DIVISION/MCGRAW-HILL		151-200
IJ	SKLKIT	+10 VOCABULARY BOOSTER, LEVEL D	WEBSTER DIVISION/MCGRAW-HILL		151-200
IJ	SKLKIT	+10 VOCABULARY BOOSTER, LEVEL E	WEBSTER DIVISION/MCGRAW-HILL		151-200
IJ	WKBOOK	WORDS	CHANNING L. BETE COMPANY, INC.		<5
IJ	WKBOOK	SEQUENTIAL SKILLS DEVELOPMENT ACTIVITIES FOR READING	T.S. DENISON & COMPANY	4	6-10
IJ	WKBOOK	MCP BUILDING WORD POWER, LEVEL B	MODERN CURRICULUM PRESS		<5
IJ	WKBOOK	MCP BUILDING WORD POWER C	MODERN CURRICULUM PRESS		<5
IJ	WKBOOK	MCP BUILDING WORD POWER D	MODERN CURRICULUM PRESS		<5
IJ	WKBOOK	MCP BUILDING WORD POWER E	MODERN CURRICULUM PRESS		<5
IJ	WKBOOK	MCP BUILDING WORD POWER F	MODERN CURRICULUM PRESS		<5
IJS	AUDKIT	HITS SKILLBOOK SERIES, BOOK A (RL 1 - 2)	MODULEARN, INC.		<5
IJS	AUDKIT	HITS SKILLBOOK SERIES, BOOK B (RL 2 - 3)	MODULEARN, INC.		<5
IJS	AUDKIT	HITS SKILLBOOK SERIES, BOOK C (RL 3 - 4)	MODULEARN, INC.		<5
IJS	AUDKIT	HITS SKILLBOOK SERIES, BOOK D (RL 4 - 5)	MODULEARN, INC.		<5
IJS	MULTIU	CORRECTIVE SPELLING THROUGH MORPHOGRAPHS, TEACHER'S BOOK	SRA		31-50
IJS	MULTIM	VOCABULARY SKILLS (R.L. 5.1 - 5.3)	CORONET MULTI MEDIA		151-200
IJS	PUPILB	CORRECTIVE SPELLING THROUGH MORPHOGRAPHS, STUDENT BOOK	SRA		<5
IJS	SKLKIT	VOCABULAB 3 KIT	SRA		101-150
IJS	TEXTBK	101 WAYS TO LEARN VOCABULARY	AMSCO SCHOOL PUBLICATIONS, INC.		<5
J	AUDKIT	SRA LISTENING LANGUAGE LABORATORY: INTERMEDIATE KIT 2A	SRA		301-400
J	AUDKIT	SRA LISTENING LANGUAGE LABORATORY: INTERMEDIATE KIT 2B	SRA		301-400
J	AUDKIT	SRA LISTENING LANGUAGE LABORATORY: INTERMEDIATE KIT 2C	SRA		301-400
J	DITTO	WORDSEARCH VOCABULARY BUILDERS, GRADE 7	INSTRUCTIONAL FAIR		<5
J	DITTO	WORDSEARCH VOCABULARY BUILDERS, GRADE 8	INSTRUCTIONAL FAIR		<5
J	DITTO	ENRICHMENT ROUSERS: VOCABULARY BUILDING	IDEAL SCHOOL SUPPLY COMPANY		6-10
J	GUIDE	WORDS ARE IMPORTANT: GREEN LEVEL 7, KEY	HAMMOND, INC.		<5
J	GUIDE	WORDS ARE IMPORTANT: ORANGE LEVEL 8, KEY	HAMMOND, INC.		<5
J	GUIDE	WORDS ARE IMPORTANT: PURPLE LEVEL 9, KEY	HAMMOND, INC.		<5
J	PUPILB	ACCENT ON READING, READER D	HOLT, RINEHART AND WINSTON, INC.		<5
J	PUPILB	ACCENT ON READING, READER E	HOLT, RINEHART AND WINSTON, INC.		<5
J	SKLKIT	SPELLING WORD POWER LABORATORY KIT	SRA		151-200
J	TEXTBK	INCREASE YOUR VOCABULARY, BOOK 1	CAMBRIDGE BOOK CO.		<5
J	WKBOOK	WORDS ARE IMPORTANT: GREEN LEVEL 7	HAMMOND, INC.		<5
J	WKBOOK	WORDS ARE IMPORTANT: ORANGE LEVEL 8	HAMMOND, INC.		<5
J	WKBOOK	WORDS ARE IMPORTANT: PURPLE LEVEL 9	HAMMOND, INC.		<5
J	WKBOOK	TROUBLESHOOTER II: BOOK 2, VOCABULARY	HOUGHTON MIFFLIN COMPANY		<5
JS	A/VKIT	EXPANDING YOUR VOCABULARY	SVE		101-150
JS	CL SET	PLAN: READING IN THE CONTENT AREAS	WESTINGHOUSE LEARNING CORP.		101-150
JS	DITTO	VOCABULARY BOOSTERS	J. WESTON WALCH PUBLISHING		11-20
JS	DITTO	VOCABULARY BUILDERS	J. WESTON WALCH PUBLISHING		11-20
JS	GAME	VOCABULARY BINGO	J. WESTON WALCH PUBLISHING		6-10
JS	MULTIM	WORDS IN CONTEXT, SET 1	LISTENING LIBRARY, INC.		76-100
JS	MULTIM	WORDS IN CONTEXT, SET 2	LISTENING LIBRARY, INC.		76-100
JS	MULTIM	WORDS IN CONTEXT, SET 3	LISTENING LIBRARY, INC.		76-100
JS	PI/PRT	SKILLS IN LANGUAGE, BOOK 2	CAMBRIDGE BOOK CO.		<5
JS	PUPILB	DEVELOPING READING EFFICIENCY	BURGESS PUBLISHING CO.		6-10
JS	SKLKIT	READING VOCABULARY LABORATORIES G	BFA EDUCATIONAL MEDIA		101-150
JS	VISKIT	VERSA-TILES, LANGUAGE ARTS COMPETENCY KIT	EDUCATIONAL TEACHING AIDS		51-75
JS	WKBOOK	VOCABULARY BUILDING EXERCISES FOR YOUNG ADULTS, BOOK A	DORMAC, INC.		<5
JS	WKBOOK	VOCABULARY BUILDING EXERCISES FOR YOUNG ADULTS, BOOK B	DORMAC, INC.		<5
JS	WKBOOK	VOCABULARY BUILDING EXERCISES FOR YOUNG ADULTS, BOOK C	DORMAC, INC.		<5
S	GUIDE	WORDS ARE IMPORTANT: BROWN LEVEL 10, KEY	HAMMOND, INC.		<5
S	GUIDE	WORDS ARE IMPORTANT: PINK LEVEL 11, KEY	HAMMOND, INC.		<5
S	GUIDE	WORDS ARE IMPORTANT: GRAY LEVEL 12, KEY	HAMMOND, INC.		<5
S	GUIDE	VOCABULARY	NATIONAL LEARNING CORPORATION		6-10
S	PUPILB	BARRON'S DEV. SKILLS FOR H.S. EQUIV. EXAM (GED) IN GRAMMAR	BARRON'S EDUCATIONAL SERIES, INC.		<5
S	PUPILB	PERSONALIZING READING EFFICIENCY	BURGESS PUBLISHING CO.		6-10
S	TEXTBK	INCREASE YOUR VOCABULARY, BOOK 2	CAMBRIDGE BOOK CO.		<5
S	WKBOOK	WORDS ARE IMPORTANT: BROWN LEVEL 10	HAMMOND, INC.		<5
S	WKBOOK	WORDS ARE IMPORTANT: PINK LEVEL 11	HAMMOND, INC.		<5
S	WKBOOK	WORDS ARE IMPORTANT: GRAY LEVEL 12	HAMMOND, INC.		<5

84 - SKILL: SIGHT VOCABULARY

LEVEL	FORMAT	TITLE	PUBLISHER	NT	$PRICE
R	DITTO	SOUND, WRITE, READ, SPELL	HAYES SCHOOL PUBLISHING COMPANY		<5
R	PUPILB	LADYBIRD BOOK: 1A, PLAY WITH US	IDEAL SCHOOL SUPPLY COMPANY		<5

LEVEL	FORMAT	TITLE	PUBLISHER	NT	$PRICE

84 - SKILL: SIGHT VOCABULARY

LEVEL	FORMAT	TITLE	PUBLISHER	NT	$PRICE
R	PUPILB	LADYBIRD BOOK: 2A, WE HAVE FUN	IDEAL SCHOOL SUPPLY COMPANY		<5
R	PUPILB	LADYBIRD BOOK: 11B, LOOK AT THIS	IDEAL SCHOOL SUPPLY COMPANY		<5
R	PUPILB	LADYBIRD BOOK: 2B, HAVE A GO	IDEAL SCHOOL SUPPLY COMPANY		<5
R	PUPILB	LADYBIRD BOOK: 1C, READ & WRITE	IDEAL SCHOOL SUPPLY COMPANY		<5
R	PUPILB	LADYBIRD BOOK: 2C, I LIKE TO READ	IDEAL SCHOOL SUPPLY COMPANY		<5
R	WKBOOK	LADYBIRD: WORKBOOK 1	IDEAL SCHOOL SUPPLY COMPANY		<5
R	WKBOOK	LADYBIRD: WORKBOOK 2	IDEAL SCHOOL SUPPLY COMPANY		<5
RP	ACTCRD	TUTORGRAM: BASIC WORD RECOGNITION	ENRICHMENT READING CORP OF AMER.		11-20
RP	ACTCRD	TUTORGRAM: COMMON TERMS	ENRICHMENT READING CORP OF AMER.		11-20
RP	ACTCRD	TUTORGRAM: MORE BASIC WORDS	ENRICHMENT READING CORP OF AMER.		11-20
RP	ACTCRD	PICTURE WORD CARDS	GARRARD PUBLISHING COMPANY		<5
RP	ACTCRD	SIGHT WORD PACER	DM EDUCATIONAL PUBLICATIONS		<5
RP	AUDKIT	EARLY PRIMARY SKILLS SERIES	MEDIA MATERIALS, INC.	7	51-75
RP	DITTO	NUMBER & COLOR BOOK	CHILDREN'S LEARNING CENTER, INC.		<5
RP	DITTO	LEARN THE COLORS	CHILDREN'S LEARNING CENTER, INC.		<5
RP	DITTO	SIGHT WORD RECOGNITION	CHILDREN'S LEARNING CENTER, INC.		<5
RP	FILMST	READING READINESS	ENCYCLOPEDIA BRITANNICA		76-100
RP	FILMST	BEGINNING TO LEARN: I CAN READ SIGNS	URBAN MEDIA MATERIALS, INC.		31-50
RP	FILMST	BEGINNING TO LEARN: MORE SIGNS TO READ	URBAN MEDIA MATERIALS, INC.		31-50
RP	GAME	PHONIC RUMMY CARD GAMES, READINESS	KENWORTHY EDUCATIONAL SERVICE		<5
RP	PUPILB	I CAN READ	BEHAVIORAL RESEARCH LABORATORIES	8	51-75
RP	PUPILB	I CAN READ, BOOK 1	BEHAVIORAL RESEARCH LABORATORIES		<5
RP	PUPILB	I CAN READ, BOOK 2	BEHAVIORAL RESEARCH LABORATORIES		<5
RP	PUPILB	I CAN READ, BOOK 3	BEHAVIORAL RESEARCH LABORATORIES		<5
RP	PUPILB	I CAN READ, BOOK 4	BEHAVIORAL RESEARCH LABORATORIES		<5
RP	PUPILB	I CAN READ, BOOK 5	BEHAVIORAL RESEARCH LABORATORIES		<5
RP	PUPILB	I CAN READ, BOOK 6	BEHAVIORAL RESEARCH LABORATORIES		<5
RP	PUPILB	I CAN READ, BOOK 7	BEHAVIORAL RESEARCH LABORATORIES		<5
RP	PUPILB	I CAN READ, BOOK 8	BEHAVIORAL RESEARCH LABORATORIES		<5
RP	PUPILB	LADYBIRD: PICTURE DICTIONARY 1	IDEAL SCHOOL SUPPLY COMPANY		<5
RP	PUPILB	FUN WITH WORDS	WESTERN PUBLISHING EDUC. SERVICE		6-10
RP	PUPILB	MY FIRST BOOK OF WORDS	WALKER EDUCATIONAL BOOK CORP.		<5
RP	SKLKIT	AIMS: VOWELS KIT	CONTINENTAL PRESS, INC.		51-75
RP	SKLKIT	SWEET PICKLES READING READINESS PROGRAM	BFA EDUCATIONAL MEDIA		101-150
RP	VISKIT	WORDS TO GROW ON	IDEAL SCHOOL SUPPLY COMPANY		31-50
RP	VISKIT	ALPHABET SERIES	WALKER EDUCATIONAL BOOK CORP.		31-50
RP	WKBOOK	ADVENTURES IN READING	JENN PUBLICATIONS		<5
RP	WKBOOK	PRIMARY PHONICS WORKBOOK 1	EDUCATORS PUBLISHING SERVICE		<5
RP	WKBOOK	FUN WITH WORDS & PICTURES	HAYES SCHOOL PUBLISHING COMPANY		<5
RPI	WKBOOK	LADYBIRD: WORKBOOKS	IDEAL SCHOOL SUPPLY COMPANY	6	6-10
P	ACTCRD	LINGUISTIC DRILL CARDS	KENWORTHY EDUCATIONAL SERVICE		<5
P	ACTCRD	SENTENCES SWING	ORE PRESS, INC.		<5
P	ACTCRD	ILLUSTRATED SIGHT WORDS	IDEAL SCHOOL SUPPLY COMPANY		<5
P	ACTCRD	BASIC SKILLS KIT- SIGHT READING K	EDUCATIONAL PERFORMANCE ASSOC.		31-50
P	ACTCRD	BASIC SKILLS KIT- SIGHT READING L	EDUCATIONAL PERFORMANCE ASSOC.		31-50
P	ACTCRD	SIGHT WORD LAB	DEVELOPMENTAL LEARNING MATERIALS		21-30
P	ACTCRD	WORD COVER	HOUGHTON MIFFLIN COMPANY		<5
P	ACTCRD	VEGETABLES & FRUITS POSTER CARDS	MILTON BRADLEY/PLAYSKOOL		6-10
P	AUDCAS	SIMPLE SIGHT VOCABULARY	EDUCATIONAL TEACHING AIDS		21-30
P	AUDCAS	SIGHT WORD FUN	UNITED LEARNING		31-50
P	AUDCAS	LEARNING SIGHT WORDS	UNITED LEARNING		31-50
P	AUDCRD	BASIC VOCABULARY BUILDING I	AUDIOTRONICS CORPORATION		21-30
P	AUDCRD	BASIC VOCABULARY BUILDING II	AUDIOTRONICS CORPORATION		21-30
P	AUDCRD	SIGHT WORDS FOR BEGINNING READERS	AUDIOTRONICS CORPORATION		21-30
P	AUDKIT	EARLY PRIMARY LANG. ARTS: SIGHT WORDS WITH SOUND & FUN	EYE GATE MEDIA		6-10
P	AUDKIT	KIT 11: READ-ALONG	EDUCATIONAL RESEARCH, INC.		101-150
P	AUDKIT	KIT 12: SIGHT WORDS	EDUCATIONAL RESEARCH, INC.		101-150
P	AUDKIT	SIGHT & SOUND PHONICS	WEBER COSTELLO COMPANY		21-30
P	AUDKIT	ICE CREAM COLOR-CONES	MEDIA MATERIALS, INC.		6-10
P	AUDKIT	WINKY'S WEEK	MEDIA MATERIALS, INC.		6-10
P	AUDKIT	WINKY'S TWELVE WISHES	MEDIA MATERIALS, INC.		6-10
P	AUDKIT	SIGHT WORDS WITH SOUND AND FUN	MEDIA MATERIALS, INC.		6-10
P	AUDKIT	FRIENDLY SIGHT WORDS	MEDIA MATERIALS, INC.		6-10
P	AUDKIT	TRICKY SIGHT WORDS	MEDIA MATERIALS, INC.		6-10
P	AUDKIT	SIGHT WORD FUN	HAMPDEN PUBLICATIONS, INC.		21-30
P	A/VKIT	SIGHT-WORDS, GRADE TWO	MEDIA MARKETING, INC.		51-75
P	CL SET	PICTO-CABULARY, BASIC WORD SET A	BARNELL LOFT, LTD.		76-100
P	DITTO	READ, THINK, COLOR	FRANK SCHAFFER PUBLICATIONS, INC		<5
P	DITTO	WORD RECOGNITION	INSTRUCTOR PUBLICATIONS, INC.		<5
P	DITTO	VOCABULARY, BOOK A (GRADE 2)	INSTRUCTOR PUBLICATIONS, INC.		<5
P	DITTO	VOCABULARY, BOOK B (GRADE 3)	INSTRUCTOR PUBLICATIONS, INC.		<5
P	DITTO	COLOR	EDUCATORS PUBLISHING SERVICE		6-10
P	DITTO	EARLY WORDS	MILTON BRADLEY/PLAYSKOOL		<5
P	FLASH	POPPER WORDS, SET 1	GARRARD PUBLISHING COMPANY		<5
P	FLASH	POPPER WORDS, SET 2	GARRARD PUBLISHING COMPANY		<5
P	FLASH	PICTURE FLASH WORDS FOR BEGINNERS	MILTON BRADLEY/PLAYSKOOL		<5
P	GAME	BASIC SIGHT WORDS	FRANK SCHAFFER PUBLICATIONS, INC		<5
P	GAME	BASIC WORD LOTTO	CONSTRUCTIVE PLAYTHINGS		6-10
P	GAME	PHONIC RUMMY CARD GAMES, PRIMARY	KENWORTHY EDUCATIONAL SERVICE		<5

LEVEL	FORMAT	TITLE	PUBLISHER	NT	$PRICE

---

84 - SKILL: SIGHT VOCABULARY

LEVEL	FORMAT	TITLE	PUBLISHER	NT	$PRICE
P	GAME	GROUP WORD TEACHING GAME	GARRARD PUBLISHING COMPANY		<5
P	GAME	GROUP-SIZE POPPER WORDS, SET 1	GARRARD PUBLISHING COMPANY		<5
P	GAME	GROUP-SIZE POPPER WORDS, SET 2	GARRARD PUBLISHING COMPANY		<5
P	GAME	START YOUR ENGINES	IDEAL SCHOOL SUPPLY COMPANY		6-10
P	GAME	VOWEL BEES	GOOD APPLE, INC.		6-10
P	GAME	SIGHT-WORDS, GRADE ONE	MEDIA MARKETING, INC.		51-75
P	GAME	SIGHT WORD SNAP 1	LAKESHORE CURRICULUM MATERIALS		6-10
P	GAME	SIGHT WORD SNAP 2	LAKESHORE CURRICULUM MATERIALS		6-10
P	GAME	SIGHT WORD MATCH, ETTES	JUDY COMPANY		11-20
P	GAME	SPLICE	STANWIX HOUSE, INC.		6-10
P	GAME	GET SET: GAMES FOR BEGINNING READERS	HOUGHTON MIFFLIN COMPANY	8	101-150
P	GAME	GET SET: PICTURE WORDS	HOUGHTON MIFFLIN COMPANY		11-20
P	GAME	GET SET: SENTENCE TRAIN	HOUGHTON MIFFLIN COMPANY		11-20
P	GAME	EDUCATIONAL PASSWORD	MILTON BRADLEY/PLAYSKOOL		<5
P	MANIPU	PHONICS E-Z LANGUAGE LEARNING SLIDE RULES	E-Z GRADER COMPANY	5	6-10
P	MANIPU	PHONICS E-Z LANGUAGE LEARNING SLIDE RULES, WORD-BUILDING	E-Z GRADER COMPANY		<5
P	MANIPU	ETA BASIC WOOD LOTTO	EDUCATIONAL TEACHING AIDS		21-30
P	MANIPU	ETA APPROACH PICTURE & WORD-BUILDING CARDS	EDUCATIONAL TEACHING AIDS		31-50
P	MANIPU	ETA EARLY WORD PICTURE & WORD MATCHING CARDS	EDUCATIONAL TEACHING AIDS		21-30
P	MANIPU	WORD PICTURE DOMINOES, SIGHT WORDS	DEVELOPMENTAL LEARNING MATERIALS		<5
P	MANIPU	SIGHT READING: NOUNS	AERO PUBLISHERS, INC.		6-10
P	MANIPU	SIGHT READING: VERBS	AERO PUBLISHERS, INC.		6-10
P	MANIPU	SIGHT READING: ADJECTIVES	AERO PUBLISHERS, INC.		6-10
P	MANIPU	SIGHT READING: ADVERBS	AERO PUBLISHERS, INC.		6-10
P	MULTIU	EPIC: EMPHASIZING PHONICS IN CONTEXT	MCCORMICK-MATHERS PUBLISHING CO.		151-200
P	MULTIM	DEVELOPING READING SKILLS, PART I: WORD RECOGNITION	EDUCATIONAL ENRICHMENT MATERIALS		101-150
P	PUPILB	LADYBIRD BOOK: 3A, THINGS WE LIKE	IDEAL SCHOOL SUPPLY COMPANY		<5
P	PUPILB	LADYBIRD BOOK: 4A, THINGS WE DO	IDEAL SCHOOL SUPPLY COMPANY		<5
P	PUPILB	LADYBIRD BOOK: 5A, WHERE WE GO	IDEAL SCHOOL SUPPLY COMPANY		<5
P	PUPILB	LADYBIRD BOOK: 6A, OUR FRIENDS	IDEAL SCHOOL SUPPLY COMPANY		<5
P	PUPILB	LADYBIRD BOOK: 7A, HAPPY HOLIDAY	IDEAL SCHOOL SUPPLY COMPANY		<5
P	PUPILB	LADYBIRD BOOK: 8A, SUNNY DAYS	IDEAL SCHOOL SUPPLY COMPANY		<5
P	PUPILB	LADYBIRD BOOK: 9A, GAMES WE LIKE	IDEAL SCHOOL SUPPLY COMPANY		<5
P	PUPILB	LADYBIRD BOOK: 10A, ADVENTURES ON ISLAND	IDEAL SCHOOL SUPPLY COMPANY		<5
P	PUPILB	LADYBIRD BOOK: 3B, BOYS & GIRLS	IDEAL SCHOOL SUPPLY COMPANY		<5
P	PUPILB	LADYBIRD BOOK: 4B, FUN AT THE FARM	IDEAL SCHOOL SUPPLY COMPANY		<5
P	PUPILB	LADYBIRD BOOK: 5B, OUT IN THE SUN	IDEAL SCHOOL SUPPLY COMPANY		<5
P	PUPILB	LADYBIRD BOOK: 6B, WE LIKE TO HELP	IDEAL SCHOOL SUPPLY COMPANY		<5
P	PUPILB	LADYBIRD BOOK: 7B, FUN & GAMES	IDEAL SCHOOL SUPPLY COMPANY		<5
P	PUPILB	LADYBIRD BOOK: 8B, THE BIG HOUSE	IDEAL SCHOOL SUPPLY COMPANY		<5
P	PUPILB	LADYBIRD BOOK: 9B, JUMP FROM THE SKY	IDEAL SCHOOL SUPPLY COMPANY		<5
P	PUPILB	LADYBIRD BOOK: 10B, ADVENTURE AT CASTLE	IDEAL SCHOOL SUPPLY COMPANY		<5
P	PUPILB	LADYBIRD BOOK: 9C, ENJOYING READING	IDEAL SCHOOL SUPPLY COMPANY		<5
P	PUPILB	LADYBIRD BOOK: 10C, LEARNING IS FUN	IDEAL SCHOOL SUPPLY COMPANY		<5
P	RECORD	BUILDING VERBAL POWER, VOLUME 5	CLASSROOM MATERIALS CO.		6-10
P	SND FS	WORDS TO WORK WITH I	LEARNING TREE FILMSTRIPS		51-75
P	SND FS	WORDS TO WORK WITH II	LEARNING TREE FILMSTRIPS		51-75
P	SND FS	WORDS TO WORK WITH III	LEARNING TREE FILMSTRIPS		51-75
P	SP EQT	FUNCTIONAL WORD RECOGNITION (SP. ED.)	MAST DEVELOPMENT COMPANY		301-400
P	VISKIT	BASIC VOCABULARY PROGRAM, STAGE 2	EDUCATIONAL TEACHING AIDS		11-20
P	VISKIT	COLOR CHARTS	INSTRUCTOR PUBLICATIONS, INC.		6-10
P	WKBOOK	FROM WORDS TO SENTENCES	CREATIVE TEACHING ASSOCIATES		<5
P	WKBOOK	READ, THINK, COLOR	FRANK SCHAFFER PUBLICATIONS, INC		<5
P	WKBOOK	MORE READ, THINK, COLOR	FRANK SCHAFFER PUBLICATIONS, INC		<5
P	WKBOOK	LADYBIRD: WORKBOOK 3	IDEAL SCHOOL SUPPLY COMPANY		<5
P	WKBOOK	LADYBIRD: WORKBOOK 4	IDEAL SCHOOL SUPPLY COMPANY		<5
P	WKBOOK	LADYBIRD: WORKBOOK 5	IDEAL SCHOOL SUPPLY COMPANY		<5
P	WKBOOK	LADYBIRD: WORKBOOK 6	IDEAL SCHOOL SUPPLY COMPANY		<5
P	WKBOOK	COLOR WORDS	JENN PUBLICATIONS		<5
P	WKBOOK	PRIMARY PHONICS WORKBOOK 3	EDUCATORS PUBLISHING SERVICE		<5
P	WKBOOK	FUN WITH WORDS, GRADE 1	HAYES SCHOOL PUBLISHING COMPANY		<5
P	WKBOOK	FUN WITH WORDS, GRADE 2	HAYES SCHOOL PUBLISHING COMPANY		<5
P	WKBOOK	MORE FUN WITH WORDS, GRADE 3	HAYES SCHOOL PUBLISHING COMPANY		<5
PI	ACTCRD	READING FUN FACTORY	KIDS & COMPANY		<5
PI	ACTCRD	TUTORGRAM: WORD COMPLETION I	ENRICHMENT READING CORP OF AMER.		11-20
PI	ACTCRD	TUTORGRAM: WORD COMPLETION II	ENRICHMENT READING CORP OF AMER.		11-20
PI	ACTCRD	LEARNING CENTER PAK (GRADES 2 - 4)	WISE OWL PUBLICATIONS		31-50
PI	AUDKIT	PRIMARY VOCABULARY	HAMPDEN PUBLICATIONS, INC.		101-150
PI	AUDKIT	BLENDS & SIGHT WORDS AUDIO LESSONS	SVE		101-150
PI	A/VKIT	BLENDS & SIGHT WORDS, GROUP 1	SVE		76-100
PI	A/VKIT	BLENDS & SIGHT WORDS, GROUP 2	SVE		76-100
PI	CL SET	SOUNDER CLASSROOM SET	EDMARK ASSOCIATES		301-400
PI	CL SET	ESSENTIAL SIGHT WORDS PROGRAM, LEVEL I	TEACHING RESOURCES CORPORATION		76-100
PI	DITTO	LEARNING CENTER ACTIVITIES, GRADES 3-4	INSTRUCTIONAL FAIR		<5
PI	DITTO	VOCABULARY MASTERY	INCENTIVE PUBLICATIONS, INC.		<5
PI	DITTO	VOCABULARY, INTERMEDIATE	MILTON BRADLEY/PLAYSKOOL		<5
PI	GAME	77 GAMES FOR READING GROUPS	FEARON PITMAN PUBLISHERS, INC.		<5
PI	GAME	READING GAMES THAT TEACH	FERN TRIPP		<5
PI	GAME	SOC-O	FERN TRIPP		<5

LEVEL	FORMAT	TITLE	PUBLISHER	NT	$PRICE

84 – SKILL: SIGHT VOCABULARY

LEVEL	FORMAT	TITLE	PUBLISHER	NT	$PRICE
PI	GAME	BASIC WORDS SNAP GAME	EDUCATIONAL TEACHING AIDS		11-20
PI	GAME	SPELLO	IDEAL SCHOOL SUPPLY COMPANY		11-20
PI	GAME	JUNIOR WORBAGE	IDEAL SCHOOL SUPPLY COMPANY		6-10
PI	GAME	SIGN CARD GAMES (SP. ED.)	ST. JOHN SCHOOL FOR THE DEAF		6-10
PI	GAME	WORD RECOGNITION	PAUL S. AMIDON & ASSOC., INC.		<5
PI	GUIDE	VOCABULARY MAGIC	INCENTIVE PUBLICATIONS, INC.		<5
PI	MANIPU	POPEYE'S SPECIAL LANGUAGE BUILDER: BALLOON PUZZLES (SP.ED.)	KING FEATURES		11-20
PI	MANIPU	PHONICS E-Z LANGUAGE LEARNING SLIDE RULES, 3RD & 4TH	E-Z GRADER COMPANY		<5
PI	MANIPU	AERO SIGHT READING LAB	AERO PUBLISHERS, INC.		76-100
PI	PUPILB	LADYBIRD BOOK: 11A, MYSTERY ON ISLAND	IDEAL SCHOOL SUPPLY COMPANY		<5
PI	PUPILB	LADYBIRD BOOK: 12A, HOLIDAY CAMP MYSTERY	IDEAL SCHOOL SUPPLY COMPANY		<5
PI	PUPILB	LADYBIRD BOOK: 11B, THE CARNIVAL	IDEAL SCHOOL SUPPLY COMPANY		<5
PI	PUPILB	LADYBIRD BOOK: 12B, MOUNTAIN ADVENTURE	IDEAL SCHOOL SUPPLY COMPANY		<5
PI	PUPILB	LADYBIRD BOOK: 11C, BOOKS ARE EXCITING	IDEAL SCHOOL SUPPLY COMPANY		<5
PI	PUPILB	LADYBIRD BOOK: 12C, OPEN DOOR TO READING	IDEAL SCHOOL SUPPLY COMPANY		<5
PI	PUPILB	LADYBIRD: DICTIONARY 2	IDEAL SCHOOL SUPPLY COMPANY		<5
PI	REFBK	SPECIAL NEEDS: SPECIAL ANSWERS	BOOK-LAB, INC.		11-20
PI	SKLKIT	EDMARK READING PROGRAM (FOR NONREADERS)	EDMARK ASSOCIATES		301-400
PI	SND FS	WORDS WE NEED	UNITED LEARNING		51-75
PI	TEXTBK	WORDS, FROM PRINT TO MEANING	ADDISON-WESLEY PUBLISHING CO.		6-10
PI	TUTORL	SOUNDER RESOURCE SET	EDMARK ASSOCIATES		51-75
PI	VISKIT	BASIC VOCABULARY PROGRAM, STAGE 3	EDUCATIONAL TEACHING AIDS		11-20
PI	WKBOOK	WORDS FOR WRITING	CHILD FOCUS COMPANY		6-10
PI	WKBOOK	PRIMARY PHONICS WORKBOOK 4	EDUCATORS PUBLISHING SERVICE		<5
PIJ	DITTO	VOCABULARY SCAVENGER HUNTS	PAUL S. AMIDON & ASSOC., INC.		11-20
PIJ	FLASH	BASIC VOCABULARY STUDY CARDS, UNIT I	DORMAC, INC.		31-50
PIJ	FLASH	BASIC VOCABULARY STUDY CARDS, UNIT II	DORMAC, INC.		21-30
PIJ	GAME	WORD CHALLENGE	IDEAL SCHOOL SUPPLY COMPANY		6-10
PIJS	GUIDE	3,000 INSTANT WORDS	JAMESTOWN PUBLICATIONS, INC.		<5
I	AUDCAS	SIMPLE SIGHT VOCABULARY	WEBER COSTELLO COMPANY		21-30
I	AUDKIT	A WORM CAN WIGGLE ANYWHERE	MEDIA MATERIALS, INC.		6-10
I	AUDKIT	IF THE SHOE FITS	MEDIA MATERIALS, INC.		6-10
I	AUDKIT	WORD RECOGNITION ACTIVITIES	MEDIA MATERIALS, INC.		6-10
I	CL SET	WORDS AROUND THE HOUSE	BARNELL LOFT, LTD.		31-50
I	CL SET	WORDS AROUND THE NEIGHBORHOOD	BARNELL LOFT, LTD.		31-50
I	CL SET	WORDS TO EAT	BARNELL LOFT, LTD.		31-50
I	CL SET	WORDS TO WEAR	BARNELL LOFT, LTD.		31-50
I	CL SET	WORDS TO MEET	BARNELL LOFT, LTD.		31-50
I	DITTO	READING ESSENTIALS: VOCABULARY DEVELOPMENT, GRADE 6	CONTINENTAL PRESS, INC.		<5
I	DITTO	VOCABULARY, BOOK C (GRADE 4)	INSTRUCTOR PUBLICATIONS, INC.		<5
I	GAME	PHONIC RUMMY CARD GAMES, INTERMEDIATE	KENWORTHY EDUCATIONAL SERVICE		<5
I	GUIDE	BETTER READING & SPELLING THROUGH PHONICS	FEARON PITMAN PUBLISHERS, INC.		<5
I	MULTIM	VOCABULARY DEVELOPMENT	MILTON BRADLEY/PLAYSKOOL		76-100
I	RECORD	BUILDING VERBAL POWER IN THE UPPER GRADES, VOLUME 5	CLASSROOM MATERIALS CO.		6-10
I	VISKIT	BASIC VOCABULARY PROGRAM, STAGE 4	EDUCATIONAL TEACHING AIDS		11-20
I	VISKIT	BASIC VOCABULARY PROGRAM, STAGE 5	EDUCATIONAL TEACHING AIDS		11-20
I	VISKIT	BASIC VOCABULARY PROGRAM, STAGE 6	EDUCATIONAL TEACHING AIDS		11-20
I	VISKIT	BASIC VOCABULARY PROGRAM, STAGE 7	EDUCATIONAL TEACHING AIDS		11-20
IJ	AUDCRD	DESCRIPTIVE WORDS	AUDIOTRONICS CORPORATION		11-20
IJ	A/VKIT	VOCABULARY DEVELOPMENT: WORDS, WORDS, WORDS	TROLL ASSOCIATES		101-150
IJ	CL SET	PICTO-CABULARY SERIES, SET 222	BARNELL LOFT, LTD.		31-50
IJ	CL SET	BIG ADVENTURE BOX	XEROX EDUCATION PUBLICATIONS		101-150
IJ	DITTO	VOCABULARY, ADVANCED	MILTON BRADLEY/PLAYSKOOL		<5
IJ	MULTIU	TROLL JAM SESSIONS: JAZZ	TROLL ASSOCIATES		31-50
IJ	MULTIU	TROLL JAM SESSIONS: FOLK	TROLL ASSOCIATES		31-50
IJ	MULTIU	TROLL JAM SESSIONS: ROCK	TROLL ASSOCIATES		31-50
IJ	MULTIU	TROLL JAM SESSIONS: COUNTRY	TROLL ASSOCIATES		31-50
IJ	MULTIM	COMMUNICATION POWER SERIES: BE A WORD DETECTIVE	UNITED LEARNING		51-75
IJS	AUDCRD	ACTION WORDS	AUDIOTRONICS CORPORATION		11-20
IJS	GAME	PAL READING SKILL GAME, RALLY 1	XEROX EDUCATION PUBLICATIONS		51-75
IJS	GAME	PAL READING SKILLS GAME, RALLY 2	XEROX EDUCATION PUBLICATIONS		51-75
IJS	PICTUR	SOCIAL SIGNS	LAKESHORE CURRICULUM MATERIALS		6-10
IJS	PICTUR	CUC PICTURE-WORD PROGRAM	PAUL S. AMIDON & ASSOC., INC.		11-20
IJS	WKBOOK	PHOTOCABULARY	ODDO PUBLISHING, INC.		<5
IJS	WKBOOK	SOUND WAY, BOOK 1	HAYES SCHOOL PUBLISHING COMPANY		<5
IJS	WKBOOK	SOUND WAY, BOOK 2	HAYES SCHOOL PUBLISHING COMPANY		<5
J	WKBOOK	WORD CLUES, BOOK G	EDL/MCGRAW-HILL		<5
J	WKBOOK	WORD CLUES, BOOK H	EDL/MCGRAW-HILL		<5
J	WKBOOK	WORD CLUES, BOOK I	EDL/MCGRAW-HILL		<5
J	WKBOOK	TROUBLESHOOTER I	HOUGHTON MIFFLIN COMPANY	8	11-20
J	WKBOOK	TROUBLESHOOTER I: BOOK 5, WORD MASTERY	HOUGHTON MIFFLIN COMPANY		<5
JS	AUDKIT	SIGHT VOCABULARY SERIES	MEDIA MATERIALS, INC.		76-100
JS	CHART	SPEED READING CHARTS	BOOK-LAB, INC.		<5
JS	DITTO	SURVIVAL READING SKILLS	J. WESTON WALCH PUBLISHING		11-20
JS	SND FS	WORDS! WORDS! WORDS!	ENCORE VISUAL EDUCATION, INC.		101-150
JS	WKBOOK	VOCABULARY BUILDING EXERCISES FOR YOUNG ADULTS, BOOK A	DORMAC, INC.		<5
JS	WKBOOK	VOCABULARY BUILDING EXERCISES FOR YOUNG ADULTS, BOOK B	DORMAC, INC.		<5
JS	WKBOOK	VOCABULARY BUILDING EXERCISES FOR YOUNG ADULTS, BOOK C	DORMAC, INC.		<5
S	AUDKIT	READ-O-MAT	NATIONAL BOOK COMPANY		31-50

LEVEL	FORMAT	TITLE	PUBLISHER	NT	$PRICE

---

84 - SKILL: SIGHT VOCABULARY

LEVEL	FORMAT	TITLE	PUBLISHER	NT	$PRICE
S	AUDKIT	VOCABULARY BUILDING, LEVEL III	NATIONAL BOOK COMPANY		51-75
S	AUDKIT	VOCABULARY BUILDING, LEVEL IV	NATIONAL BOOK COMPANY		51-75
S	MULTIM	RELEVANCE SERIES	CAMBRIDGE BOOK CO.	5	>450
S	MULTIM	RELEVANCE SERIES: INDEPENDENCE THROUGH READING	CAMBRIDGE BOOK CO.		201-300
S	WKBOOK	WORD CLUES, BOOK J	EDL/MCGRAW-HILL		<5

---

85 - SKILL: FUNCTIONAL VOCABULARY

LEVEL	FORMAT	TITLE	PUBLISHER	NT	$PRICE
R	DITTO	SOUND, WRITE, READ, SPELL	HAYES SCHOOL PUBLISHING COMPANY		<5
R	MULTIU	EXPERIENCES IN READING READINESS	MILTON BRADLEY/PLAYSKOOL		76-100
RP	ACTCRD	TUTORGRAM: COMMON TERMS	ENRICHMENT READING CORP OF AMER.		11-20
RP	AUDKIT	EARLY PRIMARY SKILLS SERIES	MEDIA MATERIALS, INC.	7	51-75
RP	FILMST	READING READINESS	ENCYCLOPEDIA BRITANNICA		76-100
RP	FILMST	BEGINNING TO LEARN: I CAN READ SIGNS	URBAN MEDIA MATERIALS, INC.		31-50
RP	FILMST	BEGINNING TO LEARN: MORE SIGNS TO READ	URBAN MEDIA MATERIALS, INC.		31-50
P	ACTCRD	VEGETABLES & FRUITS POSTER CARDS	MILTON BRADLEY/PLAYSKOOL		6-10
P	AUDCRD	BASIC VOCABULARY BUILDING I	AUDIOTRONICS CORPORATION		21-30
P	AUDCRD	BASIC VOCABULARY BUILDING II	AUDIOTRONICS CORPORATION		21-30
P	AUDKIT	EARLY PRIMARY LANG. ARTS: EASY FUNCTIONAL READING	EYE GATE MEDIA		6-10
P	AUDKIT	PRIMARY LANGUAGE ARTS	EYE GATE MEDIA	4	31-50
P	AUDKIT	PRIMARY LANGUAGE ARTS: FUNCTIONAL READING WITH SOUND & FUN	EYE GATE MEDIA		6-10
P	AUDKIT	SOUND-ALIKE TWINS	MEDIA MATERIALS, INC.		6-10
P	AUDKIT	EASY FUNCTIONAL READING	MEDIA MATERIALS, INC.		6-10
P	FLASH	PICTURE FLASH WORDS FOR BEGINNERS	MILTON BRADLEY/PLAYSKOOL		<5
P	PUPILB	SUPPORTIVE READING SKILLS: READING SCHEDULES, B	BARNELL LOFT, LTD.		11-20
P	PUPILB	SUPPORTIVE READING SKILLS: READING SCHEDULES, C	BARNELL LOFT, LTD.		11-20
P	PUPILB	SUPPORTIVE READING SKILLS: READING ADS, A	BARNELL LOFT, LTD.		11-20
P	PUPILB	SUPPORTIVE READING SKILLS: READING ADS, B	BARNELL LOFT, LTD.		11-20
P	PUPILB	SUPPORTIVE READING SKILLS: READING ADS, C	BARNELL LOFT, LTD.		11-20
P	RECORD	BUILDING VERBAL POWER, VOLUME 5	CLASSROOM MATERIALS CO.		6-10
P	SP EQT	FUNCTIONAL WORD RECOGNITION (SP. ED.)	MAST DEVELOPMENT COMPANY		301-400
PI	ACTCRD	INTERNATIONAL SIGNS & SYMBOLS	DEVELOPMENTAL LEARNING MATERIALS		<5
PI	DITTO	LEARNING CENTER ACTIVITIES, GRADES 3-4	INSTRUCTIONAL FAIR		<5
PI	DITTO	MARK ON-WIPE OFF: WORLD HIGHWAY OF SIGNS	IDEAL SCHOOL SUPPLY COMPANY		6-10
PI	DITTO	VITAL WORDS	IDEAL SCHOOL SUPPLY COMPANY		6-10
PI	DITTO	VOCABULARY MASTERY	INCENTIVE PUBLICATIONS, INC.		<5
PI	DITTO	VOCABULARY, INTERMEDIATE	MILTON BRADLEY/PLAYSKOOL		<5
PI	GAME	READING GAMES THAT TEACH	FERN TRIPP		<5
PI	GAME	SOC-O	FERN TRIPP		<5
PI	GUIDE	VOCABULARY MAGIC	INCENTIVE PUBLICATIONS, INC.		<5
PI	MULTIM	VOCABULARY SKILLS PROGRAM	TROLL ASSOCIATES		201-300
PI	SP EQT	LANGUAGE SKILLS PROGRAM: WORD GAMES & PUZZLES	SPELLBINDER, INC.		51-75
PIJ	ACTCRD	FUNCTIONAL SIGNS	DEVELOPMENTAL LEARNING MATERIALS		<5
PIJ	ACTCRD	SURVIVAL SIGNS	DEVELOPMENTAL LEARNING MATERIALS		6-10
PIJ	CL SET	SUPPORTIVE READING SKILLS: READING ADS (MULTI COPIES)	BARNELL LOFT, LTD.	14	21-30
PIJ	GAME	FUNCTIONAL SIGNS MATCH-UPS	DEVELOPMENTAL LEARNING MATERIALS		<5
PIJ	VISKIT	TOUCH TYPE, SET 2: COMMON SIGNS	MODERN EDUCATION CORPORATION		11-20
PIJS	FILMST	SIGNS	EDUCATIONAL ACTIVITIES, INC.		21-30
PIJS	GUIDE	3,000 INSTANT WORDS	JAMESTOWN PUBLICATIONS, INC.		<5
I	ACTCRD	SURVIVAL READING TASK CARDS	CREATIVE TEACHING ASSOCIATES		<5
I	AUDKIT	EVERYDAY VOCABULARY	EBSCO CURRICULUM MATERIALS		51-75
I	CHART	SURVIVAL SIGNS	IDEAL SCHOOL SUPPLY COMPANY		6-10
I	DITTO	READING ESSENTIALS: VOCABULARY DEVELOPMENT, GRADE 6	CONTINENTAL PRESS, INC.		<5
I	GUIDE	BETTER READING & SPELLING THROUGH PHONICS	FEARON PITMAN PUBLISHERS, INC.		<5
I	PUPILB	SUPPORTIVE READING SKILLS: READING ADS, D	BARNELL LOFT, LTD.		11-20
I	PUPILB	SUPPORTIVE READING SKILLS: READING ADS, E1-E2	BARNELL LOFT, LTD.		11-20
I	PUPILB	SUPPORTIVE READING SKILLS: READING ADS, F1-F4	BARNELL LOFT, LTD.		11-20
I	PUPILB	SUPPORTIVE READING SKILLS: READING SCHEDULES, D	BARNELL LOFT, LTD.		11-20
I	PUPILB	SUPPORTIVE READING SKILLS: READING SCHEDULES, E1-E2	BARNELL LOFT, LTD.		11-20
I	PUPILB	SUPPORTIVE READING SKILLS: READING SCHEDULES, F1-F2	BARNELL LOFT, LTD.		11-20
I	RECORD	BUILDING VERBAL POWER IN THE UPPER GRADES, VOLUME 5	CLASSROOM MATERIALS CO.		6-10
I	VISKIT	READING FORMS & LABELS, GRADE 3	INSTRUCTO/MCGRAW-HILL		6-10
I	VISKIT	READING FORMS & LABELS, GRADE 4	INSTRUCTO/MCGRAW-HILL		6-10
I	VISKIT	READING FORMS & LABELS, GRADE 5	INSTRUCTO/MCGRAW-HILL		6-10
I	VISKIT	READING FORMS & LABELS, GRADE 6	INSTRUCTO/MCGRAW-HILL		6-10
I	WKBOOK	MOTT BASIC SKILLS: LANG., GRAMMAR & SURVIVAL SKILLS, BK 1608	ALLIED EDUCATION COUNCIL		<5
I	WKBOOK	MOTT BASIC SKILLS: LANG., GRAMMAR & SURVIVAL SKILLS, BK 1609	ALLIED EDUCATION COUNCIL		<5
I	WKBOOK	MOTT BASIC SKILLS: LANG., GRAMMAR & SURVIVAL SKILLS, BK 604	ALLIED EDUCATION COUNCIL		<5
I	WKBOOK	MOTT BASIC LANG. SKILLS: LANG./GRAMMAR SKILLS, BK 1607	ALLIED EDUCATION COUNCIL		<5
IJ	A/VKIT	VOCABULARY DEVELOPMENT: WORDS, WORDS, WORDS	TROLL ASSOCIATES		101-150
IJ	DITTO	WORD SKILLS: THE POWER OF WORDS, BOOK I	T.S. DENISON & COMPANY		6-10
IJ	DITTO	WORD SKILLS: LIVING WITH WORDS, BOOK II	T.S. DENISON & COMPANY		6-10
IJ	DITTO	VOCABULARY, ADVANCED	MILTON BRADLEY/PLAYSKOOL		<5
IJ	MULTIU	TROLL JAM SESSIONS: JAZZ	TROLL ASSOCIATES		31-50
IJ	MULTIU	TROLL JAM SESSIONS: FOLK	TROLL ASSOCIATES		31-50
IJ	MULTIU	TROLL JAM SESSIONS: ROCK	TROLL ASSOCIATES		31-50
IJ	MULTIU	TROLL JAM SESSIONS: COUNTRY	TROLL ASSOCIATES		31-50
IJ	MULTIM	COMMUNICATION POWER SERIES: BE A WORD DETECTIVE	UNITED LEARNING		51-75
IJ	SND FS	SITUATIONAL LANGUAGE	UNITED LEARNING		76-100
IJ	WKBOOK	WORDS	CHANNING L. BETE COMPANY, INC.		<5

LEVEL	FORMAT	TITLE	PUBLISHER	NT	$PRICE

85 - SKILL: FUNCTIONAL VOCABULARY

LEVEL	FORMAT	TITLE	PUBLISHER	NT	$PRICE
IJS	PICTUR	SOCIAL SIGNS	LAKESHORE CURRICULUM MATERIALS		6-10
IJS	WKBOOK	SOUND WAY, BOOK 1	HAYES SCHOOL PUBLISHING COMPANY		<5
IJS	WKBOOK	SOUND WAY, BOOK 2	HAYES SCHOOL PUBLISHING COMPANY		<5
J	PUPILB	SUPPORTIVE READING SKILLS: READING ADS, ADV. 1-ADV. 4	BARNELL LOFT, LTD.		11-20
J	PUPILB	SUPPORTIVE READING SKILLS: READING SCHEDULES, ADV. 1-ADV. 4	BARNELL LOFT, LTD.		11-20
J	WKBOOK	COMMUNICATION COMPETENCY IN READING & WRITING (RL 7-9)	BENEFIC PRESS		<5
J	WKBOOK	LIFELINE (RL 7-9)	BENEFIC PRESS		<5
J	WKBOOK	IMPACT (RL 7-9)	BENEFIC PRESS		<5
J	WKBOOK	MOTT BASIC LANG. SKILLS: ADV. LANG./GRAMMAR SKILLS, BK 1912	ALLIED EDUCATION COUNCIL		<5
J	WKBOOK	MOTT BASIC LANG. SKILLS: ADV. LANG./GRAMMAR SKILLS, BK 1913	ALLIED EDUCATION COUNCIL		<5
JS	HI INT	READING FOR PROGRESS (RL 1 - 2)	CAMBRIDGE BOOK CO.		<5
JS	HI INT	READING FOR RESULTS (RL 2 - 3)	CAMBRIDGE BOOK CO.		<5
JS	PUPILB	ABSOLUTELY ESSENTIAL WORDS	BARRON'S EDUCATIONAL SERIES,INC.		<5
JS	PUPILB	SIGNS SERIES (RL 2)	NEW READERS PRESS		<5
JS	PUPILB	EDL CORE VOCABULARIES BOOK	EDL/MCGRAW-HILL		<5
JS	TEXTBK	READING PERFORMANCE	CAMBRIDGE BOOK CO.		<5
JS	TEXTBK	READING ACHIEVEMENT	CAMBRIDGE BOOK CO.		<5
JS	WKBOOK	ROAD SIGNS	FERN TRIPP		<5
JS	WKBOOK	VOCABULARY BUILDING EXERCISES FOR YOUNG ADULTS, BOOK A	DORMAC, INC.		<5
JS	WKBOOK	VOCABULARY BUILDING EXERCISES FOR YOUNG ADULTS, BOOK B	DORMAC, INC.		<5
JS	WKBOOK	VOCABULARY BUILDING EXERCISES FOR YOUNG ADULTS, BOOK C	DORMAC, INC.		<5
JS	WKBOOK	SIGN LANGUAGE, BOOK A	JANUS BOOK PUBLISHERS		<5
JS	WKBOOK	SIGN LANGUAGE, BOOK B	JANUS BOOK PUBLISHERS		<5
JS	WKBOOK	SIGN LANGUAGE, BOOK C	JANUS BOOK PUBLISHERS		<5
JS	WKBOOK	SIGN LANGUAGE, BOOK D	JANUS BOOK PUBLISHERS		<5
S	AUDKIT	READ-O-MAT	NATIONAL BOOK COMPANY		31-50
S	AUDKIT	VOCABULARY BUILDING, LEVEL III	NATIONAL BOOK COMPANY		51-75
S	AUDKIT	VOCABULARY BUILDING, LEVEL IV	NATIONAL BOOK COMPANY		51-75
S	WKBOOK	MOTT BASIC LANG. SKILLS: ADV. LANG./GRAMMAR SKILLS, BK 1914	ALLIED EDUCATION COUNCIL		<5

86 - SKILL: SYNONYMS

LEVEL	FORMAT	TITLE	PUBLISHER	NT	$PRICE
RP	GAME	SOLO GAMES: ANTONYMS, SYNONYMS, HOMONYMS	WISE OWL PUBLICATIONS		<5
RP	PUPILB	USING WORDS SERIES	CHILD'S WORLD	5	21-30
RP	PUPILB	LOUD-NOISY, DIRTY-GRIMY, BAD & NAUGHTY TWINS	CHILD'S WORLD		<5
RP	PUPILB	MORE SYNONYMS	CHILD'S WORLD		<5
RP	PUPILB	JOAN HANSON WORD BOOKS	CHILD'S WORLD	16	51-75
RP	PUPILB	BRITISH-AMERICAN SYNONYMS	CHILD'S WORLD		<5
RP	SND FS	STORIES ABOUT WORDS	CORONET MULTI MEDIA		101-150
RPI	MULTIM	ABSTRACT LANGUAGE CONCEPTS	LISTEN & LEARN CORPORATION		76-100
P	ACTCRD	TUTORGRAM: SYNONYMS I	ENRICHMENT READING CORP OF AMER.		11-20
P	ACTCRD	SYNONYMS/ANTONYMS PACER	DM EDUCATIONAL PUBLICATIONS		<5
P	AUDKIT	KIT 58: BUILDING WORD POWER, LEVEL 3	EDUCATIONAL RESEARCH, INC.		101-150
P	AUDKIT	KIT 84: BASIC PHONICS, LEVEL 4	EDUCATIONAL RESEARCH, INC.		101-150
P	AUDKIT	ADD A DASH OF SYNONYMS FOR SPICE	MEDIA MATERIALS, INC.		6-10
P	CHART	WORD MEANING CARDS: SYNONYMS	KENWORTHY EDUCATIONAL SERVICE		<5
P	CHART	HORSE OF A DIFFERENT COLOR	IDEAL SCHOOL SUPPLY COMPANY		<5
P	CHART	SYNONYM POSTER CARDS	MILTON BRADLEY/PLAYSKOOL		6-10
P	DITTO	WORD SPY, GRADE 2	CONTINENTAL PRESS, INC.		<5
P	DITTO	NEW LANGUAGE PATTERNS & USAGE: GRADE 2, PART 3	CONTINENTAL PRESS, INC.		<5
P	DITTO	READING ESSENTIALS: VOCABULARY DEVELOPMENT, GRADE 3, BOOK 2	CONTINENTAL PRESS, INC.		<5
P	DITTO	JUMBO SPELLING YEARBOOK 3	EBSCO CURRICULUM MATERIALS		11-20
P	DITTO	WORD ATTACK SKILLS: SYNONYMS, ANTONYMS & HOMONYMS	EDL/MCGRAW-HILL		6-10
P	DITTO	BASIC READING SKILLS	XEROX EDUCATION PUBLICATIONS		<5
P	DITTO	PHONICS IIIB	HAYES SCHOOL PUBLISHING COMPANY		<5
P	DITTO	PHONICS IVA	HAYES SCHOOL PUBLISHING COMPANY		<5
P	GAME	CHECKMATE: SYNONYMS	DM EDUCATIONAL PUBLICATIONS		<5
P	GAME	HOMONYMS, SYNONYMS & ANTONYMS	ACTIVITY RESOURCES COMPANY, INC.		<5
P	MANIPU	TRAY PUZZLES: GRAMMAR	IDEAL SCHOOL SUPPLY COMPANY		11-20
P	MANIPU	SHAPE-UPS: SYNONYMS	READING JOY, INC.		<5
P	MANIPU	ANTONYM & SYNONYM BOARDS	DEVELOPMENTAL LEARNING MATERIALS		6-10
P	MULTIM	DEVELOPING READING SKILLS, PART I: WORD RECOGNITION	EDUCATIONAL ENRICHMENT MATERIALS		101-150
P	MULTIM	READING SKILLS SUPPORT SYSTEM, BOX 1	EDL/MCGRAW-HILL		301-400
P	PUPILB	BRITISH-AMERICAN SYNONYMS	LERNER PUBLICATIONS COMPANY		<5
P	PUPILB	MORE SYNONYMS	LERNER PUBLICATIONS COMPANY		<5
P	SP EQT	DEVELOPING LANGUAGE SKILLS, KIT B	BORG-WARNER EDUCATIONAL SYSTEMS		201-300
P	SP EQT	DEVELOPING LANGUAGE SKILLS, KIT C	BORG-WARNER EDUCATIONAL SYSTEMS		201-300
P	SP EQT	DEVELOPING LANGUAGE SKILLS, KIT D	BORG-WARNER EDUCATIONAL SYSTEMS		201-300
P	SP EQT	CHARLIE: SYNONYMS	EDUCATIONAL INSIGHTS, INC.		6-10
P	WKBOOK	MORE SOUNDS & SYMBOLS, BOOK F	GINN & COMPANY		<5
P	WKBOOK	LANGUAGE ARTS, GRADE 2	JENN PUBLICATIONS		<5
PI	ACTCRD	ANTONYMS, SYNONYMS, HOMONYMS	FRANK SCHAFFER PUBLICATIONS, INC		<5
PI	ACTCRD	LANGUAGE LOLLIPOP	KIDS & COMPANY		<5
PI	ACTCRD	SYNONYM PUZZLES	INCENTIVES FOR LEARNING, INC.		6-10
PI	ACTCRD	CREATURE FEATURES: ACTIVITY CARDS	EDUCATIONAL ACTIVITIES, INC.		6-10
PI	ACTCRD	WORD POWER SKILL CARDS	MILTON BRADLEY/PLAYSKOOL		<5
PI	AUDKIT	BEGINNING VOCABULARY	EBSCO CURRICULUM MATERIALS		51-75
PI	AUDKIT	TOTAL BUILDING WORK POWER (KITS 58 - 61)	EDUCATIONAL RESEARCH, INC.	4	>450
PI	AUDKIT	FUN WITH WORDS	MEDIA MATERIALS, INC.		6-10

LEVEL	FORMAT	TITLE	PUBLISHER	NT	$PRICE

86 - SKILL: SYNONYMS

LEVEL	FORMAT	TITLE	PUBLISHER	NT	$PRICE
PI	AUDKIT	PRIMARY VOCABULARY	HAMPDEN PUBLICATIONS, INC.		101-150
PI	DITTO	VOCABULARY SKILLS 1	ACTIVITY RESOURCES COMPANY, INC.		<5
PI	GAME	MEM-O-MATCH	CREATIVE TEACHING ASSOCIATES		6-10
PI	GAME	ANTONYMS, SYNONYMS, HOMONYMS	FRANK SCHAFFER PUBLICATIONS, INC		<5
PI	GAME	GAMEBOARD KIT C	READING JOY, INC.		6-10
PI	MULTIM	TROLL READ-ALONG: I CAN READ ABOUT SYNONYMS & ANTONYMS	TROLL ASSOCIATES		11-20
PI	PUPILB	SUPPORTIVE READING SKILLS: DISCOVERING WORD PATTERNS, BASIC	BARNELL LOFT, LTD.		11-20
PI	SKLKIT	TARGET GREEN: VOCABULARY DEVELOPMENT KIT I	ADDISON-WESLEY PUBLISHING CO.		151-200
PI	SND FS	WORD ANALYSIS SKILLS: WORD MEANINGS III	LEARNING TREE FILMSTRIPS		51-75
PI	SND FS	WORKING WITH WORDS	TROLL ASSOCIATES		101-150
PI	TRANSP	SKILL RECOGNITION: MULTIPLE MEANING VOCABULARY	UNITED TRANSPARENCIES, INC.		151-200
PI	WKBOOK	GOING BANANAS OVER LANGUAGE SKILLS	GOOD APPLE, INC.		6-10
PIJ	MULTIU	CREATURE FEATURES: VOCABULARY DEVELOPMENT	EDUCATIONAL ACTIVITIES, INC.		31-50
PIJ	PUPILB	SUPPORTIVE READING SKILLS: DISCOVERING WORD PATTERNS	BARNELL LOFT, LTD.	9	11-20
PIJ	SND FS	MORE ROADS TO MEANING	ENCYCLOPEDIA BRITANNICA		101-150
PIJ	WKBOOK	ANTONYMS, SYNONYMS, HOMONYMS	FRANK SCHAFFER PUBLICATIONS, INC		<5
I	ACTCRD	WORD ANALYSIS: SYNONYMS & ANTONYMS	INSTRUCTIONAL FAIR		<5
I	ACTCRD	WORD ANALYSIS PAK	INSTRUCTIONAL FAIR		21-30
I	AUDKIT	KIT 59: BUILDING WORD POWER, LEVEL 4	EDUCATIONAL RESEARCH, INC.		101-150
I	AUDKIT	KIT 60: BUILDING WORD POWER, LEVEL 5	EDUCATIONAL RESEARCH, INC.		101-150
I	AUDKIT	KIT 61: BUILDING WORD POWER, LEVEL 16	EDUCATIONAL RESEARCH, INC.		101-150
I	AUDKIT	PRO'S & CON'S	MEDIA MATERIALS, INC.		6-10
I	AUDKIT	EXPANDING VOCABULARY	HAMPDEN PUBLICATIONS, INC.		21-30
I	AUDKIT	WORDPLAY	CORONET MULTI MEDIA		76-100
I	DITTO	READING ESSENTIALS: VOCABULARY DEVELOPMENT, GRADE 4	CONTINENTAL PRESS, INC.		<5
I	DITTO	READING ESSENTIALS: VOCABULARY DEVELOPMENT, GRADE 5	CONTINENTAL PRESS, INC.		<5
I	DITTO	READING ESSENTIALS: VOCABULARY DEVELOPMENT, GRADE 6	CONTINENTAL PRESS, INC.		<5
I	DITTO	WORD SPY, GRADE 4	CONTINENTAL PRESS, INC.		<5
I	DITTO	WORD SPY, GRADE 5	CONTINENTAL PRESS, INC.		<5
I	DITTO	NEW LANGUAGE PATTERNS & USAGE: GRADE 4, PART 3	CONTINENTAL PRESS, INC.		<5
I	DITTO	NEW LANGUAGE PATTERNS & USAGE: GRADE 5, PART 3	CONTINENTAL PRESS, INC.		<5
I	DITTO	NEW LANGUAGE PATTERNS & USAGE: GRADE 6, PART 3	CONTINENTAL PRESS, INC.		<5
I	DITTO	WORD ANALYSIS: SYNONYMS & ANTONYMS	INSTRUCTIONAL FAIR		<5
I	DITTO	WORD ANALYSIS PAK	INSTRUCTIONAL FAIR		21-30
I	DITTO	FOURTH GRADE LANGUAGE DRILLS	HAYES SCHOOL PUBLISHING COMPANY		<5
I	DITTO	FIFTH GRADE LANGUAGE DRILLS	HAYES SCHOOL PUBLISHING COMPANY		<5
I	DITTO	VOCABULARY SKILLS B	ACTIVITY RESOURCES COMPANY, INC.		<5
I	GAME	CREATURE CLUES TO WORDS	CREATIVE TEACHING ASSOCIATES		<5
I	GAME	CREATURE CLUES TO WORDS	ENRICH, INC.		<5
I	GAME	CHECKMATE: SYNONYMS	DM EDUCATIONAL PUBLICATIONS		<5
I	GAME	LEMON TREE	XEROX EDUCATION PUBLICATIONS		51-75
I	GAME	PRESS & CHECK BINGO GAMES: SYNOYNYMS & ANTONYMS	MILTON BRADLEY/PLAYSKOOL		6-10
I	GAME	VOCABULARY QUIZMO	MILTON BRADLEY/PLAYSKOOL		<5
I	MULTIM	VOCABULARY DEVELOPMENT	MILTON BRADLEY/PLAYSKOOL		76-100
I	PUPILB	SUPPORTIVE READING SKILLS: DISCOVERING WORD PATTERNS, INTER.	BARNELL LOFT, LTD.		11-20
I	WKBOOK	MOTT BASIC SKILLS: LANG., GRAMMAR & SURVIVAL SKILLS, BK 1608	ALLIED EDUCATION COUNCIL		<5
I	WKBOOK	LANGUAGE ARTS FOR THE INTERMEDIATE GRADES (4, 5, 6)	JENN PUBLICATIONS		<5
IJ	AUDCRD	DESCRIPTIVE WORDS	AUDIOTRONICS CORPORATION		11-20
IJ	AUDKIT	VOCABULARY STUDY	EBSCO CURRICULUM MATERIALS		51-75
IJ	AUDKIT	DEVELOPING ENGLISH SKILLS	EDUCATIONAL ACTIVITIES, INC.		51-75
IJ	AUDKIT	INTERMEDIATE VOCABULARY	HAMPDEN PUBLICATIONS, INC.		101-150
IJ	A/VKIT	VOCABULARY BUILDERS	EYE GATE MEDIA		51-75
IJ	GAME	GAMEBOARD KIT D	READING JOY, INC.		6-10
IJ	GAME	LIME TREE	XEROX EDUCATION PUBLICATIONS		51-75
IJ	WKBOOK	DEVELOPING LANGUAGE ARTS SKILLS: VOCABULARY ENRICHMENT	WILSON EDUCATIONAL MEDIA		6-10
IJ	WKBOOK	BOOK TWO: VOCABULARY DEVELOPMENT ACTIVITIES	T.S. DENISON & COMPANY		6-10
IJ	WKBOOK	LANGUAGE 940, GRADES 4 - 8	STECK-VAUGHN COMPANY		<5
IJS	AUDCRD	ACTION WORDS	AUDIOTRONICS CORPORATION		11-20
IJS	AUDKIT	HITS, LEVEL 1: PRATT & MCCLAIN, HAPPY DAYS	MODULEARN, INC.		11-20
IJS	AUDKIT	HITS, LEVEL 1: AMERICA, TODAY'S THE DAY	MODULEARN, INC.		11-20
IJS	AUDKIT	HITS, LEVEL 1: THREE DOG NIGHT, ONE MAN BAND	MODULEARN, INC.		11-20
IJS	AUDKIT	HITS, LEVEL 1: AMERICA, LONELY PEOPLE	MODULEARN, INC.		11-20
IJS	AUDKIT	HITS, LEVEL 1: SANTANA, LET IT SHINE	MODULEARN, INC.		11-20
IJS	AUDKIT	HITS, LEVEL 1: DOOBIE BROTHERS, IT KEEPS YOU RUNNING	MODULEARN, INC.		11-20
IJS	AUDKIT	HITS, LEVEL 1: AMERICA, TIN MAN	MODULEARN, INC.		11-20
IJS	AUDKIT	HITS, LEVEL 1: AMERICA, VENTURA HIGHWAY	MODULEARN, INC.		11-20
IJS	AUDKIT	HITS, LEVEL 1: BLACKBYRDS, YOU'VE GOT THAT SOMETHING	MODULEARN, INC.		11-20
IJS	AUDKIT	HITS, LEVEL 2: B.J. THOMAS, HEY WON'T YOU PLAY	MODULEARN, INC.		11-20
IJS	AUDKIT	HITS, LEVEL 2: FLEETWOOD MAC, OVER MY HEAD	MODULEARN, INC.		11-20
IJS	AUDKIT	HITS, LEVEL 2: SPINNERS, GAMES PEOPLE PLAY	MODULEARN, INC.		11-20
IJS	AUDKIT	HITS, LEVEL 2: BELLAMY BROTHERS, LET YOUR LOVE FLOW	MODULEARN, INC.		11-20
IJS	AUDKIT	HITS, LEVEL 2: JOHN SEBASTIAN, WELCOME BACK	MODULEARN, INC.		11-20
IJS	AUDKIT	HITS, LEVEL 2: ABBA, KNOWING ME, KNOWING YOU	MODULEARN, INC.		11-20
IJS	AUDKIT	HITS, LEVEL 2: EARTH WIND & FIRE, SHINING STAR	MODULEARN, INC.		11-20
IJS	AUDKIT	HITS, LEVEL 2: SIDE EFFECT, S.O.S.	MODULEARN, INC.		11-20
IJS	AUDKIT	HITS, LEVEL 3: HARRY CHAPIN, CIRCLE	MODULEARN, INC.		11-20
IJS	AUDKIT	HITS, LEVEL 3: JAMES TAYLOR, SHOWER THE PEOPLE	MODULEARN, INC.		11-20
IJS	AUDKIT	HITS, LEVEL 3: DOOBIE BROTHERS, LISTEN TO THE MUSIC	MODULEARN, INC.		11-20
IJS	AUDKIT	HITS, LEVEL 3: EMOTION, BEST OF MY LOVE	MODULEARN, INC.		11-20

LEVEL	FORMAT	TITLE	PUBLISHER	NT	$PRICE

86 - SKILL: SYNONYMS

LEVEL	FORMAT	TITLE	PUBLISHER	NT	$PRICE
IJS	AUDKIT	HITS, LEVEL 3: THREE DOG NIGHT, THE FAMILY OF MAN	MODULEARN, INC.		11-20
IJS	AUDKIT	HITS, LEVEL 3: SPINNERS, JUST CAN'T GET YOU OUT OF MY MIND	MODULEARN, INC.		11-20
IJS	AUDKIT	HITS, LEVEL 4: AMERICA, I NEED YOU	MODULEARN, INC.		11-20
IJS	AUDKIT	HITS, LEVEL 4: PAUL SIMON, I AM A ROCK	MODULEARN, INC.		11-20
IJS	AUDKIT	HITS, LEVEL 4: DAVE LOGGINS, PLEASE COME TO BOSTON	MODULEARN, INC.		11-20
IJS	AUDKIT	HITS, LEVEL 4: FLEETWOOD MAC, DREAMS	MODULEARN, INC.		11-20
IJS	AUDKIT	HITS, LEVEL 4: PAUL SIMON, BRIDGE OVER TROUBLED WATERS	MODULEARN, INC.		11-20
IJS	AUDKIT	HITS, LEVEL 4: ARETHA FRANKLIN, BRIDGE OVER TROUBLED WATERS	MODULEARN, INC.		11-20
J	PUPILB	SUPPORTIVE READING SKILLS: DISCOVERING WORD PATTERNS, ADV.	BARNELL LOFT, LTD.		11-20
J	WKBOOK	WORD CLUES, BOOK H	EDL/MCGRAW-HILL		<5
J	WKBOOK	WORD CLUES, BOOK I	EDL/MCGRAW-HILL		<5
JS	AUDKIT	LEARNING BASIC VOCABULARY	HAMPDEN PUBLICATIONS, INC.		101-150
JS	SKLKIT	TARGET ORANGE: VOCABULARY DEVELOPMENT KIT II	ADDISON-WESLEY PUBLISHING CO.		151-200
JS	TEXTBK	READING ACHIEVEMENT	CAMBRIDGE BOOK CO.		<5
S	AUDKIT	VOCABULARY BUILDING, LEVEL III	NATIONAL BOOK COMPANY		51-75
S	AUDKIT	VOCABULARY BUILDING, LEVEL IV	NATIONAL BOOK COMPANY		51-75
S	PUPILB	A BASIC DICTIONARY OF SYNONYMS & ANTONYMS	ELSEVIER/NELSON BOOKS		6-10
S	WKBOOK	WORD CLUES, BOOK J	EDL/MCGRAW-HILL		<5

87 - SKILL: ANTONYMS

LEVEL	FORMAT	TITLE	PUBLISHER	NT	$PRICE
RP	ACTCRD	OPPOSITES	MILTON BRADLEY/PLAYSKOOL		<5
RP	CL SET	SEE YOUR WORDS: LEARNING WORDS THROUGH OPPOSITES	MAFEX ASSOCIATES, INC.		51-75
RP	GAME	ETA DISCOVERING OPPOSITES	EDUCATIONAL TEACHING AIDS		11-20
RP	GAME	SOLO GAMES: ANTONYMS, SYNONYMS, HOMONYMS	WISE OWL PUBLICATIONS		<5
RP	GAME	PICTURE CARD GAMES, SET II	MILTON BRADLEY/PLAYSKOOL		6-10
RP	PUPILB	USING WORDS SERIES	CHILD'S WORLD	5	21-30
RP	PUPILB	STILL MORE ANTONYMS	CHILD'S WORLD		<5
RP	PUPILB	OPPOSITE ODELIA	CHILD'S WORLD		<5
RP	PUPILB	JOAN HANSON WORD BOOKS	CHILD'S WORLD	16	51-75
RP	PUPILB	ANTONYMS	CHILD'S WORLD		<5
RP	PUPILB	MORE ANYTONYMS	CHILD'S WORLD		<5
RP	SND FS	STORIES ABOUT WORDS	CORONET MULTI MEDIA		101-150
RPI	MULTIM	ABSTRACT LANGUAGE CONCEPTS	LISTEN & LEARN CORPORATION		76-100
P	ACTCRD	TUTORGRAM: ANTONYMS	ENRICHMENT READING CORP OF AMER.		11-20
P	ACTCRD	MAGIC CARDS: CLASSIFICATION, OPPOSITES, SEQUENCE	IDEAL SCHOOL SUPPLY COMPANY		6-10
P	ACTCRD	ANTONYM CARDS	DEVELOPMENTAL LEARNING MATERIALS		<5
P	ACTCRD	SYNONYMS/ANTONYMS PACER	DM EDUCATIONAL PUBLICATIONS		<5
P	AUDKIT	KIT 58: BUILDING WORD POWER, LEVEL 3	EDUCATIONAL RESEARCH, INC.		101-150
P	AUDKIT	KIT 84: BASIC PHONICS, LEVEL 4	EDUCATIONAL RESEARCH, INC.		101-150
P	AUDKIT	WINKY IN THE LOST & FOUND DEPARTMENT	MEDIA MATERIALS, INC.		6-10
P	CHART	WORD MEANING CARDS: ANTONYMS	KENWORTHY EDUCATIONAL SERVICE		<5
P	CHART	CLASSIFICATIONS-OPPOSITES-SEQUENCE	IDEAL SCHOOL SUPPLY COMPANY		11-20
P	CHART	OPPOSITES	INSTRUCTO/MCGRAW-HILL		<5
P	CHART	ANTONYM POSTER CARDS	MILTON BRADLEY/PLAYSKOOL		6-10
P	DITTO	READING ESSENTIALS: VOCABULARY DEVELOPMENT, GRADE 1	CONTINENTAL PRESS, INC.		<5
P	DITTO	WORD SPY, GRADE 2	CONTINENTAL PRESS, INC.		<5
P	DITTO	NEW LANGUAGE PATTERNS & USAGE: GRADE 2, PART 3	CONTINENTAL PRESS, INC.		<5
P	DITTO	JUMBO SPELLING YEARBOOK 3	EBSCO CURRICULUM MATERIALS		11-20
P	DITTO	WORD ATTACK SKILLS: SYNONYMS, ANTONYMS & HOMONYMS	EDL/MCGRAW-HILL		6-10
P	DITTO	READING ENRICHMENT ACTIVITIES	XEROX EDUCATION PUBLICATIONS		<5
P	DITTO	BASIC READING SKILLS	XEROX EDUCATION PUBLICATIONS		<5
P	DITTO	PHONICS IIIB	HAYES SCHOOL PUBLISHING COMPANY		<5
P	DITTO	PHONICS IVA	HAYES SCHOOL PUBLISHING COMPANY		<5
P	FLASH	CLASSIFICATION-OPPOSITES PICTURES FOR PEGBOARD	IDEAL SCHOOL SUPPLY COMPANY		6-10
P	GAME	MATCH ME CARDS	CREATIVE TEACHING ASSOCIATES	4	11-20
P	GAME	MATCH ME CARDS, OPPOSITES	CREATIVE TEACHING ASSOCIATES		<5
P	GAME	CHECKMATE: ANTONYMS	DM EDUCATIONAL PUBLICATIONS		<5
P	GAME	MATCH ME CARDS: OPPOSITES	TREND ENTERPRISES, INC.		<5
P	GAME	HOMONYMS, SYNONYMS & ANTONYMS	ACTIVITY RESOURCES COMPANY, INC.		<5
P	MANIPU	TRAY PUZZLES: GRAMMAR	IDEAL SCHOOL SUPPLY COMPANY		11-20
P	MANIPU	SHAPE-UPS: ANTONYMS	READING JOY, INC.		<5
P	MANIPU	ANTONYM & SYNONYM BOARDS	DEVELOPMENTAL LEARNING MATERIALS		6-10
P	MULTIM	DEVELOPING READING SKILLS, PART I: WORD RECOGNITION	EDUCATIONAL ENRICHMENT MATERIALS		101-150
P	MULTIM	READING SKILLS SUPPORT SYSTEM, BOX 1	EDL/MCGRAW-HILL		301-400
P	PUPILB	ANTONYMS	LERNER PUBLICATIONS COMPANY		<5
P	PUPILB	MORE ANTONYMS	LERNER PUBLICATIONS COMPANY		<5
P	PUPILB	STILL MORE ANTONYMS	LERNER PUBLICATIONS COMPANY		<5
P	RECORD	BUILDING VERBAL POWER, VOLUME 1	CLASSROOM MATERIALS CO.		6-10
P	SP EQT	DEVELOPING LANGUAGE SKILLS, KIT B	BORG-WARNER EDUCATIONAL SYSTEMS		201-300
P	SP EQT	DEVELOPING LANGUAGE SKILLS, KIT C	BORG-WARNER EDUCATIONAL SYSTEMS		201-300
P	SP EQT	DEVELOPING LANGUAGE SKILLS, KIT D	BORG-WARNER EDUCATIONAL SYSTEMS		201-300
P	WKBOOK	MORE SOUNDS & SYMBOLS, BOOK F	GINN & COMPANY		<5
P	WKBOOK	PHONICS & READING REVIEW	JENN PUBLICATIONS		<5
P	WKBOOK	LANGUAGE ARTS, GRADE 2	JENN PUBLICATIONS		<5
P	WKBOOK	LANGUAGE ARTS, GRADE 3	JENN PUBLICATIONS		<5
PI	ACTCRD	ANTONYMS, SYNONYMS, HOMONYMS	FRANK SCHAFFER PUBLICATIONS, INC		<5
PI	ACTCRD	ANTONYMS	INCENTIVES FOR LEARNING, INC.		<5
PI	ACTCRD	WORD OPPOSTIES PACER	DM EDUCATIONAL PUBLICATIONS		<5

LEVEL	FORMAT	TITLE	PUBLISHER	NT	$PRICE

87 - SKILL: ANTONYMS

LEVEL	FORMAT	TITLE	PUBLISHER	NT	$PRICE
PI	ACTCRD	CREATURE FEATURES: ACTIVITY CARDS	EDUCATIONAL ACTIVITIES, INC.		6-10
PI	ACTCRD	WORD DEVILS SKILL CARDS	MILTON BRADLEY/PLAYSKOOL		<5
PI	AUDKIT	BEGINNING VOCABULARY	EBSCO CURRICULUM MATERIALS		51-75
PI	AUDKIT	TOTAL BUILDING WORK POWER (KITS 58 - 61)	EDUCATIONAL RESEARCH, INC.	4	>450
PI	AUDKIT	FUN WITH WORDS	MEDIA MATERIALS, INC.		101-150
PI	AUDKIT	PRIMARY VOCABULARY	HAMPDEN PUBLICATIONS, INC.		101-150
PI	DITTO	VOCABULARY SKILLS 1	ACTIVITY RESOURCES COMPANY, INC.		<5
PI	GAME	MEM-O-MATCH	CREATIVE TEACHING ASSOCIATES		6-10
PI	GAME	ANTONYMS, SYNONYMS, HOMONYMS	FRANK SCHAFFER PUBLICATIONS, INC		<5
PI	GAME	HOMONYM & ANTONYM CASINO	JUDY COMPANY		6-10
PI	GAME	OPPOSITES GAME	JUDY COMPANY		6-10
PI	MULTIM	TROLL READ-ALONG: I CAN READ ABOUT SYNONYMS & ANTONYMS	TROLL ASSOCIATES		11-20
PI	PUPILB	SUPPORTIVE READING SKILLS: DISCOVERING WORD PATTERNS, BASIC	BARNELL LOFT, LTD.		11-20
PI	SKLKIT	TARGET GREEN: VOCABULARY DEVELOPMENT KIT I	ADDISON-WESLEY PUBLISHING CO.		151-200
PI	SND FS	WORD ANALYSIS SKILLS: WORD MEANINGS III	LEARNING TREE FILMSTRIPS		51-75
PI	SND FS	WHAT'S THE GOOD WORD?	MILLER-BRODY PRODUCTIONS, INC.		51-75
PI	SND FS	WORKING WITH WORDS	TROLL ASSOCIATES		101-150
PI	TRANSP	SKILL RECOGNITION: MULTIPLE MEANING VOCABULARY	UNITED TRANSPARENCIES, INC.		151-200
PI	WKBOOK	GOING BANANAS OVER LANGUAGE SKILLS	GOOD APPLE, INC.		6-10
PIJ	MULTIU	CREATURE FEATURES: VOCABULARY DEVELOPMENT	EDUCATIONAL ACTIVITIES, INC.		31-50
PIJ	PUPILB	SUPPORTIVE READING SKILLS: DISCOVERING WORD PATTERNS	BARNELL LOFT, LTD.	9	11-20
PIJ	WKBOOK	ANTONYMS, SYNONYMS, HOMONYMS	FRANK SCHAFFER PUBLICATIONS, INC		<5
I	ACTCRD	WORD ANALYSIS: SYNONYMS & ANTONYMS	INSTRUCTIONAL FAIR		<5
I	ACTCRD	WORD ANALYSIS PAK	INSTRUCTIONAL FAIR		21-30
I	AUDKIT	KIT 59: BUILDING WORD POWER, LEVEL 4	EDUCATIONAL RESEARCH, INC.		101-150
I	AUDKIT	KIT 60: BUILDING WORD POWER, LEVEL 5	EDUCATIONAL RESEARCH, INC.		101-150
I	AUDKIT	KIT 61: BUILDING WORD POWER, LEVEL 16	EDUCATIONAL RESEARCH, INC.		101-150
I	AUDKIT	PRO'S & CON'S	MEDIA MATERIALS, INC.		6-10
I	AUDKIT	EXPANDING VOCABULARY	HAMPDEN PUBLICATIONS, INC.		21-30
I	AUDKIT	WORDPLAY	CORONET MULTI MEDIA		76-100
I	DITTO	READING ESSENTIALS: VOCABULARY DEVELOPMENT, GRADE 4	CONTINENTAL PRESS, INC.		<5
I	DITTO	READING ESSENTIALS: VOCABULARY DEVELOPMENT, GRADE 5	CONTINENTAL PRESS, INC.		<5
I	DITTO	READING ESSENTIALS: VOCABULARY DEVELOPMENT, GRADE 6	CONTINENTAL PRESS, INC.		<5
I	DITTO	WORD SPY, GRADE 4	CONTINENTAL PRESS, INC.		<5
I	DITTO	WORD SPY, GRADE 5	CONTINENTAL PRESS, INC.		<5
I	DITTO	WORD ANALYSIS: SYNONYMS & ANTONYMS	INSTRUCTIONAL FAIR		<5
I	DITTO	WORD ANALYSIS PAK	INSTRUCTIONAL FAIR		21-30
I	DITTO	NEWSPAPER TASKS SWING INTO LANGUAGE ARTS, INTERMEDIATE	ORE PRESS, INC.		<5
I	DITTO	FIFTH GRADE LANGUAGE DRILLS	HAYES SCHOOL PUBLISHING COMPANY		<5
I	DITTO	VOCABULARY SKILLS B	ACTIVITY RESOURCES COMPANY, INC.		<5
I	GAME	CREATURE CLUES TO WORDS	CREATIVE TEACHING ASSOCIATES		<5
I	GAME	CREATURE CLUES TO WORDS	ENRICH, INC.		<5
I	GAME	CHECKMATE: ANTONYMS	DM EDUCATIONAL PUBLICATIONS		<5
I	GAME	LEMON TREE	XEROX EDUCATION PUBLICATIONS		51-75
I	GAME	PRESS & CHECK BINGO GAMES: SYNOYNYMS & ANTONYMS	MILTON BRADLEY/PLAYSKOOL		6-10
I	GAME	VOCABULARY QUIZMO	MILTON BRADLEY/PLAYSKOOL		<5
I	MULTIM	VOCABULARY DEVELOPMENT	MILTON BRADLEY/PLAYSKOOL		76-100
I	PUPILB	SUPPORTIVE READING SKILLS: DISCOVERING WORD PATTERNS, INTER.	BARNELL LOFT, LTD.		11-20
I	RECORD	BUILDING VERBAL POWER IN THE UPPER GRADES, VOLUME 1	CLASSROOM MATERIALS CO.		6-10
I	WKBOOK	MOTT BASIC SKILLS: LANG., GRAMMAR & SURVIVAL SKILLS, BK 1608	ALLIED EDUCATION COUNCIL		<5
I	WKBOOK	LANGUAGE ARTS FOR THE INTERMEDIATE GRADES (4, 5, 6)	JENN PUBLICATIONS		<5
IJ	AUDKIT	DEVELOPING ENGLISH SKILLS	EDUCATIONAL ACTIVITIES, INC.		51-75
IJ	AUDKIT	INTERMEDIATE VOCABULARY	HAMPDEN PUBLICATIONS, INC.		101-150
IJ	A/VKIT	VOCABULARY BUILDERS	EYE GATE MEDIA		51-75
IJ	GAME	GAMEBOARD KIT D	READING JOY, INC.		6-10
IJ	GAME	LIME TREE	XEROX EDUCATION PUBLICATIONS		51-75
IJ	WKBOOK	DEVELOPING LANGUAGE ARTS SKILLS: VOCABULARY ENRICHMENT	WILSON EDUCATIONAL MEDIA		6-10
IJ	WKBOOK	BOOK TWO, PART ONE: VOCABULARY DEVELOPMENT ACTIVITIES	T.S. DENISON & COMPANY		6-10
IJ	WKBOOK	LANGUAGE 940, GRADES 4 - 8	STECK-VAUGHN COMPANY		<5
IJS	AUDKIT	HITS, LEVEL 2: ABBA, S.O.S.	MODULEARN, INC.		11-20
IJS	AUDKIT	HITS, LEVEL 3: FIREFALL, LIVIN' AIN'T LIVIN'	MODULEARN, INC.		11-20
IJS	AUDKIT	HITS, LEVEL 3: FLEETWOOD MAC, DON'T STOP	MODULEARN, INC.		11-20
IJS	AUDKIT	HITS, LEVEL 3: CARLY SIMON, GROWN UP	MODULEARN, INC.		11-20
IJS	AUDKIT	HITS, LEVEL 3: SPINNERS, ONE OF A KIND LOVE AFFAIR	MODULEARN, INC.		11-20
IJS	AUDKIT	HITS, LEVEL 4: AMERICA, I NEED YOU	MODULEARN, INC.		11-20
IJS	AUDKIT	HITS, LEVEL 4: PAUL SIMON, I AM A ROCK	MODULEARN, INC.		11-20
IJS	AUDKIT	HITS, LEVEL 4: DAVE LOGGINS, PLEASE COME TO BOSTON	MODULEARN, INC.		11-20
IJS	AUDKIT	HITS, LEVEL 4: FLEETWOOD MAC, DREAMS	MODULEARN, INC.		11-20
IJS	AUDKIT	HITS, LEVEL 4: PAUL SIMON, BRIDGE OVER TROUBLED WATERS	MODULEARN, INC.		11-20
IJS	AUDKIT	HITS, LEVEL 4: ARETHA FRANKLIN, BRIDGE OVER TROUBLED WATERS	MODULEARN, INC.		11-20
J	PUPILB	SUPPORTIVE READING SKILLS: DISCOVERING WORD PATTERNS, ADV.	BARNELL LOFT, LTD.		11-20
J	WKBOOK	WORD CLUES, BOOK G	EDL/MCGRAW-HILL		<5
J	WKBOOK	WORD CLUES, BOOK H	EDL/MCGRAW-HILL		<5
J	WKBOOK	WORD CLUES, BOOK I	EDL/MCGRAW-HILL		<5
JS	AUDKIT	LEARNING BASIC VOCABULARY	HAMPDEN PUBLICATIONS, INC.		101-150
JS	SKLKIT	TARGET ORANGE: VOCABULARY DEVELOPMENT KIT II	ADDISON-WESLEY PUBLISHING CO.		151-200
JS	TEXTBK	READING PERFORMANCE	CAMBRIDGE BOOK CO.		<5
S	PUPILB	A BASIC DICTIONARY OF SYNONYMS & ANTONYMS	ELSEVIER/NELSON BOOKS		6-10
S	WKBOOK	WORD CLUES, BOOK J	EDL/MCGRAW-HILL		<5

LEVEL	FORMAT	TITLE	PUBLISHER	NT	$PRICE

88 - SKILL: HOMONYMS & HOMOGRAPHS

LEVEL	FORMAT	TITLE	PUBLISHER	NT	$PRICE
RP	GAME	SOLO GAMES: ANTONYMS, SYNONYMS, HOMONYMS	WISE OWL PUBLICATIONS		<5
RP	PUPILB	USING WORDS SERIES	CHILD'S WORLD	5	21-30
RP	PUPILB	STILL MORE HOMONYMS	CHILD'S WORLD		<5
RP	PUPILB	NEVER MONKEY WITH A MONKEY	CHILD'S WORLD		<5
RP	PUPILB	JOAN HANSON WORD BOOKS	CHILD'S WORLD	16	51-75
RP	PUPILB	HOMONYMS	CHILD'S WORLD		<5
RP	PUPILB	MORE HOMONYMS	CHILD'S WORLD		<5
RP	PUPILB	HOMOGRAPHS	CHILD'S WORLD		<5
RP	PUPILB	HOMOGRAPHIC HOMOPHONES	CHILD'S WORLD		<5
RP	SND FS	STORIES ABOUT WORDS	CORONET MULTI MEDIA		101-150
P	ACTCRD	SOUND ALIKES	TEACHING RESOURCES CORPORATION		6-10
P	ACTCRD	TUTORGRAM: HOMONYMS	ENRICHMENT READING CORP OF AMER.		11-20
P	ACTCRD	SOUND THE SAME CARDS	LAKESHORE CURRICULUM MATERIALS		6-10
P	ACTCRD	HOMONYM CARDS, HOMOGRAPHS	DEVELOPMENTAL LEARNING MATERIALS		<5
P	ACTCRD	HOMONYM CARDS, HOMOPHONES	DEVELOPMENTAL LEARNING MATERIALS		<5
P	ACTCRD	HOMONYMS PACER	DM EDUCATIONAL PUBLICATIONS		<5
P	AUDKIT	TWO WORDS IN ONE	MEDIA MATERIALS, INC.		6-10
P	CHART	WORD MEANING CARDS: HOMONYMS	KENWORTHY EDUCATIONAL SERVICE		<5
P	CHART	WORD MEANING CARDS: HOMOGRAPHS	KENWORTHY EDUCATIONAL SERVICE		<5
P	CHART	HOMONYM PEAS	IDEAL SCHOOL SUPPLY COMPANY		<5
P	CHART	SCAREY FOREST	IDEAL SCHOOL SUPPLY COMPANY		6-10
P	CHART	HOMONYM POSTER CARDS	MILTON BRADLEY/PLAYSKOOL		6-10
P	DITTO	NEW PHONICS & WORD ANALYSIS SKILLS: GRADE 3, PART 3	CONTINENTAL PRESS, INC.		<5
P	DITTO	READING ESSENTIALS: VOCABULARY DEVELOPMENT, GRADE 1	CONTINENTAL PRESS, INC.		<5
P	DITTO	WORD SPY, GRADE 2	CONTINENTAL PRESS, INC.		<5
P	DITTO	WORD SPY, GRADE 3	CONTINENTAL PRESS, INC.		<5
P	DITTO	READING ESSENTIALS: VOCABULARY DEVELOPMENT, GRADE 3, BOOK 2	CONTINENTAL PRESS, INC.		<5
P	DITTO	WORD ATTACK SKILLS: SYNONYMS, ANTONYMS & HOMONYMS	EDL/MCGRAW-HILL		6-10
P	DITTO	READING ENRICHMENT ACTIVITIES	XEROX EDUCATION PUBLICATIONS		<5
P	DITTO	PHONICS IVA	HAYES SCHOOL PUBLISHING COMPANY		<5
P	DITTO	WORD WIZARDS, BOOK 1	HAYES SCHOOL PUBLISHING COMPANY		<5
P	DITTO	THIRD GRADE LANGUAGE DRILLS	HAYES SCHOOL PUBLISHING COMPANY		<5
P	GAME	WHITE WATER RAFT TRIP	DEVELOPMENTAL LEARNING MATERIALS		6-10
P	GAME	CHECKMATE: HOMONYMS (HOMOPHONES)	DM EDUCATIONAL PUBLICATIONS		<5
P	GAME	HOMONYMS, SYNONYMS & ANTONYMS	ACTIVITY RESOURCES COMPANY, INC.		<5
P	MANIPU	TRAY PUZZLES: GRAMMAR	IDEAL SCHOOL SUPPLY COMPANY		11-20
P	MULTIM	READING SKILLS SUPPORT SYSTEM, BOX 2	EDL/MCGRAW-HILL		301-400
P	PUPILB	SUPPORTIVE READING SKILLS: READING HOMONYMS, A	BARNELL LOFT, LTD.		11-20
P	PUPILB	SUPPORTIVE READING SKILLS: READING HOMONYMS, B1-B2	BARNELL LOFT, LTD.		11-20
P	PUPILB	SUPPORTIVE READING SKILLS: READING HOMONYMS, C1-C2	BARNELL LOFT, LTD.		11-20
P	PUPILB	SUPPORTIVE READING SKILLS: MASTERING MULTIP. MEANINGS, A1-A2	BARNELL LOFT, LTD.		11-20
P	PUPILB	SUPPORTIVE READING SKILLS: MASTERING MULTI. MEANINGS, B1-B8	BARNELL LOFT, LTD.		11-20
P	PUPILB	SUPPORTIVE READING SKILLS: MASTERING MULTI. MEANINGS, C1-C16	BARNELL LOFT, LTD.		21-30
P	PUPILB	SUPPORTIVE READING SKILLS: READING HOMOGRAPHS, A	BARNELL LOFT, LTD.		11-20
P	PUPILB	SUPPORTIVE READING SKILLS: READING HOMOGRAPHS, B	BARNELL LOFT, LTD.		11-20
P	PUPILB	SUPPORTIVE READING SKILLS: READING HOMOGRAPHS, C1-C2	BARNELL LOFT, LTD.		11-20
P	PUPILB	HOMONYMS	LERNER PUBLICATIONS COMPANY		<5
P	PUPILB	HOMOGRAPHS	LERNER PUBLICATIONS COMPANY		<5
P	PUPILB	HOMOGRAPHIC HOMOPHONES	LERNER PUBLICATIONS COMPANY		<5
P	PUPILB	MORE HOMONYMS	LERNER PUBLICATIONS COMPANY		<5
P	PUPILB	STILL MORE HOMONYMS	LERNER PUBLICATIONS COMPANY		<5
P	RECORD	COMPREHENSION THROUGH LISTENING, VOLUME 4	CLASSROOM MATERIALS CO.		6-10
P	SP EQT	DEVELOPING LANGUAGE SKILLS, KIT B	BORG-WARNER EDUCATIONAL SYSTEMS		201-300
P	SP EQT	DEVELOPING LANGUAGE SKILLS, KIT C	BORG-WARNER EDUCATIONAL SYSTEMS		201-300
P	SP EQT	DEVELOPING LANGUAGE SKILLS, KIT D	BORG-WARNER EDUCATIONAL SYSTEMS		201-300
P	WKBOOK	LANGUAGE ARTS, GRADE 3	JENN PUBLICATIONS		<5
P	WKBOOK	PHONICS & WORD POWER, BOOK 3	XEROX EDUCATION PUBLICATIONS		<5
P	WKBOOK	SOUNDS WE USE, BOOK 3	HAYES SCHOOL PUBLISHING COMPANY		<5
PI	ACTCRD	ANTONYMS, SYNONYMS, HOMONYMS	FRANK SCHAFFER PUBLICATIONS, INC		<5
PI	ACTCRD	HOMONYMS	INCENTIVES FOR LEARNING, INC.		<5
PI	ACTCRD	HOMOPHONES	INCENTIVES FOR LEARNING, INC.		<5
PI	ACTCRD	CREATURE FEATURES: ACTIVITY CARDS	EDUCATIONAL ACTIVITIES, INC.		6-10
PI	ACTCRD	WORD DEVILS SKILL CARDS	MILTON BRADLEY/PLAYSKOOL		<5
PI	AUDKIT	BEGINNING VOCABULARY	EBSCO CURRICULUM MATERIALS		51-75
PI	AUDKIT	PRIMARY VOCABULARY	HAMPDEN PUBLICATIONS, INC.		101-150
PI	DITTO	VOCABULARY SKILLS 2	ACTIVITY RESOURCES COMPANY, INC.		<5
PI	DITTO	SOUND-ALIKE WORDS	ACTIVITY RESOURCES COMPANY, INC.		<5
PI	GAME	NEW GNU	CREATIVE TEACHING ASSOCIATES		<5
PI	GAME	BARE BEAR	CREATIVE TEACHING ASSOCIATES		<5
PI	GAME	MEM-O-MATCH	CREATIVE TEACHING ASSOCIATES		6-10
PI	GAME	ANTONYMS, SYNONYMS, HOMONYMS	FRANK SCHAFFER PUBLICATIONS, INC		<5
PI	GAME	HOMONYM & ANTONYM CASINO	JUDY COMPANY		6-10
PI	GAME	PLUM TREE	XEROX EDUCATION PUBLICATIONS		51-75
PI	GUIDE	VOCABULARY MAGIC	INCENTIVE PUBLICATIONS, INC.		<5
PI	MANIPU	E-Z PHONIC HOMONYM SLIDE RULE	E-Z GRADER COMPANY		<5
PI	MULTIU	HOMONYMS	GEL-STEN, INC.		6-10
PI	MULTIM	TROLL READ-ALONG: I CAN READ ABOUT HOMONYMS	TROLL ASSOCIATES		11-20
PI	RECORD	PHONICS & WORD DEVELOPMENT	EDUCATIONAL ACTIVITIES, INC.		31-50
PI	SKLKIT	TARGET GREEN: VOCABULARY DEVELOPMENT KIT I	ADDISON-WESLEY PUBLISHING CO.		151-200

LEVEL	FORMAT	TITLE	PUBLISHER	NT	$PRICE

88 - SKILL: HOMONYMS & HOMOGRAPHS

LEVEL	FORMAT	TITLE	PUBLISHER	NT	$PRICE
PI	SND FS	WORD ANALYSIS SKILLS: WORD MEANINGS III	LEARNING TREE FILMSTRIPS		51-75
PI	SND FS	WHAT'S THE GOOD WORD?	MILLER-BRODY PRODUCTIONS, INC.		51-75
PI	TRANSP	SKILL RECOGNITION: MULTIPLE MEANING VOCABULARY	UNITED TRANSPARENCIES, INC.		151-200
PI	VISKIT	HOMONYMS	INSTRUCTO/MCGRAW-HILL		11-20
PI	WKBOOK	GOING BANANAS OVER LANGUAGE SKILLS	GOOD APPLE, INC.		6-10
PIJ	CL SET	SUPPORTIVE READING SKILLS: READING HOMONYMS (MULTI COPIES)	BARNELL LOFT, LTD.	42	51-75
PIJ	CL SET	SUPPORTIVE READING SKILLS: READING HOMOGRAPHS (MULTI COPIES)	BARNELL LOFT, LTD.	26	31-50
PIJ	MULTIU	CREATURE FEATURES: VOCABULARY DEVELOPMENT	EDUCATIONAL ACTIVITIES, INC.		31-50
PIJ	WKBOOK	ANTONYMS, SYNONYMS, HOMONYMS	FRANK SCHAFFER PUBLICATIONS, INC		<5
I	ACTCRD	WORD ANALYSIS: HOMONYMS & HOMOGRAPHS	INSTRUCTIONAL FAIR		<5
I	AUDKIT	EVERYDAY VOCABULARY	EBSCO CURRICULUM MATERIALS		51-75
I	AUDKIT	LET'S ALL (AWL) TAKE A BOW (BOW)	MEDIA MATERIALS, INC.		6-10
I	AUDKIT	TAKE YOUR PICK	MEDIA MATERIALS, INC.		6-10
I	AUDKIT	HOMONYMS	MEDIA MATERIALS, INC.		6-10
I	AUDKIT	EXPANDING VOCABULARY	HAMPDEN PUBLICATIONS, INC.		21-30
I	AUDKIT	WORDPLAY	CORONET MULTI MEDIA		76-100
I	DITTO	READING ESSENTIALS: VOCABULARY DEVELOPMENT, GRADE 3	CONTINENTAL PRESS, INC.		<5
I	DITTO	READING ESSENTIALS: VOCABULARY DEVELOPMENT, GRADE 4	CONTINENTAL PRESS, INC.		<5
I	DITTO	READING ESSENTIALS: VOCABULARY DEVELOPMENT, GRADE 5	CONTINENTAL PRESS, INC.		<5
I	DITTO	WORD SPY, GRADE 4	CONTINENTAL PRESS, INC.		<5
I	DITTO	WORD SPY, GRADE 5	CONTINENTAL PRESS, INC.		<5
I	DITTO	NEW LANGUAGE PATTERNS & USAGE: GRADE 4, PART 3	CONTINENTAL PRESS, INC.		<5
I	DITTO	NEW LANGUAGE PATTERNS & USAGE: GRADE 5, PART 3	CONTINENTAL PRESS, INC.		<5
I	DITTO	NEW LANGUAGE PATTERNS & USAGE: GRADE 6, PART 3	CONTINENTAL PRESS, INC.		<5
I	DITTO	WORD ANALYSIS: HOMONYMS & HOMOGRAPHS	INSTRUCTIONAL FAIR		<5
I	DITTO	WORD WIZARDS, BOOK 2	HAYES SCHOOL PUBLISHING COMPANY		<5
I	DITTO	WORD WIZARDS, BOOK 3	HAYES SCHOOL PUBLISHING COMPANY		<5
I	DITTO	VOCABULARY SKILLS A	ACTIVITY RESOURCES COMPANY, INC.		<5
I	DITTO	VOCABULARY SKILLS B	ACTIVITY RESOURCES COMPANY, INC.		<5
I	GAME	CREATURE CLUES TO WORDS	CREATIVE TEACHING ASSOCIATES		<5
I	GAME	CREATURE CLUES TO WORDS	ENRICH, INC.		<5
I	GAME	CHECKMATE: HOMONYMS (HOMOPHONES)	DM EDUCATIONAL PUBLICATIONS		<5
I	GAME	LEMON TREE	XEROX EDUCATION PUBLICATIONS		51-75
I	GAME	PRESS & CHECK BINGO GAMES: HOMONYMS	MILTON BRADLEY/PLAYSKOOL		6-10
I	MULTIM	SELECT-A-SKILL KIT, UNIT 3: SPORTS	IMPERIAL INTERNATIONAL LEARNING		51-75
I	MULTIM	SELECT-A-SKILL KIT, UNIT 3: SPORTS	IMPERIAL INTERNATIONAL LEARNING		51-75
I	MULTIM	VOCABULARY DEVELOPMENT	MILTON BRADLEY/PLAYSKOOL		76-100
I	PUPILB	SUPPORTIVE READING SKILLS: MASTERING MULTI. MEANINGS, D1-D16	BARNELL LOFT, LTD.		21-30
I	PUPILB	SUPPORTIVE READING SKILLS: READING HOMONYMS, D1-D8	BARNELL LOFT, LTD.		11-20
I	PUPILB	SUPPORTIVE READING SKILLS: READING HOMONYMS, E1-E8	BARNELL LOFT, LTD.		11-20
I	PUPILB	SUPPORTIVE READING SKILLS: READING HOMONYMS, F1-F8	BARNELL LOFT, LTD.		11-20
I	PUPILB	SUPPORTIVE READING SKILLS: READING HOMOGRAPHS, D1-D4	BARNELL LOFT, LTD.		11-20
I	PUPILB	SUPPORTIVE READING SKILLS: READING HOMOGRAPHS, E1-E8	BARNELL LOFT, LTD.		11-20
I	PUPILB	SUPPORTIVE READING SKILLS: READING HOMOGRAPHS, F1-F8	BARNELL LOFT, LTD.		11-20
I	RECORD	BUILDING VERBAL POWER IN THE UPPER GRADES, VOLUME 1	CLASSROOM MATERIALS CO.		6-10
IJ	AUDKIT	VOCABULARY STUDY	EBSCO CURRICULUM MATERIALS		51-75
IJ	AUDKIT	DEVELOPMENTAL VOCABULARY	EBSCO CURRICULUM MATERIALS		51-75
IJ	AUDKIT	INTERMEDIATE VOCABULARY	HAMPDEN PUBLICATIONS, INC.		101-150
IJ	A/VKIT	PROBLEM WORDS MADE EASY	EYE GATE MEDIA		76-100
IJ	A/VKIT	VOCABULARY BUILDERS	EYE GATE MEDIA		51-75
IJ	GAME	GAMEBOARD KIT D	READING JOY, INC.		6-10
IJ	GAME	LIME TREE	XEROX EDUCATION PUBLICATIONS		51-75
IJ	WKBOOK	DEVELOPING LANGUAGE ARTS SKILLS: VOCABULARY ENRICHMENT	WILSON EDUCATIONAL MEDIA		6-10
IJ	WKBOOK	BOOK TWO, PART ONE: VOCABULARY DEVELOPMENT ACTIVITIES	T.S. DENISON & COMPANY		6-10
IJ	WKBOOK	LANGUAGE 940, GRADES 4 - 8	STECK-VAUGHN COMPANY		<5
IJS	AUDCRD	LOOK-ALIKES & SOUND-ALIKES	AUDIOTRONICS CORPORATION		21-30
IJS	AUDKIT	HITS, LEVEL 4: FOUR TOPS, KEEPER OF THE CASTLE	MODULEARN, INC.		11-20
IJS	AUDKIT	HITS, LEVEL 4: PAUL SIMON, AMERICAN TUNE	MODULEARN, INC.		11-20
J	PUPILB	SUPPORTIVE READING SKILLS: READING HOMONYMS, ADV. 1-ADV. 13	BARNELL LOFT, LTD.		11-20
J	PUPILB	SUPPORTIVE READING SKILLS: READING HOMOGRAPHS, ADV. 1-ADV. 2	BARNELL LOFT, LTD.		11-20
JS	AUDKIT	LEARNING BASIC VOCABULARY	HAMPDEN PUBLICATIONS, INC.		101-150
JS	SKLKIT	TARGET ORANGE: VOCABULARY DEVELOPMENT KIT II	ADDISON-WESLEY PUBLISHING CO.		151-200

89 - SKILL: HOMOPHONE

LEVEL	FORMAT	TITLE	PUBLISHER	NT	$PRICE
RP	PUPILB	USING WORDS SERIES	CHILD'S WORLD	5	21-30
RP	PUPILB	NEVER MONKEY WITH A MONKEY	CHILD'S WORLD		<5
RP	PUPILB	WHAT DID YOU SAY?	CHILD'S WORLD		<5
RP	PUPILB	JOAN HANSON WORD BOOKS	CHILD'S WORLD	16	51-75
RP	PUPILB	HOMOGRAPHIC HOMOPHONES	CHILD'S WORLD		<5
P	ACTCRD	HOMONYM CARDS, HOMOPHONES	DEVELOPMENTAL LEARNING MATERIALS		<5
P	ACTCRD	HOMONYMS PACER	DM EDUCATIONAL PUBLICATIONS		<5
P	AUDKIT	TWO WORDS IN ONE	MEDIA MATERIALS, INC.		6-10
P	DITTO	NEW PHONICS & WORD ANALYSIS SKILLS: GRADE 3, PART 3	CONTINENTAL PRESS, INC.		<5
P	DITTO	NEW LANGUAGE PATTERNS & USAGE: GRADE 2, PART 3	CONTINENTAL PRESS, INC.		<5
P	DITTO	READING ESSENTIALS: VOCABULARY DEVELOPMENT, GRADE 3, BOOK 2	CONTINENTAL PRESS, INC.		<5
P	GAME	CHECKMATE: HOMONYMS (HOMOPHONES)	DM EDUCATIONAL PUBLICATIONS		<5
P	RECORD	COMPREHENSION THROUGH LISTENING, VOLUME 4	CLASSROOM MATERIALS CO.		6-10
PI	SND FS	WORD ANALYSIS SKILLS: WORD MEANINGS III	LEARNING TREE FILMSTRIPS		51-75
PI	TRANSP	SKILL RECOGNITION: MULTIPLE MEANING VOCABULARY	UNITED TRANSPARENCIES, INC.		151-200

LEVEL	FORMAT	TITLE	PUBLISHER	NT	$PRICE

89 - SKILL: HOMOPHONE

LEVEL	FORMAT	TITLE	PUBLISHER	NT	$PRICE
I	AUDKIT	LET'S ALL (AWL) TAKE A BOW (BOW)	MEDIA MATERIALS, INC.		6-10
I	AUDKIT	TAKE YOUR PICK	MEDIA MATERIALS, INC.		6-10
I	AUDKIT	MINISYSTEMS: MULTIPLE MEANINGS	CORONET MULTI MEDIA		11-20
I	AUDKIT	WORDPLAY	CORONET MULTI MEDIA		76-100
I	DITTO	READING ESSENTIALS: VOCABULARY DEVELOPMENT, GRADE 3	CONTINENTAL PRESS, INC.		<5
I	GAME	CHECKMATE: HOMONYMS (HOMOPHONES)	DM EDUCATIONAL PUBLICATIONS		<5
IJ	AUDKIT	INTERMEDIATE VOCABULARY	HAMPDEN PUBLICATIONS, INC.		101-150
IJ	A/VKIT	PROBLEM WORDS MADE EASY	EYE GATE MEDIA		76-100
JS	AUDKIT	LEARNING BASIC VOCABULARY	HAMPDEN PUBLICATIONS, INC.		101-150

90 - SKILL: ANALOGIES, SIMILIES, METAPHORS

LEVEL	FORMAT	TITLE	PUBLISHER	NT	$PRICE
RP	MULTIM	AMELIA BEDELIA	EDUCATIONAL ENRICHMENT MATERIALS		76-100
RP	MULTIM	COME BACK, AMELIA BEDELIA	EDUCATIONAL ENRICHMENT MATERIALS		21-30
RP	PUPILB	USING WORDS SERIES	CHILD'S WORLD	5	21-30
RP	PUPILB	SIMILIES	CHILD'S WORLD		<5
RP	PUPILB	MORE SIMILIES	CHILD'S WORLD		<5
RP	PUPILB	MORE SIMILIES	CHILD'S WORLD		<5
RP	PUPILB	YOU DANCE LIKE AN OSTRICH	CHILD'S WORLD		<5
RP	PUPILB	JOAN HANSON WORD BOOKS	CHILD'S WORLD	16	51-75
RP	SND FS	ANALOGAMES	CHILDREN'S BOOK & MUSIC CENTER		31-50
RPI	MULTIM	ABSTRACT LANGUAGE CONCEPTS	LISTEN & LEARN CORPORATION		76-100
P	AUDKIT	KIT 58: BUILDING WORD POWER, LEVEL 3	EDUCATIONAL RESEARCH, INC.		101-150
P	AUDKIT	IT'S RAINING CATS & DOGS	MEDIA MATERIALS, INC.		6-10
P	AUDKIT	LITTLE RIDDLES	MEDIA MATERIALS, INC.		6-10
P	CL SET	SUPPORTIVE READING SKILLS: PHONIC ANALOGIES (MULTI COPIES)	BARNELL LOFT, LTD.	24	31-50
P	DITTO	COMPREHENSION SKILLS 2	ACTIVITY RESOURCES COMPANY, INC.		<5
P	PUPILB	SUPPORTIVE READING SKILLS: PHONIC ANALOGIES, A1-A8	BARNELL LOFT, LTD.		11-20
P	PUPILB	SUPPORTIVE READING SKILLS: PHONIC ANALOGIES, B1-B8	BARNELL LOFT, LTD.		11-20
P	PUPILB	SUPPORTIVE READING SKILLS: PHONIC ANALOGIES, C1-C8	BARNELL LOFT, LTD.		11-20
P	PUPILB	SIMILES	LERNER PUBLICATIONS COMPANY		<5
P	PUPILB	MORE SIMILES	LERNER PUBLICATIONS COMPANY		<5
P	PUPILB	SMILES	INSTRUCTO/MCGRAW-HILL		<5
P	RECORD	BUILDING VERBAL POWER, VOLUME 3	CLASSROOM MATERIALS CO.		6-10
P	WKBOOK	WORKING WITH WORDS, BOOK G	GINN & COMPANY		<5
PI	ACTCRD	WORD DEVILS SKILL CARDS	MILTON BRADLEY/PLAYSKOOL		<5
PI	AUDKIT	BEGINNING VOCABULARY	EBSCO CURRICULUM MATERIALS		51-75
PI	AUDKIT	TOTAL BUILDING WORK POWER (KITS 58 - 61)	EDUCATIONAL RESEARCH, INC.	4	>450
PI	AUDKIT	AS HUNGRY AS A BEAR	MEDIA MATERIALS, INC.		6-10
I	AUDKIT	KIT 59: BUILDING WORD POWER, LEVEL 4	EDUCATIONAL RESEARCH, INC.		101-150
I	AUDKIT	KIT 60: BUILDING WORD POWER, LEVEL 5	EDUCATIONAL RESEARCH, INC.		101-150
I	AUDKIT	KIT 61: BUILDING WORD POWER, LEVEL 16	EDUCATIONAL RESEARCH, INC.		101-150
I	AUDKIT	PAINT WITH PENCIL	MEDIA MATERIALS, INC.		6-10
I	GAME	VOCABULARY QUIZMO	MILTON BRADLEY/PLAYSKOOL		<5
I	MULTIM	SELECT-A-SKILL KIT, UNIT 5: FAMOUS PEOPLE	IMPERIAL INTERNATIONAL LEARNING		51-75
I	MULTIM	SELECT-A-SKILL KIT, UNIT 5: FAMOUS PEOPLE	IMPERIAL INTERNATIONAL LEARNING		51-75
I	PUPILB	FUNNY BUSINESS	INSTRUCTO/MCGRAW-HILL		<5
I	RECORD	BUILDING VERBAL POWER IN THE UPPER GRADES, VOLUME 3	CLASSROOM MATERIALS CO.		6-10
IJ	AUDKIT	VOCABULARY STUDY	EBSCO CURRICULUM MATERIALS		51-75
IJ	AUDKIT	DEVELOPMENTAL VOCABULARY	EBSCO CURRICULUM MATERIALS		51-75
IJ	AUDKIT	GETTING INTO FIGURATIVE LANGUAGE	MEDIA MATERIALS, INC.		6-10
IJ	PUPILB	IN OTHER WORDS	INSTRUCTO/MCGRAW-HILL		<5
IJ	WKBOOK	DEVELOPING LANGUAGE ARTS SKILLS: VOCABULARY ENRICHMENT	WILSON EDUCATIONAL MEDIA		6-10
J	WKBOOK	WORD CLUES, BOOK H	EDL/MCGRAW-HILL		<5
J	WKBOOK	WORD CLUES, BOOK I	EDL/MCGRAW-HILL		<5
S	WKBOOK	WORD CLUES, BOOK J	EDL/MCGRAW-HILL		<5

91 - SKILL: IDIOMS

LEVEL	FORMAT	TITLE	PUBLISHER	NT	$PRICE
RPI	MULTIM	ABSTRACT LANGUAGE CONCEPTS	LISTEN & LEARN CORPORATION		76-100
P	DITTO	COMPREHENSION SKILLS 2	ACTIVITY RESOURCES COMPANY, INC.		<5
P	PUPILB	SUPPORTIVE READING SKILLS: INTERPRETING IDIOMS, A	BARNELL LOFT, LTD.		11-20
P	PUPILB	SUPPORTIVE READING SKILLS: INTERPRETING IDIOMS, B	BARNELL LOFT, LTD.		11-20
P	PUPILB	SUPPORTIVE READING SKILLS: INTERPRETING IDIOMS, C1-C2	BARNELL LOFT, LTD.		11-20
PI	DITTO	PRACTICE IN VOCABULARY BUILDING, BOOK A (GRADES 3 - 4)	INSTRUCTOR PUBLICATIONS, INC.		<5
PI	SP EQT	PROGRAMMED LANGUAGE/READING, LEVEL II: SET 15, HOME	INSTRUCTIONAL INDUSTRIES (G.E.)		101-150
PI	WKBOOK	RAINING CATS & DOGS	DORMAC, INC.		<5
PIJ	CL SET	SUPPORTIVE READING SKILLS: INTERPRETING IDIOMS (MULT COPIES)	BARNELL LOFT, LTD.	18	21-30
I	DITTO	PRACTICE IN VOCABULARY BUILDING, BOOK B (GRADES 4 - 5)	INSTRUCTOR PUBLICATIONS, INC.		<5
I	PUPILB	SUPPORTIVE READING SKILLS: INTERPRETING IDIOMS, D1-D4	BARNELL LOFT, LTD.		11-20
I	PUPILB	SUPPORTIVE READING SKILLS: INTERPRETING IDIOMS, E1-E4	BARNELL LOFT, LTD.		11-20
I	PUPILB	SUPPORTIVE READING SKILLS: INTERPRETING IDIOMS, F1-F4	BARNELL LOFT, LTD.		11-20
IJ	AUDKIT	BLAST!	MEDIA MATERIALS, INC.		6-10
IJ	DITTO	PRACTICE IN VOCABULARY BUILDING, BOOK C (GRADES 5 - 7)	INSTRUCTOR PUBLICATIONS, INC.		<5
J	PUPILB	SUPPORTIVE READING SKILLS: INTERPRETING IDIOMS, ADV.1-ADV.2	BARNELL LOFT, LTD.		11-20

92 - SKILL: WORD COMPREHENSION

LEVEL	FORMAT	TITLE	PUBLISHER	NT	$PRICE
R	WKBOOK	WORDS WE USE, BOOK I (RL K-3)	BENEFIC PRESS		<5
RP	MULTIU	READING STEP BY STEP, UNIT 2	IMPERIAL INTERNATIONAL LEARNING		51-75
RP	PUPILB	LADYBIRD: PICTURE DICTIONARY 1	IDEAL SCHOOL SUPPLY COMPANY		<5

LEVEL	FORMAT	TITLE	PUBLISHER	NT	$PRICE

92 - SKILL: WORD COMPREHENSION

LEVEL	FORMAT	TITLE	PUBLISHER	NT	$PRICE
RP	PUPILB	FUN WITH WORDS	WESTERN PUBLISHING EDUC. SERVICE		6-10
RP	PUPILB	MY FIRST BOOK OF WORDS	WALKER EDUCATIONAL BOOK CORP.		<5
RP	SND FS	BASIC RELATIONSHIPS	CLEARVUE, INC.	6	76-100
RP	SND FS	BASIC RELATIONSHIPS: SAGE & TRIP'S FOREST GAMES	CLEARVUE, INC.		11-20
RP	SND FS	BASIC RELATIONSHIPS: PICNIC SITE	CLEARVUE, INC.		11-20
RP	SND FS	BASIC RELATIONSHIPS: ANIMAL CARNIVAL	CLEARVUE, INC.		11-20
RP	SND FS	BASIC RELATIONSHIPS: FOREST JOB BOARD	CLEARVUE, INC.		11-20
RP	SND FS	BASIC RELATIONSHIPS: ANDY'S NEW HOME	CLEARVUE, INC.		11-20
RP	SND FS	BASIC RELATIONSHIPS: PLAYING THE DAY AWAY	CLEARVUE, INC.		11-20
RP	SP EQT	CONCEPT DEVELOPMENT: BEGINNING LANGUAGE CONCEPTS, KIT C	BORG-WARNER EDUCATIONAL SYSTEMS		101-150
RP	SP EQT	CONCEPT DEVELOPMENT: BEGINNING LANGUAGE CONCEPTS, KIT D	BORG-WARNER EDUCATIONAL SYSTEMS		101-150
RP	SP EQT	CONCEPT DEVELOPMENT: BEGINNING LANGUAGE CONCEPTS, KIT E	BORG-WARNER EDUCATIONAL SYSTEMS		101-150
RP	SP EQT	CONCEPT DEVELOPMENT: BEGINNING LANGUAGE CONCEPTS, KIT H	BORG-WARNER EDUCATIONAL SYSTEMS		101-150
RP	SP EQT	CONCEPT DEVELOPMENT: BEGINNING LANGUAGE CONCEPTS, KIT I	BORG-WARNER EDUCATIONAL SYSTEMS		101-150
RP	WKBOOK	COLOR WORDS, LEFT & RIGHT: PROBLEM SOLVING, PHONICS, OPPOS.	JENN PUBLICATIONS		<5
RP	WKBOOK	ADVENTURES IN READING	JENN PUBLICATIONS		<5
RPI	WKBOOK	LADYBIRD: WORKBOOKS	IDEAL SCHOOL SUPPLY COMPANY	6	6-10
P	ACTCRD	ONE TOO MANY, KIT A	BARNELL LOFT, LTD.		6-10
P	ACTCRD	ONE TOO MANY, KIT B	BARNELL LOFT, LTD.		6-10
P	ACTCRD	FUN WITH WORDS, A	BARNELL LOFT, LTD.		6-10
P	ACTCRD	FUN WITH WORDS, B	BARNELL LOFT, LTD.		6-10
P	ACTCRD	FUN WITH WORDS, C	BARNELL LOFT, LTD.		6-10
P	ACTCRD	ETA WORD CLASSIFICATION CARDS	EDUCATIONAL TEACHING AIDS		11-20
P	ACTCRD	LADYBIRD: COMPREHENSION CARDS, SET 1	IDEAL SCHOOL SUPPLY COMPANY		6-10
P	ACTCRD	LADYBIRD: COMPREHENSION CARDS, SET 2	IDEAL SCHOOL SUPPLY COMPANY		6-10
P	ACTCRD	FIND THE MISSING WORD	IDEAL SCHOOL SUPPLY COMPANY		6-10
P	ACTCRD	LANGUAGE ACTIVITY CARDS: BASIC WORD COMPREHENSION	WEBER COSTELLO COMPANY		6-10
P	AUDKIT	PRIMARY BASIC READING COMPREHENSION	EYE GATE MEDIA	5	31-50
P	AUDKIT	YOUR OWN LOAD OF WORDS	EYE GATE MEDIA		6-10
P	AUDKIT	FUN WITH WORD USAGE	EYE GATE MEDIA		6-10
P	AUDKIT	KIT 58: BUILDING WORD POWER, LEVEL 3	EDUCATIONAL RESEARCH, INC.		101-150
P	CHART	WORD CONCEPT CARDS: WORDS THAT TELL "WHERE"	KENWORTHY EDUCATIONAL SERVICE		<5
P	CHART	WORD CONCEPT CARDS: WORDS THAT TELL "HOW"	KENWORTHY EDUCATIONAL SERVICE		<5
P	CHART	WORD CONCEPT CARDS: WORDS THAT TELL "WHEN"	KENWORTHY EDUCATIONAL SERVICE		<5
P	CHART	WORD CONCEPT CARDS: WORDS THAT TELL "HOW MUCH"	KENWORTHY EDUCATIONAL SERVICE		<5
P	CL SET	PICTO-CABULARY, BASIC WORD SET A	BARNELL LOFT, LTD.		76-100
P	CL SET	SUPPORTIVE READING SKILLS: PHONIC ANALOGIES (MULTI COPIES)	BARNELL LOFT, LTD.	24	31-50
P	DITTO	PHONICS IVB	HAYES SCHOOL PUBLISHING COMPANY		<5
P	DITTO	WORD WIZARDS, BOOK 1	HAYES SCHOOL PUBLISHING COMPANY		<5
P	FLASH	COLOR NAME CARDS	IDEAL SCHOOL SUPPLY COMPANY		<5
P	GAME	INSTRUCTIONAL AID PACKS: TACK ON! A	BARNELL LOFT, LTD.		6-10
P	GAME	INSTRUCTIONAL AID PACKS: TACK ON! B	BARNELL LOFT, LTD.		6-10
P	GAME	INSTRUCTIONAL AID PACKS: TACK ON! C	BARNELL LOFT, LTD.		6-10
P	GAME	INSTRUCTIONAL AID PACKS: TACK ON! D	BARNELL LOFT, LTD.		6-10
P	GAME	INSTRUCTIONAL AID PACKS: SWAP! A	BARNELL LOFT, LTD.		6-10
P	GAME	INSTRUCTIONAL AID PACKS: SWAP! B	BARNELL LOFT, LTD.		6-10
P	GAME	INSTRUCTIONAL AID PACKS: SWAP! C	BARNELL LOFT, LTD.		6-10
P	GAME	INSTRUCTIONAL AID PACKS: TURN ABOUT! A	BARNELL LOFT, LTD.		6-10
P	GAME	INSTRUCTIONAL AID PACKS: TURN ABOUT! B	BARNELL LOFT, LTD.		6-10
P	GAME	INSTRUCTIONAL AID PACKS: TURN ABOUT! C	BARNELL LOFT, LTD.		6-10
P	GAME	INSTRUCTIONAL AID PACKS: STRIKE OUT! A	BARNELL LOFT, LTD.		6-10
P	GAME	INSTRUCTIONAL AID PACKS: STRIKE OUT! B	BARNELL LOFT, LTD.		6-10
P	GAME	INSTRUCTIONAL AID PACKS: STRIKE OUT! C	BARNELL LOFT, LTD.		6-10
P	MANIPU	WORD BUILDERS: LARGE LETTER CARDS	KENWORTHY EDUCATIONAL SERVICE		<5
P	MANIPU	WORD BUILDERS: SMALL LETTER CARDS	KENWORTHY EDUCATIONAL SERVICE		<5
P	MANIPU	PHONICS E-Z LANGUAGE LEARNING SLIDE RULES, WORD-BUILDING	E-Z GRADER COMPANY		<5
P	MANIPU	ETA WHAT-AM-I?	EDUCATIONAL TEACHING AIDS		<5
P	MULTIM	DEVELOPING READING SKILLS, PART I: WORD RECOGNITION	EDUCATIONAL ENRICHMENT MATERIALS		101-150
P	PUPILB	SERIES C EXERCISES	BEHAVIORAL RESEARCH LABORATORIES		<5
P	PUPILB	SUPPORTIVE READING SKILLS: PHONIC ANALOGIES, A1-A8	BARNELL LOFT, LTD.		11-20
P	PUPILB	SUPPORTIVE READING SKILLS: PHONIC ANALOGIES, B1-B8	BARNELL LOFT, LTD.		11-20
P	PUPILB	SUPPORTIVE READING SKILLS: PHONIC ANALOGIES, C1-C8	BARNELL LOFT, LTD.		11-20
P	SKLKIT	FOKES SENTENCE BUILDER	TEACHING RESOURCES CORPORATION		51-75
P	SKLKIT	FOKES SENTENCE BUILDER EXPANSION	TEACHING RESOURCES CORPORATION		31-50
P	SND FS	WORDS TO WORK WITH I	LEARNING TREE FILMSTRIPS		51-75
P	SND FS	WORDS TO WORK WITH II	LEARNING TREE FILMSTRIPS		51-75
P	SND FS	WORDS TO WORK WITH III	LEARNING TREE FILMSTRIPS		51-75
P	VISKIT	PICTURE/WORD CONCEPTS: CLOTHING	INSTRUCTOR PUBLICATIONS, INC.		<5
P	VISKIT	PICTURE/WORD CONCEPTS: HOUSEHOLD ITEMS	INSTRUCTOR PUBLICATIONS, INC.		<5
P	VISKIT	PICTURE/WORD CONCEPTS: CLOTHING ACCESSORIES	INSTRUCTOR PUBLICATIONS, INC.		<5
P	VISKIT	PICTURE/WORD CONCEPTS: DISHES & UTENSILS	INSTRUCTOR PUBLICATIONS, INC.		<5
P	VISKIT	PICTURE/WORD CONCEPTS: SCHOOL ITEMS	INSTRUCTOR PUBLICATIONS, INC.		<5
P	WKBOOK	WORDS WE USE, BOOK II (RL 1-3)	BENEFIC PRESS		<5
P	WKBOOK	WORDS WE USE, BOOK III (RL 1-3)	BENEFIC PRESS		<5
P	WKBOOK	WORDS WE USE, BOOK IV (RL 1-3)	BENEFIC PRESS		<5
P	WKBOOK	WORDS WE USE, BOOK V (RL 1-3)	BENEFIC PRESS		<5
P	WKBOOK	MOTT BASIC LANG. SKILLS: BOOK 1302	ALLIED EDUCATION COUNCIL		<5
P	WKBOOK	WORKING WITH WORDS, BOOK G	GINN & COMPANY		<5
P	WKBOOK	COLOR WORDS	JENN PUBLICATIONS		<5

LEVEL	FORMAT	TITLE	PUBLISHER	NT	$PRICE

92 - SKILL: WORD COMPREHENSION

LEVEL	FORMAT	TITLE	PUBLISHER	NT	$PRICE
P	WKBOOK	PHONICS & READING REVIEW	JENN PUBLICATIONS		<5
PI	ACTCRD	VOCABULARY	FRANK SCHAFFER PUBLICATIONS, INC		<5
PI	ACTCRD	READING FUN FACTORY	KIDS & COMPANY		<5
PI	ACTCRD	BUILDING STORIES WITH JULIE & JACK	ST. JOHN SCHOOL FOR THE DEAF		<5
PI	ACTCRD	EGGHEAD JAZZ	LESWING PRESS		11-20
PI	ACTCRD	STANDARD BASIC WORD POWER PACER	DM EDUCATIONAL PUBLICATIONS		6-10
PI	ACTCRD	LEARNING CENTER PAK (GRADES 2 - 4)	WISE OWL PUBLICATIONS		31-50
PI	AUDKIT	TOTAL BUILDING WORK POWER (KITS 58 - 61)	EDUCATIONAL RESEARCH, INC.	4	>450
PI	AUDKIT	FUN WITH WORDS	MEDIA MATERIALS, INC.		6-10
PI	AUDKIT	BEGINNING STRUCTURAL ANALYSIS	HAMPDEN PUBLICATIONS, INC.		101-150
PI	CL SET	AEVAC STARTER 101 (NON-READERS)	AEVAC, INC.	10	11-20
PI	DITTO	MYSTERY READING RIDDLES	FRANK SCHAFFER PUBLICATIONS, INC		<5
PI	DITTO	READING ACTIVITIES & SKILLS	XEROX EDUCATION PUBLICATIONS		<5
PI	DITTO	VOCABULARY SKILLS 1	ACTIVITY RESOURCES COMPANY, INC.		<5
PI	DITTO	VOCABULARY SKILLS 2	ACTIVITY RESOURCES COMPANY, INC.		<5
PI	GAME	ANIMAL FAMILIES	CREATIVE TEACHING ASSOCIATES		<5
PI	GAME	VOCABULARY DEVELOPMENT	FRANK SCHAFFER PUBLICATIONS, INC		<5
PI	GAME	77 GAMES FOR READING GROUPS	FEARON PITMAN PUBLISHERS, INC.		<5
PI	GAME	INSTRUCTIONAL AID PACKS - VOCABULARY GAMES	BARNELL LOFT, LTD.	20	101-150
PI	GUIDE	100 INDIVIDUALIZED ACTIVITIES FOR READING	FEARON PITMAN PUBLISHERS, INC.		<5
PI	PUPILB	LADYBIRD: DICTIONARY 2	IDEAL SCHOOL SUPPLY COMPANY		<5
PI	TEXTBK	WORDS, FROM PRINT TO MEANING	ADDISON-WESLEY PUBLISHING CO.		6-10
PI	WKBOOK	ADVENTURES IN READING COMPREHENSION	FRANK SCHAFFER PUBLICATIONS, INC		<5
PI	WKBOOK	BUILDING STORIES WITH JULIE & JACK	ST. JOHN SCHOOL FOR THE DEAF		<5
I	ACTCRD	FUN WITH WORDS, D	BARNELL LOFT, LTD.		6-10
I	ACTCRD	FUN WITH WORDS, E	BARNELL LOFT, LTD.		6-10
I	ACTCRD	FUN WITH WORDS, F	BARNELL LOFT, LTD.		6-10
I	AUDKIT	EVERYDAY VOCABULARY	EBSCO CURRICULUM MATERIALS		51-75
I	AUDKIT	KIT 59: BUILDING WORD POWER, LEVEL 4	EDUCATIONAL RESEARCH, INC.		101-150
I	AUDKIT	KIT 60: BUILDING WORD POWER, LEVEL 5	EDUCATIONAL RESEARCH, INC.		101-150
I	AUDKIT	KIT 61: BUILDING WORD POWER, LEVEL 16	EDUCATIONAL RESEARCH, INC.		101-150
I	AUDKIT	IF THE SHOE FITS	MEDIA MATERIALS, INC.		6-10
I	AUDKIT	MINISYSTEMS: MULTIPLE MEANINGS	CORONET MULTI MEDIA		11-20
I	CL SET	WORDS AROUND THE HOUSE	BARNELL LOFT, LTD.		31-50
I	CL SET	WORDS AROUND THE NEIGHBORHOOD	BARNELL LOFT, LTD.		31-50
I	CL SET	WORDS TO EAT	BARNELL LOFT, LTD.		31-50
I	CL SET	WORDS TO WEAR	BARNELL LOFT, LTD.		31-50
I	CL SET	WORDS TO MEET	BARNELL LOFT, LTD.		31-50
I	DITTO	WORD WIZARDS, BOOK 2	HAYES SCHOOL PUBLISHING COMPANY		<5
I	DITTO	WORD WIZARDS, BOOK 3	HAYES SCHOOL PUBLISHING COMPANY		<5
I	DITTO	VOCABULARY BUILDING, UPPER INTERMEDIATE	HAYES SCHOOL PUBLISHING COMPANY		<5
I	DITTO	WORD DISCOVERY	HAYES SCHOOL PUBLISHING COMPANY		<5
I	DITTO	VOCABULARY SKILLS A	ACTIVITY RESOURCES COMPANY, INC.		<5
I	GAME	INSTRUCTIONAL AID PACKS: TACK ON! E	BARNELL LOFT, LTD.		6-10
I	GAME	INSTRUCTIONAL AID PACKS: SWAP! D	BARNELL LOFT, LTD.		6-10
I	GAME	INSTRUCTIONAL AID PACKS: SWAP! E	BARNELL LOFT, LTD.		6-10
I	GAME	INSTRUCTIONAL AID PACKS: TURN ABOUT! D	BARNELL LOFT, LTD.		6-10
I	GAME	INSTRUCTIONAL AID PACKS: TURN ABOUT! E	BARNELL LOFT, LTD.		6-10
I	GAME	INSTRUCTIONAL AID PACKS: STRIKE OUT! D	BARNELL LOFT, LTD.		6-10
I	GAME	INSTRUCTIONAL AID PACKS: STRIKE OUT! E	BARNELL LOFT, LTD.		6-10
I	GAME	VOCABULARY QUIZMO	MILTON BRADLEY/PLAYSKOOL		<5
I	PUPILB	SERIES F EXERCISES	BEHAVIORAL RESEARCH LABORATORIES		<5
I	SND FS	MAKING WORDS WORK	CORONET MULTI MEDIA		101-150
I	WKBOOK	WORDS WE USE, BOOK VI (RL 4-6)	BENEFIC PRESS		<5
I	WKBOOK	WORDS WE USE, BOOK VII (RL 4-6)	BENEFIC PRESS		<5
I	WKBOOK	WORDS WE USE, BOOK VIII (RL 4-6)	BENEFIC PRESS		<5
IJ	AUDKIT	VOCABULARY STUDY	EBSCO CURRICULUM MATERIALS		51-75
IJ	A/VKIT	VOCABULARY BUILDERS	EYE GATE MEDIA		51-75
IJ	A/VKIT	WORD BUILDERS	EYE GATE MEDIA		76-100
IJ	CL SET	PICTO-CABULARY SERIES, SET III	BARNELL LOFT, LTD.		31-50
IJ	CL SET	PICTO-CABULARY SERIES, SET 222	BARNELL LOFT, LTD.		31-50
IJ	GAME	WORD SPEEDWAY	CREATIVE TEACHING ASSOCIATES		6-10
IJ	VISKIT	VERSA-TILES, VOCABULARY SET	EDUCATIONAL TEACHING AIDS		11-20
IJ	WKBOOK	BOOK TWO, PART TWO: COMPREHENSION ACTIVITIES	T.S. DENISON & COMPANY		6-10
IJS	AUDKIT	REACH	ECONOMY COMPANY		151-200
IJS	AUDKIT	HITS, LEVEL 4: COVEN, ONE TIN SOLDIER	MODULEARN, INC.		11-20
IJS	AUDKIT	HITS, LEVEL 4: PAUL SIMON, HOMEWARD BOUND	MODULEARN, INC.		11-20
IJS	AUDKIT	HITS, LEVEL 4: PAUL SIMON, FLOWERS NEVER BEND W/THE RAINFALL	MODULEARN, INC.		11-20
IJS	AUDKIT	HITS, LEVEL 4: DAVE LOGGINS, PLEASE COME TO BOSTON	MODULEARN, INC.		11-20
IJS	AUDKIT	HITS, LEVEL 4: FLEETWOOD MAC, DREAMS	MODULEARN, INC.		11-20
IJS	AUDKIT	HITS, LEVEL 4: PAUL SIMON, BRIDGE OVER TROUBLED WATERS	MODULEARN, INC.		11-20
IJS	AUDKIT	HITS, LEVEL 4: ARETHA FRANKLIN, BRIDGE OVER TROUBLED WATERS	MODULEARN, INC.		11-20
IJS	AUDKIT	HITS, LEVEL 4: FOUR TOPS, KEEPER OF THE CASTLE	MODULEARN, INC.		11-20
IJS	AUDKIT	HITS, LEVEL 4: PAUL SIMON, AMERICAN TUNE	MODULEARN, INC.		11-20
IJS	GAME	PAL READING SKILL GAME, RALLY 1	XEROX EDUCATION PUBLICATIONS		51-75
IJS	GAME	PAL READING SKILLS GAME, RALLY 2	XEROX EDUCATION PUBLICATIONS		51-75
IJS	WKBOOK	PHOTOCABULARY	ODDO PUBLISHING, INC.		<5
J	WKBOOK	TROUBLESHOOTER I: BOOK 5, WORD MASTERY	HOUGHTON MIFFLIN COMPANY		<5
JS	AUDKIT	LEARNING BASIC VOCABULARY	HAMPDEN PUBLICATIONS, INC.		101-150

LEVEL	FORMAT	TITLE	PUBLISHER	NT	$PRICE

92 - SKILL: WORD COMPREHENSION

LEVEL	FORMAT	TITLE	PUBLISHER	NT	$PRICE
JS	PUPILB	EDL CORE VOCABULARIES BOOK	EDL/MCGRAW-HILL		<5
JS	SP EQT	WORD RECOGNITION & SPELLING DEFA-COMBO-8	EDL/MCGRAW-HILL		151-200
JS	SP EQT	WORD RECOGNITION & SPELLING DEFA-35MM TACH-X	EDL/MCGRAW-HILL		151-200
JS	WKBOOK	A SKILL AT A TIME: VOCABULARY IN CONTEXT 1	JAMESTOWN PUBLICATIONS, INC.		<5
JS	WKBOOK	A SKILL AT A TIME: USING THE SIGNAL WORDS 2	JAMESTOWN PUBLICATIONS, INC.		<5
JS	WKBOOK	SIGN LANGUAGE, BOOK A	JANUS BOOK PUBLISHERS		<5
JS	WKBOOK	SIGN LANGUAGE, BOOK B	JANUS BOOK PUBLISHERS		<5
JS	WKBOOK	SIGN LANGUAGE, BOOK C	JANUS BOOK PUBLISHERS		<5
JS	WKBOOK	SIGN LANGUAGE, BOOK D	JANUS BOOK PUBLISHERS		<5
S	MULTIM	RELEVANCE SERIES: INDEPENDENCE THROUGH READING	CAMBRIDGE BOOK CO.		201-300
S	PUPILB	BARRON'S VOCABULARY BUILDER (REVISED EDITION)	BARRON'S EDUCATIONAL SERIES,INC.		<5

93 - SKILL: WORD RELATIONSHIPS

LEVEL	FORMAT	TITLE	PUBLISHER	NT	$PRICE
RP	MANIPU	ALPHABET MATCHMATES	CONSTRUCTIVE PLAYTHINGS		6-10
RP	PUPILB	FUN WITH WORDS	WESTERN PUBLISHING EDUC. SERVICE		6-10
RP	PUPILB	MY FIRST BOOK OF WORDS	WALKER EDUCATIONAL BOOK CORP.		<5
RP	PUPILB	SOUND WORDS	CHILD'S WORLD		<5
RP	PUPILB	SOUND WORDS	CHILD'S WORLD		<5
RP	PUPILB	MORE SOUND WORDS	CHILD'S WORLD		<5
RPI	MULTIM	ABSTRACT LANGUAGE CONCEPTS	LISTEN & LEARN CORPORATION		76-100
P	ACTCRD	WE READ SENTENCES, A1	BARNELL LOFT, LTD.		6-10
P	ACTCRD	WE READ SENTENCES, A2	BARNELL LOFT, LTD.		6-10
P	ACTCRD	WE READ SENTENCES, A3	BARNELL LOFT, LTD.		6-10
P	ACTCRD	WE READ SENTENCES, A4	BARNELL LOFT, LTD.		6-10
P	ACTCRD	WE READ SENTENCES, A5	BARNELL LOFT, LTD.		6-10
P	ACTCRD	ETA WORD CLASSIFICATION CARDS	EDUCATIONAL TEACHING AIDS		11-20
P	ACTCRD	FIND THE MISSING WORD	IDEAL SCHOOL SUPPLY COMPANY		6-10
P	AUDCAS	FROM PHONICS TO READING	UNITED LEARNING		31-50
P	AUDKIT	PHONICS: FUN WITH WORDS	EYE GATE MEDIA		6-10
P	AUDKIT	PRIMARY LANGUAGE ARTS	EYE GATE MEDIA	4	31-50
P	AUDKIT	PRIMARY LANGUAGE ARTS: WORD GAMES	EYE GATE MEDIA		6-10
P	CL SET	PICTO-CABULARY, BASIC WORD SET A	BARNELL LOFT, LTD.		76-100
P	DITTO	WORD RELATIONSHIPS: CUT & PASTE	FRANK SCHAFFER PUBLICATIONS, INC		<5
P	GAME	WORD RELATIONSHIPS	FRANK SCHAFFER PUBLICATIONS, INC		<5
P	MANIPU	THINKER PUZZLES, SET 4	ACADEMIC THERAPY PUBLICATIONS		6-10
P	MANIPU	THINKER PUZZLES, SET 5	ACADEMIC THERAPY PUBLICATIONS		6-10
P	MANIPU	SENTENCE-BUILDING WORD CARDS	EDUCATIONAL TEACHING AIDS		<5
P	MANIPU	ETA PICTURE SENTENCE-MAKING CARDS	EDUCATIONAL TEACHING AIDS		<5
P	PUPILB	SUPPORTIVE READING SKILLS: UNDERSTANDING WORD GROUPS, A	BARNELL LOFT, LTD.		11-20
P	PUPILB	SUPPORTIVE READING SKILLS: UNDERSTANDING WORD GROUPS, B	BARNELL LOFT, LTD.		11-20
P	PUPILB	SUPPORTIVE READING SKILLS: UNDERSTANDING WORD GROUPS, C	BARNELL LOFT, LTD.		11-20
P	SND FS	WORDS TO WORK WITH I	LEARNING TREE FILMSTRIPS		51-75
P	SND FS	WORDS TO WORK WITH II	LEARNING TREE FILMSTRIPS		51-75
P	SND FS	WORDS TO WORK WITH III	LEARNING TREE FILMSTRIPS		51-75
P	VISKIT	WORD FAMILY FABLES	INSTRUCTOR PUBLICATIONS, INC.		6-10
PI	ACTCRD	EGGHEAD JAZZ	LESWING PRESS		11-20
PI	ACTCRD	CLASSIFYING WORD PACER	DM EDUCATIONAL PUBLICATIONS		<5
PI	CHART	WORD FUNCTION & SENTENCE PATTERNS	IDEAL SCHOOL SUPPLY COMPANY		11-20
PI	DITTO	VOCABULARY SKILLS 2	ACTIVITY RESOURCES COMPANY, INC.		<5
PI	GAME	VOCABULARY DEVELOPMENT	FRANK SCHAFFER PUBLICATIONS, INC		<5
PI	PUPILB	SUPPORTIVE READING SKILLS: DISCOVERING WORD PATTERNS, BASIC	BARNELL LOFT, LTD.		11-20
PI	PUPILB	SUPPORTIVE READING SKILLS: RECOGNIZING WORD RELAT., BASIC	BARNELL LOFT, LTD.		11-20
PI	SND FS	TIME SKILLS: VOCABULARY CONCEPTS	B. L. WINCH & ASSOCIATES		76-100
PIJ	FLASH	BASIC VOCABULARY STUDY CARDS, UNIT I	DORMAC, INC.		31-50
PIJ	FLASH	BASIC VOCABULARY STUDY CARDS, UNIT II	DORMAC, INC.		21-30
PIJ	PUPILB	SUPPORTIVE READING SKILLS: UNDERSTANDING WORD GROUPS	BARNELL LOFT, LTD.	7	11-20
PIJ	PUPILB	SUPPORTIVE READING SKILLS: DISCOVERING WORD PATTERNS	BARNELL LOFT, LTD.	9	11-20
PIJ	PUPILB	SUPPORTIVE READING SKILLS: RECOGNIZING WORD RELAT.	BARNELL LOFT, LTD.	9	11-20
I	AUDKIT	READING CASSETTES: WORD FUNCTION & SENTENCE PATTERNS	IDEAL SCHOOL SUPPLY COMPANY		51-75
I	AUDKIT	IF THE SHOE FITS	MEDIA MATERIALS, INC.		6-10
I	AUDKIT	PLAIN AS THE NOSE ON YOUR FACE	MEDIA MATERIALS, INC.		6-10
I	CL SET	WORDS AROUND THE HOUSE	BARNELL LOFT, LTD.		31-50
I	CL SET	WORDS AROUND THE NEIGHBORHOOD	BARNELL LOFT, LTD.		31-50
I	CL SET	WORDS TO EAT	BARNELL LOFT, LTD.		31-50
I	CL SET	WORDS TO WEAR	BARNELL LOFT, LTD.		31-50
I	CL SET	WORDS TO MEET	BARNELL LOFT, LTD.		31-50
I	DITTO	WORD DISCOVERY	HAYES SCHOOL PUBLISHING COMPANY		<5
I	DITTO	VOCABULARY SKILLS A	ACTIVITY RESOURCES COMPANY, INC.		<5
I	GAME	VOCABULARY QUIZMO	MILTON BRADLEY/PLAYSKOOL		<5
I	PUPILB	SUPPORTIVE READING SKILLS: UNDERSTANDING WORD GROUPS, D	BARNELL LOFT, LTD.		11-20
I	PUPILB	SUPPORTIVE READING SKILLS: UNDERSTANDING WORD GROUPS, E	BARNELL LOFT, LTD.		11-20
I	PUPILB	SUPPORTIVE READING SKILLS: UNDERSTANDING WORD GROUPS, F	BARNELL LOFT, LTD.		11-20
I	PUPILB	SUPPORTIVE READING SKILLS: DISCOVERING WORD PATTERNS, INTER.	BARNELL LOFT, LTD.		11-20
I	PUPILB	SUPPORTIVE READING SKILLS: RECOGNIZING WORD RELAT., INTER.	BARNELL LOFT, LTD.		11-20
IJ	CL SET	PICTO-CABULARY SERIES, SET III	BARNELL LOFT, LTD.		31-50
IJ	CL SET	PICTO-CABULARY SERIES, SET 222	BARNELL LOFT, LTD.		31-50
IJ	VISKIT	VERSA-TILES, VOCABULARY SET	EDUCATIONAL TEACHING AIDS		11-20
IJ	WKBOOK	BOOK TWO, PART TWO: COMPREHENSION ACTIVITIES	T.S. DENISON & COMPANY		6-10

LEVEL	FORMAT	TITLE	PUBLISHER	NT $PRICE

93 - SKILL: WORD RELATIONSHIPS

LEVEL	FORMAT	TITLE	PUBLISHER	NT	$PRICE
IJS	AUDCRD	LOOK-ALIKES & SOUND-ALIKES	AUDIOTRONICS CORPORATION		21-30
J	PUPILB	SUPPORTIVE READING SKILLS: UNDERSTANDING WORD GROUPS, ADV.	BARNELL LOFT, LTD.		11-20
J	PUPILB	SUPPORTIVE READING SKILLS: DISCOVERING WORD PATTERNS, ADV.	BARNELL LOFT, LTD.		11-20
J	PUPILB	SUPPORTIVE READING SKILLS: RECOGNIZING WORD RELAT., ADV.	BARNELL LOFT, LTD.		11-20
JS	PUPILB	EDL CORE VOCABULARIES BOOK	EDL/MCGRAW-HILL		<5
S	MULTIM	RELEVANCE SERIES: INDEPENDENCE THROUGH READING	CAMBRIDGE BOOK CO.		201-300
S	PUPILB	BARRON'S VOCABULARY BUILDER (REVISED EDITION)	BARRON'S EDUCATIONAL SERIES,INC.		<5

94 - SKILL: CAREER AWARENESS & EXPLORATION - GENERAL

LEVEL	FORMAT	TITLE	PUBLISHER	NT	$PRICE
RP	MANIPU	COMMUNITY WORKERS	CONSTRUCTIVE PLAYTHINGS		6-10
RP	MANIPU	VARIED CAREER PEOPLE	CONSTRUCTIVE PLAYTHINGS		6-10
RP	MANIPU	WOMEN WORKERS	CONSTRUCTIVE PLAYTHINGS		6-10
RP	MANIPU	SERVICE CAREER PEOPLE	CONSTRUCTIVE PLAYTHINGS		6-10
RP	MANIPU	PROFESSION & SITUATION LOTTO	NIENHUIS MONTESSORI, INC.		31-50
RP	MANIPU	FLOOR PUZZLES: OCCUPATIONS	TREND ENTERPRISES, INC.		6-10
RP	MANIPU	ADVANCED PUZZLES: PLAYING DOCTORS	PLAYSKOOL, INC.		<5
RP	MANIPU	ADVANCED PUZZLES: FLYING HIGH	PLAYSKOOL, INC.		<5
RP	SND FS	JOBS AT HOME & AT SCHOOL	CORONET MULTI MEDIA		76-100
RP	SND FS	JOBS & THE COMMUNITY	CORONET MULTI MEDIA		76-100
RP	SND FS	JOBS & THINGS	CORONET MULTI MEDIA		76-100
RP	SND FS	JOBS & PEOPLE	CORONET MULTI MEDIA		76-100
RP	SND FS	JOBS & SERVICES	CORONET MULTI MEDIA		76-100
P	ACTCRD	OCCUPATION MATCH-UPS	DEVELOPMENTAL LEARNING MATERIALS		<5
P	ACTCRD	CAREER IDENTITY CARDS	DEVELOPMENTAL LEARNING MATERIALS		<5
P	ACTCRD	CAREER ASSOCIATION CARDS	DEVELOPMENTAL LEARNING MATERIALS		6-10
P	AUDKIT	JUST RIGHT JOB STORIES	CORONET MULTI MEDIA		101-150
P	CHART	COMMUNTIY WORKERS	TREND ENTERPRISES, INC.		<5
P	CHART	CAREERS	TREND ENTERPRISES, INC.		<5
P	DITTO	OCCUPATIONS 1	JUDY COMPANY		6-10
P	DITTO	OCCUPATIONS 2	JUDY COMPANY		6-10
P	FLNLBD	WHEN I GROW UP, I WANT TO BE	INSTRUCTO/MCGRAW-HILL		6-10
P	GAME	CAREERS LOTTO	MILTON BRADLEY/PLAYSKOOL		6-10
P	GUIDE	CAREER AWARENESS ACTIVITY GUIDE	JUDY COMPANY		<5
P	MANIPU	JOB PUZZLES	DEVELOPMENTAL LEARNING MATERIALS		6-10
P	MANIPU	BUILDING MATCH-UPS	DEVELOPMENTAL LEARNING MATERIALS		<5
P	MANIPU	JOB INSET PUZZLE	DEVELOPMENTAL LEARNING MATERIALS		<5
P	MANIPU	OCCUPATIONS	JUDY COMPANY		11-20
P	MANIPU	OUR HELPERS PLAY PEOPLE	MILTON BRADLEY/PLAYSKOOL		6-10
P	MULTIU	CAREER AWARENESS	JUDY COMPANY		31-50
P	MULTIM	CAREER KITS FOR THE KIDS	ENCYCLOPEDIA BRITANNICA		151-200
P	PICTUR	CAREERS CARDS	MILTON BRADLEY/PLAYSKOOL		<5
P	SND FS	WORKERS	CORONET MULTI MEDIA		101-150
PI	ACTCRD	WRITTEN LANGUAGE CARDS, CAREERS	DEVELOPMENTAL LEARNING MATERIALS		6-10
PI	MANIPU	POPEYE'S SPECIAL LANGUAGE BUILDER: MATCHING DOMINOES(SP.ED.)	KING FEATURES		11-20
PI	MULTIU	PEOPLE WHO WORK, UNIT 1	SCHOLASTIC BOOK SERVICE		76-100
PI	MULTIU	PEOPLE WHO WORK, UNIT 2	SCHOLASTIC BOOK SERVICE		76-100
PI	MULTIU	GOAL, LEVEL II: LANGUAGE DEVELOPMENT	MILTON BRADLEY/PLAYSKOOL		151-200
PI	MULTIM	WORLD OF WORK	ASSOCIATED EDUCATIONAL MATERIALS		76-100
I	CL SET	LEARNING UNITS ON CAREERS	INSTRUCTO/MCGRAW-HILL		6-10
I	DITTO	OCCUPATION WORD HUNT I	DEVELOPMENTAL LEARNING MATERIALS		<5
I	DITTO	OCCUPATION WORD HUNT II	DEVELOPMENTAL LEARNING MATERIALS		<5
I	DITTO	CAREER CROSS WORDS	DEVELOPMENTAL LEARNING MATERIALS		<5
I	PICTUR	OCCUPATION PHOTOGRAPHS	DEVELOPMENTAL LEARNING MATERIALS		<5
I	VISKIT	EXPANDING CAREER AWARENESS	INSTRUCTO/MCGRAW-HILL		6-10
IJ	GAME	WHAT SHALL I BE?	CONSTRUCTIVE PLAYTHINGS		<5
IJ	PICTUR	EXPLORING CAREERS	CONSTRUCTIVE PLAYTHINGS		6-10
IJS	ACTCRD	CAREER EDUCATION ACTIVITIES FOR SUBJECT AREA TEACHERS	ABT PUBLICATIONS		11-20
IJS	PICTUR	CONSUMER SEQUENTIAL CARDS	DEVELOPMENTAL LEARNING MATERIALS		<5
IJS	PUPILB	VERY IMPORTANT PEOPLE SERIES	CHILDREN'S PRESS, INC.	11	51-75
JS	AUDCAS	CAREER AWARENESS PROGRAM	EYE GATE MEDIA	23	>450
JS	CL SET	EXPLORING CAREERS	ABT PUBLICATIONS		31-50
JS	MULTIU	DISCOVERY	SCHOLASTIC BOOK SERVICE		151-200

APPENDIX A --

Alphabetical List of Titles
(with skills taught by each title)

TITLE	SKILL NUMBERS						
"R" CONTROLLED & VARIANT VOWELS PEEK-A-BOO	61						
+10 VOCABULARY BOOSTER, LEVEL A	83	64	35				
+10 VOCABULARY BOOSTER, LEVEL B	83	64	35				
+10 VOCABULARY BOOSTER, LEVEL C	83	64	35				
+10 VOCABULARY BOOSTER, LEVEL D	83	64	35				
+10 VOCABULARY BOOSTER, LEVEL E	83	64	35				
+4 READING BOOSTER	48	50	75				
1, 2, 3 & A ZING, ZING, ZING	2						
1,620 POWER WORDS (HARDCOVER)	64	68					
1,620 POWER WORDS, T.E.	64	68					
100 INDIVIDUALIZED ACTIVITIES FOR READING	75	8	26	92			
101 LANGUAGE ARTS ACTIVITIES	2	3	4	29	41		
101 WAYS TO LEARN VOCABULARY	83						
3,000 INSTANT WORDS	84	85					
3,140 IMPORTANT WORDS (HARDCOVER)	64	68					
3,140 IMPORTANT WORDS, T.E.	64	68					
3-D ALPHABET COLORING BOOK	49						
3-D PUZZLE: PIRATE	25	14					
30,000 SELECTED WORDS ORGANIZED BY LETTER, SOUND & SYLLABLE	4	5	69				
40-FOURS, SET 1: S SOUND	5	4	53				
40-FOURS, SET 2: R SOUND	5	4	53				
77 GAMES FOR READING GROUPS	75	84	92				
A BASIC DICTIONARY OF SYNONYMS & ANTONYMS	86	87					
A DAY AT SCHOOL, LOGIC SEQUENCE CARDS	23						
A MAFEX PROGRAM TO DEVELOP BASIC SKILLS	49						
A MAFEX PROGRAM TO DEVELOP BASIC SKILLS: ALPHA-BITS	49						
A MAFEX PROGRAM TO DEVELOP BASIC SKILLS: LET'S WRITE & SPELL	50	66					
A MANUAL FOR THE TRAINING OF SEQUENTIAL MEMORY & ATTENTION	23	24	31	32			
A PROGRAM TO ESTABLISH FLUENT SPEECH	5						
A SKILL AT A TIME: USING THE SIGNAL WORDS 2	92						
A SKILL AT A TIME: VOCABULARY IN CONTEXT 1	92						
A SPELLING WORKBOOK	65	66	67	69			
A TO Z PANEL - CAPITAL LETTERS	49						
A TO Z PANEL - LOWER CASE LETTERS	49						
A WORD RECOGNITION SYSTEM	81	75	82				
A WORLD OF COLOR	10						
A WORLD OF COLOR	10	15					
A WORM CAN WIGGLE ANYWHERE	84						
A-APPLE PIE	49						
A-Z POSTERS: ALLIGATORS TO ZOMBIES	49						
ABC	49						
ABC BOOK, GRADE 1	49						
ABC COLORING BOOK	49						
ABC LOTTO	49						
ABC MAZES	9						
ABC OF PHONICS	50						
ABC RHYMES	49	51					
ABC SKILL BUILDER	49						
ABC'S OF PHONICS PROGRAM 1: CONSONANT LETTERS B-L W/CASSETTE	52						
ABC'S OF PHONICS PROGRAM 1: CONSONANT LETTERS B-L W/RECORDS	52						
ABC'S OF PHONICS PROGRAM 2: CONSONANT LETTERS M-Z W/CASSETTE	52						
ABC'S OF PHONICS PROGRAM 2: CONSONANT LETTERS M-Z W/RECORDS	52						
ABC'S OF PHONICS PROGRAM 3: CONSONANT DIGRAPHS W/CASSETTES	53	57					
ABC'S OF PHONICS PROGRAM 3: CONSONANT DIGRAPHS W/RECORDS	53	57					
ABC'S OF PHONICS PROGRAMS 1 - 3 W/CASSETTES	53	57	58				
ABC'S OF PHONICS PROGRAMS 1 - 3 W/RECORDS	52	53	54	58			
ABC: AN ALPHABET OF MANY THINGS	49						
ABSOLUTELY ESSENTIAL WORDS	85						
ABSTRACT LANGUAGE CONCEPTS	86	87	90	91	93		
ACCENT ON READING, READER D	83						
ACCENT ON READING, READER E	83						
ACQUIRING LANGUAGE SKILLS, BOOK A	64	1	35				
ACTION CARDS, SET 1	4	46	72				
ACTION CARDS, SET 2	4	46	71				
ACTION CARDS, SET 3	4	46	70				
ACTION PHOTOS	5						
ACTION READING: THE PARTICIPATORY APPROACH	48	75					
ACTION SONGS FOR RHYTHMIC ACTIVITIES: HOLIDAY ACTION SONGS	7	29	36	38			
ACTION SONGS FOR RHYTHMIC ACTIVITIES: SING A SONG OF ACTION	7	29	36	38			
ACTION VERB BOARDS	72	14					
ACTION WORDS	86	84	72				
ACTIVITY CARDS: KINDERGARTEN VISUAL PERCEPTION	8						
ACTIVITY RHYTHMIC MOVEMENTS OF ZOO ANIMALS	2						
ADD A DASH OF SYNONYMS FOR SPICE	86						
ADDING PREFIXES	80						
ADJECTIVE MOON BASE ALARM	73						
ADJECTIVES & ADVERBS	73						
ADVANCED PHONICS PAK	51	52	53	59	60		
ADVANCED PHONICS PAK	51	52	53	59	60		
ADVANCED PHONICS: ADVANCED INITIAL & FINAL BLENDS	53						
ADVANCED PHONICS: ADVANCED INITIAL & FINAL BLENDS	53						
ADVANCED PHONICS: ADVANCED RHYMING FAMILIES	51						
ADVANCED PHONICS: ADVANCED RHYMING FAMILIES	51						
ADVANCED PHONICS: CONSONANT DIGRAPHS	53						
ADVANCED PHONICS: CONSONANT DIGRAPHS	53						
ADVANCED PHONICS: DIPHTHONGS & VOWEL DIGRAPHS	59	60					
ADVANCED PHONICS: DIPHTHONGS & VOWEL DIGRAPHS	59	60					
ADVANCED PHONICS: MULTI-SYLLABLE WORDS	82						
ADVANCED PHONICS: MULTI-SYLLABLE WORDS	82						
ADVANCED PREFIX & SUFFIX PUZZLES	80	81					
ADVANCED PUZZLES: A BIRTHDAY PARTY	9						
ADVANCED PUZZLES: AT THE BEACH	9						
ADVANCED PUZZLES: CIRCUS ELEPHANT	9						

TITLE	SKILL NUMBERS					
ADVANCED PUZZLES: FLYING HIGH	9	94				
ADVANCED PUZZLES: PLAYING DOCTORS	9	94				
ADVANCED PUZZLES: PLAYING DRESS-UP	9					
ADVANCED PUZZLES: PUPPIES	9					
ADVANCED PUZZLES: THE AQUARIUM	9					
ADVANCED PUZZLES: THE BALLOON MAN	9					
ADVANCED WORD ATTACK	53	54	57	58	55	
ADVENTURES IN LISTENING	39	40	29	36		
ADVENTURES IN READING	84	92				
ADVENTURES IN READING COMPREHENSION	2	92				
ADVENTURES IN SOUND	35					
ADVENTURES OF A, APPLE PIE	49					
AERO PHONICS LAB	53	55	54	57	58	59
AERO SIGHT READING LAB	84	71	72	73		
AERO VISUAL DISCRIMINATION LAB	23	14	19			
AEVAC PHONICS PROGRAM	48	52	53	56	57	58
AEVAC PHONICS PROGRAM, BOOK A	48	52	53	57	58	
AEVAC PHONICS PROGRAM, BOOK B	48	52	53	51		
AEVAC PHONICS PROGRAM, BOOK C	48	52	50	57	58	51
AEVAC PHONICS PROGRAM, BOOK D	53	57	58	51	57	
AEVAC PHONICS PROGRAM, BOOK E	48	52	53	57	58	55
AEVAC PHONICS PROGRAM, BOOK F	48	56	77	83		
AEVAC STARTER 101 (NON-READERS)	48	83	49	92		
AEVAC STARTER 101, BOOK 1 (NON-READERS)	49	57	50			
AEVAC STARTER 101, BOOK 10 (NON-READERS)	54	59	60	50		
AEVAC STARTER 101, BOOK 2 (NON-READERS)	49	57	50			
AEVAC STARTER 101, BOOK 3 (NON-READERS)	49	57	50			
AEVAC STARTER 101, BOOK 4 (NON-READERS)	53	49	57	50		
AEVAC STARTER 101, BOOK 5 (NON-READERS)	50	49	57			
AEVAC STARTER 101, BOOK 6 (NON-READERS)	50	49	57	53		
AEVAC STARTER 101, BOOK 7 (NON-READERS)	49	53	50	57		
AEVAC STARTER 101, BOOK 8 (NON-READERS)	49	53	50	57		
AEVAC STARTER 101, BOOK 9 (NON-READERS)	63	49	59	54		
AFFIXES PACER	76	80	81			
AGATHA'S ALPHABET	49					
AHOY! SAILING TO TREASURES THROUGH WORDS	83					
AIMS: INITIAL CONSONANTS KIT	27	52				
AIMS: VOWELS KIT	84	56	57	58		
ALADDIN CHART: RHYMING	51					
ALADDIN CHART: VOWEL SOUNDS	57	58				
ALICE IN COMMUNICATION LAND	4	7				
ALIKE & NOT ALIKE, SET 1: SIZE PICTURE CARDS	11					
ALIKE & NOT ALIKE, SET 2: PROPORTION PICTURE CARDS	11					
ALL ABOUT ME	64					
ALOYSIOUS ALLIGATOR	35					
ALPHA ONE	48	83	4			
ALPHA PHONICS PROGRAM	48	4	25			
ALPHA SET	49	50				
ALPHA TIME PLUS	48	83	9	4		
ALPHA TIME PRE-READING PROGRAM	36	4	10	27		
ALPHA TIME WITH LARGE HUGGABLES	36	48	83			
ALPHA TIME WITH SMALL HUGGABLES	36	48	83			
ALPHA WORM	49					
ALPHA, MATCH	49	10				
ALPHA-SOUND PROGRAM, GROUP 1	48	49	50			
ALPHA-SOUND PROGRAM, GROUP 2	56	57	58	59		
ALPHABET	34					
ALPHABET	49					
ALPHABET	49					
ALPHABET	49					
ALPHABET	49	50				
ALPHABET ACROBATICS	49					
ALPHABET ACTIVITIES	49					
ALPHABET ACTIVITIES	49					
ALPHABET ACTIVITIES	49					
ALPHABET ADVENTURE	49					
ALPHABET ADVENTURES	49					
ALPHABET ADVENTURES	49					
ALPHABET BINGO	49					
ALPHABET BINGO	49					
ALPHABET BOOK	49					
ALPHABET BOOK	49					
ALPHABET BOOKS	57					
ALPHABET BOOKS: PLAY WITH "A" & "T"	57					
ALPHABET BOOKS: PLAY WITH "E" & "D"	57					
ALPHABET BOOKS: PLAY WITH "I" & "G"	57					
ALPHABET BOOKS: PLAY WITH "O" & "G"	57					
ALPHABET BOOKS: PLAY WITH "U" & "G"	57					
ALPHABET CARDS	13	49				
ALPHABET CARDS	49					
ALPHABET CARDS	49					
ALPHABET CITY	49					
ALPHABET CLUE PICTURES	49	50				
ALPHABET DOG	49					
ALPHABET EXPRESS	49					
ALPHABET FLASH CARDS	49					
ALPHABET FLASH CARDS FOR STUDENTS	49					
ALPHABET FLIP BOOK	49					
ALPHABET FLIP CHART	49	50				
ALPHABET FORMS	49					
ALPHABET FUN	49					
ALPHABET FUN	49					
ALPHABET IN ACTION	49					

TITLE	SKILL NUMBERS						
ALPHABET INLAY PUZZLES: AIRPLANE	49						
ALPHABET INLAY PUZZLES: BARN	49						
ALPHABET INLAY PUZZLES: BUS	49						
ALPHABET INLAY PUZZLES: COW	49						
ALPHABET INLAY PUZZLES: DOG, TERRIER	49						
ALPHABET INLAY PUZZLES: FROG	49						
ALPHABET INLAY PUZZLES: HOUSE	49						
ALPHABET INLAY PUZZLES: TRACTOR	49						
ALPHABET INLAY PUZZLES: TRAIN	49						
ALPHABET INLAY PUZZLES: TRUCK	49						
ALPHABET INSET BOARD	49						
ALPHABET MANUSCRIPT BOOKS, LOWER CASE	49						
ALPHABET MANUSCRIPT BOOKS, UPPER CASE	49						
ALPHABET MATCH DOMINOES	49	14					
ALPHABET MATCHING FLIP BOOK	49						
ALPHABET MATCHMATES	49	93					
ALPHABET MOTOR ACTIVITIES, BOOK & TAPE	8	26	49				
ALPHABET MURAL	49	22	23				
ALPHABET PATTERN PLAQUES	49	50					
ALPHABET POSTER CARDS	42	49					
ALPHABET PUPPETS	49	50					
ALPHABET RHYMES	49						
ALPHABET ROBOTS	49						
ALPHABET SERIES	57	53	84	49			
ALPHABET SERIES	59	53	67				
ALPHABET SHOW	49	50					
ALPHABET SOUP	49						
ALPHABET SOUP FACTORY & OTHER STORIES	49						
ALPHABET STORYLAND	49						
ALPHABET TEMPLATE	49						
ALPHABET ZOO	49						
ALPHABET ZOO	49						
ALPHABET ZOO	49						
ALPHABET ZOO ACIVITIES	49						
ALPHABET, CONSONANTS, VOWELS	49	57	58				
ALPHABET: FLIP & LEARN FLASHBOOK	49						
ALPHABET: MAGIC MAN MAKES LETTERS TALK	49	50					
ALPHABET: STARTING OFF WITH PHONICS, BOOK 2	49						
ALPHABET: STARTING OFF WITH PHONICS: BOOK 2	42	49					
ALPHABETIZING ACTIVITIES	49						
ALPHABLOCKS	49						
ALPHADART	49						
ALPHAGRAMS	49						
ALTERNATIVE CARDS	2						
AMELIA BEDELIA	90						
AN ADVENTURE IN OPEN EDUCATION	4	7	7				
AN ANIMAL ALPHABET	49						
ANALOGAMES	90						
ANCHOR, VOLUME I	48	75					
ANCHOR, VOLUME II	48	75					
AND ONE AND TWO	2						
ANIMAL BODY BLOCKS	14	25					
ANIMAL CRACKERS	19	21					
ANIMAL CUT-OUTS	4	7	36	37			
ANIMAL DOMINOES	14						
ANIMAL FAMILIES	92						
ANIMAL INSERT PUZZLES	16	25					
ANIMAL PUPPETS & TAPE	7	25					
ANIMAL PUZZLERS PHONICS ACTIVITIES	52	56					
ANIMAL PUZZLES	19	25					
ANIMAL PUZZLES WITH KNOBS: SEA HORSE	25						
ANIMAL PUZZLES WITH KNOBS: SNAIL	25						
ANIMAL SORTING GAME, FARM ANIMALS	47	24	21	18			
ANIMAL SORTING GAME, FOREST ANIMALS	47	24	21	18			
ANIMAL SORTING GAME, WILD ANIMALS	47	24	21	18			
ANIMAL-GROWTH SEQUENTIAL CARDS	23						
ANIMALS CAN TEACH	2	4	35				
ANIMALS IN PLACE	23	24	9				
ANIMATED KEY CARDS	50						
ANTONYM & SYNONYM BOARDS	86	87					
ANTONYM CARDS	87						
ANTONYM POSTER CARDS	87						
ANTONYMS	87						
ANTONYMS	87						
ANTONYMS	87						
ANTONYMS, SYNONYMS, HOMONYMS	86	87	88				
ANTONYMS, SYNONYMS, HOMONYMS	86	87	88				
ANTONYMS, SYNONYMS, HOMONYMS	86	87	88				
APPLE TREE	53	56	50	27	75		
APT (AUDITORY PERCEPTION TRAINING) DISCRIMINATION	27						
APT (AUDITORY PERCEPTION TRAINING) FIGURE GROUND	32						
APT (AUDITORY PERCEPTION TRAINING) IMAGERY	26						
APT (AUDITORY PERCEPTION TRAINING) MEMORY	33						
APT (AUDITORY PERCEPTION TRAINING): MOTOR	26						
ARE YOU LISTENING?	27	48	4	75			
ARRANGING SOUNDS WITH MAGNETIC TAPES	40						
ARTICK CARDS, SET 1: S SOUND	5						
ARTICK CARDS, SET 2: R SOUND	5						
ARTICULATION MODIFICATION /1/ AMP	5						
ARTICULATION MODIFICATION /E/ /A/ AMP	5						
ARTICULATION MODIFICATION /S/ /Z/ AMP	5						
ARTICULATION MODIFICATION /S/ AMP	5						
ARTICULATION MODIFICATION /TS/ /D3/ AMP	5						

TITLE	SKILL NUMBERS					
ARTICULATION WORKSHEETS	5					
AS HUNGRY AS A BEAR	90					
ASSIST ONE & TWO & THREE	5	7	35	29		
ASSOCIATION PICTURE CARDS 1	47	19				
ASSOCIATION PICTURE CARDS 2	47	19				
ASSOCIATION PICTURE CARDS 3	47	19				
ASSOCIATION PICTURE CARDS 4	47	19	7			
ASTRO ADVERB PIRATES	73					
ATTENDING	2	3				
ATTRIBUTE BLOCKS	47					
ATTRIBUTE DOMINOES	14					
AUDIO CASSETTES AS SUPPLEMENTARY THERAPY FOR ADULT APHASICS	5					
AUDITORY DISCRIMINATION	26	27				
AUDITORY DISCRIMINATION	27	51				
AUDITORY DISCRIMINATION GAME	51	27				
AUDITORY DISCRIMINATION IN DEPTH	27					
AUDITORY FAMILIAR SOUNDS	27	28	29			
AUDITORY SKILLS: AUDITORY MEMORY	33					
AUDITORY SKILLS: CONSONANT DISCRIMINATION A	27					
AUDITORY SKILLS: CONSONANT DISCRIMINATION B	27					
AUDITORY SKILLS: FOLLOWING DIRECTIONS	37	40				
AUDITORY SKILLS: MORPHOLOGY & CLOSURE	30	76	80	81		
AUDITORY SKILLS: SYNTAX A	6	30				
AUDITORY SKILLS: SYNTAX B	6	30				
AUDITORY SKILLS: SYNTHESIS	50	82	6	30		
AUDITORY SKILLS: VOWEL DISCRIMINATION	27	56				
AUDITORY STIMULATOR CLASS KIT	39	33	26			
AUDITORY VISUAL MOTOR SKILLS: STARTING OFF W/PHONICS, BOOK 1	25	10				
AUDITORY VISUAL MOTOR SKILLS: STARTING OFF W/PHONICS, BOOK 1	25	10				
AUTO PHONICS: ALL ABOUT CONSONANTS	52					
AUTO PHONICS: PHONETIC ALPHABET	48					
AUTO PHONICS: VOWEL DIGRAPHS & DIPHTHONGS	59	60				
AUTO PHONICS: VOWEL REVIEW	56					
B T M P D R H S F KIT	10	42	5			
BACKPACK: A LANGUAGE DEVELOPMENT GAME	2	74	7			
BALLOON GAME	10	48	83			
BARE BEAR	88					
BARRON'S DEV. SKILLS FOR H.S. EQUIV. EXAM (GED) IN GRAMMAR	83	64				
BARRON'S VOCABULARY BUILDER (REVISED EDITION)	92	93				
BASE	76	80	81	77		
BASE WORD RUMMY	80	81				
BASIC ACTION POEMS & STORIES FOR EXCEPTIONAL CHILDREN, VOL 1	37	29				
BASIC ACTION POEMS & STORIES FOR EXCEPTIONAL CHILDREN, VOL 2	37	29				
BASIC COLORS	13	15				
BASIC COLORS	10	13	15			
BASIC COLORS: MAGICAL FOREST, YELLOW	13	15				
BASIC COLORS: MAGICIAN, RED	13	15				
BASIC COLORS: MR. BLUE JEANS, ORANGE	13	15				
BASIC COLORS: THREE WISHES, BLUE	13	15				
BASIC COLORS: TRAVELLER, GREEN	13	15				
BASIC COLOS DUPLICATING MASTERS	13	15				
BASIC COLOS: COLOR FULL WORLD	13	13				
BASIC COMMUNICATION GAMES	2					
BASIC COMMUNICATION SKILLS	2	4	7			
BASIC CONCEPTS	49	12	11			
BASIC ENGLISH USAGE, THE SENTENCE	74					
BASIC LANGUAGE SKILLS: ADJECTIVES & ADVERBS	73					
BASIC LANGUAGE SKILLS: NOUNS & PRONOUNS	71					
BASIC LANGUAGE SKILLS: VERBS	72					
BASIC LANGUAGE STIMULATOR	2	35	38			
BASIC PHONETIC SKILL DRILLS	52	57	58	61		
BASIC PHONICS PAK	52	53	58	57		
BASIC PHONICS PAK	52	53	58	57		
BASIC PHONICS: BASIC RHYMING FAMILIES	51					
BASIC PHONICS: BASIC RHYMING FAMILIES	51					
BASIC PHONICS: LONG VOWELS	58					
BASIC PHONICS: LONG VOWELS	58					
BASIC PHONICS: SHORT VOWELS	57					
BASIC PHONICS: SHORT VOWELS	57					
BASIC PRACTICE IN LISTENING	39	37	29	36	38	
BASIC READING SKILLS	52	56	75			
BASIC READING SKILLS	80	81	76	86	87	70
BASIC RELATIONSHIPS	42	43	92			
BASIC RELATIONSHIPS: ANDY'S NEW HOME	42	43	92			
BASIC RELATIONSHIPS: ANIMAL CARNIVAL	42	43	92			
BASIC RELATIONSHIPS: FOREST JOB BOARD	42	43	92			
BASIC RELATIONSHIPS: PICNIC SITE	42	43	92			
BASIC RELATIONSHIPS: PLAYING THE DAY AWAY	42	43	92			
BASIC RELATIONSHIPS: SAGE & TRIP'S FOREST GAMES	42	43	92			
BASIC RHYMING WORDS	51					
BASIC SHAPES	12	17				
BASIC SHAPES	12	17				
BASIC SHAPES DUPLICATING MASTERS	12	17				
BASIC SHAPES: CIRCULAR CIRCUS ON PARADE	12	17				
BASIC SHAPES: FALLING STAR & THE CLEVER CLOWNS	12	17				
BASIC SHAPES: SAM SHAPE & THE CLUMSY CAR	12	17				
BASIC SHAPES: SAM SHAPE MEETS MAGIC MAN	12	17				
BASIC SHAPES: SHAPELESSVILLE "SHAPES" UP	12	17				
BASIC SHAPES: STAR OF TRIANGLE TRAPEZE	12	17				
BASIC SIGHT WORDS	84					
BASIC SKILLS KIT- PHONICS H	55	50				
BASIC SKILLS KIT- SIGHT READING K	71	72	70	84		
BASIC SKILLS KIT- SIGHT READING L	70	71	73	84		

TITLE	SKILL NUMBERS						
BASIC SPELLING 1	64						
BASIC SPELLING 2	64						
BASIC SPELLING, GRADE I	64						
BASIC SPELLING, GRADE II	64						
BASIC SPELLING, GRADE III	64						
BASIC SPELLING: PROBLEM WORDS	69						
BASIC TRAINING IN AUDITORY PERCEPTION: FIGURE-GROUND	32						
BASIC TRAINING IN AUDITORY PERCEPTION: SPEECH ELEMENTS	26						
BASIC VOCABULARY BINGO GAME	83	72					
BASIC VOCABULARY BUILDING I	85	84					
BASIC VOCABULARY BUILDING II	85	84					
BASIC VOCABULARY PROGRAM, STAGE 2	84						
BASIC VOCABULARY PROGRAM, STAGE 3	84						
BASIC VOCABULARY PROGRAM, STAGE 4	84						
BASIC VOCABULARY PROGRAM, STAGE 5	84						
BASIC VOCABULARY PROGRAM, STAGE 6	84						
BASIC VOCABULARY PROGRAM, STAGE 7	84						
BASIC VOCABULARY STUDY CARDS, UNIT I	84	93					
BASIC VOCABULARY STUDY CARDS, UNIT II	84	93					
BASIC VOCABULARY WORKSHEETS, BOOK 1	83						
BASIC VOCABULARY WORKSHEETS, BOOK 2	83						
BASIC VOCABULARY WORKSHEETS, BOOK 3	83	72					
BASIC VOCABULARY WORKSHEETS, BOOK 4	83						
BASIC VOCABULARY WORKSHEETS, BOOK 5	83						
BASIC VOCABULARY WORKSHEETS, BOOK 6	83	72					
BASIC WORD ATTACK	53	57	58	59	60		
BASIC WORD ATTACK SKILLS	53	56	80	81			
BASIC WORD LIST	75						
BASIC WORD LOTTO	84						
BASIC WORDS SNAP GAME	84						
BASIC-CUT PEOPLE PUZZLES	19	25					
BASIC-CUT, PUZZLE 1	19	25					
BASIC-CUT, PUZZLE 2	19	25					
BE A STAR	2						
BE SAFE WTIH SYLLABLES	82						
BEADS & LACES PATERN CARDS	23	25	47	24			
BEFORE-AFTER SEQUENTIAL CARDS	23						
BEGINNING BLENDS	53						
BEGINNING DISCOVERY	8	26					
BEGINNING EXPERIENCES IN LOGICAL THINKING	46						
BEGINNING PHONICS	48						
BEGINNING PHONICS	49	50					
BEGINNING PHONICS, BOOK 1	52						
BEGINNING PHONICS, BOOK 2	52	53					
BEGINNING PHONICS, LOWER CASE	34	50					
BEGINNING PHONICS, UPPER CASE	34	50					
BEGINNING READINESS	8	13	26	10	42		
BEGINNING SOUND WORD HUNT I	27	9	20				
BEGINNING SOUND WORD HUNT II	27	9	20				
BEGINNING SOUNDS	50						
BEGINNING SOUNDS, LEVEL A	52						
BEGINNING SOUNDS, LEVEL B	52						
BEGINNING SOUNDS, LEVEL C	52						
BEGINNING STRUCTURAL ANALYSIS	79	92	78	80	81	82	
BEGINNING TO LEARN: ALPHABET HOUSE	49						
BEGINNING TO LEARN: ALPHABET ZOO	49						
BEGINNING TO LEARN: I CAN READ SIGNS	85	84					
BEGINNING TO LEARN: MORE SIGNS TO READ	84	85					
BEGINNING TO LEARN: PICTURES & LETTERS	14	49					
BEGINNING TO LEARN: THE ALPHABET CITY	49						
BEGINNING TO READ, WRITE & LISTEN	49	50	35	35	52		
BEGINNING VOCABULARY	83	90	88	86	87	81	77
BELONGING	47	42	46				
BETTER READING & SPELLING THROUGH PHONICS	75	84	85	65	64	83	
BETTER SPELLING	65	66	69	68			
BIG ADVENTURE BOX	48	83	84				
BIG LOOK AT BEGINNING CONSONANTS	52						
BIG LOOK AT LONG & SHORT VOWELS	57	58					
BILLY BUILDS A SENTENCE	74	70					
BILLY THE LONELY WORD	70	71	72	73			
BIRDS-EYE VIEW OF LANGUAGE ARTS	48	70					
BLACK ABC'S STUDY PRINTS	49						
BLAST!	91						
BLEND DOMINOES	53						
BLENDING SOUNDS WITH COCO & CHARLIE	52	56	8	26			
BLENDS & DIGRAPHS	53						
BLENDS & DIGRAPHS	53						
BLENDS & DIGRAPHS	53						
BLENDS & DIGRAPHS	53						
BLENDS & DIGRAPHS PICTURES FOR PEGBOARD	53						
BLENDS & SIGHT WORDS AUDIO LESSONS	48	84					
BLENDS & SIGHT WORDS, GROUP 1	48	84					
BLENDS & SIGHT WORDS, GROUP 2	48	84					
BLENDS PUZZLES	53						
BLOCK BASICS	26	5					
BLUE-BLOODED SUFFIXES	81						
BODY LANGUAGE	3						
BODY PARTS CARDS & GAMEBOARD	2	4	36	42			
BOLD BEGINNING: CUT & PASTE ALPHABET BOOK	49	50					
BOLD BEGINNING: DISCOVER & DO	47						
BOLD BEGINNING: DRAW-A-SOUND	49	50					
BOLD BEGINNING: IDENTIFYING SOUNDS OF THE ALPHABET	50						
BOMB-SCARE MYSTERY	5						

TITLE	SKILL NUMBERS						
BOOK ONE, PART ONE: PHONIC ANALYSIS ACTIVITIES	53	57	58	59			
BOOK ONE, PART TWO: STRUCTURAL ANALYSIS ACTIVITIES	76	78	79	82			
BOOK REPORTING	4						
BOOK TWO, PART ONE: VOCABULARY DEVELOPMENT ACTIVITIES	86	87	88				
BOOK TWO, PART TWO: COMPREHENSION ACTIVITIES	92	93	93				
BOY WHO DIDN'T LISTEN	29	36	37	35			
BREAK THROUGH FILM STRIPS: CONSONANT SOUND ASSOCIATION	53						
BREAKTHROUGH TO LITERACY	4	6	65				
BRITISH-AMERICAN SYNONYMS	86						
BRITISH-AMERICAN SYNONYMS	86						
BUILD A SENTENCE	74						
BUILD A SHAPE GAME	17						
BUILD-A-WORD SKILL CARDS	75						
BUILDING AUDITORY & VISUAL PERCEPTION SKILLS	26	8					
BUILDING BETTER SENTENCES	74						
BUILDING BETTER SENTENCES	74						
BUILDING LANGUAGE SKILLS, BOOK B	64	1	35				
BUILDING LANGUAGE USAGE POWER, VOLUEM 6	70	71					
BUILDING LANGUAGE USAGE POWER, VOLUME 1	70	74					
BUILDING LANGUAGE USAGE POWER, VOLUME 2	77	70					
BUILDING LANGUAGE USAGE POWER, VOLUME 3	70						
BUILDING LANGUAGE USAGE POWER, VOLUME 4	71						
BUILDING LANGUAGE USAGE POWER, VOLUME 5	74						
BUILDING LANGUAGE USAGE POWER, VOLUME 7	71						
BUILDING LANGUAGE USAGE POWER, VOLUME 8	70	71					
BUILDING MATCH-UPS	94						
BUILDING SENTENCES	74						
BUILDING SENTENCES STEP-BY-STEP	74	72					
BUILDING STORIES WITH JULIE & JACK	74	92					
BUILDING STORIES WITH JULIE & JACK	74	92					
BUILDING VERBAL POWER IN THE UPPER GRADES, VOLUME 1	87	88					
BUILDING VERBAL POWER IN THE UPPER GRADES, VOLUME 2	71	47					
BUILDING VERBAL POWER IN THE UPPER GRADES, VOLUME 3	90	47					
BUILDING VERBAL POWER IN THE UPPER GRADES, VOLUME 4	73						
BUILDING VERBAL POWER IN THE UPPER GRADES, VOLUME 5	84	85					
BUILDING VERBAL POWER, VOLUME 1	14	87					
BUILDING VERBAL POWER, VOLUME 3	90	46					
BUILDING VERBAL POWER, VOLUME 4	71						
BUILDING VERBAL POWER, VOLUME 5	84	85					
BUILDING VOCABULARY	71	72	73				
BUILDING WORD POWER	80	81	76				
BUSINESS COMMUNICATIONS	70	74	64				
BUSINESS COMMUNICATIONS: ENGLISH THE EASY WAY	70	74	64				
BUZZER BOARD PATTERN CARDS	9	27	33				
BUZZER BOARDS	27	33					
C & G TRIO	54						
CALICO CAT LOOKS AROUND	12						
CALICO CAT'S RAINBOW	10						
CAMOUFLAGED ANIMAL CARDS	9	20					
CAN YOU DO THIS?	83						
CAN YOU FIND MY MOTHER?	29	36	37	35			
CANTANKEROUS CONSONANTS	53	54	55				
CAR MATCH-UPS	14						
CAR-RALLY GAME	47						
CAREER ASSOCIATION CARDS	94						
CAREER AWARENESS	94						
CAREER AWARENESS ACTIVITY GUIDE	94						
CAREER AWARENESS PROGRAM	94						
CAREER AWARENESS STICKERS	4						
CAREER CROSS WORDS	94						
CAREER EDUCATION ACTIVITIES FOR SUBJECT AREA TEACHERS	94						
CAREER IDENTITY CARDS	94						
CAREER KITS FOR THE KIDS	94						
CAREERS	94						
CAREERS CARDS	94						
CAREERS LOTTO	94						
CARTOON BOARD POSTERS	4						
CARTOON BOARDS	4						
CARTOON STORY STARTERS	4						
CATCH A CONSONANT	51						
CATEGORY CARDS	47						
CATEGORY WORD HUNT I	9	20					
CATEGORY WORD HUNT II	9	20					
CAVEMAN PLURALS	77						
CAVEMAN PLURALS CENTER	77						
CHANGEABLE CONSONANTS	54	55					
CHAPBOOK ABC'S	49						
CHARLIE: ALPHABET, UPPER & LOWER CASE	14	49					
CHARLIE: PHONICS, BEGINNING & ENDING CONSONANT BLENDS	53						
CHARLIE: PHONICS, LONG & SHORT VOWELS	57	58					
CHARLIE: SYNONYMS	86						
CHATTERBOARDS: ANIMALS	4	6	7				
CHATTERBOARDS: TOYS	4	6	7				
CHECKER GAME BOOK NO. 1 /S/ SOUND	5						
CHECKER GAME BOOK NO. 2 /S/ SOUND	5						
CHECKLIST OF BASIC SOUNDS	67	66	69	80	81		
CHECKMATE: AFFIXES	80	81					
CHECKMATE: AFFIXES	80	81					
CHECKMATE: ANTONYMS	87						
CHECKMATE: ANTONYMS	87						
CHECKMATE: BLENDS	53						
CHECKMATE: COMPOUND WORDS	79						
CHECKMATE: COMPOUND WORDS	79						

TITLE	SKILL NUMBERS						
CHECKMATE: CONTRACTIONS	78						
CHECKMATE: DIGRAPHS	59						
CHECKMATE: DIPHTHONGS	60						
CHECKMATE: HOMONYMS (HOMOPHONES)	88	89					
CHECKMATE: HOMONYMS (HOMOPHONES)	88	89					
CHECKMATE: SYNONYMS	86						
CHECKMATE: SYNONYMS	86						
CHECKMATE: THE ALPHABET	49						
CHECKMATE: VARIANT VOWEL SOUNDS	62						
CHECKMATE: VARIANT VOWEL SOUNDS	62						
CHECKMATE: VOWELS FOLLOWED BY R	61						
CHECKMATE: WORD ENDINGS	77						
CHECKMATE: WORD ENDINGS	77						
CHEST OF ACTION (RL 1-6)	48	75					
CHEST OF FUN (RL 1-3)	48	75					
CHEST OF SUCCESS (RL 4-9)	48	75					
CHESTS OF BOOKS (RL 1-9)	48	75					
CHEVES PROGRAM, PART 4: PHONICS PUZZLES & GAMES	51						
CHILDCRAFT INTERLOCKING RUBBER ANIMALS	22	14	25				
CHIP MATES	25	9					
CHUMPY'S WORD GAMES	51	83					
CIRCLE-SQUARE FIT-INS	10	11	15	16			
CIRCLES, TRIANGLES, SQUARES	12	17					
CIRCUS DAYS READING ACTIVITIES	51	57	58				
CLASSIFICATION CARDS, PEOPLE & THINGS	47						
CLASSIFICATION GAME	47						
CLASSIFICATION GAME	47	19					
CLASSIFICATION-OPPOSITES PICTURES FOR PEGBOARD	87	47					
CLASSIFICATION-OPPOSITES-SEQUENCE	47	23					
CLASSIFICATIONS-OPPOSITES-SEQUENCE	47	14	87				
CLASSIFYING WORD PACER	47	93					
CLUES TO CONSONANTS, WORKTAPES	49	50					
CLUES TO WORDS	48	82					
COGNITIVE CHALLENGE CARDS	45	46					
COLA (CONCEPTUAL ORAL LANGUAGE ACTIVITY KIT)	2						
COLOR	10	15					
COLOR	84						
COLOR & SHAPE BINGO	15	17					
COLOR & SHAPE BINGO	13						
COLOR & SHAPE BOARD	10	12	15	17			
COLOR & SHAPE MEMORY GAME	24	15	17				
COLOR & SHAPE SET	47	15	17	10	12	18	
COLOR ASSOCIATION PICTURE CARDS	10	15					
COLOR CARDS	13						
COLOR CATS	13	10					
COLOR CHARTS	10	15	84	19			
COLOR CONCEPTS	10	15					
COLOR DISCOVERY CARDS	10	15					
COLOR DISCRIMINATION	10						
COLOR DOMINOES	10						
COLOR GRADATION CARDS	10	15					
COLOR LOTTO	10	15					
COLOR MATCHING PUZZLE	15						
COLOR MIX & MATCH	10	15					
COLOR NAME CARDS	10	15	92				
COLOR PADDLES	10						
COLOR RECOGNITION	2	42	4				
COLOR RECOGNITION	10	15	19				
COLOR RECOGNITION CHART	10	15					
COLOR SEQUENCING CARDS	23						
COLOR TABLETS: FIRST BOX	10	15					
COLOR TABLETS: SECOND BOX	10	15					
COLOR TABLETS: THIRD BOX	10	15					
COLOR TRAIN	10	15					
COLOR WHEEL	13	10	15				
COLOR WORDS	84	92					
COLOR WORDS, LEFT & RIGHT: PROBLEM SOLVING, PHONICS, OPPOS.	92	21	42	46	44	49	50
COLOR WORMS	13						
COLOR, CUT & PASTE VOWEL	57	58					
COLOR, CUT & READ	10						
COLOR, SHAPE, TEXTURE, SIZE	9	14					
COLOR-CUT-CREATE	13	25					
COLOR/SHAPE ABACUS	18	47					
COLORCOLOR	10	15					
COLORED INCH CUBE DESIGNS	10						
COLORED INCH CUBES	10						
COLORGRAM ENGLISH	70	74					
COLORS	10	15					
COLORS & SHAPES	10	12	15	17			
COLORS & SHAPES: FLIP & LEARN FLASHBOOK	10	12	15	17			
COLORS AT A PARTY	10	15					
COLORS EVERYWHERE	10	15					
COLORS FLIP BOOK	13	10					
COLORS WE SEE	10	15					
COME BACK, AMELIA BEDELIA	90						
COMMUNICARDS	2	41	47				
COMMUNICATING THROUGH SYMBOLS	5						
COMMUNICATION COMPETENCY IN READING & WRITING (RL 7-9)	85						
COMMUNICATION POWER SERIES	4	76	74	7			
COMMUNICATION POWER SERIES: BE A WORD DETECTIVE	76	82	84	85			
COMMUNICATION POWER SERIES: ORAL COMMUNICATION	4	7					
COMMUNICATION POWER SERIES: SENTENCE POWER	74						
COMMUNICATION SKILLS (ORAL)	4						

TITLE	SKILL NUMBERS						
COMMUNICATION SKILLS IN ACTION	29	36	38	42	43	45	
COMMUNICATION: INTERACTING THROUGH SPEECH	4	5	7				
COMMUNICATION: INTERACTING THROUGH SPEECH	4	5	7				
COMMUNICATION: PROBLEMS APPROACH	4						
COMMUNICATIONS	23						
COMMUNICATIONS: THE BUSINESS OF ORAL COMMUNICATIN	7	35	4				
COMMUNICATIVE COMPETENCE	2	4	6	41	42	43	47
COMMUNITY WORKERS	94						
COMMUNTIY WORKERS	94						
COMPLEMENTARY OBJECT LOTTO	14						
COMPLETE BOOK OF SPELLING DEMONS	69						
COMPOUND WORD GAME	79						
COMPOUND WORD PUZZLES	79						
COMPOUND WORD PUZZLES	79						
COMPOUND WORD, PRELIMINARY	79						
COMPOUND WORDS	79						
COMPOUND WORDS	79						
COMPOUND WORDS	79						
COMPOUND-A-WORD	79						
COMPOUND-WORD PICTURE MATCHING CARDS	79						
COMPOUNDS, A	79						
COMPOUNDS, ADVANCED	79						
COMPOUNDS, B	79						
COMPOUNDS, C	79						
COMPOUNDS, D	79						
COMPOUNDS, E	79						
COMPOUNDS, F	79						
COMPREHENSION SKILLS 1	47						
COMPREHENSION SKILLS 2	42	90	91				
COMPREHENSION THROUGH LISTENING, VOLUME 1	39	40	29	36	38		
COMPREHENSION THROUGH LISTENING, VOLUME 3	39	40	29	36	38		
COMPREHENSION THROUGH LISTENING, VOLUME 4	39	40	88	89	29	36	
CONCEPT DEVELOPMENT: BEGINNING LANGUAGE CONCEPTS, KIT C	8	92					
CONCEPT DEVELOPMENT: BEGINNING LANGUAGE CONCEPTS, KIT D	8	92					
CONCEPT DEVELOPMENT: BEGINNING LANGUAGE CONCEPTS, KIT E	8	92					
CONCEPT DEVELOPMENT: BEGINNING LANGUAGE CONCEPTS, KIT H	8	92					
CONCEPT DEVELOPMENT: BEGINNING LANGUAGE CONCEPTS, KIT I	92	47					
CONCEPT DEVELOPMENT: LETTER NAMES THROUGH SOUNDS, KIT F	49						
CONCEPT DEVELOPMENT: LETTER NAMES THROUGH SOUNDS, KIT G	49						
CONCEPT FORMATION: STEPS UP TO LANG. FOR LEARNING IMPAIRED	42	43	7				
CONCEPT MATCH	47	46	42				
CONCEPT TOWN	33	31					
CONCEPT UNDERSTANDING PROGRAM: VOCABULARY OF DIRECTIONS	4	2					
CONCEPTO-CHARTS	2						
CONCEPTO-PUZZLES	2	22					
CONCEPTO-SORT	2	83	47	18			
CONCEPTS & LANGUAGE	8	26	46	2			
CONCEPTS FOR COMMUNICATION, UNIT 1: LISTEN. W/UNDERSTANDING	29	36	37	38	40		
CONCEPTS FOR COMMUNICATION, UNIT 2, CONCEPT BUILDING	47						
CONCEPTS FOR COMMUNICATION, UNIT 3, COMMUNICATION	36	37	38				
CONFIGURATIONS, BOOK 1	12	13	17				
CONFIGURATIONS, BOOK 2	12	13	17				
CONFIGURATIONS, BOOK 3	12	13	17				
CONFUSED WORDS	83	9					
CONFUSING CONSONANTS	52	54	55				
CONFUSION, SET 1	5	7					
CONFUSION, SET 2	5	7					
CONFUSION, SET 3	5	7					
CONNECT	13	24					
CONQUERING COMPOSITION SERIES	74						
CONQUERING COMPOSITION SERIES: SENTENCE PROBLEMS I	74						
CONQUERING COMPOSITION SERIES: SENTENCE PROBLEMS II	74						
CONSONANT & VOWEL LAB	57	58	53				
CONSONANT BINGO	52						
CONSONANT BLEND JUNGLE	53						
CONSONANT BLEND JUNGLE	53						
CONSONANT BLENDS	53						
CONSONANT BLENDS	53						
CONSONANT BLENDS & DIGRAPHS	53						
CONSONANT BLENDS & DIGRAPHS PLAYING CARDS	53						
CONSONANT BLENDS & DIGRAPHS, PART II	53						
CONSONANT BLENDS PEEK-A-BOO	53						
CONSONANT BLENDS, PART I	53						
CONSONANT BOOK	52	53					
CONSONANT CAPERS	53	55					
CONSONANT CAPERS	52						
CONSONANT CLUSTER FUN	53						
CONSONANT DIGRAPH GAMES	53						
CONSONANT DIGRAPHS	53						
CONSONANT DIGRAPHS	53						
CONSONANT FLIP BOOKS	52	53					
CONSONANT FLIPSTRIPS	52						
CONSONANT PICTURE PACK	53						
CONSONANT SOUNDS	27	53	61				
CONSONANT SOUNDS & SYMBOLS, BOOK B	49	50	77				
CONSONANT SOUNDS: STARTING OFF WITH PHONICS, BOOK 3	52						
CONSONANT SOUNDS: STARTING OFF WITH PHONICS, BOOK 3	52						
CONSONANT WHEELS	53						
CONSONANT WORKBOOK: SEE, HEAR, SAY, DO	52						
CONSONANTS	49						
CONSONANTS	53						
CONSONANTS	53						
CONSONANTS & DIGRAPHS	52	53					

TITLE	SKILL NUMBERS						
CONSONANTS COUNT	54	55					
CONSONANTS: HOW THEY LOOK & SOUND	50						
CONSUMER SEQUENTIAL CARDS	23	2	94				
CONTINUING LANGUAGE SKILLS, BOOK C	64	1	35				
CONTINUOUS PROGRESS IN SPELLING, INTERMEDIATE	64	68	69	65	66		
CONTINUOUS PROGRESS IN SPELLING, PRIMARY	64	68	69	65	66		
CONTINUOUS PROGRESS IN SPELLING, VARIETY DAY KIT 1	64	68	69	65	66		
CONTINUOUS PROGRESS IN SPELLING, VARIETY DAY KIT 2	64	68	69	65	66		
CONTRACTION BOARDS	78						
CONTRACTION CONCENTRATION	78						
CONTRACTION PUZZLES	78						
CONTRACTION SATISFACTION	78						
CONTRACTIONS	78						
CONTRACTIONS	78						
CONTRACTIONS	78						
CONTRACTIONS MAGIC SHOW	78						
CONTRACTIONS: WHAT ARE THEY?	78						
COORDINATION BOARD	17						
CORRECT SPELLING MADE EASY	64						
CORRECTING COMPOSITION ERRORS	70	64					
CORRECTIVE SPELLING THROUGH MORPHOGRAPHS, SPIRIT MASTERS	75	64					
CORRECTIVE SPELLING THROUGH MORPHOGRAPHS, STUDENT BOOK	75	83	64				
CORRECTIVE SPELLING THROUGH MORPHOGRAPHS, TEACHER'S BOOK	75	83	64				
COUNTDOWN FOR LISTENING	39	40	29	36	37		
COUNTING & ABC'S	49						
COUNTING & SORTING TRAY	47	18					
COUNTING & SORTING: ANIMAL SHAPES	47	18					
COUNTING & SORTING: COUNTERS	47	18					
COUNTING & SORTING: MIXED SHAPES	47	18					
COUNTING & SORTING: TRANSPORT SHAPES	47	18					
COUNTING LOTTO	2						
COVE SCHOOL READING PROGRAM	48	52	57	53			
CRACKING THE CODE: STUDENT READER (CLOTH)	48						
CRACKING THE CODE: STUDENT WORKBOOK	48						
CRACKING THE CODE: TEACHER HANDBOOK	48						
CREATING CHARACTERIZATION	3	7					
CREATING WORD PICTURES	4						
CREATIVE DIALOGUE	7						
CREATIVE DRAMATICS PROGRAM	7						
CREATIVE EXPRESSION: ADVENTURES OF A 3-SPINED STICKLEBACK	7						
CREATIVE EXPRESSION: COOK-UP TALES	7						
CREATIVE EXPRESSION: DINOSAUR BONES	7						
CREATIVE EXPRESSION: GHOST SHIPS	7						
CREATIVE EXPRESSION: JUNGLE SOUNDS	7						
CREATIVE READING PROGRAM I	4	6	7				
CREATIVE READING PROGRAM II	4	6	7				
CREATIVE READING PROGRAM III	4	6	7				
CREATIVE READING PROGRAM IV	4	6	7				
CREATIVE STORY STARTERS I	7						
CREATIVE STORY STARTERS II	7						
CREATURE CLUES TO WORDS	86	87	88				
CREATURE CLUES TO WORDS	86	87	88				
CREATURE FEATURES: ACTIVITY CARDS	86	87	88				
CREATURE FEATURES: STRUCTURAL ANALYSIS	75	70	56				
CREATURE FEATURES: VOCABULARY DEVELOPMENT	71	72	73	86	87	88	78
CREATURE TEACHERS	48	52	56				
CREEPING RUG CARD PROGRAMS: ALPHABET-LANGUAGE DEVELOPMENT	49	4					
CREEPY CREATURES (RL 2)	53						
CRONIN LETTER BOX	50	23	31				
CROSSTIES PROGRAM	35	35	2				
CROSSTIES PROGRAM: GRAND CENTRAL BOOKS, APRIL	35	35	2				
CROSSTIES PROGRAM: GRAND CENTRAL BOOKS, DECEMBER	35	35	2				
CROSSTIES PROGRAM: GRAND CENTRAL BOOKS, FEBRUARY	35	35	2				
CROSSTIES PROGRAM: GRAND CENTRAL BOOKS, JANUARY	35	35	2				
CROSSTIES PROGRAM: GRAND CENTRAL BOOKS, MARCH	35	35	2				
CROSSTIES PROGRAM: GRAND CENTRAL BOOKS, MAY	35	35	2				
CROSSTIES PROGRAM: GRAND CENTRAL BOOKS, NOVEMBER	35	35	2				
CROSSTIES PROGRAM: GRAND CENTRAL BOOKS, OCTOBER	35	35	2				
CROSSTIES PROGRAM: GRAND CENTRAL BOOKS, SEPTEMBER	35	35	2				
CROSSTIES PROGRAM: GRAND CENTRAL BOOKS, SUMMER	35	35	2				
CROSSWORD PUZZLES FOR PHONICS: BLENDS I	53						
CROSSWORD PUZZLES FOR PHONICS: BLENDS II	53						
CROSSWORD PUZZLES FOR PHONICS: PICTURE CLUES	52	57	58				
CROSSWORD PUZZLES FOR PHONICS: SPECIAL SOUNDS I	75	64	59				
CROSSWORD PUZZLES FOR PHONICS: SPECIAL SOUNDS II	75	64	59				
CROSSWORD PUZZLES FOR PHONICS: VOWELS I	57	58					
CROSSWORD PUZZLES FOR PHONICS: VOWELS II	57	58					
CROSSWORD PUZZLES FOR PHONICS: WORD/PICTURE CLUES	52	57	58				
CUBES IN COLOR	10	23	15				
CUBES IN COLOR DESIGN CARDS	10	23	15				
CUC PICTURE-WORD PROGRAM	84	56	53				
CUES & SIGNALS I	53	13					
CUES & SIGNALS II	53	13					
CUES & SIGNALS III	56	52	13				
CUES & SIGNALS IV	75	13					
CURIOUS GEORGE LEARNS THE ALPHABET	49						
CURIOUS GEORGE LEARNS THE ALPHABET	49						
CURVES & CORNERS	17	12					
CUTTING CORNERS WITH CONTRACTIONS	78						
DECIDE WHERE TO DIVIDE	82						
DECODING & COMPREHENSION SKILLS 1	48						
DECODING & COMPREHENSION SKILLS 2	48						
DECODING & COMPREHENSION SKILLS 3	48						

TITLE	SKILL NUMBERS						
DECODING SKILLS 1	9	49					
DECODING SKILLS 2	78	51	50				
DECODING SKILLS 3	54	53	79				
DECODING SKILLS 4	57	58	62	77			
DECODING SKILLS 5	76	81	82				
DECODING SKILLS A	54	53					
DECODING SKILLS B	53	79					
DECODING SKILLS C	79	78	77	76			
DECODING SKILLS D	57	58	62	61	60		
DECODING SKILLS E	59	62	81	80	82		
DELL HOME ACTIVITY: COLOR & SPELL	64						
DELL HOME ACTIVITY: MAKE ZOUP, AN ALPHABET BOOK	49						
DELL HOME ACTIVITY: PARTS OF SPEECH	70						
DELL HOME ACTIVITY: PHONICS	48						
DELL HOME ACTIVITY: PHONICS BOOK 2	48						
DELL HOME ACTIVITY: PHONICS BOOK 3	48						
DELL HOME ACTIVITY: RHYMING ROOTS	51	76					
DELL HOME ACTIVITY: SPELLING BOOK 1	64						
DELL HOME ACTIVITY: SPELLING BOOK 2	64						
DELL HOME ACTIVITY: VOCABULARY BOOK 1	83						
DEMON SPELLING WORDS	69						
DESCRIPTIVE WORDS	86	84	73				
DESCRIPTO CARDS	5	2	7				
DESIGN BOARD	10						
DESIGN DOMINOES	14	9					
DESIGN FORM BOARD	17						
DESIGN SEQUENCE CARDS	23	24					
DEVELOPING ALPHABET SKILLS	49	50	28				
DEVELOPING BASIC SKILLS: WHAT DO YOU SEE?	9						
DEVELOPING BASIC SKILLS: WHAT IS IT?	9						
DEVELOPING BASIC SKILLS: WHERE IS IT?	9	13					
DEVELOPING ENGLISH SKILLS	86	87	72	71	73		
DEVELOPING FUNDAMENTAL LANGUAGE PATTERNS, VOLUME 1: TO HAVE	72						
DEVELOPING FUNDAMENTAL LANGUAGE PATTERNS, VOLUME 2: TO BE	72						
DEVELOPING FUNDAMENTAL LANGUAGE PATTERNS, VOLUME 3: TO SEE	72						
DEVELOPING FUNDAMENTAL LANGUAGE PATTERNS, VOLUME 4: TO GO	72						
DEVELOPING FUNDAMENTAL LANGUAGE PATTERNS, VOLUME 5: TO SAY	72						
DEVELOPING FUNDAMENTAL LANGUAGE PATTERNS, VOLUME 6: TO DO	72						
DEVELOPING LANGUAGE ARTS SKILLS: VOCABULARY ENRICHMENT	90	86	87	88			
DEVELOPING LANGUAGE SKILLS, KIT B	72	86	87	88			
DEVELOPING LANGUAGE SKILLS, KIT C	72	86	87	88			
DEVELOPING LANGUAGE SKILLS, KIT D	72	86	87	88			
DEVELOPING LANGUAGE SKILLS: CAN YOU DESCRIBE IT?	8						
DEVELOPING LANGUAGE SKILLS: CAN YOU DO IT?	72						
DEVELOPING LANGUAGE SKILLS: CAN YOU NAME IT?	71						
DEVELOPING LISTENING SKILLS WITH "THE GINGERBREAD BOY"	33						
DEVELOPING LISTENING SKILLS WITH "THREE BILLY GOATS GRUFF"	29	36	33				
DEVELOPING READING EFFICIENCY	83						
DEVELOPING READING SKILLS, PART I: WORD RECOGNITION	9	27	51	87	86	84	92
DEVELOPING READING SKILLS, PART II: PHONICS, VOWEL SOUNDS	58	57	61				
DEVELOPING SENTENCE SKILLS	74						
DEVELOPING STRUCTURAL ANALYSIS SKILLS, KIT I	77	78	79				
DEVELOPING STRUCTURAL ANALYSIS SKILLS, KIT J	77						
DEVELOPING STRUCTURAL ANALYSIS SKILLS, KIT K	76	80	81	82			
DEVELOPING TECHNIQUES IN CONCENTRATION	25	20	17	24			
DEVELOPING THE LISTENING SKILLS	35	35	26				
DEVELOPMENTAL LANGUAGE LESSONS	2						
DEVELOPMENTAL READING SKILLS: DECODING	48						
DEVELOPMENTAL STORY BOOKS	36	2	29				
DEVELOPMENTAL SYNTAX PROGRAM	71	73	72	70	74		
DEVELOPMENTAL VOCABULARY	90	88	76	77	80	81	
DI-TRI BLENDER	5						
DIFFICULT PLURALS	77						
DIGRAPH DISCO	53						
DIGRAPHS & FINAL BLENDS, B	53						
DIMENSIONAL SEQUENCING CARDS	23						
DINOSAURS & SPATIAL RELATIONSHIPS	21						
DIRECTING LANGUAGE SKILLS, BOOK D	64	1	35				
DISCOVER NEW WAYS	48	7					
DISCOVERING LETTERS	74	9					
DISCOVERY	94						
DISNEY PUZZLES: DONALD DUCK	9						
DISNEY PUZZLES: DOPEY	9						
DISNEY PUZZLES: GOOFY	9						
DISNEY PUZZLES: HUEY, DEWEY & LOUIE	9						
DISNEY PUZZLES: MICKEY & DONALD	9						
DISNEY PUZZLES: MICKEY MOUSE	9						
DISNEY PUZZLES: MINNIE MOUSE	9						
DISNEY PUZZLES: PLUTO	9						
DISNEY PUZZLES: THREE LITTLE PIGS	9						
DISNEY WOOD BLOCKS	49						
DISNEYLAND LANGUAGE ARTS SKILL BUILDING KIT	2	7					
DISTAR ACTIVITY KIT: LANGUAGE	2	41	36				
DISTAR ACTIVITY KIT: READING	48	35	83	75			
DO'S & DON'T'S FOR BEGINNING SPEAKERS	7						
DOG TALES GAME	7						
DOODLE DOLLY & HER DAN DISCOVER SHAPES	12	17					
DOODLE DOLLY & HER DAO GAN DISCOVER COLORS	10	15					
DOTS & COLOR	10	12	15				
DOUBLE TAKE	14						
DOUBLE TROUBLE	53						
DR. SPELLO	64						
DR. SPELLO, T.E.	64						

TITLE	SKILL NUMBERS						
E-Z PHONIC HOMONYM SLIDE RULE	88						
E-Z PHONIC WORD-BUILDING SLIDE RULE	76	80	81				
EAR TRAINING FOR MIDDLE GRADES	29	36	38				
EAR-ING THE ACCENT	82						
EARLY LANGUAGE SKILLS	74						
EARLY PRIMARY LANG. ARTS: EASY FUNCTIONAL READING	85						
EARLY PRIMARY LANG. ARTS: SIGHT WORDS WITH SOUND & FUN	84						
EARLY PRIMARY LANG. ARTS: TRAVELING WITH THE ALPHABET	49						
EARLY PRIMARY SKILLS SERIES	9	49	25	84	85		
EARLY READING RECOGNITION SKILLS	51	52	53	57	58		
EARLY WORDS	84	4					
EARS	37	35	29	36			
EASEL LISTENING GAMES	39	40	29	36	38		
EASY CROSSWORD PUZZLES	76	80	81	77			
EASY FUNCTIONAL READING	85						
ECONOMO SENTENCE BUILDER	74	83					
EDL CORE VOCABULARIES BOOK	85	92	93				
EDMARK READING PROGRAM (FOR NONREADERS)	84	4					
EDUCATIONAL PASSWORD	19	84					
EFFECTIVE LISTENING	35	35					
EGGHEAD JAZZ	49	79	82	92	93		
EIGHT PARTS OF SPEECH	70	71	72	73			
EMERGING LANGUAGE 2	2	4	6	7			
ENDINGS/SUFFIXES, ADVANCED 1	77	81					
ENDINGS/SUFFIXES, ADVANCED 2	77	81					
ENDINGS/SUFFIXES, ADVANCED 3	77	81					
ENDINGS/SUFFIXES, B	77	81					
ENDINGS/SUFFIXES, C	77	81					
ENDINGS/SUFFIXES, D	77	81					
ENDINGS/SUFFIXES, E	77	81					
ENDINGS/SUFFIXES, F	77	81					
ENGLISH COMES ALIVE SERIES	70	83	4	75			
ENGLISH COMES ALIVE: ADVENTURES IN COMMUNICATION	4						
ENGLISH COMES ALIVE: ADVENTURES IN WORDS	75	83					
ENGLISH COMES ALIVE: PARTS OF SPEECH	70						
ENGLISH GRAMMAR, VOLUME I	74						
ENGLISH GRAMMAR, VOLUME II	74						
ENGLISH TOPICS I & II: SIMPLE SENTENCES & COMPLEX SENTENCES	74						
ENRICHMENT ROUSERS: SHORT VOWEL	57						
ENRICHMENT ROUSERS: SPELL STUMPERS	69						
ENRICHMENT ROUSERS: VOCABULARY BUILDING	83						
EPIC: EMPHASIZING PHONICS IN CONTEXT	48	84					
ESSENTIAL SIGHT WORDS PROGRAM, LEVEL I	84						
ETA ADJECTIVE LOTTO GAME	73						
ETA ALPHABET PICTURE & SOUND MATCHING CARDS	50						
ETA APPROACH PICTURE & WORD-BUILDING CARDS	84	50					
ETA BASIC WOOD LOTTO	84						
ETA CARNIVAL OF BEGINNING SOUNDS	27						
ETA COLOR BINGO	15	10					
ETA DIAL & SPELL	64						
ETA DISCOVERING OPPOSITES	87						
ETA DISCOVERY BLOCKS	11	12	16	17			
ETA EARLY WORD PICTURE & WORD MATCHING CARDS	84						
ETA FUN WITH RHYMES	51						
ETA JUMBO FORM BOARD	12	17					
ETA JUMBO POUND AWAY	25						
ETA LET'S LEARN SEQUENCE	23						
ETA LETTER DISCRIMINATION INSET BOARDS	49	12					
ETA MAKE-A-WORD SPELLING GAMES	64						
ETA MOTSPUR SINGULARS-AND-PLURALS CARDS	77						
ETA PHONICS COUPLETS	50						
ETA PHONOGRAM PICTURE & WORD GROUPING CARDS	48	50					
ETA PICTORIAL ALPHABET FR1EZE	49	50					
ETA PICTURE & SHAPE SORTING CARDS	10	12					
ETA PICTURE SENTENCE-MAKING CARDS	74	93					
ETA POSITIONAL WORD & PICTURE MATCHING CARDS	74						
ETA PRE-READING VISUAL DISCRIMINATION BOARDS	12						
ETA SEE & SOUND ALPHABET CARDS	49	50					
ETA SORT & SOUND VOWEL DIGRAPH CARDS	59						
ETA SORT & SOUND WORD-MAKING CARDS	50						
ETA SPELLING GAME	64						
ETA SPIN-AND-SPELL	65	66					
ETA SUFFIX CHANGING CARDS	81						
ETA VERB LOTTO GAME	72						
ETA VISUAL DISCRIMINATION INSTRUCTION SET	9						
ETA WHAT-AM-I?	92						
ETA WHAT-IS-MY-COLOR? MATCHING CARDS	15	10					
ETA WORD CLASSIFICATION CARDS	92	93					
EVERYBODY WINS!	42	47					
EVERYDAY VOCABULARY	85	83	88	80	81	77	92
EXPANDING CAREER AWARENESS	94						
EXPANDING VOCABULARY	76	80	81	86	87	88	
EXPANDING YOUR VOCABULARY	83						
EXPERIENCES IN READING READINESS	19	33	10	52	85		
EXPERIENCES WITH PERCEPTION	9	13	14	12	20		
EXPLODE THE CODE, BOOK 1	57						
EXPLODE THE CODE, BOOK 2	53						
EXPLODE THE CODE, BOOK 3	63	59	60				
EXPLODE THE CODE, BOOK 4	63	82					
EXPLODE THE CODE, BOOK 5	53	55					
EXPLODE THE CODE, BOOK 6	60	61					
EXPLORING CAREERS	94						
EXPLORING CAREERS	94						

TITLE	SKILL NUMBERS					
EXPLORING WITH RIDDLES & RHYMES	51					
EXPRESSIVE LANGUAGE CARDS	72	73				
EYE-EAR-HAND PHONICS, SET B: CONSONANT DIGRAPHS & BLENDS	53					
EYE-EAR-HAND PHONIS, SET C: LONG & SHORT VOWELS	57	58				
FACE & FIGURE PUZZLES	25	14				
FAMILIAR THINGS PUZZLE	17	12				
FAR OUT STORY STARTERS	4					
FAR-OUT WORDS	69					
FARM PEGS	25					
FAT CAT & EBENEZER GEESER, THE TEENY TINY MOUSE	35					
FAT CAT'S DISH WISH	51					
FICKLE VOWELS	62	57	58			
FIFTH GRADE LANGUAGE DRILLS	86	87	72	71	74	
FIGURE-GROUND ACTIVITY CARDS	20					
FIGURE-GROUND TRANSPARENCIES	32					
FILL THE CONE	79					
FINAL CONSONANT BLENDS	53					
FINAL CONSONANT BLENDS	53					
FINAL CONSONANT DISCS	52					
FIND IT LOTTO	20					
FIND THE MISSING WORD	92	93				
FIND-A-WORD	83	9				
FINTON THE FISH	9					
FIRST BOX OF COLORS	10	15				
FIRST CONCEPTS FILMSTRIP LIBRARY	48	49	2			
FIRST JIGSAWS	25					
FIRST PHONICS, PART 1	57	53				
FIRST PHONICS, PART 2	57	62	59	53		
FIRST PUZZLES: COLORS I SEE	9					
FIRST PUZZLES: FARM ANIMALS	9					
FIRST PUZZLES: FAVORITE FRUITS	9					
FIRST PUZZLES: FOR MY BATH	9					
FIRST PUZZLES: MY HOUSE	14					
FIRST PUZZLES: MY PETS	9					
FIRST PUZZLES: MY TOYS	9					
FIRST PUZZLES: THINGS THAT FLY	9					
FIRST PUZZLES: THINGS WITH WHEELS	9					
FIRST TALKING ALPHABET: PART 1, CONSONANTS	52					
FIRST TALKING ALPHABET: PART 2, VOWELS	57	58				
FIT-A-SHAPE	17	12	10	15		
FIT-A-SIZE	16	11				
FIT-A-SQUARE, FIT-A-CIRCLE	17	12				
FITZHUGH PLUS PROGRAM, BOOK 102: SHAPE COMPLETION	22					
FITZHUGH PLUS PROGRAM, BOOK 104: SHAPE ANALYSIS & SEQUENC.	18					
FITZHUGH PLUS PROGRAM, BOOK 201: COMMON NOUNS	71					
FITZHUGH PLUS PROGRAM, BOOK 202: ACTION VERBS	72					
FITZHUGH PLUS PROGRAM, BOOK 207: GRAMMAR & GENL. KNOWLEDGE	70					
FIVE COMPONENTS FOR ARTICULATION MODIFICATION	5					
FIVE SENSE STORE	40	12	17			
FLANNEL BOARD MANUSCRIPT LETTERS, CAPITALS	49					
FLANNEL BOARD MANUSCRIPT LETTERS, LOWER CASE	49					
FLASH CARDS, SET B	60	62	81			
FLASH-X-SET 1: READING PICTURES	71	47	46	50	51	
FLIGHT TIME (RL 2)	53					
FLOOR PUZZLES, FARM	23					
FLOOR PUZZLES, ZOO	23					
FLOOR PUZZLES: INNER CITY CONSONANTS	52					
FLOOR PUZZLES: OCCUPATIONS	94					
FLOOR PUZZLES: RURAL VOWELS	58					
FOAM LETTERS	49	25				
FOCUS ON PHONICS 1: SOUNDS & NAMES OF LETTERS	50					
FOCUS ON PHONICS 1: TEACHER'S EDITION	50					
FOCUS ON PHONICS 2A	57					
FOCUS ON SKILLS: THE SPELLING BOX, INTERMEDIATE	64					
FOCUS ON SKILLS: THE SPELLING BOX, PRIMARY	64					
FOCUS ON SKILLS: THE VOCABULARY BOX, INTERMEDIATE	83					
FOCUS ON SKILLS: THE VOCABULARY BOX, PRIMARY	83					
FOKES SENTENCE BUILDER	6	74	92	70		
FOKES SENTENCE BUILDER EXPANSION	6	92	70			
FORE & AFT	80	81				
FORM BLOCKS	12	10				
FORM PUZZLE	14	12				
FORM-A-SOUND	53	57	58	5		
FOURTH GRADE LANGUAGE DRILLS	78	86	71	72		
FREQUENT ERROR PAIRS	5					
FRIENDLY SIGHT WORDS	84					
FROGGIE	49	16				
FROM COLOR TO WORDS	9	15				
FROM PHONICS TO READING	75	48	83	93		
FROM WORDS TO SENTENCES	84					
FRUIT & VEGETABLE INSERT PUZZLES	16	25				
FULL SPEED AHEAD, COMMUNICATION 3	2					
FUN PHONIC JINGLES, BOOK I	51	50				
FUN PHONIC JINGLES, BOOK II	53	51				
FUN SOUNDS (RL K-3)	4	35	7			
FUN WITH AFFIXES	80	81				
FUN WITH BLENDS & DIGRAPHS	53					
FUN WITH COLORS	10					
FUN WITH COLORS	10	15				
FUN WITH CONSONANT BLENDS	53					
FUN WITH CONSONANT BLENDS	53					
FUN WITH CONSONANTS	52					
FUN WITH RHYMES	51					

TITLE	SKILL NUMBERS						
FUN WITH SUPER SHAPES	13						
FUN WITH VOWEL SOUNDS	57	58					
FUN WITH VOWEL SOUNDS	56						
FUN WITH VOWEL SOUNDS, GRADES 1 & 2	57	58					
FUN WITH WORD USAGE	92						
FUN WITH WORDS	84	92	93				
FUN WITH WORDS	82	86	87	92			
FUN WITH WORDS & PICTURES	84						
FUN WITH WORDS, A	92	48					
FUN WITH WORDS, B	92	48					
FUN WITH WORDS, C	92	48					
FUN WITH WORDS, D	92	48					
FUN WITH WORDS, E	92	48					
FUN WITH WORDS, F	92	48					
FUN WITH WORDS, GRADE 1	84						
FUN WITH WORDS, GRADE 2	84						
FUNCTIONAL SIGNS	85						
FUNCTIONAL SIGNS MATCH-UPS	85						
FUNCTIONAL SPEECH & LANGUAGE TRAINING	4	5	7				
FUNCTIONAL WORD RECOGNITION (SP. ED.)	84	85					
FUNNY BUSINESS	90						
FUNNY FACE PHONICS	57	58	63	59	60	54	
FUNNY-FACE PHONICS	48						
FUNTACTICS: MOVEMENT & SPEECH ACTIVITIES FOR YOUNG CHILDREN	4	7					
GAMEBOARD KIT A	51	50	57				
GAMEBOARD KIT C	86	47					
GAMEBOARD KIT D	76	80	81	82	87	88	86
GAMEBOARD KIT F	13	9	12	51	35	26	27
GAMEBOARD KIT G	52	48	61	50			
GAMEBOARDS FOR EARLY CHILDHOOD EDUCATION	2	29	42	47			
GAMEBOARDS FOR SPEECH & LANGUAGE DEVELOPMENT	5	50	42	29	2		
GAMES & MORE GAMES KIDS LIKE	5	29	4	6			
GAMES 'N' FRAMES: AL'S PIT STOP	78	77	70				
GAMES 'N' FRAMES: COOKING WITH CONSONANTS	52						
GAMES 'N' FRAMES: DR. DIGRAPH'S HOCUS-POCUS	59	60					
GAMES 'N' FRAMES: GETTING TO KNOW THE UNKNOWN	55						
GAMES 'N' FRAMES: SOUL TRIP	57	58	82				
GAMES 'N' FRAMES: STRENGTHENING SUFFIXES WITH GRIMN & BARRET	76	81					
GAMES 'N' FRAMES: THE HOUSE OF FORTUNE	82						
GAMES 'N' FRAMES: THE STRANGE CASE OF THE VANISHING VOWELS	58	57	61				
GAMES 'N' FRAMES: VICENT VAN BLEEP	53						
GAMES 'N' FRAMES: WORD NEWS ROUNDUP	76	80					
GAMES MAKE SPELLING FUN	64						
GATEWAYS TO CORRECT SPELLING	64						
GAY SOUNDS (RL K-3)	4	35	7				
GENERAL CLASSIFICATION	47						
GENERAL SEQUENCING CARDS	23						
GEO-SHAPE BOARD	17						
GEOMETRIC SORTING BOARD	18	14	9	25			
GET SET: BROKEN LETTERS	49						
GET SET: GAMES FOR BEGINNING READERS	28	50	49	84			
GET SET: PICK A FIT	50						
GET SET: PICTURE WORDS	84						
GET SET: SENTENCE TRAIN	84						
GET SET: SILLY SENTENCES	28						
GET SET: TREASURE CAPTURE	28						
GETTING INTO FIGURATIVE LANGUAGE	90						
GETTING READY TO READ	9	25	49	51	23		
GETTING STARTED, COMMUNICATION 1	2						
GETTING TO KNOW WORDS	75	83					
GIANT ALPHABET TAPE	49						
GILLIGAN MILLIGAN	48	75	83				
GLAD SOUNDS (RL 1-3)	4	35	7				
GO TOGETHER LOTTO	2	19					
GO-TOGETHER: CLASSIFYING & MATCHING	47	14	18				
GOAL, LEVEL I: LANGUAGE DEVELOPMENT	22	30	33	42			
GOAL, LEVEL II: LANGUAGE DEVELOPMENT	9	24	26	30	33	42	94
GOING BANANAS OVER LANGUAGE SKILLS	86	87	88	78			
GOING PLACES BY AIR	23						
GOING PLACES BY LAND	23						
GOING PLACES BY WATER	23						
GOLDMAN-LYNCH SOUNDS & SYMBOLS DEVELOPMENT KIT	26	35	50	5			
GOOD APPLE SPELLING BOOK	64						
GOOD SPEECH POSTERS, SET 1	5	7					
GOOD SPEECH POSTERS, SET 2	5	7					
GOT TO BE ME, 48 CARDS	1	35					
GOT TO BE ME, WORKBOOK	1	35					
GRADED CYLINDER BLOCKS WITH KNOBS	11						
GRAMMAR	70						
GRAMMAR	70						
GRAMMAR GRAB BAG	70	74					
GRAPHIC DOMINOES	10						
GREAT BIG ALPHABET PICTURE BOOK	49						
GREAT COSMIC TREATY AGREEMENT OF SUBJECT: VERB	71	72	74				
GROUP SOUNDING GAME	82						
GROUP WORD TEACHING GAME	84						
GROUP-SIZE CONSONANT CARDS	52	53					
GROUP-SIZE PICTURE WORD CARDS	71						
GROUP-SIZE POPPER WORDS, SET 1	84						
GROUP-SIZE POPPER WORDS, SET 2	84						
GROUP-SIZE VOWEL CARDS	57	58	59	60			
GUESS WHOSE EARS	42	45					
GUESS WHOSE FEET	42	45					

TITLE	SKILL NUMBERS						
GUESS WHOSE TAIL	42	45					
HALF ANIMAL LOTTO	23						
HANDBOOK FOR SPEECH THERAPY	5	7					
HANDS ON	3						
HAPPY BIRTHDAY CARDS	5						
HAPPY ENDING	77						
HAPPY SOUNDS (RL 1-3)	4	35	7				
HAPPY TIME LISTENING	39	40	35				
HAPPY TIME LISTENING	39	40	35				
HAPPY WORLD OF COLOR	10	13	15				
HARD & SOFT C & G	54						
HAYES PHONETIC ALPHABET	49	50					
HEAR HOW, SET 1	35	29	36	37			
HEAR HOW, SET 2	35	29	36	37			
HEAR YE! HEAR YE! (RL 4-6)	4	35	7				
HEAR-SEE-SAY, PHONICS READING COURSE	48	49	50	57	58	53	
HELP: BLENDS & DIGRAPHS	53						
HELP: CASUAL RELATIONSHIPS	46						
HELP: PATTERN DETECTION	23	19					
HELP: PERCEPTUAL DIFFERENCES	9						
HELP: RHYMING WORDS	51						
HELP: TIME SEQUENCES	23	31					
HELP: VOWELS	57	58					
HELPING CHILDREN LEARN	2						
HELPING VERB	72						
HEY, LOOK AT ME!	49						
HIDDEN PICTURE PUZZLES, BOOK I	51	50					
HIDDEN PICTURE PUZZLES, BOOK II	53	51	50				
HILLTOP SERIES, BOOK 1 & THE HILLTOP SERIES COLORING BOOK	49	50					
HILLTOP SERIES, BOOK 2 & GOGO	49	50					
HILLTOP SERIES, BOOK 3 & JO JO	49	50					
HILLTOP SERIES, BOOK 4 & FLO	49	50					
HILLTOP SERIES, BOOK 5 & SALTY	49	50					
HITS SKILLBOOK SERIES, BOOK A (RL 1 - 2)	48	75	83				
HITS SKILLBOOK SERIES, BOOK B (RL 2 - 3)	48	75	83				
HITS SKILLBOOK SERIES, BOOK C (RL 3 - 4)	48	75	83				
HITS SKILLBOOK SERIES, BOOK D (RL 4 - 5)	83						
HITS, LEVEL 1: AMERICA, LONELY PEOPLE	53	57	58	86			
HITS, LEVEL 1: AMERICA, TIN MAN	53	57	58	59	60	86	
HITS, LEVEL 1: AMERICA, TODAY'S THE DAY	53	86					
HITS, LEVEL 1: AMERICA, VENTURA HIGHWAY	61	53	57	58	59	60	86
HITS, LEVEL 1: BLACKBYRDS, YOU'VE GOT THAT SOMETHING	53	57	58	59	60	61	86
HITS, LEVEL 1: DOOBIE BROTHERS, IT KEEPS YOU RUNNING	57	58	59	86			
HITS, LEVEL 1: JAMES TAYLOR, SWEET BABY JAMES	53	57	58	59	60	61	
HITS, LEVEL 1: PAUL SIMON, EL CONDOR PASA	53	57	58	59	60	61	
HITS, LEVEL 1: PRATT & MCCLAIN, HAPPY DAYS	86						
HITS, LEVEL 1: SANTANA, LET IT SHINE	53	57	58	86			
HITS, LEVEL 1: THREE DOG NIGHT, ONE MAN BAND	57	86					
HITS, LEVEL 2: ABBA, KNOWING ME, KNOWING YOU	57	58	60	65	86	78	
HITS, LEVEL 2: ABBA, S.O.S.	57	58	59	60	61	65	87
HITS, LEVEL 2: B.J. THOMAS, HEY WON'T YOU PLAY	86						
HITS, LEVEL 2: BELLAMY BROTHERS, LET YOUR LOVE FLOW	53	57	58	59	65	86	
HITS, LEVEL 2: DONNIE & MARIE OSMOND, IT TAKES TWO	53	57	58	59	60	61	
HITS, LEVEL 2: EARTH WIND & FIRE, SHINING STAR	57	58	59	60	61	65	86
HITS, LEVEL 2: FLEETWOOD MAC, OVER MY HEAD	57	58	65	86			
HITS, LEVEL 2: JOHN SEBASTIAN, WELCOME BACK	53	57	58	59	60	65	86
HITS, LEVEL 2: PAUL SIMON, STILL CRAZY AFTER ALL THESE YEARS	57	58	59	60	61	65	78
HITS, LEVEL 2: SIDE EFFECT, S.O.S.	57	58	59	60	61	65	86
HITS, LEVEL 2: SPINNERS, COULD IT BE I'M FALLING IN LOVE	57	58	59	60	61	65	78
HITS, LEVEL 2: SPINNERS, GAMES PEOPLE PLAY	53	57	58	59	65	86	
HITS, LEVEL 3: CARLY SIMON, GROWN UP	57	58	59	60	65	78	87
HITS, LEVEL 3: DOOBIE BROTHERS, LISTEN TO THE MUSIC	57	58	59	60	61	65	86
HITS, LEVEL 3: EMOTION, BEST OF MY LOVE	57	58	59	60	61	65	86
HITS, LEVEL 3: FIREFALL, LIVIN' AIN'T LIVIN'	53	57	58	59	61	65	87
HITS, LEVEL 3: FLEETWOOD MAC, DON'T STOP	57	58	59	60	61	65	87
HITS, LEVEL 3: HARRY CHAPIN, CIRCLE	86	33					
HITS, LEVEL 3: JAMES TAYLOR, SHOWER THE PEOPLE	53	57	58	65	86		
HITS, LEVEL 3: JOHNNY NASH, I CAN SEE CLEARLY NOW	53	57	58	59	60	61	65
HITS, LEVEL 3: PAUL SIMON, 50 WAYS TO LEAVE YOUR LOVER	57	58	59	60	61	65	78
HITS, LEVEL 3: SPINNERS, JUST CAN'T GET YOU OUT OF MY MIND	57	58	59	60	61	65	86
HITS, LEVEL 3: SPINNERS, ONE OF A KIND LOVE AFFAIR	57	58	59	60	61	65	87
HITS, LEVEL 3: THREE DOG NIGHT, THE FAMILY OF MAN	57	58	59	60	61	65	86
HITS, LEVEL 4: AMERICA, I NEED YOU	65	86	87				
HITS, LEVEL 4: ARETHA FRANKLIN, BRIDGE OVER TROUBLED WATERS	65	92	86	87			
HITS, LEVEL 4: COVEN, ONE TIN SOLDIER	65	80	81	92			
HITS, LEVEL 4: DAVE LOGGINS, PLEASE COME TO BOSTON	65	86	87	92			
HITS, LEVEL 4: FLEETWOOD MAC, DREAMS	65	92	87	86			
HITS, LEVEL 4: FOUR TOPS, KEEPER OF THE CASTLE	65	80	92	88			
HITS, LEVEL 4: PAUL SIMON, AMERICAN TUNE	65	80	92	88			
HITS, LEVEL 4: PAUL SIMON, BRIDGE OVER TROUBLED WATERS	65	92	86	87			
HITS, LEVEL 4: PAUL SIMON, FLOWERS NEVER BEND W/THE RAINFALL	65	80	92				
HITS, LEVEL 4: PAUL SIMON, HOMEWARD BOUND	65	80	92				
HITS, LEVEL 4: PAUL SIMON, I AM A ROCK	65	80	86	87			
HITS, LEVEL 4: PAUL SIMON, LEAVES THAT ARE GREEN	65						
HOMOGRAPHIC HOMOPHONES	88						
HOMOGRAPHIC HOMOPHONES	88	89					
HOMOGRAPHS	88						
HOMOGRAPHS	88						
HOMONYM & ANTONYM CASINO	87	88					
HOMONYM CARDS, HOMOGRAPHS	88						
HOMONYM CARDS, HOMOPHONES	88	89					
HOMONYM PEAS	88						
HOMONYM POSTER CARDS	88						

TITLE	SKILL NUMBERS						
HOMONYMS	88						
HOMONYMS	88						
HOMONYMS	88						
HOMONYMS	88						
HOMONYMS	88						
HOMONYMS	88						
HOMONYMS PACER	88	89					
HOMONYMS, SYNONYMS & ANTONYMS	86	87	88				
HOMOPHONES	88						
HORSE OF A DIFFERENT COLOR	86						
HOUND DOG PUPPET	7	25					
HOW ARE THEY ALIKE?	9	47					
HOW TO PREPARE FOR H.S. EQUIV. EXAM: WRITING SKILLS TEST	74	64					
HOWDY PARTNER	17						
HOWDY PARTNER, AGAIN	12						
HOWL FOR OWL, LEVEL I	60	61					
HOWL FOR OWL, LEVEL II	60	61					
I CAN DO IT	21	11	16	19	15	17	
I CAN DO IT, PART ONE	14	9	18				
I CAN DO IT, PART TWO	19	23					
I CAN READ	50	84					
I CAN READ, BOOK 1	50	84					
I CAN READ, BOOK 2	50	84					
I CAN READ, BOOK 3	50	84					
I CAN READ, BOOK 4	50	84					
I CAN READ, BOOK 5	50	84					
I CAN READ, BOOK 6	50	84					
I CAN READ, BOOK 7	50	84					
I CAN READ, BOOK 8	50	84					
I CAN SPELL	64						
I HEAR A RHYME	51						
I HEAR A RHYME	51						
I HEARD IT WITH MY OWN TWO EARS	35	29	36	37			
I LEARN MY ABC'S	49						
I READ & I UNDERSTAND, LEVEL TWO	83	48	75				
I READ & I UNDERSTAND, LEVELS THREE & FOUR	83	48	75				
ICE CREAM COLOR-CONES	15	84					
IDENTIFICATION CARDS	4	2					
IDENTIFICATION PUZZLES	4	2					
IDENTIFYING PARTS OF SPEECH	70						
IF THE SHOE FITS	84	92	93				
IF YOUR CHILD STUTTERS	5						
ILLUSTRATED SIGHT WORDS	84						
IMAGINATIVE ADJECTIVES & PREPOSITIONS	73	70					
IMAGINATIVE ADJECTIVES & PREPOSITIONS, SET 1	73	70					
IMAGINATIVE ADJECTIVES & PREPOSITIONS, SET 10	73	70					
IMAGINATIVE ADJECTIVES & PREPOSITIONS, SET 11	73	70					
IMAGINATIVE ADJECTIVES & PREPOSITIONS, SET 12	73	70					
IMAGINATIVE ADJECTIVES & PREPOSITIONS, SET 13	73	70					
IMAGINATIVE ADJECTIVES & PREPOSITIONS, SET 14	73	70					
IMAGINATIVE ADJECTIVES & PREPOSITIONS, SET 2	73	70					
IMAGINATIVE ADJECTIVES & PREPOSITIONS, SET 3	73	70					
IMAGINATIVE ADJECTIVES & PREPOSITIONS, SET 4	73	70					
IMAGINATIVE ADJECTIVES & PREPOSITIONS, SET 5	73	70					
IMAGINATIVE ADJECTIVES & PREPOSITIONS, SET 6	73	70					
IMAGINATIVE ADJECTIVES & PREPOSITIONS, SET 7	73	70					
IMAGINATIVE ADJECTIVES & PREPOSITIONS, SET 8	73	70					
IMAGINATIVE ADJECTIVES & PREPOSITIONS, SET 9	73	70					
IMPACT (RL 7-9)	85						
IMPROVING COMMUNICATION SKILLS THROUGH SPEECH CORRECTION	5	4					
IMPROVING COMMUNICATION SKILLS THROUGH SPEECH CORRECTION	5						
IMPROVING COMPOSITION	74	70					
IN OTHER WORDS	90						
INCREASE YOUR VOCABULARY, BOOK 1	83						
INCREASE YOUR VOCABULARY, BOOK 2	83						
INCREDIBLE "R" BLENDS	53						
INDEPENDENT DRILL FOR MASTERY, FUNDAMENTALS OF SPELLING	64						
INDEPENDENT LANGUAGE ARTS ACTIVITIES: PRIMARY	64						
INDEPENDENT WORD PERCEPTION	83	26	52	56			
INDIVIDUAL CORRECTIVE ENGLISH, GRADE 2	2						
INDIVIDUAL CORRECTIVE ENGLISH, GRADE 3	2						
INDIVIDUAL CORRECTIVE ENGLISH, GRADE 4	2						
INDIVIDUAL CORRECTIVE ENGLISH, GRADE 4, T.M.	2						
INDIVIDUAL CORRECTIVE ENGLISH, GRADE 5	2						
INDIVIDUAL CORRECTIVE ENGLISH, GRADE 5, T.M.	2						
INDIVIDUAL CORRECTIVE ENGLISH, GRADE 6	2						
INDIVIDUAL CORRECTIVE ENGLISH, GRADE 6, T.M.	2						
INDIVIDUAL CORRECTIVE ENGLISH, GRADES 2 - 3, T.M.	2						
INDIVIDUAL LANGUAGE ARTS, GRADE 1	51						
INDIVIDUAL LANGUAGE ARTS, GRADE 2	48						
INDIVIDUAL LANGUAGE ARTS, GRADE 3	48						
INDIVIDUAL LANGUAGE ARTS, GRADE 4	48						
INDIVIDUAL LANGUAGE ARTS, GRADE 5	48						
INDIVIDUAL LANGUAGE ARTS, GRADE 6	48						
INDIVIDUAL LANGUAGE ARTS, PHONICS	50						
INDIVIDUAL LETTER & WORD CARDS, SET 2	77						
INDIVIDUAL LISTENING GAMES	38	39	40	29	36		
INDIVIDUALIZED ENGLISH, SET H	6						
INDIVIDUALIZED ENGLISH, SET J	6						
INDIVIDUALIZED INSTRUCTION IN SPELLING	65	67	66				
INDIVIDUALIZED READING DEVELOPMENT ACTIVITIES	52	57	58	47			
INDIVIDUALIZED SPELLING	69						
INITIAL BLENDS	53						

TITLE	SKILL NUMBERS						
INITIAL CONSONANT BINGO	53						
INITIAL CONSONANT BLENDS, B	53						
INITIAL CONSONANT BLENDS, PART 1	53						
INITIAL CONSONANT BLENDS, PART 2	53						
INITIAL CONSONANT BLENDS, PART 3	53						
INITIAL CONSONANT DISCS	52						
INITIAL CONSONANT SUBSTITUTION	51						
INITIAL CONSONANTS DIGRAPHS/CLUSTERS (GRADES 1 - 2)	53						
INITIAL CONSONANTS, PART 1	52						
INITIAL CONSONANTS, PART 2	52						
INSTEAD, SET 1	5						
INSTEAD, SET 2	5						
INSTEAD, SET 3	5						
INSTRUCTIONAL AID PACKS - VOCABULARY GAMES	83	92					
INSTRUCTIONAL AID PACKS: STRIKE OUT! A	83	92					
INSTRUCTIONAL AID PACKS: STRIKE OUT! B	83	92					
INSTRUCTIONAL AID PACKS: STRIKE OUT! C	83	92					
INSTRUCTIONAL AID PACKS: STRIKE OUT! D	83	92					
INSTRUCTIONAL AID PACKS: STRIKE OUT! E	83	92					
INSTRUCTIONAL AID PACKS: SWAP! A	83	92					
INSTRUCTIONAL AID PACKS: SWAP! B	83	92					
INSTRUCTIONAL AID PACKS: SWAP! C	83	92					
INSTRUCTIONAL AID PACKS: SWAP! D	83	92					
INSTRUCTIONAL AID PACKS: SWAP! E	83	92					
INSTRUCTIONAL AID PACKS: TACK ON! A	83	92					
INSTRUCTIONAL AID PACKS: TACK ON! B	83	92					
INSTRUCTIONAL AID PACKS: TACK ON! C	83	92					
INSTRUCTIONAL AID PACKS: TACK ON! D	83	92					
INSTRUCTIONAL AID PACKS: TACK ON! E	83	92					
INSTRUCTIONAL AID PACKS: TURN ABOUT! A	83	92					
INSTRUCTIONAL AID PACKS: TURN ABOUT! B	83	92					
INSTRUCTIONAL AID PACKS: TURN ABOUT! C	83	92					
INSTRUCTIONAL AID PACKS: TURN ABOUT! D	83	92					
INSTRUCTIONAL AID PACKS: TURN ABOUT! E	83	92					
INTEGRATED TOTAL LANGUAGE	50						
INTERMEDIATE SPELLING	67	69					
INTERMEDIATE STRUCTURAL ANALYSIS	80	81	82	78	72		
INTERMEDIATE VOCABULARY	86	87	88	89	80	81	
INTERNATIONAL SIGNS & SYMBOLS	85						
INTERSENSORY PHONICS READINESS KIT	50						
INTERSENSORY READING PROGRAM, BLEND - IT	28						
INTRODUCING ATTRIBUTES, SPINNERS WITH BLOCKS	14						
INTRODUCING ATTRIBUTES, TASK CARDS WITH BLOCKS	14						
IT'S RAINING CATS & DOGS	90						
JACK & THE BEANSTALK MEMORY GAME	24						
JELLY JAR BLUES & OTHER STORIES	54						
JOAN HANSON WORD BOOKS	70	87	88	89	86	90	77
JOB INSET PUZZLE	94						
JOB PUZZLES	94						
JOBS & PEOPLE	94						
JOBS & SERVICES	94						
JOBS & THE COMMUNITY	94						
JOBS & THINGS	94						
JOBS AT HOME & AT SCHOOL	94						
JOHNNY LEARNS TO READ FOR FUN & QUICKLY	48						
JOIN THE VOWEL QUINTET	57	58					
JR. HI LANGUAGE DRILLS, BOOK 1	71	72	73				
JR. HI LANGUAGE DRILLS, BOOK 2	71	72	73				
JUMBO ANIMAL DOMINOES	15						
JUMBO HUNDRED PEGBOARD	13	21	15	17			
JUMBO SPELLING YEARBOOK	64						
JUMBO SPELLING YEARBOOK 3	64	65	66	67	86	87	
JUNIOR LISTEN-HEAR PROGRAM	27						
JUNIOR WORBAGE	84						
JUST RIGHT JOB STORIES	94						
K-SPEECH NEWS	5	2					
KALEIDOSCOPE	4						
KERNEL SENTENCES	74	71	72	73			
KEYS & LOCKS KNOB PUZZLE	9						
KEYS & LOCKS KNOB PUZZLE	25						
KINDERGARTEN KEYS: LANGUAGE DEVELOPMENT CARDS, GROUP A	8	83	4				
KINDERGARTEN KEYS: LANGUAGE DEVELOPMENT CARDS, GROUP B	49	2	4				
KINDERGARTEN KEYS: MOCKINGBIRD FLIGHT	51						
KINDERGARTEN KEYS: THE CATERPILLAR CAPER	9	27	51				
KING LOUIE HOLIDAY STORIES FOR SPEECH & LANG. REMEDIATION	5						
KIT 11: READ-ALONG	83	84					
KIT 12: SIGHT WORDS	84						
KIT 17: SPELLING, LEVEL 1	64						
KIT 18: SPELLING, LEVEL 2	64						
KIT 19: SPELLING, LEVEL 3	64						
KIT 1: BUILDING READING SKILLS, LEVEL 2	48	75					
KIT 20: SPELLING, LEVEL 4A	64						
KIT 21: SPELLING, LEVEL 4B	64						
KIT 22: BASIC SKILLS IN FOLLOWING DIRECTIONS	37						
KIT 23: READING READINESS STORY STARTERS	4						
KIT 2: BUILDING READING SKILLS, LEVEL 3	48	75					
KIT 30: IMPROVING SPEECH PATTERNS	5						
KIT 31: BUILDING PHONICS SKILLS	48						
KIT 32: BUILDING READING COMPREHENSION & VOCABULARY SKILLS	83						
KIT 3: BUILDING READING SKILLS, LEVEL 4	48	75					
KIT 4: BUILDING READING SKILLS, LEVEL 5	48	75					
KIT 58: BUILDING WORD POWER, LEVEL 3	86	87	92	90	79	80	81
KIT 59: BUILDING WORD POWER, LEVEL 4	86	87	92	90	79	80	81

TITLE	SKILL NUMBERS						
KIT 5: BUILDING READING SKILLS, LEVEL 6	48	75					
KIT 60: BUILDING WORD POWER, LEVEL 5	86	87	92	90	79	80	81
KIT 61: BUILDING WORD POWER, LEVEL 16	86	87	92	90	79	80	81
KIT 7: BASIC WORD ATTACK - BEG., END. CONSONANT BLENDS	53						
KIT 80: BASIC PHONICS, READINESS LEVEL	49	50	51				
KIT 81: BASIC PHONICS, LEVEL 1	49	50	51				
KIT 82: BASIC PHONICS, LEVEL 2	52	56					
KIT 83: BASIC PHONICS, LEVEL 3	52	56					
KIT 84: BASIC PHONICS, LEVEL 4	52	56	76	86	87		
KIT 8: BASIC WORD ATTACK - LONG, SHORT VOWELS	57	58	63				
KIT 9: BASIC WORD ATTACK - STRUCTURAL ANALYSIS, PREFIXES	80	81					
KNIGHT INDIVIDUALIZED SPELLING PROGRAM KIT	67	65	66	76	80	81	
KNOB PUZZLES: ACTIVITIES	25						
KNOB PUZZLES: CIRCUS TIME	25						
KNOB PUZZLES: CITY TRAFFIC	25						
KNOB PUZZLES: CLASSROOM	25						
KNOB PUZZLES: FAMILIAR SUBJECTS	25						
KNOB PUZZLES: FARM LIFE	25						
KNOB PUZZLES: FRIENDLY ANIMALS	25						
KNOB PUZZLES: GARAGE	25						
KNOB PUZZLES: TOYS 'N' STUFF	25						
KNOB PUZZLES: TRANSPORTATION VEHICLES	25						
KNOB PUZZLES: WILDLIFE	25						
KNOBBED ALPHA WORM PUZZLE	49						
KNOW 'N' SHOW ALPHABET	49						
LAC CARDS, SET 1: VERBS, SPORTS IN ACTION	2	4					
LAC CARDS, SET 2: GENERAL VERBS	2	4	72				
LACE-A-SHAPE, ANIMAL FRIENDS & PETS	49						
LACE-A-SHAPE, TOYS & FAVORITE THINGS	49						
LACING BOARDS	11	12					
LADYBIRD BOOK: 10A, ADVENTURES ON ISLAND	84						
LADYBIRD BOOK: 10B, ADVENTURE AT CASTLE	84						
LADYBIRD BOOK: 10C, LEARNING IS FUN	84						
LADYBIRD BOOK: 11A, MYSTERY ON ISLAND	84						
LADYBIRD BOOK: 11B, LOOK AT THIS	84						
LADYBIRD BOOK: 11B, THE CARNIVAL	84						
LADYBIRD BOOK: 11C, BOOKS ARE EXCITING	84						
LADYBIRD BOOK: 12A, HOLIDAY CAMP MYSTERY	84						
LADYBIRD BOOK: 12B, MOUNTAIN ADVENTURE	84						
LADYBIRD BOOK: 12C, OPEN DOOR TO READING	84						
LADYBIRD BOOK: 1A, PLAY WITH US	84						
LADYBIRD BOOK: 1C, READ & WRITE	84						
LADYBIRD BOOK: 2A, WE HAVE FUN	84						
LADYBIRD BOOK: 2B, HAVE A GO	84						
LADYBIRD BOOK: 2C, I LIKE TO READ	84						
LADYBIRD BOOK: 3A, THINGS WE LIKE	84						
LADYBIRD BOOK: 3B, BOYS & GIRLS	84						
LADYBIRD BOOK: 4A, THINGS WE DO	84						
LADYBIRD BOOK: 4B, FUN AT THE FARM	84						
LADYBIRD BOOK: 4C, SAY THE SOUND	50						
LADYBIRD BOOK: 5A, WHERE WE GO	84						
LADYBIRD BOOK: 5B, OUT IN THE SUN	84						
LADYBIRD BOOK: 5C, MORE SOUNDS TO SAY	50						
LADYBIRD BOOK: 6A, OUR FRIENDS	84						
LADYBIRD BOOK: 6B, WE LIKE TO HELP	84						
LADYBIRD BOOK: 6C, READING WITH SOUNDS	50						
LADYBIRD BOOK: 7A, HAPPY HOLIDAY	84						
LADYBIRD BOOK: 7B, FUN & GAMES	84						
LADYBIRD BOOK: 7C, EASY TO SOUND	50						
LADYBIRD BOOK: 8A, SUNNY DAYS	84						
LADYBIRD BOOK: 8B, THE BIG HOUSE	84						
LADYBIRD BOOK: 8C, FUN WITH SOUNDS	50						
LADYBIRD BOOK: 9A, GAMES WE LIKE	84						
LADYBIRD BOOK: 9B, JUMP FROM THE SKY	84						
LADYBIRD BOOK: 9C, ENJOYING READING	84						
LADYBIRD BOOK: ACTION RHYMES	51						
LADYBIRD BOOK: ANIMALS	4	6					
LADYBIRD BOOK: BABY	4	6					
LADYBIRD BOOK: BEDTIME	4	6					
LADYBIRD BOOK: CLOTHES	4	6					
LADYBIRD BOOK: DANCING RHYMES	51						
LADYBIRD BOOK: FINGER RHYMES	51						
LADYBIRD BOOK: GARDENS	4	6					
LADYBIRD BOOK: HOLIDAYS	4	6					
LADYBIRD BOOK: HOME	4	6					
LADYBIRD BOOK: MEMORY RHYMES	51						
LADYBIRD BOOK: NUMBER RHYMES	51						
LADYBIRD BOOK: PLAYBOOK 1	37	36	35	29			
LADYBIRD BOOK: PLAYBOOK 2	37	36	35	29			
LADYBIRD BOOK: PLAYBOOK 3	37	36	35	29			
LADYBIRD BOOK: PLAYBOOK 4	37	36	35	29			
LADYBIRD BOOK: SHOPPING	4	6					
LADYBIRD BOOK: STARTING SCHOOL	4	6					
LADYBIRD BOOK: TALKING RHYMES	51						
LADYBIRD BOOK: THE BEACH	4	6					
LADYBIRD BOOK: THE PARK	4	6					
LADYBIRD: COMPREHENSION CARDS, SET 1	92	65					
LADYBIRD: COMPREHENSION CARDS, SET 2	92	65					
LADYBIRD: DICTIONARY 2	84	92					
LADYBIRD: PICTURE DICTIONARY 1	84	92					
LADYBIRD: WORKBOOK 1	84						
LADYBIRD: WORKBOOK 2	84						
LADYBIRD: WORKBOOK 3	84						

TITLE	SKILL NUMBERS					
LADYBIRD: WORKBOOK 4	84	50				
LADYBIRD: WORKBOOK 5	84	50				
LADYBIRD: WORKBOOK 6	84	50				
LADYBIRD: WORKBOOKS	84	92	50			
LADYBUG, LADYBUG & MORE CHILDREN'S SONGS	2					
LANGUAGE	2	70				
LANGUAGE 720, GRADES 4 - 8	71	72				
LANGUAGE 830, GRADES 4 - 8	70					
LANGUAGE 940, GRADES 4 - 8	73	86	87	88		
LANGUAGE ACTIVITY CARDS: BASIC WORD COMPREHENSION	92					
LANGUAGE ACTIVITY CARDS: KNOW YOUR ALPHABET	49					
LANGUAGE ACTIVITY CARDS: PLURALS & CONTRACTIONS	78	77				
LANGUAGE ACTIVITY CARDS: SUFFIXES & PREFIXES	80	81				
LANGUAGE ACTIVITY CARDS: SYLLABLES & COMPOUND WORDS	79	82				
LANGUAGE ACTIVITY CARDS: VOWELS & CONSONANTS	52	56				
LANGUAGE ARTS ACTIVITIES	7					
LANGUAGE ARTS FOR THE INTERMEDIATE GRADES (4, 5, 6)	74	70	86	87		
LANGUAGE ARTS, GRADE 2	49	74	76	86	87	
LANGUAGE ARTS, GRADE 3	49	87	88			
LANGUAGE ARTS-SKILL DRILLS WITH MOTIVATORS	49	50	9	14		
LANGUAGE ARTS: SPELLING AIDS	65	66	67			
LANGUAGE ASSOCIATION BOARD NO. 1	70	2	4			
LANGUAGE ASSOCIATION BOARD NO. 2	72	2	4			
LANGUAGE ASSOCIATION BOARD NO. 3	73	2	4	71		
LANGUAGE CATEGORY GAMES	47					
LANGUAGE CENTER 1	35	35	7			
LANGUAGE CENTER 2	35	35	7			
LANGUAGE DEVELOPMENT & READING SKILLS	13	51	42	48	52	53	75
LANGUAGE DEVELOPMENT PROJECT	2					
LANGUAGE EXPERIENCES IN READIN (LEIR), LEVEL III	64	1	35	41		
LANGUAGE EXPERIENCES IN READING (LEIR), LEVEL I	64	1	35	41		
LANGUAGE EXPERIENCES IN READING (LEIR), LEVEL II	64	1	35	41		
LANGUAGE EXPERIENCES IN READING (LEIR), LEVEL IV	64	1	35	41		
LANGUAGE LOLLIPOP	81	76	82	86	79	
LANGUAGE MAKING ACTION CARDS	5					
LANGUAGE PATTERNS	74	70				
LANGUAGE PATTERNS/SELF-INSTRUCTIONAL MODALITIES APPROACH	8	26	47	48		
LANGUAGE REHABILITATION PROGRAM	74	70	72			
LANGUAGE REMEDIATION & EXPANSION	4	5	35	41	74	
LANGUAGE SCOOP	75	48				
LANGUAGE SKILLS PROGRAM: INTRODUCTION TO SPELLING	52	57	58	64		
LANGUAGE SKILLS PROGRAM: READINESS SKILLS (YY)	14	13	52	47	22	
LANGUAGE SKILLS PROGRAM: READING-SPELLING COMPREHENSION	58	64				
LANGUAGE SKILLS PROGRAM: READING-SPELLING COMPREHENSION	53	64				
LANGUAGE SKILLS PROGRAM: READING-SPELLING COMPREHENSION	64	52	56			
LANGUAGE SKILLS PROGRAM: READING-SPELLING COMPREHENSION (RP)	53	64				
LANGUAGE SKILLS PROGRAM: WORD GAMES & PUZZLES	51	52	53	59	85	70
LANGUAGE SKILLS STEP BY STEP, KIT A	2					
LANGUAGE SKILLS STEP BY STEP, KIT B	2					
LANGUAGE STIMULATION: ADJECTIVES	73	4	6			
LANGUAGE STIMULATION: NOUNS, ANIMALS & INSECTS	71	4	6			
LANGUAGE STIMULATION: NOUNS, FOOD	71	4	6			
LANGUAGE STIMULATION: NOUNS, HOUSEHOLD ITEMS	71	4	6			
LANGUAGE STIMULATION: VERBS	72	4	6			
LANGUAGE USAGE SKILLS FOR UPPER GRADES, VOLUME 1	72					
LANGUAGE USAGE SKILLS FOR UPPER GRADES, VOLUME 2	77	70	71			
LANGUAGE USAGE SKILLS FOR UPPER GRADES, VOLUME 3	70	72				
LANGUAGE USAGE SKILLS FOR UPPER GRADES, VOLUME 4	71					
LANGUAGE USAGE SKILLS FOR UPPER GRADES, VOLUME 6	70	71	72			
LANGUAGE USAGE SKILLS FOR UPPER GRADES, VOLUME 8	70	72				
LANGUAGE VISUALS	4	6				
LANGUAGE WORKSHOP (RL 4 - 5)	70	74				
LANGUAGE: PLURAL ACTION PICTURES	72	5				
LANGUAGE: VERB ACTION PICTURES	72	5				
LARC (LANGUAGE ARTS RESOURCE CENTER) PROGRAM	4					
LARC: MODULE O: ORDER & SEQUENCE SKILLS	37	74	72			
LARC: MODULE W: WORD SKILLS	83	75	36			
LARGE PARQUETRY BLOCKS, WOOD	21	23	15	19		
LARGE PARQUETRY DESIGNS CARDS	21	23	15	19		
LARGE PARQUETRY INSET BOARDS	25	17				
LARGE PEGBOARD	25					
LARGE SYMMETRICAL MATCH-UPS	9					
LARRY THE LEARNING LION	49	57	58	59		
LAUGH & LEARN WITH JACK & JULIE	4					
LAZY LETTERS	55	64				
LEARN THE ALPHABET	52	49	55			
LEARN THE COLORS	10	84				
LEARN TO LISTEN	39	40	29	36	38	37
LEARNING ABOUT OUR LANGUAGE, SET 1	39	50	51			
LEARNING ABOUT OUR LANGUAGE, SET 2	53	77				
LEARNING ABOUT OUR LANGUAGE, SET 3	57					
LEARNING ABOUT OUR LANGUAGE, SET 4	58	59	60	61	62	
LEARNING ACTION WORDS	72					
LEARNING ACTIVITIES FOR THE LEARNING DISABLED	24	2				
LEARNING ACTIVITY CARDS FOR CHILDREN	37	4				
LEARNING BASIC VOCABULARY	92	86	87	88	89	80	81
LEARNING CENTER ACTIVITIES, GRADES 3-4	82	84	85			
LEARNING CENTER ACTIVITIS, GRADES 2-3	53	59				
LEARNING CENTER PAK (GRADES 2 - 4)	8	84	92	48		
LEARNING CENTER PAK (GRADES 3 - 5)	48	33				
LEARNING CENTER PAK (GRADES 4 - 7)	70					
LEARNING CENTER PAK (GRADES K - 3)	49	8				
LEARNING COLORS	13	10	15			

TITLE	SKILL NUMBERS					
LEARNING COMMUNICATION SKILLS	4	38				
LEARNING LANGUAGE AT HOME, LEVEL I	35	8	1			
LEARNING LANGUAGE AT HOME, LEVEL II	26	8	1			
LEARNING LANGUAGE SKILLS 1	2	5	26	83	35	35
LEARNING LANGUAGE SKILLS 2	2	5	26	83	35	35
LEARNING LANGUAGE SKILLS 3	2	5	26	83	35	35
LEARNING LANGUAGE SKILLS 4	2	5	26	83	35	35
LEARNING LETTER NAMES, KIT A	49					
LEARNING LETTER NAMES, KIT B	49					
LEARNING LETTER SOUNDS, KIT E	53					
LEARNING LETTER SOUNDS, KIT EE	53					
LEARNING LETTER SOUNDS, KIT F	53					
LEARNING LETTER SOUNDS, KIT FF	53					
LEARNING LETTER SOUNDS, KIT G	58					
LEARNING LETTER SOUNDS, KIT GG	58					
LEARNING LETTER SOUNDS, KIT H	57					
LEARNING LETTER SOUNDS, KIT HH	57					
LEARNING LETTERS FROM A TO Z	49					
LEARNING PHONICS	49	78	79	55	82	56
LEARNING PHONICS	53	59	60	61	55	
LEARNING PREDICTABLE LANGUAGE	48					
LEARNING SHORT VOWELS	57					
LEARNING SIGHT WORDS	84					
LEARNING SLATE: ANIMALS (NOUNS)	71					
LEARNING SLATE: AT HOME (NOUNS)	71					
LEARNING SLATE: CHILDREN (VERBS)	72					
LEARNING SLATE: PHONICS	57	58	53			
LEARNING SPEECH SOUNDS, SET 1	35	5	29	36	37	
LEARNING SPEECH SOUNDS, SET 2	35	5	29	36	37	
LEARNING SPEECH SOUNDS, SET 3	35	5	29	36	37	
LEARNING STRUCTURAL ANALYSIS	79	77	78	76	80	81	82
LEARNING SYLLABLES	82					
LEARNING THE ALPHABET WITH AMOS & HIS FRIENDS	49					
LEARNING THE CONSONANT BLENDS WITH AMOS & HIS FRIENDS	53					
LEARNING THE LETTERS, BOOK I	49	50				
LEARNING THE LETTERS, BOOK II	57	58				
LEARNING THE LETTERS, BOOK III	57	58				
LEARNING THE LETTERS, BOOK IV	57	58	53			
LEARNING THE LETTERS, BOOK V	57	58	53	55		
LEARNING THE LETTERS, BOOK VI	57	58	53	55		
LEARNING THROUGH SONG	47	2				
LEARNING TO LEARN SERIES, SET 1	4	6				
LEARNING TO LEARN SERIES, SET 2	4	6				
LEARNING TO LISTEN	35	39	40	36	37	38
LEARNING TO SPELL CORRECTLY	64	65	66	67	68	
LEARNING UNITS ON CAREERS	94					
LEMON TREE	75	82	86	87	88	76
LESSONS IN SYNTAX: STUDENT'S WORKBOOK	6					
LESSONS IN SYNTAX: TEACHER'S MAUNAL	6					
LESSONS TO GROW ON, BOOK 1	49	25	12	21	50	
LESSONS TO GROW ON, BOOK 3	49	50	25			
LET'S ALL (AWL) TAKE A BOW (BOW)	88	89				
LET'S COMMUNICATE	4					
LET'S FIND SOME ROOT WORDS: INFLECTIONAL ENDINGS	76					
LET'S FIND SOME ROOT WORDS: PREFIXES	76	80				
LET'S FIND SOME ROOT WORDS: SUFFIXES	76	81				
LET'S FIND SYLLABLES IN WORDS	82					
LET'S LEARN SEQUENCE	23					
LET'S LEARN THE ALPHABET	49					
LET'S LISTEN	29	36	38			
LET'S LISTEN	40	29	36	39		
LET'S LOOK FOR ACTION WORDS	72					
LET'S LOOK FOR COMPOUND WORDS	79					
LET'S LOOK FOR MORE ACTION WORDS	72					
LET'S SING & ACT TOGETHER	7					
LET'S TALK	7					
LET'S TALK ABOUT FAMILIES	4	38				
LET'S TALK ABOUT LEARNING	4	38				
LET'S TALK ABOUT MAKING FRIENDS	4	38				
LET'S TALK ABOUT RULES	4	38				
LET'S TALK WITH WINNIE THE POOH	4	7				
LET'S WRITE A LETTER	74					
LETTER CARDS	49	50				
LETTER KNOWLEDGE DUPLICATING MASTERS	13	49				
LETTER NAMES & SOUNDS	49	50				
LETTER RECOGNITION	13	49				
LETTER SOUND ASSOCIATION, PART I	50					
LETTER SOUND ASSOCIATION, PART II	50					
LETTER SOUNDS ALL AROUND	49	50				
LETTER-PICTURE SOLITAIRE	50					
LETTERS & SOUNDS, INTERMEDIATE	52	57	58	76		
LETTERS & SOUNDS, PRIMARY	52	57	58	50		
LETTERS & SYLLABLES	82					
LETTERS & SYLLABLES, WORKTAPES	82					
LETTERS FROM CALICO CAT	49					
LETTERS OF THE ALPHABET, KIT I	49					
LETTERS, SOUNDS & WORDS	49	50				
LETTO	49					
LIFE CYCLE OF A FROG	23					
LIFE CYCLE OF A MONARCH BUTTERFLY	23					
LIFE CYCLE OF A ROBIN	23					
LIFELINE (RL 7-9)	85					
LIGHT & LEARN CARDS: BEGINNING & ENDING SOUNDS	48					

TITLE	SKILL NUMBERS						
LIGHT & LEARN CARDS: SENTENCE SENSE	74						
LIME TREE	80	81	82	86	87	88	
LINE GAME CUBES	10						
LINES 'N DOTS CARD GAME	4	7	42	43			
LINGUISTIC DRILL CARDS	84						
LINK LETTERS	74	49					
LINQUISTIC PACER	75	50	57	58	76		
LISTEN & DO: CONSONANTS	53						
LISTEN & DO: VOWELS	57	58					
LISTEN & SPEAK TO READ	5	29	2				
LISTEN HERE	35	29	36	37			
LISTEN, HEAR	39	40	29	36	38		
LISTEN, SPEAK, READ, & SPELL	48	12	35	1			
LISTEN-HEAR PROGRAM	27						
LISTENING	35	35					
LISTENING & LEARNING	29	36	38	35	35		
LISTENING & LEARNING	35	29	36	37	29		
LISTENING ACTIVITIES RECORD ALBUM	39	40	29	36	38		
LISTENING ACTIVITIES: A MANUAL OF LISTENING ACTIVITIES	39	40	29	36	38		
LISTENING ACTIVITY BOOK	39	40	29	36	38		
LISTENING EARS	39	40	29	36	38		
LISTENING EARS CARD SET	39	40	29	36	38		
LISTENING FOR SOUNDS	50	52	56	77	79	82	
LISTENING GAMES	39	40	29	36	38		
LISTENING SKILLS	35	39	40	37	29	36	
LISTENING SKILLS	35	35					
LISTENING SKILLS	35	39	40	29	36	38	
LISTENING SKILLS FOR PRE-READERS	39	40	29	36	37		
LISTENING SKILLS FOR PRE-READERS, VOLUME 1	39	40					
LISTENING SKILLS FOR PRE-READERS, VOLUME 1	39	40					
LISTENING SKILLS FOR PRE-READERS, VOLUME 2	39	40	47				
LISTENING SKILLS FOR PRE-READERS, VOLUME 2	27	40	47				
LISTENING SKILLS FOR PRE-READERS, VOLUME 3	39	40	24				
LISTENING SKILLS FOR PRE-READERS, VOLUME 4	39	40					
LISTENING SKILLS FOR PRE-READERS, VOLUME 4	39	40					
LISTENING SKILLS FOR PRE-READERS, VOLUME 5	39	40					
LISTENING SKILLS FOR PRE-READERS, VOLUME 5	39	40					
LISTENING SKILLS PROGRAM, GRADES 1-3 (RL 1-3)	35	29	38	36	37		
LISTENING SKILLS PROGRAM, GRADES 4-8 (RL 4-9)	35	29	38	36	37		
LISTENING SKILLS PROGRAM, UNIT I: EASY EARS	36	29	37	38			
LISTENING SKILLS PROGRAM, UNIT II: EAR POWER	29	36	37	38			
LISTENING SKILLS, ADVANCED LEVEL	26	35	35				
LISTENING SKILLS, INTERMEDIATE LEVEL	26	35	35				
LISTENING SKILLS, LEVEL 1	35	35					
LISTENING SKILLS, LEVEL 2	35	35					
LISTENING SKILLS, LEVEL 3	35	37	35				
LISTENING SKILLS, PRIMARY LEVEL	35	35					
LISTENING SKILLS, SERIES 7/8/9 LEVEL	26	35	35				
LISTENING TIME	35	35					
LISTENING TO THE WORLD	26	35	35	1			
LISTENING WITH A PURPOSE	35	35					
LISTENING YOUR WAY TO BETTER READING	35	26	48	52	56	57	58
LISTENING YOUR WAY TO UNDERSTANDING WORD PROBLEMS	35	36					
LISTENING-DOING-LEARNING TAPES	35	39					
LITTLE MONSTER'S ALPHABET BOOK	49						
LITTLE PICTURE CARDS	13	42	47				
LITTLE RIDDLES	90						
LITTLE TROLLY BOOKS & TAPES	35	35	2				
LOCKING SHAPES	12	17					
LOGIC CARDS	46	45					
LOGOS 1A	48	75	83				
LONG & SHORT OF IT	57	58					
LONG & SHORT OF IT	57	58					
LONG & SHORT VOWEL PUZZLES	57	58					
LONG & SHORT VOWEL SOUNDS KIT	57	58					
LONG & SHORT VOWELS	57	58					
LONG & SHORT VOWELS	57	58					
LONG & SHORT VOWELS	57	58					
LONG & SHORT VOWELS	57	58					
LONG & SHORT VOWELS	57	58	63				
LONG & SHORT VOWELS DESK TAPES	57	58					
LONG & SHORT VOWELS, GRADES 1 & 2	58	57					
LONG & SHORT VOWELS, PART I	57	58					
LONG & SHORT VOWELS, PART II	57	58					
LONG VOWEL DISCS	58						
LONG VOWEL SOUND FUN	58						
LONG VOWEL SOUNDS	58						
LONG VOWELS	58						
LONG VOWELS	58						
LONG VOWELS	58						
LONG VOWELS	58						
LONG VOWELS	58						
LONG VOWELS: STARTING OFF WITH PHONICS, BOOK 6	58						
LONG VOWELS: STARTING OFF WITH PHONICS, BOOK 6	58						
LONG, SHORT & COMBINED VOWEL SOUNDS	57	58	59	60			
LOOK & LISTEN	35	35					
LOOK FOR WORDS THAT COMPARE	73						
LOOK IN THE MIRROR	72						
LOOK SHARP	8						
LOOK SHARP	10	11	12	13			
LOOK-ALIKES & SOUND-ALIKES	88	93					
LOOK-LISTEN-SAY STORY CARDS	4	6					

TITLE	SKILL NUMBERS						
LOOKING AT WORDS A	64	70	75				
LOOKING FOR ROUND SHAPES	12	17					
LOOKING FOR SQUARE SHAPES	12	17					
LOTS MORE TELL & DRAW STORIES	34	10	42	40			
LOUD & CLEAR (RL 4-6)	4	35	7				
LOUD-NOISY, DIRTY-GRIMY, BAD & NAUGHTY TWINS	86						
MACMILLAN TUTORIAL SYSTEM KIT, GRADE 1	48	75					
MACMILLAN TUTORIAL SYSTEM KIT, GRADE 2	48	75					
MACMILLAN TUTORIAL SYSTEM KIT, GRADE 3	48	75					
MAGIC CARDS: BLENDS & DIGRAPHS	53						
MAGIC CARDS: CLASSIFICATION, OPPOSITES, SEQUENCE	23	87	47				
MAGIC CARDS: VOWELS	57	58					
MAGIC MONSTERS LOOK FOR COLORS	10	15					
MAGIC MONSTERS LOOK FOR SHAPES	12	17					
MAGIC TEACHER PUZZLE-PLANS (NOUNS), LEVEL 1	71						
MAGIC TEACHER PUZZLE-PLANS: PHONICS (CONSONANT BLENDS)	53						
MAGIC TEACHER PUZZLE-PLANS: PHONICS (CONSONANT SOUNDS)	52						
MAGIC TEACHER PUZZLE-PLANS: PHONICS (VOWEL SOUNDS)	57	58					
MAGIC TEACHER PUZZLE-PLANS: READING (NOUNS), LEVEL 2	71						
MAGIC TEACHER PUZZLE-PLANS: READING (NOUNS), LEVEL 3	71						
MAGIC TEACHER PUZZLE-PLANS: READING (VERBS)	72						
MAGICAL SILENT E	63	57	58				
MAINSTREAMING CHILDREN'S GAMES	35	39	31				
MAKE & TELL: COUNTRY THINGS KIT	35	83	40				
MAKE & TELL: LIVING THINGS KIT	35	83	40				
MAKE & TELL: TOWN THINGS KIT	35	83	40				
MAKE IT MANY: IRREGULAR PLURALS	77						
MAKE-A-WORD CARDS	13	83					
MAKING ENGLISH WORK FOR YOU	74						
MAKING WORDS WORK	92						
MANUSCRIPT ABC CARDS	49						
MANUSCRIPT LETTERS, UPPER & LOWER CASE	29	50					
MANY & FEW	8						
MARK ON-WIPE OFF CARDS: LOOK ALIKES	14	19					
MARK ON-WIPE OFF CARDS: MATCHING COLORS	15	19					
MARK ON-WIPE OFF CARDS: MATCHING MOTHERS & BABIES	19						
MARK ON-WIPE OFF CARDS: SEQUENCING PICTURE STORIES	23						
MARK ON-WIPE OFF CARDS: TRACING SHAPES	25						
MARK ON-WIPE OFF CARDS: VOWEL SOUNDS	57	58					
MARK ON-WIPE OFF CARDS: WHAT GOES TOGETHER?	19	14					
MARK ON-WIPE OFF CARDS: WHAT'S MISSING?	22						
MARK ON-WIPE OFF: SCRAMBLED WORDS	65						
MARK ON-WIPE OFF: WORLD HIGHWAY OF SIGNS	85						
MASTERING PARTS OF SPEECH	70						
MASTERING THE SENTENCE	74						
MASTERING THE SENTENCE IN SEVEN STEPS	70	74					
MASTERING THE SENTENCE IN SEVEN STEPS	70	74					
MASTERING THE SHORT VOWEL	57						
MASTERING THE SHORT VOWELS	57						
MATCH & CHECK, LEVEL 2	9	42					
MATCH & CHECK, LEVEL 3	9	42					
MATCH & CHECK, LEVEL 4	9	42					
MATCH & MEMORY, BOOK 1: MATCHING OBJECTS & SHAPES	17	14					
MATCH & MEMORY, BOOK 2: VISUAL DISCRIMINATION & PERCEPTION	10	12					
MATCH & MEMORY, BOOK 3: VISUAL MEMORY, POSITION IN SPACE	24						
MATCH & MEMORY, BOOK 4: VISUAL MEMORY SEQUENTIAL, LEVEL I	23						
MATCH & MEMORY, BOOK 5: VISUAL MEMORY SEQUENTIAL, LEVEL II	23						
MATCH GAMES, SET 1	14	19	71				
MATCH GAMES, SET 2	14	19	71				
MATCH ME CARDS	51	77	87				
MATCH ME CARDS, OPPOSITES	87						
MATCH ME CARDS, RHYMING WORDS	51						
MATCH ME CARDS, SINGULAR/PLURAL	77						
MATCH ME CARDS: BEGINNING SOUNDS	52						
MATCH ME CARDS: OPPOSITES	87						
MATCH ME CARDS: RHYMING WORDS	51						
MATCH ME CARDS: SINGULAR/PLURAL	77						
MATCH THE ANIMALS, TELL & DRAW WORKBOOK	17						
MATCH THREE	69						
MATCH-N-FIT: CIRCLES	11	12					
MATCH-N-FIT: MIXED	11	12					
MATCH-N-FIT: SQUARES	11	12					
MATCH-N-FIT: TRIANGLES	11	12					
MATCH-N-STAMP	12						
MATCHING LETTERS & WORDS, A	14	50					
MATCHING LETTERS, A	14	49					
MATCHING UPPER & LOWER CASE LETTERS, A	49	14					
MATCHING WORDS, A	14						
MAZES	21	45					
MCP BUILDING WORD POWER C	83						
MCP BUILDING WORD POWER D	83						
MCP BUILDING WORD POWER E	83						
MCP BUILDING WORD POWER F	83						
MCP BUILDING WORD POWER, LEVEL B	83						
MCP PHONICS WORKBOOKS: LEVEL A	52	57	58	75	49	81	
MCP PHONICS WORKBOOKS: LEVEL B	53	79	80	81	78	83	60
MCP PHONICS WORKBOOKS: LEVEL C	53	57	58	80	81	82	83
MEET MR. MIX-UP	39	40	29	36	37		
MEET MR. MIX-UP	39	40	29	36	37		
MEM-O-MATCH	78	86	87	88			
MERRILL PHONICS SKILL TEXT: COSTUME BOOK, LEVEL R	49	50	51	8			
MERRILL PHONICS SKILL TEXT: COSTUME BOOK, LEVEL R	49	50	51	8			
MERRILL PHONICS SKILL TEXT: COSTUME KIDS, LEVEL B	53	58					

TITLE	SKILL NUMBERS						
MERRILL PHONICS SKILL TEXT: COSTUME KIDS, LEVEL B	53	58					
MERRILL PHONICS SKILL TEXT: COSTUME SHOP, LEVEL A	52	57					
MERRILL PHONICS SKILL TEXT: COSTUME SHOP, LEVEL A	52	57					
MERRILL PHONICS SKILL TEXT: DETECTIVE CLUB, LEVEL E	53	58	55	80	81	82	
MERRILL PHONICS SKILL TEXT: DETETIVE CLUB, LEVEL E	53	58	55	80	81	82	
MERRILL PHONICS SKILL TEXT: SIGN MAKERS, LEVEL D	55	53	60	54			
MERRILL PHONICS SKILL TEXT: SIGN MAKERS, LEVEL D	55	53	60	54			
MERRILL PHONICS SKILL TEXT: SPACE VISITORS, LEVEL C	53	58	58	57			
MERRILL PHONICS SKILL TEXT: SPACE VISITORS, LEVEL C	53	58	58	57			
MERRILL PHONICS SKILL TEXT: WHIZ KID, LEVEL F	81	82	80	52	56	50	
MERRILL PHONICS SKILL TEXT: WHIZ KID, LEVEL F	80	81	82	52	56	50	
MERRY CHRISTMAS CARDS	5						
MIGHT "L" BLENDS	53						
MIGHTY CONSONANTS	52						
MILL /L/ SOUND	5						
MILL /R/ SOUND	5						
MILL /S/ SOUND	5						
MILLER PICTURE INDEX	5						
MINISYSTEMS: B WITH L & R	55						
MINISYSTEMS: BUILDING POWER VOCABULARY A,E,I	57						
MINISYSTEMS: BUILDING POWER VOCABULARY A,E,I,O	57						
MINISYSTEMS: BUILDING VOCABULARY, BLENDS, VOWELS, CONSONANTS	52	53	57	58			
MINISYSTEMS: C WITH L & R	55						
MINISYSTEMS: CHANGING SHORT a TO SHORT i	57						
MINISYSTEMS: COMPOUND WORDS	79						
MINISYSTEMS: CONSONANT DIGRAPHS	53						
MINISYSTEMS: CONTRACTIONS	78						
MINISYSTEMS: D WITH L & R	55						
MINISYSTEMS: DIPHTHONGS, EA,AI,OA	60						
MINISYSTEMS: DIPHTHONGS, EA,OU,OO	60						
MINISYSTEMS: ENDING S, 'S, ES, ING	77						
MINISYSTEMS: F WITH L & R	55						
MINISYSTEMS: FINAL CONSONANTS PLUS ENDINGS	77						
MINISYSTEMS: FROM SPELLING TO WRITING I	77	71					
MINISYSTEMS: FROM SPELLING TO WRITING II	77	71					
MINISYSTEMS: G WITH L & R	55						
MINISYSTEMS: HARD & SOFT C & G	54						
MINISYSTEMS: LEFT TO RIGHT PROGRESSION	34						
MINISYSTEMS: LETTER MATCHING GAMES	14	49					
MINISYSTEMS: LETTER RECOGNITION	49	13					
MINISYSTEMS: LETTERS B,M,S,H	49	13					
MINISYSTEMS: LETTERS D,A,E,C	49	13					
MINISYSTEMS: LETTERS L,T,O,W,U,V	49	13					
MINISYSTEMS: LETTERS N,P,F,R	49	13					
MINISYSTEMS: LETTERS Y,G,J,K	49	13					
MINISYSTEMS: LISTENING TO RHYMES	51						
MINISYSTEMS: LISTENING, SEEING, SRITING M,B,K,S,G,SH	53						
MINISYSTEMS: LISTENING, SEEING, WRITING D,N,L,P,T,CH	53						
MINISYSTEMS: LONG VOWELS A,E	58						
MINISYSTEMS: LONG VOWELS I,O,U	58						
MINISYSTEMS: MATCHING LETTERS PAIRS Aa,Ee,Hh,Nn	14	49					
MINISYSTEMS: MATCHING LETTERS, LIKE PAIRS Cc,Ii,Kk,Pp,Tt	14	49					
MINISYSTEMS: MATCHING LETTERS, LIKE PAIRS Ll,Jj,Oo,Ss,Ww	14	49					
MINISYSTEMS: MATCHING LETTERS, UNLIKE PAIRS Bb,Mm,Rr,Ff	14	49					
MINISYSTEMS: MATCHING LETTERS, UNLIKE PAIRS Dd,Gg,Qq	14	49					
MINISYSTEMS: MEDIAL SHORT TO LONG VOWELS PLUS E	63						
MINISYSTEMS: MULTIPLE MEANINGS	92	89					
MINISYSTEMS: ORIENTATION TO LETTERS	13	19					
MINISYSTEMS: ORIENTATION TO SHAPES	13	19					
MINISYSTEMS: P WITH L & R	55						
MINISYSTEMS: PARTICIPATING IN RHYMES	51						
MINISYSTEMS: PREFIXES	80						
MINISYSTEMS: REVIEW OF BLENDS	53						
MINISYSTEMS: REVIEW OF CONSONANT DIGRAPHS	53						
MINISYSTEMS: REVIEW, VOWELS CONTROLLED BY R,W,L	61						
MINISYSTEMS: RHYMING REVIEW	51						
MINISYSTEMS: RHYMING WORDS WITH PICTURES I	51						
MINISYSTEMS: RHYMING WORDS WITH PICTURES II	51						
MINISYSTEMS: RHYMING, ALL,AT,AY	51						
MINISYSTEMS: RHYMING, OW,OY,OI	51						
MINISYSTEMS: ROOTS, PREFIXES, SUFFIXES	76	80	81				
MINISYSTEMS: SHORT a	57						
MINISYSTEMS: SHORT e	57						
MINISYSTEMS: SHORT i	57						
MINISYSTEMS: SHORT o	57						
MINISYSTEMS: SHORT u	57						
MINISYSTEMS: SPELLING WITH SHORT a	57	66					
MINISYSTEMS: SPELLING WITH SHORT e	57	66					
MINISYSTEMS: SPELLING WITH SHORT i	57	66					
MINISYSTEMS: SPELLING WITH SHORT o	57	66					
MINISYSTEMS: SPELLING WITH SHORT u	57	66					
MINISYSTEMS: SPELLING WITH VOWELS & CONSONANTS	66	57	58				
MINISYSTEMS: SUFFIXES	81						
MINISYSTEMS: SYLLABICATION	82						
MINISYSTEMS: THE BLENDS OF S	53						
MINISYSTEMS: THREE-LETTER BLENDS	53						
MINISYSTEMS: VOWELS CONTROLLED BY R	61						
MINISYSTEMS: VOWELS CONTROLLED BY W & L	61						
MISSING MATCH-UPS	14						
MIX & MATCH MONSTER PUZZLES	4	6	12				
MIX 'N' MATCH PUZZLES: ANIMALS & THEIR YOUNG	14						
MIX 'N' MATCH PUZZLES: BEFORE & AFTER	14						
MIX 'N' MATCH PUZZLES: COLORS	13						

TITLE	SKILL NUMBERS						
MIX 'N' MATCH PUZZLES: CONSONANTS	52						
MIX 'N' MATCH PUZZLES: CONSONANTS	52						
MIX 'N' MATCH PUZZLES: GO-TOGETHERS	14						
MIX 'N' MATCH PUZZLES: INITIAL CONSONANTS, LEVEL 2	52						
MIX 'N' MATCH PUZZLES: LONG VOWELS	58						
MIX 'N' MATCH PUZZLES: LONG VOWELS	58						
MIX 'N' MATCH PUZZLES: MAKING PAIRS	14						
MIX 'N' MATCH PUZZLES: MATCHING THINGS	14						
MIX 'N' MATCH PUZZLES: MONEY	14						
MIX 'N' MATCH PUZZLES: RHYMING WORDS, LEVEL 1	51						
MIX 'N' MATCH PUZZLES: SEQUENCE, LEVEL 1	23						
MIX 'N' MATCH PUZZLES: SHORT VOWELS	57						
MIX 'N' MATCH PUZZLES: SHORT VOWELS	57						
MIX 'N' MATCH PUZZLES: SMALL, MEDIUM, LARGE	11						
MIX 'N' MATCH PUZZLES: THINGS OF A KIND	47						
MIX 'N' MATCH PUZZLES: WHAT'S MISSING?	14						
MIXED SHAPE-FINDING	12	17					
MODCOM: MODULES IN SPEECH COMMUNICATIONS	7						
MONSTER BOOKS, SERIES I	83	74					
MONSTER BOOKS, SERIES II	83	74					
MONSTER HUNT	48	82	80	81			
MONSTER LACING CARDS	2	7					
MORE ANTONYMS	87						
MORE ANYTONYMS	87						
MORE CONSONANT SOUNDS: STARTING OFF WITH PHONICS, BOOK 4	52						
MORE CONSONANT SOUNDS: STARTING OFF WITH PHONICS, BOOK 4	52						
MORE EASY CROSSWORD PUZZLES	76	80	81	77			
MORE FUN WITH WORDS, GRADE 3	84						
MORE HOMONYMS	88						
MORE HOMONYMS	88						
MORE NEW WORDS	48	75	83				
MORE PHONICS	53	59	60	61	54	55	
MORE PROGRAMMED ARTICULATION SKILLS CARRYOVER STORIES	5						
MORE READ, THINK, COLOR	52	56	51	84			
MORE ROADS TO MEANING	75	83	86				
MORE SEQUENCE PICTURES FOR STORY TELLING	7	5					
MORE SIMILES	90						
MORE SIMILIES	90						
MORE SIMILIES	90						
MORE SOUND WORDS	93						
MORE SOUNDS & SYMBOLS, BOOK F	82	80	81	86	87		
MORE SYNONYMS	86						
MORE SYNONYMS	86						
MORE TELL & DRAW STORIES	34	10	42	40			
MORE VOWELS & VARIANTS, BOOK D	58	59	61	63	60		
MORE-THAN-ONE, FUN FROM HEADQUARTERS	77						
MOST USED WORDS FOR SPELLING	64						
MOTHER'S PICTURE ALPHABET	49						
MOTIVATIONAL CARD GAMES /s/-/r/-/l/	5	7					
MOTOR EXPRESSIVE LANGUAGE PICTURE CARDS I	2						
MOTOR EXPRESSIVE LANGUAGE PICTURE CARDS II	2						
MOTT BASIC LANG. SKILLS: ADV. LANG./GRAMMAR SKILLS, BK 1912	85	70					
MOTT BASIC LANG. SKILLS: ADV. LANG./GRAMMAR SKILLS, BK 1913	85	70					
MOTT BASIC LANG. SKILLS: ADV. LANG./GRAMMAR SKILLS, BK 1914	85	70					
MOTT BASIC LANG. SKILLS: BOOK 1301	50						
MOTT BASIC LANG. SKILLS: BOOK 1302	57	92					
MOTT BASIC LANG. SKILLS: BOOK 1303	53	77					
MOTT BASIC LANG. SKILLS: BOOK 1304	58	59	60				
MOTT BASIC LANG. SKILLS: BOOK 1305	62	63					
MOTT BASIC LANG. SKILLS: BOOK 1306	54	55	63	75			
MOTT BASIC LANG. SKILLS: LANG./GRAMMAR SKILLS, BK 1607	85	79	80	81			
MOTT BASIC SKILLS: LANG., GRAMMAR & SURVIVAL SKILLS, BK 1608	85	86	87	70			
MOTT BASIC SKILLS: LANG., GRAMMAR & SURVIVAL SKILLS, BK 1609	85	70					
MOTT BASIC SKILLS: LANG., GRAMMAR & SURVIVAL SKILLS, BK 604	85	70					
MR. PHUN PHONICS	50	48					
MS. GOOD-BODY: ALPHABET	49						
MUCH & LITTLE	13						
MUG SHOTS	24						
MULTI-CONCEPT SQUARES	15	16	17	19	42	43	
MULTI-SOUNDS	5						
MULTI-STORY SEQUENCE PADS	7						
MULTIMOES	17	12					
MULTIPLE PHONEME APPROACH	5						
MUSIC TIME WITH CHARITY BAILEY	2						
MWM PROGRAM FOR DEVELOPING LANGUAGE ABILITIES	2	83	8	26			
MY ABC BOOK	49						
MY ALPHABET BOOK	9	49					
MY EVERYTHING BOOK	83						
MY EVERYTHING PRACTICE BOOK	2	83					
MY FIRST BOOK OF WORDS	92	93	84				
MY OWN READING BOOK, VOLUME 1	50						
MY OWN READING BOOK, VOLUME 2	48						
MY PHONICS PRACTICE BOOK	49	50					
MY PHONICS PRACTICE BOOK, T.E.	49	50					
MY SOUND BOOK: G	5						
MY SOUND BOOK: K	5						
MY SOUND BOOK: L	5						
MY SOUND BOOK: R	5						
MY SOUND BOOK: S	5						
MY SOUND BOOK: SH	5						
MY SOUND BOOK: TH	5						
MY SPEECH BOOK (SP. ED.)	71						
MY SPELLING BOOK	64						

TITLE	SKILL NUMBERS						
MY STREET BEGINS AT MY HOUSE	2						
MYSTERY READING RIDDLES	64	92					
NAME-A-LETTER: MATCH-A-SOUND	50	49					
NAMING ACTIONS	4						
NAMING NAMES	4						
NATURAL LANGUAGE	2	3	4				
NEITHER LONG NOR SHORT	62						
NES LINGUISTIC BLOCK SERIES, SET 1W	70	71	72	73			
NEVER MONKEY WITH A MONKEY	88	89					
NEW ADVENTRURES IN LANGUAGE	65	2	74	70			
NEW GNU	88						
NEW GOALS IN LISTENING, GRADES 1-3	39	40	51	53	57	58	
NEW GOALS IN LISTENING, GRADES 2-4	39	40	76	80	81		
NEW HOUSE & HOW MONEY HELPED	2						
NEW LANGUAGE PATTERNS & USAGE: GRADE 2, PART 2	74						
NEW LANGUAGE PATTERNS & USAGE: GRADE 2, PART 3	74	86	87	89			
NEW LANGUAGE PATTERNS & USAGE: GRADE 4, PART 3	88	86					
NEW LANGUAGE PATTERNS & USAGE: GRADE 5, PART 2	74						
NEW LANGUAGE PATTERNS & USAGE: GRADE 5, PART 3	88	86					
NEW LANGUAGE PATTERNS & USAGE: GRADE 6, PART 3	88	86					
NEW PHONICS & WORD ANALYSIS SKILLS: GRADE 1, PART 1	52	48					
NEW PHONICS & WORD ANALYSIS SKILLS: GRADE 1, PART 2	52	78	77				
NEW PHONICS & WORD ANALYSIS SKILLS: GRADE 1, PART 3	53	77					
NEW PHONICS & WORD ANALYSIS SKILLS: GRADE 2, PART 1	52	53	57	58			
NEW PHONICS & WORD ANALYSIS SKILLS: GRADE 2, PART 2	53	57	58	60	77		
NEW PHONICS & WORD ANALYSIS SKILLS: GRADE 2, PART 3	78	79	80	81	82		
NEW PHONICS & WORD ANALYSIS SKILLS: GRADE 3, PART 1	52	53	58	57	60	64	
NEW PHONICS & WORD ANALYSIS SKILLS: GRADE 3, PART 2	77	76	80	81	82		
NEW PHONICS & WORD ANALYSIS SKILLS: GRADE 3, PART 3	48	78	79	82	89	88	
NEW PHONICS WE USE LEARNING GAMES KITS, KIT ONE	52	53	49	57	58		
NEW PHONICS WE USE LEARNING GAMES KITS, KIT TWO	53	61	82	54	57	58	
NEW PHONICS WORKBOOK, BOOK A	48	79	62	9			
NEW PHONICS WORKBOOK, BOOK B	48	52	57	58	83	75	
NEW PHONICS WORKBOOK, BOOK C	48	52	56	83	76	80	81
NEW PHONICS WORKBOOK, BOOK D	56	52	76	78	83	75	82
NEW SPECIFIC SKILL SERIES: WORKING WITH SOUNDS, BOOK A	48						
NEW SPECIFIC SKILL SERIES: WORKING WITH SOUNDS, BOOK B	48						
NEW SPECIFIC SKILL SERIES: WORKING WITH SOUNDS, BOOK C	48						
NEW SPECIFIC SKILL SERIES: WORKING WITH SOUNDS, BOOK D	48						
NEW SPECIFIC SKILL SERIES: WORKING WITH SOUNDS, BOOK E	48						
NEW SPECIFIC SKILL SERIES: WORKING WITH SOUNDS, BOOK F	48						
NEW SPECIFIC SKILL SERIES: WORKING WITH SOUNDS, BOOK G	48						
NEW SPECIFIC SKILL SERIES: WORKING WITH SOUNDS, BOOK I	48						
NEW SPECIFIC SKILL SERIES: WORKING WITH SOUNDS, BOOK J	48						
NEW SPECIFIC SKILL SERIES: WORKING WITH SOUNDS, BOOK K	48						
NEW SPECIFIC SKILL SERIES: WORKING WITH SOUNDS, BOOK L	48						
NEW STREAMLIND ENGLISH SERIES: SKILL BOOK 4	59	60	61				
NEW STREAMLINED ENGLISH SERIES: FLASH CARDS	57						
NEW STREAMLINED ENGLISH SERIES: PHONICS CARDS	49	50					
NEW STREAMLINED ENGLISH SERIES: SKILL BOOK 1	49	50					
NEW STREAMLINED ENGLISH SERIES: SKILL BOOK 2	53	57					
NEW STREAMLINED ENGLISH SERIES: SKILL BOOK 3	58						
NEW STREAMLINED ENGLISH SERIES: SKILL BOOK 5	54	55					
NEW WORD GAME SAFARI	62	61	57	53	58		
NEWSPAPER TASKS SWING INTO LANGUAGE ARTS, INTERMEDIATE	87	77	80	81			
NEWSPAPER TASKS SWING INTO LANGUAGE ARTS, PRIMARY	57	58	78	77			
NOAH'S ARK ABC & 8 OTHER ALPHABET BOOKS	49						
NON-SLIP KIT	3	4	5				
NON-VERBALL COMMUNICATION	3						
NONVERBAL COMMUNICATION	3						
NONVERBAL COMMUNICATION & INTERACTION	3						
NOUN BOARDS	71						
NOUN PUZZLES	71						
NOUN-SENSE IN FAR OFF SPACE	71						
NOUNS	71						
NOUNS, ADJECTIVES & VERBS COLOR 'N' LEARN	71	72	73				
NOW HEAR THIS (RL 4-6)	4	35	7				
NUMBER & COLOR BOOK	84						
NURSERY RHYMES FOR LITTLE PEOPLE	51	7	29	36	38		
OBJECTS THAT RHYME	51						
OBSERVING & DESCRIBING COLOR	10						
OBSERVING & DESCRIBING SHAPE	12	47					
OBSERVING & DESCRIBING SIZE	11						
OCCUPATION MATCH-UPS	94						
OCCUPATION PHOTOGRAPHS	94						
OCCUPATION WORD HUNT I	94						
OCCUPATION WORD HUNT II	94						
OCCUPATIONS	94						
OCCUPATIONS 1	94						
OCCUPATIONS 2	94						
OLD FASHIONED ALPHABETS	49						
OLD FASHIONED ALPHABETS	49	50					
OLD TIME SONGS FOR CHILDREN	2						
OLIVE THE OSTRICH	4	7	36	37			
ON LOCATION WITH LANGUAGE	3	4	7				
ON THE WAY, COMMUNICATION 2	2						
ON-WORDS	70	76	77	80	81		
ONE TOO MANY, KIT A	92						
ONE TOO MANY, KIT B	92	48					
ONE TWO THREE & AWAY PHONIC CARD GAME	50	51					
OPPOSITE ODELIA	87						
OPPOSITES	87						
OPPOSITES	9	87					

TITLE	SKILL NUMBERS						
OPPOSITES GAME	87						
ORAL LANGUAGE CONTINUUM CHECKLIST	4	36	46	5	7		
ORAL LANGUAGE EXPANSION	4						
ORAL LANGUAGE SKILLS THROUGH "ALMOST JUST ALIKE"	7						
ORAL LANGUAGE SKILLS THROUGH "BRAVE THE DRAGON"	4	5	7				
ORAL READING & LINGUISTICS PROGRAM (RL 1-6)	4	35	7				
ORANGE IS A COLOR	13	15					
OUR HELPERS PLAY PEOPLE	94						
OVER, UNDER & ALL AROUND	21						
PAINT WITH PENCIL	90						
PAIRS	14						
PAIRS WORD GAME	14	19	51				
PAL READING SKILL GAME, RALLY 1	48	75	84	92			
PAL READING SKILLS GAME, RALLY 2	48	75	84	92			
PALS: PERCEPTUAL AUDITORY LEARNING SERIES	50	28	31				
PARADE LOTTO	23						
PARADE OF SHAPES	12						
PARADE OF SHAPES	12	17					
PARADE OF VOWELS	57	58					
PARADE OF VOWELS	57	58					
PARADE OF VOWELS	57	58					
PARQUETRY DESIGN BLOCK PATTERNS	12	25					
PARQUETRY DESIGN BLOCKS	12	10					
PARQUETRY PLUS	12	19	17				
PARQUETRY PLUS DESIGNS	17	19	12				
PART/WHOLE LOTTO	19	22					
PARTS OF SPEECH	70						
PARTS OF SPEECH	70	71	72	73			
PARTS OF SPEECH BINGO	70						
PARTS OF SPEECH MOBILE	70						
PARTS OF SPEECH RUMMY	70						
PARTS OF SPEECH SERIES	71	72	73				
PARTS OF SPEECH SKILL BOX	70						
PARTS OF SPEECH: ADJECTIVE CONCEPTS	73						
PARTS OF SPEECH: ADVERB CONCEPTS	73						
PARTS OF SPEECH: NOUN CONCEPTS	71						
PARTS OF SPEECH: VERB CONCEPTS	72						
PASTING PARADE	57	58					
PASTING PARTY	50						
PASTING TIME	78	79	53				
PATHWAYS TO SPEECH	3	4	7	6			
PATTERN BLOCKS TASK CARDS	12	17					
PATTERNS	65						
PATTERNS	5						
PATTERNS IN COMMUNICATION	7						
PAY ATTENTION	39	29	37				
PEABODY ARTICULATION CARDS KIT	5						
PEABODY ARTICULATION DECKS	5						
PEABODY ARTICULATION DECKS: DECK 1, (B-M-P)	5						
PEABODY ARTICULATION DECKS: DECK 10, (L-R-S BLENDS)	5						
PEABODY ARTICULATION DECKS: DECK 2, (CH-SH)	5						
PEABODY ARTICULATION DECKS: DECK 3, (F-V)	5						
PEABODY ARTICULATION DECKS: DECK 4, (G,K)	5						
PEABODY ARTICULATION DECKS: DECK 5, (L)	5						
PEABODY ARTICULATION DECKS: DECK 6, (R)	5						
PEABODY ARTICULATION DECKS: DECK 7, (S)	5						
PEABODY ARTICULATION DECKS: DECK 8, (TH)	5						
PEABODY ARTICULATION DECKS: DECK 9, (Z)	5						
PEABODY EARLY EXPERIENCES KIT	4	42	43	45	14	18	26
PEABODY LANGUAGE DEVELOPMENT KIT, LEVEL #1	2	4	43	45	46	47	42
PEABODY LANGUAGE DEVELOPMENT KIT, LEVEL #2	2	4	7	42	43	47	46
PEABODY LANGUAGE DEVELOPMENT KIT, LEVEL #3	4	35	44	45	46	7	37
PEABODY LANGUAGE DEVELOPMENT KIT, LEVEL #P	2	35	4	44	42	47	
PEANUTS PUZZLES: BE A FRIEND	9						
PEANUTS PUZZLES: HEAD BEAGLE	9						
PEANUTS PUZZLES: I CAN CURE ANYTHING	9						
PEANUTS PUZZLES: NATIONAL DOG WEEK	9						
PEANUTS PUZZLES: SCHROEDER & SNOOPY	9						
PEANUTS PUZZLES: SIGH!	9						
PEANUTS PUZZLES: SMAK!	9						
PEANUTS PUZZLES: SMILE!	9						
PEANUTS PUZZLES: SNOOPY SUPERSTAR	9						
PEEL & PUT (SPEECH THERAPY & LANGUAGE DEVELOPMENT)	2	5	7				
PEEL & PUT READING PROGRAM	1	35	41				
PEEL & PUT: DIALECTAL PHONEMES	5						
PEEL & PUT: SIBILANT PHONEMES	5						
PEG PADS	15	10					
PEGBOARD	15	10					
PEGBOARD DESIGNS	15	10					
PEGS	15	10					
PEOPLE PUPPETS & SCRIPTS, BLACK	7	25					
PEOPLE PUPPETS & SCRIPTS, WHITE	7	25					
PEOPLE WHO WORK, UNIT 1	94						
PEOPLE WHO WORK, UNIT 2	94						
PEOPLE, PLACES & THINGS: OCCUPATIONS	19	42	7				
PEOPLE, PLACES & THINGS: RECREATION	42	7	19				
PEOPLE, PLACES & THINGS: SPORTS	42	7	19				
PEOPLE, PLACES & THINGS: STORIES	19	42	7				
PEP, VOLUME I	33						
PEP, VOLUME II	33	37					
PEP, VOLUME III	27						
PEP, VOLUME IV	39	40	29	36	37	38	
PERCEIVE & RESPOND, VOLUME I	27	28					

TITLE	SKILL NUMBERS					
PERCEIVE & RESPOND, VOLUME II	27	57	58	32	53	
PERCEIVE & RESPOND, VOLUME III	31	33	37			
PERCEPTION CARDS: BUSES	9	46				
PERCEPTION CARDS: CLOWNS	9	46				
PERCEPTION CARDS: COGITO	9	46				
PERCEPTION CARDS: TOM TURNIP	9	46				
PERCEPTION CARDS: TRUCKS	9	46				
PERCEPTION LOTTO	2					
PERCEPTION OF COLOR	10	15				
PERCEPTION TASK CARDS	9	13	14	12		
PERCEPTUAL ENHANCEMENT: DIRECTIONALITY & LATERALITY	21					
PERCEPTUAL ENHANCEMENT: EYE-MOTOR COORDINATION	25					
PERCEPTUAL ENHANCEMENT: FIGURE-GROUND	20					
PERCEPTUAL ENHANCEMENT: SPATIAL RELATIONS	21					
PERCEPTUAL ENHANCEMENT: VISUAL CLOSURE	22					
PERCEPTUAL TRAINING FILMSTRIPS	9	13	14	20	21	
PERCEPTUAL TRAINING, SET 6: BEGINNING ADDITIONS	10	11	12			
PERPLEXING PREFIXES	80					
PERPLEXITY	5					
PERSONALIZED FLUENCY CONTROL THERAPY	5					
PERSONALIZING READING EFFICIENCY	83					
PHONEME BASELINE RECORDING FORMS	5					
PHONETIC DRILL CARDS	48					
PHONETIC QUIZMO	48					
PHONETIC READER	71					
PHONETIC VOWELS	56					
PHONETICS FACTORY	57	58	59			
PHONIC DOMINO GAME	50	48				
PHONIC HELPERS	57	53				
PHONIC PICTURE CARDS	53	57	58	60		
PHONIC RUMMY CARD GAMES, INTERMEDIATE	48	84				
PHONIC RUMMY CARD GAMES, PRIMARY	48	84				
PHONIC RUMMY CARD GAMES, READINESS	48	84				
PHONIC TALKING LETTERS	49	50				
PHONIC WIPE OFF CARDS	50	57	58	59	60	
PHONIC WORD DRILL CARDS, ADVANCED	48					
PHONIC WORD DRILL CARDS, INTERMEDIATE	48					
PHONIC WORD DRILL CARDS, PRIMARY	48					
PHONICS	57	58	53	55	82	80
PHONICS & READING	19	48	52	57	58	
PHONICS & READING REVIEW	87	92				
PHONICS & WORD DEVELOPMENT	56	66	78	76	88	
PHONICS & WORD POWER, BOOK 1	48	75	51	49		
PHONICS & WORD POWER, BOOK 2	48	75				
PHONICS & WORD POWER, BOOK 3	48	75	49	88		
PHONICS ANALYSIS	48					
PHONICS BOOK C: SHORT VOWEL SOUNDS	57					
PHONICS BOOK D: LONG VOWEL SOUNDS, VOWEL DIGRAPHS	58	59				
PHONICS BOOK E: CONSONANT BLENDS	53					
PHONICS COME FIRST	50	49	51			
PHONICS CONSONANT DIGRAHS, 2 SOUNDS OF C & G	53	54				
PHONICS DISCOVERY	52	57	58	53	59	
PHONICS E-Z LANGUAGE LEARNING SLIDE RULES	52	82	57	58	53	84	75
PHONICS E-Z LANGUAGE LEARNING SLIDE RULES, 1ST & 2ND	52	82	57	58		
PHONICS E-Z LANGUAGE LEARNING SLIDE RULES, 3RD & 4TH	53	57	58	84		
PHONICS E-Z LANGUAGE LEARNING SLIDE RULES, 5TH	61	79	82	60		
PHONICS E-Z LANGUAGE LEARNING SLIDE RULES, WORD-BUILDING	48	75	92	84		
PHONICS FAST & EASY	50	53	57	58		
PHONICS FILM STRIP SERIES 2	53	59	60			
PHONICS FILMSTRIP SERIES 1	57	58				
PHONICS FOR FUN	48	9				
PHONICS FOR READING & SPELLING, GRADE 2	66	48				
PHONICS FOR READING & SPELLING, GRADE 3	66	48				
PHONICS FOR READING & SPELLING, GRADE 4	66	48				
PHONICS FOR THE INTERMEDIATE GRADES (4, 5, 6)	58	57	59	60	62	61	82
PHONICS FUN, GRADE 1	52					
PHONICS FUN: CONSONANT	52					
PHONICS FUN: VOWEL	56					
PHONICS GAMES	57	58	53	59	60	
PHONICS IA	52					
PHONICS IB	52	53	77			
PHONICS IC	57	58				
PHONICS IIA	52	53	57	58	61	
PHONICS IIB	53	57	58	79	76	80	81
PHONICS IIIA	48	53	76	82		
PHONICS IIIB	57	58	62	77	82	86	87
PHONICS IN CONTEXT, SET I	53	57	58	62	59	61
PHONICS IN CONTEXT, SET II	53	57	58	62	59	61
PHONICS INITIAL CONSONANT BLENDS	53					
PHONICS IS FUN, BOOK 1	49	52	53	57	58	9
PHONICS IS FUN, BOOK 1	49	52	53	57	58	9
PHONICS IS FUN, BOOK 2	58	57	61	78	80	81	83
PHONICS IS FUN, BOOK 2	58	57	61	78	80	81	83
PHONICS IS FUN, BOOK 3	53	80	81	82	83	49
PHONICS IS FUN, BOOK 3	53	80	81	82	83	49
PHONICS IVA	62	76	81	82	86	87	88
PHONICS IVB	48	81	82	92		
PHONICS LONG VOWELS	58					
PHONICS OTHER VOWEL SOUNDS, REVIEW LONG & SHORT VOWELS	57	58				
PHONICS PROGRAM	48					
PHONICS PROGRAM	48					
PHONICS PROGRAM, BOOK 11	53					
PHONICS PROGRAM, BOOK 12	53					

TITLE	SKILL NUMBERS						
PHONICS PROGRAM, BOOK 7	57						
PHONICS PROGRAM, BOOK 8	57						
PHONICS PROGRAM, BOOK 9	58						
PHONICS PUZZLES & GAMES	27	50	53	51			
PHONICS R CONTROLLED VOWELS & Y AS A VOWEL	61	62					
PHONICS SERIES	57	58	53	55	59	60	
PHONICS SERIES 1	57	58					
PHONICS SERIES 1	57	58					
PHONICS SERIES 2	53	59	60				
PHONICS SERIES 2	53	59	60				
PHONICS SHORT VOWELS	57						
PHONICS SILENT INITIAL CONSONANTS-FINAL CONSONANTS CLUSTERS	55	53					
PHONICS SOUND & SYMBOL	50						
PHONICS SOUP	56	53	51				
PHONICS SOUP GAME PACKAGES: BLENDS	53						
PHONICS SOUP GAME PACKAGES: DIGRAPHS	53						
PHONICS SOUP GAME PACKAGES: LONG VOWELS	58						
PHONICS SOUP GAME PACKAGES: RHYMING, SET A	51						
PHONICS SOUP GAME PACKAGES: RHYMING, SET B	51						
PHONICS SOUP GAME PACKAGES: SHORT VOWELS	57						
PHONICS SOUP, BLEND GAMES	53						
PHONICS SOUP, DIGRAPH GAMES	53						
PHONICS SOUP, LONG VOWEL GAMES	58						
PHONICS SOUP, RHYMIN GAMES SET B	51						
PHONICS SOUP, RHYMING GAMES SET A	51						
PHONICS SOUP, SHORT VOWEL GAMES	57						
PHONICS STORIES	57	58	77				
PHONICS WHEEL	9	27	14	53			
PHONICS WORKBOOK, BOOK D	56	52	76	78	83	75	82
PHONICS WORKTEXT: ANSWER KEY (6)	52	57	58				
PHONICS WORKTEXT: CONSONANTS 1	52						
PHONICS WORKTEXT: CONSONANTS 2	52						
PHONICS WORKTEXT: LONG VOWELS	58						
PHONICS WORKTEXT: SHORT VOWELS 1	57						
PHONICS WORKTEXT: SHORT VOWELS 2	57						
PHONICS WORKTEXT: VARIANT VOWELS	57	58	62				
PHONICS, GRADE 3	54	53	57	58	62	63	55
PHONICS-VOWEL SOUNDS (INITIAL & MEDIAL)	48	52					
PHONICS: CONSONANT CLUSTER FUN	53						
PHONICS: FUN WITH AFFIXES	80	81					
PHONICS: FUN WITH WORDS	93						
PHONICS: INITIAL & FINAL BLENDS, GRADE 2	53						
PHONICS: LONG VOWEL SOUND FUN	58						
PHONICS: MANUSCRIPT	50						
PHONICS: SHORT VOWEL SOUND FUN	57						
PHONICS: SYLLABLE FUN	82						
PHONICS: THE F.I.R.S.T. APPROACH TO READING	50	57	58				
PHONICS: VARIENTS & SILENT LETTERS	55						
PHONICS: VOWEL CLUSTER FUN	59	60					
PHONICS: VOWELS, GRADE 2	57	58					
PHONICS: VOWELS-BLENDS READING REVIEW	57	53	58				
PHONO JUNIOR GAME	50						
PHONO SENIOR GAME	48						
PHONOGAMES SERIES: THE PHONICS EXPLORER	48	83					
PHONOGAMES SERIES: THE PHONICS EXPRESS	48	83					
PHONOGAMES SERIES: THE READINESS STAGE	48	83					
PHONOGRAMS	48						
PHONOVISUAL LEARNING GAMES 1	52						
PHONOVISUAL LEARNING GAMES 2	52						
PHOTO RESOURCE KIT	2	4					
PHOTO SEQUENCE CARDS, SET 1: OCCUPATIONS	31						
PHOTO SEQUENCE CARDS, SET 2: RECREATION	31						
PHOTO SEQUENCE CARDS, SET 3: DAILY LIVING ACTIVITIES	31						
PHOTOCABULARY	84	92					
PICK-PAIRS CARD GAME	14	35					
PICTO-CABULARY SERIES, SET 222	84	93	92				
PICTO-CABULARY SERIES, SET III	93	92					
PICTO-CABULARY, BASIC WORD SET A	84	93	92				
PICTURE A VOWEL SOUND	57	58					
PICTURE A VOWEL SOUND II	56						
PICTURE CARD GAMES, SET I	14	18	4	47			
PICTURE CARD GAMES, SET II	14	18	87	47			
PICTURE CARDS	9	18	4	47			
PICTURE COMMUNICATION CARDS	2	3					
PICTURE COMPOSITE	5	13	9	49			
PICTURE COMPOSITE CHART	5	13	9	49			
PICTURE FLASH WORDS FOR BEGINNERS	19	84	85	48	24		
PICTURE FLASHCARD SET	5	13	9	49			
PICTURE LACING BOARD	2						
PICTURE READINESS GAME	29						
PICTURE SEQUENCE CARDS, SET 1	23						
PICTURE SEQUENCE CARDS, SET 2	23						
PICTURE WORD CARDS	19	65	84				
PICTURE WORKBOOKS: CIRCUS SOUNDS	5						
PICTURE WORKBOOKS: HOLIDAY SOUNDS	5						
PICTURE WORKBOOKS: SOUNDS IN FANTASY LAND	5						
PICTURE/WORD CONCEPTS: CLOTHING	92	19					
PICTURE/WORD CONCEPTS: CLOTHING ACCESSORIES	92	19					
PICTURE/WORD CONCEPTS: DISHES & UTENSILS	92	19					
PICTURE/WORD CONCEPTS: HOUSEHOLD ITEMS	92	19					
PICTURE/WORD CONCEPTS: SCHOOL ITEMS	92	19					
PICTURES & SOUNDS ALPHABET BOOK	50						
PICTURES FOR SOUNDS	4	50					

TITLE	SKILL NUMBERS						
PICTURES THAT RHYME	51	14					
PICTURES, PLEASE!	2	73	3	42	43	47	72
PIPER: WHISPERS UNIT	2						
PLAIN AS THE NOSE ON YOUR FACE	93						
PLAN: LITERATURE, LANGUAGE & COMMUNICATION	4	6	7	35			
PLAN: READING IN THE CONTENT AREAS	83	48					
PLANNING INDIVIDUALIZED SPEECH & LANGUAGE INTERVENTION PROG.	3	7	35				
PLASTIC OBJECTS, SET 1	50						
PLASTIC OBJECTS, SET 2	50						
PLASTIC OBJECTS, SET 3	50	53					
PLAY & SAY, SET A	5						
PLAY & SAY, SET B	5						
PLAY & SAY, SET C	5						
PLAY & SAY, SET D	5						
PLAY IT BY SIGN	3						
PLAY PLANKS	25	14					
PLAY SCENES LOTTO	9	4					
PLAY TRAY PUZZLES	9						
PLAY-ALL	18						
PLAYBOARD PUZZLES	25						
PLAYMATES	49						
PLEASANT PLURALS	77						
PLUM TREE	27	53	56	88	82	75	
PLURALS	77						
PLURALS	71	77					
POCKET PUZZLES	25						
POLY-STRIP SENTENCES	74						
POPEYE'S SPECIAL LANGUAGE BUILDER: BALLOON PUZZLES (SP.ED.)	84	4	79				
POPEYE'S SPECIAL LANGUAGE BUILDER: MATCHING DOMINOES(SP.ED.)	15	94					
POPEYE'S SPECIAL LANGUAGE BUILDER: STORY BUILDERS (SP.ED.)	4	74					
POPPER WORDS, SET 1	84						
POPPER WORDS, SET 2	84						
PORTFOLIO OF RUB-ON REBUSES	4	5	7	48	75		
POSITIVELY PHONICS: LONG VOWELS	58						
POSITIVELY PHONICS: SHORT VOWELS	57						
POSSESSIVES	70						
POSSESSIVES - TEN FINGERS & THEY'RE ALL MINE	71	77					
POWER OF WORDS	1	4	5	7			
POWERPAC I	52						
POWERPAC II	52						
POWERPAC III	57	58	59				
POWERPAC IV	57	58	59				
POWERPAC PROGRAM	57	58	59	52			
PRACTICAL LANGUAGE SKILLS	37						
PRACTICE IN BASIC LANGUAGE SKILLS, BOOK 1 (GRADE 1)	70	74	7				
PRACTICE IN BASIC LANGUAGE SKILLS, BOOK 2 (GRADE 2)	70	74	7				
PRACTICE IN BASIC LANGUAGE SKILLS, BOOK 3 (GRADE 3)	70	74	7				
PRACTICE IN BASIC LANGUAGE SKILLS, BOOK 4 (GRADE 4)	70	74	7				
PRACTICE IN BASIC LANGUAGE SKILLS, BOOK 5 (GRADE 5)	70	74	7				
PRACTICE IN BASIC LANGUAGE SKILLS, BOOK 6 (GRADE 6)	70	74	7				
PRACTICE IN VOCABULARY BUILDING, BOOK A (GRADES 3 - 4)	76	80	81	91			
PRACTICE IN VOCABULARY BUILDING, BOOK B (GRADES 4 - 5)	76	80	81	91			
PRACTICE IN VOCABULARY BUILDING, BOOK C (GRADES 5 - 7)	76	80	81	91			
PRE- READING SKILLS SERIES	35	9	27				
PRE-ALPHABET PUZZLE	25	49					
PRE-READING EXERCISES & PERCEPTUAL SKILLS	25	9	13	14			
PREFIX POW-WOW	80						
PREFIX PUZZLES	80						
PREFIXES	80						
PREFIXES	80						
PREFIXES	80						
PREFIXES	80						
PREFIXES & SUFFIXES	80	81					
PREFIXES & SUFFIXES	80	81					
PREFIXES, ADVANCED 1	80						
PREFIXES, ADVANCED 2	80						
PREFIXES, ADVANCED 3	80						
PREFIXES, D	80						
PREFIXES, E	80						
PREFIXES, F	80						
PREFIXES, SUFFIXES, SYLLABLES	80	81	82				
PREFIXES, SUFFIXES, SYLLABLES	80	81	82	79	77	53	
PREPOSITION 500 SPACE RACE	70						
PREPOSTEROUS PHONICS POSTERS	52	50					
PRESENTING...PARTS OF SPEECH	71	72	73				
PRESS & CHECK BINGO GAMES: ABBREVIATIONS & CONTRACTIONS	78						
PRESS & CHECK BINGO GAMES: HOMONYMS	88						
PRESS & CHECK BINGO GAMES: PREFIXES & SUFFIXES	81	80					
PRESS & CHECK BINGO GAMES: SYNOYNYMS & ANTONYMS	87	86					
PRIMARY BASIC READING COMPREHENSION	92	64					
PRIMARY COLOR BOX	10	15					
PRIMARY CONCEPTS II	8						
PRIMARY LANGUAGE ARTS	85	93					
PRIMARY LANGUAGE ARTS: FUNCTIONAL READING WITH SOUND & FUN	85						
PRIMARY LANGUAGE ARTS: WORD GAMES	93						
PRIMARY PATTERN BLOCKS TASK CARDS	17						
PRIMARY PHONICS WORKBOOK 1	57	84					
PRIMARY PHONICS WORKBOOK 2	53	58	59				
PRIMARY PHONICS WORKBOOK 3	53	57	58	59	79	84	
PRIMARY PHONICS WORKBOOK 4	53	61	59	57	58	84	
PRIMARY PHONICS WORKBOOK 5	77	79	82	59			
PRIMARY PHONICS-SKILL DRILLS WITH MOTIVATORS	48	52	56				
PRIMARY READER, SET 3: BLENDS	53						

TITLE	SKILL NUMBERS						
PRIMARY READER, SET 4: DIGRAPHS	53						
PRIMARY READERS, SET 2: LONG VOWELS	58						
PRIMARY READERS: SET 1, SHORT VOWELS	57						
PRIMARY SPELLING	65	66	69				
PRIMARY THINKING BOX (RL 1-3)	41	43	47	45	46		
PRIMARY VOCABULARY	84	86	87	88			
PRIMARY WORK RECOGNITION	52	56	53	59	60	75	
PRO'S & CON'S	87	86					
PROBLEM SOLVING CARDS, SET 1: S SOUND	5	2	4				
PROBLEM SOLVING CARDS, SET 2: R SOUND	5	2	4				
PROBLEM WORDS MADE EASY	83	89	88				
PROFESSION & SITUATION LOTTO	94						
PROGRAMMED ARTICULATION CONTROL KIT	5						
PROGRAMMED ARTICULATION SKILLS CARRYOVER STORIES	5						
PROGRAMMED ENRICHMENT SONGS FOR EXCEPTIONAL CHILDREN	35	2					
PROGRAMMED LANGUAGE/READING, LEVEL I	77	71	73	72	70		
PROGRAMMED LANGUAGE/READING, LEVEL I: SET 1, SELF	71	77	72				
PROGRAMMED LANGUAGE/READING, LEVEL I: SET 2, ANIMALS	77	73	71				
PROGRAMMED LANGUAGE/READING, LEVEL I: SET 3, FOODS	71	72					
PROGRAMMED LANGUAGE/READING, LEVEL I: SET 4, PLAYTHINGS	71	72					
PROGRAMMED LANGUAGE/READING, LEVEL I: SET 5, ACTIVITIES	71						
PROGRAMMED LANGUAGE/READING, LEVEL I: SET 6, SELF	73						
PROGRAMMED LANGUAGE/READING, LEVEL I: SET 7, CLOTHING	77	70					
PROGRAMMED LANGUAGE/READING, LEVEL I: SET 8, SHELTER	70						
PROGRAMMED LANGUAGE/READING, LEVEL II	70						
PROGRAMMED LANGUAGE/READING, LEVEL II: SET 10, SELF	70						
PROGRAMMED LANGUAGE/READING, LEVEL II: SET 11, SELF	70	72	73				
PROGRAMMED LANGUAGE/READING, LEVEL II: SET 12, COMMUNITY	73	70	72				
PROGRAMMED LANGUAGE/READING, LEVEL II: SET 13, FOODS	72	70	73				
PROGRAMMED LANGUAGE/READING, LEVEL II: SET 14, HOME	70	72	71				
PROGRAMMED LANGUAGE/READING, LEVEL II: SET 15, HOME	91						
PROGRAMMED LANGUAGE/READING, LEVEL II: SET 16, CLOTHING	72	73					
PROGRAMMED LANGUAGE/READING, LEVEL II: SET 9, SCHOOL	70	72					
PROGRAMMED LANGUAGE/READING, LEVEL IV	70	74					
PROGRAMMED LANGUAGE/READING, LEVEL IV: SET 25,NATURE/ECOLOGY	73	71					
PROGRAMMED LANGUAGE/READING, LEVEL IV: SET 26,SCHOOL PROJECT	73	74					
PROGRAMMED LANGUAGE/READING, LEVEL IV: SET 27, LIFE IN U.S.	74	73					
PROGRAMMED LANGUAGE/READING, LEVEL IV: SET 28, NORTH AMERICA	74						
PROGRAMMED LANGUAGE/READING, LEVEL IV: SET 29, SAFETY	74						
PROGRESSION LOTTO	2	21					
PROJECT ALPHABETIZING	49						
PRONOUN PAGES	71						
PRONOUN PARADE, A	71						
PRONOUN PARADE, B	71						
PRONOUN PARADE, C	71						
PRONOUN PARADE, D	71						
PRONOUN PARADE, E	71						
PRONOUN PINCH HITTER	71						
PRONOUN SPACE SHUTTLE	71						
PRONOUNS	71						
PRONUNCIATION SKILLS	50	2					
PROSPECTING IN PHONICS	57	58	59	60	61	62	
PRS: THE PRE-READING SKILLS PROGRAM	48	75	26				
PRS: VOCABULARY SEGMENT	83						
PS: PREFIX-SUFFIX LANGUAGE-BUILDING GAME	4	66					
PUBLIC SPEAKING	7						
PUNCH-THRU CARDS: CONSONANT BLENDS	53						
PUNCH-THRU CARDS: FINAL CONSONANTS	52						
PUNCH-THRU CARDS: INITIAL CONSONANTS	52						
PUNCH-THRU CARDS: LONG VOWELS	58						
PUNCH-THRU CARDS: LONG VOWELS	58						
PUNCH-THRU CARDS: RHYMING WORDS	51						
PUNCH-THRU CARDS: SHORT VOWELS	57						
PUNCH-THRU CARDS: SHORT VOWELS	57						
PUNCH-THRU CRDS: CONSONANT BLENDS	53						
PURSUIT	80						
PUT-ONS	81						
PUTTING WORDS IN ORDER / SENTENCE STRUCTURE	74	70					
PUZZLE CUBES	9	25					
PUZZLE POSTERS: ALPHABET BOATING	49						
PUZZLE POSTERS: ALPHABET VILLAGE	13	49					
PUZZLE POSTERS: DINOSAURS & SHAPES	12						
PUZZLE POSTERS: DONKEY TRAIL	21						
PUZZLERS	4	64					
PUZZLES & SUCH	4						
QUIZZLE: CONTRACTIONS	78						
QUIZZLE: PLURALS	77						
R-SOUND WORKBOOK	5						
R.E.A.C.H. (READING EXERCISES AND COMPOSITION HELP)	7						
RAINBOW ROLLS	10						
RAINBOW WORD BUILDERS	52	53	57	58			
RAINING CATS & DOGS	91						
RAISED ALPHABET PUZZLE	49	50					
REACH	92						
READ & REASON	78	81					
READ ALONG BEGINNING PHONICS, SET 1	57						
READ ALONG BEGINNING PHONICS, SET 2	58						
READ, THINK, COLOR	52	56	51	84			
READ, THINK, COLOR	52	56	51	84			
READ-ALONG BEGINNING PHONICS, SET 1	48						
READ-ALONG BEGINNING PHONICS, SET 2	48						
READ-O-MAT	84	85					
READ-THE-PICTURE STORYBOOKS	53	5					

TITLE	SKILL NUMBERS						
READER IN THE KITCHEN	35	83					
READINESS BOOK: COME TO MY PARTY	50	51					
READINESS DISCOVERY	23	9	51				
READINESS TASK CARDS: ALPHABET	49						
READINESS TASK CARDS: SEQUENCING	23						
READINESS: ALPHABET	49						
READINESS: ALPHABET	49						
READINESS: SEQUENCING	23						
READINESS: SEQUENCING	23						
READINESS: SHAPES & DESIGN REPRODUCTION	13	25					
READINESS: SHAPES & DESIGN REPRODUCTION	13	25					
READINESS: SIZE DISCRIMINATION & CLASSIFICATION	11						
READINESS: SIZE DISCRIMINATION & CLASSIFICATION	11						
READING	74						
READING & LANG. ARTS COMPLETE SET OF 50 JOY ACT. CARDS KITS	48	75	83				
READING ACHIEVEMENT	85	86					
READING ACTIVITIES & SKILLS	83	92					
READING ACTIVITIES FOR LEARNING CENTERS	74	9	64	83	82		
READING BOX	35	48	7				
READING BRIDGE	48	49	50				
READING CASSETTES: BLENDS	53						
READING CASSETTES: BLENDS & DIGRAPHS	53						
READING CASSETTES: CONSONANTS & DIGRAPHS	53	54	55	52			
READING CASSETTES: LEARN TO LISTEN	39	40	29	36	37		
READING CASSETTES: PHONIC ANALYSIS	63	59	60	61	62		
READING CASSETTES: READING READINESS	51	10	42	40			
READING CASSETTES: SPELLING GENERALIZATIONS	65						
READING CASSETTES: SYLLABLE RULE & ACCENT CLUE	82						
READING CASSETTES: VOWEL ENRICHMENT	57	58	63				
READING CASSETTES: VOWELS	57	58	63				
READING CASSETTES: VOWELS	56	57	58	59	60	61	62
READING CASSETTES: WORD BUILDING	78	77	79	76	80	81	
READING CASSETTES: WORD FUNCTION & SENTENCE PATTERNS	93						
READING ENRICHMENT ACTIVITIES	64	51	56	87	88		
READING ESSENTIALS: CONTEXT CLUES, GRADE 1	47	52					
READING ESSENTIALS: VOCABULARY DEVELOPMENT, GRADE 1	79	87	88	47			
READING ESSENTIALS: VOCABULARY DEVELOPMENT, GRADE 3	77	79	81	88	47	89	88
READING ESSENTIALS: VOCABULARY DEVELOPMENT, GRADE 3, BOOK 2	83	86	88	89	80	47	81
READING ESSENTIALS: VOCABULARY DEVELOPMENT, GRADE 4	83	80	81	88	87	86	
READING ESSENTIALS: VOCABULARY DEVELOPMENT, GRADE 5	80	81	87	86	88		
READING ESSENTIALS: VOCABULARY DEVELOPMENT, GRADE 6	80	81	87	86	84	85	
READING FOR PROGRESS (RL 1 - 2)	85	76	77	78	69		
READING FOR RESULTS (RL 2 - 3)	85	58	63	59	61		
READING FORMS & LABELS, GRADE 3	85						
READING FORMS & LABELS, GRADE 4	85						
READING FORMS & LABELS, GRADE 5	85						
READING FORMS & LABELS, GRADE 6	85						
READING FUN FACTORY	9	84	92	25			
READING GAMES THAT TEACH	84	85					
READING LANTERNS: AMUSEMENT PARK	80						
READING LANTERNS: PLAY BALL!	81						
READING PERFORMANCE	85	80	81	87			
READING READINESS	50						
READING READINESS	47	49	27	9			
READING READINESS	9	13	14	84	85		
READING READINESS	49	50	13	27	28		
READING READINESS	13	22	20	23	24	33	
READING READINESS, TEXTBOOK A	50						
READING READINESS, TEXTBOOK B	50						
READING READINESS, TEXTBOOK C	50						
READING READINESS, TEXTBOOK D	50						
READING READINESS: PARTS I, II, III, IV, V, VI	52	57	58	53	51	83	27
READING RIDDLES	83						
READING SELF-CHECK: SHORT VOWELS, LONG VOWELS	57	58					
READING SELF-CHECK: SPECIAL VOWELS & CONSONANTS	54	55	62				
READING SKILLS SUPPORT SYSTEM, BOX 1	77	51	79	78	86	87	
READING SKILLS SUPPORT SYSTEM, BOX 2	53	54	57	58	82	88	
READING SKILLS SUPPORT SYSTEM, BOX 3	56	76	77	82	80	81	79
READING SKILLS: DRAWING CONCLUSIONS	46						
READING STAND UPS RHYMING	51						
READING STEP BY STEP, KIT A	9	27	42	52			
READING STEP BY STEP, UNIT 2	57	58	53	92			
READING TO LEARN: FOCUS ON LEISURE TIME	83						
READING VOCABULARY LABORATORIES C	83						
READING VOCABULARY LABORATORIES D	83						
READING VOCABULARY LABORATORIES E	83						
READING VOCABULARY LABORATORIES F	83						
READING VOCABULARY LABORATORIES G	83						
READING WITH PHONICS A	48						
READING WITH PHONICS B	48						
READING WITH PHONICS C	48						
READING ZINGO	53	78					
READING-LISTENING COMPREHENSION SKILLS, LEVEL 3	39						
READING-LISTENING COMPREHENSION SKILLS, LEVEL 4	39						
READY GO ALPHABET	49	13					
READY STEPS	27	29	31	23	49	4	
REALLY READING	2						
REALLY READING	2						
REBUS GLOSSARY CARDS	4	5	7	48	75		
REBUS SOUND-CENTERED PICTURE PUZZLES	5	8	53				
RECIPE FOR READING	59	53	67				
RECOGNIZING & USING SHAPES	11	16					
RED HEN & SLY FOX	37	29	36	33	35		

TITLE	SKILL NUMBERS						
RED-BLOODED PREFIXES	80						
RELEVANCE SERIES	70	66	35	48	75	84	
RELEVANCE SERIES: INDEPENDENCE THROUGH READING	84	92	93				
RELEVANCE SERIES: RELEVANCE OF LISTENING	35	35					
RELEVANCE SERIES: RELEVANCE OF PATTERNS	70						
RELEVANCE SERIES: RELEVANCE OF SOUND	48	75					
RELEVANCE SERIES: RELEVANCE OF WORDS	66						
REPTILES, FROM DINOSAURS TO ALLIGATORS	23						
RESCUE, VOLUME I	9	48					
RETELLING FAVORITE STORIES	23	31	40				
RHETORIC READINESS	7						
RHYME ME A RHYME	51						
RHYME-O BOX II	51						
RHYMES I KNOW CAN MAKE DOGS GROW	51						
RHYMING	51						
RHYMING & READING	51	77					
RHYMING ALPHABET	51						
RHYMING BINGO	51						
RHYMING CARDS	51						
RHYMING GAME	51						
RHYMING KITTENS	51						
RHYMING PAIRS	51						
RHYMING PICTURES	51	13					
RHYMING PICTURES FOR PEGBOARD	51						
RHYMING PUZZLE	25	51					
RHYMING PUZZLES	51						
RHYMING PUZZLES	51						
RHYMING READER, BOOK A	51						
RHYMING SOUNDS	51						
RHYMING WHEEL	51						
RHYMING WORD GAME	51						
RHYMING WORD PUZZLES	51						
RHYMING WORDS	51						
RHYMING WORDS	51						
RHYMING WORDS	51						
RHYMING WORDS & VARIANT CONSONANTS	51	54	55				
RHYMING ZIG ZAG	51						
RHYMING, LEVEL A	51						
RHYMING, LEVEL B	51						
RHYMING, LEVEL C	51						
RHYMING: CUT & PASTE	25	51					
RHYTHMS TO READING	51						
RIDDLE RIDDLE RHYME TIME, KIT A: INITIAL CONSONANTS	51						
RIDDLE RIDDLE RHYME TIME, KIT B: INITIAL BLENDS & DIGRAPHS	53	51					
RIDDLE-A-RHYME	33	51	52	56			
RIDING THE PLURALS TRAIN	77						
RIGHT-TO-READ PROGRAM, LEVEL I	50	48	64				
RIGHT-TO-READ PROGRAM, LEVEL II	50	48	64				
ROAD SIGNS	85						
ROAD TO READING, PHONICS PROGRAM, LANGUAGE SKILLS	57	58	54	55			
ROLE-PLAYING UNIT FOR GRADES K-6	7						
ROLLING PHONICS	53	57	58				
ROLLING READER	74						
ROOT WORDS	76						
ROOT WORDS	76						
ROOT WORDS, THE HEART OF IT ALL	76						
ROOTS/STEMS, ADVANCED 1	76	77					
ROOTS/STEMS, ADVANCED 2	76	77					
ROOTS/STEMS, ADVANCED 3	76	77					
ROOTS/STEMS, ADVANCED 4	76	77					
ROOTS/STEMS, ADVANCED 5	76	77					
ROOTS/STEMS, ADVANCED 6	76	77					
ROOTS/STEMS, F1	76	77					
ROOTS/STEMS, F2	76	77					
ROXY THE ROBIN	23	24					
ROYAL ROAD READING APPARATUS	14						
RR (REMEDIAL READING)	48	75					
RR (REMEDIAL READING), T.M.	48	75					
RUBBER DIFFERENCES PUZZLES	14	25					
RUFUS RABBIT'S RHYME TIME	51	50					
S-I PROGRAM TO INCREASE FLUENCY	5						
S.T.A.R.T, BOOK 10	56						
S.T.A.R.T, BOOK 4	53						
S.T.A.R.T., BOOK 1	57						
S.T.A.R.T., BOOK 11	56						
S.T.A.R.T., BOOK 12	57	58					
S.T.A.R.T., BOOK 13	62	59	60				
S.T.A.R.T., BOOK 14	82	59	60	62			
S.T.A.R.T., BOOK 15	57	58					
S.T.A.R.T., BOOK 16	57	58					
S.T.A.R.T., BOOK 17	57	58					
S.T.A.R.T., BOOK 18	56						
S.T.A.R.T., BOOK 2	57						
S.T.A.R.T., BOOK 3	53	57					
S.T.A.R.T., BOOK 7	57	58					
S.T.A.R.T., BOOK 8	59	60					
S.T.A.R.T., BOOK 9	61						
SADDLE UP (RL 3)	59	60	62				
SAME OR DIFFERENT COLOR CARDS	10	15					
SAME OR DIFFERENT DESIGN CARDS	9	13	25				
SAME OR DIFFERENT PORPORATION CARDS	8	11	13	25			
SAME OR DIFFERENT SIZE CARDS	11	13	25				
SAME OR DIFFERENT WORD CARDS	13	18					

TITLE	SKILL NUMBERS						
SAY & DO	72						
SAY & HEAR (RL 1-3)	4	35	7				
SAY IT RIGHT: ARTICULATION KIT FOR "L"	5						
SAY IT RIGHT: ARTICULATION KIT FOR "R"	5						
SAY IT RIGHT: ARTICULATION KIT FOR "S"	5						
SAY THE SOUNDS	52	53	57	58	60	61	
SCARECROW CARD GAME	4	7	42	43			
SCAREY FOREST	88						
SCHOOL & HOME PROGRAM	2	35	41	65			
SCHOOLHOUSE: SPELLING PATTERNS A	65						
SCHOOLHOUSE: SPELLING PATTERNS B	65						
SCHOOLHOUSE: WORD ATTACK 1C	48	75					
SCHOOLHOUSE: WORD ATTACK SKILLS KIT	48	75					
SEA OF VOWELS	57	58	59	60	61		
SEASON LOTTO	2						
SECOND BOX OF COLORS	10	15					
SEE HOW YOU FEEL	41	4					
SEE IT, SAY IT	4	71	72	7			
SEE YOUR WORDS: LEARNING WORDS THROUGH OPPOSITES	87						
SEE-LISTEN-THINK	35	41	8				
SEEING CLEARLY: VISUAL READINESS	9	13					
SELECT-A-SKILL KIT, UNIT 1: MYSTERY ADVENTURE	52	53	60				
SELECT-A-SKILL KIT, UNIT 1: MYSTERY ADVENTURE	52	53	60				
SELECT-A-SKILL KIT, UNIT 2: PIONEER LIFE	57	58					
SELECT-A-SKILL KIT, UNIT 2: PIONEER LIFE	57	58					
SELECT-A-SKILL KIT, UNIT 3: SPORTS	78	77	79	88			
SELECT-A-SKILL KIT, UNIT 3: SPORTS	78	77	79	88			
SELECT-A-SKILL KIT, UNIT 4: ANIMALS	76	80	82				
SELECT-A-SKILL KIT, UNIT 4: ANIMALS	76	80	82				
SELECT-A-SKILL KIT, UNIT 5: FAMOUS PEOPLE	81	90	80				
SELECT-A-SKILL KIT, UNIT 5: FAMOUS PEOPLE	81	90	80				
SELECT-A-SKILL KIT, UNIT 8: LEGENDS, TALES & POETRY	57	58	81	82			
SELF-CARE SEQUENTIAL CARDS	23						
SELF-THERAPY FOR THE STUTTER	5						
SEMANTICS	3	4	2				
SEMANTICS	3	4	2				
SEMEL AUDITORY PROCESSING PROGRAM (ADVANCED BASE)	8	26					
SEMEL AUDITORY PROCESSING PROGRAM (BEGINNING BASE)	8	26					
SEMEL AUDITORY PROCESSING PROGRAM (INTERMEDIATE BASE)	8	26					
SENSE OF SENTENCES	74						
SENTENCE BUILDER	74						
SENTENCE BUILDER	74						
SENTENCE BUILDING KIT	74						
SENTENCE FAMILY	74						
SENTENCE GAME A	74						
SENTENCE GAME B	74						
SENTENCE GAME FOR JUNIORS	74						
SENTENCE IMPROVEMENT SKILLS & DRILLS, LEVEL B	74						
SENTENCE IMPROVEMENT SKILLS & DRILLS, LEVEL C	74						
SENTENCE PATTERNS	74						
SENTENCE PATTERNS	74	71	72	73			
SENTENCE SATELLITE	74						
SENTENCE SENSE	74						
SENTENCE SENSE	74						
SENTENCE SHARPIES, LEVEL 1	74						
SENTENCE SHARPIES, LEVEL 2	74						
SENTENCE SKILLS	74						
SENTENCE STRUCTURE	74						
SENTENCE STRUCTURE	74						
SENTENCE STRUCTURE	74						
SENTENCE STRUCTURE	74						
SENTENCE-BUILDING SEQUENTIAL CARDS	4	23					
SENTENCE-BUILDING WORD CARDS	74	93					
SENTENCES SWING	74	84					
SEQUENCE BINGO	13	23					
SEQUENCE CARDS	23						
SEQUENCE CHARTS	23						
SEQUENCE PICTURES FOR STORY TELLING	5						
SEQUENCE PUZZLES	23						
SEQUENCE PUZZLES: SEQUENCE 3	23						
SEQUENCE PUZZLES: SEQUENCE 4	23						
SEQUENCING	23						
SEQUENCING BEADS & DESIGN CARDS	10	12	24	15	17		
SEQUENCING STORIES	23						
SEQUENTIAL CARDS, A FAMILY'S DAY	23						
SEQUENTIAL CARDS, BY SIZE	12	17	23				
SEQUENTIAL CARDS, FROM-TO SERIES	23						
SEQUENTIAL CARDS, HEALTH & SAFETY	23						
SEQUENTIAL CARDS, LEVEL I	23						
SEQUENTIAL CARDS, LEVEL II	23						
SEQUENTIAL CARDS, LEVEL III	23						
SEQUENTIAL SKILLS DEVELOPMENT ACTIVITIES FOR READING	48	75	83				
SEQUENTIAL SORTING BOX	12	17	23				
SEQUENTIAL SORTING BOX	18	12	25				
SEQUENTIAL SORTING BOX	18						
SEQUENTIAL STRIPS	23						
SERIES C EXERCISES	92						
SERIES F EXERCISES	92						
SERVICE CAREER PEOPLE	94						
SESAME STREET LOOK-INSIDE PUZZLES: BIG BIRD PRESENTS COLORS	9						
SESAME STREET LOOK-INSIDE PUZZLES: COOKIE'S NUMBER TRAIN	9						
SESAME STREET LOOK-INSIDE PUZZLES: GOIN' FOR A RIDE	9						
SESAME STREET LOOK-INSIDE PUZZLES: GROVER'S BLOCKS	9						

TITLE	SKILL NUMBERS						
SESAME STREET LOOK-INSIDE PUZZLES: PEOPLE IN NEIGHBORHOOD	9						
SESAME STREET LOOK-INSIDE PUZZLES: WHERE DO THINGS COME FROM	9						
SESAME STREET MATCH-UPS	51	49					
SESAME STREET PUZZLES: BERT'S "B"	9						
SESAME STREET PUZZLES: BIG & LITTLE	9						
SESAME STREET PUZZLES: COOKIE'S "C"	9						
SESAME STREET PUZZLES: ERNIE	9						
SESAME STREET PUZZLES: FOUR MONSTERS	9						
SESAME STREET PUZZLES: NIGHT & DAY	9						
SESAME STREET PUZZLES: WE'RE FRIENDS	9						
SHAPE & PATTERNS	12	17					
SHAPE BOARD: FARM SHAPES	17	47	12				
SHAPE BOARD: SEA SHAPES	17	47	12				
SHAPE DOMINOES	17	12					
SHAPE IN A SHAPE	12	17					
SHAPE PUZZLES	17	12					
SHAPE RELATIONSHIPS	12	17					
SHAPE SORTING CUBES	12	17					
SHAPE-UPS: ANTONYMS	87						
SHAPE-UPS: CLASSIFICATION	47						
SHAPE-UPS: COMPOUND WORDS	79						
SHAPE-UPS: SYLLABICATION, S - U	82						
SHAPE-UPS: SYNONYMS	86						
SHAPERINO	17						
SHAPES	12	17					
SHAPES BOARD	17	12					
SHAPES GAME	15	17					
SHAPES IN THINGS	17	12					
SHAPES SORTING BOX	11	12	17	18			
SHAPES, COLORS & FORMS	10	11	12	15	16	17	
SHARPEN THEIR EARS!	35	35	33	26	27	34	
SHELLY HELPS MOTHER SHOP	29	36	37	35	33	31	
SHIFTING SHAPES, SET 1	12	17	25				
SHORT "A" & LONG "A" PLAY A GAME	57	58					
SHORT "E" & LONG "E" PLAY A GAME	57	58					
SHORT "I" & LONG "I" PLAY A GAME	57	58					
SHORT "O" & LONG "O" PLAY A GAME	57	58					
SHORT "U" & LONG "U" PLAY A GAME	57	58					
SHORT & LONG A	57	58					
SHORT & LONG A	57	58					
SHORT & LONG E	57	58					
SHORT & LONG E	57	58					
SHORT & LONG I	57	58					
SHORT & LONG I	57	58					
SHORT & LONG O	57	58					
SHORT & LONG O	57	58					
SHORT & LONG U	57	58					
SHORT & LONG U	57	58					
SHORT & LONG VOWELS	57	58					
SHORT & LONG VOWELS	57	58					
SHORT & LONG VOWELS	57	58					
SHORT & LONG VOWELS	57	58					
SHORT & LONG VOWELS	57	58					
SHORT & LONG VOWELS PEEK-A-BOO KID	57	58					
SHORT & LONG VOWELS PLAY A GAME	57	58					
SHORT PLAYS: FRIENDS INDEED, KIT B	7						
SHORT PLAYS: FUN WITH FANTASY, KIT D	7						
SHORT PLAYS: SCRIPTS ON SOCIETY, KIT C	7						
SHORT PLAYS: THE ADULT SCENE, KIT A	7						
SHORT VOWEL DISCS	57						
SHORT VOWEL SOUND FUN	57						
SHORT VOWEL SOUNDS	57						
SHORT VOWEL TAPE PROGRAM	57						
SHORT VOWEL TIC TAC TOE	57						
SHORT VOWELS	57						
SHORT VOWELS	57						
SHORT VOWELS	57						
SHORT VOWELS	57						
SHORT VOWELS POSTER	57						
SHORT VOWELS: STARTING OFF WITH PHONICS, BOOK 5	57						
SHORT VOWELS: STARTING OFF WITH PHONICS, BOOK 5	57	58					
SIGHT & SOUND DISCOVERY TRIPS: LISTENING & SIGHT EXPERIENCE	35	34					
SIGHT & SOUND PHONICS	53	59	60				
SIGHT & SOUND PHONICS	84	50	48				
SIGHT READING: ADJECTIVES	73	84					
SIGHT READING: ADVERBS	73	84					
SIGHT READING: NOUNS	71	84					
SIGHT READING: VERBS	72	84					
SIGHT VOCABULARY SERIES	84						
SIGHT WORD FUN	84						
SIGHT WORD FUN	84						
SIGHT WORD LAB	84						
SIGHT WORD MATCH, ETTES	84						
SIGHT WORD PACER	84						
SIGHT WORD RECOGNITION	84						
SIGHT WORD SNAP 1	84						
SIGHT WORD SNAP 2	84						
SIGHT WORDS FOR BEGINNING READERS	84						
SIGHT WORDS WITH SOUND AND FUN	84						
SIGHT-WORDS, GRADE ONE	84						
SIGHT-WORDS, GRADE TWO	84						
SIGHTS & SOUNDS, SET 1	35	26	9				

TITLE	SKILL NUMBERS						
SIGHTS & SOUNDS, SET 2	35	26	9				
SIGN CARD GAMES (SP. ED.)	72	84					
SIGN LANGUAGE	3						
SIGN LANGUAGE ALPHABET WALL CARDS	3						
SIGN LANGUAGE FOR EVERYONE	3						
SIGN LANGUAGE THESAURUS	3						
SIGN LANGUAGE, BOOK A	85	92					
SIGN LANGUAGE, BOOK B	85	92					
SIGN LANGUAGE, BOOK C	85	92					
SIGN LANGUAGE, BOOK D	85	92					
SIGNS	85						
SIGNS & SOUNDS	27						
SIGNS SERIES (RL 2)	85						
SILENT CONSONANTS	55						
SILENT E ON THE END OF A WORD	63						
SILENT LETTERS	55						
SILLY SOUNDING RHYMES, SET 1	51						
SILLY SOUNDING RHYMES, SET 2	51						
SILLY SOUNDING RHYMES, SET 3	51						
SILLY SOUNDING RHYMES, SET 4	51						
SILLY SOUNDS	52	71	72	73			
SIMILES	90						
SIMILIES	90						
SIMPLE LONG VOWEL SOUNDS	58						
SIMPLE SENTENCE IN SEVEN STEPS	70	74					
SIMPLE SENTENCE IN SEVEN STEPS	70	74					
SIMPLE SIGHT VOCABULARY	84						
SIMPLE SIGHT VOCABULARY	84						
SIMPLIFIED LUMMI STICK ACTIVITIES	29	36	38				
SING A SONG OF SOUND	35	40	33				
SING CHILDREN'S SONGS & GAMES FROM THE SOUTHERN MOUNTAINS	2						
SINGING ABOUT COLOR	35	27					
SINGING SOUNDS	50						
SINGLE SOUNDS	50						
SINGLE SOUNDS: INFANT PROGRAM	50						
SINGLE SOUNDS: SECOND PROGRAM	50						
SINGULAR - PLURAL PUZZLES	77						
SINGULAR, PLURAL DOMINOES	77						
SITUATIONAL LANGUAGE	85						
SIXTH GRADE LANGUAGE DRILLS	72	71	73	74			
SIXTY DEMONS	69						
SIZE & SHAPE PUZZLE	11	12					
SIZE & SHAPE PUZZLES WITH KNOBS: BIRDS IN A FRUIT TREE	11	12	16	17			
SIZE & SHAPE PUZZLES WITH KNOBS: FLOWER POT	11	12	16	17			
SIZE & SHAPE PUZZLES WITH KNOBS: FOUR DUCKS	11	12	16	17			
SIZE & SHAPE PUZZLES WITH KNOBS: KITES	11	12	16	17			
SIZE & SHAPE PUZZLES WITH KNOBS: SNOWMAN	11	12	16	17			
SIZE & SHAPE PUZZLES WITH KNOBS: THREE FISH	11	12	16	17			
SIZE & SHAPE PUZZLES WITH KNOBS: TOAD STOOL	11	12	16	17			
SIZE & SHAPE PUZZLES WITH KNOBS: TWO LADYBUGS	12	11	16	17			
SIZE DISCRIMINATION CIRCUS	11						
SIZE FIT-INS	12	17					
SIZE INSERT PUZZLES	16	25					
SIZE SEQUENCING CARDS	14						
SKANEATELES ALPHABET BLOCKS	49						
SKETCH-A-PUZZLE	25	9	22				
SKILL BUILDING SERIES: CODE BOOK	13	12	49				
SKILL BUILDING SERIES: WORD SHAPES	22	19	13				
SKILL RECOGNITION: MULTIPLE MEANING VOCABULARY	88	89	86	87			
SKILLBUILDERS	52	56					
SKILLS IN LANGUAGE, BOOK 1	83	70					
SKILLS IN LANGUAGE, BOOK 2	83	70					
SKITS FOR SKILLS: FRIENDS INDEED, KIT B	7	29					
SKITS FOR SKILLS: FUN WITH FANTASY, KIT D	7	29					
SKITS FOR SKILLS: SCRIPTS ON SOCIETY, KIT C	7	29					
SKITS FOR SKILLS: THE ADULT SCENE, KIT A	7	29					
SLY SPY & OTHER STORIES	48						
SMALL PARQUETRY BLOCKS	45	21	23	15	19		
SMALL PARQUETRY, DESIGN I	21	23	15	19			
SMALL PARQUETRY, DESIGN II	21	23	15	19			
SMALL PARQUETRY, DESIGN III	21	23	15	19			
SMALL WONDER	2	5					
SMALL/LARGE MATCH PUZZLES	11						
SMILES	90						
SNEAKY SUFFIXES	81						
SNOOPY SNAKE & OTHER STORIES	5						
SOC-O	84	85					
SOCIAL SIGNS	84	85					
SOLAR SWAMP VERB	72						
SOLO GAMES: ANTONYMS, SYNONYMS, HOMONYMS	86	87	88				
SOLO GAMES: RHYMING	51						
SOLVING THE PHONICS MYSTERY: CASE OF THE LONG & SHORT VOWELS	57	58					
SOLVING THE PHONICS MYSTERY: CLUE OF THE COMBINING LETTERS	49	50	53	59	60		
SONG & PLAY TIME	2						
SONGS TO GROW ON, VOLUME 2: SCHOOL DAYS	2						
SONGS TO GROW ON, VOLUME 3: AMERICAN WORK SONGS	2						
SORTING & GROUPING SET	18	47					
SORTING BOX & ACCESSORIES	15	17	18				
SORTING FLIP BOOK	18						
SOUND & SYMBOL PUZZLES	50	49					
SOUND 'N' SPELL ALPHABET PUZZLE	65	57	58				
SOUND ABSURDITIES	31	39	40				
SOUND ALIKES	88						

TITLE	SKILL NUMBERS						
SOUND BOXES	27	28	33	29			
SOUND BOXES	27						
SOUND CHECKERS /L/ (SP. ED.)	5						
SOUND CHECKERS /R/ (SP. ED.)	5						
SOUND CHECKERS /S/ (SP. ED.)	5						
SOUND CHECKERS /SH/ (SP. ED.)	5						
SOUND CLOSURE	30	53	23	24			
SOUND DISCRIMATION SET: SECOND SET	27						
SOUND DISCRIMINATION SET: FIRST SET	27						
SOUND DOMINO GAME	27	64	83	4			
SOUND FOUNDATION PROGRAM III	48	75					
SOUND FOUNDATION, PROGRAM 1	58	59	53	14	51		
SOUND FOUNDATION, PROGRAM 2	57	58	75	83			
SOUND GAMES THROUGH THE GRADES, VOLUME 1	26	48					
SOUND GAMES THROUGH THE GRADES, VOLUME 2	26	48					
SOUND GAMES THROUGH THE GRADES, VOLUME 3	26	48					
SOUND GAMES THROUGH THE GRADES, VOLUME 4	26	48					
SOUND IT!	10	24	33				
SOUND IT, UNIT 1	52	53	54	55	35		
SOUND IT, UNIT 2	56	57	58	59	60	61	35
SOUND LOTTO 1	26	42	50				
SOUND LOTTO 2	26	42	50				
SOUND MATCHING	26	27	28				
SOUND OFF & READ	50	53	57	58	62	59	
SOUND OFF & READ GAMES	57	58	60	61	62		
SOUND OUT: LISTENING SKILLS PROGRAM	35	35					
SOUND PUZZLES	27	50					
SOUND PUZZLES	48						
SOUND SEARCH	53						
SOUND SKILLS FOR UPPER GRADES	53	54	57	58	82	79	80
SOUND SKILLS FOR UPPER GRADES, VOLUME 1	53	54					
SOUND SKILLS FOR UPPER GRADES, VOLUME 2	57	58	63				
SOUND SKILLS FOR UPPER GRADES, VOLUME 3	82	76	80	79			
SOUND SODA	53						
SOUND SODA	53	60					
SOUND STORIES	31	39	40				
SOUND STORIES CARDS	31						
SOUND THE SAME CARDS	88						
SOUND WAY, BOOK 1	84	48	85	70			
SOUND WAY, BOOK 2	48	84	85	70			
SOUND WE USE, BOOK 1	19	48	52	57	58		
SOUND WHEEL (SP. ED.)	5						
SOUND WORDS	93						
SOUND WORDS	93						
SOUND, PICTURE MATCH-UP	8	26					
SOUND, WRITE, READ, SPELL	13	84	85	37	64		
SOUND-ALIKE TWINS	85						
SOUND-ALIKE WORDS	88						
SOUND-OFF 2	57						
SOUND-OFF 3	53						
SOUND-OFF 4	63						
SOUND-OFF 5	58	59	60				
SOUND-SIGHT SKILLS	25						
SOUND-SIGHT SKILLS, SET I	35	35					
SOUND-SIGHT SKILLS, SET II	35	35					
SOUNDER CLASSROOM SET	48	75	84				
SOUNDER RESOURCE SET	48	75	84				
SOUNDS & LETTERS, KIT II	49	50					
SOUNDS & SIGNALS A	48						
SOUNDS & SIGNALS B	48						
SOUNDS & SIGNALS C	48						
SOUNDS & SIGNALS D	48						
SOUNDS & SIGNALS E	48						
SOUNDS & SYLLABLES, BOOK E	79	82	59	60	77		
SOUNDS & SYMBOLS	49	53	57	58	50		
SOUNDS AROUND US	9	35	35				
SOUNDS FOR YOUNG READERS, VOLUME 1	51	50					
SOUNDS FOR YOUNG READERS, VOLUME 1	51	50					
SOUNDS FOR YOUNG READERS, VOLUME 2	52	53	57	58			
SOUNDS FOR YOUNG READERS, VOLUME 2	52	53	57	58			
SOUNDS FOR YOUNG READERS, VOLUME 3	58	57					
SOUNDS FOR YOUNG READERS, VOLUME 3	58	57					
SOUNDS FOR YOUNG READERS, VOLUME 4	53	75					
SOUNDS FOR YOUNG READERS, VOLUME 4	53	75					
SOUNDS FOR YOUNG READERS, VOLUME 5	79	80	81	82			
SOUNDS FOR YOUNG READERS, VOLUME 5	79	80	81	82			
SOUNDS FOR YOUNG READERS, VOLUME 6	60	61					
SOUNDS FOR YOUNG READERS, VOLUME 6	60	61					
SOUNDS I SAY	50						
SOUNDS IN MY WORLD	27	33					
SOUNDS IN WORDS, BOOK 1	50						
SOUNDS IN WORDS, BOOK 10	53	55	54	55	57	58	63
SOUNDS IN WORDS, BOOK 11	53	57	58	59	63		
SOUNDS IN WORDS, BOOK 12	76	82	79	80			
SOUNDS IN WORDS, BOOK 13	82	80	81	76			
SOUNDS IN WORDS, BOOK 14	57	58	59	60	61		
SOUNDS IN WORDS, BOOK 15	76	80	81	82			
SOUNDS IN WORDS, BOOK 16	53	55	54	57	58	59	60
SOUNDS IN WORDS, BOOK 17	57	58	59	60	61		
SOUNDS IN WORDS, BOOK 18	79	76	80	81	82		
SOUNDS IN WORDS, BOOK 2	50						
SOUNDS IN WORDS, BOOK 3	63						
SOUNDS IN WORDS, BOOK 4	53	56	63				

TITLE	SKILL NUMBERS						
SOUNDS IN WORDS, BOOK 5	53	56	63				
SOUNDS IN WORDS, BOOK 6	57	58	53				
SOUNDS IN WORDS, BOOK 7	53	55	54				
SOUNDS IN WORDS, BOOK 8	57	58	59				
SOUNDS IN WORDS, BOOK 9	79	76	80	81	82		
SOUNDS MAKE WORDS	50						
SOUNDS WE USE, BOOK 2	52	53	59				
SOUNDS WE USE, BOOK 3	48	57	58	61	77	82	88
SOUNDS, VOL. 1	51						
SOUNDS, VOL. 2	53	57					
SOUNDS, VOL. 3	57	58					
SOUNDS, WORDS & ACTIONS	39	40	29	36	38		
SPACE ADVENTURES READING SERIES	2	29	41	65			
SPACE FIREWORKS: REGULAR VERBS VS. IRREGULAR	72						
SPACE FLIGHT	53						
SPACETALK	5	2					
SPAR	64						
SPEAK FOR YOURSELF	2						
SPEAK OUT!	4						
SPEAKEASY /S/ (SP. ED.)	5						
SPEAKING BY DOING	35	4	7				
SPEAKING EFFECTIVELY	7						
SPEAKING OF LANGUAGE	2						
SPEAKING OF SPELLING	64						
SPECIAL KIDS' STUFF, PART IV: WORK STUDY SKILLS (SP. ED.)	48	75	83				
SPECIAL NEEDS: SPECIAL ANSWERS	9	35	48	84			
SPECIAL VOWEL PATTERNS, PART I	59	57	58	61			
SPECIAL VOWEL PATTERNS, PART II	57	58	59	61			
SPECIAL VOWELS	59	60	61	62			
SPECTRUM OF SKILLS: VOCABULARY DEVELOPMENT, LEVEL 1	83						
SPECTRUM OF SKILLS: VOCABULARY DEVELOPMENT, LEVEL 2	83						
SPECTRUM OF SKILLS: VOCABULARY DEVELOPMENT, LEVEL 3	83						
SPECTRUM OF SKILLS: VOCABULARY DEVELOPMENT, LEVEL 4	83						
SPECTRUM OF SKILLS: VOCABULARY DEVELOPMENT, LEVEL 5	83						
SPECTRUM OF SKILLS: VOCABULARY DEVELOPMENT, LEVEL 6	83						
SPECTRUM OF SKILLS: WORD ANALYSIS, LEVEL 1	48	75					
SPECTRUM OF SKILLS: WORD ANALYSIS, LEVEL 2	48	75					
SPECTRUM OF SKILLS: WORD ANALYSIS, LEVEL 3	48	75					
SPECTRUM OF SKILLS: WORD ANALYSIS, LEVEL 4	48	75					
SPECTRUM OF SKILLS: WORD ANALYSIS, LEVEL 5	48	75					
SPECTRUM OF SKILLS: WORD ANALYSIS, LEVEL 6	48	75					
SPECTRUM SERIES	75	83					
SPECTRUM, UNIT 1 (RL 3.5 - 4.4)	76	80	81				
SPEECH & HEARING	5						
SPEECH & PUBLIC SPEAKING: COMMUNICATION GAMES	7	4					
SPEECH - AN IMPORTANT SKILL PUPIL TEXT (RL 4-6)	7	6					
SPEECH FUN WITH A CHALKBOARD (SP. ED.)	5						
SPEECH LINGO	4	6					
SPEECH PENCILS	5						
SPEECH SOUNDS PICTURE CARDS: CONSONANTS & VOWELS	57	58					
SPEECH SOUNDS PICTURE CARDS: DIGRAPHS & DIPTHONGS	59	60					
SPEECH SOUNDS PICTURE CARDS: INITIAL CONSONANT BLENDS	53						
SPEECH SOUNDS PICTURE CARDS: VOWEL-R BLENDS	61						
SPEECH THERAPY	7	5	2				
SPEECH THERAPY WITH BEGINNING SOUNDS	5						
SPEECH THERAPY WORKBOOKS: B SOUND	5						
SPEECH THERAPY WORKBOOKS: CH SOUND	5						
SPEECH THERAPY WORKBOOKS: D SOUND	5						
SPEECH THERAPY WORKBOOKS: F SOUND	5						
SPEECH THERAPY WORKBOOKS: G SOUND	5						
SPEECH THERAPY WORKBOOKS: J SOUND	5						
SPEECH THERAPY WORKBOOKS: K SOUND	5						
SPEECH THERAPY WORKBOOKS: L SOUND	5						
SPEECH THERAPY WORKBOOKS: P SOUND	5						
SPEECH THERAPY WORKBOOKS: R SOUND	5						
SPEECH THERAPY WORKBOOKS: S SOUND	5						
SPEECH THERAPY WORKBOOKS: SH SOUND	5						
SPEECH THERAPY WORKBOOKS: T SOUND	5						
SPEECH THERAPY WORKBOOKS: TH SOUND	5						
SPEECH THERAPY WORKBOOKS: V SOUND	5						
SPEECH THERAPY WORKBOOKS: Z SOUND	5						
SPEECH-TO-PRINT PHONICS: A PHONICS FOUNDATIN FOR READING	48						
SPEECH: AN IMPORTANT SKILL AUDIO PACK (RL 4-6)	4	7	6				
SPEED READING CHARTS	84						
SPELL CHECK: LONG VOWELS, SET 1	66	57					
SPELL CHECK: LONG VOWELS, SET 2	66	57					
SPELL IT OUT, BOOK 1 (RL 3 - 5)	64						
SPELL IT OUT, BOOK 2 (RL 3 - 5)	64						
SPELL IT WRITE	64	66					
SPELL MASTER	64						
SPELL OF WORDS	66						
SPELL POWER	81	64	80				
SPELLBINDING 1	67	69					
SPELLBINDING 2	67	69					
SPELLBOUND	64						
SPELLING	64	66					
SPELLING	65	66					
SPELLING	64						
SPELLING	64						
SPELLING	64						
SPELLING & WRITING PATTERNS BOOK A	65						
SPELLING & WRITING PATTERNS BOOK A, T.E.	65						
SPELLING & WRITING PATTERNS BOOK B	65						

TITLE	SKILL NUMBERS						
SPELLING & WRITING PATTERNS BOOK B, T.E.	65						
SPELLING & WRITING PATTERNS BOOK C	65						
SPELLING & WRITING PATTERNS BOOK C, T.E.	65						
SPELLING & WRITING PATTERNS BOOK D	65						
SPELLING & WRITING PATTERNS BOOK D, T.E.	65						
SPELLING & WRITING PATTERNS BOOK E	65						
SPELLING & WRITING PATTERNS BOOK E, T.E.	65						
SPELLING & WRITING PATTERNS BOOK F	65						
SPELLING & WRITING PATTERNS BOOK F, T.E.	65						
SPELLING BOX, LEVEL 3	64						
SPELLING BOX, LEVEL 4	64						
SPELLING EXPRESS	65	66	67				
SPELLING FILMSTRIPS 1	64						
SPELLING FILMSTRIPS 2	64						
SPELLING FOR THE MILLIONS	69						
SPELLING GAMES	64	66	68				
SPELLING GAMES & PUZZLES FOR JUNIOR HIGH	64						
SPELLING GENERALIZATIONS	64	65	66				
SPELLING GENERALIZATIONS	65						
SPELLING MAGIC	64						
SPELLING MASTERY	64						
SPELLING MASTERY & DIAGNOSTIC REFERENCE KIT	64	74					
SPELLING MONSTERS, UNIT A	64						
SPELLING MONSTERS, UNIT B	64						
SPELLING MONSTERS, UNIT C	64						
SPELLING MONSTERS, UNIT D	64						
SPELLING PATTERNS	65						
SPELLING POWER	65						
SPELLING PROGRAM, BOOK A	66	57					
SPELLING PROGRAM, BOOK B	66	57					
SPELLING PROGRAM, BOOK C	66	57					
SPELLING PROGRAM, BOOK D	66	57					
SPELLING PROGRAM, BOOK E	66	57					
SPELLING PROGRAM, BOOK F	66	57					
SPELLING PROGRAM, BOOK G	66	51					
SPELLING PROGRAM, BOOK H	66	58					
SPELLING PROGRAM, BOOK I	66	53					
SPELLING PROGRAM, BOOK J	66	59	60				
SPELLING PROGRAM, BOOK K	66	61					
SPELLING PROGRAM, BOOK L	66	53	77				
SPELLING REFERENCE BOOK	64						
SPELLING WITH SPORTS	64						
SPELLING WORD POWER LABORATORY KIT	75	83	64				
SPELLING WORD POWER LABORATORY KIT 2A	75	83	64				
SPELLING WORD POWER LABORATORY KIT 2B	75	83	64				
SPELLING WORD POWER LABORATORY KIT 2C	75	83	64				
SPELLING WORDS IN USE	67	68	69				
SPELLING WORDS IN USE DEVELOPMENTAL	67	68	69				
SPELLING, ADVANCED	64						
SPELLING, CAPITALIZATION & PUNCTUATION	64						
SPELLING, INTERMEDIATE	64						
SPELLING/LANGUAGE LEARNING GAMES KITS, KIT ONE	51	53	64				
SPELLING/LANGUAGE LEARNING GAMES KITS, KIT TWO	76	81	64				
SPELLING: A MNEMONICS APPROACH	67	69	68				
SPELLING: BASIC SPELLING	64						
SPELLING: SOUND TO LETTER, BOOK A	66	67					
SPELLING: SOUND TO LETTER, BOOK A, T.E.	66	67					
SPELLING: SOUND TO LETTER, BOOK B	66	67					
SPELLING: SOUND TO LETTER, BOOK B, T.E.	66	67					
SPELLING: SOUND TO LETTER, BOOK C	66	67					
SPELLING: SOUND TO LETTER, BOOK C, T.E.	66	67					
SPELLING: SOUND TO LETTER, BOOK D	66	67					
SPELLING: SOUND TO LETTER, BOOK D, T.E.	66	67					
SPELLING: SOUND TO LETTER, BOOK E	66	67					
SPELLING: SOUND TO LETTER, BOOK E, T.E.	66	67					
SPELLING: SOUND TO LETTER, BOOK F	66	67					
SPELLING: SOUND TO LETTER, BOOK F, T.E.	66	67					
SPELLO	84	64					
SPELLTAPES SERIES	64						
SPELLTAPES: DIAGNOSIS & IMPROVEMENT OF SPELLING SKILLS, TR 1	64						
SPELLTAPES: HOMONYMS & BIG DEMONS, TRAY 8	69						
SPELLTAPES: LONG VOWELS & VOWEL DIGRAPHS, TRAY 3	66						
SPELLTAPES: OTHER VOWELS & OTHER SPELLING TOPICS, TRAY 4	66						
SPELLTAPES: PREFIXES, PLURALS & POSSESSIVES, TRAY 6	65						
SPELLTAPES: SHORT VOWELS & CONSONANTS, TRAY 2	66						
SPELLTAPES: SPECIAL SPELLING TOPICS, TRAY 7	69	67					
SPELLTAPES: WORD ENDINGS, TRAY 5	65						
SPICE SERIES: ANCHOR	48	75					
SPICE SERIES: RESCUE	48	75					
SPICE SERIES: SPICE	48	75					
SPICE, VOLUME I	48						
SPICE, VOLUME II	48	75					
SPIDER CRAWL	49	23	33				
SPIN & SEE GAMES	14	19					
SPIN-A-WORD	27	4	64	50	83		
SPIN-N-MATCH	14	49					
SPIRIT MASTER WORKBOOKS: SPELLING GENERALIZATIONS	65						
SPIRIT MASTER WORKBOOKS: SYLLABLE RULE & ACCENT CLUE	82						
SPIRIT MASTER WORKBOOKS: VOWELS	56						
SPLICE	57	84	25	24			
SPLIT WORDS	48	65					
SPORT SCRAMBLE (RL 3)	53						
SPORTS LOTTO	2						

TITLE	SKILL NUMBERS						
SPOTLIGHT ON SENTENCES, BOOK ONE	74						
SPOTLIGHT ON SENTENCES, BOOK TWO	74						
SPOTLIGHT ON SPELLING, BOOK ONE	65	66	67				
SPOTLIGHT ON SPELLING, BOOK TWO	65	66	67				
SPREAD I	56	52	14				
SPRINGBOARDS FOR WRITING	74						
SRA LISTENING LANGUAGE LABORATORY: INTERMEDIATE KIT 2A	35	29	36	37	38	83	35
SRA LISTENING LANGUAGE LABORATORY: INTERMEDIATE KIT 2B	35	29	36	37	38	83	35
SRA LISTENING LANGUAGE LABORATORY: INTERMEDIATE KIT 2C	29	35	36	37	38	83	35
SRA LISTENING LANGUAGE LABORATORY: PRIMARY KIT 1A	35	29	36	37	38	83	35
SRA LISTENING LANGUAGE LABORATORY: PRIMARY KIT 1B	35	29	36	37	38	83	35
SRA LISTENING LANGUAGE LABORATORY: PRIMARY KIT 1C	29	35	36	37	38	83	35
SRA SKILLS SERIES: PHONICS	48						
SRA SKILLS SERIES: STRUCTURAL ANALYSIS	75						
STANDARD BASIC WORD POWER PACER	83	74	92				
STANDARD REBUS GLOSSARY	50	4	5	7	48	75	
STAR BOOKS	83	10	13	47	12		
STAR TRAILS /r/-/s/-/l/-/th/-/sh/-/ch/	5						
STAR TRIP (RL 2)	53						
START YOUR ENGINES	84						
STARTER SET: SHAPES, COLORS, SIZES, LETTERS, NUMBERS	10	11	12	49	14		
STEP	42	43	45	46			
STEPPING STONES, WALK-ON ALPHABET CAPITALS	49	25					
STEPPING STONES, WALK-ON ALPHABET LOWERCASE	49	25					
STEPS TO SPELLING BREAKTHROUGH, LEVEL 1	64						
STEPS TO SPELLING BREAKTHROUGH, LEVEL 2	64						
STEPS TO SPELLING BREAKTHROUGH, LEVEL 3	64						
STEPTEXT	2						
STILL MORE ANTONYMS	87						
STILL MORE ANTONYMS	87						
STILL MORE HOMONYMS	88						
STILL MORE HOMONYMS	88						
STIMULATION CARDS, SET 1: S SOUND	5						
STIMULATION CARDS, SET 2: R SOUND	5	4					
STIMULATION CARDS, SET 3: TH SOUND	5	4					
STIMULATION CARDS, SET 4: L SOUND	5	4					
STIMULATION CARDS, SET 5: SH SOUND	5	4					
STIMULATION CARDS, SET 6: K SOUND	5	4					
STIMULATION CARDS, SET 7: G SOUND	5	4					
STIMULATION CARDS, SET 8: CH SOUND	5	4					
STIMULATION CARDS, SET 9: Z SOUND	5	4					
STIMULUS SHIFT ARTICULATION KIT	5						
STOP THAT WORM!	50						
STORIES ABOUT COLORS	15	10					
STORIES ABOUT LETTERS	49	14					
STORIES ABOUT SHAPES	12	17					
STORIES ABOUT WORDS	87	86	88	79	80	81	
STORIES FROM SOUND, LEVEL A	53	57					
STORIES FROM SOUNDS, LEVEL B	53	57					
STORIES FROM SOUNDS, LEVEL C	53	57					
STORIES FROM SOUNDS, LEVEL D	53	57					
STORIES FROM SOUNDS, LEVEL E	53	57					
STORIES TO FINISH MIDDLE GRADES	7						
STORIES TO FINISH PRIMARY GRADES	7						
STORY BOARDS	4	7					
STORY BOARDS	4	6					
STORY CARDS TELL WHAT PART IS MISSING	19	22	9	13			
STORY OF A, E, O	57	58					
STORY OF C	54						
STORY OF CH & SCH	53						
STORY OF CORN	23						
STORY OF F & PH	55						
STORY OF G	54						
STORY OF GH	55						
STORY OF H & WH	53						
STORY OF I & Y	57	58					
STORY OF NG	55	53					
STORY OF Q	55						
STORY OF R & R CONTROLLER	61						
STORY OF SH	53						
STORY OF TH	53						
STORY OF U, W & W CONTROLLER	57	58	61				
STORY OF X	55						
STORY STARTERS	7	40					
STORY STARTERS: BIRTHDAY PARTY	7	40					
STORY STARTERS: CARNIVAL	7	40					
STORY STARTERS: FIREHOUSE	7	40					
STORY STARTERS: IT'S MAGIC	7	40					
STORY STARTERS: LOST DOG	7	40					
STORY STARTERS: MYSTERY HAT	7	40					
STORY STARTERS: PLAYGROUND	7	40					
STORY STARTERS: SECRET MESSAGE	7	40					
STORY STARTERS: UP, UP, UP	7	40					
STORY STARTERS: WAITING	7	40					
STORY STARTERS: WINTER HIKE	7	40					
STORY STIMULUS CARDS	7						
STORY TELLING	1						
STORYBOOK PUZZLES: CINDERELLA	9						
STORYBOOK PUZZLES: HANSEL & GRETEL	9						
STORYBOOK PUZZLES: HUMPTY-DUMPTY	9						
STORYBOOK PUZZLES: LITTLE RED RIDING HOOD	9						
STORYBOOK PUZZLES: OLD WOMAN IN THE SHOE	9						
STORYBOOK PUZZLES: RUB-A-DUB-DUB	9						

TITLE	SKILL NUMBERS						
STORYBOOK PUZZLES: RUMPELSTILTSKIN	9						
STORYBOOK PUZZLES: THREE BEARS	9						
STORYBOOK PUZZLES: TORTOISE & THE HARE	9						
STRAIGHT TALK	5						
STRAIGHT TALK CARD SET	5						
STRING ALONG	20						
STRING ALONG ADVANCED PATTERNS	20						
STRUCTO BRICKS	34						
STRUCTURAL ANALYSIS	78	76	80	81	82		
STRUCTURAL ANALYSIS FILMSTRIP SERIES	78	76	80	81	82		
STRUCTURAL ANALYSIS FOR BEGINNING READERS	78	77	79	76	75		
STRUCTURAL ANALYSIS SERIES	78	76	80	81	82		
STRUCTURE OF WORDS	66	76	80	81	65	67	
STRUCTURE WORDS	40						
STRUCTURED SYNTAX	74						
STRUCTURED SYNTAX PROGRAM FOR AUDIO CARD READER	74						
STUCK NO. 1 (SP. ED.)	5						
STUCK NO. 2 (SP. ED.)	5						
STUTTERING WORDS	5						
SUCCEED IN SPELLING	68						
SUE GOES TO THE ZOO	29	36	37	33	35		
SUFFIX PEDRO	81						
SUFFIX PUZZLES	81						
SUFFIXES	81						
SUFFIXES	81						
SUFFIXES	81						
SUFFIXES	81						
SUFFIXES	81						
SUFFIXES -ABLE -ION AND FRIENDS	81						
SUFFIXES -ER -ENT AND FRIENDS	81						
SUFFIXES TO WATCH	81						
SUGGESTIONS FOR TEACHING LANGUAGE SKILLS	5						
SULLIVAN DECODING KIT	50						
SULLIVAN READING GAMES	48						
SUPER "S" BLENDS	53						
SUPER EARS	26	35					
SUPER SPELLING FUN	65						
SUPER STOCK	48	82	80	81			
SUPER SUFFIXES	81						
SUPER SUFFIXES	81						
SUPER SUFFIXES	81						
SUPPORTIVE READING SKILLS: DISCOVERING WORD PATTERNS	86	87	93				
SUPPORTIVE READING SKILLS: DISCOVERING WORD PATTERNS, ADV.	86	87	93				
SUPPORTIVE READING SKILLS: DISCOVERING WORD PATTERNS, BASIC	86	87	93				
SUPPORTIVE READING SKILLS: DISCOVERING WORD PATTERNS, INTER.	86	87	93				
SUPPORTIVE READING SKILLS: INTERPRETING IDIOMS (MULT COPIES)	91						
SUPPORTIVE READING SKILLS: INTERPRETING IDIOMS, A	91						
SUPPORTIVE READING SKILLS: INTERPRETING IDIOMS, ADV.1-ADV.2	91						
SUPPORTIVE READING SKILLS: INTERPRETING IDIOMS, B	91						
SUPPORTIVE READING SKILLS: INTERPRETING IDIOMS, C1-C2	91						
SUPPORTIVE READING SKILLS: INTERPRETING IDIOMS, D1-D4	91						
SUPPORTIVE READING SKILLS: INTERPRETING IDIOMS, E1-E4	91						
SUPPORTIVE READING SKILLS: INTERPRETING IDIOMS, F1-F4	91						
SUPPORTIVE READING SKILLS: MASTERING MULTI. MEANINGS, B1-B8	88						
SUPPORTIVE READING SKILLS: MASTERING MULTI. MEANINGS, C1-C16	88						
SUPPORTIVE READING SKILLS: MASTERING MULTI. MEANINGS, D1-D16	88						
SUPPORTIVE READING SKILLS: MASTERING MULTIP. MEANINGS, A1-A2	88						
SUPPORTIVE READING SKILLS: PHONIC ANALOGIES (MULTI COPIES)	90	92					
SUPPORTIVE READING SKILLS: PHONIC ANALOGIES, A1-A8	90	92					
SUPPORTIVE READING SKILLS: PHONIC ANALOGIES, B1-B8	90	92					
SUPPORTIVE READING SKILLS: PHONIC ANALOGIES, C1-C8	90	92					
SUPPORTIVE READING SKILLS: READING ADS (MULTI COPIES)	85						
SUPPORTIVE READING SKILLS: READING ADS, A	85						
SUPPORTIVE READING SKILLS: READING ADS, ADV. 1-ADV. 4	85						
SUPPORTIVE READING SKILLS: READING ADS, B	85						
SUPPORTIVE READING SKILLS: READING ADS, C	85						
SUPPORTIVE READING SKILLS: READING ADS, D	85						
SUPPORTIVE READING SKILLS: READING ADS, E1-E2	85						
SUPPORTIVE READING SKILLS: READING ADS, F1-F4	85						
SUPPORTIVE READING SKILLS: READING HOMOGRAPHS (MULTI COPIES)	88						
SUPPORTIVE READING SKILLS: READING HOMOGRAPHS, A	88						
SUPPORTIVE READING SKILLS: READING HOMOGRAPHS, ADV. 1-ADV. 2	88						
SUPPORTIVE READING SKILLS: READING HOMOGRAPHS, B	88						
SUPPORTIVE READING SKILLS: READING HOMOGRAPHS, C1-C2	88						
SUPPORTIVE READING SKILLS: READING HOMOGRAPHS, D1-D4	88						
SUPPORTIVE READING SKILLS: READING HOMOGRAPHS, E1-E8	88						
SUPPORTIVE READING SKILLS: READING HOMOGRAPHS, F1-F8	88						
SUPPORTIVE READING SKILLS: READING HOMONYMS (MULTI COPIES)	88						
SUPPORTIVE READING SKILLS: READING HOMONYMS, A	88						
SUPPORTIVE READING SKILLS: READING HOMONYMS, ADV. 1-ADV. 13	88						
SUPPORTIVE READING SKILLS: READING HOMONYMS, B1-B2	88						
SUPPORTIVE READING SKILLS: READING HOMONYMS, C1-C2	88						
SUPPORTIVE READING SKILLS: READING HOMONYMS, D1-D8	88						
SUPPORTIVE READING SKILLS: READING HOMONYMS, E1-E8	88						
SUPPORTIVE READING SKILLS: READING HOMONYMS, F1-F8	88						
SUPPORTIVE READING SKILLS: READING SCHEDULES, ADV. 1-ADV. 4	85						
SUPPORTIVE READING SKILLS: READING SCHEDULES, B	85						
SUPPORTIVE READING SKILLS: READING SCHEDULES, C	85						
SUPPORTIVE READING SKILLS: READING SCHEDULES, D	85						
SUPPORTIVE READING SKILLS: READING SCHEDULES, E1-E2	85						
SUPPORTIVE READING SKILLS: READING SCHEDULES, F1-F2	85						
SUPPORTIVE READING SKILLS: RECOGNIZING WORD RELAT.	93						
SUPPORTIVE READING SKILLS: RECOGNIZING WORD RELAT., ADV.	93						

TITLE	SKILL NUMBERS						
SUPPORTIVE READING SKILLS: RECOGNIZING WORD RELAT., BASIC	93						
SUPPORTIVE READING SKILLS: RECOGNIZING WORD RELAT., INTER.	93						
SUPPORTIVE READING SKILLS: RHYME TIME (MULTI COPIES)	51						
SUPPORTIVE READING SKILLS: RHYME TIME, A1-A4	51						
SUPPORTIVE READING SKILLS: RHYME TIME, B	51						
SUPPORTIVE READING SKILLS: SYLLABICATION (MULTI COPIES)	82						
SUPPORTIVE READING SKILLS: SYLLABICATION, ADV. 1-ADV. 3	82						
SUPPORTIVE READING SKILLS: SYLLABICATION, B1-B2	82						
SUPPORTIVE READING SKILLS: SYLLABICATION, C1-C3	82						
SUPPORTIVE READING SKILLS: SYLLABICATION, D1-D3	82						
SUPPORTIVE READING SKILLS: SYLLABICATION, E1-E3	82						
SUPPORTIVE READING SKILLS: SYLLABICATION, F1-F3	82						
SUPPORTIVE READING SKILLS: UNDERSTANDING WORD GROUPS	93						
SUPPORTIVE READING SKILLS: UNDERSTANDING WORD GROUPS, A	93						
SUPPORTIVE READING SKILLS: UNDERSTANDING WORD GROUPS, ADV.	93						
SUPPORTIVE READING SKILLS: UNDERSTANDING WORD GROUPS, B	93						
SUPPORTIVE READING SKILLS: UNDERSTANDING WORD GROUPS, C	93						
SUPPORTIVE READING SKILLS: UNDERSTANDING WORD GROUPS, D	93						
SUPPORTIVE READING SKILLS: UNDERSTANDING WORD GROUPS, E	93						
SUPPORTIVE READING SKILLS: UNDERSTANDING WORD GROUPS, F	93						
SURVIVAL READING SKILLS	84						
SURVIVAL READING TASK CARDS	85						
SURVIVAL SIGNS	85						
SURVIVAL SIGNS	85						
SWEET PICKLES PHONICS PROGRAM	57	58	53	59			
SWEET PICKLES READING READINESS PROGRAM	4	84	49				
SYLLABLE FUN	82						
SYLLABLE PUZZLES	82						
SYLLABLE RULE & ACCENT CLUE	82						
SYLLABLE RULES & ACCENT CLUE	82						
SYLLABLE SAFARI	82						
SYLLABLE SCORE BOARD	82						
SYLLABLE SCRAMBLE	82						
SYLLABLES	82						
SYLLABLES	82						
SYLLABLES	82						
SYLLABLES	82						
SYLLABLES	82						
SYLLABLES & WORDS, WORKTAPES	82						
SYLLABLES, DIVIDE & CONQUER	82						
SYMBOL DISCRIMINATION & SEQUENCING	9	25					
SYMBOL DISCRIMINATION SERIES, BOOK I	9						
SYMBOL DISCRIMINATION SERIES, BOOK II	9						
SYMBOL DISCRIMINATION SERIES, BOOK III	9						
SYMBOL DISCRIMINATION SERIES, BOOK IV	9						
SYMBOL DISCRIMINATION SERIES, BOOK V	9						
SYMBOL DISCRIMINATION SERIES, BOOK VI	9						
SYMMETRICAL MATCH-UP	9	13	14				
SYMPTOMATIC VOICE THERAPY	5						
SYNONYM POSTER CARDS	86						
SYNONYM PUZZLES	86						
SYNONYMS/ANTONYMS PACER	86	87					
SYNTAX CODES ARE, ARE VERBING	72	6	74				
SYNTAX CODES IRREGULAR PAST TENSE VERBS, I	72	6	74				
SYNTAX CODES IRREGULAR PAST TENSE VERBS, II	72	6	74				
SYNTAX CODES IRREGULAR PAST TENSE VERBS, III	72	6	74				
SYNTAX CODES IRREGULAR PAST TENSE VERBS, IV	72	6	74				
SYNTAX CODES IS, IS VERBING	72	6	74				
SYNTAX CODES REGULAR PAST TENSE VERBS	72	6	74				
SYNTAX CODES SINGULAR NOUN PRESENT TENSE VERB	72	71	6	74			
SYNTAX GAME	74						
SYNTAX ONE	6						
SYNTAX TWO	6	35					
SYSTEMATIC SENTENCE BUILDER, LEVEL ONE	6	74	72				
SYSTEMATIC SENTENCE BUILDER, LEVEL THREE	6	74	71	72			
SYSTEMATIC SENTENCE BUILDER, LEVEL TWO	6	74	71	72	73		
SYSTEMATIC SPELLING	64	77	80	81	79		
TABLET GAMES: BEGINNING CONSONANTS	52						
TABLET GAMES: LONG VOWELS	58						
TABLET GAMES: SHORT VOWELS	57						
TAC-MATES PROGRAMS: SEEING & WRITING WORDS	24	13	19				
TAKE	77	75	48				
TAKE A WALK IN FALL	23						
TAKE A WALK IN SPRING	23						
TAKE A WALK IN SUMMER	23						
TAKE A WALK IN WINTER	23						
TAKE YOUR PICK	88	89					
TALES FOR TRANSFER SKILL SERIES	53	59	60				
TALK & TURN	5	7					
TALK ABOUT IT	48	75	4				
TALK ABOUT IT SERIES	83	7					
TALK TALK TALK	10	73	40				
TALKING PICTURE DICTIONARY	48	75	83				
TARGET 180, GRADES 1 - 2	65	66	68	69			
TARGET 360, GRADES 2 - 3	65	66	68	69			
TARGET 540, GRADES 3 - 4	65	66	68	69			
TARGET BLUE: STRUCTURAL ANALYSIS KIT	75						
TARGET GREEN: VOCABULARY DEVELOPMENT KIT I	76	81	86	87	88	80	
TARGET MECHANICS KIT: CAPITALIZATION & PUNCTUATION	71	73					
TARGET MECHANICS KIT: GUIDES FOR STANDARD ENGLISH	70	72	74				
TARGET ORANGE: VOCABULARY DEVELOPMENT KIT II	80	81	86	87	88		
TARGET RED: AUDITORY-VISUAL DISCRIMINATION KIT	34						
TARGET YELLOW: PHONIC ANALYSIS KIT	48						

TITLE	SKILL NUMBERS						
TASK CARDS: KINDERGARTEN VISUAL PERCEPTION	8						
TASK CARDS: PRIMARY LANGUAGE ARTS	48	83					
TEACHING A CHILD TO IMITATE	3	4	5				
TEACHING MORPHOLOGY DEVELOPMENTALLY	2						
TEACHING OF /R/ BY A SEQUENCED METHOD	5						
TEACHING READING THROUGH CREATIVE MOVEMENT	29	36	38				
TEACHING SPEECH TO A NONVERBAL CHILD	3	4	5				
TEACHING VERB TENSE THROUGH CREATIVE CALENDAR ACTIVITIES	72						
TEAM CHECKERS: LONG VOWELS	58						
TEAM CHECKERS: SHORT VOWELS	57						
TEDDY BEAR BINGO	13	37	15	3			
TELEPHONE TALK	7						
TELL & DRAW PAPER BAG PUPPET BOOK 1	35						
TELL & DRAW PAPER BAG PUPPET BOOK 2	35						
TELL & DRAW STORIES	34	10	42	40			
TELL AGAIN NURSERY RHYMES CARDS	23	51	2				
TELL-A-STORY CARDS	7	45					
TELL-A-TALE CARDS, SET 1	4						
TELL-A-TALE CARDS, SET 2	4						
THE COMMUNICATION SCREEN	5	2					
THERAPY FOR STUTTERS	5						
THINK AWHILE STORY CARDS	46	7					
THINK PATTERNS, BLENDS TASK CARDS	53						
THINK PATTERNS, CONSONANTS & BLENDS	53						
THINK PATTERNS, VOWELS	56						
THINK PATTERNS, VOWELS TASK CARDS	56						
THINKER PUZZLES, SET 1	17	49					
THINKER PUZZLES, SET 2	17	49					
THINKER PUZZLES, SET 3	17	49					
THINKER PUZZLES, SET 4	14	93					
THINKER PUZZLES, SET 5	14	93					
THINKER PUZZLES, SET 6	14						
THINKERTHINGS: A STUDENT GENERATED APPROACH TO LANGUAGE EXP.	49	74					
THINKING SKILLS	41	42	47	46			
THIRD BOX OF COLORS	10	15					
THIRD CONSONANT BOOK	53	55					
THIRD GRADE LANGUAGE DRILLS	88	72					
THIS IS THE WAY I GO	83						
THIS IS YOUR YEAR	2						
THREE LANGUAGE GAMES	35	37	35				
THREE-DIMENSIONAL SHAPES	12	17					
THREE-LETTER CONSONANT BLENDS	53						
TICK TOCK TIME & OTHER STORIES	54	57					
TIGER CUB READERS	48						
TIME FOR PHONICS, BOOK A	48	35	1				
TIME FOR PHONICS, BOOK A, T.E.	48	35	1				
TIME FOR PHONICS, BOOK B	48	35	1				
TIME FOR PHONICS, BOOK B, T.E.	48	35	1				
TIME FOR PHONICS, BOOK C	48	35	1				
TIME FOR PHONICS, BOOK C, T.E.	48	35	1				
TIME FOR PHONICS, BOOK R	48	35	1				
TIME FOR PHONICS, BOOK R, T.E.	48	35	1				
TIME FOR SOUNDS, KIT B: INITIAL BLENDS & DIGRAPHS	53						
TIME SKILLS: VOCABULARY CONCEPTS	93						
TIME TO RHYME	51						
TIME TO RHYME	51						
TIME TO RHYME	51						
TIME TO RHYME WITH CALICO CAT	51						
TO THE STUTTER	5						
TOK-BACH	5	26					
TOK-BACK	5						
TONGUE POSITION CHARTS	5						
TONGUE THRUST THERAPY	5						
TOTAL BUILDING READING SKILLS (KITS 1 - 5)	48	75					
TOTAL BUILDING WORK POWER (KITS 58 - 61)	86	87	92	90	79	80	81
TOTAL SPELLING (KITS 17 - 21)	64						
TOUCH TYPE, SET 2: COMMON SIGNS	85						
TOY CHEST OF BEGINNING SOUNDS	27						
TR LARGE PICTURE CARDS, SET 1	2	83	47	74			
TR LARGE PICTURE CARDS, SET 2	2	83	47	74			
TRACE-A-LETTER: MATCH-A-SOUND	50						
TRACE-A-LETTER: SAY-A-SOUND	50						
TRANSFORMATIONS	74	73	72				
TRANSITION BOOK: I CAN & NOW I CAN READ	50	51					
TRANSPORTATION PUZZLE	23	83					
TRAVELING WITH THE ALPHABET	49						
TRAY PUZZLES: GRAMMAR	88	86	87				
TRAY PUZZLES: PHONICS	57	58	53				
TREASURE SPELL	64						
TRIAD	80	81	76				
TRICKY SIGHT WORDS	84						
TROLL JAM SESSIONS: COUNTRY	75	84	85				
TROLL JAM SESSIONS: FOLK	75	84	85				
TROLL JAM SESSIONS: JAZZ	75	84	85				
TROLL JAM SESSIONS: ROCK	75	84	85				
TROLL READ-ALONG: I CAN READ ABOUT HOMONYMS	88						
TROLL READ-ALONG: I CAN READ ABOUT SYNONYMS & ANTONYMS	86	87					
TROUBLESHOOTER I	48	65	66	75	84	74	
TROUBLESHOOTER I: BOOK 5, WORD MASTERY	84	92					
TROUBLESHOOTER I: BOOK 6, SENTENCE STRENGTH	74						
TROUBLESHOOTER II: BOOK 2, VOCABULARY	83						
TROUBLESHOOTER II: BOOK 3, SPELLING & PARTS OF SPEECH	64	70					
TRY: EXPERIENCES FOR YOUNG CHILDREN	25	49					

TITLE	SKILL NUMBERS						
TURTLE PUPPET	7	25					
TUTORGRAM: ALPHABET RECOGNITION & SEQUENCING	23	49					
TUTORGRAM: ANTONYMS	87						
TUTORGRAM: BASIC WORD RECOGNITION	13	84					
TUTORGRAM: BODY PARTS & EVERYDAY THINGS	19						
TUTORGRAM: COMMON NOUNS	14	71					
TUTORGRAM: COMMON TERMS	84	85					
TUTORGRAM: CONCEPTUAL DISCRIMINATION	9	42	43				
TUTORGRAM: CONTRACTIONS	78						
TUTORGRAM: HOMONYMS	88						
TUTORGRAM: LANGUAGE ARTS READINESS	14	13					
TUTORGRAM: LANGUAGE ARTS READINESS	13	15	17				
TUTORGRAM: MATCHING	14						
TUTORGRAM: MATCHING UPPER & LOWER CASE LETTERS	14	35					
TUTORGRAM: MATCHING VOWEL SOUNDS	57	58					
TUTORGRAM: MORE BASIC WORDS	13	84					
TUTORGRAM: NOUNS, VERBS, ADJECTIVES, ADVERBS	71	72	73				
TUTORGRAM: PAST TENSE IRREGULAR VERBS	72						
TUTORGRAM: PAST TENSE VERBS	72						
TUTORGRAM: PREFIX MEANINGS, INTERMEDIATE LEVEL	80						
TUTORGRAM: PRIMARY SUFFIXES	81						
TUTORGRAM: PRONOUN REFERENCE	71						
TUTORGRAM: PUZZLES I	10	11	12				
TUTORGRAM: RHYMING	51						
TUTORGRAM: RHYMING ELEMENTS	51						
TUTORGRAM: SIMILARITIES & DIFFERENCES	9						
TUTORGRAM: SYLLABICATION	82						
TUTORGRAM: SYNONYMS I	86						
TUTORGRAM: VOWELS	57	58					
TUTORGRAM: WORD COMPLETION I	84	13					
TUTORGRAM: WORD COMPLETION II	84	13					
TWO PART MATCH-UPS: ANIMAL, VEGETABLE, MINERAL	9						
TWO WORDS IN ONE	88	89					
TWOS COMPANY	53						
UN "FAMILIAR" FABLES FOR /S/ CARRYOVER	5						
UNDERSTANDING CONSONANTS	50						
UNDERSTANDING CONSONANTS	50						
UNDERSTANDING SENTENCE	74						
UNDERSTANDING THE SENTENCE	74	70					
UNDERSTANDING WHAT WE READ, LEVEL A	36	4	5	6	7		
UNIVERSAL ARTICULATION PROGRAM	5						
USAGE SLEUTH	70						
USE YOUR SENSES	4	47					
USING CONSONANT BLENDS	53						
USING CONSONANT BLENDS	53						
USING GOOD ENGLISH	74	6					
USING LETTERS	74	9					
USING PHONICS	49	52	57	55	82	75	83
USING PHONICS	49	50	52	55			
USING PHONICS SERIES	57	58	53	59	61	54	
USING PREFIXES & SUFFIXES	80	81					
USING PREFIXES & SUFFIXES	80	81					
USING PRONOUNS	71						
USING STRUCTURAL ANALYSIS SERIES	79	77	78	76	80	81	82
USING VERB TENSES	72						
USING VOWEL DIGRAPHS	59						
USING VOWEL DIGRAPHS	59						
USING VOWEL DIPHTHONGS	60						
USING VOWEL DIPHTHONGS	59						
USING WORDS SERIES	86	88	89	87	90		
V2 VOWELS & VALUES, SET 1: SHORT VOWEL WORDS	57						
V2 VOWELS & VALUES, SET 2: LONG VOWEL WORDS	58						
VARI-SHAPE BEADS	25	12	17				
VARIANT VOWEL SOUNDS, GRADES 2 & 3	57	58					
VARIANTS AND SILENT LETTERS	55						
VARIED CAREER PEOPLE	94						
VEE'S VERBS	72						
VEGETABLES & FRUITS POSTER CARDS	13	84	85	4			
VENTURE IN VOWELS	59	60					
VERB PUZZLE	72						
VERB TENSE BOARDS	72						
VERB USAGE	72						
VERBAL ABILITIES	7						
VERBS	72						
VERBS - VERBS - VERBS	72						
VERBS, MUSCLES IN ACTION	72						
VERBS: PAST, PRESENT, FUTURE	72						
VERSA-TILES	8	14					
VERSA-TILES, BEGINNING READING SET	9	24					
VERSA-TILES, EARLY CHILDHOOD SET	9	13	14				
VERSA-TILES, LANGUAGE ARTS & GRAMMAR SETS	70						
VERSA-TILES, LANGUAGE ARTS COMPETENCY KIT	83						
VERSA-TILES, LANGUAGE ARTS LAB 1	83	48					
VERSA-TILES, LANGUAGE ARTS LAB 2	83	48					
VERSA-TILES, LANGUAGE ARTS LAB 3	83	48					
VERSA-TILES, VOCABULARY SET	92	93					
VERSATILES	80						
VERY IMPORTANT PEOPLE SERIES	94						
VIEW ON VOWELS	57	58	59	60			
VIEW ON VOWELS, WORKTAPES	57	58	59	60			
VIP ADJECTIVES	73	6					
VIP NOUNS, BOX 1	71	6					
VIP VERBS, BOX 1	72	6					

TITLE	SKILL NUMBERS						
VISUAL AURAL DISCRIMINATIONS, BOOK I	10	53					
VISUAL AURAL DISCRIMINATIONS, BOOK II	53						
VISUAL AURAL DISCRIMINATIONS, BOOK III	53						
VISUAL AURAL DISCRIMINATIONS, BOOK IV	60						
VISUAL AURAL DISCRIMINATIONS, BOOK V	53	55					
VISUAL CLOSURE & DISCRIMINATION PUZZLE KIT	22	14	9				
VISUAL CLOSURE CARDS	22						
VISUAL DISCRIMINATIN LEARNING- SEQUENCING M	23						
VISUAL DISCRIMINATION	9	11	12	13			
VISUAL DISCRIMINATION	9	49					
VISUAL DISCRIMINATION	10	11	12	21			
VISUAL DISCRIMINATION	9						
VISUAL DISCRIMINATION BOARDS	9						
VISUAL DISCRIMINATION GAMES	9	49	24				
VISUAL DISCRIMINATION LEARNING- MATCHING CAPITALS	14	49					
VISUAL DISCRIMINATION LEARNING- MATCHING LETTERS N	14	9					
VISUAL DISCRIMINATION LEARNING-BEG. LETTER WORDS	14	48					
VISUAL DISCRIMINATION, BOOK 1: PICTURES	12						
VISUAL DISCRIMINATION, BOOK 2: SHAPES	12						
VISUAL DISCRIMINATION, BOOK 3: LINES & SHAPES	12						
VISUAL MATCHING, MEMORY & SEQUENCING EXERCISES	15	23	24				
VISUAL MEMORY CARDS, SET I, COLORS	24	23					
VISUAL MEMORY CARDS, SET II, OBJECTS	24	23					
VISUAL MEMORY CARDS, SET III, SHAPES	24	23					
VISUAL MEMORY CARDS, SET IV, LETTERS	24	23					
VISUAL MOTOR & CLOSURE DUPLICATING KIT	30	28	29				
VISUAL PERCEPTION	10	11	12	15	16	17	
VISUAL PERCEPTION CARDS	12	13	17				
VISUAL, MATCHING, MEMORY & SEQUENCING, BOOKS 4, 5, 6	15	23	24				
VISUAL, MATHING, MEMORY & SEQUENCING, BOOKS 1, 2, 3	15	23	24				
VITAL WORDS	85						
VOCAB-TRACKS	13						
VOCABULAB 3 KIT	83						
VOCABULARY	83	92					
VOCABULARY	83						
VOCABULARY BINGO	83						
VOCABULARY BOOSTERS	83						
VOCABULARY BOX, INTERMEDIATE	83						
VOCABULARY BOX, PRIMARY	83						
VOCABULARY BUILDERS	83	86	87	88	92		
VOCABULARY BUILDERS	83						
VOCABULARY BUILDING	83						
VOCABULARY BUILDING EXERCISES FOR YOUNG ADULTS, BOOK A	83	84	85	82	70		
VOCABULARY BUILDING EXERCISES FOR YOUNG ADULTS, BOOK B	83	85	82	70	84		
VOCABULARY BUILDING EXERCISES FOR YOUNG ADULTS, BOOK C	83	85	82	70	84		
VOCABULARY BUILDING, INTERMEDIATE	16	71	72	73			
VOCABULARY BUILDING, LEVEL III	84	85	86				
VOCABULARY BUILDING, LEVEL IV	84	85	86				
VOCABULARY BUILDING, UPPER INTERMEDIATE	92	71	72	73			
VOCABULARY DEVELOPMENT	93	92					
VOCABULARY DEVELOPMENT	78	77	81	86	87	88	84
VOCABULARY DEVELOPMENT: WORDS, WORDS, WORDS	84	85					
VOCABULARY MAGIC	88	84	85				
VOCABULARY MASTERY	84	85					
VOCABULARY QUIZMO	83	86	87	90	92	93	
VOCABULARY SCAVENGER HUNTS	83	84					
VOCABULARY SKILLS (R.L. 5.1 - 5.3)	83						
VOCABULARY SKILLS 1	92	86	87				
VOCABULARY SKILLS 2	92	88	93				
VOCABULARY SKILLS A	92	93	88				
VOCABULARY SKILLS B	86	87	88				
VOCABULARY SKILLS PROGRAM	85	64					
VOCABULARY STUDY	86	90	76	77	88	92	
VOCABULARY, ADVANCED	84	85					
VOCABULARY, BOOK A (GRADE 2)	84						
VOCABULARY, BOOK B (GRADE 3)	84						
VOCABULARY, BOOK C (GRADE 4)	84						
VOCABULARY, INTERMEDIATE	84	85					
VOCABULARY-SKILL DRILLS WITH MOTIVATORS	83						
VOICE DISORDERS	5						
VOICE, VOCABULARY DELIVERY	4	5	6	7			
VOWEL BEES	57	58	84				
VOWEL BINGO	56	57	58				
VOWEL BINGO	57	58					
VOWEL CLUSTER FUN	59	60	61				
VOWEL COMBINATIONS	59						
VOWEL COMBINATIONS PLAYING CARDS	59	60					
VOWEL COMBINATIONS: CITY SOUNDS	59	60					
VOWEL DIGRAPHS & DIPHTHONGS	59	60					
VOWEL DIGRAPHS & DIPHTHONGS	59	60					
VOWEL DIGRAPHS AND DIPHTHONGS	59	60					
VOWEL ENRICHMENT	56	57	58				
VOWEL FLIPSTRIPS	56						
VOWEL HOWL	56						
VOWEL IN THE MIDDLE	57						
VOWEL LOTTO	59	60	56				
VOWEL OWL	56						
VOWEL OWL	56	57	58	60	59		
VOWEL OWL	57	58					
VOWEL PACER	57	58	59	63			
VOWEL PICTURE PACK	56						
VOWEL PICTURES FOR PEGBOARD	57	58	63				
VOWEL POSTER CARDS	42	57	58	59			

TITLE	SKILL NUMBERS						
VOWEL QUARTET	56						
VOWEL SKILL CARDS	56						
VOWEL SOLITAIRE	57	58					
VOWEL SORTING & WORD CARDS	57	58					
VOWEL SOUNDS	57	58	59	60			
VOWEL SOUNDS & SILENT LETTERS	57	58	55	60	62		
VOWEL SOUNDS AUDIO LESSONS	56						
VOWEL SOUNDS KIT	57	58					
VOWEL SOUNDS WORD SLIDES	57	58					
VOWEL SOUNDS/SELF-INSTRUCTIONAL MODALITIES APPROACH	52	57	58				
VOWEL SOUNDS: LONG A	58						
VOWEL SOUNDS: LONG E	58						
VOWEL SOUNDS: LONG I	58						
VOWEL SOUNDS: LONG O	58						
VOWEL SOUNDS: LONG U	58						
VOWEL SOUNDS: R-CONTROLLED VOWELS	61						
VOWEL SOUNDS: SHORT A	57						
VOWEL SOUNDS: SHORT E	57						
VOWEL SOUNDS: SHORT I	57						
VOWEL SOUNDS: SHORT O	57						
VOWEL SOUNDS: SHORT U	57						
VOWEL SOUNDS: VOWEL DIGRAPHS	59						
VOWEL SOUNDS: VOWEL DIPHTHONGS	60						
VOWEL VACATION	56						
VOWEL VACATION	58						
VOWEL WHEELS	57	58					
VOWEL WORKBOOK: SOUND, SPELL, READ	57	58					
VOWELS	56	57	58	61			
VOWELS	56						
VOWELS	57	58					
VOWELS	57	58					
VOWELS & CONSONANTS	52	56					
VOWELS & VARIANTS, BOOK C	57	63	58	61			
VOWELS (IMMEDIATE-SECONDARY)	56	57	58	61			
VOWELS I (GRADE 1)	57	58					
VOWELS II (GRADE 2)	57	58					
VOWELS THAT ARE NEITHER LONG NOR SHORT	62						
VOWELS, B	56						
VOWELS: FLIP & LEARN FLASHBOOK	56						
VOWELS: HOW THEY LOOK & SOUND	57	58					
W L N K J C G V Q Y Z X KIT	4	5	7				
WALK-ON ALPHABET	49	25					
WALKING INTO THE PICTURE	7						
WANTED EARS... FOR RHYMING	51						
WAY TO SPELL LONG VOWEL SOUNDS	58						
WE READ SENTENCES, A1	93	74					
WE READ SENTENCES, A2	93	74					
WE READ SENTENCES, A3	93	74					
WE READ SENTENCES, A4	93	74					
WE READ SENTENCES, A5	93	74					
WEBSTER WORD WHEELS	53	80	81				
WHAT BELONGS WHERE?	42	45					
WHAT CAN YOU DO WITH A PENNY?	33	31	35	29	36	37	
WHAT COMES FIRST? NEXT? LAST?	23						
WHAT DID YOU SAY?	89						
WHAT DO THEY BECOME?	42	45					
WHAT FOLLOWS NEXT? SEQUENCE PICTURE CARDS	23						
WHAT GOES WITH WHAT?	42	45					
WHAT I HEAR	35	35					
WHAT IS BIG? WHAT IS SMALL?	43	8	11	17	13		
WHAT IS IT? SPATIAL RELATIONSHIP CARDS	21						
WHAT SHALL I BE?	94						
WHAT SIZE LOTTO	16						
WHAT TO DO ABOUT BILL?	2	65					
WHAT'S FUNNY CARDS	5						
WHAT'S GOING ON?	4						
WHAT'S GOING THROUGH THE TUNNEL?	42	45					
WHAT'S HAPPENING?	41	4					
WHAT'S IN THE SQUARE?	15	16	17	22			
WHAT'S NEXT?	11	16	18				
WHAT'S PART OF WHAT?	42	45					
WHAT'S THE GOOD WORD?	88	87	77				
WHAT'S THE MEANING OF THIS?	76	80	81				
WHAT'S THE OPPOSITE?	42	45					
WHAT'S THE SOLUTION?	2	3					
WHAT'S THE WORD? GAME	70	74	71	72			
WHAT'S WRONG HERE?, LEVEL 1	4	13	45				
WHAT'S WRONG HERE?, LEVEL 2	4	13	45				
WHAT'S YOUR STORY?	14	9	12	27	51		
WHEN I GROW UP, I WANT TO BE	94						
WHEN R CONTROLS THE VOWEL	61						
WHICH PIECE FITS?	42	45					
WHITE WATER RAFT TRIP	88						
WHO SAID IT?	39	40	29	36	37		
WHO SAID IT?	39	40	29	36	37		
WHO, WHAT, WHEN, WHERE, WHY	2						
WHO, WHAT, WHEN, WHERE, WHY	2						
WHY DON'T PEOPLE SAY WHAT THEY MEAN?	4						
WIDE, WIDE WORLD OF GRAMMAR: BASKETWORD	80	76	70				
WIDE, WIDE WORLD OF GRAMMAR: GOAL WORD SOCCER	81	76	70				
WIDE, WIDE WORLD OF GRAMMAR: GREAT GRAMMATICAL GOLF TOURN.	70	72	73	74			
WINDOWS TO READING, BOOK A	57	52					
WINDOWS TO READING, BOOK B	52						

TITLE	SKILL NUMBERS						
WINDOWS TO READING, BOOK C	52						
WINDOWS TO READING, BOOK D	59	60					
WINKY IN THE LOST & FOUND DEPARTMENT	87						
WINKY'S TWELVE WISHES	84						
WINKY'S WEEK	84						
WIPE-OFF CARDS: BEGINNING SOUNDS	50						
WIPE-OFF CARDS: BEGINNING SOUNDS	52						
WIPE-OFF CARDS: BEGINNING SOUNDS, LEVEL 2	52						
WIPE-OFF CARDS: BLENDS, LEVEL 1	53						
WIPE-OFF CARDS: DRAW WHAT'S MISSING	22						
WIPE-OFF CARDS: FINDING PAIRS	14						
WIPE-OFF CARDS: INITIAL CONSONANTS	52						
WIPE-OFF CARDS: LONG VOWELS	58						
WIPE-OFF CARDS: LONG VOWELS	58						
WIPE-OFF CARDS: RHYMING WORDS	51						
WIPE-OFF CARDS: RHYMING WORDS	51						
WIPE-OFF CARDS: RHYMING WORDS, LEVEL 2	51						
WIPE-OFF CARDS: SHORT VOWELS	57						
WIPE-OFF CARDS: SHORT VOWELS	57						
WIPE-OFF CARDS: WORD PATTERNS, LEVEL 2	65						
WITCH'S BREW	4						
WOG'S LOG BOOK I	57						
WOG'S LOG BOOK II	57						
WOG'S LOG BOOK III	54	57					
WOG'S LOG BOOK IV	53	57					
WOG'S LOG BOOK V	59	60	61	63	78	80	81
WOG'S LOG BOOK VI	59	60	61	63	78	80	81
WOG'S LOG BOOK VII	55	54	59	60	81	62	
WOG'S LOG BOOK VIII	55	54	59	60	81	62	
WOMEN WORKERS	94						
WOODEN LETTERS	49						
WORD ANALYSIS	80	81	82				
WORD ANALYSIS PAK	78	79	76	81	82	86	87
WORD ANALYSIS PAK	78	79	76	81	82	86	87
WORD ANALYSIS SKILLS: WORD FORMS II	77	78	79				
WORD ANALYSIS SKILLS: WORD MEANINGS III	86	87	88	89			
WORD ANALYSIS SKILLS: WORD PARTS I	80	81	82				
WORD ANALYSIS: COMPOUND WORDS & CONTRACTIONS	78	79					
WORD ANALYSIS: COMPOUND WORDS & CONTRACTIONS	78	79					
WORD ANALYSIS: HOMONYMS & HOMOGRAPHS	88						
WORD ANALYSIS: HOMONYMS & HOMOGRAPHS	88						
WORD ANALYSIS: ROOT WORDS	76						
WORD ANALYSIS: ROOT WORDS	76						
WORD ANALYSIS: SUFFIXES & PREFIXES	81	80					
WORD ANALYSIS: SUFFIXES & PREFIXES	81	80					
WORD ANALYSIS: SYLLABICATION	82						
WORD ANALYSIS: SYLLABICATION	82						
WORD ANALYSIS: SYNONYMS & ANTONYMS	87	86					
WORD ANALYSIS: SYNONYMS & ANTONYMS	86	87					
WORD ATTACK JOY	52	57	58	75	48		
WORD ATTACK SKILLS: CONSONANT BLENDS & DIGRAPHS	53						
WORD ATTACK SKILLS: INFLECTIONAL ENDINGS	77						
WORD ATTACK SKILLS: MODIFIED VOWEL SOUNDS	61						
WORD ATTACK SKILLS: READINESS, BOOK 1	48						
WORD ATTACK SKILLS: READINESS, BOOK 2	48						
WORD ATTACK SKILLS: SHORT & LONG VOWEL SOUNDS	57	58					
WORD ATTACK SKILLS: SYLLABICATION & SPELLING PATTERNS, BK.1	82	65					
WORD ATTACK SKILLS: SYLLABICATION & SPELLING PATTERNS, BK.2	82	65					
WORD ATTACK SKILLS: SYNONYMS, ANTONYMS & HOMONYMS	86	87	88				
WORD BOOK	64						
WORD BUILDERS	80	81	77	78	79	92	
WORD BUILDERS	63	82	76				
WORD BUILDERS: LARGE LETTER CARDS	49	92					
WORD BUILDERS: SMALL LETTER CARDS	49	92					
WORD BUILDING	75						
WORD CHALLENGE	84						
WORD CIRCUS	53						
WORD CLUES	48	75	82				
WORD CLUES, BOOK G	84	87					
WORD CLUES, BOOK H	84	86	87	90			
WORD CLUES, BOOK I	84	86	87	90			
WORD CLUES, BOOK J	84	86	87	90			
WORD COMPUTER	76	80	81				
WORD CONCEPT CARDS: WORDS THAT TELL "HOW MUCH"	92						
WORD CONCEPT CARDS: WORDS THAT TELL "HOW"	92						
WORD CONCEPT CARDS: WORDS THAT TELL "WHEN"	92						
WORD CONCEPT CARDS: WORDS THAT TELL "WHERE"	92						
WORD CONFIGURATIONS	14	48					
WORD CONSERVATION GROUPING CARDS	47						
WORD COVER	84						
WORD DEVILS SKILL CARDS	87	88	90	51			
WORD DISCOVERY	92	93					
WORD ELEMENTS B3	75						
WORD ELEMENTS C2	75						
WORD ELEMENTS CA	75						
WORD ENDINGS	77						
WORD ENDINGS	77	80	81	78	76		
WORD FAMILIES	5	56					
WORD FAMILY FABLES	51	93					
WORD FAMILY FUN	51						
WORD FUN	54						
WORD FUNCTION & SENTENCE PATTERNS	93						
WORD GAMES ON GRAMMAR	70						

TITLE	SKILL NUMBERS						
WORD HUNT	83	64					
WORD KALEIDOSCOPE	53						
WORD LISTS	5	13	9				
WORD MAKING CARDS	5						
WORD MASTERY, BOOK A	83	64					
WORD MASTERY, BOOK B	83	64					
WORD MASTERY, BOOK C	83	64					
WORD MATCHING FLIP BOOKS	14	64	83				
WORD MEANING CARDS: ANTONYMS	87						
WORD MEANING CARDS: HOMOGRAPHS	88						
WORD MEANING CARDS: HOMONYMS	88						
WORD MEANING CARDS: SYNONYMS	86						
WORD OPPOSTIES PACER	87						
WORD PARADE	80	81					
WORD PARTS	80	81	75				
WORD PATTERNS	65						
WORD PERCEPTION	14	13	52	57	58		
WORD PICTURE DOMINOES, PHONICS	48						
WORD PICTURE DOMINOES, SIGHT WORDS	84						
WORD POWER PACER	74	75	83				
WORD POWER SKILL CARDS	83	86	64				
WORD PROBE SKILL CARDS	76	80	81	82			
WORD PUZZLES, GRADE 1	64						
WORD PUZZLES, GRADE 2	64						
WORD PUZZLES, GRADE 3	64						
WORD PUZZLES, GRADE 4	64						
WORD PUZZLES, GRADE 5	64						
WORD PUZZLES, GRADE 6	64						
WORD RECOGNITION	84						
WORD RECOGNITION	84	24	48	75			
WORD RECOGNITION & SPELLING DEFA-35MM TACH-X	75	92	64				
WORD RECOGNITION & SPELLING DEFA-COMBO-8	75	92	64				
WORD RECOGNITION ACTIVITIES	84						
WORD RELATIONSHIPS	93						
WORD RELATIONSHIPS: CUT & PASTE	93	83	9				
WORD SIGNALS	71	81	72	73			
WORD SKILLS: GOING PLACES, BOOK V	74						
WORD SKILLS: LIVING WITH WORDS, BOOK II	85	71	72	73			
WORD SKILLS: LOOKING INTO THE FUTURE, BOOK IV	72	73					
WORD SKILLS: THE POWER OF WORDS, BOOK I	85	70					
WORD SKILLS: THE TIME OF YOUR LIFE, BOOK III	72	73					
WORD SKILLS: TIME ON YOUR HANDS, BOOK VI	72	71	73				
WORD SPEEDWAY	92						
WORD SPY, GRADE 1	13	51	79	51			
WORD SPY, GRADE 2	51	87	86	88			
WORD SPY, GRADE 3	51	88					
WORD SPY, GRADE 4	51	87	86	88			
WORD SPY, GRADE 5	76	87	86	88	47		
WORD STUDIES	4	5	67	7			
WORD TREK, BLENDS & DIGRAPHS	53	77					
WORD WIZARDS, BOOK 1	88	79	78	92			
WORD WIZARDS, BOOK 2	88	79	78	92			
WORD WIZARDS, BOOK 3	88	79	78	92			
WORDFACTS GAMES	55	77	82	70	83		
WORDPLAY	88	89	51	86	87		
WORDS	70	83	64				
WORDS	5	85	70	83	64		
WORDS & SOUND SERIES, SET 1	52	57	58	75	83		
WORDS & SOUND SERIES, SET 2	52	57	58	75	83		
WORDS & SOUND SERIES, SET 3	52	57	58	80	83		
WORDS & SOUND SERIES, SET 4	52	57	58	75	83		
WORDS ARE FUN	71	72	73				
WORDS ARE IMPORTANT: BLUE LEVEL 5	75	83					
WORDS ARE IMPORTANT: BLUE LEVEL 5, KEY	75	83					
WORDS ARE IMPORTANT: BROWN LEVEL 10	75	83					
WORDS ARE IMPORTANT: BROWN LEVEL 10, KEY	75	83					
WORDS ARE IMPORTANT: GRAY LEVEL 12	75	83					
WORDS ARE IMPORTANT: GRAY LEVEL 12, KEY	75	83					
WORDS ARE IMPORTANT: GREEN LEVEL 7	75	83					
WORDS ARE IMPORTANT: GREEN LEVEL 7, KEY	75	83					
WORDS ARE IMPORTANT: ORANGE LEVEL 8	75	83					
WORDS ARE IMPORTANT: ORANGE LEVEL 8, KEY	75	83					
WORDS ARE IMPORTANT: PINK LEVEL 11	75	83					
WORDS ARE IMPORTANT: PINK LEVEL 11, KEY	75	83					
WORDS ARE IMPORTANT: PURPLE LEVEL 9	75	83					
WORDS ARE IMPORTANT: PURPLE LEVEL 9, KEY	75	83					
WORDS ARE IMPORTANT: RED LEVEL 6	75	83					
WORDS ARE IMPORTANT: RED LEVEL 6, KEY	75	83					
WORDS ARE IMPORTANT: TAN LEVEL 4	75	83					
WORDS ARE IMPORTANT: TAN LEVEL 4, KEY	75	83					
WORDS AROUND THE HOUSE	84	93	92				
WORDS AROUND THE NEIGHBORHOOD	84	93	92				
WORDS FOR WRITING	84						
WORDS IN CONTEXT, SET 1	83						
WORDS IN CONTEXT, SET 2	83						
WORDS IN CONTEXT, SET 3	83						
WORDS IN MOTION, KIT A	48	75	83				
WORDS IN MOTION, KIT B	48	75	83				
WORDS IN MOTION, KIT C	48	83					
WORDS THAT DESCRIBE	73						
WORDS THAT MEAN MORE THAN ONE	77						
WORDS THAT NAME	71						
WORDS THAT SHOW OWNERSHIP	70						

TITLE	SKILL NUMBERS						
WORDS THAT TELL ACTION	72						
WORDS TO EAT	84	93	92				
WORDS TO GROW ON	84						
WORDS TO MEET	84	93	92				
WORDS TO WEAR	84	93	92				
WORDS TO WORK WITH I	84	92	93				
WORDS TO WORK WITH II	84	92	93				
WORDS TO WORK WITH III	84	92	93				
WORDS WE NEED	84						
WORDS WE USE, BOOK I (RL K-3)	48	75	92				
WORDS WE USE, BOOK II (RL 1-3)	48	75	92				
WORDS WE USE, BOOK III (RL 1-3)	48	75	92				
WORDS WE USE, BOOK IV (RL 1-3)	48	75	92				
WORDS WE USE, BOOK V (RL 1-3)	48	75	92				
WORDS WE USE, BOOK VI (RL 4-6)	48	75	92				
WORDS WE USE, BOOK VII (RL 4-6)	48	75	92				
WORDS WE USE, BOOK VIII (RL 4-6)	48	75	92				
WORDS! WORDS! WORDS!	84	71	72	73			
WORDS, FROM PRINT TO MEANING	48	84	92				
WORDSEARCH VOCABULARY BUILDERS, GRADE 2	83						
WORDSEARCH VOCABULARY BUILDERS, GRADE 3	83						
WORDSEARCH VOCABULARY BUILDERS, GRADE 4	83						
WORDSEARCH VOCABULARY BUILDERS, GRADE 5	83						
WORDSEARCH VOCABULARY BUILDERS, GRADE 6	83						
WORDSEARCH VOCABULARY BUILDERS, GRADE 7	83						
WORDSEARCH VOCABULARY BUILDERS, GRADE 8	83						
WORDWORLD	2	4	6	7			
WORKBOOK M1	57						
WORKBOOK M2	58	63					
WORKERS	94						
WORKING WITH CONSONANTS	52						
WORKING WITH PHONICS	48	52	53	57	58		
WORKING WITH VOWELS	58	57	60	59			
WORKING WITH WORDS	79	80	82	81	87	86	
WORKING WITH WORDS, BOOK G	82	74	90	92			
WORKING WTH BLENDS & DIGRAPHS	53	48					
WORKSHOPS FOR PARENTS & TEACHERS	2						
WORLD OF WORK	35	94					
WRITE-ON WORKSHEETS AA	4	65					
WRITE-ON WORKSHEETS BA	4	65					
WRITE-ON WORKSHEETS CA	4	65					
WRITING SKILLS WORKSHOPS II	74						
WRITING SKILLS WORKSHOPS III	74						
WRITTEN LANGUAGE CARDS, CAREERS	94						
WRITTEN LANGUAGE CARDS, GENERAL	4	25					
YOU DANCE LIKE AN OSTRICH	90						
YOUR OWN LOAD OF WORDS	92						

APPENDIX B --

List of Publishers

PUBLISHER	ADDRESS	CITY	ST	ZIP
ABT PUBLICATIONS	55 WHEELER STREET	CAMBRIDGE	MA	02138
ACADEMIC THERAPY PUBLICATIONS	28 COMMERCIAL BOULEVARD	NOVATO	CA	94947
ACADIA PRESS, INC.	438 ALDER STREET	SCRANTON	PA	18501
ACTIVITY RESOURCES COMPANY, INC.	P.O. BOX 4875	HAYWARD	CA	94545
ADDISON-WESLEY PUBLISHING CO.	2725 SAND HILL ROAD	MENLO PARK	CA	94025
AERO PUBLISHERS, INC.	329 WEST AVIATION ROAD	FALLBROOK	CA	92028
AEVAC, INC.	1500 PARK AVENUE	SOUTH PLAINFIELD	NJ	07080
ALLIED EDUCATION COUNCIL	P.O. BOX 78	GALIEN	MI	49113
ALLYN AND BACON, INC.	470 ATLANTIC AVENUE	BOSTON	MA	02210
AMERICAN BOOK COMPANY	7625 EMPIRE DRIVE	FLORENCE	KY	41042
AMERICAN GUIDANCE SERVICE, INC.	PUBLISHERS' BUILDING	CIRCLE PINES	MN	55014
AMSCO SCHOOL PUBLICATIONS, INC.	315 HUDSON STREET	NEW YORK	NY	10013
ANN ARBOR PUBLISHERS	P.O. BOX 7249	NAPLES	FL	33940
ARISTA CORPORATION	2440 ESTRAND WAY, P.O. BOX 6146	CONCORD	CA	94524
ASSOCIATED EDUCATIONAL MATERIALS	P.O. BOX 28167	RALEIGH	NC	27611
AUDIOTRONICS CORPORATION	P.O. BOX 3997	NORTH HOLLYWOOD	CA	91609
AV CONCEPTS CORPORATION	30 MONTAUK BOULEVARD	OAKDALE	NY	11769
B. L. WINCH & ASSOCIATES	P.O. BOX 1185	TORRANCE	CA	90505
BARNELL LOFT, LTD.	958 CHURCH STREET	BALDWIN	NY	11510
BARR FILMS	P.O. BOX 5667	PASADENA	CA	91107
BARRON'S EDUCATIONAL SERIES,INC.	113 CROSSWAYS PARK DRIVE	WOODBURY	NY	11797
BEHAVIORAL RESEARCH LABORATORIES	P.O. BOX 577	PALO ALTO	CA	94302
BEMISS-JASON CORPORATION	P.O. BOX 11486-STATION A	PALO ALTO	CA	94306
BENEFIC PRESS	1900 N. NARRAGANSETT	CHICAGO	IL	60639
BFA EDUCATIONAL MEDIA	P.O. BOX 1795	SANTA MONICA	CA	90406
BOOK-LAB, INC.	1449 37TH STREET	BROOKLYN	NY	11218
BORG-WARNER EDUCATIONAL SYSTEMS	600 W. UNIVERSITY DRIVE	ARLINGTON HEIGHTS	IL	60004
BOWMAR/NOBLE PUBLISHERS, INC.	4563 COLORADO BOULEVARD	LOS ANGELES	CA	90039
BRADBURY PRESS, INC.	2 OVERHILL DRIVE	SCARSDALE	NY	10583
BURGESS PUBLISHING CO.	7108 OHMS LANE	MINNEAPOLIS	MN	55435
C.C. PUBLICATIONS, INC.	P.O. BOX 23699	TIGARD	OR	97223
CADACO	310 WEST POLK STREET	CHICAGO	IL	60607
CAMBRIDGE BOOK CO.	888 7TH AVENUE	NEW YORK	NY	10019
CENTER FOR EARLY LEARNING	PRIMROSE LANE	LACONIA	NH	03246
CHANNING L. BETE COMPANY, INC.	45 FEDERAL STREET	GREENFIELD	MA	01301
CHARLES E. MERRILL PUBLISHING CO	1300 ALUM CREEK DRIVE	COLUMBUS	OH	43216
CHILD FOCUS COMPANY	1230 KEATS STREET	MANHATTAN BEACH	CA	90266
CHILD'S WORLD	P.O. BOX 681	ELGIN	IL	60120
CHILDCRAFT EDUCATION CORPORATION	20 KILMER ROAD	EDISON	NJ	08817
CHILDREN'S BOOK & MUSIC CENTER	5373 WEST PICO BOULEVARD	LOS ANGELES	CA	90019
CHILDREN'S LEARNING CENTER, INC.	4660 E. 62ND STREET	INDIANAPOLIS	IN	46220
CHILDREN'S PRESS, INC.	1224 W. VAN BUREN STREET	CHICAGO	IL	60607
CHRONICLE GUIDANCE PUBLICATIONS		MORAVIA	NY	13118
CLASSROOM MATERIALS CO.	93 MYRTLE DRIVE	GREAT NECK	NY	11021
CLEARVUE, INC.	6666 N. OLIPHANT AVENUE	CHICAGO	IL	60631
COLORCO	P.O. BOX 1000	GARLAND	TX	75040
COMENIUS, INC.		WESTON	CT	06883
COMMUNICATION SKILL BUILDERS,INC	3130 N. DODGE BOULEVARD	TUCSON	AZ	85733
COMMUNITY PLAYTHINGS		RIFTON	NY	12471
CONCEPT RECORDS	P.O. BOX 171	CENTERS CONWAY	NH	03813
CONSTRUCTIVE PLAYTHINGS	1040 E. 85TH STREET	KANSAS CITY	MO	64108
CONTINENTAL PRESS, INC.	520 E. BAINBRIDGE STREET	ELIZABETHTOWN	PA	17022
CORONET MULTI MEDIA	65 SOUTH WATER STREET EAST	CHICAGO	IL	60601
COUNCIL FOR EXCEPTIONAL CHILDREN	1920 ASSOCIATION DRIVE	RESTON	VA	22091
CREATIVE STORYTIME PRESS	P.O. BOX 572	MINNEAPOLIS	MN	55440
CREATIVE TEACHING ASSOCIATES	P.O. BOX 7766	FRESNO	CA	93727
CREATIVE TEACHING PRESS, INC.	514 HERMOSA VISTA AVENUE	MONTEREY PARK	CA	91754
DELL PUBLISHING COMPANY, INC.	750 THIRD AVENUE	NEW YORK	NY	10017
DELTA EDUCATION, INC.	P.O. BOX M	NASHUA	NH	03061
DEVELOPMENTAL LEARNING MATERIALS	7440 NATCHEZ AVENUE	NILES	IL	60648
DICK BLICK COMPANY	BOX 1267	GALESBURGH	IL	61401
DISCOVERY LEARNING	P.O. BOX 3987	BELLEVUE	WA	98009
DIVERSIFIED PRODUCTION RESOURCES	NORTHWEST BOULEVARD	NEWFIELD	NJ	08344
DM EDUCATIONAL PUBLICATIONS	5502 EAST CALLE DEL PAISANO	PHOENIX	AZ	85018
DORMAC, INC.	P.O. BOX 752	BEAVERTON	OR	97005
DOVER PUBLICATIONS	180 VARICK STREET	NEW YORK	NY	10014
E-Z GRADER COMPANY	P.O. BOX 24040	CLEVELAND	OH	44124
EBSCO CURRICULUM MATERIALS	P.O. BOX 1943	BIRMINGHAM	AL	35201
ECONOMY COMPANY	P.O. BOX 25308	OKLAHOMA CITY	OK	73125
EDL/MCGRAW-HILL	1221 AVENUE OF THE AMERICAS	NEW YORK	NY	10020
EDMARK ASSOCIATES	P.O. BOX 3903	BELLEVUE	WA	98009
EDUCATIONAL ACTIVITIES, INC.	P.O. BOX 87	BALDWIN	NY	11510
EDUCATIONAL DIMENSIONS CORP.	P.O. BOX 126	STAMFORD	CT	06904
EDUCATIONAL ENRICHMENT MATERIALS	357 ADAMS STREET	BEDFORD HILLS	NY	10507
EDUCATIONAL INSIGHTS, INC.	20435 S. TILLMAN	CARSON	CA	90746
EDUCATIONAL MEDIA, INC.	P.O. BOX 39	ELLENBURG	WA	98926
EDUCATIONAL PERFORMANCE ASSOC.	563 WESTVIEW AVENUE	RIDGEFIELD	NJ	07657
EDUCATIONAL PROGRAMMERS, INC.	P.O. BOX 332	ROSEBURG	OR	97470
EDUCATIONAL PROGRESS CORPORATION	P.O. BOX 45663	TULSA	OK	74145
EDUCATIONAL PROJECTIONS COMPANY	P.O. BOX 50276	JACKSONVILLE	FL	32250
EDUCATIONAL RESEARCH, INC.	1768 WILLOW POINT DRIVE	SHREVEPORT	LA	71119
EDUCATIONAL SERVICE, INC.	P.O. BOX 219	STEVENSVILLE	MI	49127
EDUCATIONAL TEACHING AIDS	159 W. KINZIE STREET	CHICAGO	IL	60610
EDUCATORS PUBLISHING SERVICE	75 MOULTON STREET	CAMBRIDGE	MA	02138
ELSEVIER/NELSON BOOKS	2 PARK AVENUE	NEW YORK CITY	NY	10016
EMC CORPORATION	180 EAST 6TH STREET	ST. PAUL	MN	55101
ENCORE VISUAL EDUCATION, INC.	1235 SOUTH VICTORY BLVD.	BURBANK	CA	91502
ENCYCLOPEDIA BRITANNICA	425 N. MICHIGAN AVENUE, TENTH FL	CHICAGO	IL	60611
ENGLISH LANGUAGE SERVICES	5761 BUCKINGHAM PKWY	CULVER CITY	CA	90230
ENRICH, INC.	760 KIFER ROAD	SUNNYVALE	CA	94086
ENRICHMENT READING CORP OF AMER.		IRON RIDGE	WI	53035
EYE GATE MEDIA	146-01 ARCHER AVENUE	JAMAICA	NY	11435
FEARON PITMAN PUBLISHERS, INC.	6 DAVIS DRIVE	BELMONT	CA	94002

PUBLISHER	ADDRESS	CITY	ST	ZIP
FERN TRIPP	2035 E. SIERRA WAY	DINUBA	CA	93618
FOLKWAYS RECORDS & SERVICE CORP.	43 W. 61ST STREET	NEW YORK	NY	10023
FOLLETT PUBLISHING COMPANY	1010 W. WASHINGTON BOULEVARD	CHICAGO	IL	60607
FRANK SCHAFFER PUBLICATIONS, INC	26616 INDIAN PEAK ROAD	RANCHO PALOS VERDES	CA	90274
FREDERICK WARNE & CO., INC.	101 FIFTH AVENUE	NEW YORK	NY	10003
GARRARD PUBLISHING COMPANY		CHAMPAIGN	IL	61820
GEL-STEN, INC.	P.O. BOX 2248	PALM SPRINGS	CA	92262
GINN & COMPANY	P.O. BOX 2649	COLUMBUS	OH	43216
GLENCOE PUBLISHING COMPANY, INC.	17337 VENTURA BOULEVARD	ENCINO	CA	91316
GLOBE BOOK COMPANY, INC.	50 W. 23RD STREET	NEW YORK	NY	10010
GOOD APPLE, INC.	P.O. BOX 299	CARTHAGE	IL	62321
GROSSET & DUNLAP, INC.	51 MADISON AVENUE	NEW YORK	NY	10010
GUIDANCE ASSOCIATES	COMMUNICATIONS PARK, P.O. BOX 30	WHITE PLAINS	NY	10602
H & H ENTERPRISES, INC.	P.O. BOX 1070	LAWRENCE	KS	66044
HAMMOND, INC.	515 VALLEY STREET	MAPLEWOOD	NJ	07040
HAMPDEN PUBLICATIONS, INC.	P.O. BOX 4873, DEPT. AHP3	BALTIMORE	MA	21211
HARCOURT BRACE JOVANOVICH, INC.	757 THIRD AVENUE	NEW YORK	NY	10017
HARPER & ROW PUBLISHERS, INC.	10 E. 53RD STREET	NEW YORK	NY	10022
HAYES SCHOOL PUBLISHING COMPANY	321 PENNWOOD AVENUE	WILKINSBURG	PA	15221
HERBERT M. ELKINS COMPANY	10031 COMMERCE AVENUE	TUJUNGA	CA	91042
HOLT, RINEHART AND WINSTON, INC.	383 MADISON AVENUE	NEW YORK	NY	10017
HOUGHTON MIFFLIN COMPANY	1 BEACON STREET	BOSTON	MA	02107
IDEAL SCHOOL SUPPLY COMPANY	11000 S. LAVERGNE AVENUE	OAK LAWN	IL	60453
IDEAS	P.O. BOX 741	TEMPE	AZ	85281
IMPERIAL INTERNATIONAL LEARNING	P.O. BOX 548	KANKAKEE	IL	60901
INCENTIVE PUBLICATIONS, INC.	P.O. BOX 120189	NASHVILLE	TN	37212
INCENTIVES FOR LEARNING, INC.	600 WEST VAN BUREN STREET	CHICAGO	IL	60607
INDIVIDUALIZED LEARNING MATERIAL	2741 BROADWAY	NEW YORK	NY	10025
INSTRUCTIONAL FAIR	P.O. BOX 1650	GRAND RAPIDS	MI	49501
INSTRUCTIONAL INDUSTRIES (G.E.)	EXECUTIVE PARK	BALLSTON LAKE	NY	12019
INSTRUCTO/MCGRAW-HILL	CEDAR HOLLOW & MATHEWS ROADS	PAOLI	PA	19301
INSTRUCTOR PUBLICATIONS, INC.	INSTRUCTOR PARK	DANSVILLE	NY	14437
INTERPRETIVE EDUCATION	2306 WINTERS DRIVE	KALAMAZOO	MI	49002
INVICTA PLASTICS LTD.	200 FIFTH AVENUE, SUITE 940	NEW YORK	NY	10010
J. WESTON WALCH PUBLISHING	P.O. BOX 658	PORTLAND	ME	04104
JABBERWOCKY	4 COMMERCIAL BOULEVARD	NOVATO	CA	94947
JAMESTOWN PUBLICATIONS, INC.	P.O. BOX 6743	PROVIDENCE	RI	02940
JANUARY PRODUCTIONS	124 REA AVENUE	HAWTHORNE	NJ	07506
JANUS BOOK PUBLISHERS	3541 INVESTMENT BLVD., SUITE 5	HAYWARD	CA	94545
JENN PUBLICATIONS	815-825 E. MARKET STREET, BOX 32	LOUISVILLE	KY	40232
JUDY COMPANY	250 JAMES STREET	MORRISTOWN	NJ	07960
KENWORTHY EDUCATIONAL SERVICE	P.O. BOX 3031	BUFFALO	NY	14205
KIDS & COMPANY	P.O. BOX 49034	LOS ANGELES	CA	90049
KIMBO EDUCATIONAL	P.O. BOX 477	LONG BRANCH	NJ	07740
KING FEATURES	235 E. 45TH STREET	NEW YORK	NY	10017
LAKESHORE CURRICULUM MATERIALS	P.O. BOX 6261	CARSON	CA	90749
LANSFORD PUBLISHING COMPANY	P.O. BOX 8711	SAN JOSE	CA	95155
LAURI, INC.	P.O. BOX F	PHILLIPS-AVON	ME	04966
LEARNCO, INC.	P.O. BOX L	EXETER	NH	03833
LEARNING HANDBOOKS	530 UNIVERSITY AVENUE	PALO ALTO	CA	94301
LEARNING STUFF	P.O. BOX 4123	MODESTO	CA	95352
LEARNING TREE FILMSTRIPS	P.O.B OX 1590	BOULDER	CO	80306
LERNER PUBLICATIONS COMPANY	241 FIRST AVENUE NORTH	MINNEAPOLIS	MN	55401
LESWING PRESS	P.O. BOX 3577	SAN RAFAEL	CA	94901
LISTEN & LEARN CORPORATION	13366 PESCADERO ROAD	LA HONDA	CA	94020
LISTENING LIBRARY, INC.	1 PARK AVENUE	OLD GREENWICH	CT	06870
LITTLE KENNY PUBLICATIONS, INC.	1315 W. BELMONT AVENUE	CHICAGO	IL	60657
LOVE PUBLISHING COMPANY	6635 E. VILLANOVA PLACE	DENVER	CO	80222
MACMILLAN PUBLISHING CO., INC.	23 ORINDA WAY	ORINDA	CA	94563
MAFEX ASSOCIATES, INC.	P.O. BOX 519	JOHNSTOWN	PA	15902
MARLON CREATIONS, INC.	P.O. BOX 1530	LONG ISLAND CITY	NY	11101
MAST DEVELOPMENT COMPANY	2212 EAST 12TH STREET	DAVENPORT	IA	52803
MCCORMICK-MATHERS PUBLISHING CO.	7625 EMPIRE DRIVE	FLORENCE	KY	41042
MCDOUGAL, LITTEL & COMPANY	P.O. BOX 1667	EVANSTON	IL	60204
MEDIA MARKETING, INC.	5307 LEE HIGHWAY, P.O. BOX 7184	ARLINGTON	VA	22207
MEDIA MATERIALS, INC.	2936 REMINGTON AVENUE	BALTIMORE	MD	21211
MELODY HOUSE PUBLISHING COMPANY	819 N.W. 92ND STREET	OKLAHOMA CITY	OK	73114
MILLER-BRODY PRODUCTIONS, INC.	342 MADISON AVENUE	NEW YORK	NY	10017
MILTON BRADLEY/PLAYSKOOL		SPRINGFIELD	MA	01101
MODERN CURRICULUM PRESS	13900 PROSPECT ROAD	CLEVELAND	OH	44136
MODERN EDUCATION CORPORATION	P.O. BOX 721	TULSA	OK	74101
MODULEARN, INC.	P.O. BOX 667	SAN JUAN CAPISTRANO	CA	92693
MOSIER MATERIALS	P.O. BOX 3036	SAN BERNARDINO	CA	92413
NATIONAL BOOK COMPANY	333 S.W. PARK AVENUE	PORTLAND	OR	97205
NATIONAL EDUCATIONAL LABORATORY	P.O. BOX 1003	AUSTIN	TX	78767
NATIONAL LEARNING CORPORATION	212 MICHAEL DRIVE	SYOSSET	NY	11791
NATIONAL TEXTBOOK COMPANY	8259 NILES CENTER ROAD	SKOKIE	IL	60077
NEW READERS PRESS	P.O. BOX 131	SYRACUSE	NY	13210
NIENHUIS MONTESSORI, INC.	320 PIONEER WAY	MOUNTAIN VIEW	CA	94041
NYSTROM	3333 ELSTON AVENUE	CHICAGO	IL	60618
ODDO PUBLISHING, INC.	BEAUREGARD BLVD.	FAYETTEVILLE	GA	30214
OPPORTUNITIES FOR LEARNING, INC.	8950 LURLINE AVENUE	CHATSWORTH	CA	91311
ORE PRESS, INC.	P.O. BOX 61688	SUNNYVALE	CA	94088
P.S. ASSOCIATES	6461 LUANNE DRIVE	FLUSHING	MI	48433
PAUL S. AMIDON & ASSOC., INC.	1966 BENSON AVENUE	ST. PAUL	MN	55116
PEEK PUBLICATIONS	P.O. BOX 11065	PALO ALTO	CA	94306
PERFECTION FORM COMPANY	1000 N. SECOND AVENUE	LOGAN	IA	51546
PHONOVISUAL PRODUCTS, INC.	12216 PARKLAWN DRIVE	ROCKVILLE	MD	20852
PLAYSKOOL, INC.		SPRINGFIELD	MA	01101
PRESCHOOL LEARNING CORPORATION	P.O. BOX 6244	OVERLAND PARKS	KS	66207
Q-ED PRODUCTIONS	P.O. BOX 4029	WESTLAKE VILLAGE	CA	91359
RAND MCNALLY & COMPANY	P.O. BOX 7600	CHICAGO	IL	60680
READERS DIGEST SERVICES, INC.	EDUCATIONAL DIVISION	PLEASANTVILLE	NY	10570

PUBLISHER	ADDRESS	CITY	ST	ZIP
READING JOY, INC.	P.O. BOX 404	NAPERVILLE	IL	60540
REGENTS PUBLISHING COMPANY	2 PARK AVENUE	NEW YORK	NY	10016
SCHOLASTIC BOOK SERVICE	P.O. BOX 2002	ENGLEWOOD CLIFFS	NJ	07632
SCOTT RESOURCES, INC.	P.O. BOX 2121	FORT COLLINS	CO	80522
SCOTT, FORESMAN & CO.	1900 E. LAKE AVENUE	GLENVIEW	IL	60025
SOUND MATERIALS	P.O. BOX 453	KNOXVILLE	TN	37901
SOUTH-WESTERN PUBLISHING CO.	5101 MADISON ROAD	CINCINNATI	OH	45227
SPECIAL CHILD PUBLICATIONS	4535 UNION BAY PLACE, N.E.	SEATTLE	WA	98105
SPECIAL LEARNING CORPORATION	42 BOSTON POST ROAD	GUILFORD	CT	06437
SPEECH FOUNDATION OF AMERICA	152 LOMBARDY ROAD	MEMPHIS	TN	38111
SPELLBINDER, INC.	33 BRADFORD STREET	CONCORD	MA	01742
SPOKEN ARTS, INC.	59 LOCUST AVENUE	NEW ROCHELLE	NY	10800
SRA	155 N. WACKER DRIVE	CHICAGO	IL	60606
ST. JOHN SCHOOL FOR THE DEAF	3680 S. KINNICKINNIC AVENUE	MILWAUKEE	WI	53207
STANWIX HOUSE, INC.	3020 CHARTIERS AVENUE	PITTSBURGH	PA	15204
STECK-VAUGHN COMPANY	P.O.B OX 2028	AUSTIN	TX	78768
SVE	1345 DIVERSEY PARKWAY	CHICAGO	IL	60614
T.S. DENISON & COMPANY	9601 NEWTON AVENUE SOUTH	MINNEAPOLIS	MN	55431
TEACHING RESOURCES CORPORATION	50 POND PARK ROAD	HINGHAM	MA	02043
TREND ENTERPRISES, INC.	P.O. BOX 3073	ST. PAUL	MN	55165
TROLL ASSOCIATES	320 ROUTE 17	MAHWAH	NJ	07430
UNITED LEARNING	6633 WEST HOWARD STREET	NILES	IL	60648
UNITED TRANSPARENCIES, INC.	BOX 688	BINGHAMTON	NY	13902
URBAN MEDIA MATERIALS, INC.	315 WALT WHITMAN ROAD	HUNTINGTON STATION	NY	11746
WALKER EDUCATIONAL BOOK CORP.	720 FIFTH AVENUE	NEW YORK	NY	10019
WALT DISNEY EDUCATIONAL MEDIA	500 S. BUENA VISTA STREET	BURBANK	CA	91521
WEBER COSTELLO COMPANY	1900 NORTH NARRAGANSETT AVENUE	CHICAGO	IL	60639
WEBSTER DIVISION/MCGRAW-HILL	1221 AVENUE OF THE AMERICAS	NEW YORK	NY	10020
WENKART	4 SHADY HILL SQUARE	CAMBRIDGE	MA	02138
WESTERN PUBLISHING EDUC. SERVICE	150 PARISH DRIVE	WAYNE	NJ	07470
WESTINGHOUSE LEARNING CORP.	5005 W. 110TH STREET	OAK LAWN	IL	60453
WHITEHAVEN PUBLISHING COMPANY	P.O. BOX 2	NEW RICHMOND	WI	54017
WILSON EDUCATIONAL MEDIA		SOUTH HOLLAND	IL	60473
WISE OWL PUBLICATIONS	P.O. BOX 3816	LOS ANGELES	CA	90028
WORD MAKING PRODUCTIONS, INC.	P.O. BOX 15038	SALT LAKE CITY	UT	84115
XEROX EDUCATION PUBLICATIONS	1250 FAIRWOOD AVENUE	COLUMBUS	OH	43216

PHONEME BASELINE RECORDING FORMS   *by Mary Pizzuti (1979)*

A series of tests designed to determine phoneme baselines for helping clinicians correctly pinpoint the level at which the student should begin speech therapy. All on duplicating masters, the tests are easy to administer and score — approximately seven minutes per phoneme. They're also great for making clinical comparisons during and after therapy; determining which phonemes will respond most quickly to therapy; and developing IEPs. Baselines consist of tests for phonemes in isolation, syllables, words, sentences, stories (reading and retelling), and spontaneous speech. Duplicating masters for /r/, /ar/, /ir/, /or/, /er/, /l/, /th/, /ch/, /k/, /s/, /sh/, /f/, /h/, and data recording sheets. Total of 92 spirit masters, 8½" x 11", softbound.

No. 3055 $15

PRE-SCISSOR SKILLS: Skill Starters for Motor Development   *by Marsha Lee Dunn (1979)*

A success learning program for teaching sequential scissor training to pre-school and developmentally delayed children, outlining a variety of pre-scissor experiences and classroom teaching activities with provisions necessary for the student to succeed. Designed as a workbook for the teacher or clinician to use as a self-learning tool, with specific objectives and a pre/post-test for before and after reading to assess information gain. 80 pages, 8½" x 11", softbound.   **No. 3101 $10**

COLOR RECOGNITION: Steps Up To Language for the Learning Impaired
by Vickie Simmons and Irene Williams (1979)

Very young children or students with severe learning disabilities may not be able to separate the property of color from an object's other properties. This manual is a success training program for teaching color recognition. Students can name solid colors and the basic color patterns of their environment after they complete the program. Teachers working with deaf students may utilize procedures described in these programs through the use of signed cues included in the appendix. Reproducible recording data sheets to measure progress are included. 96 pages, 8½" x 11", softbound.   **No. 3100 $8**

MORE PROGRAMMED ARTICULATION SKILLS CARRYOVER STORIES
by Judith Sonderman and Daniel H. Zwitman (1979)

Many times you're working with a child who articulates sounds perfectly in clinical and classroom sessions, only to fall back into old habits on the playground or at home. This manual attacks the problem by covering four sounds — /l/, /s/, /r/, and /th/ — often misarticulated by children in everyday conversation. Each story consists of five pictures, described by short sentences. The book is printed so the text faces you while the picture faces the student. Great for sending home with the child — complete instructions to the parent are included. 176 pages, 8½" x 11", softbound.   **No. 3107 $16.50**

PROGRAMMED ARTICULATION CARRYOVER STORIES
by Judith C. Sonderman and Daniel H. Zwitman (1976)

Same as MORE PROGRAMMED ARTICULATION SKILLS CARRYOVER STORIES, except covering these sounds — /p/, /b/, /d/, /t/, /k/, /g/, /f/, /v/, /sh/, /ch/, and /j/. Sentences are length-controlled, consist of basic vocabulary and structures, and contain the target sounds in two to four words. Tested in a controlled longitudinal study, these stories have been effective in articulation carryover. Complete with administration and parental instructions. 220 pages, 8½" x 11", softbound.   **No. 2029 $16.50**

KING LOUIE HOLIDAY STORIES FOR SPEECH AND LANGUAGE REMEDIATION
by Dorothy Jean Soule (1979)

A series of eight warmhearted tales about "King Louie" — a little white poodle — and the family with whom he lives. These stories are geared for children in primary grades and may be utilized for remediation of speech, language, and listening problems. Worksheets accompany each story and are filled with crossword puzzles, fill-in-the-blanks drills, matching exercises, or picture stories. Each set of worksheets targets the sounds /f-v/, /th/, /s-z/, /l/, /r/, /sh-ch-j/, and /k-g/. All materials can be reproduced for classroom and carryover use. 176 pages, 8½" x 11", looseleaf binder with tab indexes, 10" hand puppet. **No. 3098 $35**

LANGUAGE REMEDIATION AND EXPANSION   *by Catharine S. Bush (1979)*

100 skill-building reference lists. Designed to provide resource material for speech-language pathologists, specialists, and classroom teachers involved in language remediation and/or expansion. Included are lists of examples and exercises for major skill areas. Suggested activities that precede each list emphasize communicative interaction and experience-based language. Because most of the skills lists are sequenced in order of difficulty, the teacher may begin at the appropriate level for the individual student or group. 216 pages, 8½" x 11", softbound.   **No. 3052 $15**

101 LANGUAGE ARTS ACTIVITIES   *by Trudy Aarons and Francine Koelsch (1979)*

Includes 101 different step-by-step directions for making games, gameboards, and learning centers that can be used by reading, as well as nonreading, children. Because each game is geared to reach a specific performance objective, the materials are ideal for developing IEPs. 134 pages, 8½" x 11", softbound.

No. 3053 $10

**Communication
Skill Builders, Inc.**®
3130 N. Dodge Blvd./P.O. Box 42050
Tucson, Arizona 85733